Wildlife in Britain

A GUIDE TO NATURAL HABITATS, SAFARI PARKS AND ZOOS

THE AUTOMOBILE ASSOCIATION

Wildlife in Britain

How to use this book	In this book, Britain's wildlife is described in ten regional surveys. The regions are defined on the map on page 2 of the Introduction. Each region is described in a similar way, as follows.
The region	This is an essay by a naturalist who has detailed local knowledge of the area in question. It describes the wildlife to be seen and how to see it, as well as the effects on natural history of the climate, geology, topography and land-use of the region.
Regional map	On the third page of each essay is a map of the region, showing the sites where animals can be seen in the wild or in captivity. These are the symbols which distinguish the different types of site:

	Zoo		Bird Collection		Farm Park
	Safari Park		Forest nature reserve		National Trust
	Aquarium		National nature reserve		National Park and Forest Park
	Dolphinarium		Other nature reserves		

Guide to natural habitats	Following the regional article is a county-by-county gazetteer of the important sites where animals and sometimes plants may be encountered in their natural wild habitat. Reserves, sanctuaries and other designated areas are listed, their limitations described and their locations clearly stated in the form of road directions and National Grid references. All these sites appear on the regional map. This gazetteer also lists the addresses of the organisations, local and national, which are concerned with and sometimes administer the region's wildlife.
Animal collections	As well as being plotted on the regional map, the zoos, safari parks, bird-gardens, aquaria, dolphinaria etc. are listed alphabetically and very fully described. In each case, the collection's scope and purpose are outlined; the reader is guided through its layout, picking up fascinating information about the animals, their behaviour, their distribution in the wild, and their place in the collection as a whole. Great emphasis is placed on the role that collections perform in preserving and breeding animals whose wild existence is in danger.

For each collection, practical details for the visitor's guidance, such as opening-times, facilities and locations, are displayed in a buff-coloured panel accompanying the description. Please note that the animal collections change constantly; therefore some details of them may differ from those given in this book.

Names of species and subspecies of animals are capitalised in the text.

Abbreviations	AONB	Area of Outstanding Natural Beauty
	BC	Borough Council
	BTO	British Trust for Ornithology
	CC	County Council
	For Comm	Forestry Commission
	FNR	Forest Nature Reserve
	FP	Forest Park
	LNR	Local Nature Reserve
	MDC	Metropolitan District Council
	NCC	Nature Conservancy Council
	NNR	National Nature Reserve
	NT	National Trust
	NTS	National Trust for Scotland
	RSPB	Royal Society for the Protection of Birds
	SPNR	Society for the Promotion of Nature Reserves
	SWT	Scottish Wildlife Trust
	TC	Town Council
	WAGBI	Wildfowlers' Association of Great Britain and Ireland

Contents

The front cover of this book shows a buck Red Deer, the back cover shows three doe Red Deer. The endpapers show a male Dartford Warbler attending to its young at the nest in the middle of a gorse bush. On the title-page an Osprey flies on to its tree-top nest.

Kenneth Williamson (general editor of the Wildlife sections of this book) has been a Senior Research Officer of the British Trust for Ornithology since 1958, at first co-ordinating the migration studies of the Bird Observatory network, and later taking charge of bird populations work. He served in the Faeroes from 1941 to 1945, returning with a wife and daughter and the manuscript of *The Atlantic Islands* — a book about people in relation to their natural environment. He and his wife spent eight years at Fair Isle developing the Bird Observatory, his chief contribution to ornithology being the correlation of bird migration with meteorological events. He had a season in 1957 as NCC Warden at St Kilda. Four of his books reflect an obsession with the ecology and human history of remote islands; otherwise his main pursuit, shared with his son Robin, is archaeology and ancient history. He edits the BTO journal *Bird Study* and has published many papers on bird-life in scientific journals. He was elected a Fellow of the Royal Society of Edinburgh in 1960 and awarded the Union Medal of the British Ornithologists' Union in 1976.

Geoffrey Schomberg (general editor of the Animal Collections parts of this book) has had a life-long interest in zoos and in the problems of keeping wild animals in captivity throughout Europe, America, Africa and the Far East. He was secretary of the Federation of Zoological Gardens of Great Britain and Ireland for nine years, and since 1974 he has been editor of *International Zoo News*, a magazine for zoo directors. He has written two books on British zoos and numerous articles on zoo subjects. Aged 48, he is married, lives in Suffolk and is a director of a zoo-planning consultancy which designs zoos, mainly for overseas governments. He has compiled all the zoo entries in this book.

This book was devised and produced by Park and Roche Establishment, Schaan.

First published in Great Britain in 1976 by The Automobile Association, Fanum House, Basingstoke, Hampshire, RG21 2EA.

Designed by Crispin Fisher
Picture research by Juliet Brightmore

Maps produced by the Cartographic Services Unit of the Automobile Association, and based upon the Ordnance Survey Maps, with the sanction of the Controller of Her Majesty's Stationery Office, Crown Copyright Reserved. Copyright © 1976 The Automobile Association.

Printed in England by Jarrold and Sons Ltd, Norwich, England.

ISBN 09 126390 5

A growing number of people are now aware that wildlife and wild places are seriously threatened throughout the world. The threats are many - but in almost every case they are directly or indirectly the result of man's activities.

Two of the most densely populated countries in the world are my own country, the Netherlands, and the United Kingdom. But, despite this intense human pressure, there is a surprising wealth and variety of wildlife still surviving in both our countries. This is largely due to the constant vigilance and dedication of voluntary conservation organisations, of which there are many such bodies in Britain, both large and small and devoted to virtually every aspect of wildlife and nature study. I am happy to say that every year the World Wildlife Fund grants a substantial amount of money to their conservation projects.

However, ever greater sums of money are needed to continue the vital work of safeguarding Britain's rich natural heritage. This money comes from the public - and there is no doubt that the public will be much more inclined to support our conservation activities if they can be introduced to Britain's wildlife at first hand, and encouraged to look at it with enhanced perception.

This book, with its copious illustrations and expert and informed text, will enable many people to enjoy the countryside and its wildlife, and appreciate the importance of saving it for future generations to enjoy. I warmly welcome its publication, and hope that it reaches a very wide readership.

The Prince of the Netherlands,
President of the World Wildlife Fund.

Introduction KENNETH WILLIAMSON

For many centuries man has lived uneasily with wildlife. Rather like a wild animal himself, he is jealous of his territory — the ground he has won from nature — and intolerant of competition. With singularly few exceptions those birds and mammals which thrive in the countryside today are the ones that seldom did him any harm. The bigger and more competitive beasts were the first to disappear, and the chance that we shall ever have them again as wild-living neighbours is remote. There is no place in our crowded isle, other than in zoos, for Brown Bears, Wolves and Wild Boars; and even the anciently wild White Cattle have to be contained within extensive parks. The Fox has managed to survive and so have the Badger and the Otter, though the last is currently a threatened species in England. Some smaller mammals which barely escaped elimination — Wild Cat, Pine Marten and Polecat — are showing definite signs of increase and seem likely to be reprieved now that man's attitude to wildlife is becoming more positively sympathetic.

Today's Briton is more in tune with his natural environment than ever before. A lot of this has to do with centuries of animal husbandry and cultivation of the soil, but also with the mediaeval chase — that sublimation of the primaeval hunting economy translated into social occasion. Surprising though it may seem, this hunting was an early form of conservation that secured for later generations the beauty and elegant grace of several kinds of deer and the White Cattle of the Chillingham herd. During past centuries the landscape has altered remarkably, but throughout this long period of change we have never really become divorced from the elemental wonder of the natural scene and the mystery of natural events. The more that we of the modern world live withdrawn into our urban shell, the greater is our need for a little wilderness. In years past the rich man surrounded his home with a park, the farmer planted an orchard, and other men tended their gardens; and if they did not actively release animals for sport or to adorn their quiet acres, they were at least tolerant of those that came of their own accord. Since the Second War more people have had to make do with fewer gardens, but an increased standard of living has brought greater leisure, a higher level of education, a mass-media which has capitalised on the attraction of the great outdoors, and a national fleet of cars.

The countryside has come closer to everyone — so much so that national parks, country parks, forest parks, nature trails, farm walks and such-like have been designed to absorb and edify more and more folk, either for brief visits or, if you are one of those who trail a temporary home behind you, for longer stays. Four million people visit the National Trust's houses and gardens each year; four million people enjoy the Peak District National Park every summer. The anomalous situation has arisen that we are now in danger of destroying the quiet and the solitude, the beauty and the wildness, that we need more than ever before and seek so eagerly. A gulf has opened between those of us who want to snatch more land for human-oriented development, and those who feel that wilderness is a rare resource essential to our mental and physical well-being. Oddly enough, this division is less an individual than a group phenomenon, the planners versus the conservationists, or bureaucracy versus the people, as when a new airport or reservoir is required to further the nation's progress but can only be built at the price of a rural way of life or a rich wildlife haunt.

It seems that a communion with nature is something which, despite 4,000 years of 'civilisation' in Britain, we cannot or would rather not escape. It is not just the fresh air, the wide skies, the swelling hills, the restful green — it is a complex amalgam of the myriad components which go to make up the natural scene. We are all aware of the beauty of form and colour of a whole host of flowers and trees; it may not register, but the need is there, and the consciousness inspires us even though we cannot give each one a name. When we listen to bird-song in a wood most of us neither know nor care what the species are which so please us, and what is their way of life — yet the experience comforts us

Max Nicholson writes:

If we are to keep Britain teeming with wildlife, an understanding as well as a love of animals and plants and of nature generally must go on growing and spreading more strongly and deeply.

The exploding pressures of human population, the many and diverse impacts of modern technology, and the pervasive changes which we inflict on habitats, make it unrealistic to decline responsibility for active management. Such management must be based on thorough research and experiment, to make sure that we know what we are doing and where it will lead.

In this perspective we can draw no hard line between what we used to regard as 'natural', and the many habitats which are humanly modified or artificial.

Zoos, once little better than crowds of small cages and cramped paddocks, where the animals were on strike against breeding, are becoming more spacious, and affording their inmates an approximation to their essential habitat. Research in the wild has made this possible, and growing public sensibility demands it. Breeding in captivity is bringing closer the day when most zoos will be mainly stocked from their own populations. Whatever our views about the rights and wrongs of zoos, we must give credit to those zoo directors who have done so much to make them more acceptable on both sides of the barriers, and to enhance their contribution to scientific knowledge and general education.

There are still plenty of shortcomings, but the authors of this book are justified, as they would not have been some years ago, in including zoos with nature reserves as part of the British wildlife scene.

I commend this book to all those who love wildlife and wish to see it flourish in Britain.

Max Nicholson C.B., C.V.O., former Director-General of the Nature Conservancy, the official body created to study and conserve wildlife throughout Britain, has been for many years an outstanding influence and force in the development of modern ecological conservation. Active in all leading organisations devoted to the study and protection of nature, he is the author of many authoritative works on environmental questions.

Opposite The memorable sight of a Badger foraging on the woodland floor could so easily reward a keen and patient watcher at dusk (see page 194).

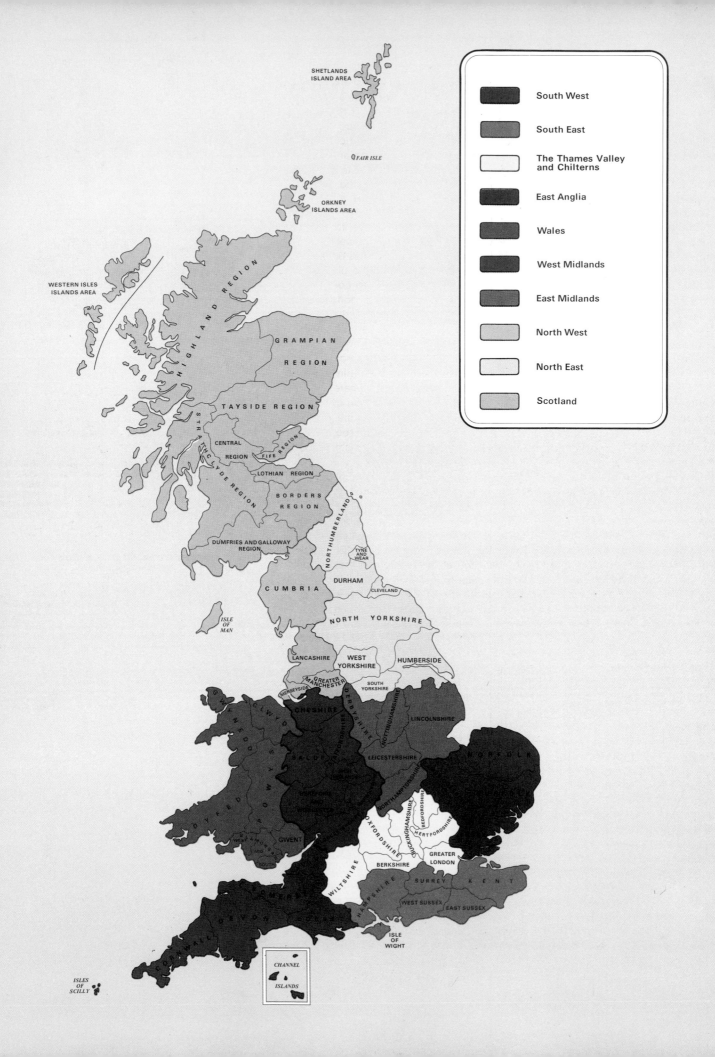

Legend:
- South West
- South East
- The Thames Valley and Chilterns
- East Anglia
- Wales
- West Midlands
- East Midlands
- North West
- North East
- Scotland

SHETLANDS ISLAND AREA

FAIR ISLE

ORKNEY ISLANDS AREA

WESTERN ISLES ISLANDS AREA

HIGHLAND REGION

GRAMPIAN REGION

TAYSIDE REGION

STRATHCLYDE REGION

CENTRAL REGION

FIFE REGION

LOTHIAN REGION

BORDERS REGION

DUMFRIES AND GALLOWAY REGION

NORTHUMBERLAND

TYNE AND WEAR

ISLE OF MAN

CUMBRIA

DURHAM

CLEVELAND

NORTH YORKSHIRE

LANCASHIRE

WEST YORKSHIRE

HUMBERSIDE

GREATER MANCHESTER

MERSEYSIDE

SOUTH YORKSHIRE

CHESHIRE

DERBYSHIRE

NOTTINGHAMSHIRE

LINCOLNSHIRE

GWYNEDD

CLWYD

SALOP

STAFFORDSHIRE

LEICESTERSHIRE

NORFOLK

DYFED

POWYS

HEREFORD AND WORCESTER

WARWICKSHIRE

NORTHAMPTONSHIRE

BEDFORDSHIRE

HERTFORDSHIRE

OXFORDSHIRE

BUCKINGHAMSHIRE

GLAMORGAN

GWENT

WILTSHIRE

BERKSHIRE

GREATER LONDON

SURREY

KENT

SOMERSET

HAMPSHIRE

WEST SUSSEX

EAST SUSSEX

DORSET

DEVON

CORNWALL

ISLE OF WIGHT

ISLES OF SCILLY

CHANNEL ISLANDS

just the same. We thrill to a glimpse of deer through the trees, the bark of a Fox in the night, the honking of wild geese against the vivid sunset of an estuary. This prodigal from nature, man, has a primordial sense of belonging; the need to return is in all of us, and because it is primitive it is especially strong in our children. Often it is they, unconsciously responding to the call, who need the company of pets and a romantic association with the animal dreamworld of Beatrix Potter and Alison Uttley and many more besides. Often it is they who later tempt us into the countryside and supply the inquiring mind; and the opportunity to explore and discover animal reality with them is a powerful catalyst for cementing family ties.

Our book is designed to foster this relationship, to bring the family into contact with wildlife, whether in zoos or in the countryside. Animals are not just curiosities, they are our neighbours and essential companions on this planet, and there is satisfaction in seeking to know more about them and the places they fill in nature's scheme. It may seem odd to mix zoos and the open country in a book, but we have done it deliberately (and have brought in domesticated animals too) because we believe that basically it is *knowing animals* that counts. The zoos can show us what a wonderful range of creatures there are in the world as a whole (the great majority of them creatures we would not otherwise meet); and the countryside, if we have a patient and inquiring approach and a sympathy for the needs of our subjects, can teach us how some animals live.

Zoos are finite locations and can be listed; wildlife is everywhere and the writers of this book have set out to make a comprehensive selection of the best and most easily accessible places. However, many good places are privately owned and there is no public access; and some nature reserves are too sensitive to disturbance and must remain sacrosanct to the flowers, birds, mammals and insects for which they were set apart.

The great Swedish naturalist Linnaeus, who described many plants and animals for the first time and gave them accepted scientific names (the international language of biology), prefaced his *Systema Naturae* with the remark that a name is the beginning of knowledge. We have not tried here to give detailed descriptions which will enable you to identify birds and beasts; there are a number of excellent field-guides which will help you to solve this problem. They are a valuable asset if you really want to get the best out of family forays in the country, and any one will fit into a jacket or anorak pocket. Binoculars of 7× or 8× magnification should be part of your equipment, and a more powerful telescope is a very useful aid to seabird, estuary or reservoir bird-watching.

There have been a number of powerful developments in the field of habitat and species conservation in recent years. Since 1949 ten National Parks have been confirmed in England and Wales (there is none in Scotland, but several Scottish nature reserves are vast by English standards). Over 140 National Nature Reserves, some of them open to the public, have been declared and are managed by the Nature Conservancy Council; the research on which this management is based is largely undertaken by the Institute of Terrestrial Ecology. The National Trust for Places of Historic Interest and Natural Beauty, besides owning many fine residences and estates, has a very large number of properties which are in effect nature reserves, including long reaches of Heritage Coast. The Royal Society for the Protection of Birds owns over 50 reserves, not always entirely ornithological in merit, in the United Kingdom. In the Forestry Commission's 1,500,000 acres of state forests there are seven Forest Parks and walking and riding are encouraged in many others. A number of Forest Nature Reserves are managed by the NCC for scientific research and conservation by agreement with the owners, the Forestry Commission, the Crown Estates Commissioners and the Duchy of Cornwall.

Local Nature Reserves are declared by Local Authorities after consultation with the NCC and some are managed for the authorities by the appropriate County Naturalists' Trust. Regional Wildfowl Refuges are statutory bird sanctuaries created under the Protection of Birds Act of 1954. Other refuges and sanctuaries are administered by independent organisations, such as the Wildfowl Trust and the Wildfowlers' Association of Great Britain and Ireland. The

Sunset over Hilbre Island in the estuary of the River Dee, one of the biggest areas of tidal mud-flats in Britain, and a haven for feeding waders.

National Parks *Areas in square miles*

Dartmoor   365
Exmoor   265
Pembrokeshire Coast   225
Brecon Beacons   519
Snowdonia   845
Peak District   542
Yorkshire Dales   680
North York Moors   553
Lake District   866
Northumberland   398

3

Scottish Wildlife Trust owns or has agreements in respect of many fine areas in Scotland, where stretches of magnificent mountain country as well as a number of smaller sites belong to the National Trust for Scotland. The Manx Museum and National Trust looks after the Isle of Man. The Society for the Promotion of Nature Reserves, which has been hard at work since 1916, is the parent body of the County Naturalists' Trusts, maintaining a cohesion of interests and aims and providing contact with government departments. Indeed, it may be said to service conservation organisations all over the country through its Conservation Liaison Committee, which provides a forum for discussion and a spur to action where this is deemed to be necessary.

The countryside is a highly sensitive place. The combined experience of those who have used it for leisure and research is embodied in a number of Codes of Conduct, chief among which is *The Country Code* published by H.M. Stationery Office. These Codes are brief and succinct, and compliance with them will greatly increase your own and others' enjoyment of the countryside. Respect land ownership and use footpaths and bridleways; leave field gates (whether open or closed) as you find them, and if you have to climb them, then do so as close to the hinged upright as possible. Do not damage stone walls, river banks, the vegetation, or indeed any part of the habitat — and be careful if you light a fire. If you want to take a photograph of a flower or a bird's nest avoid 'gardening' to expose your subject to the lens (if you do this with a nest, you may well give the site away to a predator). Do not pick flowers just because they're there — leave them for others to enjoy, and to provide seeds for next year's growth. Please resist the temptation to collect — in other words, do not remove or destroy anything which is likely to give pleasure to others. There are times when you can even improve on what the Codes tell you: if you spot a Hedgehog or Hare in the road ahead when driving at night, slow down, stop if it is safe to do so, and switch off your headlights. It will disappear, and you'll feel better for having secured its life.

Admission is free to many NNRs and other nature reserves, but you may find that access is controlled, either to preserve the habitat or to avoid disturbance of particular mammals, birds or insects at critical periods in their life-cycle. Please respect such restrictions — they are for the long-term benefit of us all. For many reserves owned by independent organisations you will require a permit, or the

The Country Code
Prepared by the Countryside Commission

Leave no litter — take it home.
Guard against all risk of fire.
Fasten all gates.
Keep dogs under proper control.
Avoid damaging fences, hedges and walls.
Keep to the paths across farm land.
Safeguard water supplies.
Go carefully on country roads.
Protect wild life, wild plants and trees.
Respect the life of the countryside.

Left: New Forest, a stand of oak trees that have been neither coppiced nor pollarded; below: pollarded beeches in Epping Forest; right: an overgrown former charcoal hearth in Glen Nant, Argyllshire, surrounded by coppiced hazel trees.

facility of entry may depend upon your being a member. A National Trust membership card, be it English or Scottish, is the open sesame to all NT and NTS properties everywhere, except to certain areas which are farmed, or which are held under protective covenants. There are several organisations which need active help for their conservation projects — the BTO, the RSPB, the SPNR and County Naturalists' Trusts — and by identifying yourself with this important and rewarding work it is easier to gain an understanding of the countryside, and so enjoy nature reserve visiting to the full.

Until a few centuries BC, a mixed broad-leaved forest, dominated by oak, but with a good mixture of beech and ash on chalk and limestone soils, covered roughly two-thirds of Britain. By Roman times clearing for agriculture was under way, and the forest became increasingly fragmented. The Norman nobility set aside the best remnants, such as the New Forest, as hunting preserves, but within a few generations even these were being eroded to make room for an expanding agriculture, and soon there were growing fears of a timber shortage.

Some mediaeval mind, conscious of this rapid depletion of reserves, hit upon the idea of rotational coppicing, and the 'sustained yield' principle which is the keystone of modern conservation was born. This had important and far-reaching effects on bird-life. The trees were cut close to the ground, and their stumps or 'stools' were left for a number of years to sprout new timber. The pole-growth was prolific, several stems arising from each stool, and the periodic harvest of this renewable resource was adequate for most domestic and industrial uses, such as fence and hurdle making, turnery, the production of bark for tanning, and of charcoal for the furnaces of the glass-blowers and iron-smelters. Woods or copses were divided into 'coupes' of a few acres each, and these were cut on a 12–15 years' rotation, though oak coppice for the tanneries was allowed to grow for 20 years or more. Usually the coppice was hazel, though in different areas sweet chestnut, ash, hornbeam or field maple might be favoured.

Since much larger timbers were required for the beams and rafters of castles, churches and dwellings, as well as for ship-building, some oaks were left to grow as 'standards', and care was taken that these were uneven-aged so that there were always replacements for those which were felled. Another way of securing a sustained yield of timber was by 'pollarding', the bole being cut at a

The tangled form of limbs sprouting from coppiced and pollarded timber provides an ideal nest-site for the Wren.

Pollarding. Pollarding is the art of topping broad-leaved trees, at a height of about six feet; it was done where animals were present in numbers, as a useful alternative to coppicing trees at ground level. Where trees were coppiced, fences had to be put up to exclude livestock for several years whilst the 'young spring' was growing. Pollarding was done just above the browsing level — the greatest height that a cow, or an acrobatic deer standing on its hind-legs, could reach. So no fences were needed. The word originates in the Norman French *poil*, meaning head, since the trees were 'beheaded'. Three kinds of produce were secured by repeated pollarding. (1) Small poles or pliant rods useful for fence repairs, hedge stakes, thatching spars and other odd jobs. (2) Fuel, cheaply won at low transport cost in the days before coal was available. (3) Fodder; at the end of a long winter tree bark and fresh green foliage were fed to farm stock, and even deer, before the grass began to grow.

H. L. Edlin, *Woodland Notebook — Goodbye to the Pollards*; Q. Jour. Roy. Forestry Soc., vol. 65, pp. 157–165 (April 1971).

height of six feet or so to ensure that the new growth was out of reach of browsing deer and cattle. This cutting stimulated a bushy growth of dense new shoots at the base of the sprouting limbs, ideal nesting cover for Wrens, thrushes and other birds. The limbs grew large and strong, giving the trees wide crowns. There are many fine old pollarded oaks and beeches in the New Forest and other former royal forests, but they are an anachronism and this picturesque type of woodland will disappear as existing veterans are windthrown or felled.

Coppice-with-standards management brought about a radical change in the physical structure of the forest habitat, and therefore in the numbers and distribution of birds. It did not favour the Wood Warbler and Pied Flycatcher which like a continuous high canopy, nor the woodpeckers, Nuthatch and Treecreeper which take their food from the massive boles of mature trees. Pollarding, on the other hand, did not deprive such birds of their requirements. Some species that had existed in rather low numbers in the primaeval forest, because they need the pioneer growth along wood edges and in clearings, became vastly more abundant and widespread as coppice management increased. Year after year the practice introduced large areas of young growth and there was a greater amount of 'edge' between coupes at various stages of development, from open ground through scrub to the final thicket of low leafy canopy. The standards were given plenty of room to develop spreading crowns and fine arched limbs suitable for building timbers, and were never numerous enough to exclude light and warmth from the woodland floor. In the earlier years this encouraged a rich and varied flora of bluebells, primroses, cowslips and yellow archangel, and of course an abundant insect life. Ground-feeders like the Robin, Nightingale, Blackbird, Song Thrush and Dunnock all thrived as they had never been able to do in the dense natural forest.

The English Robin's easy and engaging familiarity, known to all gardeners, doubtless harks back to a time when Robins learned to attend the woodcutters' families as they dragged the poles together after the spring cut, disturbing insects for their feathered companions to gather. Chaffinches, which love sunlight and tall trees, found the scattered standards to their liking; Wrens scurried mouse-like through the brash and the stacked poles. Research at Ham Street Woods in Kent has shown that coppice becomes increasingly attractive to Nightingales until the canopy begins to close in about the eighth year; and there can be little doubt that the rapid decline of this marvellous songster is due in large part to the demise of active coppicing. Blue Tits, which take most of their insect food from the leaves, were at home in the dense low canopy and soon outnumbered the Great Tit, which tends to take more food from the twigs and branches and is the dominant 'high forest' species. Over much of the Continent, where more forest survived and there has not been a strong coppicing tradition, the Great Tit outnumbers the Blue, and the Robin remains a rather uncommon recluse. Coppice made excellent Pheasant covert, and the abrupt irregularities in woodland structure were well suited to the dashing, surprise hunting tactics of the Sparrowhawk.

From early mediaeval times the custom of coppicing prepared many species for the move into open countryside which the enclosures of the late eighteenth and nineteenth centuries permitted on such an enormous scale. Hedges had existed from early times, marking parish boundaries or enclosing the woods, but with the enclosures an intricate network of quickset hawthorn, elm and beech grew up. It has been estimated that these field-boundaries stretch for 600,000 miles and embrace 73 million trees — one-fifth of the standing timber of Britain in 1954. These hedgerows were really a linear coppice-with-standards, and adaptation to this new feature of the English landscape presented the woodland avifauna with absolutely no problem.

The common hedgerow species of today are precisely those which flourished best in mediaeval coppice — Robin, Wren, Chaffinch, Blackbird, Song Thrush and Dunnock. The network made available to them vast feeding areas which hitherto had been too remote from cover, and therefore too hazardous to exploit; it provided safe highways for pairs looking for nesting areas in spring, and family parties dispersing in autumn; it offered song-posts, insect food,

The coppicing of woodlands suits the Nightingale.

Oaks. The pristine British forest was dominated by oaks — the English or pedunculate oak in the midlands, east and south, and the durmast or sessile oak in the west and north. The distinction between the two species is often an academic one, since they hybridise freely, and because English oaks were often planted to replace worn-out coppice 'stools' of durmast oaks in western woods. The tallest oaks are sessile, up to 135 feet; but pedunculate oaks are usually bigger in girth, 32 feet or more. The pedunculate oak has a leaf growing almost flush with its twig, and with prominent lobes at its base. The acorns grow on a stalk. The sessile oak has a leaf-stalk or petiole but none supporting the acorn, and the leaf is without basal lobes. The sessile oak has a more open crown as the leaves are evenly spread; in the English oak they tend to be densely bunched in various parts of the tree.

Robin, Britain's 'national bird'.

and nest-sites for the excess population unable to squeeze into the crowded remnants of woodland; and the berried shrubs were an added winter food supply.

Because this centuries-long succession from high forest through coppice-with-standards to field hedgerow is unique to the English countryside, we have a variety and richness of bird-life which cannot be matched anywhere else in western Europe. And pre-adaptation to these successive changes goes far to explain why the same woodland birds are now also the dominant colonists in the newest major habitat we have created in the lowlands, the mosaic of suburban gardens on the outskirts of our cities and towns.

Hedgerows, like this one in Surrey, may be thought of as very long thin wood-lands, in terms of the wildlife which they support.

Most mammals enjoy the security offered by woods — Fox, Badger, Hedgehog, the deer and the squirrels. Apart from the last, which make nests or dreys of dead leaves and twigs, the size of a football, these mammals have their homes on or in the ground. The bird-life of a wood is influenced by many factors, not least the geographical distribution within Britain of the species themselves. Food resources are dependent upon climate, altitude, exposure, and soil and vegetation types; the availability of nesting places is determined to a large extent by the woodland structure, and this is the result of centuries of human exploitation. For some species this can be limiting, even though food is there in abundance. The historical aspect is usually more important than the kinds of trees in determining the make-up of the bird community. Almost every wood in Britain today is an artefact in the sense that the limits within which bird popula-tions can thrive have been set by man. The nature of a wood is so complex that it is true to say that no two are alike, and in no two is the bird community quite the same.

Robin and Wren are usually the most successful species in English lowland woods; Blue and Great Tits, Blackbird and Song Thrush, are high on the list. The Dunnock may be reasonably common if there is a vigorous field-layer of brambles, and secondary growth such as hazel and hawthorn attracts Bullfinch, Garden Warbler, Long-tailed Tit and a number of other species. If the wood has a 'high forest' character with a closed canopy and little secondary growth, the Great Spotted Woodpecker, Nuthatch, Treecreeper, Wood Warbler, Jay and Blackcap are likely to be there. The dominant birds are those which flourished in the old coppices; today the overspill from these highly successful and numerous species makes for a certain uniformity in the bird community, whatever the kind of wood, in the Midlands and the south.

It is quite different in oak/ash woods in Scotland; there the Chaffinch is easily the dominant bird, followed by the Wren. In the pioneer growth of birch and sallow in glades or along wood edges the Willow Warbler is important. Some woods which have been coppiced in the past — for example, those around Loch Lomond — have an intrusion of Robins and Blackbirds, and sometimes Dunnocks, but usually in western Scotland Blackbirds and Dunnocks are birds of the settlements. Characteristic birds of the western oakwoods, especially those open to grazing animals, are Wood Warbler, Redstart, Tree Pipit and (in the Lake District and Wales) Pied Flycatcher. Some relatively uncommon species like the Treecreeper, Coal Tit, Jay, Tawny Owl and Mistle Thrush are found in both types of oakwood.

The Willow Warbler, though well distributed over the country as a whole, is most abundant in the west and north. It is essentially a birch-wood bird and in many hillside birch woods in Scotland it amounts to one-third of the breeding bird community. Even among the birches on English commons it is well repre-

The Willow Warbler is the dominant breeding bird of birch woods like Crathie Wood (below) in Aberdeenshire.

sented and in good years may outnumber the Robin. Since the birch is a pioneer tree everywhere, springing up in glades opened by windthrow or felling, the Willow Warbler is much the commonest of our summer visitors.

The old Caledonian Forest of Scots pines was the home of some rather special birds and mammals, among which Capercaillie, Goshawk, Osprey, Crossbill, Crested Tit, Roe Deer and Pine Marten are worth mentioning. In the wetter west, Scots pine harbours fewer species than in the east, and it is only where it is well mixed with birch, and occasionally juniper, that a varied bird-life is found. Ash is the dominant tree in limestone regions, such as the White Peak of the southern Pennines, while beech is characteristic of the English chalk; their bird-life does not appear to differ significantly from that of the mixed oak-woods. Yew occasionally forms woods on both soils but, unless it is in mixture with ash or oak, the birds are few and include more Goldcrests and Coal Tits than are found in deciduous woods.

The generous admixture of stately conifers, mature broad-leaved trees and ornamental shrubs which we have inherited from what has been called the Great Plantation Period early in the nineteenth century harbours a rich assortment of birds. This was a time of botanical exploration and discovery and many travelling naturalists sent home seeds of exotic trees and shrubs which landowners planted in full knowledge that trees grow slowly, so that the ultimate triumph of their achievement would be for later generations to enjoy. Their unselfish foresight is worth a passing thought as we explore the parks and gardens of National Trust houses and 'stately homes'. Such places abound in that most important attribute of habitat, 'edge effect', the frequent and often abrupt change from one vegetation type to another which offers such wide opportunities for settlement by birds. The combination of a varied and abundant — and musical — bird-life with a setting of noble trees and beautiful flowering shrubs makes such gardens exciting places for the naturalist.

The Crested Tit is confined to Caledonian pine forest, such as on the shores of Loch Morlich (below) in the Cairngorms.

INTRODUCTION

When we think of wilderness, it is often moorland we see in the mind's eye, the great hills lifting the clouds, remote and brown as a desert. Indeed, the greater part of our moorland *is* man-made desert: once clothed with trees and shrubs, centuries of peat-cutting, burning and excessive grazing by sheep have reduced these uplands to the least productive habitat we have. Climate has also played a part: once the tree-cover disappeared, erosion followed quickly; and an excess of cool, sunless summers has kept the evaporation of moisture to a minimum, encouraging the growth of blanket-bogs dappled white with waving cotton-grass. Yet the very starkness of the barren scene compels admiration. Dartmoor, the Pennines, the Border Fells, the Monadhliath – each has its own special qualities of grandeur and strange, exciting beauty. As Tom Weir describes in his article on Scotland, this is the land of Red Deer and Blue Hare, and there are many splendid birds, including Dotterel, Dunlin and Golden Plover on 'the tops', and Curlew, Redshank and Lapwing lower down. The moors are where we go if we want to find Red Grouse, Ring Ousel and Wheatear.

Much of this landscape is useless, or at best marginal, for any form of agriculture, as we can readily see if we drive uphill from the Yorkshire dales, or over the Lakeland passes. Yet much of it was once fertile ground, growing trees; if you look out of the train window as it struggles across the desolate expanse of Rannoch Moor you will see the bare, blackened bones of the dead forest protruding from the bogs. Here and there fragments of the old Caledonian Forest are being rejuvenated by underplanting with young Scots pines. In Wales a lot of the hillside land is now clothed with Norway spruce and Japanese larch. Upland birch woods in parts of the Highlands will be retained within extensive new plantings of European larch and Sitka spruce. A great area of the uplands will go under the plough before the end of the century: not seeds, but seedling trees, are the new crop, and the soft mist-wreathed contours will be swallowed up by regimented rows of conifers. The soil is peaty and acid, the exposure to wind and driving rain extreme. Few trees will tolerate the harsh conditions and only one, the Sitka spruce of northwestern America, has any future on a commercial scale.

In their race to have 5 million acres of Britain afforested by the turn of the century, the Forestry Commission is planting Sitka spruce at the rate of 30,000 acres a year, and private concerns like the Economic Forestry Group are following this example. A useful tree on drier, heather-grown moor is another American, lodgepole pine, accounting for 12,000 acres a year. These two form a partnership which not only withstands the poverty of the soil and the recurrent Atlantic gales, but rapidly produces large volumes of useful timber needed for the new pulp-

Above: cotton-grass grows on a blanket-bog in the shelter of Corrie Ba, on Rannoch Moor in Perthshire.

Left: the erosion of peat reveals fragments of old fallen Caledonian pines on Rannoch Moor.

mills like the one at Corpach near Fort William. They are destined to become the forest cover of the twenty-first century over vast areas of the north and west of Britain.

A good measure of the value to wildlife of a forest is the variety of insects (and therefore of birds) which its trees will support. Generally the older native trees, like oak and birch, are the most prolific. The conifers — even our native Scots pine — come well down the list, and the introduced alien conifers are very low indeed. This Sitka spruce is a forest in search of a fauna. But Britain's timber imports are third only behind food and oil, and we must have more trees. Eventually native insects and birds will colonise but it will take time, and imaginative management is needed to speed the process. Dismal blocks of conifers could be relieved by establishing 'islands' of birch, alder and gorse at frequent intervals (and the hills would look much better for it), especially around pools, in sheltered gullies and along stream-sides. On the island of Rhum in the Hebrides the Nature Conservancy Council has shown that native trees and scrub will grow rapidly in such situations, quickly attracting Willow Warblers, Stonechats, Whinchats and Wrens. This planting on Rhum NNR is not for commercial gain, but is an experiment aimed at developing techniques for the rehabilitation of degraded uplands, by enriching the soil and increasing the 'biological turnover' through re-establishing the native woody cover. Most of the new forests are destined to be cut for pulp-wood at the very junior age of 40–50 years, and it is to be hoped that, in the interests of diversification in what might become a dull and uninspiring scene, the landowners will leave a few groups of trees here and there to grow to splendid maturity. Those who have wandered among the fells of Lapland will readily appreciate the great beauty and diversity which our own uplands have lost, but might easily regain with wise forest management.

Interestingly, ploughing in preparation for planting has the immediate effect of increasing the density of moorland birds; studies made by the British Trust for Ornithology show that the Meadow Pipit population is doubled, while more Skylarks, Snipe and Red Grouse move in. Ploughing, of course, exposes more food and creates greater shelter. As the young trees grow the rank grass around them gives cover for Short-tailed Voles, whose predators arrive. If you want to watch the magnificent hunting flight of the Hen Harrier, or the thrilling courtship display of a pair of Short-eared Owls, there is no better place than a young spruce plantation among the hills. You will see Kestrels, and perhaps a Merlin chasing the pipits — and there are always Blue Hares. There is a period in the middle age of a conifer plantation, the thicket stage after the leaf-canopy has closed in, when birds are few; but after about 25 years, and especially following the early thinnings, the plantations come to life again. The birds of prey now are Sparrowhawks and Long-eared Owls, while Goldcrests and Coal Tits dominate the smaller birds. Perhaps one of the best things that can be said about the older Sitka spruce forests is that they appear to be very attractive to Siskins, a charming greenish bird (the male black-capped) which is becoming well known in the south of England as a winter visitor to garden bird-tables.

Such forests, growing up in Scotland and Wales since the Second War, gave sanctuary to Pine Marten and Polecat just when their rapidly declining populations needed it most; and there is no doubt that they have encouraged the Buzzard and Wild Cat too. The Roe Deer and the Capercaillie, a large forest grouse which became extinct in the eighteenth century but has since been reintroduced from Sweden, have found a good home in them. New planting on lower ground encouraged the Montagu's Harrier, but this has now become one of our rarest birds, possibly due to the shooting of British-reared young when migrating in autumn through France and Spain.

The farmland which man has fashioned out of forest during the last 2,000 years is now our most important wildlife reserve. More than 80% of the land-area of Britain, some 29 million acres, supports agriculture, though about 12% of this can be considered marginal. There remains only about one-tenth of the woodland and scrub which existed when this process first began in prehistoric times, but because of the sequence of events which has brought about today's mosaic pattern of the countryside, between 80 and 85% of the birds which thrive on farms have a forest origin. The proportion is highest in the Midlands and south where this mosaic includes the fringes of woods, isolated copses and spinneys, the scrub along ditches and streams, farm-buildings and adjacent gardens and orchards, field pools, disused marl-pits, and of course that network of hedgerows — linear coppice-with-standards — dividing the fields and bordering the lanes. Since farming methods vary from region to region because of modern economics and the natural factors of soil, climate and altitude, the farm bird community differs widely from place to place.

Despite the abundance of Woodpigeons, Starlings and Rooks, bird density is much less on farms than it is in woods. The best lowland farms will have around 50 species nesting regularly, nearly twice as many as are to be found in most woods. In general, the present-day order of abundance among farm song-birds in the English lowlands is Blackbird (easily the commonest), Wren (which jumped into second place in 1973 after a long run of mild winters), Chaffinch, Dunnock, Skylark, Robin, Blue Tit, Song Thrush, Yellowhammer and Great Tit. It will be noted that only one of the top ten, the Skylark, is a bird of the open fields. In northern England it outnumbers the others, but there dry-stone

Male Red Grouse, famous gamebird of the upland moors.

Linnet, a typical farmland finch.

walls largely replace the hedges and much rough grazing or reseeded pasture has been won from the moors; so the woodland element is at a premium while the upland birds — Lapwing, Snipe, Curlew, Redshank and even Oystercatcher — are strongly in evidence.

What birds can one find on a typical lowland farm? Associated with the buildings are Barn Owl, Swift, Swallow, House Martin, Starling, House Sparrow; with the crops are the two partridges, Quail, Skylark, Corn Bunting; with the field pools, the Mallard, Moorhen, Reed and Sedge Warblers, Reed Bunting; with the rivers, Heron, Sand Martin, Kingfisher, Pied Wagtail; with the garden and orchard, Bullfinch, Greenfinch, Goldfinch, Spotted Flycatcher; with old hedgerow trees, Kestrel, Little Owl, Stockdove, Jackdaw, Green Woodpecker, Tree Sparrow; with copses and spinneys, the rookery, the woodpeckers, the thrushes, the tits, the warblers, Treecreeper and most of the common species mentioned earlier, which will also share the hedgerows with Common and Lesser Whitethroats and Linnet. The list is not exhaustive, but perhaps enough has been said to show that even if you should never set foot in a nature reserve there remains a whole world of birds awaiting discovery along the footpaths and bridleways and green country lanes.

The last decade has witnessed the growth of an agricultural revolution in England, particularly in the east but spreading to the Midlands and south, which could materially alter the numbers and distribution of many birds. The powerful effects which modern farm management can exert on bird-life made a startling impact in the early 1960s when highly toxic pesticides and weed-killers came into general use, resulting in mass 'wrecks' of birds in some areas. Concerted action on the part of the BTO and RSPB secured a 'voluntary ban' on the sowing of spring corn treated with the worst of these poisons, dieldrin and other chlorinated hydrocarbons, and later on statutory restrictions were

Lesser Whitethroat, a skulking bird of dense hedgerows and shrubberies.

The mosaic structure of English farm-land, with its hedgerows, copses and scattered trees, is well seen in this Wiltshire landscape.

imposed. But pollution of one kind or another from both agricultural and industrial sources is by no means at an end.

In some parts of England, again particularly in the east, the whole structure of farming is undergoing change from a pastoral or mixed farming to the production of cereals and root-crops such as sugar-beet, and peas and beans for the frozen food industries. The development of sophisticated and very expensive machinery has led to an increase in the size of holdings and a more highly commercialised approach, and is bringing about an increase in the size of fields to around 50 acres so that these machines can work at maximum efficiency. As a consequence, the quickset hawthorn hedges with their fine elms and oaks which have typified the English lowland scene during the past two centuries are gradually disappearing — at an estimated rate nationally of about one yard per acre per year. This same desire for greater profitability has led to a general 'tidying up' of most farms: field pools are filled in, wet rushy fields are tile-drained, scrub is cleared from odd corners, and open ditches are piped underground. The trend is towards roots and cereal production on a massive scale in a prairie countryside.

The depletion of the field hedgerow system does not mean that farm bird-life decreases by a proportional amount; a recent study of a Norfolk farm which lost one-third of its hedges in three years showed that some of the displaced birds were able to crowd into such hedges as remained, suggesting that this is a marginal habitat for most species and perhaps seldom fully occupied. Of course, there must be a limit to this kind of adjustment; but it may well be that even so drastic a reduction does less damage to bird-life than the mismanagement of hedgerows that are left. Modern cheap machine-cutting does not spare the oak, ash and elm saplings which are growing through the protective hawthorns, and when the existing trees are felled or fall they will have no successors. This is particularly unfortunate at the present time when many elms over wide tracts of the Midlands and southeast are dying from disease. Here is another development which is gradually changing the face of the English countryside which has been our pride for generations.

Our rivers and streams are under even greater threat than the land. River Authorities are concerned to 'improve' their waterways to increase the run-off from fields and so prevent undue flooding; management to this end is often overzealous, and the result is aesthetically disastrous. Reaches are deepened and straightened and made to look like canals. It is necessary to remove trees and shrubs and waterside plants to give drag-lines and other machines a chance to work. The banks are graded and bevelled and the overhangs, like the pleasant meanders, completely disappear. The recent escalation of this aspect of change is a source of grave anxiety to naturalists and country-lovers because stream birds, mammals and insects are often highly specialised, and are left with no viable alternative if their habitat is destroyed. The Sand Martins cannot make colonies in bevelled banks, and in recent years thousands must have been rendered homeless along the Trent. The Kingfisher needs the protection of an overhang for his burrow. The Common Sandpiper requires gravel beds for feeding and waterside vegetation to hide his nest. The current changes are equally disadvantageous for Water Shrew, Water Vole and Otter.

Problems arise, too, from various forms of industrial and agricultural pollution, all of which reduce the invertebrate fauna on which birds feed. Occasionally there is a brighter side, for along some streams where angling is popular deep pools are made to encourage the trout, and these are of benefit to Mallard, Moorhen, Dabchick and, in Wales and the north, the Red-breasted Merganser. They attract the Goosander, Cormorant and Heron — birds which, perhaps, the anglers feel they could well do without!

Natural wetlands have become a scarce resource all over Europe, as they are bound to do in any land which has to produce food for an expanding human population. Yet, as Ron Hickling explains in his article on the East Midlands, this very population growth has produced substitutes for the drained fens and marshes in the form of reservoirs, canals and flooded ballast pits. One of our

Dutch Elm Disease probably originated in central Asia; it was first identified in western Europe in 1918 and had reached the USA by 1930. The fungus responsible for it exists in two forms, one benign and the other much more aggressive and damaging. The latter, common in America, has been rampant in southern England and the Midlands since 1969. Two species of elm-bark beetle are vectors, flying up to the crowns with fungus spores which then attack the new shoots and, in the virulent form of DED, spread down the branches and boles into the root systems. As English elms arise from suckers growing in the protection of thorn hedgerows, the trees over a wide area soon become infected. There are an estimated 23 million elms south of a line from Monmouth to the Wash, determining the character of the English landscape, and all are currently at risk.

An elm tree showing the effects of Dutch Elm Disease.

recent colonists, the Little Ringed Plover, is almost entirely dependent on the last. Partly because of the proliferation of water-storage enterprises, the water-fowl fauna of Britain is today much more varied and abundant than it was a century ago; but the increase has also been assisted by the natural process of climatic change. During the latter part of the last century, the drying up of marshes in southeast Europe and near-Asia coincided with a climatic amelioration in northwest Europe so that many species forced to seek an extension of range found congenial conditions in our area. The Great Crested Grebe, an attractive if bizarre bird in appearance and behaviour, has managed to make valuable use of the reservoirs and flooded sand and gravel workings; the Black-headed Gull greatly expanded in numbers inland, and vast flocks now roost on many reservoirs, coming and going in impressive dusk and dawn flights. Ducks which benefited are the Tufted Duck, Pochard and Shoveler, all to be seen on most open waters, and also the less common Gadwall and Pintail. The general increase in these and other species all over northern Europe and in Iceland in this century has been reflected in the winter wildfowl gatherings on rural waters, estuaries and even in the London parks. One of the useful features of reservoirs and other waters is that, unlike woods and farms and high moors, they are most rewarding to the bird-watcher during the winter months.

Climatic change is altering the tapestry of Britain's bird-life all the time. Recent trends have been towards a southwards expansion of the polar east winds and a less vigorous atmospheric circulation over the Atlantic Ocean than we had earlier in the century. This has brought the Atlantic storm-track farther south and, because of the strong development of polar anticyclones over Scandinavia in the late winter and spring, the depressions causing the storms have also been pushed farther west. The change has coincided with a more regular appearance in this country, in greater strength than before, of a number of North American birds which, drifted out to sea from their normal migration routes, are more easily able than formerly to make a fast and direct Atlantic crossing. The meres, reservoirs, gravel-pits and estuaries are the places to look for them, in September and October: the Pectoral, White-rumped and Buff-breasted Sandpipers are the most likely, but keen and knowledgeable observation might turn up any one of a score of other waders or ducks.

The more persistent springtime anticyclone over the Scandinavian peninsula

The random and natural ecology of the unimproved River Camel (left) is obviously beneficial to waterside breeders, whereas tidily bevelled banks (right) suit few birds and mammals.

The fish-eating Cormorant.

has had another important effect on our birds. Because the anticyclone has an easterly airstream on its southern side, a number of migrant species on their way home to Sweden and Finland in spring are getting displaced to Scotland where, finding similar conditions to those at home, they are settling down. The keen bird-watcher, moving through Sutherland and Wester Ross, can hardly fail to see and hear the Redwing, a northern thrush now well established in that part of Scotland. In some places its larger, greyer relative the Fieldfare is now nesting, and on one or two lochs the Goldeneye has become a breeding duck. The Wood Sandpiper is another Scandinavian which may well have entered Scotland to stay. There can be little doubt that recent recolonisation by the Osprey, though the species has enjoyed protection, has a climatic cause, for its increase has been dramatic in recent years.

In England, too, some changes are manifest. Two new marshland birds from France are Savi's and Cetti's Warblers, and there is a wild canary — the Serin; at present they are few and all have a restricted distribution in East Anglia and the south. The Firecrest also came from the Continent; it has been here more than a decade now and its distribution in maturing conifer plantations is doubtless more widespread than is at present known. On the reverse side of the coin, a deterioration in our summer weather may cost us the Wryneck and the Red-backed Shrike before the end of the century. A selection of our summer visitors such as the Common Whitethroat, Redstart, Sedge Warbler, Swallow, Sand and House Martins, are suffering the adverse effects of a serious drought in their main wintering and springtime fattening region in the Sahel Zone on the southern fringe of the Sahara Desert, and they are less numerous than they were in the late 1960s.

If we stop by the roadside in the west of Scotland to look closely at the shaggy Highland Cattle we can glimpse something of the past splendour of our native beasts; for, with their wide upswept horns and long dun coats to throw off the rain and snow, they are the lineal descendants of the wild oxen which roamed Britain when Neolithic man was taking hesitant steps to establish a farming economy. Together with their lords and masters, the Celts, they were pushed ever northwards towards the inhospitable, undesired margins by successive invaders, and during centuries of comparative isolation have retained much of

Part of Marsworth Reservoir near Tring in Hertfordshire, where Herons breed, unusually, in the reedbeds. The expanse of open water is attractive to water birds of many species at all seasons.

The numbers of the Common Whitethroat, measured by the BTO's 'Common Bird Census' index of 100 in 1966, reached a peak in 1968 and then slumped dramatically to a low point from which there was no sign of a recovery prior to 1975. The decline is believed to be due to the onset of drought conditions in its winter quarters on the southern fringe of the Sahara Desert.

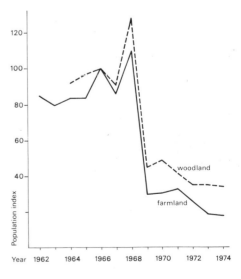

their original beauty and dignity. There can be little doubt that they gain stature from the rugged asperity of their spartan setting, but in their turn they wonderfully embellish this wilderness of rolling moor and cloud-wreathed mountain.

There are other domesticated and feral animals which are well worth a few minutes of the time we devote to our quest for the creatures of the countryside. It is curious how the value of a word can change. When we say 'feral' we imply a creature once domesticated, designed by man to fulfil a specific need, but now returned to nature; the tag has a quality of denigration as though, compared with a truly wild beast, a feral animal is a second-class citizen. Perhaps those relics of the old Caledonian Forest, the White Park Cattle of the Chillingham herd, are too majestic and dignified to fit snugly into this category, but it is a kind of limbo to which we consign our Soay Sheep of St Kilda, Manx Loghtans, and the numerous herds of goats which grace the fells and bring excitement to the craggy sea-cliffs of the north. In Britain, with her impoverished fauna of large mammals, it would be as well to return to the *Oxford English Dictionary* sense of 'feral', something 'wild, untamed, uncultivated'. They are all entirely acceptable as integral units of our faunal heritage.

Perhaps more ancient than any of these, in the sense of being unimproved, is the Soay Sheep — no whit changed today, judging by studies of its skeleton, from animals shepherded by our Neolithic forbears. For much more than a millennium it lived almost unmolested on the grassy top of uninhabited Soay in the St Kilda Islands, the most isolated, most desolate, most inaccessible refuge. James Fisher called it 'a living fossil'. The St Kildans made no effort to introduce new blood; occasionally they climbed ashore and hunted a few sheep with their dogs, for sport; and when they abandoned St Kilda in 1930, the Marquis of Bute, who then owned the islands, took a group of animals out of this cold storage and gave them the run of the main island of Hirta, where their numbers now hover around the thousand mark. They have been introduced as a novelty to a number of zoos, farm parks and similar places on the mainland.

We ought certainly to give a higher ranking among our faunal treasures to domesticated animals, those creatures with which man has been most closely associated throughout time. He has made them what they are today, often by selective breeding with a conscious aim of improving the stock for wool, for meat, for speed, for ornament in his parks, for draught or as bearers of burdens. But why the great multiplicity of breeds, even in one particular species? This perplexed Charles Darwin and he gave an additional reason in the introduction to his *The Variation of Animals and Plants Under Domestication*, '. . . man, without any intention or thought of improving the breed, by preserving in each successive generation the individuals which he prizes most, and by destroying the worthless individuals, slowly, though surely, induces great changes. As the will of man thus comes into play, we can understand how it is that domesticated breeds show adaptation to his wants and pleasures.' Thus there is hardly a region of our land that does not have (or has had in the recent past) some distinctive animal whose form and colouring reflect the cumulative foibles of generations of local farmers and breeders.

Alas, many of these breeds have become very rare, falling by the wayside in the rat-race quest for the quickest fattener, the best lean-meat carcase, the most prolific milker, and so on. Only within recent years has a strong effort been made to secure for posterity small groups of these almost forgotten animals. The wish to preserve such breeds is often a sentimental one, but beyond that is the entirely practical aim of preserving a gene-bank on which livestock breeders may draw in the event that requirements should change, and something that our forefathers built up painstakingly over generations of selective breeding will again have a value to society. Once a breed is lost its genetic material disappears forever, and we are back to square one in the search for its particular characteristics; and a not inconsiderable reason for wanting to retain them is that such animals reflect a way of life, a historical and cultural achievement, of the British people.

England's mediaeval wool trade was largely founded on the heavy fleeces of the Cotswold Sheep, and the fine abbeys, manor houses and churches of the west Midlands owe much to them. The Lincoln Longwool played a similar

A four-horned ram of the Loghtan breed, which exists in a semi-wild state on the Calf of Man.

The Soay Sheep is descended from the Mouflon or Wild Sheep; until 1930, the only place in the world where it existed was on the tiny island of Soay in the St Kilda archipelago, 50 miles outside the Outer Hebrides of Scotland.

role. The almost extinct Norfolk Horn is a product of the impoverished Brecklands; the Woodland Whiteface was evolved to combat the rigours of the southern Pennines. At nearly opposite extremes of the British Isles are the small Portland Sheep (whose progenitors are said to have swum ashore from a wrecked Spanish Armada vessel), and the ecologically fascinating North Ronaldsay breed which, confined *outside* the perimeter wall of their home island, subsist mainly on seaweed. For one good reason or another these and many others are unique to our native fauna, and should compel our attention and sympathetic care. The Cotswold Farm Park and Stoneleigh Farm and Country Centre are among the places where they can be seen and enjoyed.

Some animals and birds are not native to this country, but were introduced to fill a real or imagined human need; a few were commercial fur-bearers, others objects of the chase. There is considerable dissension among naturalists concerning the morality of introductions. Some consider it is wrong to 'interfere with nature' in this way; but then, are we not interfering with nature all the time? We are continually manipulating natural environments and creating new 'ecosystems'; should we deliberately exclude non-native birds and mammals which might help to put these systems in balance? Because of the shrinking numbers and ranges of many animals due to human mismanagement of our planet's natural resources, ought we not to afford endangered species the opportunity to acclimatise to such newly created habitats as seem appropriate?

A long-fleeced Woodland Whiteface ram: this breed was developed to withstand the hardship of life in the Pennine hills.

Whatever we may think, however, introductions should not be lightly undertaken; many in the past have proved detrimental to the native fauna and to man's own interests. Introductions from one major geographical region of the world into another seem to have been particularly hazardous, as when homesick colonists took English song-birds to New Zealand, where, being pre-adapted to farm and suburban conditions, they successfully excluded native birds. Cats, dogs, rats, mongooses and pigs released by man have wrought havoc on islands dotted around the globe, and have brought about the extinction of several endemic rails and other birds. Those birds which have proved to be the most successful commensals with man, the House Sparrow and Starling, have gone with him to the New World and beyond to Australasia, but not always as welcome guests.

The Grey Squirrel came to Britain from eastern North America, and has replaced the admittedly more handsome native Red Squirrel over most of England; more recently, the continental Red Squirrel, let loose in Epping Forest, seems to be recovering some of the lost ground. The Red-legged Partridge, introduced as a sporting bird, has spread from East Anglia as far as Dorset and the West Midlands, and is an entirely acceptable embellishment to our avifauna. Such exciting exotic creatures as Golden and Lady Amherst's Pheasants, Mandarin Duck and Red-crested Pochard, have become established locally as wild birds without apparently offending anyone; and we may soon have to accept wild-living populations of the Bobwhite Quail in East Anglia and the Ring-necked Parrakeet in the Kent and Surrey suburbs of London. A generation ago the Little Owl was still unwelcome and its rapid spread was viewed with alarm, but the population seems now to have stabilised and it is clearly not displacing a native owl.

Small populations of the Golden Pheasant have existed in the wild in one or two parts of Britain for several decades.

The Fat Dormouse is confined to a relatively small part of the Chilterns country around Tring, where it was first released; as it is already damaging young conifer plantations, farmers and foresters hope it will go no farther. The small, podgy Muntjac Deer which escaped from captivity at Woburn Park in the same part of the country about 1890 has spread somewhat farther into the Home Counties, and to Warwickshire, Dorset and Gwent. Escaped herds of Sika Deer cause concern in the Lake District and southern Ireland, because they will interbreed with Red Deer and so a native gene-pool is at risk. The Ministry of Agriculture, Fisheries and Food has managed to eliminate the Musk Rat from East Anglia and the Porcupine from Devon, but the Mink and that giant rodent the Coypu have defied man's war against them.

It is difficult to draw a clear line between introduction and natural establishment or re-establishment in these days of spirited protection and conservation.

Many native ducks have had their numbers increased by the Wildfowlers' Association of Great Britain and Ireland, as an insurance against inroads made by the guns. Falconers are known to have released Goshawks deliberately in the hope that they will breed and eventually provide young birds which can be taken for training. Some years ago single pairs of Osprey and Snowy Owl settled of their own accord in Scotland, but it is questionable if either would have become fully established without stringent protective measures organised by the RSPB, which included fostering of public sympathy through the mass-media. These are entirely laudable events like those other RSPB triumphs, the revival of British populations of Avocet, Ruff and Black-tailed Godwit at Havergate, Minsmere and the Ouse Washes.

There is always a chance that careless surveillance of animals in the smaller zoos and safari parks will put creatures of the countryside at risk, but on the whole such escapees have done much less harm than releases which have emanated from fur farms and the whims of rich landowners. Individual birds like the pink flamingos, which have a habit of showing up at sewage-farms and marshland reserves, merely add a little strangeness and colour to the familiar scene. Zoo escapes often remain very localised, as with the wallabies in the southern Pennines, and the Night Herons which nest in the trees of Edinburgh Zoological Gardens and fly down to the Forth to feed. We have said that zoos afford us an intimacy with a wide range of animals that we could not otherwise hope to encounter (it is certainly a privilege to be able to watch Pandas in Regent's Park), and therefore their educational function is great.

Many birds and mammals the world over are facing the threat of extinction; they are listed in the *Red Data Books* of the Survival Service Commission of the International Union for Nature Conservation (IUCN) — frighteningly massive documents. The most important zoos have research projects aimed at establishing successful captive breeding conditions for rare animals. Some zoos have achieved success with one species, some with another; but not all animals take kindly to a life behind bars, and some are proving intractable. This only increases the challenge and, in spite of the frustrations, such projects will always loom large in the zoos' contribution to scientific research and conservation.

Captive breeding has two important end-results: firstly, to raise sufficient stock to be able to return some of it to the wild; secondly, to have enough animals to share with other zoos, so reducing the collecting pressure on wild populations. Complete success is not realised until both aims have been met; but of course it is no use returning Oryx to Saudi Arabia or Swinhoe's Pheasants to Taiwan unless the animals are assured of a large enough reserve to enable them to continue successful reproduction under natural conditions. Politics complicate the issue, for in many of the smaller and poorer countries national parks tend to get a low priority. There have been success stories, and there will be more. In England the Wildfowl Trust saved the Nene, the Hawaiian Goose, from extinction and re-established a viable population in a new reserve on one of the islands; the Pheasant Trust has succeeded in breeding and translocating some Asiatic species of pheasants. The knowledge and expertise being gained by many zoos will at least defer the disappearance of many animal forms; and we must hope that man's growing need for true wildlife contact will be able to capitalise on this situation eventually in all the corners of the world.

The Ring-necked Parrakeet's natural range is in sub-tropical Africa and India; but recently, following escapes from captivity, groups of this parrot species have established themselves in London's suburbs, where they are nesting successfully in holes in trees.

South West England FRANK CLAFTON

The appearance of sign-boards in every town and village proffering Cream Teas or Clotted Cream by Post will signify to the traveller that he has arrived in the West Country. They epitomise the dual industries of the southwest peninsula of England — agriculture and tourism. The region is characterised by undulating farmland, mercifully still interlaced with substantial hedges and copses, for here the grubbing-out of scrub in the interests of farming productivity is progressing only slowly and is, no doubt, tempered by the necessity to provide wind-breaks. Some of these farms, particularly along the Stour and other Dorset rivers, are richly endowed with birds. Their double hedgerows, crocheted with tall trees, have a dark tunnel running between, a wonderful highway for Fox and Badger; they seem more attractive than hedgerows elsewhere to strictly woodland birds, so that there are many Chiffchaffs, Blackcaps and Garden Warblers. Inland, large areas of urbanisation are few and modern development has tended towards only a marginal expansion in what were, and in most cases remain, local market towns.

On the coast the picture is very different. The equable climate, the beaches and sheltered coves and the estuaries beloved by the yachtsman have attracted both the tourist and those seeking the best of Britain's notorious weather for a comfortable retirement. As a result the centres of population, such as Bournemouth and Torbay, are dominated by tower blocks of flats, substantial hotels and innumerable smaller private ones, surrounded by bungalow estates of considerable size, and often with a final periphery of caravan and chalet camps to provide a cheaper and less rigid mode of holiday, but with reasonable access to shops and entertainment. The resultant sprawl does nothing to enhance the area scenically, and were it to continue would engulf the coastline in all but its inaccessible stretches. Fortunately, the planning authorities are aware of the dangers and development sites are at a premium. The resident human population is quite small by nationwide standards, but it is often trebled or quadrupled during the peak of the holiday season, July to September, when roads tend to become over-busy and progress can be slow.

Although lacking the grandeur of mountain ranges, the West Country can still claim some of the finest scenery in Britain. Having escaped glaciation in the Ice Ages, the river valleys, although steep in places, lack the deep scouring found in more northerly parts. The evidence of raised beaches, at a comparatively low level, reveals that many of the estuaries are in fact river valleys drowned by the rise in sea-level which followed the 'Climatic Optimum' around 5000 BC. The absence of glaciated rock erosion and the consequent blockage of moraines has had the effect of leaving the region without natural lakes of any size, but man-made reservoirs are now tending to remedy this, to the advantage of the naturalist and the birds.

The general flow of the hills is soft but there is no monotony. In the southeast of the region, the heaths of the Poole Basin mirror many of the specialised species of the New Forest. Here in the close-knit 'islands' of gorse on windswept heather moors the tiny long-tailed Dartford Warbler has its stronghold, its survival a constant struggle against man's encroachment upon what has been considered wasteland useful only for afforestation or urban development; Dorset, in fact, has lost 10,000 acres of its heaths in the last 14 years. The near elimination of this species in two severe winters in the early 1960s highlights the necessity to preserve sufficient suitable habitat, and the existence of several National Nature Reserves in the area, as well as the RSPB reserve at Arne, indicates the seriousness of the threat.

Two other small birds, the Woodlark and Cirl Bunting, whose range in England has retreated markedly in this century, can now be considered specialities of the southwest peninsula: the Woodlark, a beautiful songster, is dependent upon these fragmented heaths, but the Cirl Bunting has a more catholic choice of habitat which embraces field hedgerows and the agricultural edge of suburbia.

Frank Clafton is Curator of the Portland Museum, Dorset. He was Warden of Bardsey Bird and Field Observatory, 1961–62, and of Portland Bird Observatory, 1963–75. He is Chairman of the Dorset Field Ornithology Group and Chairman of the Bird Observatories Council, and edited the *Dorset Bird Report* from 1967 to 1974.

Female Blackcap (top) incubates; male later feeds the young.

Opposite: the valley of the River Camel above Wadebridge, where the grubbing-out of scrub is progressing only slowly.

21

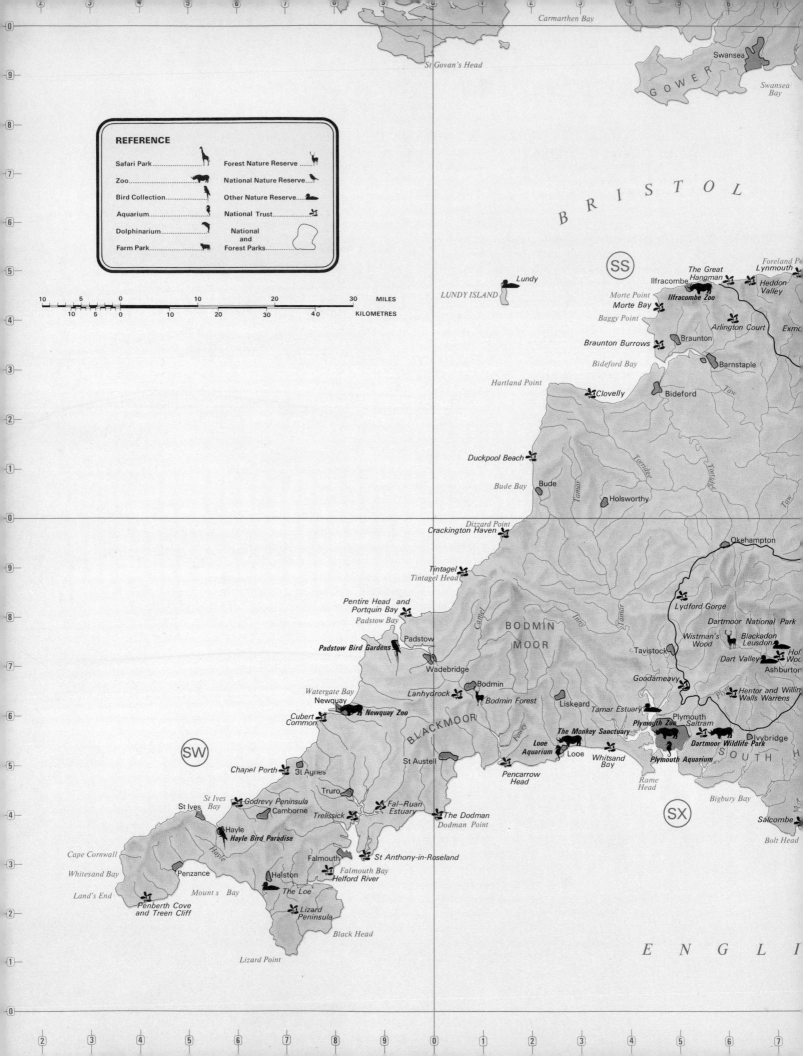

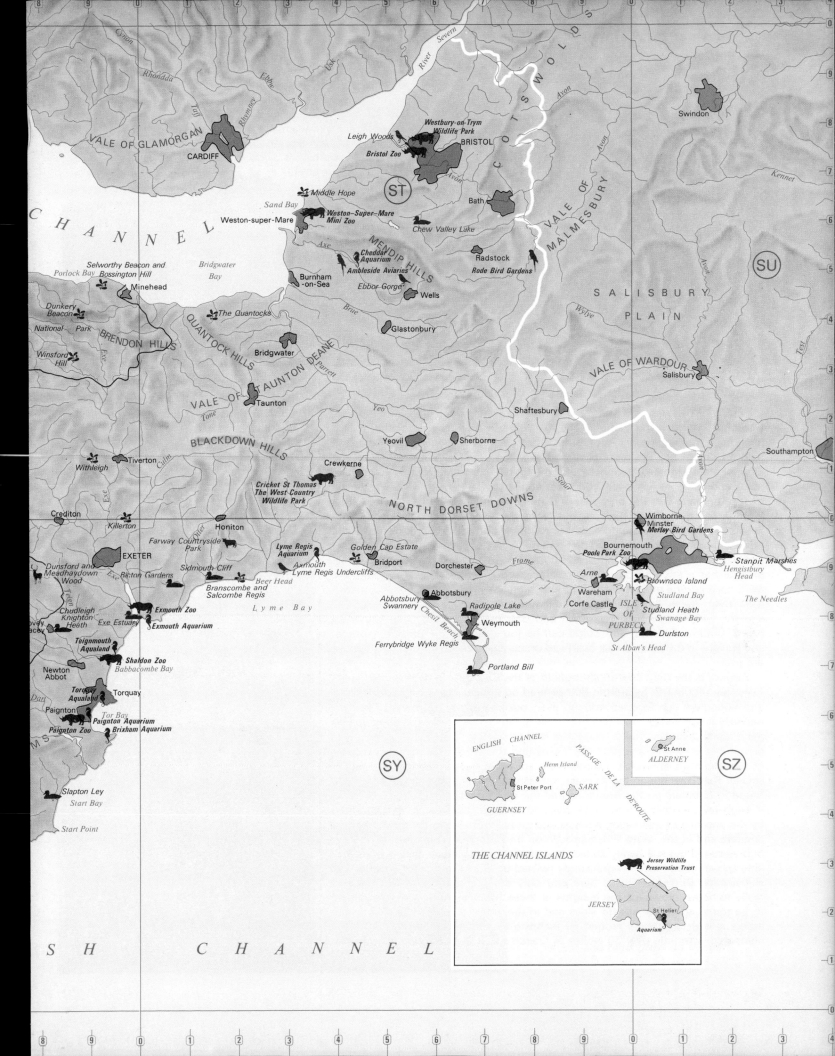

There is endless variety in structure and even in colour — the yellow sandstone, the white chalk west of Lulworth in Dorset, the light grey limestones and granites, and the dark grey Devonian. Along much of their length these cliffs stand like battlements, shattering the great Atlantic rollers into a million misty particles which drench the cliff-top grass, producing a sward of inimitable green. It is intended that there shall be a coastal footpath running the whole length of the peninsula, and long sections are already in use, making access to this wonderful coast easy.

At one time, Peregrines occupied all the suitably sheer cliffs until the sad decline of this species, apparently through its consumption of bird-prey carrying toxic contaminants, in the late 1950s. Happily, a tiny nucleus survived and would seem now to be on the road to recovery, so that the cliff walker still has a reasonable chance of seeing this most magnificent of the falcons, especially along the north Devon coast. The decline and ultimate disappearance of the Cornish population of the Chough is more difficult to explain. It occupied a number of cliffs on the north Cornwall coast, particularly near Boscastle, until 1971, but the reappearance of two birds in Cornwall in 1974 gives a glimmer of hope even now.

Wherever the topography of the cliffs prevents excessive human disturbance there remain seabird colonies of substantial size. The Herring Gull is ubiquitous, breeding not only on the cliffs but also on buildings, even in urban areas, such as the Wyke Regis district of Weymouth where gulls' nests may be seen on house chimney-stacks and on factory roofs. It has even been reported nesting in a tree. Its larger relative the Great Black-backed Gull is also widespread, but in much smaller numbers. That more delicate sea-going gull, the Kittiwake, has several breeding stations on the mainland, notably at St Agnes Head on the north Cornish coast where over 1,000 pairs are present. Smaller colonies may be seen at Durlston Head and Portland Bill in Dorset, at Berry Head and Hope's Nose in Torbay, at Scabbacombe Head in Devon, and on Gull Rock in Veryan Bay and Mullion Island in Cornwall. The superficially gull-like Fulmar can now be seen gliding on rigid horizontal wings around almost every cliff in the region, having performed a remarkable spread from the north within living memory. It now breeds at many sites in all three counties and is prospecting at countless others each spring.

The auk colonies undoubtedly stand now at only a fraction of their former strength. Cliff disturbance due to increased human pressure as man has become so much more mobile has no doubt had some effect; but pollution in the sea, particularly through oil spillage, is probably the major factor as this family of birds seems most prone to contamination. Cleaning centres where volunteers soldier on with the prolonged task of rehabilitation have been established at a number of places, but it is exacting work and the number of successful releases is depressingly small, bearing in mind that only a fraction of the birds contaminated ever reach a bird-hospital alive. Both the Guillemot and Razorbill are widespread and can be seen sharing cliffs with the Kittiwakes, as well as at other places, for instance around Combe Martin in north Devon. The Puffin's strangely comical face is more difficult to find on mainland sites and the watcher has often to be satisfied with views of these birds swimming and diving around the few remaining colonies, such as those along the Purbeck (Dorset) coast between Swanage and St Aldhelm's Head, and at Lye Rock off Tintagel (Cornwall). Cormorants and Shags can be seen throughout the year and there are a number of breeding stations.

In places where the cliffs are less severe and where landslips have occurred there is often a naturally developed scrub vegetation difficult to reach. The patient watcher can scan these patches from above and will often be rewarded by excellent views of Foxes, Badgers and Roe Deer, all taking advantage of the peaceful seclusion. Cliff-top watching will also reveal the presence of Grey Seals which still breed on the mainland of the north Cornish coast around Portreath.

The seabird enthusiast may use one of a number of watch-points for views of birds which do not breed in the area but which pass by, often in spectacular

Puffins at their grassy cliff-top colony.

Peregrines. Between 1930 and 1939 there are believed to have been over 700 Peregrines' eyries in Britain. A BTO census in 1971 revealed only 341 of these in occupation (54%) and only 157 with young birds (25%). Low as these figures are, they represent a distinct improvement on a previous census in 1963, when the figures were 44% and 16% respectively. The chief factor causing mortality and reducing breeding success is contamination of prey by persistent toxic chemical residues, such as dieldrin and DDT, widely used during the 1950s and early 1960s in agriculture. The first stages of the recovery noted in 1971 reflect an improvement in the quality of the environment following bans on the use of these chemicals; but coastal Peregrines of the north and west are still suffering from contamination of their seabird prey by PCBs and other industrial pollutants released into the marine food-chain.

D. A. Ratcliffe, *The Peregrine in Great Britain in 1971*, BTO.

A breeding colony of Herring Gulls and Shags on the Scilly island of Annet.

Adult Kittiwake at its nest on a narrow cliff ledge.

numbers, at migration times or in stormy weather. Sites which have proved well worth watching are Portland Bill in Dorset, Start Point and Prawle Point in south Devon, The Lizard and Cape Cornwall near Land's End, St Ives Island in Cornwall, and Hartland, Morte and Baggy Points in north Devon. Gannets, glinting white in the sunlight even a long distance out to sea, are regular passers-by, and the more fortunate and perhaps more patient watcher will see the dark, pigeon-sized Manx Shearwaters scudding close to the wave-tops. The Great Skua, brown and as big as a Buzzard, and its two lesser relatives, the Pomarine and Arctic Skuas, are strong possibilities; and there is a variety of terns on passage, the black Common Scoter and other winter sea-ducks, the small Storm or Leach's Petrels and even, if you are lucky, one of the rarer shearwaters. Por-poises and dolphins can be seen with some regularity from most headlands.

To the naturalist who is not restricted to the mainland, visits to two offshore islands can be highly recommended. Lundy (NT) lies in the Bristol Channel and can be visited in summer by steamer from Ilfracombe. It holds good seabird colonies including Puffins, Fulmars and Kittiwakes; in addition, Lundy is renowned for its Bird Observatory, producing rare vagrant species at migration times. It has a little sparse woodland and a veritable forest of rhododendrons, where Sika Deer lie up in daytime, along its eastern coast. There are a number of semi-domesticated animals living in a feral state, such as Soay Sheep and Wild Goats.

The Scilly Isles require a visit of longer duration but offer ample accommoda-tion, and there is ready access by boat between the islands. They are 28 miles southwest of Land's End and are fully exposed to the Atlantic weather. However, they exemplify the climatic conditions of the West Country, being warmed but moistened by the Gulf Stream. The winters are mild with rare snowfalls and frosts are unusual, hence the early bulb- and potato-growing industries. To the bird-watcher, the most interesting islands are St Mary's, Tresco and St Agnes. Annet has fine seabird colonies including Manx Shearwaters, Puffins and Storm

Petrels but, for the protection of the birds, this island is closed to visitors during the breeding season. There are accessible seabird colonies on other islands and outlying rocks, however, and a summer holiday will yield fine memories when the coast is far away. The Scillies have earned a great reputation for rare vagrants at migration times both from the east and the west. A number of American waders are seen annually and the islands can claim a considerable list of 'firsts' for Britain, including several American wood warblers. They share with Jersey and Sark in the Channel Islands the distinction of having the only British population of the Lesser White-toothed Shrew, the Scilly shrews holding sub-specific rank.

The beaches of the West Country must of necessity be given over to the holiday-maker for much of the year, and only in a few less accessible spots may one find beach-nesting birds such as Common or Little Terns and Ringed Plovers. The privately owned Chesil Beach in west Dorset still holds healthy colonies and amply demonstrates how conservation can preserve a sample of the avifauna. A cross-section of all its breeding birds can be seen well enough from the public car park at the eastern end of the beach, without the necessity to encroach into the nesting area.

Although no individual estuary in the region can claim to be of national importance as a wintering ground for wildfowl and waders, this type of habitat is so frequent in the peninsula that collectively a population of great size is supported. No single estuary can be selected as typical but a list of those that are interesting to the bird-watcher must include Christchurch harbour, Poole harbour, the Axe, the Exe, the Teign, the Tamar-Tavy, the Fal, the Hayle, the Camel and the Taw-Torridge. Similar conditions are also found in the Fleet, behind Chesil Beach, and at Salcombe-Kingsbridge, although neither is a true estuary in the strict sense. In estuary-watching it is essential to know the tides, and some familiarity is necessary in order to know which particular stretches are favoured by birds at specific stages of the tide. Naturally, the winter months are the most interesting, although the periods of both spring and autumn migration will yield sightings of waders on passage, particularly birds like Wood Sandpipers and Spotted Redshanks.

Brent Geese winter in Poole harbour and on the Exe, and the Tamar has a

American vagrants. Since they lie closer to the North Atlantic storm-track than any other part of Britain, the Scilly Islands and the southwest peninsula provide our most regular landfall for 'lost' American birds. The Scillies claim the only British records of the American Purple Gallinule (a large relative of the Moorhen), Nighthawk, Northern Waterthrush and Bobolink. Altogether ten species of New World song-birds — nearly half the number listed for Britain — have turned up in the Scillies, and the islands can boast 15 out of a score or so of vagrant American waders. It used to be thought that most American birds were unable to fly the Atlantic unaided and must get 'assisted passage' on ships; but it is now generally accepted that even the small ones do cross regularly, aided by strong westerly winds. A marked increase in the incidence of American vagrants during the last 15 years has coincided with a southwestwards displacement of the mean path taken by Atlantic depressions, giving a shorter and more direct wind-drifted route to this part of Britain.

Poole harbour at low tide: an Oyster-catcher feeds in company with Black-headed Gulls.

Groups of feeding Shelducks (left) are a familiar sight in winter on estuary mud. Right: Sanderlings (foreground) and Turnstones forced to crowd together by the rising tide.

regular flock of Avocets, probably from the Suffolk breeding colonies. Wigeon outnumber all other ducks, with particularly large numbers on the Fleet and the Exe, their shrill whistling calls echoing across the water both by day and by moonlight. Teal, Mallard, Pintail and Shoveler are well represented. Goldeneyes dive in the deeper channels, often associating with Red-breasted Mergansers. The dominant waders are Curlew, Redshank and Dunlin. Both Black-tailed and Bar-tailed Godwits are present, the former (mostly from Iceland) utilising this region for wintering to a far greater extent than anywhere else in Britain. Some waders seem to oscillate between the estuaries and the deserted beaches and rocks exposed at low tide, particularly Turnstones, Grey Plovers, Oystercatchers and Sanderlings, whilst Ringed Plovers will usually be found both on the beaches and on estuarine mud regardless of tide. A few Greenshanks are present throughout the winter in all the major estuaries.

On the sea at the estuary mouth careful scanning will usually reveal the presence of wintering divers, grebes and Eiders. Great Crested Grebes are quite widely distributed and both Black-necked and Slavonian Grebes are concentrated at some points, for instance at Poole and the Exe. The birds are usually present until well into April, and the watcher who looks for them late in the season will have the added pleasure of seeing birds well advanced in their colourful summer plumage. The distribution and numerical status of the three species of divers off southwest coasts are still not well defined, but mid-winter flighting of numbers occasionally running into hundreds has been observed at some headlands, and there is an eastward movement of Red-throated and Black-throated Divers up the English Channel in April.

In summer the estuaries change in character. The heady, shimmering air makes clear, long-distance vision difficult. Parent Shelducks and Mute Swans steer their families out of the paths of dinghies and the muddy shores are almost devoid of waders, becoming now the province of the stalking Heron, whilst the adjoining reedbeds ring with the mechanical rattle of Reed and Sedge Warblers. But the high summer period is short as the last spring migrants have barely gone before the first of the autumn waders return, and soon there is excitement for the watcher as he searches for the early Little Stint or Curlew Sandpiper on its way from the Arctic, or perhaps even an Osprey or Spoonbill or one of the rarer herons, such as the all-white Little Egret, which appear annually in the West Country.

In any present-day review of the fauna of a region there is a tendency to over-stress that which has been lost and to forget the gains. In the West Country, conservation organisations, both national and local, have been vigorously active. The latter include the Cornwall Naturalists' Trust, Devon Trust for Nature

Drake Wigeon, the most numerous wintering duck of the estuaries of the southwest.

Conservation, Somerset Trust for Nature Conservation, and the Dorset Naturalists' Trust. The Walmsley Sanctuary on the Camel estuary, the property of the Cornwall Bird-watching and Preservation Society, is one of the longest established and holds a wintering flock of White-fronted Geese; it is the only regular haunt of grey geese in the region. Some of the gains which have become apparent recently, such as the increasingly regular breeding of the Siskin, Lesser Redpoll, Firecrest and Serin, may well be due to climatic factors. A series of mild winters since 1963 has revealed surprising numbers of Chiffchaffs and Blackcaps (which normally migrate to the Mediterranean countries) utilising coastal gardens and scrub, these tree-loving warblers frequently dropping to the ground in their perpetual search for insects. At this time of year they may hop on heaps of rotting seaweed in some south-facing sheltered coves, mingling with Black Redstarts, Stonechats, Rock Pipits and Pied Wagtails.

Persistent efforts are being made to research fully into the strange life-cycle of the Large Blue butterfly which relies upon ants to adopt and feed its caterpillars. Its population has been reduced to a precarious level, confined to Devon and Cornwall, but its decline may well be unconnected with man's activities. Visitors to the southwest are agreeably surprised by the wealth of butterflies still to be found, an indication of the favourable climate but more particularly of the retention of natural grassland beneath the hedgerows, along the precarious cliff-edges and on some of the high, steep-sided escarpments. Here, species like the Marsh and Dark Green Fritillaries and the electric-shaded Adonis Blue may be seen, and the more drably coloured Wall and Grayling abound. Migratory species like the Painted Lady and Red Admiral occur in substantial numbers in most years, whilst the exciting Clouded Yellow sometimes arrives in strength in the late summer and autumn. The County Naturalists' Trusts have done much to preserve the general abundance of butterflies by the creation of small reserves where specialised food-plants are common, and also by negotiating with local councils the specially timed cutting of roadside verges.

The Marsh Fritillary, a rare butterfly of patchy distribution in Britain, may be seen in southwest England.

Studland Heath National Nature Reserve, an ever-expanding sand-dune system with lakes at the mouth of Poole harbour.

No catalogue of sites of interest to the wildlife enthusiast in the West Country could hope to be fully comprehensive, but some areas are particularly important. In the southwest, Poole can boast the second largest natural harbour in the world and it possesses an astonishing diversity of interests. The harbour mouth may be crossed by car-ferry to reach Studland Heath NNR, based on an ever-expanding sand-dune system which has isolated a chain of freshwater but rather acid lakes which support good numbers of diving and surface-feeding ducks in winter. The Poole Basin heaths hold the bulk of the small British populations of the harmless Smooth Snake and the Sand Lizard.

Brownsea Island, situated centrally in Poole harbour and open to the public from Easter until the end of September, is owned by the National Trust with a substantial portion leased as a nature reserve by the Dorset Naturalists' Trust. The large, shallow lagoon inside the reserve has ducks and waders bustling about their business, and tiny islands built by voluntary labour hold flourishing colonies of Common and sometimes Sandwich Terns. The heronry is among the largest in the country. But perhaps Brownsea's greatest joy is its Red Squirrels. Untroubled by competition from the introduced Greys, the Red Squirrels revel in the isolation given by the island and seem able to maintain a population level high enough for the animals to be seen without difficulty. The Arne reserve (RSPB) may be visited by permit and gives a fairly certain promise of views of Dartford Warblers (and perhaps of a Hobby), as well as a fine cross-section of heath and estuarine birds.

The Weymouth and Portland area of south Dorset is another Mecca for the bird-watcher. The Bird Observatory at the Old Lower Light at Portland Bill has a history spanning 25 years of intensive migration study and is an excellent watch-point for the movements of seabirds and for gatherings of migrant land-birds, the 'island' list containing first British records of the Calandra Lark and Desert Warbler amongst many other rarities. At Ferrybridge, at the base of the isthmus joining Portland to the 'mainland', waders and terns can be well seen, and good views can be had across Portland harbour where Red-breasted Mergansers, grebes and divers gather in winter. In the heart of Weymouth is Radipole Lake, another reserve on which the ducks reward man for the protection he gives them by becoming particularly confiding and easy to see. The reedbeds hold a healthy number of Bearded Reedlings (which colonised in 1965) and, in summer, Reed and Sedge Warblers. Study has revealed that the lake is utilised by very large numbers of these two species as a resting place on passage, individually marked birds from many other parts of England having been found there whilst preparing for the next stage of their journey to distant African wintering areas; amongst them small numbers of the rare Aquatic Warbler from across the English Channel have been found in recent autumn seasons.

The Poole Basin heaths form the British headquarters of two scarce reptiles. Above: the very timid Sand Lizard. Below: a pair of water-loving Smooth Snakes.

Within easy reach of Weymouth are the marshes at Lodmoor where waders and terns on passage are interesting, and occasionally one of the rarer herons and wintering Bitterns may be seen. To the westward are the Fleet shores and, at the western end of the Fleet, the unique Abbotsbury Swannery, which is open to the public throughout the summer months. The precise origin of this colonial-breeding herd of Mute Swans is not known, but there are records of its existence in the fourteenth century, and at peak periods as many as 1,500 birds have been present. Without doubt it was created for culinary purposes, but the swans now enjoy rigid protection.

Of all the south Devon estuaries, the Exe must have pride of place if for no other reason than for the sheer quantity of birds it supports, particularly through the winter. Along its five miles it exhibits a classic gradient in plant communities relative to salt tolerance, with a healthy eel-grass growth on the estuary floor providing food for all ducks, geese and swans which utilise this National Wildfowl Refuge. Wigeon sometimes exceed 5,000 and Brent Geese, mainly the dark-bellied Siberian race, regularly reach a three-figure total. At the mouth of the estuary, on the western side, the eroding sand-bar of Dawlish Warren provides a useful watch-point. There are convenient access points on the eastern shore at Topsham, Powderham and in Exmouth itself.

Braunton Burrows: the largest sand-dune system in the southwest.

Within a 15-mile radius eastwards of Exeter and the Exe, there are a number of heathland commons which can provide an interesting contrast to the estuary birds. Woodbury Common is probably the most productive and holds birds such as Nightjar, Tree Pipit, Redstart and Lesser Redpoll, all of only local distribution in the West Country.

It is not possible to appreciate the birds and animals of Dartmoor in a casual way as a great deal of travelling and, in particular, walking, has to be done. Some planning is necessary and the weather needs to be considered for the National Park is wild enough to present a serious risk to anyone who is lost. Two reservoirs are used by numbers of wildfowl — at Burrator in the southwest and at Fernworthy which is more central, situated near the village of Chagford. The latter has a pleasant woodland setting, and will provide the more interesting variety. The Dart valley between Buckfastleigh and Dartmeet has fine oakwoods along much of its length, including Holne Wood (NT). However, to see the high moorland specialities such as the Red Grouse there is no escaping a walk over the wind-swept tops, and one would be fortunate indeed to see many of them without leaving the comfort of the car.

The combined estuaries of the rivers Tamar, Tavy, Plym and Lynher are situated on the county boundary between Devon and Cornwall at Plymouth. Here again there is a varied estuarine habitat with good numbers of waders and wildfowl and the added attraction of a wintering flock of Avocets, usually found in the Tamar between Cargreen and Weirquay, mingling with the commoner Curlews, Redshanks, Oystercatchers and Dunlins. The stark black-and-white wing and tail pattern will distinguish the Black-tailed Godwit from its relative the Bar-tailed Godwit in flight; and tail-bobbing Common Sandpipers are to be seen not infrequently, even in winter when the bulk of the population has departed to warmer waters. The southern end of the estuary, including St John's Lake and the River Lynher, can be watched from the Torpoint area.

Freshwater marshes and lakes are few in the southwest but three sites are worthy of mention. On the south Devon coast between Dartmouth and Start Point is Slapton Ley, the largest area of open fresh water in the region. It is shallow and is separated from the sea by a sand- and shingle-bar. The Ley, which has extensive reedbeds with Reed Warblers at its northern end, is controlled and managed by the Field Studies Council which has a Field Centre there. The Devon Bird Watching and Preservation Society runs a ringing and migration station on a part-time basis. Access is restricted, but views over the Ley are easily obtained from the road which runs along the sand-bar. Two smaller but basically similar areas are to be found in south Cornwall, at Loe Pool near Helston and Marazion Marsh near Penzance. Both have a similar sand- or shingle-bar which has impounded fresh water, extensive at Loe Pool and haunted by ducks; whilst Marazion, based on a submerged forest, is more of a true marsh with only small pools. All three sites have yielded excellent lists of uncommon and vagrant birds, including a number of American waders.

The Cornish estuaries, particularly those of the Camel and the Fal, are something of an enigma to the bird-watcher as they extend to a considerable length and have innumerable side creeks and inlets all of which can prove rewarding when the tide happens to be right; but all too frequently this is not so and some frustration can result, although the absence of the main bulk of the waders is quickly tempered by the scenic delights of the winding creeks with woodland along the shore often filled with the calls of tits, Goldcrests and, in summer, the warblers. The comparatively tiny Hayle estuary has the advantage of being within easy reach of the seabird watch-point at St Ives, thus providing a fine centre for a great variety of birds, with Marazion and the Land's End peninsula only a short distance away.

The north Devon coast can boast two special features, its mighty cliffs and the largest sand-dune system in the southwest, at Braunton Burrows. These lie at the confluence of the rivers Taw and Torridge, and part of the area has NNR status. The dunes on the south side of the estuary are known as Northam Burrows and form a similar habitat. In addition to the usual waterfowl, wintering Short-eared Owls and Hen Harriers are frequent, gliding on stiffened wings whilst scouring the dunes for mice and voles. Merlins hunt over the dunes in winter endeavouring to outfly a lark or pipit. The breeding birds include Shelduck and Wheatear, both utilising the Rabbit burrows as nest-sites.

Turning the corner to complete a circuit of the peninsula, one is soon climbing into the Exmoor foothills. Three woodland areas in the Ilfracombe-Lynton region are worth visiting for their charm and beauty: Chapel Wood (RSPB), Arlington Court (NT) and Combe Park (NT). Ravens and Buzzards use these for nesting and there is a heronry at Arlington Court.

The high Exmoor plateau drops very steeply to the sea along the north coast of Devon, giving cliffs over 1,000 feet in height at Holdstone Barrows and Great Hangman. Seabird colonies, including Razorbills, Guillemots and Fulmars, may be seen by those with a head for heights, whilst the moors may be searched for Red Grouse and the occasional Black Grouse which Devon shares with Somerset in this southerly outpost on Exmoor.

Somerset is a county of contrasts. The Mendips in the north form a magnificent range of limestone hills which dip into the sea at Brean Down (NT). Interesting gorges cleave the hills on the southern side, the most famous being Cheddar, but there are many others which have great wildlife interest such as Ebbor Gorge and Rodnay Stoke NNRs, the latter containing one of the finest surviving remnants of Mendips ashwood.

A male Wheatear with food for its young; at Braunton this species nests in disused rabbit-burrows.

The steep and wooded Ebbor Gorge, rich in wildlife, cleaves the limestone of the Mendip Hills in Somerset.

Wild ponies on the Quantock Hills; in the distance is Bridgwater Bay in the Bristol Channel.

The Quantock Hills form another designated AONB, providing splendid walking country with fine views of the Bristol Channel and the Somerset lowlands. Buzzards are frequent overhead and Red Deer are present in good numbers. The Somerset Trust for Nature Conservation has its headquarters at the eastern end of the hills at Fyne Court, Broomfield, where there is an Interpretive Centre for the Quantocks, and walks of various lengths are open to visitors. To the west the Tone valley leads into the Brendons, fine rolling red sandstone hills with narrow sunken lanes, good sheep pastures and large areas of woodland. The Brendons merge imperceptibly into the Exmoor National Park with Dunkery Beacon as its highest point.

Somerset and Avon also provide extensive moors and mud-flats which, with the comparative mildness of the winters, attract ducks and geese from the north in great numbers. They can be seen on the water-meadows bordering the Severn estuary, and on the extensive mud-flats of Bridgwater Bay NNR, which in late summer is the major moulting ground in the southwest for thousands of Shelduck, mostly from Ireland. Wildfowl and waders may also be viewed in good numbers on Chew Valley Lake near Bristol, which has a fine record of aquatic rarities, such as the American Pied-billed Grebe. Durleigh Reservoir near Bridgwater and Sutton Bingham Reservoir near Yeovil are other excellent bird-watching haunts.

Somerset and Avon have proved fruitful areas in the search for the tiny and now very scarce Harvest Mouse; so keep a look-out among tall vegetation for its summer nest, a compact tangle of grass blades about the size of a cricket ball.

Although the naturalist will tend to gravitate towards the coast or the highlands in the West Country, the rural countryside on the way should not be ignored as the quieter lanes with their characteristic high hedgerows still abound with life, as any resident in the farming districts will testify. It is a truly green and pleasant land.

The County Naturalists' Trusts in the region work unceasingly to prevent unnecessary destruction of habitat and unwarranted culling of deer and Badgers, and frequently succeed in preserving specialised animals and flowers by leasing quite small areas, for example old quarries near the Purbeck coast of Dorset where bats abound. It is fascinating and worth-while work, and visitors and newcomers would do well to support these Trusts and reap the benefits which members receive in being allowed access to reserves.

The West Country is a happy place to be. Whether one's interest in wildlife is general or specialised, casual or deep, there is a bit of everything, clothed in a mantle of mild air off a sea which can never be more than 30 miles away.

Britain's smallest mouse, the Harvest Mouse, is now very scarce; but can be seen in southwest England.

Guide to wildlife habitats in South West England

This Appendix provides a selected but varied list of places of wildlife interest. It is emphasised that nature reserves exist primarily for the conservation of animals and plants and in some cases for environmental experiments and research. They are not 'public open spaces' in the recreational sense. Access to many is therefore restricted and some, because of their sensitivity to disturbance, have been omitted from this list, in deference to the wishes of conservation organisations. Even with 'open' reserves visitors are earnestly requested to keep to the paths and bridleways and so avoid damage to the habitat and undue disturbance to wildlife. *There is no public access to the enclosed farmland which is part of many National Trust properties.*

Application to visit a National Nature Reserve (NNR) should be made to the appropriate Regional Office of the Nature Conservancy Council (NCC) at the address given. Intention to visit reserves of the Royal Society for the Protection of Birds (RSPB) should be notified to the Warden (whose address is shown) as far in advance as possible. In all cases where an address is shown, it is wise to contact the Warden to avoid disappointment.

CORNWALL

Bodmin Forest SX 12 65. State forest, mainly conifers, but also oak/beech, incl. stretch of Fowey valley. 6000 a. 2 mls s.e. of Bodmin on A38. For Comm.

Chapel Porth SW 70 49. Cliffs and heather-covered moor surrounding wild valley of Chapel Coombe, 363 a. Nearby is St Agnes Beacon, 628 ft, at SW 71 51. 5 mls n. of Redruth A30 – B3277, s.w. of St Agnes. Car park, cafe. NT.

Cornwall Naturalists' Trust, Trendrine, Zennor, St Ives, Cornwall, TR26 3BW.

Crackington Haven SX 14 97. Cliffs and foreshore incl. rugged headlands and highest cliff in Cornwall, 731 ft. 8 mls s.w. of Bude, 6 mls n.e. of Boscastle, on w. side of A39. NT.

Cubert Common SW 77 60. Cliffs, commonland and sand-dunes behind beaches of Porth Joke and Holywell. Nearby is the Gannel, s. bank of a sandy estuary, and sand-dunes behind Crantock beach SW 79 61. 3 mls s.w. of Newquay, between Crantock and Holywell Bay, on w. side of A3075. Car parks at West Pentire, and at Treago Mill in valley leading to Porth Joke. NT.

The Dodman SX 00 39. Coast of Dodman Point and Hemmick Beach and Coves. 8 mls s. of St Austell, 4 mls s. of Mevagissey. Car parks at Penare and Lamledra Farm SX 015 414. NT.

Duckpool Beach SS 20 12. Steep cliffs rising to Steeple Point, 300 ft, behind large sandy beach. Footpath along $2\frac{1}{2}$ mls of coast. 5 mls n. of Bude, on w. side of A39. Car park at Sandymouth. NT.

Fal-Ruan Estuary SW 89 42. Muddy foreshore and saltmarsh at Ardevora and Trelonk. Gulls, waders, wildfowl incl. Shelduck. 3 mls s.w. of Tregoney, A3078, then minor roads to Trelonk and Ardevora. NT/Cornwall Nats T.

Godrevy Peninsula SW 58 43. Cliffs and coastal footpath extending over 6 mls on Godrevy peninsula. Small beaches and numerous coves. Grey Seals. 5–8 mls n.e. of Hayle, on n. side of B3301. NT.

Helford River SW 78 28. Wooded valleys, coastal footpaths and cliffs s. of Mawnan Smith, incl. headlands of Mawnan Sheer and Rosemullion. 3 mls s.w. of Falmouth. Car parks at Bosloe Farm and Mawnan church. NT.

Lanhydrock SX 09 64. Park and woodland in Fowey valley, 540 a. 2 mls s. of Bodmin, on e. side of B3268, or w. side of A38 at Cutmadoc. NT.

Lizard Peninsula SW 66 19. Coastal heath and cliffs incl. heather-covered Predannack and Lower Predannack Downs, Pollurrian Cove, Marconi Memorial, Mullion Cove and Island. Nearby are Kynance Cove and Lizard Downs SW 69 13, w. of Lizard, Inglewidden Cliffs and Devil's Frying Pan SW 72 14, s. of Cadgwith. 6 mls s. of Helston A3083, on coast to w. of Mullion, and e. and w. of Lizard. NT/Cornwall Nats T.

The Loe SW 64 24. Lagoon with well-wooded sides. Waterfowl. 1 ml s.w. of Helston A394, on e. side of Porthleven.

The National Trust Cornwall, Regional Office, The Friaries, Mount Folly, Bodmin, Cornwall.

Penberth Cove and Treen Cliff SW 40 23. Granite headland of Treryn Dinas and valley. 7 mls s.w. of Penzance, 4 mls s.e. of Land's End, on s. side of B3315. NT.

Pencarrow Head SX 15 51. Cliffs, coves and beaches on Lantic and Lantivet Bays. 5–8 mls w. of West Looe A387 and minor roads between Polperro and Polruan. Footpaths from Polruan to Lansallos and Polruan to Pont roads, car parks at Frogmore and Lansallos. NT.

Pentire Head and Portquin Bay SW 93 81. Cliffs, incl. Carnweather Point SW 95 80, Doyden Point and Portquin Harbour SW 97 81, Epphaven Cove SW 96 80 and Pentire Point SW 93 80. 6 mls n.w. of Wadebridge B3314. Car park at Pentire Farm. Warden and access path at Pentireglaze Farm. NT.

St Anthony-in-Roseland SW 86 32. Coastal land and beaches surrounding the hamlet of Bohortha, incl. Porthmellin and Killigerran Heads. Also St Anthony Head 1 ml to the w. 1 ml s.e. of St Mawes (ferry), 3 mls e. of Falmouth (steamer), 10 mls s.w. of Tregony (via A3078 and minor road through Gerrans). Car park at St Anthony Head. NT.

Tamar Estuary SX 43 62. Mudflats, saltmarsh. Waders and waterfowl. 2 mls n.w. of Plymouth A38, via A388 at Saltash and minor roads to Landulph. Duchy of Cornwall/Cornwall Nats T.

Tintagel SX 04 88. Cliffs and beaches incl. Glebe Cliff on either side of Dunderhole Point, Penhallick Point to s., and Trebarwith Strand, high cliffs overlooking fine beach. w. of Tintagel and

Sea-shore near Duckpool on Cornwall's north coast.

B3263, on w. side of A39 via Camelford. NT.

Trelissick SW 83 39. Parkland, gardens and woods overlooking Fal estuary. 4 mls s. of Truro, on e. side of A39 astride B3289. NT.

Whitsand Bay SX 39 53. Coastland and cliffs. Also Trethill Cliffs 1 ml to w. 3 mls s.w. of Torpoint, on s. side of A374 at Antony. NT.

DEVON

Arlington Court SS 61 40. Parkland with lake, also hills and steep, wooded valleys, wildfowl refuge. Two-mile circular walk by R. Yeo and lake. Shetland Ponies, Jacob Sheep. Buzzard, Raven, heronry. 7 mls n.e. of Barnstaple, on e. side of A39. NT.

Axmouth–Lyme Regis Undercliffs NNR SY 30 90. Shrub vegetation on major landslip undercliffs, incl. spontaneous ash wood in chasm near Dowlands. 794 a. 4 mls w. of Lyme Regis, on coast s. of A3052. (Best seen from public footpath.) NCC.

Bicton Gardens SY 07 86. Formal gardens and famous pinetum. Waterfowl. 6 mls n.e. of Exmouth e. of A376, East Budleigh.

Blackadon, Leusdon SX 71 73. Grass moorland around Blackadon Tor, and oakwoods. 4 mls n.w. of Ashburton, n. of A384 near Buckland-in-the-Moor. Devon T for Nature Conservation.

Branscombe and Salcombe Regis SY 20 88. Wooded valley, cliffs and foreshore, stretching for 4 mls from Branscombe Mouth to Dunscombe Cliff. Several miles of footpaths connecting Lincombe, Western Combe and Branscombe, beaches reached from Branscombe and Weston Mouths. Between Seaton and Sidmouth, s. of A3052. NT.

Braunton Burrows NNR SS 45 35. Sanddunes and shore, estuary of Rs Taw and Torridge, 1492 a. 7 mls w. of Barnstaple A361, w. of Braunton. NT/NCC.

Chudleigh Knighton Heath SX 84 77. Wet and dry heath with scrub, woodland and small ponds. 5 mls n.w. of Newton Abbot, A382 and A38. Devon T for Nature Conservation.

Clovelly SS 32 25. Woodland and footpath access to cliffs and Mouth Mill Beach. Access nearby to Fatacott Cliff 1½ mls w. of Clovelly. 10 mls w. of Bideford A39. NT.

Dartmoor National Park, Devon. 365 sq. mls. Heather moorland and upland bogs, with massive granite tors weathered into fantastic shapes; steep-sided combes with hanging oakwoods of Rs. Teign, Bovey, Tavy, Dart, Meavy and Erme. Incl. Wistman's Wood FNR SX 61 77, Black Tor Copse FNR SX 57 70, Yarner Wood NNR SX 77 78 and Bovey Valley Woodlands NNR. Information centre at Two Bridges (caravan near Two Bridges Hotel SX 608 750). Flanked by A30 Exeter–Okehampton; A386 Okehampton–Tavistock; A38 Exeter–Plymouth. Traversed by A382 Bovey Tracey–Moretonhampstead; A384 Ashburton–Two Bridges; B3212 Princetown–Moretonhampstead; and many minor roads. Recommended leaflets: Dartmoor National Park, Animals and Birds of the Dartmoor National Park, and a series on mammals by H. G. Hurrell.

Dart Valley SX 70 71. Moorland and old oak-coppice woods, marsh and valley bogs on both sides of the R. Dart, 900 a. Adjoins Holne Woods (NT) in the south. 4 mls n.w. of Ashburton, on s. side of A384 near Poundsgate. Devon T for Nature Conservation.

Devon Trust for Nature Conservation, 2 Pennsylvania Road, Exeter, EX4 6BQ.

Dunsford and Meadhaydown Wood SX 81 88. Predominantly sessile oakwood on e. slope of Teign valley, 140 a. Mink. Raven, Dipper, Grey Wagtail. 6 mls w. of Exeter, s. of Dunsford at junction of B3212 – B3193. Devon T for Nature Conservation.

Exe Estuary SX 97 80. National Wildfowl Refuge, 1022 a. Western section of estuary incl. Dawlish Warren. Wintering Brent Geese, Wigeon, Shelduck, Teal and other waterfowl, visited by Eider, Avocet, Spoonbill. 10 mls s. of Exeter, on e. side of A379.

Farway Countryside Park SY 18 96. Parkland in Coly valley. Deer enclosure, free-roaming rare breeds of domesticated animals, Donkey sanctuary. 6 mls s. of Honiton A375 – B3174. Car park, trails, picnic area, refreshments, facilities for children. Adm. fee. Holnest Farm/ Rare Breeds Survival T.

The Great Hangman SS 60 48. Cliffs and moorland rising to 1046 ft. Fulmars and auk colonies. 5 mls e. of Ilfracombe, n.e. of Combe Martin A399. NT.

Goodameavy SX 53 64. In the s.w. corner of Dartmoor, incl. Dewerstone and Cadworthy Woods, part of Wigford Down, all accessible by footpaths. 6 mls n.e. of Plymouth, 2 mls s. of Yelverton, e. side of A386. NT.

Heddon Valley SS 65 48. Woods and moorland leading down from Trentishoe Common to the sea, 941 a., incl. steep oakwoods on w. side of valley above Hunters Inn. 3 mls n. of Parracombe. NT.

Hentor and Willings Walls Warrens SX 60 65. On the s.w. flank of Dartmoor, moorland rising to 1600 ft overlooking headwaters of R. Plym. 2847 a. 9 mls n.e. of Plymouth A386 and minor roads e. of Yelverton. NT.

Holne Woods SX 70 71. Oakwoods extending for 2½ mls on s. bank of R. Dart upstream of New Bridge. Footpaths along and above river. 10 mls w. of Newton Abbot, 3½ mls w. of Ashburton, on s. side of A384. NT.

Killerton SS 97 01. Ashclyst Forest 600 a. and Killerton Gardens and Park 300 a., incl. fine arboretum and woods. 7 mls n.e. of Exeter, e. of B3185, off A38 at Budlake. NT.

Lundy SS 13 45. Island, 1200 a. Sika Deer, Soay Sheep. Seabirds on granite cliffs at n. end, migrant birds. 11 mls n. of Hartland Point. Access by boat from Bideford (25 mls), Ilfracombe (23 mls) and Tenby (30 mls). NT.

Lydford Gorge SX 51 85. Deep ravine of R. Lyd emerging into steep-sided valley with oakwoods and 90 ft high White Lady Waterfall. Half-way between Okehampton and Tavistock, 1 ml w. of A386. NT.

Lynmouth SS 74 48. Steep wooded valleys of R. East Lyn upstream to Rockford Bridge and Hoar Oak Water as far as Hillsford Bridge. The two rivers unite at Watersmeet and flow to sea beneath Lyn and Myrtleberry Cleaves. Incl. Butter Hill 994 ft and Foreland Point, also precipitous Coddow Combe. 1265 a. E. of Lynmouth, astride A39. Car parks at Barna Barrow above Countisbury and at Hillsford Bridge. Refreshments, information centre at Watersmeet House. NT.

Morte Bay SS 45 45. Cliffs, beaches, coastal heath and sand-dunes. Incl. Woolacombe Warren SS 45 43, sanddunes along shore of s. Woolacombe, and Morte Point SS 44 45 to w. of Mortehoe. Nearby is Baggy Point SS 42 41 on s.w. arm of bay. All are accessible by coastal footpaths. 4 mls s.w. of Ilfracombe B3231, to n. and s. of Woolacombe. NT.

The National Trust Devonshire, Regional Office, Killerton Estate Office, Budlake, Exeter, Devonshire.

Salcombe SX 73 36. Coast on both sides of harbour. On w. side 6 mls from Bolt Head SX 73 36 to Bolt Tail SX 66 39, on e. side 5 mls of cliff walks and sandy coves. S. of Salcombe A381.

Saltram SX 52 55. House, parkland and Sawpit Hill on n. side with Wixenford Bottom and Sellar Acres woods. 2 mls w. of Plympton, 3½ mls s.e. of Plymouth centre, between A38 and A379. NT.

Sidmouth Cliff SY 15 88. Cliff-face and landslip area overgrown with scrub, mainly blackthorn in e. section. (The reserve is in 2 sections, SY 150 878 and SY 133 874, separated by private land.) E. of Sidmouth, on s. side of A3052. Access by footpath from Sidmouth, trail. Devon T for Nature Conservation.

Slapton Ley SX 82 44. Lagoon with reedbeds. Waterfowl and Reed Warblers. Field Studies Council Centre. 5 mls s.w. of Dartmouth, 5 mls e. of Kingsbridge A379. Viewable from road.

Wistman's Wood SX 61 77. High-level pedunculate oakwood on boulder-strewn hillside. 3 mls n.e. of Princetown, w. of B3212.

Withleigh SS 91 12. Woodland, water-meadows and steep pastures in valley of R. Little Dart. 3 mls w. of Tiverton to s. of A373. NT.

SOMERSET

Dunkery Beacon SS 90 43. High moorland of Dunkery Hill 1403 ft and Dunkery Beacon 1705 ft. 2 mls s. of Porlock on minor roads via Luccombe. NT.

Ebbor Gorge NNR ST 53 48. Dry Carboniferous limestone gorge on s. face of Mendip Hills above Wookey Hole, woodland of oak/ash/wych elm and varied shrub growth on rocky slopes. 142 a. Fox, Badger. Buzzard, Sparrowhawk, Kestrel. 2 mls n.w. of Wells, via minor roads e. of A371. Car park, picnic area. (Visitors should use waymarked footpaths.) NT/NCC.

Exmoor National Park, Somerset, intruding into Devon. 265 sq. mls. Magnificent coast between Heddon's Mouth and Foreland Point and on both sides of Porlock Bay; heathery plateau over 1000 ft rising to Dunkery Beacon (NT) 1705 ft and Winsford Hill (NT); farming country of northern reach of Brendon Hills; wooded combes of Rs. Exe, Barle and Haddeo. Information centres at Combe Martin (caravan in Beach car park), Lynton (Lyn and Exmoor Museum) and Minehead (Market House, The Parade). Traversed by A39 Dunster–Lynton; A396 Dunster–Bampton; B3223 Dulverton–Exford–Lynton. Recommended leaflets: Safety, Animals on Exmoor, Bird Life, Plant Life, Geology, Archaeology, Touring Caravan and Tent Sites.

Nature Conservancy Council, South West Regional Office, Roughmoor, Bishops Hull, Taunton, Somerset, TA1 5AA.

The Quantocks ST 15 41. Woods and moorland of Willoughby Cleeve at the foot of the Quantocks, and adjoining moorland of Longstone Hill ST 14 41.

Nearby is Shervage Wood, oak coppice and moorland, ST 16 40. 9 mls w. of Bridgwater A39, near Dodington and Holford. NT.

Selworthy Beacon and Bossington Hill SS 93 47. Moorland rising to 1013 ft and 4 mls of coast overlooking Bristol Channel. 3 mls w. of Minehead on n. side of A39. NT.

Somerset Trust for Nature Conservation Fyne Court, Broomfield, Bridgwater, TA5 2EQ.

Winsford Hill SS 87 34. Moorland, 1288 a. 4 mls n.w. of Dulverton B3223. NT.

AVON

Chew Valley Lake ST 57 60. Regional Wildfowl Refuge. Waterfowl, especially in winter. Nearby to w. is Blagdon Lake ST 52 60. 8 mls s. of Bristol between A368 and B3114.

Leigh Woods NNR ST 56 74. Broad-leaved woods with fine panorama of Avon Gorge NNR, on s. side of R. Avon. Incl. Nightingale valley. W. of Bristol A369 – B3129, n.w. of Clifton Suspension Bridge. NT/NCC.

Middle Hope ST 33 66. Coast stretching over 2 mls between Kewstoke and Sand Point, overlooking Somerset Marshes. 3–5 mls n. of Weston-super-Mare by minor roads. NT.

DORSET

Abbotsbury Swannery SY 57 85. Historic herd of Mute Swans at w. end of Chesil Beach. 7 mls n.w. of Weymouth, 9 mls s.e. of Bridport B3157.

Arne SY 97 88. Relict Wessex heathland; heather, gorse and Scots pines, 739 a. Nightjar, Stonechat, Dartford and Grasshopper Warblers. Ducks and waders in autumn and winter. 3 mls e. of Wareham off A351. Trail. Permits required for escorted visits. (Warden – Syldata, Arne, Wareham, Dorset.) RSPB.

Brownsea Island SZ 03 88. Woodland and wetland, lagoons. 250 a. Red Squirrels. Big heronry, Sandwich and Common Terns, waders and waterfowl. Poole Harbour. Boats 1st April–30th Sept from Sandbanks and Poole Quay. Guided tours only 14.00–15.00 hrs. Nature trail and explanatory leaflet available. (Warden – The Villa, Brownsea Island, Poole.) NT/Dorset Nats T.

Dorset Naturalists' Trust, Island View, 58 Pearce Avenue, Parkstone, Poole, Dorset, BH14 8EH.

Durlston SZ 03 77. Coast and cliffs of Durlston Head, 261 a. Country Park. S. of Swanage. Dorset CC.

Ferrybridge, Wyke Regis SY 66 75. Tidal pools, sandflats and shingle ridge at e. end of Chesil Beach. Gulls, terns and wading birds, incl. interesting migrants. 2 mls s. of Weymouth, on w. side of A354. Public car park.

Golden Cap Estate SY 40 92. Hill, cliff, undercliff and beach. Has 15 mls of footpaths incl. through route of 6 mls. Incl. Chardown Hill SY 395 930, Hardown Hill SY 405 945, undercliffs on either side of Seatown SY 415 920, undercliff and cliff-top at St Gabriel's SY 401 924, Stonebarrow Hill SY 383 928. Access from A35 by car to sea at Charmouth, Seatown and Eypemouth, to viewpoints and picnic places at Chardown and Stonebarrow Hills from Morcombe Lake and Charmouth respectively. Camping for youth organisations at Downhouse Farm SY 440 915. and St Gabriel's SY 401 924. NT.

Portland Bill SY 68 68. Bird Observatory at Old Lower Light. Seabirds, small migrants in scrub in fields and old quarries. 6 mls s. of Weymouth A354, at s. end of Portland Bill.

Radipole Lake SY 68 80. Lake with large reedbeds; regional wildfowl refuge. 70 a. Bearded Reedlings, Reed Warblers. In autumn migrant waterfowl, waders and marsh terns. Weymouth A354, near harbour. Car park. Weymouth Corporation/RSPB.

Stanpit Marshes LNR SZ 16 93. Saltmarsh, wet grassland, brackish pools, sand-banks. Mute Swans, Shelducks, Goldeneye, Red-breasted Merganser and other ducks in winter and waders on passage. W. of Christchurch, on s. side of B3059. Car parks by gasworks and at Stanpit road. Christchurch BC/ Hants and IOW Nats T.

Studland Heath NNR SZ 01 84. Beach and sand-dunes, freshwater lagoon and marsh, heath and acid bog, 429 a. Harvest Mouse. Stonechat, Whitethroat and other warblers. 5 mls s. of Poole B3369 (ferry at Sandbanks); 7 mls s.e. of Wareham A351 – B3351. Trail, hide. NCC.

Animal collections in South West England

Ambleside Water Gardens and Aviaries

This small mixed collection mainly consists of birds, with parrots, parrakeets, including Princess of Wales Parrakeets and rosellas, mynahs, glossy starlings, Budgerigars, lovebirds, touracos, Fantail Pigeons and ducks – some 280 birds in all. The half-dozen mammal species include a monkey, gerbils, Rabbits, guinea-pigs and white mice. There is also a lake stocked with fish. The Gardens are owned by Mr L. J. Davenport, and they were opened in 1935.

Ambleside Water Gardens and Aviaries. **Address** Lower Weare, Axbridge, Somerset. **Telephone** Axbridge 362. **Open** 10.30–18.30 Tues–Sat, 14.00–18.30 Sun, summer; closed in winter. **Catering** unlicensed restaurant, snack bar. **Acreage** 1½. **Car** 2 mls s.w. of Lower Weare on A38 Bristol–Bridgwater road. **Bus** stops 100 yds from Gardens. **Train** to Weston-super-Mare (8 mls). Public allowed to feed animals with food prepared and sold in Zoo only.

Aqualand

This Aquarium has one of the largest collections of tropical marine fish in the country, and there is a good variety of freshwater fish, as well as one of the best exhibitions of local marine life. The Aquarium has its own collecting boat and diver to serve the marine section. You can also see penguins and two marine turtles, the Loggerhead and the Hawksbill. This exhibition was opened in 1954, and in the last four years it has been rebuilt and is now one of the most modern in the country.

Aqualand. **Address** Beacon Quay, Torquay, Devon. **Telephone** Torquay 24439. **Open** 10.00–20.00 1st April–31st Oct. Gift shop. **Car** park on Beacon Quay, near Torquay Harbour Clock Tower. **Bus** stops 400 yds from entrance. **Train** to Torquay (2 mls). **Taxis** available. Public **not allowed** to feed exhibits.

Aqualand Aquarium

This Aquarium exhibits locally caught marine fish, including Moray Eels, sharks and rays, and a collection of corals and invertebrate species (animals without a backbone). There are also tropical marine fish from the Gulf of Cortes, Cuba, and from the Caribbean, Red Sea, Indian Ocean and the mid-Pacific Ocean. You can also see living coral reefs with the marine life associated with them, and other tanks display Hawksbill Turtles, crocodiles and caimans. The Aquarium was opened in 1957.

Aqualand Aquarium. **Address** The Den, Sea-front, Teignmouth, Devon. **Telephone** Teignmouth 3383. **Open** 10.00–22.00 daily summer, 10.00–22.00 weekends winter. **Guided tours** by arrangement. **Acreage** 1. **Car** Sea-front closed to cars Easter–Sept, nearest car park at station. **Bus** to Triangle, Teignmouth, then 100 yds to Aquarium. **Train** to Teignmouth (¼ ml). Public **not allowed** to feed exhibits.

The Aquarium, Guernsey

This Aquarium exhibits a large collection of temperate marine fish, and small collections of locally caught freshwater species such as Perch, Tench, carp and Rudd. There is also a tropical marine section and a few reptiles. The temperate seawater fish include Conger Eels weighing up to 30 lb., Greater Spotted and Lesser Spotted Dogfish, ray, bass and bream, in a 10,000-gallon pool, and smaller tanks housing wrasse, gurnard, mullet, blennies, gobies, lobsters and usually octopus. There is a small collection of invertebrates (animals with no backbone) such as anemones, Triton, Fan Mussel and hermit crabs. Hermit crabs, whose own ectoskeleta are not strong, live in the shells of whelks, winkles and other shellfish, taking occupation after the original occupant has died. The tropical sea-fish tanks contain anemone fish with anemones, dragonfish, squirrel fish, surgeon fish, damsels, monos and scats. The tropical freshwater fish include African Lungfish, piranha, Giant Gourami, Archer Fish, cichlids, barbs, characins, and a small collection of tropical catfish. The reptile collection, to be increased, at present includes caimans, terrapins and one lizard species, the tegu. The Aquarium was opened in 1967 and it is housed in three tunnels, remnants of the Second World War.

The Aquarium. **Address** La Valette, St Peter Port, Guernsey. **Telephone** 23301. **Open** 10.00–sunset summer, 10.00–16.00 winter. **Bus** to terminus, then 10 mins' walk to Aquarium. **Taxis** available. Public **not allowed** to feed exhibits.

The Aquarium

Plymouth Aquarium, opened in 1885, is a small section of the Marine Biological Association, which carries out independent research on many aspects of marine biology. It houses one of the best collections of temperate marine fish in the country, including sharks, bass, bream, octopus, cuttlefish, starfish and many other species. All these are caught by the Association's own boats. Dogfish, cuttlefish and several other species of invertebrates (without backbones) breed here regularly and are reared in the Aquarium.

The Aquarium. **Address** The Laboratory, Citadel Hill, Plymouth, Devon. **Telephone** Plymouth 21761. **Open** 10.00–18.00 summer and winter. **Guide-book**. **Car** on sea-front at e. end of The Hoe. **Bus** 28 from city centre stops outside Aquarium. **Train** to Plymouth (1½ mls). **Taxis** available. No pets. Public **not allowed** to feed exhibits.

Bird Paradise and Children's Zoo

This is a bird collection specialising in breeding rare species and those endangered in the wild. The rarest here are White-eared Pheasants, which bred in 1974, this being the first time the species has bred in Great Britain outside Jersey Zoo. Other rare species are St Vincent Amazon Parrots, Rothschild's Grackles, which breed regularly, Thick-billed Parrots and Wattled Cranes. The St Vincent Amazons here are two of only seven in the world outside the island of St Vincent. Other birds in the collection include Palm Cockatoos, Hyacinthine Macaws, Plum-crowned Parrots, Duyvenboides Lories, Sun Conures, Argus Pheasants and Viellot's Fireback Pheasants. A number of macaws, cockatoos and other birds are at liberty in the gardens, which were opened in 1973 by Mr M. W. Reynolds.

Bird Paradise and Children's Zoo. **Address** Hayle, Cornwall. **Telephone** Hayle 3365. **Open** 10.00–1 hr before dark summer and winter. **Catering** snack bar. Zoo shop. **Acreage** 13. **Car** s.e. of Hayle on B3302 Helston road. **Bus** stops at Foundry Square, Hayle, ½ ml from Zoo. **Train** to Hayle (¾ ml). **Taxis** available. Public allowed to feed animals but not birds with food prepared and sold in Zoo only.

Bristol Zoo

Bristol Zoo is the second oldest in Great Britain, and although it covers only a small area it houses one of the major British collections. It is specially noted for its breeding groups of great apes, White Tigers and Okapis, and many other species breed regularly. There is a good bird collection, a Reptile House and an Aquarium which contains some rare species. Most of the animal houses are arranged round the perimeter of the Zoo, with a lake in the middle. The Zoo is also noted for its gardens, which contain attractive herbaceous borders and many fine specimen trees. This is a zoological garden in the strict sense of the term, that is, a zoo set in a garden, and a delightful place in which to spend a day away from the bustle of Bristol.

The Zoo's Gorillas made history in 1971 when the first Gorilla to be born in a British zoo was delivered. The adults, Samson and Delilah, arrived at the Zoo in 1966, and a second female, Caroline, in 1968. On 6th March 1971 Caroline gave birth to a male infant, and for the first few days all went well, the two females sharing the duties of caring for it. However, Caroline was not quite ready for the responsibilities of motherhood and she abandoned her baby, which did not survive. On 10th April Delilah gave birth, also to a male infant, and being more mature she looked after it better and it became the first Gorilla to be reared successfully in this country. The Gorillas in the Zoo are the Lowland species, which come from the rain-forests of central and West Africa. In the wild, they live in family groups of an adult male with several wives and young. Although a Gorilla can bend a steel bar three inches thick, it is not an aggressive animal unless attacked, and most of its time is spent quietly feeding or resting. At night they nest in the low branches of trees, the big males weaving a nest of branches on the ground.

There are also breeding groups of Orang utans and Chimpanzees, and both species bred in the same year as the Gorillas, which is in itself a record. In 1934 the Zoo bred and reared the first Chimpanzee to be bred in Europe. The father,

Bristol Zoo. **Address** Clifton, Bristol, Somerset. **Telephone** Bristol 38951. **Open** 09.00–19.00 weekdays, 10.00–19.00 Sun, summer; 09.00–16.30 weekdays, 10.00–16.30 Sun, winter. **Guide-book**. **Catering** licensed restaurant, self-service cafeteria, snack bar, kiosk. Zoo shop. **Acreage** 12. **Car** near Clifton Down, Clifton by A4 Bristol–Avonmouth road. **Bus** 7, 8, 34 or 42 to Zoo. **Train** to Clifton Down station (¾ ml). **Other facilities** first-aid post, lost children's room. No pets. Public **not allowed** to feed animals.

40

Ko-Ko, later went to London Zoo, where he became the father of London's first Chimpanzee baby, Jubilee. Chimpanzees come from central Africa, living in large family groups and nesting in trees at night. They are noisy, inquisitive animals, and while delightful when young, they develop uncertain tempers when they mature at about seven years of age and they can be dangerous, flying into sudden rages, when they use their teeth and hands to attack. Orang utans, confined to Borneo and Sumatra, live high in the trees of thick forest and seldom visit the ground. They are more solitary animals, living singly or with one or two offspring. The adult male grows enormous cheek pads which make its head look larger than it is. Like Gorillas, Orang utans are exclusively vegetarian, while Chimpanzees will sometimes kill and eat young baboons or young Bush Pigs.

The Zoo's newest exhibit is the Ape House, built on the site of the old Lion House, and completed in 1976. The three outdoor landscaped enclosures, one for each group, are an innovation here, where space has always been at a premium. There is also a utility exhibit, where mothers and infants or young male animals can be isolated and displayed separately from the main groups.

The gibbons are in a large outdoor cage which enables them to demonstrate their ability in swinging rapidly from branch to branch, using their very long arms with which they can generate considerable speed through their native forests in southeast Asia and India. Gibbons are the smallest of the anthropoid, or man-like apes and they have loud voices which carry a great distance. There are Ring-tailed and Mongoose Lemurs, which belong to the most primitive group of primates, Spider Monkeys and capuchins, baboons, macaques and guenons in the Monkey House. Lemurs are found only in Madagascar, the Ring-tailed Lemur being a large grey species with a beautifully ringed black and white tail. In the wild it lives in thinly wooded, rocky country, unlike other lemur species which are forest animals. There is another smaller species here, the Mongoose Lemur, which is endangered in the wild, as are most animals in Madagascar, where forest clearance is destroying their natural habitat.

Unlike the gibbons, which they resemble, the Spider Monkeys of South America have prehensile tails, used for grasping branches as an aid to their hands. Another South American species here is the Brown Capuchin, a sturdy little monkey, with a long prehensile tail, which has been bred here successfully. Some of them have lived in the Zoo for over 20 years before dying. There are several species of baboon here, the most colourful being the Mandrill, a large species with brightly coloured facial markings and behind. The Drill, slightly smaller, is not so brightly coloured, nor is the Yellow Baboon, a more slender species distributed across central Africa. The Drill and the Mandrill are found only in West Africa, where they live in forest but on the ground during the day, searching for nuts, seeds and fallen fruit. They climb trees only to look for fruit, to rest for the night or to escape danger, their main natural enemy being the leopard. Baboons are sociable, living in troops varying in size from 12 up to 100 or 200, according to the available food supply. They are mainly vegetarian, noisy, and fierce fighters, a party of baboons being capable of defending themselves against most animals.

The monkey collection also has several species of macaque, the group of monkeys inhabiting India and southeast Asia. The species exhibited include the Pig-tailed Macaque, the largest of the family, from Burma and Sumatra, where it is trained to climb palm trees and throw down coconuts; the Stump-tailed, a species from southern Asia; the Crab-eating Macaque from Malaya, which lives among mangrove trees and eats shellfish; the Lion-tailed Macaque of India, a shy forest species, and the Rhesus Macaque, the commonest monkey in India, where it has for long been regarded as a sacred animal and has therefore increased in numbers. However, it has been much in demand in Europe and America in recent years for laboratory use, and huge importations have reduced its numbers. You can see a colony of Rhesus in the Monkey Temple, which recalls the 'banderlog' of Kipling's books. The guenons, the largest group of Old World monkeys, found in central Africa, are represented in the Zoo by the Green, Mona, Patas and De Brazza Monkeys. The Green Monkey, or Vervet, is commonly seen in East African game parks, while the Mona Monkey comes from

Ring-tailed Lemur: lemurs are found wild only in Madagascar, and are some of the most primitive of the primates.

West Africa, and the Patas from northern Africa. All have long tails, live in troops, and spend most of their time in trees. They are shy but not aggressive, and are often found in groups of mixed species.

There is an interesting collection of the larger cats at Bristol, including Lions, Tigers, Leopards, Jaguars and Pumas. But the pride of the cat collection is the group of white Tigers, which are the only ones in Europe. Only nine white Tigers have been seen in the wild since the First War, the most recent being Mohan, a white male which was captured as a cub in 1951 and kept by the Maharajah of Rewa in India. When this Tiger reached maturity he was mated with a normal-coloured tigress, which produced normal-coloured cubs. Mohan was then mated with one of his daughters, who produced white offspring, and all the white Tigers in captivity are descended from these. In 1963, Bristol Zoo received a pair from India, 'Champa' and 'Chameli', and their stock is descended from these two, and from their normal-coloured sister which accompanied them. Since 1964, all white Tigers found in India have become the property of the Indian Government, and there are only a few in zoos other than Bristol, and those are mostly in India. White Tigers have greyish-brown stripes on a cream background, pink noses and pink pads.

Amongst the Zoo's bear exhibits, the Polar Bears and European Brown Bears breed regularly, and in 1958, when a Polar Bear cub was born, Bristol Zoo became only the second in Britain to breed this species and rear it successfully. In the wild, Polar Bears hibernate to give birth to their cubs, making a den under the Arctic ice which is kept warm by the mother's body. They usually give birth to two cubs, each weighing no more than 2 lb. as against the mother's weight of at least 700 lb. The cubs remain in the den until spring, when they are strong enough to follow their mother. In zoos it is necessary to provide complete seclusion for breeding, as well as some background heating in the den to ensure that the cubs do not become chilled. Failure to provide complete peace and quiet results in the mother killing her cubs, from a sense of insecurity. Polar Bears feed mainly on seals and they are strong swimmers. Their numbers have dwindled owing to hunting by white men, often in planes. They are now afforded protection by most northern countries, and they are bred regularly in a number of zoos. European Brown Bears breed regularly in zoos, although they are now extremely rare in the wild in Europe, being confined to a few mountainous districts in the Pyrenees, in Italy and central Europe. They were exterminated in the British Isles by about the eighth century AD.

The large animals in the Zoo include elephants, rhinoceroses, Pygmy Hippopotamuses, camels, deer, antelopes, zebras, Giraffes and Okapis, the rarest and most valuable animals in the collection. The two elephants are African and Indian respectively, the African species being easily recognised by its larger ears and sloping forehead. The Indian Elephant has been used for centuries, both for riding and pack transport, and as a draught animal in forestry. Attempts have been made to domesticate the African Elephant, but they have not been very successful, partly because it is the wrong shape for pulling heavy objects such as logs, with its back sloping upwards towards the hind quarters. Both elephants here are female, as they are in most zoos, since the bulls are difficult to handle and dangerous when adult.

The Black Rhinoceros can move very quickly in spite of its size, and it has an uncertain temper. The Zoo obtained a pair in 1952 which bred the first calf of this species to be born in this country, in 1958. This, and the other calves they bred, were sent to other zoos to form new breeding pairs. Bristol is only one of five zoos in the British Isles to exhibit the Pygmy Hippopotamus. This is a pig-sized relation of the Common Hippopotamus, with a small head, found in the swampy forests of Liberia along streams and rivers. Unlike its massive cousin, it lives singly or in pairs, spending much more time on land. It is nocturnal, and has probably never been a numerous species.

There are two species of zebra here, Grévy's and the Damara, or Chapman's Zebra. Grévy's Zebra is the largest of all zebras, with big ears and well-defined black stripes. It is found in Somaliland, Ethiopia and northern Kenya. The Damara Zebra is a race of the Common Zebra of southern Africa, and it has a creamy

Three animals which can be seen at Bristol: above, Common Hippopotamus; below, Collared Peccary; right, White-lipped Peccary. Peccaries are the wild pigs of the New World.

coat with shadow stripes between its better-defined stripes.

The Okapi is related to the Giraffe, but it is found only in dense rain-forest in Zaire. It was unknown to science until 1901, when it was classified by Sir Ray Lankester, after examining a skin and two skulls sent from the Congo by Sir Henry Johnson. Johnson had been told of the existence of a 'wild donkey' deep in the forests of central Africa by the explorer H. M. Stanley in 1899, and in the following year he heard his first account of this strange animal from pygmies, who described it as a cross between a zebra and a mule. They called it the 'O'api'. The first live animal was exhibited in Antwerp Zoo in 1919, and since then more than 125 have been exhibited in zoos in Europe and the United States. Nevertheless, only a few zoos have been able to breed it regularly, and one of these is Bristol Zoo. Their first pair began breeding in 1966, and since then a number have been born, and with occasional importations of new blood lines the small herd is increasing satisfactorily. In the wild, Okapis live in pairs or small family groups, feeding mainly on leaves, with the addition of seeds and fruit. They are very shy, and at the Zoo they are not disturbed before giving birth, the mother being watched by closed-circuit television.

There is a varied selection of the smaller mammals, and the Zoo has for several years maintained a colony of kangaroos and wallabies. The largest species are the Red Kangaroo and the Great Grey Kangaroo. The Bennett's Wallabies are a small species of kangaroo, and they breed regularly in captivity. Kangaroos give birth to one young, which is born naked and only partially developed. The mother smooths a path with her tongue to the pouch, and the infant crawls up this into the pouch, where it grasps a nipple in its mouth. The nipple swells in its mouth, holding it secure until it has grown larger. The 'joey' does not emerge from the pouch until it is fully developed, and it returns to the pouch when older for as long as the mother will accept it. Another interesting animal, now endangered in the wild, is the Giant Anteater. This has a tubular, toothless mouth, a long sticky tongue and a large claw on the third toe of each front foot, used for digging out termites. It comes from the tropical forests of Central and South America. It is seldom bred in captivity, probably because not enough is yet known about the conditions necessary to induce it to breed; but another animal which breeds regularly here is the peccary. This is the wild pig of South America, Mexico and the western United States. There are two species, the Collared Peccary, which lives in small herds of up to a dozen in open scrub, and the White-lipped Peccary, which lives in forests. It is interesting that in captivity the Collared Peccary tends not to breed once the herd reaches a certain size, and it then becomes necessary to remove some of the animals before breeding is resumed.

The Zoo's bird collection is distributed all round the gardens – in the Plant House where various small birds and butterflies are kept, in the bird of prey aviary, the pheasant runs, the wading-bird aviary, the new aviary (a semi-walk-through range of outdoor aviaries containing a variety of exotic species), the Bird House containing the parrot collection, and the lake, on which there is a variety of waterfowl. Among the more interesting species to be seen are the Snowy Owl, which ranges into the Arctic Circle and breeds in Iceland, Norway, northern Russia, Alaska and Greenland. It occasionally strays southwards to the British Isles, where one pair has been nesting in the Shetland Islands since 1967. One of the most magnificent-looking birds which breeds regularly in the Zoo is the Victoria Crowned Pigeon, one of the giants of the pigeon family which is found in New Guinea. In the past they have been hunted for their flesh, but they are now protected and are still fairly common.

One of the rarer species is Rothschild's Mynah, a member of the starling family which is confined to the island of Bali. Another species endangered in the wild is the Red Bird of Paradise, with its orange and red plumage, which occurs only on the island of Waigeu, off the northwestern coast of New Guinea. Bird of paradise plumes have been used by the tribesmen of New Guinea for centuries and there was a trade in their skins from the sixteenth century onwards. In the nineteenth century their feathers were much in demand by the fashion trade, until trading was prohibited by law in the 1920s. By then, many formerly common species had become rare. Another endangered species is the Red-cheeked Ibis, a member of the graceful family of wading birds which is found throughout most of the warm climatic regions.

A rare gamebird, now endangered in the wild, is the Ocellated Turkey (a smaller bird than the common American Turkey) which has a bare blue head and prominent eyespot markings at the end of its tail feathers. It comes from Yucatan, Guatemala and Honduras. The rarest pheasant in the Zoo is the Palawan Peacock Pheasant, one of the smallest and most beautiful members of its group. It has a metallic green crown and a long green crest, which is brown in the female. It is found only on Palawan Island in the Philippines, high up in the damp tropical forests. It is bred only occasionally in captivity, the first successful breeding being in California in 1930. The Green Peafowl in the Zoo breed regularly, the long train feathers, which are not true tail feathers, being used in courtship displays. Peafowl are one of the oldest domesticated birds, and they were bred as table birds by the Romans.

There are three species of crane, all endangered in the wild, which you can see here. These are the Manchurian or Japanese Crane from Manchuria and northern Japan; the Hooded Crane, another Asiatic species; and the Wattled Crane of South Africa, which has a conspicuous red growth on its face. In Japan and Korea cranes have been strictly protected for many years, but their numbers were reduced by poaching after the Second War, and by battles in the Korean War which took place on their wintering grounds.

Two waterfowl of interest are the Cereopsis or Cape Barren Goose, found on the islands off western and southern Australia, and the Black Swan of Australia and Tasmania, which has been introduced into New Zealand and Sweden. Both birds breed regularly in the Bristol Zoo. The penguin collection exhibits the King, the Gentoo and the Macaroni species from Antarctica, Humboldt's Penguin from the west coasts of South America, and the South African Black-footed Penguin which breeds at the Zoo regularly. The penguin pool represents an inlet in an Antarctic island of volcanic origin, and it was copied from a design in plasticine made by a little girl in 1951.

Three species which have become rare in recent years will be found in the Reptile House. These are the American Alligator, the Nile Crocodile and the Spectacled Caiman. All the crocodile family have been hunted for sport and for their skins to such an extent that they are now far less numerous than they were, even 20 years ago. The American Alligator is now protected in Florida, where it was in danger of extinction partly because it was caught for the American pet trade, and partly because of the drainage schemes in the Everglades, the huge area of mangrove swamps in Florida. The Nile Crocodile is now only found in numbers in game reserves on the Upper Nile and in eastern Africa. The Spectacled Caiman, from Central and tropical South America, is a smaller species, up to eight feet long. The upper eyelids are wrinkled, often giving the impression of a pair of spectacles. Crocodiles and caimans are regarded as vicious, active animals, whereas alligators tend to be quieter and altogether less aggressive.

The Aquarium exhibits tropical freshwater fish in heated tanks, some seawater fish found off the western coasts of the British Isles, and freshwater fish from the temperate regions. The major part of the collection consists of various members of the carp family, several species of which have been bred traditionally as ornamental fish. These include the Goldfish, Shubunkins, Fantails and Veiltails, Golden Orfe and Golden Rudd, which has been bred selectively for its colours. You can also see South American Electric Eels, which have tail muscles modified to develop electric shocks of several hundred volts.

The gardens contain a fine collection of trees, some of which were planted when the grounds were laid out in the early nineteenth century. There are two cedars of Lebanon, five deodar cedars and one Mount Atlas cedar, a wellingtonia and some Californian redwoods, the largest tree in the world, which can grow to 300 feet. There is a maidenhair tree introduced into England in 1754 from China, two monkey puzzle or Chilean pine trees, a tree of heaven — a flowering species from China — and a tulip tree from North America. There are also colourful herbaceous borders and a rock garden.

The rare Nile Crocodile from East Africa.

American Alligator, an endangered species.

Spectacled Caiman from South America.

Bristol Zoo is owned by the Bristol, Clifton and West of England Zoological Society, founded in 1845 by a group of Bristol citizens who agreed that there was a need for a scientific society in the city, since at the time science was 'cultivated by a few within the circle of their Closets — but out of that circle, studied only upon a holiday in the travelling booth of a fair, or in the prisons of the Tower, or in the disgusting receptacles of Exeter Change, by a class of gazers as innocent of science as the miserable objects of their vacant curiosity'! (The royal menagerie in the Tower of London was closed in 1831, and the animals distributed between the newly opened London Zoo and Dublin Zoo. Exeter Change refers to a zoo run by a dealer off the Strand, London.) But the Society always envisaged many other attractions besides a zoo in the' gardens, to provide the necessary income to support an animal collection. This policy was developed, until the gardens were hired out for all kinds of annual carnivals and 'grand re-unions' and many attractions such as croquet, concerts, archery, fire-works, roller-skating and ice-skating, with a flooded rink in winter. Despite these activities, the Zoo was losing money, and after 1927 the Society concentrated again on its animal collection, since when it has grown into one of the best zoos in the country. In 1954 the Society received a grant of arms, and its coat of arms can be seen at the entrance gates. These combine elephants' heads, a Chimpanzee and a Gorilla with a Cross of Botany, representing the Zoo's main successes. In 1963, the Society bought the Hollywood Towers estate, seven miles from Clifton, where some of the rarest and most valuable animals are bred in seclusion. The exhibition of animals is not always compatible with the conditions needed for breeding, and this is an ideal way of ensuring that endangered species are bred and preserved.

Cuttlefish can be seen at the Aquaria in Brixham and Cheddar.

Brixham Aquarium

The Brixham Aquarium, opened in 1954, is devoted entirely to sea fish found within a radius of 40 miles from Brixham by local trawlers and crabbers. Species you can see here include rays and skates, sharks and dogfish, Conger Eel, Cod, Whiting, Pollack, bass, mullet, wrasse, Mackerel, blennies, gobies, bullheads and gurnards — and the flat fish such as Plaice, dab, Sole, Turbot and Brill. There is also an excellent selection of invertebrate marine animals (those with no backbone) such as sea-anemones, corals, jellyfish (including the Portuguese Man-of-war, a rare visitor to our coasts with a nasty sting), lobsters, crabs, prawns and shrimps. The molluscs include whelk, scallop, cuttlefish, squid and the Common Octopus, and you can also see starfishes and sea-urchins.

Brixham has always been the most important fishing port in the West Country, and it was once the largest in Great Britain with over 200 fishing vessels. Depending on the weather, the tide and other factors, you can generally see the trawlers bringing in their catch between 6 p.m. and 9 p.m. during the summer months.

The Brixham Aquarium. **Address** 12 The Quay, Brixham, Devon. **Telephone** Brixham 2204. **Open** 10.00–22.00 summer, closed winter. **Guide-book**. **Car** to The Quay, Brixham. **Bus** 12 Newton Abbot – Torquay – Paignton – Brixham route. **Train** to Paignton (6 mls). Public **not allowed** to feed exhibits.

Cheddar Marineland Aquarium

This Aquarium displays tropical and temperate marine fish and invertebrates (animals without backbones), and temperate freshwater fish. One section is devoted to British marine species, from rays and sharks down to Pipefish and blennies, and crustaceans and invertebrates such as lobsters, crabs, shellfish, cuttlefish and anemones. Another section has British freshwater species. The tropical marine tanks mainly display fish of the coral reefs, with invertebrates and living corals, and the tropical freshwater section always has some unusual exhibits. Marine species which breed here include perch and Lesser Dogfish. Sea-horses have been bred, but not reared.

The Aquarium is owned by Mr P. J. Pittman. It was opened in 1960 and rebuilt in 1975.

Cheddar Marineland Aquarium. **Address** Cheddar Gorge, Somerset. **Telephone** Cheddar 742854. **Open** 09.30–21.00 Easter–Oct, closed in winter. **Guide-book**. Zoo shop. **Car** 2½ mls s.e. of Axbridge on A371. **Bus** 371 from Weston-super-Mare stops outside Aquarium. **Train** to Weston-super-Mare. **Taxis** available. Public **not allowed** to feed exhibits.

Dartmoor Wildlife Park

This little Zoo, started by Mr E. B. Daw in 1968, specialises in British and European animals. You can see Red and Fallow Deer and three introduced species, the Chinese Water Deer, Sika and Muntjac. Smaller British mammals include the Badger, Fox, Grey Squirrel, Polecat and Wild Cat, and there is a pool for Grey Seals, and for Coypus, another introduced species which is now found wild in Great Britain. Exotic animals here include Palm Civets and Malayan Otters. The Long Pen contains the Grey Heron and some ornamental pheasants, and there are aviaries for more pheasants, Kestrels, Eagle Owls, Tawny Owls and Barn Owls, all of which have bred here, and Ravens and Buzzards. The waterfowl pool contains Mute Swans, Black Swans from Australia, various species of goose and duck, and some flamingos and herons. The open-air vivarium exhibits the Adder (or Viper), the only British poisonous snake, European Dice Snakes and terrapins, and some amphibians and fish.

There is a Pet House, where small mammals and birds are kept, a walk-in enclosure for Rabbits, lambs and ducks and a nursery enclosure for hand-reared fawns, ducks and pheasants. Permanent residents in this enclosure are Purple Herons, Night Herons and Curlews on a pond. Several peafowl and ornamental pheasants are at liberty in the grounds and there is an observation tower and an animal graveyard with epitaphs to animals dating back to 1820.

Dartmoor Wildlife Park. **Address** Sparkwell, Plymouth. **Telephone** Cornwood 209. **Open** 10.00–dusk summer and winter. **Guide-book. Catering** snack bar, kiosk. Information centre, gift shop. **Guided tours** by arrangement. **Acreage** 25. **Car** 8 mls e. of Plymouth n. of A38, near Plympton. **Bus** 58 and 59 from Bretonside bus station stop at entrance. **Train** to Plymouth then bus to Park. **Other facilities** push-chairs. Public allowed to feed animals with food prepared and sold in Park only.

Exmouth Aquarium

The Aquarium has a mixed collection of local marine and freshwater fish, as well as tropical marine and freshwater species. There are also some turtles and terrapins, including a very large Loggerhead Turtle, believed to be the largest exhibited in the British Isles. Many species breed regularly here, including seahorses, although these have not yet been reared. The Aquarium was opened in 1955.

Exmouth Aquarium. **Address** Sea-front, Exmouth, Devon. **Telephone** Exmouth 3016. **Open** 10.00–dusk daily summer, 10.00–17.30 Tues, Fri, Sat, Sun winter. Aquarium shop. **Car** to sea-front – The Esplanade – just e. of clock tower. **Bus** stops 100 yds from Aquarium. **Train** to Exmouth ($\frac{1}{4}$ ml). **Taxis** available. Public **not allowed** to feed exhibits.

Exmouth Zoo

Exmouth Zoo is a small mixed collection of mammals, birds and reptiles. Although on a small scale, this is a carefully chosen collection containing some very choice exhibits. Emphasis is placed on small mammals, amongst which you can see Kinkajous, which breed here regularly – they were the first to be bred in captivity in Great Britain – and Olingos, mongooses, Tayras and bushbabies; the Senegal Bushbabies here also breed regularly. You can also see the Slender Loris, which breeds here occasionally, and there is a Chimpanzee and several species of monkey. The only larger mammals here are Pumas, which are also regular breeders. Among the birds, the collection is strong on hornbills and toucans, and you can also see peafowl, macaws, parrots, cockatoos and conures. There are curassows and Crested Screamers, and the birds of prey here are caracaras and Savannah Hawks. Caracaras, of which there are nine species in the wild, are large falcon-like birds of prey. The reptiles exhibited include the Yellow Anaconda, Carpet Pythons and Blood Pythons, tree boas from Haiti and the only poisonous lizards in the world, the Gila Monster and the Mexican Beaded Lizard. There are also a few amphibians, and altogether the collection has over 100 mammals and about 50 birds and reptiles.

The Zoo was started in 1957 by Paignton Zoological and Botanical Gardens and it was taken over in 1962 by Mr Kenneth Smith, an experienced animal collector and zoo superintendent. Enthusiastic naturalists need not wait for the rain clouds when they find themselves in Exmouth.

Exmouth Zoo. **Address** Sea-front, Exmouth, Devon. **Telephone** Exmouth 5756. **Open** 10.00–dusk summer, 10.00–17.00 winter. **Guide-book.** Zoo shop. **Guided tours** by arrangement. **Acreage** 1. **Car** to sea-front – The Esplanade – e. of Carlton Hill. **Bus** 52 stops 200 yards from Zoo. **Train** to Exmouth ($\frac{1}{2}$ ml). **Taxis** available. Public allowed to feed animals with food prepared and sold in Zoo only.

Ilfracombe Tropical Wildlife Corner

This small Zoo has a selection of about 50 mammals and over 100 birds. The mammals include monkeys, Leopard Cats, Raccoons, Muntjac and African Goats. Birds you can see include flamingos, penguins, cranes, peafowl, hornbills, toucans, parrots, macaws, cockatoos and fishing owls. The Zoo was opened in 1974 by Mr C. H. Trevisick, who moved it from Comyn Hill, where he had another small zoo from 1949 to 1973.

Jersey Zoological Park

Jersey Zoological Park was founded in 1959 by Mr Gerald Durrell — author of many best-selling books on wildlife — with the object of establishing breeding colonies of animals which are threatened with extinction in the wild. The Park is remarkable for its collection of some of the world's rarest animals, many of which breed regularly. Some of them have bred here for the first time anywhere in captivity. 48% of the mammals have been zoo-bred, and controlled breeding programmes of the rarer species have top priority. Most of the animal accommodation has been redesigned in recent years, and the Park is noted for its breeding groups of Lowland Gorillas, Orang utans, lemurs, marmosets and rare pheasants. At the Park entrance is a model of the Dodo, which became extinct in the seventeenth century and is the Jersey Zoological Park's symbol of survival. Some of the exhibits in the Park have this Dodo symbol displayed, indicating that if it is not bred in captivity it will become 'as dead as the Dodo'.

One of the first buildings you come to is the Lemur House where several species are exhibited, their outdoor cages having glass panels for better viewing. Lemurs are found only in Madagascar, where they are threatened because of forest clearance by timber contractors. They have survived in isolation owing to the absence of predatory animals on the island. The species exhibited here are the Ruffed Lemur, the Mayotte Brown Lemur which has bred regularly in the Park, the Mouse Lemur, the Mongoose Lemur and the Fat-tailed Dwarf Lemur. Fat-tailed Lemurs have the ability to store fat in their tails, and they sleep during the dry season.

There are spacious outdoor enclosures for Brazilian Tapirs and Cheetahs, the latter being endangered in Africa, almost its last remaining range. Cheetahs were once common in India and Asia Minor, but they have become extinct in those parts of the world, except for a few in Iran. Tapirs live in the tropical jungles of South America, spending much time near water.

The Brian Park Gorilla Complex contains the Park's Gorillas. The two females were joined by a male which had been bred in the Basle Zoo, Switzerland, and in 1973 two babies were born, making this only the second British zoo to breed the Lowland Gorilla. Two subsequent births put the Park amongst the select few, among British zoos, which can boast of a group which breeds regularly. Only five other zoos in Europe have bred even one Gorilla. The Gorilla Complex was completed in 1972, and it contains breeding accommodation and a glass-panelled outdoor enclosure. The Ape Range is the home of the Orang utans, which are also breeding regularly. Both races are exhibited, the Bornean and the Sumatran. The Sumatran Orang utan has longer hair, and both races are fast disappearing in the wild, partly because of poaching but also, like so many wild animals, because of the destruction of their forest habitat.

Several species of monkey are exhibited in the Park, including Mandrills, Gelada Baboons, which breed regularly, Diana Monkeys and the Celebes Black Ape, which also breeds here. The Gelada Baboon is sometimes called the 'bleeding heart' baboon because of the bare red patch on its chest. It is found only in the mountainous regions of Ethiopia, and with such a confined distribution it could be in danger of extinction. There is a fine breeding colony of the

Ilfracombe Tropical Wildlife Corner. **Address** Bicclescombe Park, Ilfracombe. **Telephone** Ilfracombe 62702. **Open** 11.00—dusk summer, closed in winter. **Acreage** ½. **Car** 1 ml s. of town in Bicclescombe Park Road, off A361. **Bus** to Cider Apple Club, then ¼ ml to Park. **Train** to Barnstaple (9 mls). **Taxis** available. Public allowed to feed animals with food sold in Zoo only.

Jersey Zoological Park. **Address** Les Augres Manor, Trinity, Jersey, Channel Islands. **Telephone** Jersey 61949. **Open** 10.00—dusk summer and winter. **Guide-book**. **Catering** self-service cafeteria. Zoo shop. **Guided tours** for educational groups by arrangement. **Acreage** 20. **Bus** frequent service from St Helier to Zoo. **Taxis** available. Public **not allowed** to feed animals.

Mother and baby tapir at Jersey Zoological Park. Tapirs are normally shy creatures, but they can be aggressive if threatened.

Ursine Black and White Colobus monkey here. This is a beautiful West African species from the forests of Guinea, with black and white hair. As soon as the animals here were breeding regularly, a second group was established away from the original group to ensure that the colony would survive should there be an outbreak of disease. One of the most recent buildings is the Marmoset House, where four species of marmoset are shown, the policy being to keep a few species in breeding groups, rather than a large number in small units where the chances of breeding are minimal. Marmosets come from South America, where several species are in danger of extinction. The male takes charge of the infant, returning it to its mother at feeding time.

The Park has always placed emphasis on the preservation of the smaller mammals, many of which lack the glamour of the larger, more popular animals in zoos. Many of the small creatures here are rare in the wild, and also seldom seen in captivity. Three of these are the Jamaican Hutia, the Crested Rat and the Hedgehog Tenrec. The hutia is a primitive rodent which lives on the ground. There are several species, found only in the West Indies, where their restricted island range makes them an easy prey to man, domestic dogs and cats, and the mongoose. They bred here for the first time in captivity. The Crested Rat, also bred here for the first time in a zoo, is a stoutly built species about a foot long. It lives in rocky terrain in Ethiopia and northern Kenya, and is a slow-moving nocturnal animal although it is a good climber. The Hedgehog Tenrec is a small insect-eating animal, with spines like a hedgehog but less than half its size. The tenrec family, comprising several species, is restricted to Madagascar and the Comoro Islands, and those in the Park have been bred successfully for some years. You can also see another spiny animal, the echidna, which belongs to the most primitive order of mammals. It lays eggs and then suckles the young when hatched. It is toothless, and has hard ridges on its palate which help to grind up food. One of the most successful breeding groups among the small mammals is the Sierra Leone Striped Squirrel, of which 42 were bred in seven years. On the upper waterfowl pond is an island for tamarins, small squirrel-like monkeys which closely resemble marmosets but with large canine teeth. Two tamarin species in the collection, an Emperor Tamarin and a Geoffroy's Tamarin, which arrived in 1961, each set a record for the oldest of their species in captivity.

There is a large grass enclosure for White-throated or Parma Wallabies, which they share with Cape Barren Geese, also known as Cereopsis. In order to create a natural environment for the wallabies, patches of long grass have been left, and the enclosure is planted with more than 20 species of eucalyptus. The Cereopsis is a large goose from the small islands off southern Australia and Tasmania. It is the fourth rarest goose in the world, and it is protected in the wild. Another enclosure exhibits a thriving herd of peccaries, the wild pig of South America. It lives in small groups in the wild, and when the numbers increased in the Park breeding stopped, but was resumed when the herd was divided into two, thus relieving the population pressure.

The carnivorous animals in the Park include African Civets, a powerful animal with a gland under the tail which contains the oily discharge used by the cosmetic industry in making scent; Servals, a small African species of cat which, like the Civets, breeds regularly here; leopards and Asiatic Lions. Lions were once common in Asia Minor and India, but the last remnants of the Asiatic race are now confined to a single reserve in the Gir Forest, in the State of Gujerat, northwestern India. The pair exhibited here arrived in 1972, and they are the only ones to be seen in a European zoo.

Several rare species of pheasant are to be seen, the rarest being the White-eared Pheasant from western Szechwan in China and parts of southeastern Tibet. When the first of these birds arrived in 1969, there were only 18 specimens in the Western world. They were bred successfully in the Park, and 70 birds have now been exported to 11 different countries, where they are placed on deposit with other zoos. This species can be said to have been saved from extinction by successful breeding in Jersey. Other rare species which breed here are the Satyr Tragopan, the Palawan Peacock Pheasant, and the Brown-eared Pheasant from the mountains of northeastern China. Perhaps the most interesting bird in the Park

Jersey Zoo's male Gorilla, Jambo.

is the Congo Pheasant. The natural range of pheasants is central and southern Asia. but this lone species, the only one of the true pheasants discovered in Africa, was identified by a single feather in the 1930s. The first live bird was not found until 20 years later, in the jungle swamps of the Congo. It had survived there hitherto unknown to science, and a few birds were sent to the Antwerp Zoo which gradually built up a breeding stock. Six zoos were eventually selected to receive pairs of this rare bird to continue the breeding programme, and Jersey is the only place outside Antwerp where they have been bred in captivity.

The parrot aviaries contain several species, including the Hispanolian Parrot and Thick-billed Parrots from Mexico, both of which are rare in the wild. Two handsome birds in the owl aviaries are the Snowy Owl and the Spectacled Owl. The Snowy Owl breeds in the Arctic Circle, nesting in the open on the tundra. Spectacled Owls, found in the jungles of South America and in southern Mexico, have startling facial markings, the eyes being ringed with white and looking like spectacles. In fact, owls have very large eyes, but their vision is restricted sideways. To compensate for this they can turn their heads through 270 degrees. They also have very well-developed ears, hidden by feathers, and acute hearing. In the aviaries opposite the owl aviary, one interesting bird is the Weka Rail, a New Zealand wood rail. This is a flightless bird which preys on mice and rats which have been introduced by man, as well as on other small animals.

The Tropical Bird House is cleverly landscaped to give a natural-looking background to each exhibit, and it contains several birds which have been bred here for the first time in captivity. These include the Mexican Jay, the Grey Touraco, the Gold Coast Touraco and the Thick-billed Euphonia. Touracos come from Africa, where they live on plantains and other fruit, and insects. They mostly inhabit thick forest, in pairs or family groups, and feed their young on regurgitated fruit. Euphonias are small tanagers, found in Mexico and South America. They live along the fringes of forests, searching for berries and fruit. They too feed their young with regurgitated food. Another species which has bred here is the Speckled Mousebird. Mousebirds, or colies, are African in origin, and their name is derived from the way in which they scurry about, their bodies crouched over the branches. Physically, they are not closely related to any other birds, and they are peculiar for having reversible outer toes which can grasp a branch either forwards or backwards. Mousebirds are gregarious and they live on leaves, fruit, berries and insects. Two endangered species here are Rothschild's Mynah and Bare-faced Ibis. The former is found only on the island of Bali. Ibises are divided into 28 species, throughout most of the warmer regions of the world. Most species have been persecuted by feather hunters and they are not now seen in the wild in the large flocks which used to be commonplace.

The Reptile House is a recent development, and it contains the Nile and Cuban Crocodiles, the Mississippi Alligator, the Copperhead Snake and the Mangrove Snake, to mention a few. One of the rarest of these is the Cuban Crocodile, a small species only about eight feet long which is confined to Cuba. Although comparatively small, it is fierce and agile, able to jump three feet out of the water. One extremely rare reptile here is the Tuatara, which in the wild state exists only on a few islands off the North and South Islands of New Zealand. It is long-lived, and reputed to continue growing for up to 50 years. Another rare species is the Spine-tailed Mastigure, a lizard found in western and central Asia and North Africa. It is a plant-eater and it has spines on its tail which it uses as a means of self-defence.

Having founded the Park in 1959, Gerald Durrell established the Jersey Wildlife Preservation Trust in 1963, as a charitable trust to take over the collection and continue its objective of breeding rare animals which are endangered in the wild. The importance of the Trust's work is widely recognised, and a grant has enabled it to build and staff a nutrition research unit. Membership of the Trust entitles you to free admission with one guest to the Park, a quarterly newsletter from Gerald Durrell and a copy of the Trust's annual report. The Park is a delightful setting for this exceedingly interesting collection of animals, and Les Augrès Manor is a good example of Jersey architecture, the oldest part of which dates from the fourteenth century, and the west wing from about 1660.

Looe Aquarium

This little Aquarium exhibits local marine fish, all of which are found along the local shoreline. At the end of the summer season all the fish are returned to the sea, so the collection varies somewhat from year to year. It was opened in 1953 by Mr H. S. Tucker.

Looe Aquarium. **Address** The Quay-head, Looe, Cornwall. **Telephone** Looe 2423. **Open** 10.30–21.00 1st June–30th Sept. **Catering** kiosk. **Car** drive to Quayhead. **Train** to Looe ($\frac{1}{4}$ ml). Public **not allowed** to feed exhibits.

Lyme Regis Marine Aquarium

As its name suggests, this is a collection of marine species — local fish and shore creatures being collected each year and returned to the sea at the end of the summer season. Young dogfish are reared each year, and there is an extra large ground-level tank in the Aquarium. The exhibition was opened in 1958.

Lyme Regis Marine Aquarium. **Address** The Harbour, Lyme Regis, Dorset. **Telephone** Lyme Regis 2309. **Open** 10.00–18.00 Easter–end of Sept. **Guided tours** for schools by arrangement. **Car** to the harbour (The Cobb). Public **not allowed** to feed exhibits.

Merley Tropical Bird Gardens

Merley Bird Gardens were opened in 1968, and you can see a good selection here of tropical birds, including many members of the parrot family, such as Australian and Indian parrakeets, cockatoos, macaws, Amazon parrots, African Grey Parrots and lories. You can also see Blue Crowned Pigeons, Imperial Pigeons, Nicobar Pigeons, touracos, a wide variety of small seed-eating and soft-billed birds, as well as penguins, flamingos and cranes. Altogether there are 1,000 birds, of 150 different species.

Merley Tropical Bird Gardens. **Address** Merley, Nr Wimbourne, Dorset. **Telephone** Wimbourne 3790. **Open** 10.00–17.00 summer, closed end of Oct–Easter. **Catering** self-service cafeteria. Zoo shop. **Acreage** $3\frac{1}{2}$. **Guided tours** by arrangement. **Car** $\frac{1}{2}$ ml s. of Wimbourne on A349 Poole road. **Train** to Poole (3 mls). **Other facilities** wheelchairs. No pets. Public **not allowed** to feed birds.

The Monkey Sanctuary

The Monkey Sanctuary is not a conventional zoo, as it consists of one species — a thriving colony of Woolly Monkeys from tropical South America. The monkeys have large grassed areas and beech trees, all enclosed, providing an environment which enables these fascinating animals to behave naturally. On arrival, visitors receive an explanation of the Woolly Monkey and its way of life. During their visit there is an opportunity for people to meet some of the monkeys, including mothers with babies. The monkeys are supervised by the staff, and comments are given by experienced lecturers. After the main talk, the lecturing staff are available to explain and comment on the social behaviour of the monkeys. In bad weather all talks and demonstrations are held indoors where the monkeys have comfortable and roomy quarters.

The Sanctuary was founded in 1964 by Mr Leonard Williams who has spent many years studying and writing about Woolly Monkeys. This is not an easy species to breed in captivity, but Mr Williams is one of the few people in the world to have achieved regular breeding of it.

In fine weather you can also see a free-living colony of Prairie Marmots, and there are donkeys, macaws, Rabbits and cavies as well.

The Monkey Sanctuary. **Address** Looe, Cornwall. **Telephone** Looe 2532. **Open** 10.30–18.00 Easter–30th Sept. **Guidebook. Catering** kiosk. **Guided tours** by arrangement. **Acreage** 3. **Car** 3 mls n.e. of Looe off B3253. **Bus** to Seaton or Bindown then 2 mls to Zoo. **Train** to Looe (3 mls). **Taxis** available. Public **not allowed** to feed animals.

Newquay Zoological Gardens

This Zoo, started by Newquay U.D.C. in 1969, has a mixed collection of mammals and birds, with a few reptiles. There are Chimpanzees, various monkeys, including Crab-eating Macaques which breed here, Lions, Chinese Leopards, Asiatic Black Bears, sealions, American Bison, Red Deer, Formosan Sika Deer,

Barbary Sheep and Bennett's Wallabies, which breed here regularly. There is a small Tropical House exhibiting some constrictor snakes (such as pythons), Broad-nosed Crocodiles, caimans, terrapins, Box Turtles, lizards and toads. A few tropical birds are also shown here in aviaries. There are two small lakes, where you can see Bar-headed and Barnacle Geese, Caribbean Flamingos, several species of shelduck and pintail, Black-necked Swans from South America and pelicans. Nearby is a paddock for Sarus Cranes. There is a walk-through aviary showing touracos, starlings, whydahs, weavers, doves, parrakeets, Golden Pheasants and Scarlet Ibises; and a penguin pool.

The most interesting exhibit is for Cornish Choughs, now extinct in Cornwall, in a specially designed aviary where they are now breeding. They are the property of the Cornish Chough Society, which hopes to reintroduce these beautiful members of the crow family to the Cornish countryside. The children's section contains domestic animals, free-flying macaws, some aviaries containing parrakeets, mynahs and finches, and an enclosure for Crested Porcupines.

Padstow Bird Gardens

This is a beautifully laid out little Bird Garden, with the emphasis on soft-billed birds, but also with a cross-section of bird life. The more delicate birds are in a heated Tropical House, and there is an interesting collection of butterflies from all over the world, including live butterflies with their own food plants. A good proportion of the birds here are breeding, which is one of the main objects of the collection. It was opened by Mr J. H. Brown in 1969.

Paignton Aquarium

You can see here a general collection of marine fish and other sea creatures found in Torbay. The Aquarium concentrates on small creatures not usually exhibited in aquaria, such as barnacles, which are seen under a magnifying glass, dogfish eggs, showing the living embryo, hermit-crabs with parasitic anemone and ragworm. There is also a large number of static exhibits and models illustrating life on the sea shore. The Aquarium has been open since 1955.

Paignton Zoological and Botanical Gardens

Paignton Zoological and Botanical Gardens are the only ones in Great Britain to have been planned as a combination of animal and plant life, and as you walk through the gardens you will see a wonderful collection of trees and shrubs, some of which are so rare that they have not yet been identified. Many plants are too delicate to grow in less-sheltered parts of the country, and wherever possible, interesting plant specimens have been placed in and around the animal houses and enclosures. This is certainly one of the most beautiful zoos in the country, and its animal collection makes it one of the major British zoos and the main zoo in the West Country. Besides having the big cats, elephants and rhinoceroses, there is a good collection of monkeys, deer, antelopes and the smaller mammals, an outstanding collection of parrots, some interesting small tropical birds and rare pheasants, and a good assortment of reptiles.

One of the first houses you see on entering the Zoo is the Sub-tropical House with its high glass roof. It is in two compartments, arranged according to the source of the exhibits. The first contains plants from Europe, central Asia and South Africa. There are massive clumps of Mediterranean reed and Kashmir cypress, and colourful collections of South African bulbs. The second compartment exhibits plants from the Australian region and Central and South America.

Newquay Zoological Gardens. **Address** Trenance Park, Newquay, Cornwall. **Telephone** Newquay 3342. **Open** 10.00–21.00 summer, 10.00–17.00 winter. **Catering** self-service cafeteria, kiosk. **Guided tours** by arrangement. **Acreage** 9. **Car** ¼ ml s. of Newquay on A3075 Perranporth road (Edgecumbe Avenue). **Train** to Newquay (¼ ml). **Taxis** available. No pets. Public **not allowed** to feed animals.

Padstow Bird Gardens. **Address** Fentonluna, Padstow, Cornwall. **Telephone** Padstow 262. **Open** 10.30–1 hr before dusk summer and winter. **Guide-book**. **Catering** snack bar. Zoo shop. **Guided tours** by arrangement. **Acreage** 2. **Car** large free car park on B3276 at Padstow, then walk through Church pathway. **Bus** stops ¼ ml from Gardens. **Train** to Bodmin Road then bus from station to Padstow. **Other facilities** butterfly exhibition. Public **not allowed** to feed birds.

Paignton Aquarium. **Address** The Harbour, Paignton, Devon. **Telephone** Paignton 56927. **Open** 10.00–22.00 summer, closed winter. **Car** Dartmouth road A379 then turn e. along Sands Road B3201 for The Harbour. **Bus** open-top service passes harbour during summer months. Public **not allowed** to feed exhibits.

Paignton Zoological and Botanical Gardens. **Address** Totnes Road, Paignton, Devon. **Telephone** Paignton 57479. **Open** daily 10.00–17.30 summer, 10.00–dusk winter. **Guide-book**. **Catering** bar, self-service cafeteria, kiosks. Zoo shop. **Acreage** 75. **Car** ¼ ml from Tweensaway Cross on A385 Totnes road. **Bus** between Paignton, Totnes and Plymouth to Zoo. **Train** to Paignton (1 ml). **Taxis** available. **Other facilities** miniature train, first-aid post, children's playground, dog kennels. No pets. Public may feed animals with own food or food sold in Zoo.

Here, climbing plants are flanked by the big Australian tree ferns and mimosa. There is a walk-through aviary in this house, and several birds are breeding, including Chestnut-backed Mousebirds, Red-vented Bulbuls, Cayenne Wood Rails and Orange-headed Ground Thrushes.

The Tropical House contains a remarkable exhibit of tropical plants and there is nothing else like it in the country. One comes first to the tropical pond, designed as a pool in a tropical swamp with fantastic and brightly coloured water plants, both under the water and floating on the surface. There are fern-covered islands, plants of marshy habitats around the pool's edge, and many exotic creepers around the back and sides of the display. The main part of the house has, on one side, groups of plants arranged according to the type of environment in which they grow, including a tropical forest and a display of succulents, and on the other side, plants arranged according to their family groups. These give a fascinating insight into the variety and beauty of the plant kingdom. The founder of the Zoo, Mr Herbert Whitley, is said to have designed this house on the back of an envelope, and to have built it with his own staff.

Opening out of the Tropical House is the combined Aquarium and Reptile House. The Aquarium contains a variety of tropical fish, including several species of tetra, the Blind Cave Fish, the Higoi Carp, a domesticated species related to the Goldfish, and various species of barb. You can also see the Electric Eel, the African Lungfish and the Ampullarian Water-snail. The reptile collection contains a Snapping Turtle, several species of terrapin and the European Pond Tortoise, all of which live in fresh water, and several other tortoises, including the rare Pancake Tortoise. The crocodiles exhibited here are the Nile Crocodile, the Estuarine Crocodile, which swims in the sea as well as in the rivers of southeast Asia, the Broad-fronted Crocodile and the Smooth-fronted Crocodile. Closely related to these are the American Alligator and Spectacled Caiman, and the False Gavial, from Asia. All the members of the crocodile family are now endangered in the wild, as their hides are much in demand for leather.

The snake collection includes the Boa Constrictor and several other species of boa and python, of which the rarest are the Indian Python and the Bahama Boa, which is seldom exhibited in this country. One of the most colourful pythons is the Green Tree Python, a small species which reaches a length of six and a half feet. It lives mainly in trees, feeding on small birds and lizards. Its young are buttercup-yellow before developing the brilliant emerald-green of the adult.

There is an interesting collection of lizards, including the Gila Monster and the Mexican Beaded Lizard, the only two poisonous lizards, both of which are endangered in the wild — in the western United States and Mexico. Look out also for the Bloodsucker with its bright red throat which is probably significant in its courtship display, the High-casqued Chameleons, and the Scheltopusik, a curious snake-like reptile which is a legless lizard rather than a snake, closely related to the British Slow-worm. Do not miss the frogs and toads, which include some large species not often seen in British zoos.

Of the carnivorous animals, the first ones which you see after entering the Zoo are the Lions and Tigers, in large paddocks. The other large cat species here are the Cheetah and Leopard. All of these except the Lion are in considerable danger of extinction in the wild, and captive breeding in zoos is likely to be the only insurance that they will continue to exist, although they are now given protection in the countries where they occur — which is not easy to enforce. There are also Pumas, the Jungle Cat and the European Wild Cat, which recently bred here, a comparatively unusual event in zoos. The dog family is represented by the Arctic Fox and the Dingo. Arctic Foxes, when calling to their mates, lower their heads to the ground, so that the sound will carry along the frozen surface of snow and ice. This is in contrast to the other species of fox which raise their heads to call, so that the sound will carry through the air. The Dingo is not a truly wild species of dog, having been introduced to Australia, perhaps thousands of years ago. All the native mammals of Australia are either pouched animals or egg-laying animals, and the aboriginal people of Australia do not keep domestic animals. Presumably, the people who brought the Dingo left at a later date, leaving their dogs behind to run wild.

The marsupials include the Western Grey Kangaroo and Bennett's Wallaby, both of which breed here regularly, the Coarse-haired Wombat, and two other species. The Brush-tailed Possum has a somewhat foxy appearance with a sharp muzzle and long ears, and a long furry tail. It is nocturnal, but is the most familiar of the marsupials to Australians. The Four-eyed Opossum, on the other hand, comes from Central and South America; it too is a tree climber. The Brush-tailed Possums have bred and they can be seen in the Small Mammal House. The wombat, a native of Australia and Tasmania is a large, tailless animal with a head rather like a teddy bear. It burrows, eating roots and other vegetable matter, and it is nocturnal.

Three other interesting animals are the Giant Anteater, the armadillo and the sloth. All come from tropical South America and belong to the group of 'toothless' mammals, a misleading term since they all have teeth of some kind, except the anteater which feeds on insects, ants and termites. The Giant Anteater's very powerful claws are used to tear open termite nests, and its long tongue can penetrate narrow openings to find its prey. The Six-banded Armadillo is found in Paraguay and Brazil. It is an insect-eater and burrower. Armadillos have jointed, bony plates on their skin, which are a protection against predatory animals. One species, the Three-banded Armadillo, can roll itself into a ball when danger threatens. The Hoffmann's Sloth exhibited here is a species of two-toed sloth, found in South America from Ecuador to Costa Rica. It has two hooks on its front feet, which are used to hang on to branches, upside-down. Sloths are preyed upon by Jaguars, and despite their ponderous mode of progress they are able to swim, if they happen to fall into the water.

Three reptiles which can be seen at Paignton: above, Green Tree Python of New Guinea, well camouflaged in its leafy habitat; below, Indian Python; right, High-casqued Chameleon from Africa.

The monkeys in the Zoo show a good selection of African species, and a smaller collection of South American ones. The anthropoid apes here are Chimpanzees, Agile Gibbons and Lar Gibbons. The gibbons will be found on Gibbon Island on the lake. They live there all the year round and it is a splendid sight when they display their agility, swinging rapidly from tree to tree. Several monkeys breed regularly at the Zoo, and the female Red-faced Spider Monkey, a South American species, has produced seven young. One of the most beautiful species is the Abyssinian Colobus Monkey, which is not often seen in captivity as it is a leaf-eater and consequently presents feeding problems. At Paignton, however, these monkeys are given bamboo, large plantations of which grow naturally in Clennon Gorge, not far from the Zoo. Infant Colobus Monkeys are pure snow-white for the first few months of their lives, before acquiring the long, flowing black and white coats of the adults. The Barbary Apes are the only members of the monkey tribe found in Europe, and there is a colony of them on the Rock of Gibraltar, where they are fed daily at public expense. One of the Barbary Apes in the Zoo has given birth to 15 babies. There is a thriving colony of Hamadryas Baboons, a handsome species with a grey mantle round the shoulders, which is exhibited on the Baboon Rock. The sloping layers of the rock have been coloured to simulate the layers of volcanic rock found in rocky outcrops in North Africa. The smaller primates to be seen in the small mammal house include the Common Treeshrew, the Ring-tailed Lemur from Madagascar, the Slow Loris, Bosman's Potto and the Cameroon Potto, and the Thick-tailed Galago or Bushbaby. The pottos and bushbabies are found in Africa and the lorises in southeast Asia. Lemurs are found now only in Madagascar, where forest clearance is seriously threatening their existence. The Treeshrews have bred in the Zoo, three born in 1974 being the second generation to be born here.

Many of the rodents exhibited in the Zoo have been bred here, one of the most prolific being the Nile Rats. Other breeding species are the African Giant Pouched Rat, the Common Spiny Mouse, the Harvest-mouse and the Crested Porcupine. Harvest-mice are not often seen in zoos, and this is one of the smallest of all the rodents. It has a wide range in the wild state, from Great Britain right across Europe and Asia to Japan. A litter of up to eight young are born blind and hairless in a nest made of grass and leaves, and two litters can be born within a month. Harvest-mice have long tails which are used for balancing as they climb up grass stems. Another interesting rodent is the Mara, or Patagonian Cavy, which is a long-legged relation of the guinea-pig, found on the grasslands of South America. It is a hardy species which is quite able to live out of doors in our winter climate.

There are three 'Rodent Cities' containing groups of Crested Porcupines, Prairie Marmots and Golden Agoutis in displays which simulate their natural habitat. The Crested Porcupine is found in Sicily, North Africa and tropical East Africa. It is a burrowing, nocturnal animal which eats roots and fruit in the wild, and weighs up to 60 lb. The Black-tailed Marmot (the species exhibited here), from the western plains of the United States and Mexico, is a burrowing animal living in large colonies and coming to the surface during the day. The underground 'towns' can be of great complexity, and just after the turn of this century one colony was estimated at 400 million marmots, covering an area of 240 miles by 100 miles. When one animal gives the alarm, this is transmitted to the others, and they all disappear below ground. They are inquisitive creatures, living on grass and other vegetation, and 32 marmots can eat as much as a sheep, or 256 marmots as much as a cow. The Golden Agouti makes its nest in holes in trees, and is mainly active in early morning and evening. It has long legs and a pointed face; it runs in quick leaps and can swim well. It lives in the forests of Brazil, Guyana and Peru where it feeds on leaves, roots and fruit. Agoutis also attack banana and sugar-cane plantations so they are killed as a pest and eaten. The Zoo also has Canadian Beavers, and they have produced young.

The paddock animals include camels, antelopes, deer, Giraffes, bison, Black Rhinoceroses, zebra and tapirs. Both the Arabian and Bactrian Camels are shown; the former being the one-humped species used for riding and transport, and the latter being the pack animal of central Asia. Another member of the camel family is the Guanaco, a wild relation of the Llama of South America. The Llama is a domesticated form, not found in a wild state. The rarest antelope in the Zoo is the Red Lechwe, a species of waterbuck from Botswana and Zambia which is now endangered in the wild. The Eland is the largest of the African antelopes, and the only one to have been domesticated. In Russia, Eland have been farmed for more than 40 years for their milk and meat. The Brindled Gnu, or Wildebeeste, lives in herds of 50 or so although large concentrations may develop in times of drought. Unlike the Eland, which is a browsing animal living on bushes with a high water content, the gnu is very dependent on water. The Blackbuck and Impala are smaller, more graceful antelope species, from Asia and Africa respectively. Blackbuck live in small groups, while Impala congregate in large herds. Both are extremely fast, and both make high leaps into the air when travelling at speed. The gnu, Blackbuck and Impala have all bred in the Zoo.

You can also see the Black Rhinoceros, Grant's Zebra, Przewalski's Wild Horse, American Bison, Brazilian Tapir and elephants. The Black Rhinoceros, like all rhino species except the Southern White Rhino, is now endangered in the wild. It is a solitary, browsing animal of uncertain temper, but it is now being bred at fairly regular intervals in captivity. Grant's Zebra, a race of the Common Zebra, was once found in enormous herds in southern Africa, but like other zebras it is now confined to game reserves. It has well-defined, broad stripes, with narrow stripes down in the whole length of its legs. Przewalski's Horse, from Mongolia, may already be extinct in the wild, having been reduced drastically in numbers by having to compete for water with domestic cattle. It has also interbred with domestic ponies, thus further reducing the pure wild stock. Wild horses have a stiff, brush-like mane and a heavy head, and in winter they grow shaggy coats. There are about 200 in zoos in various parts of the world, and a studbook is kept of all these at Prague Zoo. The American Bison is a plains animal, which was numbered in countless millions until it was almost wiped out by hunters in the nineteenth century. It was given protection in time to save the species, which is now confined to a few reserves. The tapir of tropical South America is a browser, living in forests, always near water, in which it spends a good deal of time. It is a shy animal, active mainly at night, but like many nocturnal animals it adapts itself well to the daylight hours in captivity. The elephant at Paignton Zoo is the Asiatic species, distinguished from the African by its smaller ears, slightly smaller stature and rounder build.

There is a wide variety of exotic birds in the Tropical and Exotic Bird Houses,

The Brindled Gnu, or Wildebeeste, a native of Africa, may be seen at Paignton Zoological and Botanical Gardens; in the wild it is one of the main prey species of Lions.

and in aviaries around the Zoo. Among these, ten species of starling are exhibited, of which the rarest in the wild is Rothschild's Starling. The Blue-eared Glossy Starlings have bred here. Starlings are as numerous in central Africa as the Common Starling is in Great Britain, and many species are brightly coloured. They are intelligent, and our common Starling is a good mimic, though not as good as the Indian Hill Mynah, which is often kept as a pet for this talent. Two groups of birds which look somewhat alike are the toucans and hornbills. Both have very large beaks, bright plumage and a rather slow, laboured flight, and both nest in holes in trees. However, toucans come from South America and hornbills from Africa and tropical Asia. Hornbills wall up their nesting females with mud or clay until the young are hatched, leaving only a small opening through which they feed their mates. They also have long, glamorous eyelashes, which the toucans lack entirely.

Paignton Zoo has a large collection of the parrot family, which includes the macaws, cockatoos, parrakeets, lovebirds, lories and conures. The Blue and Yellow Macaws have raised a total of 14 young since they arrived in 1959. Both parents feed the young, which remain in the nest for three months and do not reach adult plumage until they are six months old. Parrots are mostly small in Africa, and India is the home of the much smaller parrakeets, with long tails. The richest areas for parrots are tropical America, Australia and New Guinea. The largest and most brightly coloured are the macaws of South America, of which six species are exhibited here. The small South American species are called conures. The crested cockatoos are only found in Australia and islands of that region, and Australia is also the home of the Budgerigar, the wild form of which is green. Budgerigars are grass parrakeets. From New Zealand comes the Kea, which nests in hollow tree trunks and holes at ground level, and a pair of these is exhibited in the Zoo. The smallest members of the parrot family are the pygmy parrots of New Guinea and the Solomon Islands, which are the size of a wren. Notice also the Golden, or Queen of Bavaria Conures, found in Bolivia, which are rare. They are in an aviary opposite the Parrot House.

The most interesting species in the British crow aviaries is the Cornish Chough, with its long, curving, red beak. It is now extinct in Cornwall, but it is still found wild in parts of Wales and Ireland. Efforts are being made to breed it in captivity and the Choughs at Paignton have bred on four occasions in the last few years. Their young can be seen in the Cottage Aviary, near the birds of prey. All the members of the crow family are difficult to rear in captivity since they are fed enormous quantities of grubs by their parents in the wild, and in zoos it is necessary to substitute large numbers of mealworms every day, which themselves are difficult to obtain regularly.

There are six species of crane in the Zoo, and a Kori Bustard, which feeds on snakes and insects in Africa. One can also see three large species of flightless bird, the Emu of Australia, the cassowary from New Guinea, and the South American rhea. It is the male of each species which rears the young, and all have strong legs which can give a powerful kick. There is a good collection of pheasants and gamebirds, the rarest being four species of pheasant which are endangered in the wild — the Cheer, Mikado, Swinhoe's and Hume's Bar-tailed Pheasant. There is a pair of Brush Turkeys, which make an enormous nest of twigs and vegetation in the wild, which incubates the eggs as it rots and generates heat. The largest birds of prey in the Zoo are the Andean Condor and the King Vulture, both South American species, and the owl collection includes the European Eagle Owl, a large species not found in Great Britain, and four British species. These are the Barn Owl, Tawny Owl, Little Owl and Long-eared Owl. The Black-footed Penguins, found in large rookeries round the coasts of South Africa, have bred in the Zoo, each pair normally laying two eggs which are incubated by both parents. The chicks do not develop their adult plumage until they are one year old. An interesting feature not seen in other zoos is the Hereditary and Poultry Exhibit, which demonstrates the principles of physical inheritance and how animals and plants transmit physical characteristics to their descendants. There are several unusual old domestic breeds of poultry, labelled to show their relationships with modern breeds.

Paignton Zoo was opened in 1923 by the late Mr Herbert Whitley, who had for several years previously kept a private collection of animals and botanical specimens. He believed that the public should be able to enjoy the chance to study natural history, but on two occasions after opening his collection he closed it down again in protest against having to pay entertainment tax, since he held that the exhibition was of educational value. After his death in 1955, the Herbert Whitley Trust was formed as an educational charity, which now owns the Zoo company. The Zoo is the only one in the British Isles to be maintained primarily for educational purposes, and it runs a full programme of lecture tours for schools. It also has a Peacock Association (the grounds have a large colony of peacocks living free) which organises monthly tours of the Zoo, lectures and special events during winter, and excursions in summer. Members of the Association have free entry to the Zoo.

Plymouth Zoological Gardens

This small Zoo, opened by Mr Jimmy Chipperfield in 1962, now acts as a quarantine station for his safari parks. It therefore has a changing population of animals, most of which are the larger African species. You can often see Lions, Bengal Tigers, Eland Antelopes, Pig-tailed Macaques and Lion-tailed Macaques.

Poole Park Zoo

Poole Park Zoo has a mixed collection of mammals and tropical birds. The mammals here, of which there are about 60, include monkeys in a Monkey House, and Pumas. The Pumas and several monkey species breed here. There are also some Soay Sheep. The bird collection includes some 400 specimens in 60 species. There is a Parrot House and a Tropical House, and a Children's Corner. The Zoo was originally opened in 1963, and the land is leased from the Local Authority.

Shaldon Children's Zoo

This little Zoo, half of which is under cover, is above Smuggler's Tunnel which leads to Ness beach, and you can visit it along the coastal walks which surround it. Under new management, the animal collection is still being assembled, and at present there are about 70 mammals and birds and a small number of reptiles, amphibians and fish. The Zoo, now owned by Mr T. J. Edwards, was originally started in 1964 by Mr Kenneth Smith of Exmouth Zoo.

Tropical Bird Gardens

These delightful gardens were established in 1962 by Mr and Mrs Donald Risdon, and you can see an excellent collection of 1,000 birds, with more than 200 different species. In a chain of lakes fed by a stream and waterfall there are Cape Penguins, pelicans and many waterfowl including Chilean and Rosy Flamingos, the latter from the Caribbean. Wading birds include spoonbills and trumpeters, and a large aviary for Scarlet Ibises with a running pool near the lake. Many of the birds are at liberty, and there are peafowl, guineafowl and ornamental pheasants in a wood. The aviaries are designed to blend with their surroundings, and beautifully planted to show off the birds to the best advantage. Many species breed here regularly, and there is a particularly good collection of the parrot

Plymouth Zoological Gardens. **Address** Central Park, Plymouth, Devon. **Telephone** Plymouth 51375. **Open** 10.00–18.00 summer, 10.00–sunset winter. **Guide-book. Catering** snack bar, kiosk. Zoo shop. **Acreage** 6. **Car** ¾ ml from city centre on A38. **Bus** 13, 17, 18, 37, 43, 44 stop 200 yds from Zoo. **Train** to Plymouth (½ ml). **Taxis** available. Dogs on leash only. Public allowed to feed most animals.

Poole Park Zoo. **Address** Poole Park, Poole, Dorset. **Telephone** Parkstone 745296. **Open** 10.00–18.00 (or sunset whichever is earlier) daily March–Oct; 10.00–sunset Sat, Sun, public holidays (daily during school holidays) Nov–Feb. **Car** drive to Parkstone Road A350 for Poole Park. **Bus** or coach to Poole Park. **Train** to Poole (1½ mls), or to Parkstone (1 ml). **Taxis** available. Public allowed to feed animals.

Shaldon Children's Zoo. **Address** The Ness, Shaldon, Teignmouth, Devon. **Telephone** Shaldon 2234. **Open** 10.00–dusk summer and winter. **Car** 2 mls s.w. of town centre along A381, turn off at The Ness on A379. **Bus** to The Ness then 3 mins walk. **Train** to Teignmouth (2 mls) then bus or ferry to Zoo. **Taxis** available. Public allowed to feed animals with food prepared in Zoo only.

Tropical Bird Gardens. **Address** Rode, Bath, Somerset. **Telephone** Beckington 326. **Open** 11.00–sunset (last admission 18.30) summer and winter. **Guide-book. Catering** self-service cafeteria (Easter to mid Oct). Gift shop. **Car** 5 mls n.e. of Frome between A36 and A361. **Bus** from Bath to Woolverton Village, or from Trowbridge to Rode Village. **Train** to Bath (10 mls) or to Frome (5 mls) or to Trowbridge (5 mls). **Taxis** available. **Other facilities** first-aid post, wheel-chairs, butterfly and insect exhibition (May–Sept.). No pets. Public allowed to feed animals with food prepared and sold at Gift shop only.

family, including breeding groups of macaws, many of which are at liberty. Apart from these, and the parrots, parrakeets, cockatoos and lories, you can see doves, pigeons, jays, touracos, weavers, whydahs, waxbills, mynahs, finches, and starlings. There are also aviaries for owls, vultures, hornbills and cranes.

The many mature ornamental trees are labelled, and the ornamental shrubs and flower gardens add to the pleasure of the bird collection. During the summer months there is a Pets' Corner with Rabbits, guinea-pigs, pigs, goats and donkeys, and you should also see the butterfly exhibition and the tropical shell exhibition. Mr Risdon is a well known expert and this collection is one of the best in the country.

The Westcountry Wildlife Park

The Park contains a mixed collection, mostly displayed in a walled garden and in a valley through which flows a chain of lakes. The walled garden contains Leopards, Pumas, European Lynx, which have bred here, civets, coatis, Raccoons, otters, Prairie Marmots and Crested Porcupines. You can also see some White-handed Gibbons and three species of macaque — Japanese, Crab-eating and Rhesus. There are aviaries for fish eagles, owls and pheasants here, and a number of macaws are at liberty in the gardens. There is a walk-through aviary, a converted greenhouse, where you can see finches, touracos, starlings, troupials and crowned pigeons.

The Indian Elephants are in the stable yard, and the lakeside paddocks exhibit Collared Peccary, Wapiti, Formosan Sika Deer, now rare in the wild, Red and Fallow Deer, Arabian Camels, Brazilian Tapirs, Llamas, zebras and Bennett's Wallabies. The lakes contain flamingos, Black Swans, geese and ducks, and sea-lions. Adjacent paddocks display Emus and Crowned Cranes. The garden court-yard is approached through a tunnel leading to a cave, which has a resident population of bats. (There is an alternative route if you do not like bats.) The courtyard contains the Pets' Corner, Aquarium, Reptile House and the penguins. The Zoo was opened in 1967, and the owners' house, Cricket House, was built in 1804 by Sir John Soane.

Cricket, The Westcountry Wildlife Park. **Address** Chard, Somerset. **Telephone** Winsham 396. **Open** 10.00–18.00 summer, 10.00–17.00 winter. **Guide-book**. **Catering** licensed restaurant, kiosk. Gift shop. **Guided tours** by arrangement. **Acreage** 40. **Car** 3 mls e. of Chard, 5 mls w. of Crewkerne on A30. **Train** Crewkerne (6 mls). **Taxis** available. **Other facilities** first-aid post, wheel-chairs, children's playground. Public **not allowed** to feed animals.

Weston-super-Mare Mini Zoo

The Aquarium and Mini-Zoo exhibits monkeys, parrots, mynahs, domestic pet animals, insects and, in the Aquarium, tropical marine and freshwater fish, as well as local marine fish and some amphibians. There are also some reptiles, including snakes, lizards and baby alligators.

The collection was opened in 1961, and it is owned by Mr and Mrs V. E. Jones.

Weston-super-Mare Mini Zoo and Aquarium. **Address** Marine Lake, Weston-super-Mare, Somerset. **Open** 10.00–18.00 Easter–Whitsun, 10.00–20.00 Whitsun onwards (high season 10.00–22.00). **Guided tours** by arrangement. **Car** about $\frac{1}{4}$ ml n. of Grand Pier. **Zoo** is on sea-front. **Bus** from bus and coach stations to Zoo. **Train** to Weston-super-Mare. Public allowed to feed animals.

Wildlife Park and British Nature Centre

The Wildlife Park displays only British mammals and birds, with observation enclosures attached to some of the main exhibits. You can see five species of deer, all of which breed here regularly, Otters, Foxes, Badgers, Common and Atlantic Seals, birds of prey and waterfowl. When available, the Director, Mr D. R. J. Chaffe, who opened the Park in 1965, lectures on birds of prey and mammals, both to schools and adult audiences. The purpose of the collection is to bring home the recent decline of British wildlife and the deterioration in many areas of our natural environment. The Park is in a wooded valley through which the River Trym flows. There are pony rides for children.

Wildlife Park and British Nature Centre. **Address** Westbury-on-Trym, Bristol, Avon. **Telephone** Bristol 625112. **Open** 09.30–sunset (or 18.00 whichever earlier) 1st April to 30th Sept summer, 09.30–sunset (or 17.00 whichever earlier) weekends, winter. Always available for group guided tours and lectures by prior arrangement. **Guide-book**. **Catering** snack bar (weekends), kiosk (weekdays). Information centre, gift shop. **Acreage** 10. **Car** 3 mls n. of Bristol city centre, w. of B4055. **Bus** frequent service from Bristol bus station. **Train** to Bristol Temple Meads or Bristol Parkway stations. **Taxis** available. Dogs on leash only. Public are allowed to feed animals with food prepared and sold in Park only.

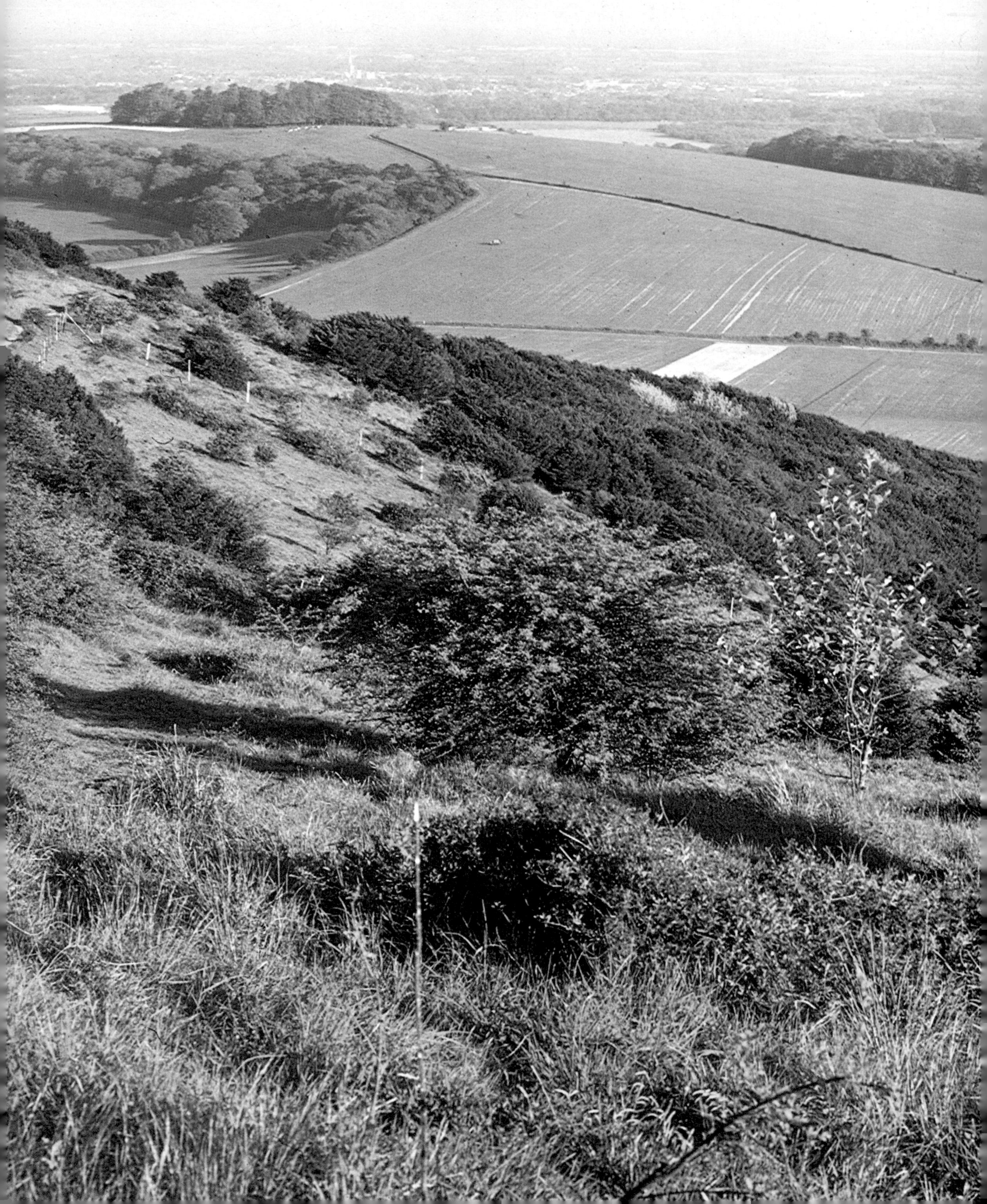

South and South East England COLIN R. TUBBS

From Dover to the Hog's Back, and from Beachy Head to Old Butser, the North and South Downs respectively reach westwards to unite with the chalk plateau of Wessex, forming as it were the topographical framework of southeast England. Though Gilbert White, the eighteenth-century parson-naturalist of Selborne in Hampshire, alluded to the South Downs as 'that chain of majestic mountains', chalkland nowhere achieves the mystic 1,000 feet, though the higher ridges lie consistently between 700 and 800 feet. White preferred his downs to more conventionally majestic terrain and must be permitted to complete his description of their unique topography given to the Hon. Daines Barrington in his letter XVII of *The Natural History of Selborne*, with the date 9th December 1733.

'I never contemplate these mountains without thinking I perceive somewhat analogous to growth in their gentle swellings and smooth, fungus-like protuberances, their fluted sides, and regular hollows and slopes, that carry at once the air of vegetative dilation and expansion. Or was there ever a time when these immense masses of calcareous matter were thrown into fermentation by some adventitious moisture; were raised and leavened into such shapes by some plastic power; and so made to swell and heave their broad backs into the sky so much above the less animated clay of the wild below?'

White's 'wild', the Weald of Kent and Sussex, is an eroded dome of Cretaceous sedimentary sands and clays lying in the encircling arms of the North and South Downs. South and north of the chalk framework of the region lie respectively the Hampshire and Thames Basins — sands and clays of more recent (Oligocene and Eocene) origin than those of the Weald but superficially similar in nature and giving rise to similar ecological conditions. Erosion of the Wealden dome has left a series of irregular, hilly ridges, some falling only just short of 1,000 feet, whilst the topography of the Hampshire and Thames Basins is that of eroded plateaux at elevations which vary from about 50 to 400 feet.

Where the chalk ridges meet the sea they terminate abruptly in white cliffs which in places rise sheer for 300–400 feet. The Dover cliffs are part of a collective image of England, but they are less spectacular than the westward march of the Seven Sisters from Beachy Head, or the ragged pinnacles of the Needles reaching into the sea from the chalk backbone of the Isle of Wight. Elsewhere, the land for the most part shelves gently into the sea. On the Hampshire and West Sussex coast and in north Kent there are extensive intertidal muds and sands accumulated in sheltered estuaries, inlets and bays — wetlands which are ornithologically of international importance for their waders and wildfowl. The East Sussex and west Kent coast includes the reclaimed levels of Pett, Pevensey and Romney Marsh, the last sheltering behind the extraordinary headland of Dungeness, the largest area of sea-borne shingle in Europe — 5,000 acres of successive ridges accumulated against the west–east longshore drift. Today the illusion of wilderness is shattered by the twin nuclear power stations which dominate its flat landscape.

From the ecological point of view, the origins and geological history of the region's parent rocks are less important than their texture and chemical composition. The sediments of the Weald and the Hampshire and Thames Basins are generally nutrient-deficient and neutral or acid in reaction, and often coarse in texture. Chalk, on the other hand, is alkaline and, although deficient in some mineral nutrients, is rich in calcium and phosphorus. These are over-simplifications, of course. Some of the clay marls of the Hampshire Basin, for instance, are highly calcareous, whilst on the chalklands there occur extensive spreads of superficial materials, usually loamy in texture and with an admixture of flints, which are often neutral or even acid in reaction.

There are other exceptions, but the broad contrast between the clays and sands and the chalklands is valid and is reflected in contrasts between their characteristic vegetation. The chalkland is species-rich, whereas the clays and sands support a comparatively impoverished vegetation. Where the land has

Colin Tubbs is an Assistant Regional Officer of the NCC, responsible for Hampshire and the Isle of Wight since 1964. He stands at the meeting-point of two disciplines, history and ecology, claiming that they are complementary approaches to a proper understanding of the nature and present circumstances of man and the environment. He has a deeply personal as well as professional commitment to conservation, and is the author of *The New Forest: An Ecological History* (1969) and *The Buzzard* (1974). His scientific papers include valuable studies of the rare Dartford Warbler.

The nuclear power station at Dungeness, built on the largest area of sea-borne shingle in Europe; the headland is a take-off point for hundreds of thousands of emigrating birds in the autumn.

Opposite: view towards Chichester and the English Channel from Kingley Vale National Nature Reserve, on the slopes of the South Downs.

Grid references (top): 2 3 4 5 6 7 8 9 0 1 2 3 4

VALE OF ST ALBANS

Watford

Chelmsford

EPPING FOREST

Crouch

Foulness I

Lea

Basildon

Canvey I

Southend-on-Sea

GREATER

LONDON

Thames

THAMES ESTUARY

Thames

Northward Hill

Sheerness

ISLE OF SHEPPEY

Gravesend

North Foreland

Margate

Queen's Hotel Dolphinarium

Rochester

Gillingham

South Swale

Blean Woods

Ramsgate

Pegwell Bay

Chatham

Darent

Queendown Warren

Stodmarsh

Chessington Zoo

N O R T H   D O W N S

Medway

Maidstone

Canterbury

Stour

Sandwich Bay

Sandwich

Leatherhead

Ranmore Common

Sevenoaks

Howletts Zoo

Reigate

Toys Hill

(TQ)

Box Hill

Bough Beech

Medway

Great Stour

Hothfield Common

Wye and Crundale Downs

(TR)

Temple Ewell

Holmwood Common

Harewoods

VALE OF KENT

South Foreland

Leith Hill

Beult

Ashford

Dover

Gatwick Garden Aviaries

East Grinstead

THE   WEALD

Tunbridge Wells

Scotney Castle

Bedgebury Forest

Crawley

Nap Wood

Ham Street Woods

Folkestone

Horsham

Wakehurst Place

ROMNEY MARSH

STRAIT OF DOVER

Haywards Heath

Ouse

Sheffield Park

Rother

Flatropers Wood

OF   SUSSEX

Heathfield Wildlife Park

Chailey Common

Rye Harbour

Dungeness

Newtimber Hill

Bentley Wildfowl Collection

Lewes

Adur

D O W N S

PEVENSEY LEVELS

Hastings

Shoreham Gap

Drusillas Zoo

Bexhill

Hove

Brighton

Ouse

Lullington Heath

Worthing

Brighton Aquarium and Dolphinarium

Newhaven

Crowlink

Eastbourne

Seven Sisters and Cuckmere Haven

Beachy Head

(TV)

10   5   0   10   20   MILES

10   5   0   10   20   30   KILOMETRES

been spared reclamation for agriculture, the chalk gives rise to woods in which ash, beech, yew and whitebeam predominate; or to grassland famed for its rich assemblage of sedges, herbs and orchids. On the loams which overlay large tracts of the chalk, oakwoods with a shrub layer of hazel and a rich ground flora occur. Oak-hazel woods are also characteristic of the sands and clays, but there the flora tends to be impoverished and many woods which have had a long history of grazing by commoners' animals — notably those of the New Forest — lack a well-developed layer of hazel, though holly may be common. In the New Forest beech has tended to replace oak as the dominant tree, at least partly because of the preferential removal of oak for ship-building from the seventeenth to nineteenth centuries. The characteristic open-ground vegetation of the more acid soils, notably the sands, is heath; and on the less acid sites, notably the clays, a species-poor grassland.

We can distinguish further contrasts in the ecology of the rivers and their flood-plains. Those which receive most of their water from chalkland catchments are highly calcareous and support an aquatic flora and fauna of unparalleled diversity. The chalk streams of Hampshire, the Avon, Test and Itchen, are biologically unique and it is no coincidence that they are famed as game-fishing rivers. The river flood-plains and the broad levels of Sussex and Kent tend to develop towards a fen vegetation once artificial drainage is withdrawn: reedbeds and wet woods dominated by alder and willows, more or less permanently waterlogged and associated with accumulations of peat. The process is arrested by drainage and the land is mostly in grass, the nature of the sward varying widely with the extent to which it has been 'improved'. In places — for example, on Romney Marsh — recently increased drainage efficiency has permitted arable cultivation for the first time, and the old sheep-dotted grasslands are going. On the other hand, there are still surprisingly extensive areas of botanically rich unimproved grazings which can be regarded as the direct derivative of the cleared and drained fen.

Implicit in this brief review of the range of habitat variability in southeast England is the concept of ecological change, whether natural or man-induced. Natural habitat is generally in a state of continuous development, even though at any point in time the nature and direction of change may not be obvious in the field. Most processes are associated in one way or another with the activities of man. Let us, therefore, look again at the present semi-natural vegetation of the southeast in an historical light, and see what processes have been at work and with what result.

In common with most of Britain below about 2,000 feet, the region was clothed mainly in deciduous forest during the 'Climatic Optimum' which drew to a close around 6,000 years ago. It is justifiable to view man's history in the context of a struggle to dominate this environment: to clear spaces for settlement, tillage, grazing and safety; and to exploit and ultimately manage deliberately the woods which remained so that they gave a sustained yield of timber and other products. The early inroads into the woodland were made on the lighter, well-drained chalk soils in Neolithic times. Succeeding periods were marked by the commencement of clearing first on the sandier sites (in the Bronze Age) and then in the river valleys and on the clays (in Saxon times). None the less, the eleventh-century record of Domesday Book shows that extensive woods then remained — indeed, that most of the Weald had escaped the settlers' axes unscathed. Remarkably few Saxon settlements were established in the Weald, and although subsequently settlement and clearance were widespread, the Weald is even today one of the most densely wooded areas of England.

Prehistoric clearance could be for tillage or grazing but the more acid soils generally failed to sustain arable agriculture for long. Clearance tended to be followed ultimately by the colonisation of acid-tolerant plants, notably ling, and we see here the formation of the extensive heaths which formerly covered much of the Hampshire and Thames Basins and part of the Weald. Clearance of the chalk uplands was succeeded by centuries of cultivation and most areas of chalk grassland probably arose because of the abandonment of tillage in favour of grazing, rather than directly from woodland clearance. Cultivation gave way to

A contrast in river ecology: above, River Itchen in Hampshire; below, Amberley Wildbrooks, a drained fen.

mainly pastoral economies on these light soils in Saxon and mediaeval times, and the species-rich chalk grasslands probably reached their greatest extent at the end of the mediaeval period. Like the heaths, they depend for perpetuation on grazing by domestic stock — traditionally sheep on the chalk, usually cattle and ponies on the heaths.

Of today's woodlands in southeast England probably a higher proportion than anywhere else in Britain can claim continuity with the natural forest cover which confronted prehistoric man, though there is possibly not a fragment which has not been modified. Much existing woodland, however, originates in modern planting or in comparatively recent recolonisation of grassland and heath from which grazing has been withdrawn.

The habitat pattern of the region is therefore closely bound up with human land-use, past and present. The secondary vegetation which succeeded the woodland has developed its own characteristic flora and fauna during long centuries of gradual development. Today, we are faced with unprecedentedly rapid changes in the countryside. We witness the agricultural reclamation or development (and in the recent past the extensive afforestation) of the heaths and chalk grasslands. We see, too, the destruction of native woods by re-afforestation with exotic trees, and the reclamation for industry of saltmarsh and mud-flat on the estuaries. Our flora and fauna are being progressively impoverished.

This continuing loss of diversity is worrying for various reasons, social and ecological, but it is perhaps appropriate to mention just one reason why it is especially significant in southeast England. This is because the region possesses a richer flora and fauna in terms of species than anywhere else in Britain: Hampshire, for example, can boast the longest plant list of any British county. This richness arises from a combination of factors. The southeast was nearest the land-bridge with continental Europe, crossed by immigrant plants and animals; its climate is mild; it possesses great variety of habitat; and it is rich in woods which support relics of the abundant flora and fauna of Atlantic times. Many species are on the edge of their European range, penetrating no farther north and west in Britain; others which appear to be retracting their range southward now hang on only in the southeast. It could be said that scientifically the region has more to lose than any other.

Climatic Optimum. Recovering from the Ice Age, Britain achieved its most advanced position towards interglacial warmth around 6000–5000 BC. No subsequent amelioration has been able to match it in intensity or duration. Summer temperatures are thought to have been 2–3 °C higher than now (though winter temperatures may have been much the same) and the sea to westward was perhaps 2 °C warmer than today. In the lowlands a broad-leaved forest of oak and elm, with lime (a warmth-loving tree) an important constituent, and much alder on the wetter ground, was developing. The tree-line in Wales rose to 2,200 feet and may have been 900 feet higher than at present in the Scottish Highlands. Woodland cover of pine, birch, alder and hazel reached the Outer Hebrides and Shetland (indicating less windy weather than now) and a number of song-birds went with it. Probably early in this Atlantic Period beech and hornbeam got into southern England just before the English Channel was formed and Britain became an island.

Agricultural reclamation of heaths and chalk grassland, seen on Cheverton Down in the Isle of Wight.

THE NEW FOREST

Through a series of historical accidents, one area largely escaped the successive tides of reclamation which have swept lowland England since the eighteenth century — the New Forest. The New Forest emerges into written history in the eleventh century when William I appropriated the district as a royal forest. In mediaeval Europe the term 'forest' had legal connotations unconnected with trees, and could best be described as an area subject to forest law as distinct from common law. The purpose of the Norman kings was the conservation of deer, both for hunting and as a source of meat and hides, and to this end the forest law regulated and controlled all other activities, though permitting grazing by commoners' animals under certain conditions. In later mediaeval times the Crown's interest turned gradually from deer to timber, and from the end of the seventeenth century successive Acts of Parliament provided for the enclosure of land for plantations. Today there are some 20,000 acres of statutory silvicultural inclosures, while about 48,000 acres remain unenclosed and are subject to the exercise of various 'rights of common' — mainly, now, those of grazing and mast (turning out pigs to feed on the fallen acorns and beech mast in the autumn).

The unenclosed common lands of the New Forest comprise the most extensive tract of unsown or semi-natural vegetation remaining in lowland Britain: a gently contoured mosaic of woods, heaths and acid grassland with bogs and fertile alluvial lawns marking the drainage pattern. Here, as elsewhere, the open habitats have succeeded an early wooded cover; the clearance apparently commencing in the Middle Bronze Age and continuing into modern times, though checked after the eleventh century by the forest law which specifically forbade clearance, if not the depredations of deer and commoners' animals. Indeed, the large number of deer maintained in the royal forest, together with the cattle and ponies, severely limited the regeneration and expansion of the woods, the present age-structure of which is closely related to fluctuations in the numbers of these animals over the past three centuries or more.

The deer of mediaeval times appear, as now, to have been mainly Fallow Deer, and huge numbers were maintained. There are still well over 1,000 Fallow

Pitts Wood in the New Forest, looking across from Hampton Ridge; this heathland is a typical breeding area for the Woodlark.

Woodlark. The fortunes of the Woodlark have varied widely. Once fairly common over much of Ireland, Wales and England north to Lancashire and Yorkshire, its numbers had fallen to a low ebb by the 1880s. It increased and spread after 1920 and had recolonised parts of Wales, the northeast Midlands and Yorkshire, and was common in East Anglia, by the 1950s. Then it declined again, its retreat hastened by the cold winters of 1962 and 1963. In the London area, where 45 pairs were known in 1950, none could be found in 1964. It has also become scarce in recent years in northern France. By 1972 its distribution in England was restricted mainly to the southwest, as shown in the map opposite, prepared by Dr J. T. R. Sharrock from the joint project of the BTO and the IWC for the forthcoming *The Atlas of Breeding Birds in Britain and Ireland.*

Fallow Deer: left, bucks in an open grassland area adjoining an enclosed wood in the New Forest; right, a fawn.

Deer, and a visitor may count himself unlucky if he fails to see some in the most casual wanderings in the New Forest. Roe Deer became extinct in England in late mediaeval times, and the present stock (of several hundred) is derived from nineteenth-century introductions into nearby Dorset. Red Deer seem also to have reached a low ebb several times in the past few hundred years; indeed, of the two small herds one is derived from the most recent of a succession of reintroductions since the 1670s.

Most of the remaining fragments of heath in lowland Britain are, or will soon become, too small to support many characteristic heathland animals indefinitely. The New Forest is thus important because it offers the best opportunity of conserving the most complete spectrum of the heathland fauna, which includes such characteristic birds as the Woodlark, Stonechat, Dartford Warbler and Nightjar. All four have declined over their respective ranges in Britain and the most important contributory factor has probably been loss of habitat. The New Forest, with 40 or more pairs, is probably now the main stronghold of the Woodlark. In 1974 it held about 400 pairs of Stonechats – the largest concentra-

Breeding distribution of the Woodlark in Britain by 10-km squares. Large dots represent proved breeding; medium dots probable breeding; small dots possible breeding.

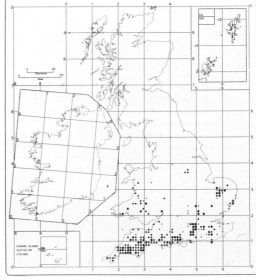

Left: a pair of Woodlarks attend to their young.

tion in Britain — and 240 pairs of Dartford Warblers, which is about half the British breeding population. With the Nightjar there is no suggestion of a decline such as seems to have occurred widely elsewhere.

In the spring the heaths and their valley bogs come alive with the calls of breeding Lapwings, Redshanks, Curlews and the aerial 'drumming' display of the Snipe. On favoured heaths in the summer, Silver-studded Blue butterflies rise in clouds, and other characteristic insects such as the Grayling butterfly and the Emperor moth abound. The New Forest bogs also support a rich invertebrate fauna which includes many rare and specialised insects such as the tiny damselflies and the impressive Large Marsh Grasshopper. Where the heath meets the woodland margins and the Tree Pipits replace Meadow Pipits another speciality occurs, the New Forest Cicada, an insect confined in Britain to the New Forest, and 'lost' for many years until 'refound' in the 1960s.

The unenclosed woods are mainly of beech and oak with a shrub layer of holly and are among the finest remnants of relatively undisturbed forest in western Europe. Their essential ecological characteristics are their generally uneven age-structure; the abundance of mature, senile and decaying trees; a wealth of lichens and mosses, and abundant insect and bird faunas. These characteristics arise from the relative lack of recent human interference: though the woods have been culled through for timber from time to time, they have seen few attempts at systematic management. The rich fauna of the unenclosed woods is directly associated with the abundance of old timber. Their large and varied bird communities arise from a rich invertebrate food supply, in turn dependent on the old decaying and fallen trees; on the plethora of nest-sites for hole- and crevice-breeders; and on the frequency with which the wood is diversified with small clearings and glades. Characteristic birds include many which tend to be local in distribution elsewhere, such as Redstart and Wood

About half the British population of Dartford Warblers breed in the New Forest.

A valley bog pond near Bull Hill in the New Forest, and two of its inhabitants: the Common Blue Damselfly, and (below) a nesting Snipe.

Warbler. Even more local species which are widespread in the New Forest are the Hawfinch and Lesser Spotted Woodpecker. Bird censuses have shown that about half the number of breeding pairs are hole- or crevice-nesters such as the woodpeckers, Nuthatch, Treecreeper, Stock Dove and the tits.

The statutory silviculture inclosures, though not to be compared with the unenclosed woods, are none the less probably ecologically more varied than other commercially managed woods in Britain. They include the relics of tree-crops planted since the eighteenth century, together with younger plantations established after the felling of the old. Because of the need to have regard for amenity, individual fellings have been small and this has led to great diversity of age-classes and species within quite limited areas. Much, if not most, of the planting in this century has been of conifers, but roughly one-third of the inclosures today remain under hardwoods and include some magnificent oak plantations whose bird-life is nearly as varied as that of the unenclosed woods. The conifer and mixed conifer-hardwood plantations include among their breeding birds the Common Crossbill, Goldcrest and Siskin. Since the mid-1960s, Firecrests have bred in many mixed woods in the New Forest, the first to do so in Britain, though they have since been discovered breeding elsewhere, as for example in spruce plantations near Wendover in Buckinghamshire.

Two further factors contribute significantly to the variety of the New Forest's wildlife. First, it is broadly true that the largest number of species occurs at habitat boundaries — the woodland edge is the classic case — whilst many species demand combinations of habitat. The Curlew, for example, needs both valley bogs for feeding and dry heath for nesting. In the New Forest, wood, heath, acid grassland and bog form intricate patterns within very small areas so that there is an abundance of habitat boundaries and combinations. Thus, in the breeding season, Curlew and Redshank, Mallard, Stonechat and Dartford Warbler, Linnet and Yellowhammer, Tree Pipit and Woodlark, can all be found within a few hundred yards.

The second important feature is that the New Forest has never been used for game rearing in the conventional sense, and to this can be attributed the survival of large numbers of birds of prey. It is doubtful whether any other area of comparable size in lowland Britain has retained such a splendid population of predatory birds — the keeper and his master have seen to that! More recently, the New Forest has enjoyed comparative freedom from the use of agricultural pesticides and has thus functioned as a 'reservoir' for species like the Sparrow-hawk which have been hard hit elsewhere by these highly toxic chemicals ingested with their prey. Today, the New Forest supports about 37 pairs of Buzzards, 30–40 pairs of Sparrowhawks, perhaps as many as 16 pairs of Hobbys, upwards of 20 pairs of Kestrels, and many Tawny Owls. This is a substantial avian predator force. Among 'lost' species is Montagu's Harrier which has disappeared as a breeding bird since about 1963 — partly, sad to record, through disturbance of the nests by bird-watchers. In winter the New Forest is depleted of its breeding birds but there is ample compensation in the Hen Harriers, Merlins and Great Grey Shrikes on the heaths and, in a good fruit year, multitudes of Redwings, Fieldfares and other thrushes in the woods and holly thickets. And the walker in quiet places can scarcely fail to see Fallow Deer, his eye perhaps drawn to a group of them by one of the conspicuous white animals which so often betray their companions.

No account of the New Forest would be complete without dwelling on its ponies. It is often not realised that the ponies which graze the heaths and woods and which, as we have seen, play an important role in the New Forest's ecology, are not wild in the sense of being ownerless but, on the contrary, are each owned by commoners with rights to depasture them. Despite domestication they exhibit distinctive behaviour traits. They live in close-knit groups, each inhabiting a surprisingly small area within which they develop daily rhythms of movement between feeding and watering grounds (often in the bogs at night) and loafing grounds (often on the higher ground or around visitors' cars by day). Their claim to be 'New Forest Ponies', however, is tenuous, and what intrinsic characters the breed may have possessed have been submerged since the late

The New Forest Cicada is found nowhere else in Britain; the species was thought to be extinct until it was rediscovered in the 1960s.

A male Hobby watches over its chicks in its nest in a pine tree; the New Forest supports an impressive array of birds of prey whose existence is widely threatened.

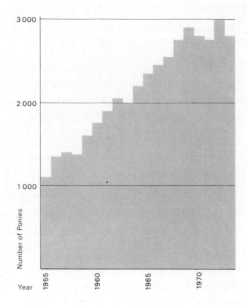

Left: New Forest Ponies in an un-enclosed area of beech and holly. Right: graph showing the total populations of Ponies in the New Forest over the last twenty years, reproduced by courtesy of the Verderers of the New Forest.

nineteenth century in blood from almost every conceivable source. They are today less New Forest Ponies than ponies in the New Forest. Paradoxically it is perhaps all the more interesting that they exhibit such distinctive patterns of feeding behaviour and social structure.

What safeguards are there for this unique area? The New Forest Acts 1877–1970 protect it from reclamation and impose on the Forestry Commission and New Forest Verderers (who are responsible for managing the commoners' animals and for protecting the amenities of the New Forest) a special requirement to conserve its flora and fauna. In 1969 the Forestry Commission and the Nature Conservancy signed an agreement which recognised the National Nature Reserve status of the New Forest and provided for consultation between the two bodies over management. In the early 1970s, however, public concern was aroused by the continued conversion of native hardwoods to conifers in the inclosures, and by the Forestry Commission's sudden insistence on exploiting the unenclosed woods. It is pleasing to record that under the direction of the Minister of Agriculture (to whom the Commission is responsible) the whole emphasis of management has now turned to the conservation of the New Forest's fine deciduous woodlands.

What of the long-term future? The most potent force for change which we can recognise today is the escalating recreational use of the area. Large-scale uncontrolled use spells disaster for wildlife and its habitats, and inevitably for the visitor seeking unspoiled nature in the New Forest. Thus, in accordance with a plan prepared jointly by Forestry Commission, Nature Conservancy, Verderers and Local Authorities, cars, campers and caravanners are being channelled to prepared sites, leaving the remainder of the New Forest vehicle-free, a wilderness in which to walk, ride and explore nature.

THE WOODLAND FAUNA

Though few woodlands possess an insect and bird fauna associated with old timber to compare with that of the New Forest, many are richer in other respects. The oak-hazel woods so widespread in the southeast support fewer hole-nesting birds (though at least one hole-nester absent from the New Forest occurs – the Willow Tit), but have a much larger and more varied small mammal fauna, including the attractive and intriguing Dormouse. With increased populations of small rodents such as Wood Mice and Bank Voles and also Rabbits, predators like Stoats and Weasels (both very scarce in the New Forest) become common, and avian predators like the Tawny Owl are more numerous. Most New Forest soils are too acid to support earthworms, so Moles are absent except on the

A Wood Mouse (or Long-tailed Field Mouse) with two young: fluctuations in the numbers of small rodents affect the populations of predators such as Stoats, Weasels and owls.

richer lawns, and it may be for a similar reason that the Hedgehog is so rare there. However, both are common in the coppices and, indeed, in all but the most acid woods in the region.

A speciality of the Isle of Wight is its Red Squirrels. Elsewhere in the region the native species has been replaced by the more thrusting, successful introduction from North America, the Grey Squirrel, which so far has failed to cross the Solent. The Red Squirrel occurs rather thinly in oak-hazel coppices but is probably most numerous in Forestry Commission plantations such as those of Parkhurst Forest near Newport. Many of the mammals mentioned here are found in open habitats but all are of woodland origin (even the Mole), and the wealth of mammals in the southeast (for to those mentioned can be added most other British species) reflects the survival there of an extensive woodland cover during the greater part of the historical period.

Regrettably few woods outside the New Forest are managed for nature conservation. Blean Woods and Ham Street Woods in north Kent, mainly mixed coppice, are National Nature Reserves. The Mens and The Cut in Sussex, a mature wood of uneven age, predominantly of beech, probably the result of natural colonisation of former open commonland, was recently acquired by the Sussex Naturalists' Trust. Hampshire County Council manages as nature reserves a fine series of chalkland woods including some magnificent beech 'hangers' and yew woods on the Wealden edge scarp west of Petersfield, and a good example of oak-hazel coppice at Crab Wood near Winchester. A fine beech 'hanger' is the one which figures in the Reverend Gilbert White's *A Natural History of Selborne*. County Naturalists' Trusts and the National Trust control other areas, mostly rather small, but in this countryside so rich in woodlands of native trees there are many other sites which deserve the accolade and ultimate safeguard of nature reserve status.

Weasels are very much more abundant in the Wealden woods than in the New Forest.

The Mens Woodland (left) has been acquired recently by the Sussex Naturalists' Trust. Blean Woods in north Kent (right) is a National Nature Reserve.

THE THAMES BASIN AND WEALDEN HEATHS

Outside the New Forest few extensive reaches of heathland are left. The tracts which once covered much of Surrey and northeast Hampshire have been greatly fragmented and much of what remains is, in the absence of grazing, being rapidly colonised by birch and Scots pine. Though many of the remaining heaths are protected, some as nature reserves (notably the Surrey Naturalists' Trust reserve at Thursley Common), some by the National Trust (e.g. Ludshott Common), and some by the Army (e.g. Woolmer Forest and Pirbright Ranges), the ultimate survival of the habitat demands the laborious removal of tree seedlings and the provision of firebreaks. The heaths, however, are worth the effort. They still support most of the birds and insects which occur on the New Forest heaths, though Dartford Warblers have only recently recolonised them after being wiped out in the severe 1962–63 winter, while populations of other species such as Stonechats and Woodlarks are small and vulnerable. The heaths also support relict populations of our two rarest reptiles, the Smooth Snake and the Sand Lizard.

Heathland is an important habitat for all six native reptiles, but in Britain these two are confined to Dorset, Hampshire, Surrey and Sussex (though there is an isolated Sand Lizard population on the Lancashire coast), where they demand mature heather on sandy, free-draining soils. The Sand Lizard also needs loose sand in which to lay its eggs. Both species have been drastically reduced in numbers and distribution in recent decades, mainly through loss of habitat but also through over-intensive heath burning, as well as collecting for the pet-shop trade. Indeed, the Sand Lizard is probably now extinct in the New Forest, where, ironically, its habitat is safest. On the heaths of the Thames Basin and western Weald they still occur widely, some colonies fostered by management involving removal of seedling trees and digging of loose sand surfaces. Whilst the patient observer still has a good chance of seeing these rare and attractive reptiles, their survival in Britain is by no means assured and demands a considerable conservation effort involving, amongst other things, the reversal of man's traditional antipathy towards reptiles which spells the death of hundreds of these harmless creatures every year.

CHALK DOWNLAND

The sheep-nibbled grasslands with their patches of scrub and scattered hawthorns, which formerly covered so much of the chalk, supported a fauna which shared many species with the heaths, but which was distinguished by the Stone Curlew and Great Bustard. The Great Bustard was exterminated by hunting at the end of the eighteenth century, and since then successive ploughing campaigns have had a drastic effect on the distribution of other species. Woodlarks, Stonechats, Whinchats, Wheatears, Tree Pipits and Red-backed Shrikes all became scarce as the sheep-walk and scrub went under the plough. The shrikes have gone completely now, but the remaining fragments of chalk grassland support relict populations of the others. Only the Stone Curlews appear to have adapted more or less successfully to the changed conditions of arable cultivation; they are still spread thinly and it is always worth while pausing in open, rolling countryside at dusk to listen for their sibilant, fluting calls. In similar areas Corn Buntings, which must have benefited from the expansion of the arable, chant their brief songs from such vantage points as telegraph posts. In the winter there is always the chance of a Hen Harrier, or even a Rough-legged Buzzard, if one is prepared to walk or wait long enough.

Chalk grassland possesses a rich invertebrate fauna, the most attractive and conspicuous members of which are the butterflies. Three species, the Silver-spotted Skipper, Chalk-hill Blue and Adonis Blue are confined to the chalk, and many which occur in other habitats are common on the downs — the Grayling, for example. The fast-flying Dark Green Fritillary, common on the chalk, also occurs in a wide variety of other open habitats. Butterfly populations, unlike birds, persist on quite small areas: Chalk-hill Blues, for example, may abound on tiny fragments of grassland, perhaps an acre or so left on a slope too

Disturbance and erosion arising from intensive public use have affected Old Winchester Hill.

steep to plough in the corner of a field. Such sites are always worth looking at.

The three chalk downland National Nature Reserves in the southeast, Old Winchester Hill (Hampshire), Kingley Vale (Sussex), and Wye and Crundale Downs (Kent), together embrace a great variety of habitats ranging from grassland through scrub to woods and including, in the first two reserves, some magnificent yew woods. The reserves are less important for open downland birds than for wood and scrub species, and for their butterflies and other invertebrates. A fourth reserve, Lullington Heath NNR in Sussex, has a mixture of heath and chalkland plants with large tracts of gorse (with breeding birds like Stonechats, Whitethroats and Linnets) growing on loamy material overlaying the chalk. At least one of these reserves, Old Winchester Hill, is faced with major problems of disturbance and soil erosion arising from intensive public use, and it is wiser for the casual visitor to seek the attractive alternative of nearby Butser Hill, managed by Hampshire County Council as part nature reserve, part public open space.

Three species of butterfly that are more or less confined to chalk grasslands: top to bottom, Silver-spotted Skipper, Chalk-hill Blue and Adonis Blue.

The bird-rich Stodmarsh: lagoons, reed-beds, and partially flooded meadows.

WETLANDS

Wetlands, whether freshmarshes or intertidal mud-flats, are biologically highly productive systems, and this is most obviously reflected in their abundant and often spectacular bird-life. Important in the river valleys, are the River Avon flood meadows in Hampshire, which support a wintering flock of 1,000 or more White-fronted Geese; the reedbeds and flanking wet meadows of the lower Test and of Titchfield Haven LNR on the River Meon in Hampshire, both supporting large wildfowl and reed-nesting bird communities; and Pulborough and Glynde Levels in Sussex, famed wildfowl resorts, though numbers today depend on the variable amount of flooding which is permitted.

Perhaps richest of all in bird-life is the 400-acre Stodmarsh NNR on the Great Stour in Kent, where mining subsidence has given rise to large shallow lagoons, reedbeds and partially flooded meadows. The meadows provide a breeding ground for Mallard, Shoveler, Teal and other ducks, and for waders like the Lapwing, Redshank and Snipe. Other waders, such as the Ruff and Black-tailed Godwit, occur during migration. The reedbeds not only support breeding communities of Reed and Sedge Warblers, Reed Buntings and Water Rails but also rarities such as Bearded Reedlings, Bitterns and two recent colonists from the Continent — Savi's Warbler and Cetti's Warbler. Marsh

New warblers. Several birds, encouraged by a warmer phase of climate earlier in this century, expanded their breeding ranges on the Continent, and a few entered southern England. Savi's Warbler, a relative of the Grasshopper Warbler, bred in the fens of East Anglia until forced out by reclamation of its haunts in the middle of the last century; it was rediscovered at Stodmarsh in Kent in 1960, and is now breeding also in Suffolk and Norfolk. Cetti's Warbler is a Mediterranean species and, like the Dartford Warbler, is not a migrant, so that its establishment in southern coastal counties has been favoured by the recent long run of mild winters.

Harriers and Hen Harriers are regular visitors and in winter the marsh supports large flocks of ducks. The maintenance of suitable conditions for this wide range of birds demands careful manipulations of water levels, whilst the wet meadows require seasonal grazing, and the reedbeds rotational burning or cutting to prevent the natural reversion to scrub which would ultimately reduce the biological interest of the reserve. There is more to managing a wetland nature reserve than immediately meets the eye!

The intertidal marshes of north Kent and the Solent (using the latter term to include the harbours and estuaries from Pagham Harbour LNR in Sussex westward to Lymington estuary in Hampshire) are wetlands of international importance for the waders and wildfowl they support on migration and during the winter. The muds abound in invertebrates – indeed, intertidal mud is biologically richer than either completely terrestrial or completely marine environments – and the huge clouds of Dunlins rising like smoke over the mud-flats on the flood tide, or the spectacle of several thousand Brent Geese on the wing, etched in lines and wedges across the low horizon, brings home the point. In north Kent and the Solent the numbers of most species have been rising steadily in recent years, partly because of mild winters and partly because of good breeding seasons in the high Arctic where so many of our wintering birds breed.

Russian Dark-bellied Brent Geese feed on estuary mud in winter.

The intertidal mud at Pagham provides abundant food for waders and wildfowl.

Most spectacular has been the increase in Dark-bellied Brent Geese. Since the mid-1950s numbers in Langstone and Chichester Harbours, on the Hampshire-Sussex border, have risen from about 200 to 14,000 in the winter of 1973–74 – 20% of the world population! Another 2,000 or so wintered in the Medway and Swale. On the south coast, at least, the flocks have also become increasingly 'tamer'. From, say, the sea-wall of Farlington Marshes LNR, a peninsula of grazing marsh in Langstone Harbour, the flocks rest and feed unconcernedly within a stone's throw of the observer.

Langstone and Chichester Harbours are amongst the ten most important intertidal wader haunts in Britain, with a peak count of over 100,000 birds of all species in the winter of 1972–73. The Swale, Medway and Thames mud-flats in north Kent supported about half that number. The Solent as a whole held nearly 100,000 Dunlins alone in that and the following winter, or about 10% of the entire European and North African winter population. Numbers of Grey Plover and Black-tailed Godwit, among others, also formed significant percentages of their European populations. Percentages, however, mean less in the imagination than the birds themselves, wave after wave pouring on to a high-water roost: being on the estuary in winter can be a cold wet business, but is seldom unrewarding.

In the breeding season the main ornithological interest of the coastal regions shifts to their breeding ducks, including the handsome pied Shelduck, and to waders and terns. The terneries are especially important because the European populations are relatively small and highly vulnerable. In the Solent about 200 pairs of Sandwich Terns, 250 pairs of Common Terns and 100 pairs of Little Terns bred in 1974, the Little Terns representing about 8% of the British breeding stock. The colonies are now mainly on saltmarshes and shell islands wardened by the County Naturalists' Trust – for a single picnic party, unwittingly landing among a colony, may bring disaster for that year. A plea for care is not out of place: disturbance can so easily wreck a ternery, or a high-water wader roost, and all too often it arises from a natural desire to see the birds close at hand.

This chapter has dwelt as much on habitats as on species. Wildlife has increased in popular appeal in recent years and acceptance of the need for its conservation has gained immeasurably. There remains, however, a tendency to regard individual species in isolation from the habitats on which they depend and, indeed, of which they are a part in the sense of occupying a place in the food-chain. The conservationist is concerned essentially with habitats – assemblages of plants and their dependent animals – rather than with individual species. It is tempting, therefore, to conclude with the exhortation to value the habitat as much as the individual bird, mammal or insect: to value the mud-flats as much as their Brent Geese, and the heaths as much as their Dartford Warblers.

Guide to wildlife habitats in South and South East England

This Appendix provides a selected but varied list of places of wildlife interest. It is emphasised that nature reserves exist primarily for the conservation of animals and plants and in some cases for environmental experiments and research. They are not 'public open spaces' in the recreational sense. Access to many is therefore restricted and some, because of their sensitivity to disturbance, have been omitted from this list, in deference to the wishes of conservation organisations. Even with 'open' reserves visitors are earnestly requested to keep to the paths and bridleways and so avoid damage to the habitat and undue disturbance to wildlife. *There is no public access to the enclosed farmland which is part of many National Trust properties.*

Application to visit a National Nature Reserve (NNR) should be made to the appropriate Regional Office of the Nature Conservancy Council (NCC) at the address given. Intention to visit reserves of the Royal Society for the Protection of Birds (RSPB) should be notified to the Warden (whose address is shown) as far in advance as possible. In all cases where an address is shown, it is wise to contact the Warden to avoid disappointment.

HAMPSHIRE

Alresford Pond SU 59 33. Pond in upper Itchen valley, with reedbeds and willows. Winter wildfowl incl. Shoveler, Pochard, Tufted Duck, also sandpipers on passage. It is n. of New Alresford. No access but viewable from B3046. Hants and IOW Nats T.

Avon Valley, Ibsley SU 15 09. River flood meadows. Wildfowl in winter incl. White-fronted Geese, Bewick's Swans. Between Ringwood and Fordingbridge A338. Private but viewable from road.

Bramshaw Commons SU 27 17. Series of commons and manorial wastes, 932 a. 10 mls n.w. of central Southampton, 5 mls s.w. of Romsey, just s. of A36 on n. edge of New Forest. NT.

Butser Hill SU 72 20. Chalk grassland yew woods. 3 mls s.w. of Petersfield, A3. Car park, trail. Hants. CC.

Chichester Harbour SU 77 98. Tidal flats. Feeding/roosting area for wildfowl and waders, incl. Black-tailed Godwits. 29 sq mls. 2 mls s.w. of Chichester, approached by A27, A286.

Crab Wood SU 44 29. Mixed woodland on 450 ft ridge, part nature reserve, 183 a. Fallow Deer. Woodpeckers, Nightjar, Nightingale. 2 mls w. of Winchester, n. of A3090 and minor road to Farley Mount. Hants CC/Hants and IOW Nats T.

Curbridge SU 52 12. Salt and fresh-water marsh, Rs. Creek and Hamble. Waders. 6½ mls e. of Southampton, 1 ml s.e. of Botley, on w. side of A3051. Car park at Horse and Jockey Inn, Curbridge. NT/Hants and IOW Nats T.

Farlington Marshes LNR SU 68 05. Peninsula in n.w. corner of Langstone harbour, wet grassland, saltmarsh, lagoon with reedbeds, 222 a. Breeding Lapwing, Yellow Wagtail, wintering waterfowl incl. Brent Geese, Shelduck, Pintail and many waders. 3½ mls n.e. of Portsmouth, s.e. of roundabout junction M27 and A2030. (Access and best viewpoints are along sea-wall.) Portsmouth City C/Hants and IOW Nats T.

Hale Purlieu SU 20 18. Heath and woodland incl. Millersford Plantation. 4 mls n.e. of Fordingbridge off B3078, 1½ mls s. of Redlynch off B3080. NT.

Hampshire and Isle of Wight Naturalists' Trust, King John's Lodge, Romsey, SO5 5BT.

Keyhaven Marshes SZ 31 92. Shingle spit, saltmarsh and mudflats, 600 a. Black-headed Gull colony, terns, shore birds; waders on passage and in winter incl. Ruff, Black-tailed Godwit. 8 mls e. of Christchurch A337 − B3058. Car parks at Keyhaven. (Access and best viewpoints are along sea-wall SZ 308 916, avoid bird nesting grounds in breeding season.) Hants and IOW Nats T.

Leigh Park SU 72 09. Gardens and shrubberies. Domesticated animals and birds incl. rare breeds. 2 mls n. of Havant B2149. Open Sat, Sun, bank holidays, April−Sept incl. from 14.00 hrs. Adm fee. City of Portsmouth/Rare Breeds Survival T.

Lepe and Calshot Foreshores SU 47 00. Country Park on shore of Solent, 123 a. 9 mls s.e. of Southampton A326, s. and s.e. of Fawley. Hants CC.

Ludshott Common and Waggoners' Wells SU 86 35. Commonland incl. a string of hammer ponds. 8 mls s. of Farnham, s.w. of Grayshott B3002, off A3, 2 mls w. of Hindhead. NT.

New Forest NNR SU 30 05. Ancient Royal Forest − oak/beech woodland, planted conifers, open heath and bog. 140 sq. mls. Fallow, Roe and Red Deer, Ponies. Birds incl. Hobby and other birds of prey, Nightjar, several warblers, Firecrest and many song-birds. It is s.w. of Southampton. Traversed by A35 Southampton−Christchurch, A337 Lyndhurst−Lymington, A31 Cadnam−Ringwood. Caravan/camp sites, picnic areas. For Comm/NCC.

Old Winchester Hill NNR SU 64 21. Chalk grassland with juniper scrub on s. slope, hawthorn scrub elsewhere, and small yew woods. 140 a. 11 mls s.e. of Winchester, 2 mls s. of West Meon on minor road off A32, to e. of Meonstoke. Trails. NCC.

Passfield Common SU 82 34. Commonland with woods. 2 mls n.w. of Liphook, astride B3004. NT.

Queen Elizabeth Country Park SU 72 19. Downs and woods, 1145 a. 13 mls n.n.e. of Portsmouth, 3½ mls s.w. of Petersfield on A3. Hants CC.

Selborne SU 74 33. Common and freehold land and the Long and Short Lythes, hanging beech woods made famous by Rev. Gilbert White in his *The Natural History of Selborne.* 4 mls s. of Alton, w. of B3006 between Selborne and Newton Valence. NT.

Stockbridge Down SU 38 35. Chalk downland. 1 ml e. of Stockbridge, on n. side of A272. Access restricted to footpaths. NT.

ISLE OF WIGHT

Bembridge and Culver Down SZ 62 86. Precipitous cliffs bordering downland rising to 343 ft. 4 mls s. of Ryde on B3395 (off A3055). NT.

Newtown Harbour LNR SZ 42 92. Tidal estuary with saltmarsh, shingle spits, rough grazing. 300 a. Wildfowl and waders on passage and in winter, incl. Brent Geese, Red-breasted Merganser, Goldeneye, Pintail, Black-tailed Godwit.

5 mls e. of Yarmouth IOW, on n. side of A3054. Trail, observation post. (Warden — Marsh Farm House, Newtown, IOW.) IOW CC/Hants and IOW Nats T.

St Boniface Down SZ 56 78. Chalk downland rising to 764 ft. Nearby are Littleton and Luccombe Downs. 115 a. Above Ventnor A3055. Footpaths from Nansen Hill and Mitchell Avenue. NT.

St Catherine's Point SZ 50 76. Cliffs at southern tip of IOW. Also chalk hill and

downland ridge to n. SZ 49 78. 1 ml w. of Niton A3055. Car park at Blackgang SZ 488 768. Access restricted to footpaths. NT.

West Wight SZ 35 86. Chalk downland rising to 500 ft stretching e. from Freshwater Bay. Incl. Afton Down SZ 354 858, 3 mls s. of Yarmouth on n. side of coast road, Compton Down SZ 370 855 adjoining on e. side, Brook Down SZ 385 853 adjoining on e. side, and Tennyson Down SZ 330 855 1 ml s.w. of Freshwater. NT.

Sunset on Cadman's Pool in the New Forest.

Yafford Mill Farm Park SZ 45 82. Farm Park with eighteenth-century watermill. Rare domesticated breeds of sheep/cattle. Waterfowl. 6 mls s.w. of Newport B3323, turn right off B3399 by Shorwell Village Hall. Open April–Oct incl. Adm. fee. Private.

SURREY

Bookham and Banks Commons TQ 12 56. Richly wooded commonland, 447 a. 2½ mls w. of Leatherhead, just n. of Bookham station, between A245 and A246. NT.

Box Hill TQ 17 51. Chalk downland and woodland incl. beech and box, 841 a. Also Mickleham Downs adjoining. 2½ mls s. of Leatherhead, 1 ml n. of Dorking, e. of A24 close to Burford Bridge. NT.

Chobham Common SU 97 65. Heathland, 1444 a. 2 mls n. of Chobham, traversed by B386 and B383. Car park. Surrey CC.

Frensham Common SU 85 40. Heathland with birch and Scots pine, incl. Frensham Great and Little Ponds and reedbeds, 943 a. Between Hindhead and Farnham, astride A287. NT/Hambledon RDC.

Harewoods TQ 33 47. Woods and Outwood Common. Outwood, 3 mls s.e. of Redhill, 2 mls e. of Salfords A23, 2 mls s.e. of Bletchingley A25. (No access to adjoining farmland.) NT.

Hindhead Common SU 89 36. Heath and woods of Hindhead, Inval and Weydown Commons, 1076 a. Incl. Devil's Punch Bowl and Gibbet Hill, 895 ft. 12 mls s.w. of Guildford, astride A3, 6 mls s. of Farnham A287. NT.

Holmwood Common TQ 17 46. Wooded common, 632 a. 2 mls s. of Dorking, astride A24. NT.

Leith Hill TQ 14 43. Woods at Leith Hill Place ¾ ml s.w. of summit (965 ft) TQ 134 424, Duke's Warren heath and woodland 193 a TQ 142 442, Mosses Wood on s. slope TQ 146 432, Severall's Copse by Friday Street Lake TQ 130 454. 3 mls s.w. of Dorking, on s. side of A25 or w. side of A24. NT.

The National Trust Surrey and West Sussex, Regional Office, Polesden Lacey, Dorking, Surrey.

Ockham and Wisley Commons TQ 07 57. Heathland, 728 a. Incl. Chatley Heath. 4 mls e. of Woking, 1 ml s.w. of Cobham traversed by A3. Car park. Surrey CC.

Puttenham Common SU 92 46. Heathland, 470 a. S. side of A31 at Puttenham midway between Guildford and Farnham. Car park. Surrey CC.

Queen Mary Reservoir TQ 08 69. Large reservoir attracting wildfowl and waders, especially in winter. Between Sunbury and Staines on s. side of A308, e. of B377.

Ranmore Common TQ 14 51. Wooded common, 470 a. on n. slope of the North Downs. 2 mls n.w. of Dorking, off A25. NT.

River Wey Navigation SU 98 47. 15½ mls from Guildford to the R. Thames at Weybridge, also Godalming Navigation 4½ mls from Guildford to Godalming. NT.

Staines Reservoir TQ 04 73. Large reservoir attracting wildfowl and waders, especially in winter. Staines, on n. side of A30, traversed by A3044.

Surrey Naturalists' Trust, Adult Education Centre, University of Surrey, Guildford.

Whitmoor Common SU 98 53. Heathland, 432 a. 1 ml n. of Guildford, between A322 and A320, e. of Worplesdon. Surrey CC.

Winkworth Arboretum SU 99 41. Hillside planted with rare exotic trees and shrubs, with two lakes. 3 mls s.e. of Godalming, on e. side of B2130. NT.

WEST SUSSEX

Arundel Wildfowl Refuge TQ 02 08. Wild area near Swanbourne Lake, incl. large reedbed. Teal, Kingfisher, Water Rail, Bearded Reedling. Arundel Park, on n. side of A27 and e. side of A284. Wildfowl T.

Black Down SU 92 30. Heath and woodland and Black Down Hill 919 ft. Nearby are Shottermill Hammer Ponds, Marley Common and Wood SU 89 32. 1 ml s. of Haslemere, on either side of A286. NT.

East Head, West Wittering SZ 77 99. Sand-dunes, saltmarsh and sandy beaches stretching for 1¼ mls on e. side of Chichester harbour. 5 mls s.w. of Chichester A286. (Access on foot from West Wittering beach.) NT.

Kingley Vale NNR SU 82 10. Finest yew wood in Europe, showing all stages of development, in dry valley rising to 670 ft on Bow Hill. 230 a. Nightingale, various warblers. 4 mls n.w. of Chichester, on n. side of B2178 at West Stoke. NCC.

The Mens TQ 03 24. Lowland deciduous high forest, dominated by beech/oak, with character of ancient Wealden woods, 360 a. Sparrowhawk, woodpeckers, Nightingale. 3 mls n.e. of Petworth alongside A272. Parking on minor roads to Bedham or Hawkhurst Court. Sussex T for Nature Conservation.

Newtimber Hill TQ 27 13. Chalk downland and woods, 238 a. 5 mls n.w. of Brighton A23, on s. side of A281. NT.

Pagham Harbour LNR SZ 87 97. Tidal mudflats and saltings enclosed by earth embankments and shingle beaches, 698 a. Feeding/roosting area for passage and wintering waders and wildfowl. 4 mls s.w. of Bognor Regis. 5 mls s. of Chichester, e. of B2145. Access from Church Norton (Information Centre), Sidlesham Ferry and Pagham Beach. (Note: It is safest to keep to public footpath which runs round the Harbour embankment.) Sussex R. Authority/W. Sussex CC.

Petworth Park SU 97 23. Parkland, 738 a. 14 mls e. of Petersfield A272, at Petworth. (No access to gardens.) NT.

Shoreham Gap TQ 24 08. Downland, 596 a, with access to Southwick Hill and Whitelot Bottom. 2 mls n.e. of Shoreham. n. of A27. NT.

Sussex Trust for Nature Conservation, Woods Mill, Henfield, Sussex, BN5 9SD.

Wakehurst Place TQ 34 31. Valley woods, gardens, pinetum and arboretum, lake. 476 a. 5 mls n. of Hayward's Heath B2028, 1½ mls n.w. of Ardingly. Car park, Adm. fee. NT/Royal Botanical Gardens.

Woolbeding Common SU 87 24. Commonland and woods. 2 mls n.w. of Midhurst, on minor road n. of A272. NT.

EAST SUSSEX

Beachy Head TV 59 95. Chalk cliffs and downland. 3 mls s.w. of Eastbourne, s. of A259. Eastbourne Corporation.

Chailey Common LNR TQ 39 19. Heath and scrub, 428 a. Nightjar, Stonechat, Grasshopper Warbler. 7 mls n. of Lewes

A275, 4 mls s.e. of Hayward's Heath A272, near Chailey. Car park, picnic areas s. of Lane End Common, on w. side of A275 at TQ 402 222, 393 218 and 378 208.

Crowlink TR 54 97. Chalk cliffs and downland, incl. part of the Seven Sisters Cliffs, 632 a. Adjoining Birling Gap. TB 555 960. 5 mls w. of Eastbourne, just s. of Friston A259. NT.

Flatropers Wood TQ 86 23. Mixed, predominantly deciduous, woodland. 4 mls n.w. of Rye A268, along Beckley Lane. Car park. Sussex T for Nature Conservation.

Lullington Heath NNR TQ 53 02. One of the largest remaining areas of chalk heath on the South Downs. Stonechat, Whitethroat, Willow Warbler. 4 mls n.e. of Seaford, 1 ml w. of Jevington off B2105. (Access on public footpaths only.) NCC.

Nap Wood TQ 58 33. Fine example of central Wealden oakwood, 110 a. Badgers. Nuthatch, Redstart, Wood Warbler. 4 mls s. of Royal Tunbridge Wells, 2 mls s. of Frant A267. Car park. NT/Sussex T for Nature Conservation.

Rye Harbour LNR TQ 94 18. Shingle beach and flooded gravel-pit. Oystercatcher, Ringed Plover, Wheatear. It is s.e. of Rye A259. Car park at Rye Harbour; hide available but prior notice is required. Kent R. Authority.

Seaford Head TV 51 98. Downland and valley of Hope Bottom running down to chalk cliffs either side of Hope Gap; saltmarsh and shingle beach. (Adjoins w. boundary of Seven Sisters Country Park.) It is s.e. of Seaford at Exceat Bridge, A259. Car park at South Hill Barn. Seaford UDC.

Seven Sisters and Cuckmere Haven TV 51 98. Chalk grassland and cliffs, river valley. Near Exceat (car park), 6 mls w. of Eastbourne, 3 mls e. of Seaford, s. of A259. Sussex CC.

Sheffield Park TQ 42 24. Woods and parkland, gardens and artificial lakes. Magnificent arboretum and pinetum. 5 mls n.w. of Uckfield on e. side of A275, midway between East Grinstead and Lewes. ($\frac{1}{2}$ ml from Sheffield Park Station). NT.

KENT

Bedgebury Forest TQ 72 33. State,

mainly conifer, forest incl. experimental exotic tree-plots. 2357 a. National Pinetum, 64 a. Information centre. 3 mls s. of Goudhurst, e. side of B2079. Car park. For Comm.

Blean Woods NNR TR 11 60. Oak/ hazel coppice-with-standards woodland, some hornbeam, sweet chestnut and birch. 165 a. Nightingale, Wood Warbler. Woodland butterflies. 3 mls n.w. of Canterbury off A290. NCC.

Bough Beech TQ 49 49. Northern end of reservoir good for migrant waders and wintering divers, grebes, geese and ducks. 6 mls w. of Tonbridge, n. of Bough Beech B2027. (*Access is by permit only* but the reservoir is viewable from the road just s. of Winkhurst Green TQ 469 494.) Kent T for Nature Conservation/E. Surrey Water Company.

Dungeness TR 06 20. Shingle accretion jutting into English Channel, with freshwater lagoons, 1193 a. Great Crested Grebe, Common Gull, Common Tern, Shelduck, Wheatear. Bird Observatory nearby. 2 mls s.e. of Lydd B2075 – 2076 off A259 at New Romney. (Warden – Boulderwall Farm, Dungeness Road, Lydd, Kent.) RSPB.

Ham Street Woods NNR TR 00 33. Mixed coppice-with-standards woodland, 240 a. Nightingale and other song-birds. Woodland butterflies. 5 mls s. of Ashford B2070. NCC.

Hothfield Common LNR TQ 97 46. Heath and acid valley-bogs, 143 a. 3 mls n.w. of Ashford off A20. Car park, picnic area, trail. Kent T for Nature Conservation/Ashford BC.

Kent Trust for Nature Conservation, Chestnut Tree Cottage, Broadoak, Mersham, Ashford, Kent.

The National Trust Kent and East Sussex, Regional Office, The Estate Office, Scotney Castle, Lamberhurst, Kent, TN3 8JN.

Nature Conservancy Council, South East Regional Office, 'Zealds', Church Street, Wye, Ashford, Kent, TN25 5BW.

Northward Hill NNR TQ 78 76. Mixed woodland, with hawthorn and bramble scrub, 130 a. Woodpeckers, Nightingale, warblers, tits. Big heronry (*c.* 190 pairs). High Halstow, n. of A228, 5 mls n.e. of Rochester. Car park TQ 790 761 Clinch Street. (Warden – Swigshole

Cottage, High Halstow, Rochester, Kent.) RSPB/NCC.

Queendown Warren LNR TQ 83 63. Chalk downland, with mature beech/ hornbeam and hawthorn scrub. 5 mls s.e. of Gillingham/Chatham on minor roads s. of M2 between junctions 4 and 5. Kent T for Nature Conservation.

Sandwich Bay TR 35 61. Sand-dunes, saltmarsh and rough grazing at the mouth of the R. Great Stour. Redshank, Ringed Plover and many migrant species. 6 mls s. of Ramsgate A256, minor road to New Downs Farm TR 342 587, thence on foot, or through toll gate at TR 351 578 and along the shore. Kent T for Nature Conservation/NT.

Scotney Castle TQ 69 35. Famous and picturesque landscape garden and park. 8 mls s.e. of Tunbridge Wells, 1$\frac{1}{2}$ mls s. of Lamberhurst, on e. side of A21. NT.

South Swale LNR TR 04 65. Estuarine shore and mudflats and rough grazing. Wintering waders, Wigeon, Brent Geese, Snow Buntings and Shorelarks. 2 mls n. of Faversham A2. 4 mls s.w. of Whitstable A299. Car park at Old Sportsman Inn TR 062 648, thence by foot westwards along shore. (*Best seen from public footpath along landward side.*) Kent T for Nature Conservation.

Stodmarsh NNR TR 22 61. Marsh, reedbeds, open water, alder carr. Bittern, Bearded Reedling, Reed and other warblers. 5$\frac{1}{2}$ mls e. of Canterbury, nr Littlebourne between A257 and A28. NCC.

Temple Ewell LNR TR 27 45. Chalk downland. 4 mls n.w. of Dover A2, between Temple Ewell and Lydden. Kent T for Nature Conservation.

Toys Hill TQ 47 52. Heath and woodland. Incl. Toys Hill Beacon, Parson's Marsh TQ 471 528 1$\frac{1}{2}$ mls s. of Brasted, Scord's Wood TQ 477 520 2 mls s. of Brasted, Ide Hill TQ 485 515 1 ml e. of Toys Hill on B2042. Car park. NT.

Wye and Crundale Downs NNR TR 07 45. Chalk grassland, scrub and mature woodland on escarpment of North Downs, incl. steep-sided valley of Devil's Kneadingtrough. 250 a. Nightingale, Lesser Whitethroat. Butterflies. 5 mls n.e. of Ashford, 2 mls s.e. of Wye on unclassified roads off A28 and A20. Trail. NCC.

Animal collections in South and South East England

Bentley Wildfowl Collection

This is one of the largest collections of waterfowl in the country, with 115 of the 147 species of waterfowl on exhibition. They are in a delightful setting and anyone with an interest in waterfowl can get Sir Peter Scott's *Coloured Key to the Wildfowl of the World* at the Pump House ticket office. You come first to the Pump House pool, where there are Greater and Lesser Flamingos, five species of whistling or tree duck, Demoiselle Cranes, peafowl, some of which are free-flying, and ornamental pheasants. On the Main Lake are three rare species — flocks of Red-breasted Geese, which breed in Siberia; Lesser White-fronted Geese, which breed between Siberia and Norway; and Ross's Snow Geese from the Arctic coasts of Canada. Here also notice the Laysan Teal, once nearly extinct but now breeding regularly in captivity, the Maned Goose, a small Australian species looking more like a duck, the Cereopsis, another rare Australian goose, and the Ne-ne Goose, which a few years ago was dying out in Hawaii. Three birds were sent to Slimbridge, home of the Wildfowl Trust, which has bred them in sufficient numbers to save the species and return many to Hawaii.

The Limes Pool contains a flock of Pacific Brent Geese, Eider Duck, and a Whistling Swan. In the Triangle Field you turn right to the Canal Pool and Canal, where you can see Shelduck, Tufted Duck, Patagonian Crested Duck, Versicolor Teal, Shoveler and others; and Black Swans, descended from birds acquired by Sir Peter Scott for Sir Winston Churchill. On the latter's death, the swans were acquired for the Bentley collection. At the Top Pool there are Whooper Swans from Iceland which breed regularly here, and Pintail. Next, a series of pens exhibit Spurwinged Geese from Africa, Abyssinian Blue-winged Geese, Bar-headed Geese from India and Swan Geese. In the Field Triangle you see Sarus Cranes from India and West African Crowned Cranes.

Turning back towards the Limes, you come to the pens, housing quarrelsome birds and those which must be separated from related species to prevent cross-breeding. Here there are more Cereopsis, which breed regularly, and Bewick's, Trumpeter, Black-necked, and Coscoroba Swans. The Bewick's Swans here are the only breeding pair in captivity in the world, and the Trumpeters are rarely seen in Great Britain. Bentley has all the swan species except our native Mute Swans, which are winter visitors as wild birds. You can also see here the Magpie Goose, an Australian species, which rarely breeds in this country.

Following the path over the stream, you come to the Goose Field with a flock of Emperor Geese from the northwest coast of Alaska. This brings you to Goose Lake, inhabited by Barnacle and Bar-headed Geese and a pair of Black-necked Swans from South America. Finally, you come to the Hay Field with a large flock of Greater Snow Geese, and Lesser or Blue Snow Geese, Taverner's Canada and Dusky Canada Geese, Greylag Geese and the pair of Whooper Swans. Returning for tea at the Pump House, do not miss the magnificent collection of bird paintings by Philip Rickman, who has illustrated all the species to be seen here.

The collection was started in 1962 by Mr Gerald Askew, who opened it to the public in 1966. He died in 1970 and Mrs Askew has continued his work, with the conservation of species of waterfowl endangered in the wild, and education, as her objectives. It is hoped that eventually the collection will be made into a trust in memory of Mr Askew.

All the ponds are artificial with water from springs, and new plantings of trees and shrubs are continually being carried out, as cover for the birds and to improve the grounds. The old-fashioned varieties of rose and masses of daffodils in spring contribute to this most attractive place, which is both fascinating and peaceful.

Bentley Wildfowl Collection. **Address** Bentley, Halland, Lewes, Sussex. **Telephone** Halland 260. **Open** 11.00–18.00 29th March–28th Sept every Sat, Sun, Wed and bank holiday Monday (also open on Tues and Thurs during June, July and Aug). **Guide-book. Catering** teas. Information centre. **Guided tours** by arrangement. **Acreage** 25. **Car** 7 mls n.e. of Lewes on B2192. **Bus** Southdown 18 Lewes–Hawkhurst or 92 Uckfield–Eastbourne (alight Iron Pear Tree Corner) or 719 and 219 Brighton–Tunbridge Wells (alight Isfield Alms Houses). **Train** to Lewes (7 mls) or Uckfield (5 mls). **Taxis** available. Public are allowed to feed the birds with their own food.

At Bentley can be seen (above) the Red-breasted Goose from Siberia, and (below) a Black Swan on its nest.

Birdworld Zoological Gardens

Birdworld is a good collection of the hardier tropical birds and penguins, birds of prey, pheasants, waterfowl and cranes. The collection was opened to the public in 1968 by Mr and Mrs Roy Harvey, and since then they have carried out many improvements and some major extensions.

The main gardens contain aviaries for hornbills, macaws, parrots, cockatoos, lories, lovebirds and Budgerigars; while a pond for the waterfowl and Greater Flamingos, as well as space for various species of exotic pheasants are found on the adjoining paddock. Other aviaries exhibit touracos, White-crested Laughing Thrushes, Bank Mynahs, starlings, and a waders' aviary for Glossy Ibises, Purple Gallinules, Indian Rollers and Cattle Egrets. This part of the garden also contains ravens, toucans, White-crested Guans, trumpeters, starlings and lorikeets. You can also see the Snowy Owls, Malayan Eagle Owls and rheas, the flightless birds of South America.

The Gardens were almost doubled in size in 1971, and here there is a double Penguin Pool, the upper one having a plate-glass side through which you can see the penguins swimming under water. The species shown here are the Jackass or Cape Penguins, Rockhoppers and Humboldt's. A range of waterfowl enclosures with ponds leads to more aviaries for hornbills, pheasants, doves and the birds of prey. These include King Vultures, Lappet-faced Vultures, Bateleur and Tawny Eagles, and Secretary Birds, which when wild in Africa feed on snakes and lizards. There are paddocks for Sarus Cranes from Asia, Crowned Cranes from Africa and Goliath Herons, one of the larger heron species from Africa.

One of the most interesting birds here is the Kori Bustard, a large bird from the grassy plains of eastern and southern Africa. Hunted as a gamebird, it is now comparatively rare. In the wild, bustards feed on small animals, birds and insects, and the Kori Bustard is one of the largest flying birds, weighing up to 50 lb.

Brighton Aquarium and Dolphinarium

The Aquarium contains tropical and freshwater fish, as well as marine fish from all over the world, including British waters. In 1968 it was extended to include sea-lions, seals and penguins, and you can also see various species of turtle and terrapin. The Dolphinarium, built in 1968 as part of a major development, exhibits six Bottle-nosed Dolphins, which perform in the morning and the afternoon.

The Aquarium, opened in 1873 by a private company, was designed by Mr E. Birch in the Italian style, and it was visited by King Edward VII and Queen Alexandra, as well as by many scientists. It was bought by Brighton Corporation in 1900, and leased to the company now operating it in 1956.

Chessington Zoo

Chessington Zoo is one of the major zoos within easy reach of London and south-east England. Without having many rare species, it has a representative collection of primates, including all the anthropoid apes, hoofed animals, elephants, Hippopotamuses, the large carnivorous animals, and many small mammal species. The bird collection includes birds of prey, waterfowl, cranes, storks and penguins, and small tropical birds. The gardens are pleasant and well kept, and you can easily spend a day here if you wish to see everything the Zoo has to offer.

The most important primates are in the modern Great Ape House, completed in 1967. The outdoor bays are separated from visitors by water moats, and indoors you see the animals through armour-plated glass. There is a pair of young

Birdworld Zoological Bird Gardens. **Address** Holt Pound, nr Farnham, Surrey. **Telephone** Bentley 2140. **Open** 09.30–18.00 (or 1 hour before dusk) summer and winter. **Guide-book. Catering** self-service cafeteria. Zoo shop. **Acreage** 5½. **Car** 2½ mls from Farnham on A325 Petersfield road. **Bus** Alder Valley 226, 228, 229 stop outside Birdworld. **Train** to Farnham (2½ mls). **Other facilities** wheel-chairs. Public allowed to feed birds with food prepared and sold in the Zoo only.

King Vulture at Birdworld; this bird of prey is a scavenger in New World tropical forests.

Brighton Aquarium and Dolphinarium. **Address** Marine Parade and Madeira Drive, Brighton, Sussex. **Telephone** Brighton 64233. **Open** 09.00–18.30 (6 shows daily summer); after 15th Sept, 09.00–17.30 (5 shows daily winter). **Guide-book. Catering** self-service cafeteria, snack bar, kiosk. Gift shop. **Acreage** 2. **Car** few yards e. of Palace Pier on A259 Marine Parade. **Bus** stops outside entrance. **Train** to Brighton (½ ml). **Taxis** available. Public **not allowed** to feed exhibits.

Lowland Gorillas, now becoming increasingly rare in Africa; Orang utans, found only in Borneo and Sumatra, which are also endangered in the wild; and Chimpanzees, the smallest of the three, which are still fairly common in tropical Africa. There is an interesting monkey range, with African, Asiatic and American species. You can see Lar and Pileated Gibbons, the smallest of the anthropoid apes, from southern Asia; the Pig-tailed Macaque from Borneo and Sumatra, which you can compare with the Stump-tailed Macaque also from southern Asia and the Crab-eating Macaque from Malaysia. African monkeys here include the Grivet, Vervet and Tantalus, which are forms of Green Monkey, and De Brazza's Monkey. One striking species is the Black Ape (which is a monkey, not an ape), found on Celebes Island. South American species here are the small stocky capuchin and the spider monkey, a long-armed tree-dwelling animal with a long tail. Other monkey exhibits in the Zoo show Yellow and Olive Baboons, both African species; Barbary Apes (again, a monkey, not an ape) from North Africa and Gibraltar; Rhesus and Lion-tailed Macaques (the latter is also called the Wanderoo Monkey in Ceylon) from India and southern Asia respectively; and Drills from Africa.

The large carnivorous animals here are Lions and Indian Tigers, both of which breed regularly, Leopards, Pumas, hyenas, and several bear species in the modern outdoor grottos built in 1970. These include the European Brown Bear and a related race, the Syrian Bear, which is now rare in the wild; the Asiatic Black Bear, which has a white V on its chest; the Sloth Bear, a long-haired species from India and Ceylon; and the Malayan Honey Bear, a small smooth-coated species, and the best tree climber of all the bears. There is also a large pool for a fine pair of Polar Bears.

The mixed collection of hoofed animals includes both wild and domestic species from Africa and the Americas. There are South American tapirs, long-snouted animals of tropical forests which are good swimmers and feed on aquatic plants; American Bison, which once covered the American prairies in huge herds, and a good selection of African animals. You can see Ankole Cattle, a domestic breed kept by the Watussi tribe, with enormous widely spread horns, and several species of antelope. The Brindled Gnu, a large antelope of central Africa, often congregates in the company of zebras. In the same paddock you can see the Collared Peccary, the wild pig of South America. Other antelopes here are the Kob, from northern and central Africa, the Blesbok of South Africa, and Maxwell's Duiker, a small species from western central Africa. The Barbary Sheep, misnamed since it is a wild goat, comes from the mountainous areas of North Africa. The zebras here are Grant's Zebra (a sub-species of the Common Zebra) found in Ethiopia, the Sudan, Somaliland, and farther southwards into Tanzania. There are also Giraffes, and a lovely mud wallow for the Hippopotamuses. Both Arabian and Bactrian Camels are exhibited, the former with one hump, and the latter being the two-humped species of central Asia. Also related to the camels are the Llama, domesticated in South America as a pack animal and for its wool, and the Guanaco, a wild South American form, closely related to the Llama.

Asiatic animals include the Blackbuck, an antelope once commonly seen in India but now depleted by the destruction of forest for agriculture; the Chinese Water Deer, a small short-tailed deer with no horns but with visible tusk-like canine teeth, from China and Korea; and the Muntjac, or Barking Deer, also with long canine teeth, found on the lower slopes of the Himalayas. You can also see Red Deer, and there is a female Indian Elephant, considerably more placid in captivity than the African species.

Many smaller mammals will be found in enclosures all over the Zoo. There are African and Indian porcupines; raccoons, which are omnivorous and agile tree climbers from North America; Arctic Foxes, small animals with dense fur which turns white in winter; and Bengal Foxes, the common foxes of open scrub and desert in India, a little smaller and slimmer than the English Red Fox. You can also see jackals, found in both Africa and Asia; Coyotes, their counterparts in North America; mongooses, and the Indian Leopard Cat, which is the size of a domestic cat but with longer legs. It is a forest animal, with spots

Chessington Zoo. **Address** Leatherhead Road, Chessington, Surrey. **Telephone** Epsom 27227. **Open** 09.30–19.30 (last admission 17.30) summer, 10.00–16.00 winter. **Guide-book**. **Catering** licensed restaurant, self-service cafeteria, snack bar, kiosk. Zoo shop. **Guided tours** by arrangement. **Acreage** 65. **Car** 13 mls s.w. of London off A243 Leatherhead road. **Bus** 468 from Epsom and Ewell or 65 from Ealing or 71 from Richmond to Zoo. **Train** from Waterloo or Wimbledon to Chessington South, then 65 bus or 10 mins' walk to Zoo. **Other facilities** first-aid post, lost children's room, pushchairs, wheel-chairs, children's playground. No pets. Public allowed to feed some animals.

Below: Syrian Bears at Chessington; these animals are endangered in the wild.

Above: at Chessington Zoo, a Sloth Bear from the Indian sub-continent.

arranged in regular lines along its body. There are three species of wallaby here – Bennett's Wallaby from Tasmania, and the Parma and Red-necked Wallabies. The Parma Wallaby is now rare on the Australian mainland, but the Red-necked Wallabies here breed regularly. There are five aquatic mammals in the Zoo. Californian Sealions; both Common and Grey Seals, which are found off British coasts; the Beaver, which frequents the rivers of North America; and the Coypu, a medium-sized rodent of South America which has become a pest in the rivers of East Anglia, having escaped from fur farms. In the fur trade it is called Nutria. Also, do not miss the bushbabies in the Small Mammal House. Bushbabies, or galagos, are small primates found in Africa and Madagascar. They are tree-dwellers, and most of them are nocturnal. Some of them can leap 20 feet or more from one branch to another.

There is plenty of variety in the bird collection, and they form some of the most attractive exhibits in the Zoo. The birds of prey here are Bateleur Eagles and Bonelli's Eagles, and three species of vulture, including the Griffon. The flamingo pool near the Zoo entrance shows Caribbean or Rosy Flamingos, which have the brightest pink plumage of all the five flamingo species, Greater Flamingos, widely distributed in Africa, Asia and Europe, and the paler Chilean Flamingos. There is a very attractive Penguin Pool, landscaped to represent the volcanic rocky outcrops of Antarctica, where you can see King Penguins, the second largest of the 17 species of penguin, and two smaller species, the Black-footed or Cape Penguin, found in the waters around South Africa, and Humboldt's Penguin, which inhabits the coastal waters of western South America. The cranes in the Zoo are the Crowned Crane, found in East and West Africa, the beautiful little Demoiselle Crane from the southern parts of central Europe and Asia, and the tall and dignified Sarus Crane from India, Burma and Thailand. The storks are represented by the Marabou, found in Africa and Asia, and the Woolly-necked Stork. In India it was called the Adjutant Stork during the British Raj, because its somewhat peppery gait reminded the troops of their less popular officers. Four large flightless birds are exhibited: the Ostrich of Africa, which is the largest flightless species, the Emu of Australia, the rhea of South America, and the cassowary of New Guinea. All these are in the early group of birds known as ratites.

There is a walk-through aviary where you can see Andean Ibises, Tiger Herons, guans, gallinules and Pied Imperial Pigeons, among others. There is a separate enclosure for Scarlet Ibises with beautiful deep red plumage. This is a wading bird which nests in trees, and it comes from tropical South America.

The pheasant aviaries contain three species which are now rare in the wild. The Cheer Pheasant, Elliot's Pheasant and Hume's Bar-tailed Pheasant. The main waterfowl ponds also exhibit pelicans, and there are several finches and lovebirds in the Tropical Bird House which regularly breed here. Other bird exhibits are Budgerigars, free-flying macaws of tropical South America, peafowl and various breeds of domestic poultry which are sometimes exhibited with hoofed animals.

Chessington Zoo was opened in 1931, two months after Whipsnade, by Mr R. S. Goddard. The house, Burnt Stub, was built in 1348, and in the sixteenth century it was used as an archery training school for officers, which Queen Elizabeth I visited to watch the archery practice. The Queen's visits usually took place on a Sunday, when archery was forbidden by law, so she passed an Act of Parliament to legalise it. During the Civil War, Burnt Stub was occupied by the Cavaliers and it was burnt down by Cromwell in 1645 – hence its name. It was rebuilt in 1660 and remained in private ownership until 1919, when it was again destroyed by fire, and not restored until Mr Goddard bought it.

Other attractions attached to the Zoo are the circus, started in 1934, Pets' Corner, a Punch and Judy show, a playground with swings and roundabouts, a Model Railway and the Model Village, bought in 1955 from the now defunct Ferndown Zoo near Bournemouth. There are several formal gardens in the grounds of Burnt Stub, and you should not miss the rose garden and the bulb walk. Overhanging the lily pond are some willow trees, grown from cuttings which were taken from the willows beside Napoleon's grave on St Helena.

Drusillas Zoo Park

Drusillas Zoo is an ideal place to visit with young children who have never seen a zoo before. Its popularity is fully justified by the healthy condition of the animals in well-designed enclosures, in a cheerful atmosphere. You can see monkeys, many small kinds of wild and domestic animals, penguins, flamingos, waterfowl and fish, and several other attractions which will delight the young.

The Small Mammal House contains marmosets, squirrels, chipmunks, porcupines, a Kestrel (which is not happy in an outdoor aviary), Kinkajous, Rabbits and chinchillas. There is also an aviary with a collection of finches here. From there you pass to an aquarium, with two tanks of tropical freshwater fish, and some seawater exhibits of fish from the English Channel. Next comes a room with a Dutch Village in which there are no less than nine different breeds of domestic Rabbit. Then you pass a picture gallery with portraits of some of the Zoo's inhabitants, as you go out of doors to Monkey Walk. Here there are seven species of monkey, including Pig-tailed Macaque, Squirrel Monkeys, Drill, Patas and Woolly Monkeys. There is also an interesting breeding unit for capuchins, a robust little monkey from South America.

A range of outdoor aviaries exhibits parrakeets, lovebirds, lories, conures and Cockatiels, and Parrot Parade has a good selection of parrots and macaws, and a hornbill. The Nursery Pen has baby farm animals, such as calves, lambs, kids or piglets which children may stroke (but not feed). There are enclosures for coatis and Raccoons, and a pool for Humboldt's Penguins. All these are in breeding groups, and if you are lucky some of them may have babies.

There is a very interesting collection of old English breeds of cattle, sheep and poultry.

As you walk towards the paddocks you pass Wagon Walk, with a fascinating collection of farm wagons which oxen used to pull on one local farm until 1925. Next you see Guinea-pig Country, a model village and farm behind glass, in which 100 guinea-pigs live. There are some more wild animal exhibits around here, including Indian Otters, Bennett's Wallabies from Tasmania, porcupines, and a Llama and Guanaco.

The lake, called Flamingo Lagoon, has Caribbean and Chilean Flamingos, Barnacle Geese, White Chinese Geese, Shelduck, Tufted Duck and Mallard. On the middle pool you can see the smaller kinds of duck which do not mix with the others. There is an illustrated board here to enable you to identify the different species. The third pool has Black Swans from Australia, and another pool has European Spoonbills, with Crowned Cranes from Africa. Wild ducks, or ducks which have not been pinioned, fly in and out of the pool enclosures.

Do not miss the train ride, which takes you round the paddocks, or the farm playground with tractors, a Landrover, a fire engine, baker's cart, swings and Jumbo Elephant climbing frame. There is also Cuckmere golf, played round obstacles representing local features of the Cuckmere Valley. Lastly there is a beautiful exhibition of tropical moths and butterflies. Drusillas was opened by the late Captain Ann in 1923, with teas and a Pets' Corner. The railway was added in 1930. The founder's two sons now run Drusillas, and they have greatly expanded and improved its attractions in recent years, making it one of the best small zoos in the country.

Flamingo Park Bird Sanctuary

This is, essentially, a Waterfowl Park with over 2,000 birds of about 80 different species, including flamingos, swans, geese and other ornamental waterfowl, as well as cranes, pheasants and peafowl. More than 500 birds are bred each year. The birds are mostly out of doors, but there is also a Bird House, and a Pets' Corner. This bird sanctuary was started by Mr P. Adams in 1971.

Drusillas Zoo Park. **Address** Alfriston, Sussex. **Telephone** Alfriston 234. **Open** 11.00–18.00 summer, 11.00–dusk winter. **Guide-book**. **Catering** licensed restaurant, snack bar, kiosk. Zoo shop. **Guided tours** by arrangement. **Acreage** 15. **Car** 4 mls n.e. of Seaford off B2108. **Bus** 126 to Zoo hourly, or 25 stops $\frac{1}{4}$ ml from Zoo. **Train** to Berwick (1$\frac{1}{2}$ mls). **Taxis** from Berwick station and Alfriston. **Other facilities** children's playground. Public **not allowed** to feed animals.

Pig-tailed Macaque from Far East Asia.

Flamingo Park Bird Sanctuary. **Address** Oakhill Road, Springvale, Seaview, Isle of Wight. **Telephone** Seaview 2153. **Open** 14.00–18.00 April, May; 10.30–18.00 June, Sept (Sun 14.00–18.00). **Guide-book**. **Catering** self-service cafeteria, kiosk. Gift shop. **Acreage** 10. **Car** 2 mls e. of Ryde on B3330. **Bus** stops 400 yds from Park. Coach tours to Park by Southern Vectis and Moss's Motor Tours, Sandown. **Taxis** available from anywhere on Island. Public allowed to feed birds with food prepared and sold at kiosk only.

Gatwick Garden Aviaries

This is a mixed collection of monkeys, parrots, waterfowl and bantams, with a children's corner. Species which breed regularly here include Black Swans from Australia, lovebirds, parrakeets and rare species of bantam. These outdoor aviaries were opened in 1973.

Heathfield Wildlife Park and Leisure Gardens

This is a small Zoo at present, designed as a general collection of mammals and birds. The mammals include zebras, Llamas, Red Deer, American Bison, some monkey species and coatis; and there are a number of aviaries in 'Bird City', exhibiting Scarlet Ibis, Great Indian Hornbill, White-backed Vulture, White-headed Vulture, Lappet-faced Vulture, caracara and Barn Owl. There are Humboldt's Penguins and Crested Pelicans on pools by the lake. There are plans for greatly expanding the Zoo over the next few years.

Other attractions here are the Gibraltar Tower, containing an interesting exhibition of military uniforms of the Napoleonic period, a veteran car museum and a children's playground. The Park and gardens were opened in 1973.

Hotham Park Children's Zoo

Opened in 1950 by the Local Authority, this is a general collection, mainly out of doors, with Red Deer, Barbary Sheep (which are really North African wild goats), Llamas, various species of monkey and some small mammals including coatis, Prairie Marmots, Crested and Brush-tailed Porcupines, Raccoons, viscachas, Kinkajous, gerbils and wallabies. The two last species are regular breeders here.

Birds include duck, geese, various pigeon and pheasant species, peafowl, penguins and pelicans, White Ibises; and in the Tropical Bird House various species of finch, weaver, small parrot, toucanet, mynah, touraco and hornbill, and Purple Gallinules. The only reptiles here are tortoises, and there are a number of domestic animals, such as Shetland and Iceland Ponies, donkeys, sheep, goats, Rabbits and guinea-pigs.

Howletts Zoo Park

Howletts Zoo Park is the private animal collection of Mr John Aspinall, who began it here in 1957. The property was part of a 1,500-acre estate, including 300 acres of parkland, until the First War, and it is now the home of a remarkable collection of Tigers and Gorillas which are famous in zoo circles all over the world. The theme of the Park is the breeding of rare species, and considerable success has been achieved, 90% of the animals kept here having been bred in the Park. An important feature is the special relationship which has been established over the years between Mr Aspinall and his staff and the wild animals. In many zoos, the policy is to suppress personal contact between animal and keeper, the theory being that wild animals which have developed a relationship with human beings will transfer their attention from others of their own species and thus fail to breed. At Howletts, an atmosphere of trust between animal and human is regarded as desirable, giving the animal a sense of confidence and security, and breeding results indicate that this approach works. Apart from the Tigers and Gorillas, you will see other members of the cat family, a number of smaller animals, elephants,

Gatwick Garden Aviaries. **Address** Russ Hill, Charlwood, Surrey. **Telephone** Norwood Hill 862312. **Open** 10.00–19.00 from Easter to end of Sept. **Catering** kiosks. **Acreage** 5½. **Car** 3 mls s.w. of Gatwick roundabout (junction of A23 and A217), turn left opposite the village hall to Russ Hill. Public allowed to feed animals and birds with own food and food prepared and sold in Gardens.

Heathfield Wildlife Park and Leisure Gardens. **Address** Hailsham Road, Heathfield, East Sussex. **Telephone** Heathfield 4656. **Open** 10.00–18.00 summer, 10.00–18.00 (dusk) winter. **Guide-book. Catering** licensed restaurant, self-service cafeteria, kiosk. Zoo shop. **Acreage** 200. **Car** on B2203 Heathfield–Horam road. **Bus** Heathfield–Horam bus stops at Park entrance. **Train** to Etchingham (5 mls). **Taxis** available. **Other facilities** children's playground and pets' corner, car museum, military museum, Chimpanzee Island, Bird City, boat rides. Public **not allowed** to feed animals.

Hotham Park Children's Zoo. **Address** Hotham Park, Bognor Regis, Sussex. **Telephone** Bognor Regis 3141 ext. 17. **Open** daily 10.00–dusk March–Nov, 10.00–16.00 weekends only Dec–Feb. **Catering** kiosk (summer only). **Guided tours** by arrangement. **Acreage** 5. **Car** entrance at junction of Upper Bognor Road (A259 to Littlehampton) and High Street. **Bus** 240, 241 to Zoo gates. **Train** to Bognor (½ ml). **Taxis** available. **Other facilities** children's playground. Public allowed to feed animals with own food.

rhinos, monkeys and hoofed animals, many of which are rare in the wild and seldom seen in British zoos.

On entering the Park you approach the large enclosures for Indian Tigers, of which there were 28 in 1975, 14 having been born in 1974. Adult animals are kept mostly in pairs, with larger groups of young animals, and mothers with their cubs. This breeding colony of Tigers is the largest in captivity in the world, and surplus animals have to be placed regularly in other zoos. Tigers originated in northern Asia and they have spread southwards into warmer parts of the world, through India, Indo-china and into southeastern Asia. Tigers in Java, Sumatra and Malaya, which live in thick tropical jungle, are smaller and darker in colour. The Indian or Bengal Tiger is a large animal with dark, short hair. All Tigers have a ruff of long hair on their cheeks, and a distinctive white spot ringed in black on the back of each ear. This is a 'marker' to enable young cubs to follow their parent through thick vegetation or long grass. The Indian race of Tiger was once numerous, but it is thought that there are now only about 1,500 in the wild, owing to shooting and forest clearance for the development of agriculture. Tigers are now protected in reserves in India, which has received financial help from the World Wildlife Fund for the setting up of protected areas. Tigers in warm climates weigh up to 500 lb. and usually produce two or three cubs, which become adult at three years old. In the wild they kill antelopes, wild pig and deer, killing one large animal every ten days or so. They are extremely fond of water and dislike great heat.

Opposite the Tigers are six Indian Elephants, including two young bull elephants, which are seldom kept in zoos since they are difficult to handle. Since the Park's policy is to breed animals, this has not been allowed to prevent the keeping of bulls, and these it is hoped will produce calves when they reach maturity. The Asiatic Elephant, found in the Indian sub-continent and southeastern Asia, is one or two feet shorter than the African Elephant, and it averages a ton and a half less in weight. It has smaller ears and tusks than the African species, and four nails on its hind feet as against the African's three. Another difference is that the Asiatic Elephant has one 'finger' at the end of its trunk whereas the African Elephant has two. Elephants are born about 21 months after conception, male calves being born a month later than females. They continue growing until they are about 25 years old.

There are five other kinds of animal in the large paddock for Indian Elephants. These are Axis Deer, Sambar Deer, Hog Deer, Nilgai and Blackbuck. Axis or Spotted Deer come from India and Ceylon, where they are becoming scarcer owing to forest clearance. The Sambar is a large deer from southeastern Asia, weighing up to 600 lb. It prefers woodland at altitudes of up to 10,000 feet, and its numbers in the wild have dwindled. It has been introduced to Australia and New Zealand. The Hog Deer is a small animal inhabiting reedbeds and swamps in India and southeastern Asia. This too has been introduced into Australia. The Nilgai is the largest of the Indian antelopes, still fairly common in northern India. The female is brown and the male, which has horns, is a greyish-blue colour. It frequents open forest in small herds, and it is a shy animal. Blackbuck are the typical antelopes of India, living in small herds on grassland in open country. Females are a light fawn colour and adult males are blackish brown, the herd leader turning a deeper brown than the other males. Bucks have long, spiralled horns.

On the left-hand side of this paddock you will see smaller paddocks for Roan Antelopes, Cheetahs, Brazilian Tapirs and a Gaur. The Roan Antelope, now endangered in the wild, is a large animal, reddish fawn in colour, with straight horns, pointing backwards. It is found in eastern, western and southwestern Africa, where it favours lightly wooded country, never straying far from water and living in herds of up to 20 animals. The herd size increases in times of drought or food shortage. Roan Antelopes are aggressive by nature, and they begin fighting while quite young.

Cheetahs live in open grassland, depending on a short burst of speed to catch their prey. If the quarry is not caught within 300 or 400 yards, the chase is given up. Cheetahs are now found only in Africa and in Iran, which is the last

Howletts Zoo Park. **Address** Bekesbourne, Nr Canterbury, Kent. **Open** 10.30–17.30 25th May–31st October. **Guide-book** and information leaflet. **Catering** self-service cafeteria, kiosk. **Acreage** 55. **Car** 2 mls s.e. of Canterbury on A2 Dover road, turn left at Bekesbourne, Zoo ½ ml on left. **Train** to Bekesbourne. **Taxis** available. No pets. Public **not allowed** to feed animals.

Axis Deer (male above) from India and Ceylon, and the Nilgai (male opposite) the largest of the Indian antelopes, two of the species which breed in Howletts Zoo Park.

remaining range of the Asiatic race. Cheetahs were trained for hunting in India and Persia for centuries, and they are the only members of the cat family which do not turn savage towards humans when they reach maturity. They are not easy to breed in captivity, the first having been bred in a zoo as recently as 1960. The tapirs in the next paddock are the Brazilian species, the commonest of those found in South America. They are shy animals living in marshland and browsing on water plants, leaves and twigs. They always live near water and are good swimmers, and their natural enemies are alligators and Jaguars. The young have spots and horizontal stripes, which disappear during growth. The Gaur is now a very rare animal in the wild. It is the largest of the wild cattle and it comes from hill-forest areas in India, Burma and Malaya. Bulls stand over six feet at the shoulder and both sexes have distinctive white 'stockings' on their legs. The animal exhibited here is the only one in Great Britain, and efforts are being made to obtain some females so that a herd can be established.

Crossing the drive and following the path towards the mansion, you pass the Black Rhinos and American Bison. The Black Rhinoceros weighs up to one and a half tons, and it has two horns. In the wild it is solitary, the sexes only meeting in the mating season, though the calves remain with their mothers for long periods. Rhinos have very poor eyesight but excellent hearing, and they will charge any intruder who disturbs them. The Black Rhino, mainly found in eastern Africa, is now an endangered species, being extensively poached wherever it occurs. The American Bison once lived in vast herds on the prairies of North America, but the development of railways across the continent brought 'buffalo' hunters in their wake and the Bison were nearly wiped out. Legal protection saved them at the end of the nineteenth century, and they are now seen in many zoos. Bull American Bison weigh up to a ton or more.

Turning to your left at the top of the drive you pass the animal nurseries where young animals are kept, and the next enclosure, opposite the Bison Paddock, exhibits the Siberian Tigers. This is the largest race of Tiger, which may measure up to 13 feet in length and weigh 650 lb. It has thicker hair, paler in colour, and with somewhat less prominent stripes than the smaller types. In their northern range Tigers do not mind frost, but like the other races these prefer to shelter from direct sunlight in hot weather. Siberian Tigers are now very rare in the wild, and the ones shown here are the first to be seen in Great Britain for many years. They have bred in the Park, and the colony stood at 11 animals in 1975. Next to the Tiger enclosures is the Ratel, or African Honey Badger. It is a member of the weasel family, but not closely related to weasels. Honey Badgers are found in India, southwestern Asia and in most parts of Africa. They live in forest, feeding on reptiles, ants and beetles, small mammals and honey. The Honey Badgers here were the first in the world to breed in captivity.

After these, you pass into a walled garden containing the Gorilla House, flanked by outdoor cages, from which overhead passages lead into a vast outdoor cage, with ropes, a slide, rubber tyres, and nesting places on the upright supports. Three tons of straw are used to cover the floor and here the Gorillas disport themselves. There are 14 Gorillas in the colony, led by two adult males, Gugis and Kisoro. Gugis has not succeeded in fathering live offspring, and Kisoro, a wild-caught male, is on extended loan from Lincoln Park Zoo, Chicago. He arrived in Chicago in 1964 at the age of three, and he sired two offspring there by different females in 1970 and 1971. In 1973, Lincoln Park Zoo agreed to send Kisoro on extended loan to Howletts and he arrived in October of that year. The Howletts colony contains four females of breeding age, and by the spring of 1974 Kisoro had been successfully introduced to them. A long-held ambition of Mr Aspinall was realised when a male baby was born to Juju, a 13-year-old female, in April 1975. Later in the same month another female, Shamba, gave birth to a female baby, and in May another male baby was born. Unlike Juju, Shamba showed no interest in her baby, which was removed to be hand-reared on the bottle. The staff are confident that Kisoro will father more babies by other females, thus establishing a thriving breeding group of these splendid animals.

Although Gorillas have been kept in European zoos since the mid-nineteenth century, the first one was not born and reared in captivity until 1956, at the

Columbus Zoo, Ohio, U.S.A. Since then, 125 Gorillas have been born in zoos including the latest animals at Howletts, and of these about 72 are still living. This is not a high enough figure to enable one to say that captive breeding will save the species from extinction, but improvements in husbandry and in our own knowledge of Gorillas' requirements are encouraging, and zoo men are increasingly confident that Gorillas can be bred in sufficient numbers to justify the belief that the species could be maintained if the wild population continued to decrease. Recent estimates put the Lowland Gorilla population in the wild in tropical West Africa at below 5,000, so there is certainly no room for complacency.

Next to the Gorillas is the Chimpanzee colony, numbering eight animals, and these also have bred here. A further range of cages beyond the walled garden contains Clouded Leopards, African Hunting Dogs and Woolly Monkeys. Clouded Leopards are beautifully marked with a mixture of large blotches, with spots and streaks on the fur of the head and legs. They have unusually long and thick tails, used for balancing on the branches of trees. They live in dense forest in Nepal, southeastern China, and southwards to southeast Asia. The animals here breed regularly, having been given the seclusion which is so important to this very shy animal, and they were the first of this species to breed in captivity in Great Britain. The African Hunting Dog lives in packs on the plains of Africa, preying on zebra and antelope. They select an old or weak animal, following it until it flags, and then falling upon it and tearing it to pieces in a very short time. Mothers with young puppies which cannot join the hunt are fed by the rest on regurgitated meat from the recent kill, and this practice of communal feeding is a feature of the species. Howletts' Woolly Monkeys are from South America, heavily built animals with a strongly prehensile tail which is an effective fifth limb used for grasping branches and swinging from them. They live in family groups in the wild, feeding on nuts, fruit and leaves, often gorging themselves to the limit when food is plentiful.

Retracing your steps past the mansion you come to the capuchin monkeys. This is another South American monkey, smaller and stockier than the Woolly Monkey, and also a tree-dweller. But its tail is not such a useful grasping organ, being used only as an aid to steady the animal while climbing. The big toe, however, is able to grasp branches, and the well-developed thumbs enable it to use its hands to the point of manipulating simple tools under experimental conditions. In the wild, these monkeys live in troops of up to 40 animals, and the Howletts colony numbers nine at present.

Turning left, past another Tiger enclosure, you come to the Snow Leopards. This is a separate species from the ordinary spotted Leopard, a pale brown in colour, with a long, bushy tail. Its coat is thick, since it comes from the Himalayas and the Altai Mountains, following the herds of wild goats, sheep, deer, gazelle and wild boar. Sometimes called the Ounce, the Snow Leopard is rare in the wild, and the animals here are the only ones to be seen in Great Britain at present. Next to these are the African Elephants. Like the Indian Elephants here, they are all young animals, and two bulls are kept.

Beyond the African Elephants is an enclosure for Fishers, the black and spotted Leopards and the wolves. The Fisher is a North American species, the largest of the martens, and one of the most sought after animals by fur trappers. It does not live on fish as far as is known, but hunts for squirrels and other small animals. It is ferocious and cunning, often taking other animals caught in traps while avoiding traps itself. It is not often seen in British zoos, and the ones shown here are the only ones exhibited in this country. The spotted Leopard, a native of Africa and Asia, makes up in strength what it lacks in size. It usually jumps on its prey from a branch, but it also catches monkeys. In Africa, Leopards often take baboons, although adult baboons can kill a Leopard, albeit losing their own lives in the process. The black Leopard, often referred to as the Panther, is simply a spotted Leopard with dark pigmentation, the spots being just visible against the dark background of the fur. It is mostly found in southeast Asia, and both black and normal-coloured cubs can occur in the same litter.

The pack of Canadian Timber Wolves is one of the largest in Great Britain, numbering 35 animals. Wolves have a clearly defined social hierarchy, with a

Serval, native of the African bush.

pack leader and a leading female. In the wild, wolves hunt in small packs, feeding on deer, carrion, small animals and occasionally fruit. Sometimes they will surround a Moose, but the size of the Moose and its ability to bulldoze its way through thick forest and to swim rivers often enables it to escape. Wolves have always been hunted mercilessly by man and their numbers are dwindling. In the United States they are now confined to northern Minnesota.

Retracing your steps past the wolves, you come to the Wild Boars in a long woodland paddock. The European Wild Boar was once common but it is now found only in woodland areas, where it is still hunted for sport. The last Boar in Great Britain was killed in 1743. Wild Boar are fierce when cornered, and in the wild they travel in small groups, staying in thick undergrowth and living on a variety of vegetation and small animals. There are a couple of dozen animals in the Howletts collection, and they are a fine sight as they charge through their enclosure. Passing a second enclosure for Clouded Leopards, you come finally to the Servals. The Serval is a slim, medium-sized cat with large ears, a native of the African bush, hunting small animals and relying more on speed than on stealth. In the large paddock enclosure for hoofed animals you will also see Emus and cassowaries, peafowl, Wild Turkeys, jungle fowl and guineafowl.

Mr Aspinall is planning to open another zoological park on the Port Lympne estate, overlooking the Romney marshes near Hythe in Kent, and it will be well worth while to keep a lookout for announcements about this, both at Howletts Zoo Park and in the press.

Marwell Zoological Park

Marwell Zoological Park is undoubtedly one of the most valuable and interesting zoological collections in the British Isles, and the number of breeding groups of animals which are endangered in the wild which you can see here makes it a zoo of world importance. This has been achieved in an incredibly short space of time, since it was only opened in 1972. Marwell is the creation of Mr John Knowles, formerly a successful poultry breeder and expert in animal genetics, who has had a lifetime interest in wild animals and is dedicated to the cause of animal conservation. The Park is unusual in two other ways: you can drive round it, stopping and alighting where you wish, as you can at Whipsnade, without being confined to your car by endless safety regulations. The animals and the public both enjoy their separate freedoms, the animals being in large paddock enclosures or, where necessary, in cages so large that you may have to look closely to discover the occupants. The other unusual and interesting feature is that the collection is arranged geographically, and you visit the wildlife of each area in turn, starting with Africa, then Eurasia, then America, and lastly Australia.

The chief conservation role of zoos is to breed stocks of animals which have become rare in the wild, and for herd animals this can only be done effectively if they are kept in large enough groups to stimulate breeding. This is exactly what has been done at Marwell, and already it has a world-famous collection of antelopes, with ten different species represented, all of which are breeding regularly. There are also excellent groups of big cats, of which seven species are shown, as well as five rare species of the horse family, six species of deer and six species of flightless birds.

After entering the Park, you come first to the African area. This is where you will see most of the antelopes. One of the most graceful of these is the Impala, a small animal of the plains which can leap ten feet at one bound. A herd of them taking great leaps when in flight gives the impression of an undulating wave, seeming to flow over every obstacle. Impalas are shy animals, not easy to keep in captivity, and for this reason are not often seen in zoos. Another beautiful antelope is the Nyala, with long horns curving slightly outwards and a mane of long hair. The males are grey and the females and young a rich chestnut-brown. It has been hunted for its hide excessively, and its numbers in the wild have declined considerably. Nyalas have not been seen in British zoos for a very long

The Hunting Dog, which preys on herds of antelope and zebra on the African plains.

Marwell Zoological Park. **Address** Colden Common, Nr Winchester, Hants. **Telephone** Owslebury 206. **Open** 10.00–19.45 (last admission 18.00) summer, 10.00–17.30 (last admission 16.00) winter. **Guide-book. Catering** self-service cafeteria with licensed bar in summer and school holidays (weekends only in winter), kiosks. **Acreage** 150. **Car** 7 mls s. of Winchester, off A333 Winchester–Portsmouth road. **Bus** to park in summer from Southampton, Winchester and Eastleigh. **Train** to Winchester and Eastleigh (7 mls). **Taxis** available. **Other facilities** children's playground, dog kennels. No pets. Public **not allowed** to feed animals.

time, and the Marwell animals were the first to breed in this country for more than 100 years. The Ellipsen or Common Waterbuck is a more heavily built animal found throughout East Africa. The males have lyre-shaped horns, and the species lives in woodland areas, never straying far from water. This is less often seen in zoos than the closely related Defassa Waterbuck, the main difference between the two being that the Ellipsen Waterbuck has a darker coat and elliptical white bands round its buttocks.

One of the most magnificent of all antelopes is the Sable, a large animal with long backward-curving horns, which are used both for defence against lions and by the males for fighting each other. Sable live in groups of one or two dozen individuals, supervised by an adult bull. They are found in the woodland and bush areas of South and East Africa. This is quite a fierce animal, requiring careful handling in captivity. It is some years since Sable have been exhibited in this country and these are almost the only ones to be seen at present in a British zoo.

The Scimitar-horned Oryx, now found only along the southern fringe of the Sahara Desert, has been reduced in numbers to the danger point by hunting, the hunters being tribesmen, soldiers and oil company employees. The ancient Egyptians kept this animal as a domestic species and it is certainly one of the handsomest antelopes, with long horns curving backwards in an arc, giving rise to the name given it by the Arabs, Abu harab, meaning the father of spears. The horns are used by bulls when fighting each other in the breeding season for leadership of the herd, and by the cows in defence of their calves. The herd at Marwell is the only one in the British Isles and also one of the largest in captivity anywhere. For these reasons, and because of the animal's beauty and rarity, it was chosen as the Park's symbol. This species can be compared with the Gemsbok, the largest of the oryx family, which is a native of the semi-arid regions in southwestern Africa. It has straight horns which may reach up to four feet in adult males. Another rare species is the White-tailed Gnu or Black Wildebeeste, which apart from its characteristic white tail is distinguished by a stiff mane and a tuft of hair on the face. It is the smallest of the wildebeeste family, and its numbers have been reduced by hunting in its native South Africa. It, too, is an aggressive animal, and seldom seen in British zoos.

The Baringo, or Rothschild's Giraffe, comes from northern Kenya where its numbers have declined, partly because of the destruction of trees by the native-owned goat population.

You can see all three species of zebra in the African section represented by Chapman's, Grévy's and Hartmann's Mountain Zebra. Chapman's Zebra is one of the four sub-species of the Plains Zebra, which is found in its various forms throughout most of eastern and southeastern Africa. It can be identified by its cream-coloured coat with 'shadow' stripes between the well-defined black stripes on its flanks. Hartmann's Zebra is now down to about 7,000 animals in the wild, and these are scattered in small groups throughout Angola and South West Africa. This zebra can be identified by the cross striping along the base of the spine and the rump. It is an unsociable animal, unlike the rest of the zebra family, living in small groups of about half a dozen. In captivity it prefers to be solitary most of the time and captive breeding therefore tends to be very slow. Grévy's Zebra is the largest of the family, standing 14 hands and distinguished by its large ears and narrow, concentrated striping pattern. It comes from northern Kenya, Somaliland and Ethiopia. Zebras have been trained for riding and as draught animals, but they are not satisfactory for these purposes because they are too highly strung: when kept with other animals in zoo paddocks they tend to bully and chivvy them, and stallions can be dangerous. When zebras are crossed with horses, the hybrids are sterile.

In some of the African enclosures you can see birds of the African plains which are found in proximity to the antelopes and zebras in their natural environment. The Ostrich, the largest flightless bird in the world, was once farmed for its plumes, which were popular as adornments. The chicks grow at an amazing speed, and the powerful legs of the adult bird can enable it to run at 40 m.p.h., besides being lethal weapons. The hen birds have brown plumage and the cocks

Three antelopes, all found in the wild in Africa, which can be seen at Marwell: Nyala (male left), Scimitar-horned Oryx (above) and Common Waterbuck (male below).

black, although the difference between the sexes cannot be distinguished until they reach adult plumage. Another ground-living bird is the Kori Bustard of East Africa, where it is found on grasslands. It feeds on seeds, insects and small mammals. There are also a number of Crowned Cranes here, distinguished by the golden feathers protruding from the tops of their heads. Both the West African and East African forms can be seen, the former having a black neck and the latter a grey neck. Crowned Cranes are popular as garden pets in Africa, because they eat insects and snakes.

The collection of predatory African animals includes the Cheetah, Leopard Serval and Hunting Dog. Cheetahs, now extinct in India and the Middle East, where they were trained to hunt in ancient times, are now found only in South West Africa, East Africa and Iran, where they are rare. They are the most difficult of all the cat family to breed in captivity and this has been achieved in only a few zoos. The two breeding pairs of Leopards here can usually be seen high up in the branches of their spacious outdoor cages, or through the windows of their indoor dens. The demand in recent years for Leopard-skin coats has caused them to become rare in both Africa and India, whereas not many years ago they were the commonest of the large cats in both continents. In zoos, they have to be kept in cages because their climbing ability makes it impossible to confine them in any other way; but at Marwell, the cages are so tall that one does not feel that they are at all restricted. The Marwell Leopard cages are certainly the best in any British zoo. The Hunting Dog inhabits the plains of central and eastern Africa, following the herds of antelope and zebra which they pursue relentlessly, singling out a weaker animal which is chased until it is exhausted. Unlike typical dogs, they have only four toes on the forefeet instead of five. When the pack goes hunting, the females with young pups are left behind and the returning pack, having killed and eaten, regurgitate some of the meat for the females. This may seem an unpleasant habit, but it is a practical way of ensuring that the nursing mothers do not starve.

The Eurasian area contains animals from Asia and Europe, which includes several species whose natural range covers both continents. The Asiatic antelopes here are the Nilgai and the Blackbuck. The Nilgai is a large Indian antelope, somewhat ungainly in appearance, whose Hindu name means 'blue bull'. In fact, only the bulls are bluish grey in colour, the cows and young animals being brown. They live in small herds in the forest, and are shy animals. The Blackbuck of northern and central India live in scrub and they are preyed upon by the Leopard and the Tiger. This used to be a common species, but like so many others, its numbers have been greatly reduced by hunting and forest clearance. At three years old, the males develop black coats along their sides and back, the females and young males being brown and white. The handsome spiralling horns are carried by the male.

The deer of Asia are represented here by the Axis Deer, the Hog Deer, Fallow Deer and three rare species – the Formosan form of the Sika Deer, the Barasingha and Père David's Deer. The Axis Deer, or Chital, has a brightly spotted coat, and it is a favourite prey of the Tiger. It is found in India and, more rarely, in Ceylon. The Hog Deer comes from northern India and Burma, living in reed-beds and marshes. It lives in small groups, except in the mating season, when it congregates in smallish herds. It is a squat animal with short horns, getting its name from its somewhat pig-like appearance. Fallow Deer, originally from Asia Minor and southern Europe, have spread all over Europe, and it may have been brought to Britain by the Romans. It is the typical animal of English parks, and it can be found wild in many parts of the country.

The Sika Deer, which is not unlike the Fallow, is found in the forests of eastern Asia, although it is now rare in the wild. The Formosan is the rarest, and it is no longer found wild in its native Taiwan. The Barasingha is a species of swamp deer, with splayed hooves adapted to marshy ground. It comes from the wet and marshy parts of Assam, although another race from central India is now found only in one reserve, where there is a small herd. Barasingha live in large herds, often associating with the much smaller Axis Deer. The coat is chestnut in summer, turning grey in winter. Père David's Deer is the rarest kind of deer in the Park. It is extinct in the wild, the last animals having been killed in the Boxer Rebellion in 1900. It was discovered near Peking by Père Armand David, a French missionary in 1865. Later a few animals were sent to zoos in Europe, but shortly before the last wild animals had been killed, the eleventh Duke of Bedford collected the existing zoo animals and founded what is still the largest remaining herd of the species. This is a swamp deer, presenting a curious appearance with its long, tufted tail, slanting eyes and odd antler formation.

It is amongst the Asiatic animals that you will see the rarest member of the horse family, Przewalski's Horse, which is the only surviving wild horse in the world. These wild horses used to roam the plains of central Asia, but the use of firearms to obtain their meat and hides has reduced their numbers, probably to the point of extinction. It is not known for certain whether any still survive in the wild, but if they do they are in all probability confined to one mountainous area in Mongolia on the Chinese frontier. Even so, as it is known that wild horses interbreed with domestic ponies, it is questionable whether any surviving wild animals would be pure bred. At the turn of the century, a few specimens were captured and sent to zoos all over the world, and there are now just over 200 in captivity, the Marwell herd being the largest in the world. Notice the characteristics which distinguish this animal from the other horses: a stiff, brush-like mane, stripes along the backbone, and the forelegs striped below the knees. In summer the wild horse has a light buff-coloured coat, which becomes darker and shaggier in winter.

Farther along, you will come to the Asiatic Wild Asses. Two races are shown, the Persian Onager and the Kulan, or Turkmenian Wild Ass. They are superficially similar, but are classified as distinct races owing to the differences in their coats and skull measurements. Wild Asses used to be found throughout the plains of Asia, but the increase in human population has isolated them in a few surviving·

Two forms of the Wild Ass: Turkmenian Kulan (above) and Persian Onager (below).

Below: Przewalski's Horse, the only surviving wild horse in the world.

herds and they are now rare all over the continent. They are tough, have immense stamina and can live on the sparsest vegetation. Fewer than 200 Kulans are in captivity, and not many more than 100 Onagers. The Kulans here are the only ones in Great Britain, and the only other Onagers in this country are at Whipsnade.

The Bactrian, or Two-humped, Camel is now probably extinct in the wild, but it has been domesticated as a pack animal for many centuries. It was found wild in the windswept deserts of northern Asia, but it is possible that a small population still exists in the Gobi Desert. The thick winter coat is shed in summer, and the splayed feet are adapted to walking on sandy terrain. The camel's hump is used for storing fat and water, and this makes it possible for it to survive for considerable periods without food. Camels cannot live for more than about ten days without water, and they normally need watering every two or three days to exist in comfort.

The most important animals in Marwell's cat collection are the Siberian and Sumatran Tigers. The Siberian Tiger is the largest race of Tiger, and after the almost extinct Javan Tiger the rarest. Its natural range extends from Siberia, through Manchuria and into Korea. There are thought to be no more than 200 animals of this race left in the wild, but there are about 250 in zoos, where they are breeding regularly, so this is an example of how captive breeding is probably saving a wild animal from extinction. Siberian Tigers weigh up to 650 lb. and because of the cold climate they inhabit in the wild, they develop immensely thick coats in winter. Two separate breeding strains were imported from zoos in the United States and Germany, and they have bred here. The Sumatran Tiger is a much smaller animal, with a darker coat and closer striping. Zoologists believe that Tigers evolved in the colder parts of the Northern Hemisphere, and as they migrated southwards into southern and eastern Asia they developed into smaller races with darker colouring. The two races exhibited here illustrate this point well.

Another handsome member of the cat family found in northern Europe is the Northern Lynx. It is a shy animal, inhabiting the less populated regions of Scandinavia and Russia. The Canadian Lynx is another race of this species, and there is a very rare race still found in Spain. In Africa and southwest Asia the Northern Lynx is replaced by another species, the Caracal, and in North America by the Bobcat. Northern Lynxes differ from other cats in having short, stubby tails, prominent tufts of hair on the points of their ears, and two tassels at the throat. They hunt mainly at night, living on small mammals, and occasionally larger ones such as Roe Deer. Their heavily padded feet equip them to hunt in deep snow, where they can even kill Reindeer.

There is a pool at Marwell for Small-clawed Otters from India and southeastern Asia. These are smaller than the European Otter and, unlike our native species, they live in family groups. You can also see Red Pandas, a beautiful small animal from the bamboo forests of the Himalayas and western China. It has a bright chestnut coat and is related to the Giant Panda of China. As in the African paddocks, you can also see in the Eurasian section a variety of the larger Asiatic birds, kept amongst the deer and antelopes. These include the Sarus Crane, one of the tallest of the cranes, standing about 5 feet 6 inches high, which comes from India, Burma and Thailand; the little Demoiselle Crane, found in southeastern Europe and across Asia; and the European Stork. There are also pheasants, including the rare Cheer Pheasant, Indian Peafowl and, near the entrance, a colony of Greater Flamingos, which share their pond with the more highly coloured Rosy Flamingos from the Caribbean.

Two purely European animals are the European Bison, or Wisent, and the Wild Boar. The Wisent formerly inhabited the deciduous forests of central and eastern Europe, but it was exterminated in the wild by 1920. However, some animals survived in zoos and these provided the nucleus of a small herd to be released in the Bialowieza Forest in eastern Poland, where they have increased under protection. A race of European Bison in the Caucasus was exterminated during the Second War, but this too survived in captivity though it has now been hybridised with other stock. It is a taller animal than the American Bison, and it is a browser, living on leaves and shoots. The Wild Boar is still common in forested areas of Europe, but the last ones in the British Isles were killed more than 250 years ago. Wherever they occur on the Continent, they are preserved for hunting. The young are striped, as with all wild species of pig.

The animals in the American section of the Park include the Jaguar, the Collared Peccary, the Llama and Guanaco, the Brazilian Tapir, and one large bird, the rhea. The Jaguar occurs throughout the forests of Central and South America, preying on deer and peccaries and also on tapirs and Capybaras, which live near water. It is a good swimmer and can even catch fish, scooping them out of the water with its paw. It is a more heavily built animal than the Leopard, and its coat pattern differs from the Leopard's in having a spot in the centre of each rosette marking. The Collared Peccary is the wild pig of South America, a small, compact animal which can live in desert scrub or thickly forested jungle. The Llama is a domestic form of the wild Guanaco, used by the mountain peoples of South America as a beast of burden as well as for its wool. The Guanaco is adapted to living in high altitudes and in the wild it is found in small herds. Both these animals are larger than the Alpaca, another domesticated member of the camel family, and the wild Vicuna, which has the finest wool of all. The Brazilian Tapir is one of three kinds of South American tapir. It lives in thick jungle swamps and is a strong swimmer. Its long mobile snout is adapted for eating aquatic plants. The rheas correspond to the Ostrich in Africa, and are considerably smaller. There are two forms here, the Grey Rhea and the White Rhea, and another much rarer species, the Darwin's Rhea, which is seldom seen in zoos.

The Australasian section of the Park contains two more flightless birds, the Emu and the cassowary, as well as Bennett's Wallaby. The Emu is found throughout the open grassland areas of Australia, living in flocks which feed on small animals including insects, and seeds and grasses. Like the rhea, the male Emu incubates the eggs, although his task is somewhat less arduous, as Emus lay 12 eggs compared with about 30 laid by the rhea. The Common Cassowary inhabits the tropical belt of northern Australia and it is also present in New Guinea. Here again, the male incubates the eggs, of which up to half a dozen are laid. Cassowaries have a bony excrescence on the forehead which is used to ram their way through thick undergrowth. The female is larger and more brightly coloured than the male.

Bennett's Wallaby is one of the many species of wallaby in Australia and one of the commonest in zoos. It is found in southeastern Australia and Tasmania. Wallabies are marsupials, giving birth to undeveloped young, which mature in the pouch where they live for nine months before becoming independent of the mother. Several kinds of duck and goose are on the ponds in the American and Australasian parts of the Park, and there are Australian Black Swans on the pond at the Park entrance.

The Children's Zoo contains donkeys, ponies, Soay Sheep, Dwarf Goats, Highland Cattle, Rabbits and guinea-pigs. One curious animal here is the Vietnamese Pot-bellied Pig. There are also aviaries for pheasants and a wide variety of exotic birds, including the Giant Hornbill. Young animals born in the Park which require artificial rearing are also kept here, and there is a glass-fronted building where some of these can be seen. Next to the Children's Zoo is the acclimatisation area, where newly arrived animals are kept and those awaiting permanent accommodation. All new animals are kept under observation to ensure that they are healthy, and some are required by law to undergo quarantine. The Park has arrangements to exchange surplus stock of endangered species with other zoos, including the London Zoo, the Jersey Wildlife Trust. Howletts Zoo Park owned by Mr John Aspinall, and the Rotterdam Zoo. You can become a member of the Marwell Zoological Society, which offers unlimited admission to the Park, a quarterly magazine and monthly meetings, except in August. There is an annual subscription, which is reduced for the 'Marwell Oryx Club', the junior section. The collection is being constantly enlarged, and new buildings appear regularly, so repeat visits to this excellent park are well worth while.

The Vicuna bears the finest wool of any animal.

Queen's Hotel Dolphinarium

This Dolphinarium exhibits three fully trained Bottle-nosed Dolphins from Florida, which give five shows daily in summer, with a continuous running commentary, and an explanation of dolphin biology. The Dolphinarium was opened in 1968.

Robin Hill-The Isle of Wight Country Park

This is a mixed collection of small mammals, birds and reptiles, but with no large animals at present. There is a ten-acre walk-through paddock with deer, wallabies, Prairie Marmots and domestic species, and several outdoor enclosures exhibiting monkeys and other smaller mammals such as Raccoons, otters, Coyotes and porcupines. The ten-acre paddock also has free-flying macaws and small parrots and there is a walk-through pond enclosure with ducks, geese, storks and cranes. Do not miss the indoor exhibits in the Jungle House, containing animals active by day, such as squirrel monkeys, chipmunks and tropical birds; nocturnal species such as bushbabies, fruit bats and Hairy Armadillos; and in the reptile section, pythons, cobras, water dragons and giant tortoises. Giant millipedes, scorpions, tarantula spiders and large butterflies are also displayed here.

There are 'contact' paddocks in which deer, wallabies and domestic animals are accessible, and a Commando-style assault course, which is popular with young and old. The Park was opened in 1969.

Southampton Zoo

This small open-air Zoo was started by Mr Jimmy Chipperfield in 1961. It has a mixed collection, including Lions, Tigers, Leopards, Jaguars, Clouded Leopards – a rare species – Chimpanzees, several species of monkey and some small mammals such as Prairie Marmots, and usually one or two large mammals such as Giraffes and elephants. A few birds are exhibited, including Ostrich, flamingo, penguin and crane. There is a small Reptile House containing snakes, lizards, small crocodiles and tortoises.

Weyhill Wildlife Park

Started in 1965 by Mr and Mrs R. D. Smith, this Zoo specialises in European wildlife, and many animals here breed regularly. The British animals to be seen include Red Foxes, Scottish Wild Cats, Polecats, Grey Squirrels, Red Deer and Fallow Deer, and Sika and Muntjac, two introduced species of deer which have become wild in this country. You can also see Arctic Foxes and Raccoon Dogs, an eastern Asiatic animal. Birds include Tawny, Barn and Little Owls, Mandarin Ducks, also found wild in Great Britain, Pintail, Tufted Duck and Wigeon; and several geese, including Canada, Snow, Barnacle and Egyptian Geese.

Queen's Hotel Dolphinarium. **Address** Queen's Hotel, Cliftonville, Kent. **Telephone** Thanet 25444. **Open** Shows daily at 11.00, 12.00, 14.00, 15.00, 16.00 (20.00 summer only). **Guidebook. Catering** kiosk. **Acreage** $\frac{1}{2}$. **Car** 1 ml from Margate along sea-front to Cliftonville. **Bus** 51 from Margate harbour. **Train** to Margate (1 ml). **Taxis** available. Public **not allowed** to feed exhibits.

Robin Hill, The Isle of Wight Country Park. **Address** Robin Hill, Arreton, I.O.W. **Telephone** Arreton 430. **Open** 10.00–18.00 summer, 10.00–16.00 winter, closed Dec–Feb. **Catering** licensed beer garden, cafeteria. Zoo shop. **Guided tours** by arrangement. **Acreage** 80. **Car** 2 mls e. of Newport and 1 ml n. off A3056 at Arreton follow 'Country Park' signs. **Bus** 13, 14a stop at Park entrance. **Train** to Ryde Esplanade (5 mls). **Taxis** available from Ryde, Sandown, Shanklin, Newport and Cowes. **Other facilities** children's playground. Public allowed to feed animals with food prepared and sold in Park.

Southampton Zoo. **Address** The Common, Southampton, Hants. **Telephone** Soton 556603. **Open** 10.00–18.00 summer, 10.00–16.30 winter. **Guide-book. Catering** snack bar. **Acreage** 3. **Car** 1 ml n. of city centre w. side of The Avenue (A33). **Bus** 15, 15a, 11. **Train** to Southampton Central (1 ml). **Taxis** available. Public **not allowed** to feed animals.

Weyhill Wildlife Park. **Address** Nr Andover, Hants. **Telephone** Weyhill 2252. **Open** 10.30–18.00 summer, 10.30–16.00 winter. **Catering** snack bar. Zoo shop. **Acreage** 13. **Car** 3 mls w. of Andover off A303. **Bus** stops $\frac{3}{4}$ ml from Park. **Train** to Andover (3 mls). **Taxis** available. **Other facilities** lectures and nature trails. Public may only feed animals with food sold in Park.

The Thames Valley and Chiltern Hills

KENNETH WILLIAMSON AND VICTOR J. SCOTT

The pleasant hobby of wildlife-watching is enjoying unprecedented popularity, and although this is encouraging to the naturalist, it generates many problems, especially in so crowded a corner of England as this. The weekend and bank-holiday explosion from Greater London nowadays encompasses the whole of the lower and middle Thames valley and the Chiltern Hills, and there is need for every care and consideration in our approach to wild creatures, and above all for a respect and regard for their habitat.

The region to the north and west of London embraces some of the most attractive scenery to be found in the English lowlands, stretching from the vast swelling downs of Wiltshire in the west, through similar Berkshire country and the Vale of the White Horse, to the green and fertile Thames valley and the beech woods of the Chiltern Hills. Eastwards there are the grassy escarpments of Dunstable Downs (NT) and Barton Hills NNR overlooking a largely arable countryside. The Vale of Aylesbury and adjoining land of north Oxfordshire offer some of the finest farmland panoramas to be found anywhere, a typically English mosaic of pastures and cornfields interlaced with rough roadside verges and an intricate network of well-grown hedgerows so richly endowed with tall ashes, oaks and elms that frequently one's impression is of a well-wooded countryside. This mosaic nature, together with the Chiltern woods and the grounds of fine residences along the Thames valley, makes this a region rich and varied in its wildlife — though in part this diversity is due to the Dukes of Bedford and the Rothschilds as we shall see! — but some species are extremely local, and a few are in urgent need of conservation.

Here, as elsewhere, the status of wildlife is prone to change, not least because large parts of the region are densely urban, and will become more so in the foreseeable future with the growth in north Buckinghamshire of the new city of Milton Keynes. There are birds, mammals and other forms of natural life which have decreased during the last few decades, but some have not only held their ground but have shown a marked tendency to grow in numbers and extend their range. Some less common members of the fauna have a degree of security by living and breeding within Ministry of Defence lands, Forestry Commission woodlands, National Trust properties, numerous private estates, and nature reserves managed by the Nature Conservancy Council and the County Naturalists' Trusts. There is one for Wiltshire, one for Gloucestershire, one for Middlesex and Hertfordshire, one for Bedfordshire and Huntingdonshire, and there is BBONT — the Berkshire, Buckinghamshire and Oxfordshire Naturalists' Trust.

THE BIRDS

Although much of the bird-life is characteristic of other parts of lowland Britain, particularly in agricultural areas, a few species are worthy of special note, being either very restricted in distribution, or virtually absent in the wild elsewhere in the country. It is likely that there are more Hawfinches in this region than in any other, simply because this is primarily a bird of hornbeam, and pure hornbeam woods are rare outside Hertfordshire and Essex. It is widely though only sparsely distributed away from Bramfield and Epping Forests, but despite its large size and massive bill (a splendid tool for cracking cherry stones) it is an elusive creature and not often seen. All three of our woodpeckers occur and of late the Lesser Spotted has been more conspicuous, and perhaps more numerous, as it searches for beetle larvae under the rotting bark of the field elms which are being destroyed by the ravages of a virulent strain of Dutch elm disease. Probably there are more Black Redstarts in the area than there are elsewhere in England (mostly in the metropolis), and may be more Little Ringed Plovers. Both are birds of man-made habitats and the Little Ringed Plover has spread far and wide since the first pair reared young at Tring Reservoirs NNR in 1938.

Victor J. Scott works on a private estate in the north Buckinghamshire village of Aston Abbots, where he was born in 1928. He is keenly interested in all aspects of natural history, especially botany, and spends much of his 'leisure' time lecturing or teaching adult classes for the Workers' Educational Association. He has travelled widely in central and southern Europe, as well as in Britain, often as leader-tutor to a WEA or similar student group.

Little Ringed Plover adjusts its eggs at its nest-scrape in the stony, sandy terrain of a working gravel-pit.

Opposite: Coots, Mute Swans and Black-headed Gulls at sunset on Wilstone Reservoir, part of the Chilterns Area of Outstanding Natural Beauty.

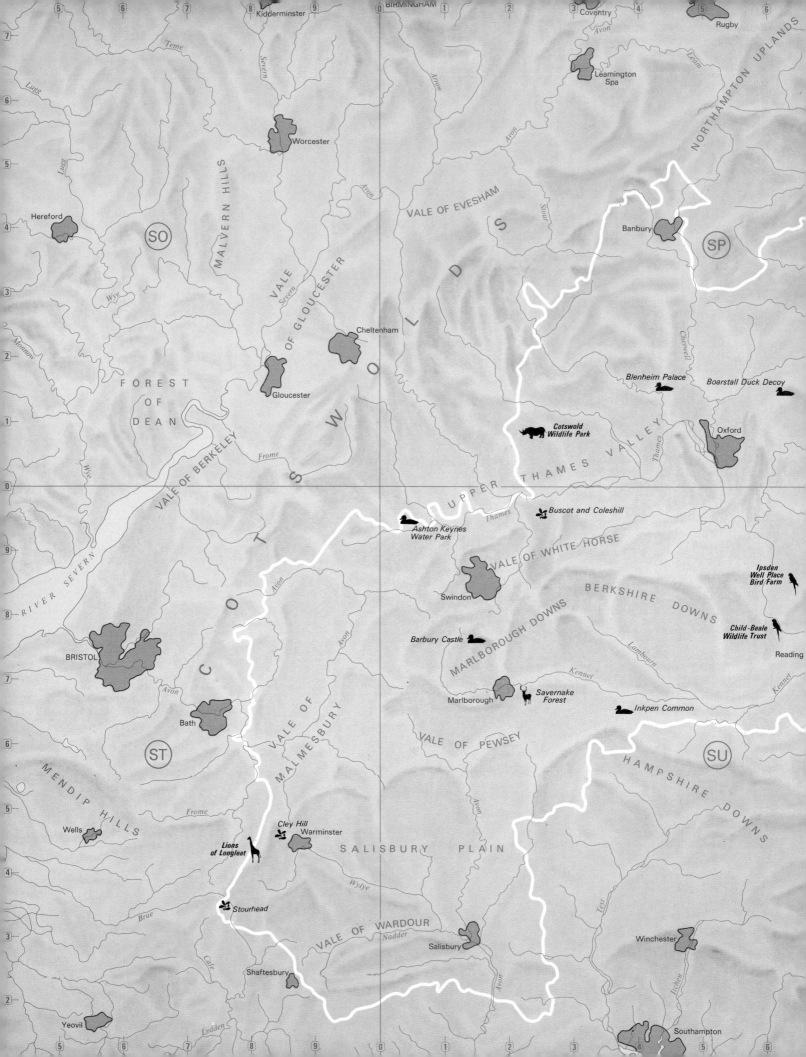

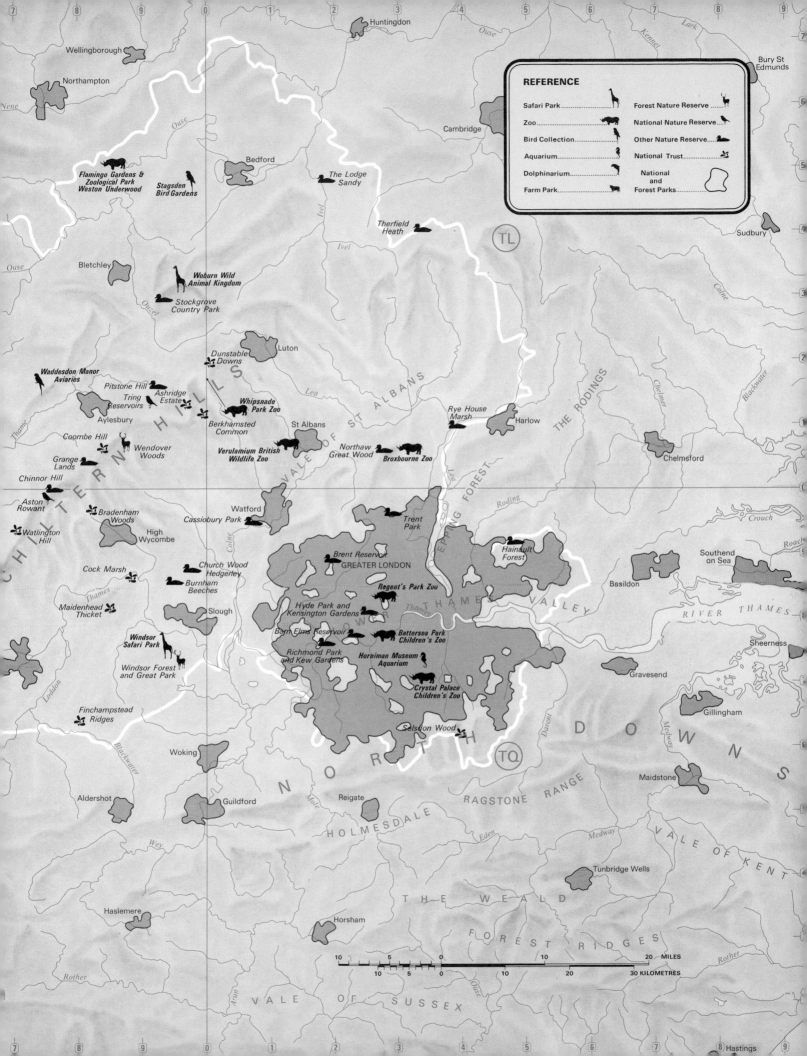

REFERENCE

Safari Park ....
Zoo ....
Bird Collection ....
Aquarium ....
Dolphinarium ....
Farm Park ....

Forest Nature Reserve ....
National Nature Reserve ....
Other Nature Reserve ....
National Trust ....
National and Forest Parks ....

Wellingborough
Northampton
Nene

Huntingdon
Ouse

Lark
Kennel

Bury St Edmunds

Ouse

Bedford

The Lodge
Sandy

Cambridge

Sudbury

**Flamingo Gardens &
Zoological Park
Weston Underwood**

**Stagsden
Bird Gardens**

Ivel

Therfield
Heath

(TL)

Bletchley

**Woburn Wild
Animal Kingdom**

**Stockgrove
Country Park**

Ouzel

Luton

Lea

Harlow

Rye House
Marsh

THE RODINGS

Chelmer

Colne

Blackwater

**Waddesdon Manor
Aviaries**

Pitstone Hill
Tring
Reservoirs

**Ashridge
Estate**

Dunstable
Downs

**Whipsnade
Park Zoo**

**Berkhamsted
Common**

St Albans

VALE OF ST ALBANS

Chelmsford

Aylesbury

Coombe Hill

Wendover
Woods

**Verulamium British
Wildlife Zoo**

Northaw
Great Wood

Broxbourne Zoo

EPPING FOREST

Roding

Grange
Lands

Chinnor Hill

CHILTERN HILLS

Thame

Aston
Rowant

Bradenham
Woods

High
Wycombe

Watford

Cassiobury Park

Colne

Trent
Park

Hainault
Forest

Southend
on Sea

Crouch

Watlington
Hill

Cock Marsh

Church Wood
Hedgerley

**Burnham
Beeches**

Slough

Brent Reservoir

GREATER LONDON

Regent's Park Zoo

LOWER THAMES VALLEY

Thames

Basildon

RIVER THAMES

Roach

Thames

Maidenhead
Thicket

**Windsor
Safari Park**

Windsor Forest
and Great Park

**Hyde Park and
Kensington Gardens**

Barn Elms Reservoir

Richmond Park
and Kew Gardens

**Battersea Park
Children's Zoo**

**Horniman Museum
Aquarium**

Sheerness

Gravesend

Loddon

Finchampstead
Ridges

**Crystal Palace
Children's Zoo**

Gillingham

Blackwater

Woking

Selsdon Wood

(TQ)

NORTH DOWNS

Darent

Medway

Maidstone

Aldershot

Guildford

Reigate

Mole

RAGSTONE RANGE

Eden

Medway

VALE OF KENT

Wey

HOLMESDALE

Haslemere

Horsham

Tunbridge Wells

Rother

THE WEALD

FOREST RIDGES

VALE OF SUSSEX

Rother

Arun

Ouse

Hastings

10   5   MILES
0   5   10   20
10   5   0   10   20   30 KILOMETRES

Some species owe their continued presence to successful acclimatisation following deliberate, or occasionally accidental, introduction by man. The Pheasant is the oldest of these by many centuries, but in quite recent years two close relatives have been found in a feral state north of the Thames — Lady Amherst's and Reeve's Pheasants. Should they thrive, they will certainly ornament our parkland and more open woods, for they are large and showy birds.

Two earlier introductions, the Red-legged Partridge and the Little Owl, are birds of farmland, though they occasionally enter woods. 'The Frenchman', distinguished from our fast-declining native Partridge by its larger size, white face and barred flanks, has spread through our region from East Anglia to the Midlands and south coastal counties. In some parts it is now commoner than the English bird which, hatching its chicks earlier in the season, has fallen victim to changes in farm technology combined with the lateness of the springs, resulting in the lack of an adequate supply of sawfly larvae to nourish the young. The Little Owl is often to be seen in daytime, perched on a telegraph pole or fence-post as he scans the ground for beetles.

Much the most conspicuous of the newcomers is the black-necked Canada Goose which haunts the London parks and breeds at many places along the Thames valley; its wild honking call as the small skeins move ground is a familiar sound at either end of the day. A singularly decorative addition to our avifauna, the more welcome here because it is a seriously threatened species in its native home in eastern China and Japan, is the gaudy Mandarin, now a well-established duck on Virginia Water and the ponds of Windsor Great Park. The most astonishing novelty is the African Ring-necked Parrakeet, small groups of which have been reported in southeast London's suburbia since 1972, the recent run of very mild winters having doubtless enabled this tropical species to colonise.

THE MAMMALS

As with most of the resident birds, the majority of the mammals found in our region are widespread throughout the southern half of Britain. There are several, however, which deserve special mention, either because they are uncommon or very local elsewhere, or because their British distribution is actually restricted to our area.

Generally speaking, looking for mammals is far less easy than looking for birds: most, certainly the larger ones, have an instinctive fear of man which, together with their mainly nocturnal habits, makes them difficult and elusive subjects. Moreover, the woodland surroundings in which many are to be found give them every advantage over the would-be watcher.

During an afternoon stroll one may expect to see a few Grey Squirrels and a few Rabbits, with very occasionally the unexpected bonus of a Stoat or Weasel earnestly pursuing a mouse or vole, quite oblivious of a close human presence. To get to know something of other mammals one must be prepared to spend hours of patient watching at those times of day when most people are disinclined to leave home comforts. As dusk falls the creatures of night come out to hunt and feed, and the countryside has few sights more rewarding than that of a family of Badgers emerging from their sett in the late evening in May or June, sometimes even before the sun has set. To get out before dawn on a still, early summer morning and sit (maybe in the comfort of one's car) at the edge of a woodland glade to watch a group of Fallow Deer, or to see a Fox returning to its earth at the start of the birds' dawn chorus, must surely be among the great experiences of life to any nature-lover.

The Fallow Deer which have long been established in many of our wooded districts are the descendants of semi-domesticated stock kept in the past on private estates. Over the last two or three decades other species have become well established, especially in the Chilterns and the more heavily wooded areas of Bedfordshire and north Buckinghamshire. The most common and widespread is the Muntjac or Barking Deer, which has extended its range from Woburn Park, the seat of the Dukes of Bedford, to include much of our region, often venturing out of the woods into open grassland and farms. It may reasonably be expected

Drake Mandarin in breeding plumage: threatened in its natural oriental range, this duck has established wild populations in the Thames valley following escapes from captivity.

Following its introduction from North America, the familiar Grey Squirrel took the place of the Red Squirrel in much of Britain's deciduous woodland.

The most widespread deer in the Chilterns is the furtive Muntjac, spreading outwards from its point of origin in Woburn Park.

wherever some cover is provided by tall vegetation and patches of thorn scrub and bramble. Its voice is a very dog-like double bark, most likely to be heard in the early morning, at any time of the year, though it is exceptionally noisy in May and June. Other escapes from Woburn Park are the Sika Deer, Siberian Roe Deer and Chinese Water Deer, all to be encountered occasionally in the extensive woods on and near the Beds.–Bucks. county boundary.

Tring, in Hertfordshire, is the site of the establishment of one mammal which, in Britain, is only found in our region. In the closing years of the last century, the late Lord Rothschild released individuals of the European Edible Dormouse (or Fat Dormouse), an animal once regarded as a table delicacy on the Continent. They thrived and gradually spread throughout the Chiltern woods around Tring, Berkhamsted and Wendover, where they now do considerable damage to young trees by removing the bark and cambium tissues vital to growth. Foresters regard them as a pest, so it is fortunate that they have so far failed to spread beyond Amersham, Chesham and Chorleywood. One often hears them called 'Glis Glis' — the only instance known to us of an animal's scientific name being taken into common usage as a vernacular.

Often they get into houses in the late autumn, seeking food and a suitable place (usually in the loft) to pass their winter hibernation, which may last for six months. They share with their English relative the Common Dormouse the distinction of being among the most nocturnal of mammals. The Fat Dormouse will often hibernate in an old woodpecker's hole, even in a nest-box, enlarging the entrance to suit its requirements. Should you discover one in such a place be cautious and resist any temptation to handle it, for it can inflict a savage and painful bite.

The more attractive English Dormouse with its sandy brown upper parts cannot be mistaken for the large, grey-backed continental animal. Although much more widely distributed, it is a rare creature, being found in very small numbers in some of the Chiltern woods, especially where hazel bushes and hedges form the woodland boundary. If found it should be left undisturbed, for it is one of our endangered species.

Along the foot of the Chilterns escarpment there occurs one of this country's most delightful small mammals, the tiny Harvest Mouse. Sometimes a diligent search will reveal its spherical nest of interwoven dry grass-blades, without any obvious entrance or exit, suspended in herbage close to the cornfield margin. It may be only a few inches above the ground and should not be mistaken for the nest, *on* the ground, of the Short-tailed Vole. The Common Shrew is another downland mammal, and in this region there is an extremely dark form with nearly black upper parts, reminiscent of the larger Water Shrew.

The small Pipistrelle and the Long-eared are our commonest bats, but some very large ones, probably Noctule Bats, occasionally hawk for insects among the martins over the reedbeds of Tring Reservoirs NNR and elsewhere.

REPTILES AND AMPHIBIANS

From time to time the walker is sure to come across one or other of the few amphibians and reptiles found within our region. Toads and frogs are distributed throughout, but the Common Frog is certainly far less common today than it was merely a few years ago; its decline is probably due to pollution and in some instances the destruction of the small farm ponds in which it likes to breed, combined with over-collecting for biological teaching and research. All three British species of newt occur, though the Palmate Newt is rather uncommon. They may be found in spring and summer in ponds and other still waters, the Palmate Newt preferring clear water, whilst the Common or Smooth Newt and Crested Newt will tolerate stagnant and quite dirty pools. The Grass Snake is well distributed and often common, preferring damp places such as stream-sides, whilst the Viper is much more local and likes drier ground; it is absent from much of the eastern half of our region, becoming progressively commoner as one travels west. The Common Lizard and the Slow-worm — a snake-like legless lizard — are fairly common on open hillsides, but can also be found in woodland clearings and on bracken and heather-clad heaths.

The Edible (or Fat) Dormouse is confined in Britain to this region alone.

Though widely distributed in England and Wales, the Common Dormouse is scarce.

Pipistrelle, the smallest and most numerous of the British bats.

THE CHALK GRASSLAND

Downland has covered large tracts of this region since early mediaeval times; in those centuries when wool was the staple of England's trade with Europe the downland was sheep-walk, carpeted with close-cropped nutritious fescue-grasses which continual grazing encourages. In many places, when wool became less important, numerous Rabbits did the work of the sheep through their constant nibbling; but since myxomatosis reduced them to a pitiful remnant in the mid-1950s, brome and coarser grasses have come to dominate the sward, and shrub growth has invaded the downs. At Porton Down in Wiltshire, Aston Rowant NNR in Buckinghamshire, and a few other sites, much of this invasive scrub is juniper, and where it is well grown it supports a high density of birds. In other places the scrub is of young pines sown by seed-parents in hill-top 'amenity' clusters planted in the last century.

Towards the northeastern end of the Chiltern Hills the main scrub growth is hawthorn, spreading outwards (doubtless helped by berry-eating thrushes) from the farm hedges below. Barton Hills NNR, Dunstable Downs (NT), Ivinghoe Beacon (NT) and Pitstone Hill (Bucks. CC) have acquired a unique breeding bird community representative of a wide spectrum of habitat tolerance. There are open-field species like the Skylark and Meadow Pipit (the latter more abundant here than anywhere in central and southern England); those which favour developing scrub, such as Grasshopper Warbler, Whinchat, Linnet, Reed Bunting and Yellowhammer; others which enjoy denser cover, like the Willow and Garden Warblers, Turtle Dove, Dunnock and Lesser Whitethroat; and 'forest' birds such as Chiffchaff and Blackcap which are colonising a few places, like Steps Hill (NT), between Ivinghoe Beacon and the Ashridge Estate, where the vegetation succession has advanced to the stage of nascent oakwood – the oaks springing, perhaps, from the acorns hidden by Jays as a winter store.

No environment can show a wider or more interesting range of song-birds, and despite immense visitor pressure, especially at weekends, all seem to do well. If you arrive early, when the car parks are still empty, the Brown Hares sit up and gaze at you in curiosity with lifted black-tipped ears, you may see a Red Fox slinking furtively into a clump of elders, and you have a fifty-fifty chance of disturbing Muntjac Deer as they browse in the open. On a warm summer's day it is all bird-song and butterflies – Small Heath, Small Copper, Ringlet, Marbled

Yellowhammer, male at nest, and the Small Heath butterfly, are two typical inhabitants of the chalk grassland and scrub.

Part of Porton Down in Wiltshire, invaded by well-grown juniper scrub.

White, Duke of Burgundy Fritillary, Common and Chalk-hill Blues. The sweet lilting songs of numerous Willow Warblers, the fluting of Blackbirds, the liquid melody of the Blackcap, and the torrent of Skylark song from above fashion an unforgettable morning. It is one of the few places where you can compare the song-flights of Tree and Meadow Pipits, for their territories overlap; and in the background there is the monotonous sewing-machine song of the secretive Grasshopper Warbler, so ventriloquial that it is almost impossible to pin-point the bird.

With minor variations you will find similar fare (though Meadow Pipits are scarce or absent) at Coombe Hill (NT) and The Grangelands (BBONT), both near Princes Risborough, and at Chinnor Hill (BBONT) and Watlington Hill (NT) over the Oxon border; and all afford similar expansive views over green miles of agricultural countryside where Corn Buntings jingle and all the hedgerow birds abound. These chalk grassland hills attract wintering thrushes such as Fieldfare and Redwing flocks, and have big autumn Linnet roosts; in spring we have seen the Hoopoe, in winter the Great Grey Shrike, and in some years at high summer you will hear the liquid whistling of Quails on the lower slopes where the grass meets the corn.

Ploughing up of old downland sheep-walks on the chalk of Wiltshire and Berkshire, and the encroachment of hawthorn and other scrub on formerly grassy hillsides, have contributed to the decline of the Stone Curlew; but a factor of some importance is the popularity of many of the traditional breeding areas with ramblers and picnickers, for the Stone Curlew is intolerant of disturbance. Fortunately there are still some large tracts of chalk like Porton Down and other Ministry of Defence lands on Salisbury Plain where this fine bird is assured of a safe habitat free from disturbance in the nesting season. It gets its name partly from its preference for bare flint-strewn ground where it feeds by night, and partly from the *cour-lee* call which features in the evening 'clamour'. During the day it likes to rest in areas of longer grass and light scrub.

Another once-familiar bird, the Red-backed Shrike which used to impale its ghoulish larder of bees, grasshoppers and even young birds on blackthorn or hawthorn spines, has virtually disappeared; it is gradually withdrawing from the most westerly parts of its European range, possibly because the wetter summers of this century have rendered the large insects on which it feeds less active and therefore difficult to find. The Wryneck too, a small brown relative of the woodpeckers which requires a large supply of ants and their larvae in the nesting season, was formerly common in the Thames valley but is now among the rarest of passing visitors. Once similarly widespread, the tuneful Woodlark is reduced to a few pairs in the Chilterns; and although the yellow Cirl Bunting with his striking black-and-green head can still be found where the fields march to the foot of the escarpment, this too has declined alarmingly in recent years.

THE WOODS AND PARKS

More recently — and we may hope only temporarily — some of our most interesting summer visitors have also decreased: they include the Whitethroat, Sedge and Reed Warblers, Whinchat and the colourful Redstart. They are migrants, and their scarcity is due to the failure of many to survive the winter season in the Sahel Zone on the southern fringe of the Sahara Desert, where calamitous droughts have prevailed since 1969. The Nightingale too has gone from many of its former haunts. The decline of active coppicing in the Thames valley and Chiltern woodlands is much to blame, for the bird is commonest during the first eight years of coppice growth, by which time the habitat no longer suits it. When woods were cut over on a regular rotation there were always suitable places for the birds to move to, but with the decline of the industry since the plastics revolution the coppice has become too densely overgrown. However, this marvellously thrilling songster can still be heard on fine, warm nights, and in daytime too, in the latter half of May and the first two weeks of June, in a few favoured localities, especially where there are blackthorn brakes.

Burnham Beeches must be one of the most visited areas in the Chilterns. The venerable gnarled beech trees, pollarded long ago to prevent the deer and

Great Bustard. The 'droves' of this stately and elegant bird were a feature of the brecklands and chalk downs of England until the close of the eighteenth century. A few lived on in East Anglia and the Yorkshire Wolds until the 1830s but (as T. A. Coward wrote) 'the bird was too big and edible to survive'. Today the only memory is 'The Bustard Hotel' near Larkhill Military Camp, north of B3086 on Salisbury Plain. A recent attempt to acclimatise birds from Europe in a large pen at Porton Down has so far met with no success: courtship and display demand a wide-ranging freedom which captivity does not permit. The Great Bustard has a relict population in Spain, northern Germany, Poland, Hungary and across south-central Asia, and fewer than ten vagrants have turned up in Britain in the last 50 years.

Brown Hares sit up and gaze at you with curiosity.

cattle from browsing the new shoots, are its pride; but there are younger woods and plantations of conifers, and tracts of rough grass and bracken as at East Burnham Common. Ponds have been made by damming a trickle of water seeping from a bog; they have willows and birches and rotting alders to the water's edge, beloved of Treecreepers, tits and woodpeckers. A rich growth of swamp vegetation gives cover for Dabchicks and Moorhens, and Muntjac and Fallow Deer leave their distinctive footprints in the mud. It is an excellent spot for dragonflies of several species, and for Smooth and Crested Newts.

Queenwood at Christmas Common near Watlington, a Forestry Commission experimental area, has younger and straighter beeches than the venerable trees at Aston Wood (NT) near Stokenchurch, and Park Wood (NT) near Bradenham; the edge of the latter is variegated with fine whitebeams and yews, and there are substantial anthills which attract the Green Woodpeckers. Salcey Forest (FC) on the Bucks.–Northants. border contains good examples of oak and ash on heavy Midlands clay, and in addition to its varied bird-life it is the haunt of interesting butterflies which include the Wood White and Purple Hair-streak. Church Wood (RSPB) at Hedgerley and Dancers End (SPNR) near Tring are both Nightingale haunts, as is Foxholes (BBONT), a young oakwood near Bruern in the Evenlode valley. This and the Warburg Reserve (BBONT), 247 acres of wood, scrub and grassland occupying the dry valley of Bix Bottom between Nettlebed and Henley-on-Thames, have Badger setts and Fallow Deer, and at Bix the birds include Sparrowhawk, Kestrel, Woodcock and Willow Tit. There are fine walks in the Ampthill Forest (FC) in Bedfordshire, and we should also mention the picturesque company of Scots pines and birches on the bracken-clothed Greensand surrounding the RSPB Headquarters above Sandy in the same county.

There are also many pollarded beeches and oaks in the outstandingly beautiful woods of the Ashridge Estate (NT), especially at Frithsden Beeches on the edge of Berkhamsted Common. So dense are the wide leafy crowns that the ground is often bare of vegetation, carpeted only with last year's russet leaves. The shade-tolerant holly is almost the only secondary growth. Young closed-canopy beech woods (such as the Forestry Commission crops at Christmas Common and Halton Woods) have a poor selection of birds; the old pollarded trees, with an abundance of cavities where winter winds and snowfall have broken heavy branches away, provide better fare because they afford homes for the hole-nesting tits, woodpeckers, Tawny Owls, Nuthatch, Redstart, Treecreeper, Stock Dove, Tree Sparrow, Jackdaw and Starling.

Ashridge is not all beech and oak; there is a fine sweet-chestnut wood (Sallow Copse) with its Nuthatches and Wood Warblers, and several former heaths now overgrown with mature birches — surely one of the most delightful of our trees, and an excellent larder for the birds. Aldbury and Pitstone Commons are really birch woods, but Berkhamsted and Northchurch Commons are more open, with Lesser Redpolls and Linnets busy in the scrub. Willow Warbler and Tree Pipit are common to both types. Both Marsh and Willow Tits, really only distinguishable by their voices, live in these woods, and among the scarcer denizens are Nightingale, Hawfinch and Sparrowhawk. Ashridge shelters some 300 Fallow Deer, and although they are best seen when you turn out to listen to the birds' dawn chorus or to watch the 'roding' flight of the Woodcocks at dusk, small groups do venture close to the roads, so that for safety as well as sheer enjoyment slow driving is essential.

On many occasions during the rutting season, from mid-September through October, we have sat in the heart of these woods into the early hours of the morning, listening to and recording the stirring noise of the bucks' bellowing as they challenge one another for supremacy. Sometimes there is a noisy battle in the moonlight, with the clashing of antlers and that deep roar shattering an impressive silence, or drowning the double hooting of the Tawny Owls.

The county boundary between Buckingham and Bedford runs through Stockgrove Country Park close to Leighton Buzzard — once a private estate but now a public open space administered by the two County Councils. There are many similar if smaller areas in the region, places like Cassiobury Park at Watford

A pollarded beech at Burnham Beeches.

Burnham Beeches. A. D. C. le Sueur, author of *Burnham Beeches* (published by the City of London Corporation), found from ring counts that many of the beeches began life about 1500. Pollarding started about 1520 and was repeated at intervals varying from 5 to 20 years, depending upon the vigour of individual trees, until about 1820. The main produce was firewood for the Manor of Allerd-in-Burnham; a manor of moderate size required 100 tons of such fuel a year, well within the capacity of this 574-acre wood. The surplus was sent by barge down the Thames to London; pollarding ceased when sea-borne coal came to London in the other direction. The pollarded hornbeams of Epping Forest, and the beeches of the Chilterns and the New Forest, are suffering fungal decay and few indeed are likely to survive the close of the century.

H. L. Edlin, *Woodland Notebook — Goodbye to the Pollards*; Q. Jour, Roy. Forestry Soc., vol. 65, pp. 157–165 (April 1971).

and Bentley Priory at Harrow, and once among the trees it is hard to appreciate that Greater London with its noise and bustle is only a few miles away. We should perhaps mention in passing Howe Park and Linford Woods, if only because they are the only woods available for recreation and conservation planning in the big new urban complex of Milton Keynes. Stockgrove is very varied with pine-clad hillsides, open grassland, a small lake and birch, beech and oak woodland, and it is rich in bird and mammal life at all seasons. Crossbills have bred, and Siskins and Bramblings come in winter. Dabchicks trill and Reed Warblers chatter in the small reedbed, while Coot, Moorhen, Mallard and Tufted Duck swim on the pool. The bracken slopes with their patches of heather and bilberry are similar to those fringing the Scots pine woods on the Greensand at Brickhill not far away; they have Grasshopper Warblers and Tree Pipits, and the Nightjar is vocal at dusk. Stockgrove is not far from the Duke of Bedford's Woburn Estate, scene of so many 'escapes', so it is not surprising that the Muntjac, Sika and the tusked Chinese Water Deer can all be found: and here, very early one June morning, one of us was thoroughly startled by a Lady Amherst's Pheasant which burst explosively from a bramble patch.

FORESTRY COMMISSION WOODS

In the wooded Chiltern Hills management has changed the status of many birds. Once clothed practically from end to end in splendid beech woods which provided the local 'bodgers', as well as the flourishing furniture industry centred on High Wycombe, with timber, many stretches have been felled by private estates and the Forestry Commission and replanted with quicker-growing softwoods such as Scots and Corsican pines, Douglas fir, European larch and Norway spruce. Here and there remnants of the old beech forest remain, such as the adjacent Naphill Common and Park Wood (NT) near Saunderton, and these provide a haven for the woodpeckers and tits and in winter the white-rumped Bramblings from Scandinavia seeking the beech mast on the brown floor.

There are many woods to choose from in this region and only a few can be mentioned. Savernake Forest near Marlborough is one of the most attractive with its many fine old oaks and beeches, intersected by numerous wide tracks and paths. The Forestry Commission's West Woods at Lockeridge nearby have a similar bird-life interest with their Redstarts, Wood Warblers, Nightingales and the occasional Nightjar; while in addition to the two common snakes, the Slow-worm and Common Lizard occur. In the Cotswold country there are remnants

Four birds whose nest-sites are typically associated with cavities in mature or rotting trees: above, Tawny Owl, adult with young; below left to right, Tree-creeper with beakful of food, Starling with food at nest-hole, and Green Woodpecker.

Left: Tree Pipit, which breeds in new conifer plantations where there is scrub. But the Goldcrest (right) moves in only at a more mature stage.

of the royal forest of Wychwood, and another royal perquisite is Windsor Great Park in Berkshire, haunt of woodpeckers and the piping Nuthatch. Sometimes the Hobby hunts over the parkland: it is a great rarity, but likely to appear suddenly on sickle-curved wings chasing the Swallows and martins (or perhaps a dragonfly) in June and July in similar park country almost anywhere in the region.

In their early years the new conifer plantations far outstrip broad-leaved woods in diversity and density of breeding birds, attracting not only the customary song-birds but also species like Grasshopper Warbler, Whitethroat, Tree Pipit and Yellowhammer which like a more open scrub-grown terrain. The unbirdlike churring of the curious Nightjar is sometimes to be heard at dusk; but, in common with these others which favour a more open habitat, the Nightjar is forced to move on in search of a new territory when the trees are 12–15 years old and the canopy begins to close in. At this, the thicket stage, few bird species remain. In more mature plantations the blue-green foliage shimmers with the pulsating song of the Goldcrest, and that new colonist the Firecrest has appeared in a few places, notably the spruce woods behind Halton and Wendover, where more than 40 singing males have been counted in mid-June. The Coal Tit is the commonest tit, and in winter small flocks of Siskins and Lesser Redpolls appear, with occasionally, in an 'irruption year', nomadic bands of Crossbills.

The whole of the Chilterns has been declared an Area of Outstanding Natural Beauty — and with this in mind, recent Forestry Commission policy has been to intermingle beech with the conifers, the aim being to remove the latter in about 40 years and allow the beech trees to grow on to maturity. Heath and Homefield Woods, in a dry valley west of Marlow, provide a particularly exciting and varied planting of this kind, the trees still young enough to harbour an astonishing variety of birds.

Great Crested Grebe on nest.

RESERVOIRS AND GRAVEL-PITS

Another aspect of human endeavour which has greatly enriched the wildlife of our region is the construction of reservoirs, partly to assuage the thirst of the metropolis, and partly to keep the network of canals topped up. The most famous canal-feeder reservoirs anywhere are those close to Tring, Weston Turville, Wilstone and Marsworth Reservoirs particularly. Together with Foxcote Reservoir (BBONT) some way to the east, and the range of Thames valley gravel-pits to the west, they are important staging-posts for wildfowl and waders crossing the country between the Wash and the Severn along the 'leading-line' of the Chilterns escarpment. The Tring Reservoirs NNR embraces four waters on any one of which you can watch the spring 'plesiosaur race' and the beautiful weed-presentation ceremonial of the Great Crested Grebes; where you can hear the loud trilling of the Dabchick in the reedbeds, momentarily silencing the chatter of the Reed Warblers; where Mallard, Teal, Shoveler, Pochard and Tufted Duck are always afloat, and every winter provides unusual visitors such as Wigeon, Gadwall, Pintail and Goosander on the water and Bearded Reedlings in the reeds.

In the passage seasons, especially if the water is low and much mud is exposed, groups of Dunlins, Ringed and Little Ringed Plovers, Lapwings, Green and Wood Sandpipers, Greenshanks and Redshanks may well be joined for a few days by some rare wader from Siberia or America. These include the Curlew Sandpiper and Little Stint, and the nearctic Pectoral Sandpiper. Black and Common Terns come regularly, Ospreys occasionally; and indeed Tring Reservoirs NNR always has that rare quality of excitement, of the unexpected just around the corner, that all great bird-watching places share.

Many would make the same claim for a whole series of London's reservoirs – the Brent, Staines, Barn Elms, King George V and Queen Mary – and in truth they are wonderfully rich in winter waterfowl, and it is always worth while eavesdropping near the anorak-clad, binocular brandishing bird-watchers on their banks. Probably there are no better waters in England for the elegant little Smew (described by one precocious young ornithologist of our acquaintance as a Panda Duck!); and one may find its larger relatives the Goosander and Red-breasted Merganser – often with a Great Northern or Red-throated Diver, or a scoter or Long-tailed Duck, in from the sea. One of the Home Counties heronries is at Tring Reservoirs NNR (there is another in Richmond Park), and you can have the unique experience in England of seeing them standing scrawnily beside their nests in reeds not trees; but it is along the Thames and its tributary streams that one looks for this gaunt and stately fisher, and for that gleaming gem among birds, the Kingfisher. This has suffered much in the recent past from pollution, the leaching into streams of dieldrin and DDT-based chemicals from farmland, and it is equally at risk from industrial chemicals such as PCB, but it is responding now to the Water Authority's efforts to create a cleaner and healthier Thames. The river has its grebes, Moorhens, Coots (though they are commoner on the reservoirs), Canada Geese and the graceful and familiar Mute Swans,

Marsh Warbler.

The **Marsh Warbler** is a rare bird which our region shares with the West Midlands along the upper reaches of the Thames and its tributaries. It haunts the sallows and other bushy growth along the banks. It is a close relative of the Reed Warbler and hardly distinguishable except by its sweeter song; it has a penchant for mimicry and makes good use of calls and song-phrases borrowed from other birds. When the osier beds were cut on a regular rotation for basket-making in the fruit-growing districts there were many more Marsh Warblers than now; but, as with the Nightingale in coppiced woods, the cessation of regular cutting has meant a considerable loss of habitat and a sad reduction in its numbers. Today intensive river management, which often removes the scrub growth along the banks so that machines can scour out the streams, poses an even greater threat to its continued existence as a British bird.

The two species of grebe which breed on Home Counties reservoirs: far left, Great Crested Grebe; left, Dabchick (or Little Grebe). Both of these grebes build their nests in semi-floating situations, and hide their conspicuous white eggs with weed if they have to leave them unattended.

all kept continually in motion by the river traffic. The water-meadows attract Snipe galore in winter, along with Lapwings, Redshanks and Golden Plovers.

Another type of wetland, ideal for winter bird-watching because the water temperature is always kept above freezing-point, is provided by the strings of watercress beds along the Chess, the Bourne, the Gade and other Hertfordshire and Buckinghamshire valleys; and if you are not too sensitive to the malodorous air, it is always worth while trying the local sewage purification works with their filter-beds and lagoons for interesting birds. The cress beds attract Pied and Grey Wagtails, migrant sandpipers and Kingfishers, and also the little-known Water Pipit, a shy grey-brown bird of high meadows in the Alps and Pyrenees which flies north to winter here.

The Cotswolds are more renowned for their beautiful villages, elegant houses and magnificent churches (symbols of the wealth formerly derived from wool) than for their birds which, however, are similar in kind to those found farther east. The rivers Windrush, Evenlode and Cherwell flow gently from the north and their valleys are well worth exploring, especially the flooded meadows alongside the Cherwell to the south of Banbury in winter time. Wildfowl are also attracted at that season to Port Meadow beside the Thames at Oxford, and to the water-meadows around Thame. In the flat country northeast of Oxford is the curious wetland area known as Otmoor; though drainage has deprived it of some of its pristine glory, the rushy fields still harbour Lapwings, Redshanks and Curlews. The best access is gained from Beckley or from Charlton-on-Otmoor, but the heavy clay of the tracks can become a morass in winter. Not far away is the interesting duck decoy at Boarstall, a ringing station of the Wildfowlers' Association of Great Britain and Ireland (WAGBI). There are fascinating disused railway lines in this part of the region, with a rich flora, many different butterflies, and a varied assortment of birds in the trees and scrub.

The enormous demands of urban and suburban building at various points along the meanders of the Thames have created countless gravel-pits, many now disused and overgrown, which in the course of their return from degraded land to natural wetland have benefited birds, mammals, reptiles, amphibia, fish and many interesting insects and plants. The Thames valley is studded with these green oases, the sanctuaries of Great Crested and Little Grebes, Little Ringed Plovers, Reed and Sedge and Willow Warblers, Coots and Moorhens and several kinds of ducks. Some of these old workings, as at Theale and Dorchester and Old Slade, are modern Meccas for botanists and bird-watchers.

Old Slade (BBONT) is an astonishing island-wilderness surrounded but by no means smothered by a vast industrial and urban complex, enveloped by the hum of traffic on the M4 and the more obtrusive, staccato noises of the railway. It has Foxes and Badgers and 45 species of breeding birds, plus the regular Bittern and Bearded Reedlings in winter — and its genesis as a nature reserve lay in the mind and the persuasive argument of a schoolboy, David Rose. If you want a cogent example of how well Nature can mind her own business in the midst of mankind, then it is here.

LONDON

The natural next step is into the metropolis itself. The concrete canyons have their House Sparrows and feral Pigeons of course, and, perhaps more surprisingly, a large population of Blackbirds which have been shown to be more successful than those in the surrounding countryside. The vast winter Starling roosts on the National Gallery and other buildings, the nightly gatherings of Pied Wagtails in the Embankment trees, the snow flurry of Black-headed Gulls over the dark Pool of London, the Tawny Owls hooting in competition with the taxi cabs, the Kestrel clutching sparrows from the gutter, the Woodpigeon walking nonchalantly away from one's feet — all qualify as natural-history wonders in a teeming, throbbing city, yet no guided tour or Odd Spot advertisement deems them worthy of a mention.

Although much disturbed by traffic and people, and at risk from rats and cats, London's birds have an enormous advantage over their rural neighbours; for London, and indeed all large towns, have a warmer climate, a 'heat-island'

The Sedge Warbler, seen here on its nest, is a common waterside breeding bird of the Thames valley.

The Black Redstart achieved fame as an early post-war colonist of London's bombed sites.

The Woodpigeon's large size distinguishes it from the London Feral Pigeon with which it often associates in the city's parklands.

effect due to vast brick and concrete buildings retaining the warmth that comes from domestic and industrial heating. The differential can be several degrees Centigrade, especially in cold winters when people are trying hard to keep warm; and this improvement on the natural climate, coupled with artificial feeding at countless bird-tables and in the parks and squares, leads to a low mortality rate among urban bird populations. We have already mentioned an exotic parrot, the Ring-necked Parrakeet, that seems destined to become a 'British bird'. One increasing species, the Black Redstart, has turned this situation to good account, and is a city-dweller throughout most of its west European range. It really 'went to town' just after the Second War, finding that the bomb-desolated areas provided many nest-sites and their flush of plants an ample supply of insect food. The last one we heard was singing merrily above the Circle Line on Paddington Station; and if you keep a sharp look-out, there is still a better chance of seeing or hearing this coal-black, fire-tailed bird in some Odd Spot in Inner London than anywhere else in Britain.

The Serpentine, St James's Park lake and other sanctuaries administered by the Ministry of Works lay audacious claim to surpass artificial waters anywhere for rich variety of waterfowl, and although the Wood Ducks and Chiloe Wigeons may be spurious, this does not make the lakes any less important to the lunch-hour relaxation of thousands of city workers. Among the waterfowl are many Tufted Ducks and Pochards which have come, and will go, of their own volition to breeding haunts in Finland and northern Russia, perhaps taking a cockney mate with them — a phenomenon well attested by bird-ringing and which ornithologists call 'abmigration'. Another good collection within easy reach of the City is at Richmond Park, where there is also a heronry and deer can be seen. The Royal Botanic Gardens at Kew also have waterfowl, but here and at Hampton Court the great attractions are the magnificent gardens laid out with innumerable exotic trees and shrubs.

Enthusiastic lunch-time bird-watchers have carried out meticulous breeding bird studies for the Common Birds Census of the British Trust for Ornithology in Hyde Park and Kensington Gardens, Bishop's Park in Fulham, and Regent's Park, and have enjoyed the same excellent bird-watching that any one of London's millions may enjoy. In 1974 a score of song-bird species held territories in the 636 acres of Hyde Park and Kensington Gardens; the Blackbird was much the commonest, and there were many Blue Tits, Song Thrushes, Robins, Wrens, Great Tits and Dunnocks, with unusually high concentrations of Coal Tits, Spotted Flycatchers, Blackcaps and Mistle Thrushes. All occur fairly regularly in other London parks, sometimes with Magpie, Jay, Treecreeper, Long-tailed Tit, Bullfinch and Goldfinch. Add to these a number of country cousins who pass through in spring and autumn, and a quiet hour, with eyes and ears attentive, can be very rewarding.

We tend to think of woods and downs and fields as natural habitats, when really the only natural thing about them is the way things grow. Man has modified practically all environments to serve his own particular needs. Yet the lesson of London, and of the gravel-pits and reservoirs, and of many other managed features of the countryside is clear — wildlife is amazingly resilient, ready and willing to adapt to and exploit the most artificial situations. But adaptation takes time, and because of the speed with which the twentieth century moves, especially in this congested region of Britain, time for birds and mammals is on the short side. They need our help: this is what active conservation is all about. It is essential to all of us that they should keep their place in the sun.

Collared Dove.

Collared Dove. A bird which has sped across Europe in the last half-century to colonise all parts except the Iberian peninsula is the Collared Dove, a sandy-buff bird with a black-and-white tail pattern and a mournful coo. Early in the century it was found in Europe only in Turkey and the Balkans, but during the 1930s spread along the Danube to Hungary, Czechoslovakia and Austria. It reached Germany and Italy in 1943–44, the Netherlands and Denmark in 1947–48, and France in 1950 — a trans-continental colonisation of over 1,000 miles in 20 years. It entered England (Norfolk) in 1955 and a second line of advance invaded Scotland (Moray) in 1957. It was recorded nesting in the Faeroe Islands and south Iceland in 1971. Robert Hudson has shown that the early colonisation of Britain was coastwise, with the species reaching the Outer Hebrides, the Isle of Man and Shetland Islands early in the 1960s, since when it has consolidated by filling in most of the inland gaps. The tremendous dynamism of its spread is something of a mystery; its preference is for low ground, below about 500 feet, where it is especially attracted to granaries, maltings, chicken farms and indeed anywhere with an abundant supply of corn. The population of Britain and Ireland may well approach 40,000 pairs, and in some areas — such as the Isle of Thanet in Kent — the new-comer is already deemed to be a pest.

Robert Hudson in *British Birds*, vol. 65, pp. 139–155 (1972).

Guide to wildlife habitats in the Thames Valley and Chiltern Hills

This Appendix provides a selected but varied list of places of wildlife interest. It is emphasised that nature reserves exist primarily for the conservation of animals and plants and in some cases for environmental experiments and research. They are not 'public open spaces' in the recreational sense. Access to many is therefore restricted and some, because of their sensitivity to disturbance, have been omitted from this list, in deference to the wishes of conservation organisations. Even with 'open' reserves visitors are earnestly requested to keep to the paths and bridleways and so avoid damage to the habitat and undue disturbance to wildlife. *There is no public access to the enclosed farmland which is part of many National Trust properties.*

Application to visit a National Nature Reserve (NNR) should be made to the appropriate Regional Office of the Nature Conservancy Council (NCC) at the address given. Intention to visit reserves of the Royal Society for the Protection of Birds (RSPB) should be notified to the Warden (whose address is shown) as far in advance as possible. In all cases where an address is shown, it is wise to contact the Warden to avoid disappointment.

GREATER LONDON

Barn Elms Reservoir TQ 23 77. Reservoir in loop of R. Thames. Smews and other wintering waterfowl. N. of Barnes on A306.

Brent Reservoir TQ 21 87. Reservoir and surrounding reeds and scrub. Waterfowl, esp. in winter. Between Neasden and Hendon on n. side of North Circular Road, A406.

Epping Forest TQ 43 97. Remnant of Royal Forest of Essex. Hornbeam, oak, beech, birch, mixed and in pure stands, mostly coppiced or pollarded. 6000 a. (4000 a. woodland, 2000 a. open land). 'Black' Fallow Deer, Fox, Badger;

Nightingale, Hawfinch. Extends from Wanstead Flats TQ 42 85 in south to the Lower Forest TL 47 03 beyond Epping in north, major part lying between Chingford and Epping in London Borough of Waltham Forest. Traversed by A11, Leytonstone–Epping. Parking, picnic places and other facilities at several points. Corporation of London.

Hainault Forest TQ 48 94 Country Park, 1108 a. East of Chigwell, A1112. Greater London Council.

Hyde Park and Kensington Gardens TQ 27 80. Parkland with lake, the Serpentine. Exotic waterfowl, many wild migrant and wintering ducks. N. of Kensington Road, Kensington.

Richmond Park and Kew Gardens TQ 20 73. Park with deer and heronry. Royal Botanic Gardens is nearby at Kew TQ 17 76. S. of Richmond, n. of Kingston upon Thames A308.

Selsdon Wood TQ 36 62. Woodland, 198 a. 3 mls s.e. of Croydon ½ m s.e. of Selsdon B268. NT/London Borough of Croydon.

Trent Park TQ 29 97. Park and woodland, 338 a. Country Park. 1½ mls w. of Enfield A110. Greater London Council.

HERTFORDSHIRE

Ashridge Estate SP 98 13. Mixed woods, chalk grassland, acid heaths. Incl. Sallow Copse, Ringshall Copse, Frithsden Beeches, Moneybury Hill, Clipper Down, and Aldbury, Pitstone and Berkhamsted Commons. 3944 a. Fallow and Muntjac Deer. Wood Warbler, Redstart, Tree Pipit and many species of song-birds. 3 mls n. of Berkhamsted astride B4506 (leaving A41 at Northchurch). Car parks Monument Drive off B4506 at SP 972 130 and elsewhere. Information centre, trails. NT.

Berkhamsted Common SP 99 11. Birch, scrub oak and gorse on bracken-covered heath, Frithsden Beeches (NT) nearby. Redpolls, Tree Pipits, woodland birds. 1–3 mls n. of Berkhamsted A41, via B4506 at Northchurch. NT.

Cassiobury Park TQ 08 96. Parkland with stream and cress-beds. Woodland

birds, Grey Wagtail, Kingfisher. W. side of Watford, on n. side of A412. Watford BC.

Hertfordshire and Middlesex Trust for Nature Conservation, Hudnall Park Environmental Studies Centre, St Margaret's Lane, Little Gaddesden, Berkhamsted, Hertfordshire, HP4 1QN.

Northaw Great Wood TL 28 04. Deciduous woodland, mainly oak/hornbeam, 247 a. Country Park. 4 mls s.e. of Hatfield A1000, via B157. Welwyn and Hatfield DC.

Rye House Marsh TL 39 10. Freshwater marsh and pools beside R. Lea. Harvest Mice. Kingfisher, Reed and Sedge Warblers, Reed Buntings. 1½ mls e. of Hoddesdon, near Rye House railway station. Car park, information centre, toilets, hide. (Warden – 32 Caxton Road, Hoddesdon, Herts) Lea Valley Regional Park Authority/RSPB.

Therfield Heath LNR TL 34 40. Chalk downland, 417 a. 2 mls w. of Royston, on s. side of A505. Car park near Pavilion at Royston end, access by foot from A505 and minor road to Therfield. Herts. and Middx. T for Nature Conservation.

Tring Reservoirs NNR SP 91 13. Canal-feeder reservoirs. Wilstone, Marsworth, Startops End, Tringford. Grebes, wildfowl, heronry at Marsworth, Reed and Sedge Warblers, rare waders and Black Terns on passage, big gull roost. 2 mls n. of Tring off A41, via B488 – B489. Restricted access off rights of way, permit required for hides at Wilstone. NCC.

BEDFORDSHIRE

Bedfordshire and Huntingdonshire Naturalists' Trust, 23 St Cuthbert's Street, Bedford, MK40 3JR.

Dunstable Downs TL 00 19. Chalk downland with thorn scrub, 285 a. Muntjac Deer, Fox, Badger. Whinchat, Grasshopper and other warblers. 2 mls s. of Dunstable, astride B4540 near Whipsnade. NT.

The Lodge, Sandy TL 19 48. Scots pines and birchwoods on Greensand, bracken-covered heath; the house and formal gardens are the RSPB Headquarters.

104 a. Woodpeckers, Nuthatch and song-birds. 9 mls e. of Bedford, 2 mls e. of Sandy, on s. side of B1042. Car park, picnic area, information centre, shop, children's discovery room, trails. (Warden — The Lodge, Sandy, Beds.) RSPB.

Stockgrove Park SP 92 29. Deciduous woodland and open areas, small lake. Country Park. Muntjac and Fallow Deer. 3 mls n. of Leighton Buzzard, on e. side of A418 beyond Heath and Reach. Beds./Bucks. CCs.

BUCKINGHAMSHIRE

Bradenham Woods SU 83 97. Mature beech woods and whitebeam on chalk. 4 mls n.w. of High Wycombe, 5 mls s. of Princes Risborough, e. side of A4010. Car park in lane from Saunderton to Speen. NT.

Burnham Beeches SU 95 85. Mature (some pollarded) beech/oak and other woodland, inc. conifers. Pools. 3 mls s. of exit 2 M40, 3 mls n. of Slough on w. side of A355. City of London Corp.

Church Wood, Hedgerley SU 97 87. Mixed oak/beech wood. Woodpeckers, Nuthatch and song-birds. 4 mls n. of Slough, on e. side of A355. RSPB.

Grange Lands, Great Kimble SP 83 04. Chalk grassland and scrub s.w. of Pulpit Hill on Chequers Estate, 450–600 ft. 50 species of birds incl. Whinchat, Nightingale, Cirl Bunting. Chalk-hill Blue and Marbled White butterflies. 1½ mls n.e. of Princes Risborough and 4 mls s.w. of Wendover B4010. E. of B4010 at Askett, car park Longdown SP 833 046. Bucks. CC/BBONT.

The National Trust Northern Home Counties, Regional Office, Hughenden Manor, High Wycombe, Buckinghamshire.

Pitstone Hill SP 95 14. Chalk grassland scrub on 700 ft hill. Whinchat, Grasshopper and Willow Warblers, Lesser Whitethroat, Meadow Pipit. 5 mls n.e. of Tring, on e. side of B488. Bucks. CC.

Wendover Woods SP 88 08. State forest, mature Norway spruce and planted beech. Firecrests, Goldcrests. 5 mls s.e. of Aylesbury A413, on e. side of A4011. Car park, picnic areas, trails. For Comm.

OXFORDSHIRE

Aston Rowant NNR SU 75 98. Chilterns escarpment chalk grassland with successional stages of scrub through to mature woodland, areas of juniper, yew and whitebeam. 200 a. Nearby is Aston Wood (NT) SU 74 97, 104 a. 9 mls w. of High Wycombe, 2 mls n.w. of Stokenchurch, near junction of A40(M) and B4009. NCC.

Berks., Bucks. and Oxon. Naturalists' Trust, Shirburn Lodge, Christmas Common, Watlington, Oxford, OX9 5HU.

Blenheim Palace SP 44 16. Gardens and parkland with lake. Great Crested and Little Grebes and other waterfowl. 7 mls n.w. of Oxford, w. of A34, entrance at Woodstock. Adm. fee, car park.

Boarstall Duck Decoy and Wildfowl Reserve SP 63 15. Ancient duck-decoy pond on which waterfowl are caught for ringing, surrounded by mixed deciduous woodland. 7 mls n.w. of Thame, on w. side of B4011, ½ ml n. of Boarstall. Car park, information centre. (Warden — Conservation Centre, Boarstall Decoy, Nr Brill, Aylesbury, Bucks.) WAGBI.

Buscot and Coleshill SU 25 95. Open space by R. Thames at Buscot Weir; also Badbury Hill and Cuckoo Pen Wood. Car park at Buscot Weir, A417; woodland between Faringdon and Coleshill, n. of B4019. NT.

Chinnor Hill SU 76 99. Chalk escarpment; hawthorn/juniper scrub below clay-with-flints plateau with beech/ash woodland. 4 mls s.w. of Princes Risborough s. of B4445, 1 ml s.e. of Chinnor. Car park at SP 763005. BBONT.

The National Trust South Midlands, Regional Office, 22 London Street, Faringdon, Oxfordshire.

Watlington Hill SU 70 93. Chalk grassland, hawthorn scrub and yew wood on Chilterns escarpment. Also beech woods surrounding Watlington Park SU 702 917, 1 ml to s. 14 mls s.e. of Oxford, 1 ml s. of Watlington. NT.

BERKSHIRE

Cock Marsh SU 89 87. Commonland extending n. to Cookham Dean, Bigfrith and Tugwood Commons. S. bank of R. Thames 1 ml n. of Winter Hill and Cookham A4094. NT.

Finchampstead Ridges SU 80 63. Heather-grown ridge and woodlands, incl. Simons Wood and Heath Pool. 1 ml w. of Crowthorne Station, 5 mls s. of Wokingham, on s. side of B3348. NT.

Inkpen Common SU 38 65. Typical heath on gravel and London Clay, with small bogs. Nightingale and Nightjar. Viper and Common Lizard. 8 mls w. of Newbury, s. of A4 via Kintbury and Inkpen. BBONT.

Maidenhead Thicket SU 85 81. Woodland, 368 a, a Nightingale haunt. Nearby to s. is Pinkneys Green. 2 mls w. of Maidenhead, traversed by A4 and A423. NT.

Nature Conservancy Council, South Regional Office, Foxhold House, Thornford Road, Crookham Common, Newbury, Berkshire, RG15 8EL.

Windsor Forest and Great Park SU 96 73. Royal deer park and woodland nature reserve. Waterfowl at Virginia Water incl. Mandarin Ducks. Incl. High Standing Hill FNR, SU 93 74. S. of Windsor, A308 – A332. HM the Queen/For Comm.

WILTSHIRE

Ashton Keynes Water Park SU 03 94. Large complex of flooded gravel-workings and associated scrub. Waterfowl, especially in winter. 4 mls w. of Cricklade, n. of B4040. Wilts. CC.

Barbury Castle SU 15 76. Country park on The Ridgeway, chalk downland overlooking Marlborough Downs. 6 mls s. of Swindon, on e. side of A361 and s. side of B4005. Wilts. CC.

Cley Hill ST 84 45. Chalk hill 800 ft high, 85 a. 3 mls w. of Warminster, on n. side of A362. NT.

The National Trust Wessex, Regional Office, Stourhead Estate Office, Stourton, Warminster, Wiltshire.

Savernake Forest SU 23 67. State forest with much oak/beech woodland. Nearby, 2 mls to w. are Hockeridge Woods. It is s.e. of Marlborough between A4 and A346. For Comm.

Stourhead ST 77 35. House and landscaped park with fine specimen trees, villages of Stourton and Kilmington, part of White Sheet Down. 2507 a. 8 mls s. of Frome, w. of Mere, B3092. NT.

Wiltshire Trust for Nature Conservation, 4 Peppercombe Close, Urchfont, Devizes, Wiltshire, SN10 4QS.

Animal collections in the Thames Valley and Chiltern Hills

Battersea Park Children's Zoo

This is a small mixed collection of animals, with special emphasis on tropical birds. Amongst these, Lady Ross's Touracos breed here regularly. The main attraction amongst the mammals is the otter exhibit and the Celebes Apes. Other mammals which breed regularly are Meerkats, Prevost's Squirrels, chipmunks and Dama Wallabies. Many small animals may be picked up and stroked, and there are pony and pony-trap rides for children.

The Zoo belongs to the Greater London Council, and it was started by the London County Council in 1951 as part of the Festival of Britain.

Battersea Park Children's Zoo. **Address** Albert Bridge Road, London SW11. **Telephone** 01–228 9957. **Open** Easter–end of Sept 13.30–17.30 Mon-Fri, 11.00–18.00 weekends, bank holidays and school holidays. **Admission free. Catering** facilities available in Park; licensed bar, self-service cafeteria. **Guided tours** for schools by arrangement. **Acreage** $\frac{1}{3}$. **Car** entrance to Park s. side of Albert Bridge (closed to motor vehicles) and Chelsea Bridge. **Bus** from central London to Chelsea Bridge, from South London 49 to Battersea, or 137 from Sloane Square. **Other facilities** pony rides. Public allowed to feed roaming animals.

Broxbourne Zoo

Broxbourne Zoo is an open-air exhibition with about 250 mammals and birds. The mixed collection has a few large animals: Lions and Leopards which breed regularly, Tigers, Pumas and Himalayan Bears. The rarest species in the collection is the European Bison; the deer species shown include Red Deer, Sika and Chinese Water Deer. You can also see Chimpanzees, Sacred and Olive Baboons, and Pig-tailed Macaques, which have bred. There are a number of small mammal species and these include porcupines, Coypus, Raccoons, coatis, Kinkajous, badgers, Dingos and Collared Peccaries. The peccary is the New World representative of the pig family, ranging from the northern parts of South America, through Central America to the southwestern parts of the United States.

A mixed collection of birds is exhibited and these include penguins, flamingos, vultures, eagles, Tawny Owls, which have bred here, pheasants, ducks and geese. There are also Demoiselle Cranes, Sarus Cranes and Emus. The Emus hatched two chicks in 1974.

The Pets' Corner contains Rabbits, guinea-pigs, both of which breed copiously, African Pygmy Goats, Llamas and three breeds of sheep — St Kilda, Soay and Jacob's. There is a drive-in picnic area and woodland walks around the Zoo, which itself is well wooded. If you wish to visit Broxbourne Zoo regularly, there is an arrangement whereby a subscription will admit two people as often as they wish within the space of one year. The Zoo was first opened in 1970.

Broxbourne Zoo. **Address** White Stubbs Lane, Broxbourne, Herts. **Telephone** Hoddesdon 62852. **Open** 10.00–18.00 summer, 10.00–16.00 winter Sun only. **Catering** self-service cafeteria, snack bar, kiosk. Zoo shop. **Guided tours** for schools by arrangement. **Acreage** 25. **Car** $2\frac{1}{2}$ mls s.w. of Hoddesdon w. off A1170 along Bell Lane for White Stubbs Lane. **Bus** to Bell Lane then $1\frac{1}{2}$ mls to Zoo. **Train** to Broxbourne (2 mls). **Taxis** available. **Other facilities** first-aid post, picnic area, woodland walks. Public allowed to feed animals.

Child-Beale Wildlife Trust

This is an attractive Garden overlooking the Thames with a small mixed collection of birds, mainly consisting of waterfowl and pheasants, and a flock of more than 200 Budgerigars. The pheasant aviaries exhibit 16 species of pheasant, including some which are rare in the wild: Mikado, Cheer, Swinhoe's, the beautiful Himalayan Monal, and Blue-eared and Brown-eared Pheasants. There are also some jungle fowl, Ring-necked Doves and peafowl, the latter breeding freely each year. The flamingo pen contains Chilean and Cuban Flamingos, as well as several species of duck, and the Big Water Aviary exhibits curlews, oyster-catchers, geese and ducks. Here you will also see Demoiselle Cranes, zebra and Bengalese Finches and Budgerigars.

Most of the geese are on the 'Three Ponds' pond, and the collection includes White-fronted and Lesser White-fronted Geese, Bar-headed, Egyptian, Pink-footed, Emperor, Snow and Canada Geese. Here, too, there is a mixed collection of duck, pochard and scaup. Next to the pond are the parrakeet aviaries. Beyond

Child-Beale Wildlife Trust. **Address** Basildon-on-Thames, Berkshire. **Telephone** Upper Basildon 325. **Open** 11.30–18.30 from Easter Sunday–Sept on Sat, Sun, Wed, Thurs. **Acreage** 15. **Car** 1 ml n.w. of Pangbourne on A329 Reading–Oxford road. **Bus** Reading-Oxford bus stops outside grounds. **Train** to Pangbourne (1 ml). Public allowed to feed animals.

Opposite: Hamadryas Baboon from northeast Africa.

this is the Moat Area, where about 30 species of waterfowl are exhibited, including Whooper Swans, geese and a wide variety of duck: teal, pintail, wigeon and shoveler. This area also contains the Maned Goose, a small grey species from Australia which can easily be mistaken for a duck.

Many of the birds here are free-winged, so they may be seen in many of the areas. There is also a large flock of peafowl, and a small flock of Soay Sheep.

The Gardens are owned by the trust founded in 1956 by Mr Gilbert Ernest Child-Beale (who died in 1967) to preserve this part of the Thames Valley and create a place which the public could enjoy and appreciate. Notice the pavilion over-looking the Moat Area, which was designed and built by Mr Child-Beale in memory of his parents. The stone is hand cut and it came from Bowood Park, Wiltshire. The garden round the pavilion contains a collection of statues, including two Jagger statues from Lord Melchett's estate and a bronze statue of the Valkyries. The fountain in the round pond is Italian and came from Witley Park, Surrey.

Cotswold Wildlife Park

The Cotswold Wildlife Park was opened in 1970 by Mr John Heyworth in the grounds of the Bradwell Grove estate. This is an excellent general collection, with a few large animals in paddocks, a beautifully laid out walled garden with aviaries and small mammal enclosures, some birds of prey, flamingos in a walk-through enclosure, a Tropical House, Reptile House and Aquarium.

As you drive up to the car park, there are Ankole Cattle, the native cattle of Uganda, and Jacob's Sheep in paddocks flanking the drive. On leaving the car park, you come to paddocks for Llamas, rheas and Sarus Cranes. The Sarus Crane is from India, Burma and Thailand, and has bred in the Park.

You next come to the walled garden, with a large pool containing Humboldt's Penguins from South America and Rockhopper Penguins, a small Antarctic species. Also here are White Pelicans from southern Europe and Asia and Brown Pelicans from the Americas. There are Common Seals in the pool. In the garden there are barless enclosures for Prairie Marmots, inquisitive little burrowing rodents of North America; coatis, related to Raccoons, which inhabit the tropical forests of South America, living on vegetables, insects, fruit and small animals; and Indian Smooth Otters, with a glass-fronted pool where you can see them swimming under water. The waterfowl pond contains a variety of ducks and some Chilean Flamingos, and there are some beautifully landscaped aviaries. The waders' aviary exhibits Scarlet and Sacred Ibises, Tiger Bitterns, Wood Ibises, European Spoonbills, Grey and Great Blue Herons. Another aviary shows the Giant Hornbill and Pied Hornbill, with Black Storks and Reeves' Pheasants. Other aviaries display toucans, touracos, Occipital Blue Pies, Emerald Toucanets, starlings, mynahs, parrakeets, mousebirds and pheasants. The Tropical House is a mass of hibiscus, rubber plants, banana palms, bougainvillea and many others. In this exotic setting you can see the Jacana, or Lily-trotter of Africa, sunbirds and white-eyes from Africa, hummingbirds from South America and the Fairy Bluebird from southeast Asia. Opposite the Tropical House is an outdoor reptilium containing various European reptiles.

In Pets' Corner you can see aviaries for macaws, African Grey Parrots and cockatoos, Rabbits, guinea-pigs, chinchillas and agoutis, all from South America; and some exhibits for more wild animals – the African Crested Porcupine, capuchin monkeys and squirrel monkeys from South America, chipmunks from North America and Prevost's Squirrels, a colourful species from Malaya and Borneo. There is a walk-through paddock for children, with ducks, poultry and sheep.

The large aviaries for birds of prey exhibit Griffon, Hooded and Lappet-faced Vultures, and great eagle owls; Bateleur Eagles from Africa and caracaras – carrion hawks from North and South America. You next come to the Badger Enclosure, where you can see them out of doors or inside their dens through glass. The Zoo's quarantine quarters are also on exhibition, where animals undergoing their six months' rabies quarantine may be seen.

The Red Panda, photographed here in the Cotswold Wildlife Park, of which it is the emblem, is related to the Giant Panda (see page 118).

The Cotswold Wildlife Park. **Address** Burford, Oxon. **Telephone** Burford 3006. **Open** 10.00–18.00 (dusk), summer and winter. **Catering** licensed self-service cafeteria, kiosks. Gift shop. **Acreage** 150. **Car** 2 mls s. of Burford off A361. **Train** to Charlbury (8 mls). **Taxis** available in Burford. **Other facilities** first-aid post, wheel-chairs, adventure playground, narrow-gauge railway. Dogs on leash only. Public **not allowed** to feed animals.

The Reptile House has an interesting collection of venomous snakes; the large constrictor snakes such as pythons and Boa Constrictors, lizards, skinks and crocodiles. The poisonous snakes include Puff Adders, the Western Diamond-backed Rattlesnake, Indian Cobra and Malayan Moccasin. The crocodiles here are the Nile Crocodile, Siamese Crocodile and the American Alligator. Next door is the Aquarium, with tanks for tropical freshwater and tropical marine fish, and a large exhibit at the far end for Asiatic Water Monitors, Anacondas — the large constrictor snake of South America — and Alligator Snapping Turtles.

You next come to outdoor exhibits for Pumas, which range from Canada to South America. Pumas feed on deer, peccaries (the South American wild pig), rats and agoutis, and they sometimes attack cattle and horses. There are also some spider monkeys which use their long tails as a fifth limb in the tropical jungles of South America. Near these, another species of otter is exhibited, the Small-clawed Otter of southeast Asia. This is a small species which spends less time in the water than other otters.

Before you enter the walk-through enclosure, there is a paddock for Secretary Birds, a bird of prey from Africa which feeds on snakes and lizards and is related to the hawks. Inside the walk-through area are Brazilian Tapirs, which breed here. This species comes from tropical South America, feeding on aquatic plants in rivers. They are good swimmers and their main natural enemy is the Jaguar. There is a lake with a flock of Chilean Flamingos, and as you walk through the woods you can see Sika Deer, an Asiatic species which has been introduced into this country and is now found wild; Bennett's Wallabies, from the brush country of Tasmania, Demoiselle Cranes from southern Europe and Asia, African Crowned Cranes, European Cranes and Sarus Cranes. There is also a variety of ducks, and geese.

The African enclosure exhibits a pair of White Rhinoceros, which arrived from Natal in 1972. The White Rhino was in danger of extinction until recently, when the Natal Parks Board protected it, and it now breeds prolifically in the South African national parks. Also here are Grévy's Zebras, the largest zebra species from Somaliland and northern Kenya, Thomson's Gazelles, which have bred here, and Ostriches. Thomson's Gazelles live in large herds on the East African plains and they migrate to follow the seasonal food supply with zebras and gnus.

Near the African paddocks are two more exhibits for animals found in Africa — the Leopard, which is also distributed throughout Asia, and the colobus Monkey, which lives high in the trees of tropical Africa, feeding on a diet of leaves. Lastly, near the restaurant and gift shop you can see one of the most interesting animals in the Park, the Red Panda. It lives in the forests of the Himalayas and western China at altitudes of between 7,000 and 12,000 feet. In the wild it feeds on bamboo shoots, mountain lichens, birds and small mammals. This beautiful chestnut-coloured animal is the emblem of the Park.

Bradwell Grove was built in 1804, the present Gothic-style house replacing a Jacobean manor house. Mr Heyworth inherited the estate in 1949. Besides the animals, you can also visit the garden centre, and there is a picnic area and, for children, an adventure playground, pony and donkey rides and a narrow-gauge railway. The courses in natural history organised for schools by an outside body are also available to individual children during the summer holidays. This is an excellent opportunity for children who are really keen to learn about animals.

Crystal Palace Children's Zoo

This small Zoo has many small animals which can be picked up and stroked by children. The domestic animals include Pygmy Goats, sheep and lambs, but there is a good little collection of wild animals, including Woolly Monkeys, Dama Wallabies, Maras or Patagonian Cavies, Chinese Water Deer and penguins. The wallabies, maras and water deer all breed here regularly. There are pony and pony-trap rides for children.

The Zoo belongs to the Greater London Council, and it was started in 1953.

Crystal Palace Children's Zoo. **Address** Thicket Road, London SE20. **Telephone** 01–778 4487. **Open** from Easter to end Sept 13.30–17.30 Mon–Fri, 11.00–18.00 Sat and Sun. During school holidays, Aug to 1st week in Sept open daily 11.00–18.00. **Admission free. Catering** self-service cafeteria. **Guided tours** by arrangement. **Acreage** ⅓. **Car** Crystal Palace (Anerley Hill entrance as for National Sports Centre) off A234. **Bus** nearest stop 10 mins' walk. **Train** from Victoria and London Bridge to Crystal Palace Parade. Public allowed to feed the animals.

Flamingo Gardens and Zoological Park

Flamingo Gardens and Zoological Park was started by Christopher Marler as a private collection of waterfowl and other birds. Having kept birds since childhood, he later became interested in the rarer birds of the world, especially those which are endangered in the wild owing to human exploitation. As a cattle farmer and well-known breeder of thoroughbred horses, he also became interested in the rarer wild hoofed animals, and in recent years the mammal collection has grown in importance. This is a major collection of more than 230 species of birds and mammals, specialising in waterfowl, flamingos, cranes, storks, birds of prey and hoofed mammals, especially bison and the camel family. The gardens were opened to the public in 1964, and are notable not only for the great variety of birds kept, but for the many rarities shown.

The formal walled garden contains flocks of flamingos, grassed enclosures with ponds for many kinds of waterfowl, and huge flight aviaries for wading birds and birds of prey. This is one of the only two collections in Great Britain where all six forms of flamingo are shown – the Rosy, Chilean, Greater, Lesser, Andean and James'. You should not miss the two rarest species, the Andean and the James'. These come from the high Andes in Peru and Bolivia, breeding in the shallow alkaline lakes up to 17,000 feet. The James' Flamingo was thought to be extinct until 1950, when it was rediscovered by a party of American ornithologists. It is a small species, with a yellow beak. Flamingos are related to waterfowl, and they congregate in enormous flocks, sometimes numbering millions. They prefer brackish water and build cone-shaped nests of mud. They feed on algae and other small organisms which they scoop up through their beaks. The beak contains a kind of sieve which retains the food, while the tongue is used to pump out the water and mud.

There are several large flight aviaries for birds of prey, with a representative collection of this group, especially of eagles and vultures. You can see here the Golden Eagle, the Imperial Eagle and the African Fish Eagle, whose harsh cry is uttered with head thrown back, even while in flight. The largest flying bird in the world is also here, the Andean Condor which may have a wing span of up to 12 feet, and weigh as much as 25 lb. Ten species of vulture are exhibited. These include the Lämmergeier, or Bearded Vulture, which has a nine-foot wing span, and the King Vulture, another huge species ranging from south Mexico to northern Argentina. It has a brightly coloured head of red, green and yellow.

There is a remarkable collection of cranes and storks, containing 11 of the world's 15 crane species, and 15 of the 17 stork species. Cranes, once numerous almost all over the world, are now facing extinction, thanks to human interference. They need a lot of space and seclusion in which to breed, and such conditions are increasingly hard for them to find. Cranes have the curious and fascinating habit of performing a stately dance as a prelude to mating in the spring. Most species have bred in captivity, and they may live for as long as 50 years. Two of the rarest can be seen here, the Siberian White Crane and the Florida Sandhill Crane. Both are endangered in the wild and this is the only place in Great Britain where the latter can be seen. In winter, cranes are gregarious, and when migrating they fly at a great height in V formation.

Storks are found in most warm parts of the world. They live near water and nest in the tops of trees and on buildings. Amongst the kinds you can see here are the European White Stork, the mythical transport of newly born babies, the Hammerhead Stork, or Hammerkop, with its head feathers protruding at front and back like a hammer, and the Saddle-billed Stork from central Africa, which has a bright shaded band of colour on its bill. The Marabou Stork, a useful scavenger of carcasses in East Africa, is rather ugly on the ground, but it becomes extremely graceful in flight. Storks have no voices, and communicate with each other by clicking their bills. They need to be kept in heated quarters during the English winter.

Flamingo Gardens and Zoological Park. **Address** The Manor House, Weston Underwood, Olney, Bucks. **Telephone** Bedford 711451. **Open** 14.00–20.00 (last admission 18.30) Wed, Thur, Sat, Sun and bank holidays from Good Friday to 30 Sept. **Guide-book**. Zoo shop. **Acreage** 12. **Car** 1 ml w. of Olney, N. Bucks., 5 mls from M1 exit 14. **Bus** Bedford–Northampton and Newport Pagnell–Northampton stop 2½ mls from Park. **Train** to Wolverton (8 mls). **Taxis** available. Public **not allowed** to feed animals.

Right: Two-wattled Cassowary, whose 'casque' protects the bird when it runs fast through undergrowth.

Below: the bills of Roseate Spoonbills are designed for feeding in shallow water.

Another interesting group of birds represented here is the bustards. These live in open country, spending most of their time on the ground, although they are good flyers. The Kori Bustard of Africa is the largest, and you can also see the Little and the Great Bustard (see p. 101), both European species.

There is an enormous aviary in the walled garden for wading birds. The aviary is 12 feet high and it measures 100 feet by 100 feet, so that the occupants can be seen flying quite freely. The most colourful birds here are Scarlet Ibises from Trinidad. Other species here are the American White, the Buff-necked Indian White, Glossy and the Black Ibises. There are also Roseate Spoonbills and the pure white European Spoonbill. Other birds here are the Black Stork, Painted Stork, several species of duck, and herons.

From the walled garden you enter the Wilderness, a delightful wild garden with woodland glades, in which aviaries are sited at intervals. You can see an interesting collection of owls here, and many species of smaller birds, including magpies, jays, starlings, and the magnificent Blue Crowned and Victoria Crowned Pigeons, and there is a large flight aviary for parrots and macaws. You will also encounter Hammerhead Storks, Buff-necked Ibises, Cattle Egrets, Stanley Cranes and Emperor Geese, all wandering at liberty. This is a peaceful and delightful spot, which was a favourite place of the poet William Cowper. His words are engraved on a number of statues and Grecian urns erected here.

The flightless birds on view here are the rhea of South America, the Australian Emu, and the Two-wattled Cassowary of New Guinea. Other birds you can see in the Park are Humboldt's Penguins, Crested Pelicans and Brown Pelicans.

The main feature of the waterfowl collection is the geese. Every known species of goose in the world is represented here (only one or two sub-species are missing). Most of them are kept in large flocks, and they include the rare Hawaiian Goose and the Red-breasted Goose, which breed in northern Siberia, migrating for the winter to southeastern Europe and Asia Minor. It is becoming scarcer in the wild, and it is not easy to breed in captivity. The flock kept here, however, breeds regularly. The collection of ducks is confined to the shelducks and whistling ducks, and a few of the surface feeders.

There is a very good collection of swans, every known species being represented. You can see the Black Swan from Australia, the Black-necked Swan of South America, the Trumpeter Swan of North America, which nearly became extinct in the 1920s but has since been protected. It is still rare, but it has bred in this collection. The Park is also visited regularly each winter by wild Bewick's Swans, which join the captive birds from November to March. This species breeds in northern Russia, migrating southwards in winter to central Asia, the Caspian Sea and northern Europe, including the British Isles.

A good selection of waterfowl is exhibited, but a further 60 acres are reserved as a waterfowl breeding area, and the Park is also the breeding station of the British Waterfowl Association, of which Christopher Marler is vice-president. The Association's object is to improve and rescue from extinction the various old breeds of domestic geese. About a dozen breeds are being kept in the Park, such as Chinese White, Toulouse, Embden, Roman and Pilgrim.

From the Wilderness you emerge into the Park paddocks where the hoofed animals are kept. The two species of bison are shown, the stocky American Bison with massive head and shoulders and steeply sloping back, and the taller, narrower European Bison. The American Bison, called Buffalo in America, is a grazing animal which once roamed the North American grasslands in countless millions. They were almost wiped out, but saved from extinction just in time at the beginning of this century. They are now fully protected by law in game reserves. The European Bison, or Wisent, is a browsing species, living in woodland. It once ranged all over Europe, but it was almost exterminated in the wild in 1920. However, a few animals survived in the Bialowieza Forest in Poland, near the Russian border, and these are now protected. Three or four hundred animals are in public zoos and private collections throughout the world, and the survival of this magnificent animal is now assured. It breeds regularly in the Park, thus contributing to the slowly increasing stock in the few British zoos which keep it.

The camel family consists of One-humped and Two-humped Camels of

Asia, and their closely related counterparts in South America, the Llama, Guanaco, Alpaca and Vicuna. In this Park you can see the heavily built Bactrian, or Two-humped Camel, originally imported by Mr Marler from Denmark. This used to be the main pack animal of northern Asia, and it can withstand extremes of both heat and cold, shedding its thick coat in great woolly tufts in the summer months. The Llama and the Alpaca are both domesticated species, developed from the wild Guanaco. Llamas are used as pack animals, and also for their wool and meat, while the Alpaca is kept for its wool. It lives in the high Andes, where large herds are kept. The Vicuna has the finest wool of all, and this has led to its slaughter in large numbers, so that it is now rare. However, it has recently been given legal protection, and its numbers are now increasing again. Export of Vicunas and their wool is now forbidden, as part of this protective legislation, and the importation of the wool into Great Britain is also illegal.

One species of deer is exhibited, the Formosan Sika Deer. It is believed to be extinct in the wild on the island of Taiwan, but it is kept in fair numbers in zoos and private collections, and several have been bred in the Park. You can also see Bennett's Wallabies, Yaks, which have been domesticated in their homeland of Tibet as well as elsewhere in central Asia, and a fine herd of Highland Cattle.

This is a most interesting collection, and because of the success achieved in regularly breeding so many species which are endangered in the wild, it is also of considerable importance. It will appeal both to the general visitor and to students of natural history.

Horniman Museum Aquarium

The Aquarium in the Museum shows tropical and temperate freshwater fish, British and tropical marine fish, and some reptiles and amphibians. Contents of the tanks vary, but you can usually see gudgeon, roach, perch, dace, eel, rudd, Mirror Carp, Goldfish, blennies, Shore and Edible crabs, anemones, lobsters, gobies and prawns. All species of British toads and frogs are exhibited, as well as African Clawed Toads, terrapins and small Mississippi Alligators. Occasional exhibits include Ribbonfish, Regal Tang and Blue-faced Angel Fish from the Pacific; and Axolotls, the larval form of the Tiger Salamander.

The Museum was founded in 1890 by Mr F. J. Horniman, M.P., because of the interest aroused by his private collection, assembled during his extensive travels.

Lions of Longleat

The 'Lions of Longleat', set in the Park surrounding Longleat House, was opened by the Marquess of Bath and Mr Jimmy Chipperfield in 1966. This was the first drive-through safari park to be established outside Africa, and it has been copied in many other countries, especially in Europe and America. The idea of constructing a closed-circuit system in which dangerous animals could be shown in comparative freedom to the motorised visitor was completely new, and the creation of an African game reserve on a small scale was only made possible by the use of a large area of parkland such as Longleat was able to offer. There were problems, of course, in the early days. For instance, large numbers of cars jammed the roads in the Lion paddocks, and it was impossible for visitors to answer the calls of nature without risk of being eaten. Traffic flow is now controlled so that cars can move freely round the circuit to the exits. Security procedures are strict, and they must be followed to the letter. Lions recognise cars as harmless moving objects, but once a human being alights, or even opens a window, he becomes a potential target for attack, or play. Whatever a Lion is thinking, the consequences are likely to be disastrous for the car's occupants. So follow the rules, and keep all windows closed.

The Park was conceived as an exhibition of African animals, and nearly all

Horniman Museum Aquarium. **Address** London Road, Forest Hill, London SE23. **Telephone** 01–699 1872. **Open** 10.30–18.00 weekdays, 14.00–18.00 Sun, summer and winter. **Admission free**. **Catering** tea rooms. **Guide-book**. **Car** South Circular Road (A205) at Forest Hill. **Bus** P4, 12, 12a, 185 stop at Museum, 63, 122, 124, 171, 194 pass close to Museum. **Train** (Southern Region) to Forest Hill ($\frac{1}{4}$ ml). Public **not allowed** to feed exhibits.

Cheetah may be seen at Longleat; it is now only found wild in Africa in any numbers.

Lions of Longleat. Address Longleat, Warminster, Wilts. **Telephone** Maiden Bradley 328. **Open** 10.00—18.00 summer, 10.00—dusk winter. **Guidebook. Catering** licensed restaurant, self-service cafeteria, kiosk. Zoo shop. **Guided tours** by arrangement. **Acreage** 300. **Car** $4\frac{1}{2}$ mls s.e. of Frome off A362 near Warminster. **Bus** nearest stop 2 mls from Park. **Train** to Warminster (4 mls). **Taxis** available. **Other facilities** children's playground, dog kennels. Public **not allowed** to feed animals.

the species here are still from Africa. In the first year 100 acres were fenced off for 40 Lions. In the following year the lake was stocked with sealions and Hippopotamus, and Chimpanzees were shown on an island. In 1968 another 100 acres were opened for Giraffes, zebras, antelopes and Ostriches, and in 1969 200 baboons were added. Since then other animals have been added, and more acreage has been brought into use in order to rest the paddocks occupied by hoofed animals. The problems encountered are the same as those familiar to livestock farmers, and fields must be rotated to prevent overgrazing, the poaching of land in wet weather and for the control of internal parasites which are present in all herbivorous animals.

The one-way road system first follows a route through the Park where unfenced animals are shown. You pass elephants, buffalo, Eland Antelopes, gnu, zebras, Giraffes, Ostriches, Ankole Cattle and White Rhinoceros. The group of young African Elephants have not yet reached breeding age, which is attained in their late teens. Very few elephants are bred in captivity, since few zoos keep bulls owing to the difficulty of controlling them. In the wild, they destroy so many trees that their numbers have to be controlled. The African Buffalo looks mild enough in a park, but it will press home an attack with great determination. The Eland is a large antelope which breeds readily in captivity, but here again the bulls are extremely fierce if provoked. The gnu, or wildebeeste, and zebras live contentedly with the Giraffes, since they often share the same territory in the wild.

Giraffes live in small herds in Africa, browsing on bushes and trees, especially the various species of acacia and other thorn trees. Despite its long neck the Giraffe has only seven neck vertebrae, like most other mammals. An adult bull weighs one to one and a half tons, and stands up to 18 feet in height. Cows weigh about half a ton, and are about two feet shorter. The longest recorded life span for a Giraffe is 28 years.

Ostriches are the largest living flightless birds, and the sexes can be distinguished in adult birds by the black plumage of the male, while the female has light brown feathers. When in breeding condition, the male's neck turns bright red. Ostriches seldom lay fertile eggs in captivity, although when they do, the eggs can be incubated successfully. Otherwise they can be eaten, and they are large enough to make about 30 omelettes. Next to the Ankole Cattle, the native cattle of the Watussi tribe in Uganda, you come to the White Rhinoceros group. White Rhinos are herd animals, and they are more likely to breed when kept in a group. They are a grazing species, and therefore well suited to conditions here.

'Monkey Jungle' is a colony of about 350 baboons, two or three species of which are shown, and this is where you have to go through the gates into the enclosed area. Baboons live on the ground in large tribal groups. They are strong, active animals which often raid plantations. Their main natural enemy is the Leopard which, however, usually takes only a young or sick animal as its victim, preferring not to attack the adult males whose teeth are formidable.

The Lion paddocks contain family groups each of which maintains its own territory, but Lions are prolific breeders and other paddocks are reserved for the young males, which in the wild would normally leave the pride in search of areas of their own. The original stock of Lions here was collected from European zoos, and a few from Ethiopia. Another enclosure contains Cheetahs, which are not often bred in zoos, although in recent years enough knowledge has been gained to breed them more frequently. Adults are solitary in the wild, and in captivity the male and female are kept apart, though within sight of each other, until they are ready to breed. This appears to stimulate breeding activity, whereas if they are kept together all the time, usually no breeding takes place.

Having completed the circuit, you can either park in the picnic area beside the lake or continue to the car park, then take a safari boat trip on the lake, which contains sealions, Hippopotamuses and the Chimpanzee Island. All these have produced young here, as have many other animals in the Park.

There is a large Pets' Corner containing an otter pool where the otters have bred, and young Lion cubs which have been hand-raised are often exhibited in this section. Beyond Pets' Corner is a children's playground and model railway.

Longleat House is also open to the public.

London Zoo

The London Zoo is by far the largest zoo in the British Isles — more than twice the size of the next largest — and it is scarcely possible to see everything properly in one visit. Everyone has favourite animals, and whatever attracts you, you are likely to be able to find it here. This is the British national collection, and there are representatives of every zoological family, with all the larger animals kept in breeding groups. Many of the exhibits can be seen under cover, so it matters far less here than in most zoos what the weather is doing. You are well advised to buy a guide-book, which contains a plan of the gardens, and then work out your own itinerary.

One exhibit you will not want to miss is the collection of apes and monkeys. These are in the Michael Sobell Pavilion for apes and monkeys near the main entrance. The prize of the collection is the pair of Lowland Gorillas, Guy and Lomie. Guy is 30 years old, and he weighs about 450 lb. He was caught in the French Cameroons, and spent six months at the Paris Zoo before arriving here, aged about 18 months. A year later, he was as strong as four men, and he now eats more than 20 lb. of food daily, including four pints of milk with eggs beaten up in it. His diet is mainly vegetables, fruit, dates, biscuits, bread and occasional delicacies such as strawberries or melon. Gorillas can live up to about 50 years old, and naturally the Zoo is hoping that he and Lomie will breed. They have a three-room suite as night quarters, and in daytime they have the choice of their day cage or the large outdoor run. In the wild, Gorillas live in bands of up to 30 individuals, consisting of an adult male known as a 'silver-back' (see p. 48) because of the greyish-silver colour developed by mature males, and several females and young of varying ages. Despite the Gorilla's alarming appearance, it is a shy, intelligent animal which avoids contact with other animals, and there is no record of a human having been killed by one when not provoked. The Gorilla's diet in the wild is vegetarian, and nests are made up each night in a different place, the large males sleeping on the ground and the others nesting in low branches. Since 1956, when the first Gorilla birth in a zoo took place, Gorillas have been bred fairly regularly in Europe and America, but it is still a comparatively rare event.

Orang utans are the next largest of the great apes, living mostly high up in the forest trees of Borneo and Sumatra. They are in great danger of extinction, but they breed quite regularly in zoos, and several have been born at London Zoo. Notice the enormous cheek pads of the large males. These are composed of fatty tissue under the skin, and have nothing to do with being old or over-weight. Orang utans are extremely inquisitive animals and they love to test every nut and bolt in their cages. Being immensely strong, they would pull their cages apart if special precautions were not taken to prevent this. The first Orang utan to be reared in captivity was born here in 1961.

There is a thriving colony of Chimpanzees, the third member of the great ape family, and they breed regularly in captivity. In the wild they live in loosely knit family groups, often moving from one group to another. Although mainly vegetarian, they also eat termites, and occasionally meat, in the form of young baboons or wild pigs. They come from the forests of Africa, and communicate noisily with each other, sometimes over considerable distances. They are good climbers, but move along the ground when travelling from one place to another.

The Sobell Pavilion also houses a good collection of monkeys, all of them in family groups. These include the capuchins and spider monkeys of South America, Mandrills, baboons and mangabeys, guenons and gibbons. The South American monkeys, including tamarins and marmosets, are all tree-dwellers, and spider monkeys have prehensile tails which are used like an extra limb to grasp the branches of trees. Baboons live on the ground, in large troops, hunting for food in grassland. The mangabeys live mainly in the trees, and their long tails are used as an aid in balancing. The guenons are found all over Africa, and the Vervet Monkeys here live in grassy bush country. There is also a breeding

London Zoo. **Address** Zoological Society of London, Regent's Park, London NW1. **Telephone** 01–722 3333. **Open** 09.00–18.00 summer (19.00 Sun and bank holidays), 10.00–sunset winter. **Guide-book. Catering** licensed restaurant, self-service cafeteriá, kiosks. Zoo shop. **Guided tours** under a formal education programme. **Acreage** 32. **Car** many routes to central London; car parking on Outer Circle and DoE car park. **Bus** Greenline (London Country) into London, then tube to Baker Street, then bus 74. **Trains** e.g. to Waterloo (3 mls), to Euston (1 ml). **Taxis** available. **Other facilities** first-aid post, nursing mothers' room, lost children's room, push-chairs, wheel-chairs, children's playground. Public **not allowed** to feed animals.

Guy, London Zoo's male Gorilla (above); Chia-Chia and Ching-Ching, the Giant Pandas (below).

group of Lar Gibbons, which come from southeast Asia. Gibbons are tree-dwellers, using their long arms to swing through the trees at great speed and seldom coming down to the ground. They live in pairs with their young, but when young males reach maturity they leave the family, and in captivity they have to be removed from their fathers to avoid fighting.

Next to the great apes are the Zoo's young pair of Giant Pandas, the most valuable animals in the collection. Chia-Chia, the male, is a month or two younger than the female, Ching-Ching. Their Chinese names mean 'Most Excellent' and 'Crystal Bright'. They were born in 1972 and arrived in London in 1974, as a gift from the Chinese people. Giant Pandas are rare in the wild, and they are found only in the bamboo forests in mountainous regions of western China. They are now strictly protected by the Chinese, and it is thought that their numbers are increasing. During the past three years, other pairs of Giant Pandas have been sent to the zoos in Paris, Tokyo and Washington, D.C., and it is hoped that these will all breed when they become mature.

The Reptile House contains the largest collection of reptiles in the country, with tortoises, turtles, terrapins, crocodiles and alligators, lizards and snakes. The giant tortoises exhibited here come from Aldabra Island in the Indian Ocean and the Galapagos Islands in the Pacific Ocean. They are very long-lived animals and they grow slowly: the largest tortoise here is over 100 years old, and still growing. It weighs more than 425 lb. Turtles live in the sea and have flippers, while terrapins have webbed feet and live in fresh water. Some turtle species have been mercilessly hunted, the Green Turtle for its fat, from which turtle soup is made, and the Hawksbill Turtle for its shell, which is used to make tortoiseshell.

Crocodilians are all carnivorous and they can be distinguished from each other by their jaws. Crocodiles have large teeth in the lower jaw which protrude when their mouths are shut, whereas alligators have a cavity in the upper jaw into which the lower teeth fit, so that no teeth are visible when the jaws are closed. The caiman from Central and South America has a shorter, wedge-shaped jaw, and the Indian Gharial has long, narrow jaws with very pronounced nostrils. Gharials live in rivers, and their main diet is fish. The others are fed twice a week in the Zoo on dead mammals, birds and fish.

Among the lizards, you can see monitor lizards, which are aggressive and carnivorous, and agama lizards, both from the Old World. Tegus, also meat-eaters, and iguanas, come from the New World. Iguanas are vegetarian, live in trees and can be identified by their ornamental crests. There are also several kinds of chameleon, which have two opposed sets of toes on each foot for gripping branches and sticky tongues which they shoot out at great speed to catch insects. The Zoo has two poisonous lizards, the Gila Monster and the Mexican Beaded Lizard from the western United States and Mexico. These are the only two species of poisonous lizard in the world.

There is a large collection of the constrictor snakes, which are the boas and pythons. These kill their prey by squeezing, and do not carry venom. The most poisonous species are the Black Mamba, the King Cobra, the Taipan and tiger snakes from Australia, the American rattlesnakes and the African Gaboon Viper.

The Stork and Ostrich House exhibits storks, cranes and flightless birds. The cranes are mostly tall, slender birds with long legs and loud calls. They live on small animals, frogs, snakes and insects which they catch with their powerful bills. Storks are also tall birds but with stockier bodies, shorter necks, and partially webbed feet since they usually live near water, where they catch small animals. The Marabou Stork is a carrion eater, which accounts for its bald head: feathers would be an encumbrance for a bird which digs into carcasses. The flightless birds include the Ostrich, rhea, Emu and cassowary. The Ostrich, from Africa, is the largest, living on a mainly vegetarian diet, but like most birds it also swallows pebbles, to aid digestion. Rheas are from South America, where they live on the plains, each male having a harem of about six females. Emus are found only in Australia, and cassowaries are from New Guinea. Cassowaries live on a mixed diet of insects, fruit and plants, and like all the flightless birds have exceedingly strong feet. They have been known to kill a man with a kick.

The Elephant and Rhino Pavilion has both Black and White Rhinos, and

Indian and African Elephants. The Black Rhino is smaller than the White, more aggressive, and it has a pointed lip which is an aid to browsing on thorn bushes. The White Rhinos, taller and heavier, may weigh two tons, and they are easily recognised by the hump over the shoulders. They are grazing animals and, unlike the Black species, they live in herds. The wide mouth is much more like a horse's mouth. The rhino's horn is made of the same material as human hair and fingernails, though in a compressed form. The horn grows continuously, but is normally worn down by being rubbed against trees.

All the elephants in the Zoo are cows, since bulls are often dangerous and can become difficult to manage. The African Elephant is taller than the Indian, and its hind quarters are higher. The other obvious difference is in the ears, the African species having much larger ones. Elephants have been known to live more than 60 years, though, like humans, they may die of old age several years earlier. The elephant's digestive system has been described as an enormous, inefficient factory, as only about half the food intake is digested. This means that in the wild they have to spend most of the day feeding, but in captivity the quantity can be reduced by feeding them a more nutritious diet. Even so, they consume an enormous amount of food, including 100 lb. of hay, as well as oats, maize, beans, vegetables, fruit, leaves, salt and cod-liver oil. The Indian Elephants here are aged 15 and 22, and the African Elephants are aged 15 and 9.

Here also are the Malayan Tapirs, members of a very early family in terms of evolution, distantly related to the rhinoceros and horse families. They are now found only in South America and southeast Asia. Tapirs are vegetarian, living near rivers, and the long nose is used for feeding. They are good swimmers. Young tapirs are spotted and the black and white marking of the Malayan species is a good camouflage in mixed shade and sunlight.

The exhibit for the big cats is the newest major development in the Zoo, replacing the Lion House which was built in 1875. When it was built, this house was the most modern of its day, with special internal corridors for moving the animals into their outdoor cages, but today much larger outside enclosures are required, and the time has come to improve technical facilities as well as those for viewing. You will see here good examples of all the big cats – Lions, Tigers, Leopards, Jaguars and Pumas. Lions were once common all over Africa, Asia Minor and western Asia, but they are now confined to southern and eastern Africa, and a small population survives in the state of Gujerat, in northwest India.

Several races of Tiger exist, the most northerly being the Siberian Tiger, which is the largest. The Tigers of India and southeast Asia are the ones most usually seen in zoos. Leopards are found in both Africa and Asia. They are smaller, better climbers, and they hunt smaller animals, although they are immensely strong. The Jaguar, more heavily built than the Leopard, comes from South America. Black forms of both the Leopard and the Jaguar occur, but the spots can be seen in their coats. The Puma of America is about the size of a Leopard, and it is the largest of the cats which yowl rather than roar. You may also see here the Cheetah and the Northern Lynx. Cheetahs are found in Africa, where they are now becoming rare, having been exterminated in Asia, except for a small population in Iran, and the Northern Lynx is found in northern Europe and western Asia. All species of cat except the Lion are now endangered in the wild, either because of the demand for their skins for the fur trade, or because man has encroached on their natural homes, cutting down forests and driving away the animals on which they prey. The big cats are bred regularly in captivity,

The Children's Zoo contains a wide variety of domestic animals, many of which can be stroked by young children. There are Rabbits, guinea-pigs, ducks and geese, goats and sheep and pigs. The guinea-pig and the Muscovy Duck both originated in South America, where they were bred for food. The domestic Rabbit came from Spain, and the hoofed animals have all been domesticated in various parts of the world for many thousands of years. In 1974 part of the Children's Zoo was developed as a farm and demonstration area, and there is a milking parlour where you can see cows being milked, with the milk passing into the cooler, and thence into the churn. There are also pony and donkey rides in summer.

Above: adult and cub American Black Bears.

Left: London Zoo's mother Polar Bear, Sally, with her cub Triplet.

Below: Himalayan or Asiatic Black Bear.

The Bird House exhibits a fascinating collection of the more brightly coloured species which require some protection from the weather. Since there are about 8,500 different species of bird known to science, it is not possible to show more than a small number of these in a zoo, but the London Zoo collection has a good cross-section of the main groups. There is a very good collection of hornbills and toucans, tropical fruit-eating species from Africa and Asia, and South America respectively. There are also wading birds, such as avocets and ibises. The Scarlet Ibis nests in trees in one of the outside aviaries attached to the Bird House. Many species of finch are represented, as well as glossy starlings and crowned pigeons, among the largest members of the pigeon family.

One of the most colourful birds here is the cock-of-the-rock, which in the wild lives in the undergrowth of tropical forests. It has a large disc of feathers on top of its head which all but conceals the bill. The cock bird of one species, from the northern Andes, is a brilliant red, while the other, from Guyana and Brazil, is a soft orange. The females of both species are brown. There are also peacocks in the outside aviaries. The peacock's long train is designed to attract the female in a mating display, and is not part of the tail feathers.

The Bird House is due for replacement by a more modern building during the next few years.

Next to this is the Tropical Bird House, where you can see the small nectar-eating birds. These include the hummingbirds, of which there are over 300 species, all found in the New World; the honey-creepers, also from the New World, and the white-eyes and sunbirds of tropical Africa and Asia. Only the hummingbirds can hover while feeding, and their diet in the wild consists of insects and nectar extracted from flowers. In the London Zoo they are given a nectar substitute, which they extract from feeding tubes. In flight, hummingbirds beat their wings up to 50 times a second, but the courting male may increase this rate to 200 wing beats a second, and this creates the hum which gives the bird its name.

The Seal Pool exhibits Grey Seals, which are found off the rocky coasts of the British Isles. Seals differ from sealions in having no ear-flaps, neither can their fore-limbs be used for locomotion on land. The Sealion Pool contains a bull and a group of females. In both seals and sealions, the adult males are very much larger than the females, and a male sealion will eat about 20 lb. of fish a day, twice as much as the females.

Several species of wild dog can be seen, in the Canine Section behind the sealion pond, in the Charles Clore Pavilion, and in the Wolf Wood, where you can see Canadian Timber Wolves. Behind the sealions you can see Cape Hunting Dogs, Coyotes, jackals, Dingos and Maned Wolves. Hunting Dogs are from southern and central Africa, and they hunt in packs, attacking the larger game animals. Coyotes, natives of North America, and jackals, which are found in Africa and Asia, are smaller, and they hunt smaller game, also scavenging on the carcasses of large animals. The Dingo of Australia is descended from domestic dogs, and has become wild. Unlike domestic dogs, it howls rather than barks. The Maned Wolf (see p. 157) is a very long-legged animal of the South American pampas, and it is now rare, both in the wild and in zoos.

There are penguins to be seen in the Penguin Pool outside the Children's Zoo and below the terrace opposite the Mappin Terraces. There are 17 species of penguin, all found in the southern hemisphere, from the Galapagos Islands on the equator down to the southern polar regions. The Mappin Terraces pool also exhibits pelicans, which, unlike penguins, are mostly found in warm climates. They fish in flocks flying low over the sea and then dipping down together, use the pouches in their bills to scoop the fish out of the water.

The Southern Aviary, next to the Sealion Pool, is landscaped to exhibit a variety of seabirds in naturalistic surroundings. You can see gannets, skuas, shags and cormorants, all of which feed on fish. In the Far East, cormorants are trained to catch fish, which are then taken by the fishermen. A ring is fitted round each bird's neck to prevent it from swallowing the fish. There are also herons in this aviary, which breed here: this is the Common Heron, and there is a small heronry of this species living in Regent's Park.

The Aquarium is divided into four halls, for freshwater fish of temperate climates, marine fish, tropical freshwater fish and amphibians. The freshwater hall contains most fish found in British rivers and lakes. There are also the primitive garfish and Bowfins from North America. The Rainbow Trout is an introduced species, having been brought over originally from America. You can also see the sturgeon, whose eggs are prized as caviare. The seawater hall has a changing population, but it usually includes many British species as well as marine fish from all over the world. There are usually rays, sharks and dogfish, and the flatfish which are eaten regularly in this country, including Plaice, Sole and flounder. These live on the sea bottom, and they change colour according to their background as camouflage. Different coloured backgrounds in the tanks are provided to illustrate this feature. Several kinds of eel are displayed, such as the big moray eel, and the smaller Conger Eel. Other groups represented are the wrasse, anemone-fish and the dragonfish, a genus from tropical oceans with poisonous spines in their dorsal fins, which can be painful and even lethal to humans. Other marine animals besides fish in this hall are lobsters, Edible Crabs, spider-crabs, octopuses, sea-urchins, starfish and sea-anemones. These last can fire barbed threads from their tentacles at shrimps and other small creatures. To supply the seawater tanks, water is imported from the Bay of Biscay, and 140,000 gallons are in constant circulation.

The tropical hall displays a huge variety of fish, many of which are in heated tanks. Some of the most curious are the lungfishes and the Electric Eel. Lung-fishes, which are found in Africa, Australia and South America, survive periods of drought by means of a primitive lung, so that they can obtain oxygen from the air as well as from water. The South American Lungfish can survive a complete absence of water in periods of severe drought by encasing itself in a kind of cocoon. The Electric Eel of the Amazon river emits electric charges for two reasons. It cannot see its food or find its way because of the muddy water, so its electric charges act like radar, rebounding from solid objects as a direction-finding mechanism. It also uses much stronger electric shocks to stun its prey. The mudskipper and Climbing Perch use their fins as temporary legs when they leave the water, and the Archer Fish shoots down flies with drops of water ex-pelled from its mouth. There is also a tank of piranhas, the South American river fish which tear to pieces with their needle-sharp teeth any animal that ventures into the water, and Blind Cavefish, which live in subterranean caves and have no eyes. Many colourful small species which are kept in home aquaria are also on show, such as angel fish, barbs and gouramis.

As you leave the Aquarium, you pass through the amphibian hall. Here you can see several species of frog, from the huge bull-frogs of the tropics to the tiny tree-frogs, which may be only an inch in length. The Poison-Arrow Frogs, as their name suggests, are used by South American Indians to extract poison, and there are also Smooth-clawed Frogs which were used in pregnancy tests before other methods were developed. The Axolotl of Central America is a kind of adult tadpole, which can live its life under water, but in certain conditions they lose their gills and move to dry land, where they become the Tiger Salamander. The Tiger Salamander is quite a familiar species in the United States, and it was not realised that it was the developed form of the Axolotl until about 100 years ago, when some Axolotls kept in Paris lost their gills and fins as the water slowly evaporated. This change can also be induced by hormone injections.

There are several attractive bird exhibits in the main part of the Zoo. The Flamingo Pool contains four species, the Rosy Flamingo, a bright pink bird from the Caribbean, and Greater and Lesser Flamingos, which are a paler pink colour, and the Chilean Flamingo. The Greater and Lesser Flamingos of Africa differ in size, and the Lesser has a deep red beak. The Chilean Flamingo has bright red knee-caps. Flamingos live in large flocks on brackish lakes, and the young are hatched on cone-shaped nests made of mud.

The Three Island Pond contains more Chilean Flamingos and a variety of waterfowl, including the rare Hawaiian Geese, which were nearly exterminated in the wild until a few pairs were taken to the Wildfowl Trust's collection in Gloucestershire, where they have been bred successfully, and have been

The Fennec Fox of North Africa and Arabia, the smallest member of the fox group, is only 16 inches long. Its enormous four-inch ears impart acute hearing, and the soles of its feet are hairy; thus, silent itself, it hunts its prey of rodents, birds, lizards and locusts by ear at night.

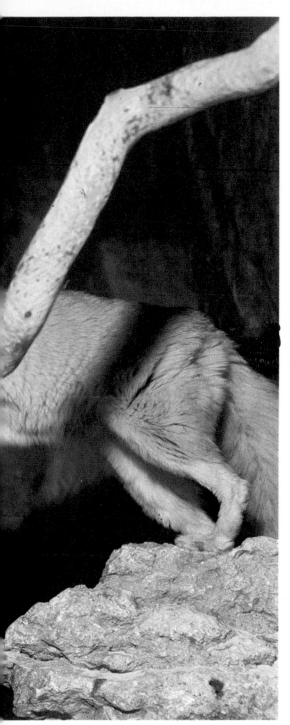

reintroduced in the Hawaiian islands. The Eastern Aviary also displays a species which is rare in the wild, the Laysan Duck, which has a distinctive white ring round its eye.

There is a large collection of birds of prey in the aviaries next to the south entrance, ranging in size from the Merlin to the Andean Condor, which has a wing span of about ten feet. Several species of eagle, vulture and hawk are shown, as well as some of the large owls of Africa and Asia. The British owl species will be found in a separate aviary in the North Gardens. Most of the owls in the Zoo breed regularly, one of the handsomest being the Snowy Owl, which ranges from the Arctic to the Shetland Islands. The British crow collection exhibits all the species of this family which are familiar in this country. One of the handsomest species is the Chough (see p. 228), which has a long, curving, orange bill and orange legs. Choughs have only been bred in two or three zoos in this country, and the crow family as a whole does not breed readily in captivity.

The parrot family can be seen in the Parrot House, in the cockatoo aviary and in the small parrot aviary adjoining the Parrot House. There are more than 300 species of parrot, found all over the world in warmer climates. They all have strong, curved bills used for opening nuts as well as a hook for climbing. Their feet are used for holding food, and most of them nest in holes in trees. The Quaker Parrakeet is unlike all other members of the parrot family in making a very large circular nest out of twigs, which contains many individual nests, one for each pair of birds. This gives the effect of a block of flats, with each pair of birds using its own front door. A large number of parrot species are found in the islands north of Australia, including the cockatoos. New Zealand is the home of the Kea, the only parrot found in a snowy climate. Many parrots, parrakeets and lovebirds come from Africa, while Central and South America is the region where macaws and conures are found.

The Mappin Terraces are on three levels, with the wild pig species at ground level, the bears in the middle, and the sheep and goats on the top terrace. Wild pigs include the Wild Boar, extinct in this country but still found in Europe, the Warthog and Bush Pig of Africa and the Collared Peccary of Central and Southern America. The Wild Boar and the smaller African Bush Pig, which has shorter tusks, live in forest, while the Warthog prefers more open bush country.

The bears in the Zoo usually include Polar Bears, Brown Bears, and the black bears of Asia and America. Polar Bears are carnivorous, living mainly on seals in the Arctic. They are amongst the most dangerous of wild animals, and are insulated against the cold by a layer of fat under the skin. They also have hair on the soles of their feet which prevents them from slipping on ice and snow. There are several races of Brown Bear, and they live in forests in temperate regions. In Europe, they are found in the wild in small numbers, in mountainous regions. The Asiatic Black Bear has a V-shaped white blaze across its chest, while the American Black Bear is entirely black.

The top terraces exhibit the Markhor, the largest kind of wild goat in the world, which comes from the Himalayas, and three species of wild sheep, the Barbary Sheep from North Africa, which is in fact a wild goat found on the African continent, the Mouflon from Sardinia and Corsica, and the North American Bighorn Sheep. Most female sheep have much smaller horns than the males, but those of the female Barbary almost compare in size.

The Cotton Terraces exhibit the Zoo's camels and hoofed animals — antelopes, Giraffes, zebra, deer, cattle and wild horses. Both the Arabian and Bactrian Camels are shown, the Arabian having one hump and the Bactrian two. Camels have been domesticated for thousands of years, and the only truly wild ones left are a small population of Bactrian Camels in Mongolia. The Bactrian is a pack animal, and coming from northern Asia it has a thick coat, which is shed, somewhat untidily, in summer. The Arabian is used as both a pack animal and for riding. The camel's hump is used for the storage of fat and water which can be drawn upon when food is scarce. The Camel House also exhibits the four other South American members of the camel family — the Llama, Guanaco, Alpaca and Vicuna. The Llama and Alpaca are domesticated species, the former being used as a pack animal as well as for its wool and meat, and the smaller Alpaca for its fine wool. The Guanaco, taller than the Llama, is a wild species. The Vicuna, also a wild species, is prized for its wool and is rare, although it is protected by law in Peru.

The antelopes exhibited here, in the paddocks overlooking the Regent Canal, are Blackbuck, waterbuck, Greater Kudu and Brindled Gnu. The Blackbuck is a small species which was once common on the plains of India, where it was the prey of Cheetahs. The females and young are fawn coloured, and the males are dark brown, except for the herd leader, which turns a very dark brown on its back. They breed well in captivity, and more than 120 have been born in the Zoo in the past ten years. They share a paddock with waterbuck, a heavily built species with long hair and a thick neck, which is found in African grasslands, usually near swamps and rivers. The Greater Kudu is another African species which lives in bush country, browsing on trees and bushes. The males have spiralling horns, and the coat marking acts as camouflage in mixed sunlight and shade. The Brindled Gnu is a plains animal, living in large herds in East Africa, and both sexes have horns. The gnu, or wildebeest, is one of the animals most frequently killed by Lions.

There is a breeding group of Giraffes here, living in one of the oldest houses in the Zoo, which has been modernised. Forty-four Giraffes have been born in this house. Giraffes live on grassland in Africa, browsing on trees with their long, prehensile tongues which can grasp leaves and twigs. They also chew bark. Several races of Giraffe exist, each with a different coat pattern, which helps to camouflage them from Lions against a background of trees. Giraffes seldom utter a sound, although they occasionally bleat or moo. The zebras which share the Giraffes' paddock are Grant's or Bohm's Zebras, a race of the Common Zebra of southern and eastern parts of Africa. As with Giraffes, the various kinds of zebra have different coat markings, although it is not certain what significance the stripes have. Possibly, they make it difficult for Lions to pick out individual animals from a closely packed herd.

The deer exhibited here are Père David's Deer, Chital, Timor Deer and Fallow Deer. Père David's Deer is a species of swamp deer from China, which was exterminated in the wild in 1900. It was discovered by Père David, a French missionary in China, in 1865. There are about 550 animals in captivity in various parts of the world, all of which are descended from the original herd collected at Woburn by the eleventh Duke of Bedford at the end of the nineteenth century. As with several other rare animals, a studbook is kept of captive stock, and the records for this deer are kept at Whipsnade. The Chital, more commonly known in zoos as the Axis Deer, lives in large herds in broken woodland areas of India, and it is the only kind of spotted deer which retains its spots throughout the year. The Timor Deer, or Rusa, distributed throughout Java, Sumatra and other East Indian islands, is related to the larger Sambar of southeast Asia, and also to the Red Deer of Europe. It inhabits tropical forests in the wild.

Fallow Deer lose their spots in winter, and both white and black forms are known. These have been kept in English parks since the Norman Conquest, and they were probably introduced into this country from southern Europe and Asia Minor. They are now found wild in many places in England. An interesting species, at present in the Stork and Ostrich House, is the Pudu, which is the smallest species of American deer. It comes from Chile and Bolivia.

At the western end of the Cotton Terraces you come to the wild horses and cattle. Przewalski's Horse may now be extinct in the wild, although there are possibly a few remaining in western Mongolia. This wild horse was discovered by western science in the nineteenth century, and a few specimens were sent to zoos in Europe. Some of the first to arrive in Europe were sent to London Zoo. Though still a rare animal, there are now more than 200 living in zoos. They breed regularly, though the numbers increase slowly. The wild asses are represented here by the Onager, a race from Persia. All wild asses are now rare in the wild, but they breed in captivity.

The wild cattle family exhibited here includes the Yak, the Cape Buffalo, the American and European Bisons, and the Anoa. Yaks have long, shaggy coats, adapted to the cold climate of Tibet and the Himalayas. They are still found in

the wild, but they are also domesticated, and valued for their milk, wool, hide and as a pack animal. The Cape Buffalo of Africa is a fierce animal inhabiting swampy grassland near rivers and waterholes. It lives in herds, and because of the size and strength of the males it is seldom preyed upon by Lions. The American Bison, a plains animal of North America, was nearly exterminated for its meat and hide in the last century, but it is now strictly protected and breeds well in captivity. Its European cousin is a taller animal, formerly inhabiting the forests of Europe. It is now extinct in the wild, but it is bred regularly in zoos, and it is protected in a forest reserve in eastern Poland. One of the other cattle species exhibited here from time to time is the Anoa, the smallest member of the cattle family, which is only found in the forests of Celebes Island in the East Indies. It is a shy animal, and seldom exhibited in this country.

The Charles Clore Pavilion for Mammals has a large collection of the smaller ones, with nocturnal animals in the Moonlight World downstairs. On the ground floor you can see the Common Treeshrews, regarded as the most primitive of the primates, the Order to which man belongs, and a variety of small monkey species. Amongst the most interesting of these are the marmosets and tamarins, tiny tree-dwellers of South America, and the Ring-tailed Lemur and Ruffed Lemur from Madagascar, which is the only place where lemurs are found in the wild. Many rodent species are exhibited, including squirrels, and Prairie Marmots from North America. These live in underground burrows, and they can be seen in these through a glass window. Other rodents here are porcupines, and the paca and agouti of South America, which are related to guinea-pigs, but also to porcupines. Carnivorous species include weasels, mongooses and several species of small cat. There are European Wild Cats here, which are still found in Scotland. Amongst the most attractive exhibits are the Red Pandas, the closest relation of the Giant Panda. This has a bright chestnut coat, and it is a good tree climber. It is found in Burma and northern India, as well as in the forests of China. You can also see the wombat, which burrows underground; the tree-kangaroos which have become adapted to a climbing existence; wallabies, which have an outdoor enclosure; and sloths, which hang upside-down on branches, rarely descending to the ground.

Downstairs, the Moonlight World shows animals which are active by night, under artificial moonlight, while the public watch them from darkened halls. At the end of the day the lighting is reversed, the animals being given artificial daylight, when they go to sleep. Several species of mice and rats are shown here, some of them in observation burrows. You can also see echidnas, which are primitive egg-laying mammals. The egg is incubated in a pouch, and when the young appear they are suckled. Echidnas, or Spiny Anteaters, are burrowing animals, found only in Australia and New Guinea.

There are several nocturnal primates here, including the Potto, and a related species, the Slow Loris. Another related animal is the galago, or bushbaby. There are several species of galago, but not all of them are entirely nocturnal. They can leap enormous distances, using their tails as a rudder. Another animal here is the Douroucouli, which is the only nocturnal species of monkey in the world. Among the small carnivorous animals here are civets, genets, and the largest member of that family, the Binturong, which has thick black hair and is a tree-dweller. The smallest member of the dog family is the Fennec Fox, a sand-coloured desert animal which hunts by night to avoid the heat of the day. It has very large ears, which are useful in detecting insects, its main item of diet.

There is a long cage for bats, containing a colony of fruit bats, and the vampire bats, some species of which live exclusively on blood. Having bitten an animal – usually a large one – the bat sucks its blood, aided by its saliva, which prevents the blood from clotting. These bats can spread disease, especially rabies, and their importation to this country is strictly controlled by law.

Outside the Charles Clore Pavilion are exhibits for three aquatic animals, Beavers, otters and Coypus. Beavers, which are vegetarian, make underground burrows or 'lodges' entered from below water level. In the wild they raise the water level of lakes by damming them with tree trunks and branches, cementing them together with mud. Coypus, like Beavers, are rodents, and they make

Three hoofed animals at Regent's Park: above, Barbary Sheep on the Mappin Terraces; left, Greater Kudu, a tree-browser of Africa; below, Blackbuck, which breed here successfully.

burrows in river banks (see p. 140). Most otters, which are related to badgers and weasels, live near rivers, feeding on fish, shellfish and other aquatic creatures. They are superb swimmers, and are exhibited to advantage in their glass-fronted pool.

The Insect House exhibits several groups of invertebrates, which form the largest section of animals in nature. Not all these creatures are classed as insects, and they include crabs, spiders, scorpions, millipedes, snails and leeches. One of the most fascinating insect exhibits here is the nest of Red Wood Ants, the largest species of ant found in Great Britain. It makes a large nest in the shape of a mound, containing a maze of passages and chambers. There are natural displays of water-boatmen, water-scorpions, damsel-fly larvae and caddis larvae. Both the Migratory and the Desert Locust are on show. You can also see stick insects — one Australian species is eight inches long — and praying mantis, which have hooks on their front legs to prevent their prey from escaping. They can be seen here catching locusts.

Several species of bird-eating spider are on view, although these are mis-named, as they hardly ever eat birds. The poisonous Black Widow Spider is also here, and the Orb-web Spider. Other exhibits are Imperial Scorpions, leeches with suckers at both ends of their bodies, the large African land snails, and Roman Snails, both of which are edible, crayfish, land crabs from the West Indies and hermit-crabs, which do not have their own hard shell, but use the discarded shells of snails.

Passing over the canal bridge to the North Gardens, you come to the aviaries for British owls, the crane and goose enclosures, the pheasantries and the Snowdon Aviary. This large flight aviary has been landscaped with shingle, a pool with running water, trees, shrubs and a cliff-face, to provide a variety of natural habitats for many different kinds of bird. The cantilevered bridge across the aviary gives visitors a good view of the inhabitants at different levels. Cattle Egrets and Sacred Ibis can be seen nesting in poplar trees during spring and summer, and herons have large nesting platforms high above the bridge, on the struts of the aviary's superstructure. Some birds, such as the Night Herons, nest in holes in the cliff-face as well as in the trees. The aviary has a changing population, but most of the birds can live there throughout the year.

There are two pheasant aviaries, by the Children's Zoo and near the Snowdon Aviary. Many rare species of pheasant are exhibited, some of which have been saved from extinction in the wild by captive breeding. Most pheasants come from Asia, including the game Pheasant found in Great Britain, which was introduced here, possibly by the Romans.

The London Zoo is not only the largest zoological collection in this country, it is also by far the oldest, as well as being one of the three oldest in the world still in existence. It was started by the Zoological Society of London, which was founded by Sir Stamford Raffles, whose name is associated with the develop-ment of the British Empire in the Far East, and especially of Singapore. The objects of the Society were 'the advancement of Zoology and Animal Physiology, and the introduction of new and curious subjects of the Animal Kingdom'. These aims hold good to this day, and the Society has been responsible for many discoveries and pioneering techniques in zoological science. Raffles died soon after the formation of the Society, but five acres of land in Regent's Park were granted by the Crown, and the Zoo was opened to holders of Fellows' tickets on 27th April 1828.

Amongst the first animals exhibited were a Griffon Vulture, which lived for 40 years, a White-headed Eagle and 'a little female deer'. Their keeper was paid a guinea a week, and he wore a uniform consisting of a top hat, a bottle-green coat, a striped waistcoat, breeches and wellington boots with painted tops. In the first year, 98,000 people visited the Zoo, but the general public was not admitted until 1847. In the early years, the Society rented offices in Mayfair, where some of the first small animals were kept until quarters for them had been built in the Zoo. On one occasion, a visiting bishop had his wig snatched off by a monkey, which promptly tried the wig on its own head.

The Society was granted its Charter by King George IV in 1829, and in 1831,

A female Slow Loris with her baby at Regent's Park; as its name suggests this animal moves in a slow, deliberate way along tree branches in search of insects and fruit.

after his death, the royal collections of wild animals at Windsor and in the Tower of London were sent to the Zoo. The architect Decimus Burton was appointed to prepare a plan for the Zoo, and although this was not followed in later years, he designed the first buildings, the Clock Tower and the original Camel House near the Fellows' Lawn. The other original features which still exist are the Three Island Pond, constructed in 1837, and the Giraffe House, built the same year, which was modernised and extended in 1963.

The Zoo has given the British public its first sight of many animals never exhibited before in this country. These include the first Indian Rhinoceros in 1834, the first Chimpanzee in 1835, and the first Giraffes in 1836, which walked from the London docks to Regent's Park. The first Giraffe ever born and reared in captivity was born in the Zoo in 1841. The first European Bison to arrive in England was presented by the Emperor of Russia in 1847, and in 1858 the Zoo received the last Quagga ever exhibited here. This was a species of zebra with no stripes on its body, which became extinct in 1883.

Obaysch, the first Hippopotamus to be seen in Europe since Roman times, was presented to Queen Victoria by the Viceroy of Egypt in 1850, and he arrived at the Zoo with an Egyptian keeper and a herd of sheep and goats to supply him with milk. A female Hippo subsequently obtained gave birth to the Zoo's first Hippo to be successfully reared. This was born on 5th November 1872, and called Guy Fawkes, although it was later discovered to be a female. Obaysch lived until 1879, and Guy Fawkes lived 36 years in the Zoo.

In 1865, the first African Elephant seen in England arrived at the Zoo from Paris. This was Jumbo, the famous elephant which grew to 11 feet 4 inches, and weighed $6\frac{1}{2}$ tons. He gave rides to children, but by 1882 his temper had become uncertain, and the Society decided to sell him to P. T. Barnum, the American circus owner. Jumbo was so popular, however, that there was a storm of public protest, and questions were asked in Parliament. Finally, Jumbo was shipped to the United States, where he was taken on an extensive tour, during the course of which he fathered two calves before meeting his death by being run down by a railway engine. It is his name that is still given to all enormous objects. In more recent times, famous stars of the Zoo have included Guy the Gorilla, who arrived in 1947; Brumas, the first Polar Bear cub to be born here, in 1949, who brought three million visitors to the Zoo; and Goldie, the Golden Eagle, which escaped for several weeks in 1962 before being recaptured.

The term 'Zoological Gardens' became shortened to 'Zoo' after a music-hall artist called Vance popularised a song which contained the chorus line, 'Walking in the Zoo is the O.K. thing to do', in 1867. By then the Zoo had become a British institution, and it was also leading the way in the art of animal husbandry.

At the beginning of this century many changes were made in the techniques of looking after animals. The Victorians had believed that animals from hot climates must be kept in over-heated houses, but Sir Peter Chalmers Mitchell, Hon. Secretary of the Society from 1903 to 1935, believed that animals would do better if acclimatised to fresh air, while being given access to heated quarters when they wished. His ideas were correct, and the health and life spans of the animals were greatly improved. This led to better designs for animal houses and enclosures, the most notable being the building of the Mappin Terraces in 1913, which were paid for by J. Newton Mappin. The concept of naturalistic rockwork exhibits divided by moats instead of bars was pioneered by Carl Hagenbeck, founder of the Hamburg Zoo, and this was copied by Mitchell. The London Zoo's first sanatorium and quarantine station was built in 1909, the present Aquarium in 1923, and the present Reptile House in 1927.

When the Second War broke out, the Zoo was closed for the first time in its history, but it reopened a fortnight later. All the poisonous snakes were destroyed as a safety precaution, but the Zoo remained open throughout the war. After the war, rebuilding was delayed by restrictions for several years, but in 1955 a new master-plan was drawn up, which has resulted in all the major developments of recent years. A new animal hospital, quarantine station and pathology laboratory were built in 1956, the new canal bridge followed in 1961, and the Cotton Terraces in 1963. The Elephant and Rhino Pavilion and the Snowdon

Aviary were completed in 1965, the Clore Pavilion in 1967, and the Sobell Pavilion for apes and monkeys in 1971.

From its earliest days, the Society has been closely associated with scientific studies in anatomy and physiology, and many famous scientists have worked on material supplied by the Zoo, including T. H. Huxley, and Sir Ray Lankester who first described the Okapi in 1900. During its recent modernisation programme the Society established the Wellcome Institute of Comparative Physiology in 1962 for research into animal reproduction, and in 1964 the Nuffield Institute of Comparative Medicine, for studies in pathology, biochemistry, radiology and infectious diseases. One benefit of these studies has been greatly improved diets for many of the animals in the Zoo.

The Zoo has always depended on private donations for capital development, and although large sums of money have been raised in this way, it became obvious that such sources of funds could not be relied on indefinitely. In 1970 the Government made a capital grant to enable capital development to continue, recognising that the Society's collections at Regent's Park and Whipsnade were a national asset. Until then, the London Zoo had been the only metropolitan zoo in the world not subsidised by public funds, and Government support has become even more necessary as capital and running costs rise. Each year, the Zoo's 6,000 animals are visited by nearly 2 million people, but expenditure is outstripping income. The annual food supply includes 220 tons of hay and clover, 40,000 eggs, 23,000 pints of milk, 95,000 lb. of fruit, 90 tons of meat, 82,000 lb. of fish and 129 tons of vegetables. Even so, at a cost of nearly £100,000 this is only a fraction of the Zoo's expenses. In 1900, the Zoo's staff numbered 105: today, more than 500 permanent staff are needed to manage the animals and conduct the Society's scientific research, educational programmes and administration.

The Zoo no longer collects animals like stamps, and the emphasis today is on fewer kinds of animal, but with each species kept in breeding groups, according to their social requirements. Keeping wild animals is as much an art as a science, and it involves great dedication and hard work.

Royal Windsor Safari Park

This Safari Park, set in a commanding position on the edge of Windsor Great Park, was opened by Smart Brothers, owners of Billy Smart's Circus, in 1969. It is the second 'drive-through' park to be established in Britain, but in one important respect it is not typical of the other British safari parks, because the greater part of the collection is seen on foot, the 'drive-through' section consisting of the five enclosures where the more dangerous animals are kept. You thus have the best of both worlds – a motorised safari route, and the freedom of the park to wander amongst the other exhibits in any order you please.

As you drive towards the main exhibition area, you see the thatched picnic shelters built to resemble the traditional native huts of Africa. The roadside exhibits in this area include pools for the sealions, flamingos, pelicans and penguins. Sealions and penguins are both well adapted to swimming under water, with streamlined contours which minimise water resistance. But while sealions undulate their hind limbs, keeping their front flippers close to the body, penguins use their flippers as underwater paddles, the forward thrust being achieved by the upward movement. Both are fast swimmers, and when travelling in search of fish, penguins 'porpoise' out of the water to breathe, without impeding their forward progress. They live on fish and plankton, and the 17 species of penguin are widely distributed in the southern hemisphere.

Sealions differ from seals in having visible ears, the construction of their flippers, and in the absence of an undercoat, which makes their pelts useless for fur.

The 'drive-through' section consists of five paddocks, showing Tigers, Lions, Cheetahs and baboons. The Tigers here are Indian, and these are now officially listed as an endangered species. Thirty years ago there were about 40,000 Tigers in the Indian sub-continent, but hunting and the disappearance of their forest

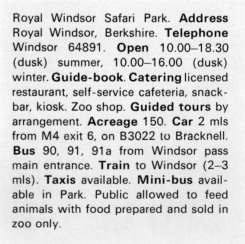

Royal Windsor Safari Park. **Address** Royal Windsor, Berkshire. **Telephone** Windsor 64891. **Open** 10.00–18.30 (dusk) summer, 10.00–16.00 (dusk) winter. **Guide-book**. **Catering** licensed restaurant, self-service cafeteria, snack-bar, kiosk. Zoo shop. **Guided tours** by arrangement. **Acreage** 150. **Car** 2 mls from M4 exit 6, on B3022 to Bracknell. **Bus** 90, 91, 91a from Windsor pass main entrance. **Train** to Windsor (2–3 mls). **Taxis** available. **Mini-bus** available in Park. Public allowed to feed animals with food prepared and sold in zoo only.

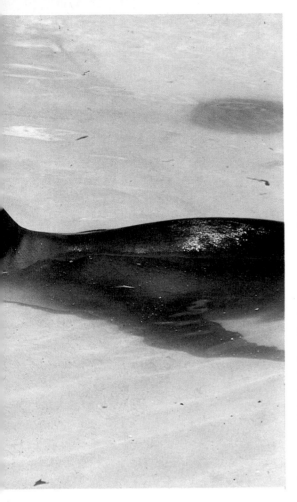

Above: Californian Sealion and pup.

Below: dolphins perform at Windsor.

habitat for expanding agriculture has reduced their numbers in the wild to danger level, and recent estimates put their number at no more than 4,000. They are now protected by the Indian Government, in reserves, and compensation is paid to owners of cattle killed by Tigers. There are two Lion enclosures, one with family groups of adults and cubs, and another where half-grown animals are kept. Lions breed prolifically in captivity, and young animals have to be removed from the pride as they become larger, otherwise there would be serious overcrowding.

The next paddock contains Cheetahs, which are the fastest land animals over a short distance. Their claws do not retract fully, like other cats' claws, and their limbs are double-jointed, which probably enables them to achieve high speeds. Cheetahs have only been bred in captivity in recent years, and cubs were not raised in Britain until 1967. The Cheetahs at Windsor have bred, and this is only the second British zoo to have achieved this.

The last 'drive-through' exhibit contains a thriving colony of Hamadryas Baboons. The gates to this paddock are open, guarded by Alsatian Dogs on long running leashes, which chase back any baboons which approach them. Hamadryas Baboons live in rocky country in the Sudan, Ethiopia and south-western Arabia. They are also called the Sacred Baboon, since they were formerly found in the Nile valley, where they were regarded as a sacred animal by the ancient Egyptians. This is the most impressive of the five species of baboon, with long, flowing hair on the head, shoulders and chest. Baboons feed on roots, and the succulent stems of plants, and they also forage for honey and insects. They live in colonies of up to 100 individuals, which enables them to ignore most other animals. With their large canine teeth they have little to fear from predators, although Leopards will sometimes kill stragglers. On chilly days, a bonfire is lit for the baboons here, and they can be seen warming themselves appreciatively beside it.

Having completed the safari circuit, you can then park your car and see the rest of the animals on foot. On the hillside can be seen the moated enclosure for a group of White Rhinoceros, a herd animal which grazes, unlike the smaller but much more dangerous Black Rhinoceros which is a browser, living a more solitary life. Rhinos have a keen sense of smell, but very poor sight, which is not important to them. Other large animals to be seen are elephants, camels, Llamas, Giraffes and zebras. The elephants here are Indian, and they are all young animals. The gestation period for elephants is twenty-one months for a female calf, and twenty-two months for a male. The newly born calf cannot use its trunk, and the mother has to hold it to one side to enable the calf to suckle. The Giraffes and zebras share a paddock, and they are often found grazing close to each other in the wild, the Giraffes acting as look-outs for the approach of hunting Lions.

There are also Chimpanzees, Raccoons, wallabies, several species of monkey and a collection of exotic birds, including Ostriches, Crowned Cranes, parrots and macaws. The monkey and macaw cage is a large walk-through exhibit with free-flying macaws, and monkeys scampering overhead, separated from visitors by a wire mesh ceiling.

There is an attractive small reptile house, showing crocodiles, snakes, lizards and tortoises; and a children's zoo and farm containing horses, donkeys, sheep and domestic pets.

The dolphinarium has a circular pool with outdoor and indoor seating. The outdoor section has glass sides so that the dolphins can be seen swimming under water. The species shown here is the Bottle-nosed Dolphin, found in most warm seas all over the world. It is the species usually exhibited, but it has not yet been bred in captivity with any success. Large numbers of dolphins are caught and killed in fishing nets, but some measure of protection is now given by U.S. Government laws, since most of the dolphins caught for exhibition are found off the coasts of Florida.

The park also offers amusements for children, with a model fortress, slides and swings, and there is a Mansion Bar in the White House, which was formerly owned by Mr Horace Dodge, the American manufacturer of the Dodge car.

Stagsden Bird Gardens

Stagsden Bird Gardens house a remarkably fine collection of pheasants, many of which are rare in the wild, and a good collection of waterfowl, exhibited in well-planted enclosures, aviaries and ponds. There is also a fine shrub rose collection. The owner, who opened the Gardens in 1965, started collecting and breeding pheasants in 1956, being specially concerned by the fact that so many species were on the brink of extinction in the wild. One of his early successes was in breeding the rare Satyr Tragopan, a brilliantly coloured species from the dense forests of the Himalayas at between 8,000 and 14,000 feet. Other rare species bred here include Edwards' Pheasant, a shy species from the bamboo forests in the mountains of Annam, whose habits in the wild are unknown; Swinhoe's Pheasant, the Cheer Pheasant, and Blue-eared and Brown-eared Pheasants. The owner achieved fame as an aviculturist when he imported some Hume's Bar-tailed Pheasants from the Naga Hills of Burma in 1961. This little-known species had never been brought alive to the Western Hemisphere, and in 1962 it was successfully bred at Stagsden. It is known to be rare in the wild, and it is therefore important to breed it in captivity.

Many species of waterfowl also breed regularly here, and you can see Red-breasted, Bar-headed, Ashy-headed and Ross's Geese, Cereopsis or Cape Barren Geese, a green-billed species which tends to be aggressive towards other geese, and many species of duck. The attractive little Chinese Bamboo Partridge is another bird which is bred here regularly, and notice the Sonnerat's Jungle Fowl from the mountainous bamboo forests of western and southern India. In the wild it lives singly or in pairs. This bird represents a link with domestic poultry, which are descended from the various wild species of jungle fowl found in Asia.

The Bird Gardens contain an interesting collection of old breeds of poultry. The breeding of ancient and unusual varieties was popular in the nineteenth century, but they became rare after the introduction of the modern breeds demanded by the poultry industry. The varieties exhibited here include Golden Bantams, Silver Sebright Bantams, Cochins, the Polish breed, and Yokohamas.

There is a group of parrakeets and a colony of Homing Budgerigars which make an interesting addition to the main collection. Notice also the fine displays of shrub roses and old-fashioned rose varieties in the gardens.

Stagsden Bird Gardens. **Address** Stagsden, Bedford. **Telephone** Oakley 2745. **Open** 11.00–18.00 summer, 11.00–dusk winter. **Catering** home-bake tea room. **Acreage** 8½. **Car** 5 mls w. of Bedford on A422, Gardens 200 yds from Stagsden Church. **Bus** 132 from Bedford stops at Royal George Inn. **Train** to Bedford (5 mls). **Taxis** available. Public **not allowed** to feed birds.

Himalayan Monal, a pheasant at Stagsden.

Verulamium British Wildlife Zoo

The Verulamium British Wildlife Zoo is almost exactly what it says — a collection of British animals which you can see eyeball to eyeball in an enclosed area of half an acre. The exceptions are the European Eagle Owl, which is not found in this country, and the Golden and Silver Pheasants, which are Asiatic in origin but have been introduced here. It is always interesting to be able to have a close look at our native animals, and this exhibition includes Badgers, which breed here regularly, Scottish Wild Cats, the Red Fox, Stoat, Weasel, Polecat-ferret (a hybrid, the Ferret being a domestic species, sometimes bred with a wild Polecat) and mink. Three small animals here that are not often seen in zoos are the Edible Dormouse, the Wood Mouse and the Fieldmouse. You can also see specimens of the Slow-worm and Grass Snake, both of which are harmless.

The British birds of prey shown here are the Golden Eagle, the Buzzard, the Barn Owl, Tawny Owl and Little Owl, and the Kestrel. These Kestrels breed regularly, and the aviaries where these species are kept are well stocked with natural undergrowth to give them the necessary seclusion. The other British species exhibited are the Black-headed Gull, the Crow, Rook and Raven.

This is a Local Authority zoo, opened in 1964 in Verulamium Park, where there is a museum of Roman exhibits on the site of the original Roman town.

Verulamium British Wildlife Zoo. **Address** Verulamium Park, St Michaels, St Albans, Herts. **Telephone** (Mon–Fri) St Albans 66100 ext. 222. **Open** 11.00–13.00 and 14.00–18.00 1st April–31st Oct. **Catering** self-service cafeteria. **Acreage** ½. **Car** 1½ mls w. of city centre on A414 Hemel Hempstead road, ¼ ml s. of junction with A5. **Bus** London Country route 330 to St Michael's Village. **Train** to St Albans City Station then bus 330 to Zoo (1½ mls). **Taxis** available. Public **not allowed** to feed animals.

National Trust Waddesdon Manor

For those interested in seeing a bird collection in this part of Buckinghamshire, the Aviary at Waddesdon Manor is well worth a visit. It is semi-circular and divided into flight cages, each with a heated inner compartment. It contains a mixed collection of about 70 soft-billed birds, seed-eaters and members of the parrot family. Amongst those exhibited are toucans, touracos, hornbills, jays and woodpeckers; while birds bred in the collection include Spreo Starlings, and a Wandering Tree Pie which is believed to be one of the first of this species bred in captivity. Probably the rarest species here, and one that is endangered in the wild, is Rothschild's Grackle. This bird has a restricted island habitat and is thus vulnerable both to encroachment by man, and to other animals. It is called after a member of the family who built the Manor.

There is also a small herd of Japanese Sika Deer in the grounds, which were introduced into Waddesdon towards the end of the last century after the house was completed.

Waddesdon Manor was built by Baron Ferdinand de Rothschild between 1874 and 1889 and it was bequeathed to the National Trust in 1957 by Mr James A. de Rothschild. The Manor contains French paintings of the seventeenth and eighteenth centuries, furniture, Savonnerie carpets, Sèvres porcelain, Dutch, Flemish and Italian paintings, portraits by Gainsborough and Reynolds, drawings, lace and personal mementoes of the Rothschild family. On Fridays only, you can also see the Bachelors' Wing, which exhibits paintings, illuminated manuscripts and a collection of small arms from various parts of Europe.

The Aviary also has interesting origins. It was designed by the French architect Gabriel-Hippolyte Destailleur in 1889 in the style of the French eighteenth century. At that time there were many collections of exotic birds and mammals in the houses and châteaux of the French nobility, including the royal aviaries at Versailles. The Waddesdon Aviary, having fallen into disrepair during the Second War, was restored and modernised by the addition of hospital cages, breeding cages and a well-equipped kitchen. It was opened to the public in 1966.

The National Trust Waddesdon Manor. **Address** Waddesdon Manor, Aylesbury. **Telephone** Waddesdon 211. **Open** 14.00–18.00 last Wed in March to last Sun in Oct, 11.00–18.00 bank holidays. **Guide-book. Catering** teas only. **Acreage** 160. **Cars** 6 mls n.w. of Aylesbury on A41 Bicester road. **Bus** Red Rover 1, 15 from Aylesbury to Waddesdon Village except Sun. **Train** to Aylesbury (6 mls). **Taxis** available. Public **not allowed** to feed animals.

Wellplace Bird Farm

There are over 100 species of bird here, with a total of 600 specimens, but you can also see about 60 mammals, including foxes, badgers, otters, Raccoons, squirrels, monkeys, deer, Llamas, and some domestic farm animals. The bird collection includes rheas, cranes, flamingos, penguins, pelicans, parrots and related species, finches, soft-billed birds, pheasants, peafowl and waterfowl. There is also a small collection of fish. The Bird Farm was opened in 1968 by Mr L. G. Holtom.

Wellplace Bird Farm. **Address** Ipsden, Oxon. **Telephone** Checkendon 680473. **Open** 10.00–18.30 Sat and Sun, 13.30–17.30 weekdays summer, 13.30–dusk Sat and Sun winter. **Catering** kiosk, tea gardens. **Acreage** 5. **Car** 4 mls s.e. of Wallingford, off A4074, turn off at Whitehouse Inn and continue for 2 mls. **Bus** to Whitehouse Inn. **Train** to Goring and Streatley (5 mls). **Other facilities** children's playground. Public allowed to feed animals with food prepared and sold at Farm only.

Whipsnade Park Zoo

Whipsnade Park Zoo is one of the major collections of large animals in the country and it has always specialised in herd animals. You can see 2,000 animals here, of which half are large mammals, nearly all in spacious moated paddocks. Many species exhibited here are rare in the wild, such as the Kodiak Bear from the offshore islands off Alaska, the Sumatran Tiger, the Cheetah, Przewalski's Wild Horse from the steppes of Asia, the Onager, a race of Asiatic Wild Ass, the Barasingha or Swamp Deer, the Formosan Sika Deer and the Musk Ox. Kodiak Bears are the largest carnivorous land animals in the world, weighing up to a ton and standing 11 feet high. They are one of the most dangerous of all wild animals, attacking man without provocation, and they live in the wild on

Whipsnade Park Zoo. **Address** Zoological Society of London, Whipsnade Park Zoo, Dunstable, Beds. **Telephone** Whipsnade 872171. **Open** 10.00–19.00 summer, 10.00–sunset winter. **Guide-book. Catering** licensed premises, self-service cafeteria, kiosks. Zoo shop. **Guided tours** under a formal education programme. **Acreage** 500. **Car** 3 mls off M1, exit 9 from London. **Bus** Greenline (London Country) 712, 713, local 43, 62. **Train** to Luton (8 mls). **Taxis** available. Public **not allowed** to feed animals.

many kinds of food, being specially fond of salmon, which they scoop out of the rivers with great dexterity. Whipsnade exhibits both the Indian and the Sumatran races of Tiger, the latter being smaller, and darker in colour. Tigers do not breed as readily as Lions in captivity, but here, in nearly natural conditions, more than 40 cubs have been bred.

The herd species of hoofed animals in which Whipsnade specialises, include some which are now extinct, or nearly so, in the wild. The Przewalski's Horse, a wild horse from northern Asia, was once common on the plains of Mongolia and the arid Gobi Desert, but no wild specimens have been sighted for many years and it will probably not survive as a wild species. These horses first came to England in 1901, and the London Zoo received its first pair from the Duke of Bedford, who established a small herd at Woburn. Whipsnade received its first animals from Woburn, though the present stock is descended from horses bred in Prague Zoo. The Père David's Deer, a species of swamp deer from China, is extinct in the wild. They were discovered in 1865 by Père David, a French missionary, in the Imperial Hunting Park outside Peking. A few were imported to Europe before the remaining wild specimens were killed in the Boxer Rebellion in 1900. The eleventh Duke of Bedford bought the animals in European zoos and built up his herd at Woburn, from which the Whipsnade stock originated. This deer is unlike other species in having backward-pointing tines in the male's antlers, unusually broad feet and a long tail. It breeds regularly at Whipsnade, and two pairs were sent to the Peking Zoo in 1973.

Other rare hoofed animals here are the Barasingha, a large species of swamp deer of northern and central India and Assam, and the Formosan race of the Sika Deer. Another animal rarely seen in European zoos is the Musk Ox, distinguished by its long, shaggy coat and spreading horns. Only distantly related to sheep and cattle, the Musk Ox is found on the Arctic tundra, where it is now rare. The bulls have a musk gland on the face and they are immensely strong, as you can guess by the heavy-duty fencing round their paddock. The European Bison is another animal here which no longer exists in the wild. Fifty years ago it nearly became extinct in the forests of Europe, but it has since been protected in reserves, especially in Poland, and it can be seen in a number of European zoos. This is a browsing animal, at home in forests. You can also see the Onager, a race of Asiatic Wild Ass, noted for its speed and stamina. Several races are known, the Onager coming from Persia, where it is now protected.

Three of the five species of rhinoceros can be seen at Whipsnade, the Black, White and the Indian. The Black Rhino, commoner than the White, is from Africa. It browses on acacia bushes and is aggressive by nature. One has been born here. The White Rhino, the other African species, is much rarer, and unlike the Black Rhino, it lives in family groups on grassland. It is larger, inoffensive and has a large hump above the shoulders. The Whipsnade White Rhinos are the southern race from Natal, another much rarer race being found west of the Nile, in Uganda, the Congo and the Sudan. At the beginning of this century, White Rhinos were nearly extinct in South Africa, and by the 1920s only 30 remained. Thanks to protection in game reserves, numbers increased to about 1,500 and the reserves were faced with over-population, so that it became necessary to send surplus animals to reserves in other parts of Africa. In 1970 Whipsnade imported 20 White Rhinos from Natal to establish the first breeding herd in Europe. The first calf was born in 1971, followed by two more in 1973 and three in 1974.

Another success story is the breeding of Indian Rhinos here. The Indian Rhino is the largest of the three Asiatic species, and only about 400 remain in the wild. It comes from Assam, Bengal and Nepal. It has only one horn, and it has been ruthlessly hunted, the horn being much in demand for its supposed medicinal value, especially as an aphrodisiac. Very few Indian Rhinos can be seen in zoos, and the first to be bred in captivity was in 1956 in Basle. A calf was born at Whipsnade in 1957, and these two calves, of opposite sexes, later went to Milwaukee Zoo. Since then, both Basle and Whipsnade have bred two calves.

More than 80% of the Whipsnade mammals have been bred in the Park and amongst them are several breeding achievements. The first White-tailed Deer,

White Rhinoceroses at Whipsnade.

the first Moose and the first Snow Leopards to be bred in this country were born here in 1959. In 1957, Whipsnade bred the first Warthog in Britain, an animal which is now rarely seen in zoos, and in 1967, the first Cheetah cubs to be bred in Britain were born. Cheetahs are the most difficult of the cat family to breed in captivity, and very few zoos have achieved it. Whipsnade's pair, Juanita and Jack, have now bred and reared four litters, which has not been achieved by any other zoo in the world. The female cub, Janica, born in 1968, has now bred herself, and this is the first time that a Cheetah has been born of captive-bred parents anywhere in the world. Whipsnade's success is owed to the fact that the male and female are kept apart until the female comes into breeding condition. The clue to this is the interest displayed by the male, who is kept in an adjoining enclosure, and the two are then put together. The latest litter produced five cubs, and other zoos have benefited from the lessons learnt in this successful breeding programme.

Other species which breed regularly here include the Red-necked Wallaby, the Northern Lynx, the Mountain Zebra, European Reindeer and Thomson's Gazelle. A herd of this graceful East African antelope has been built up over many years, and it is the largest herd of this species in Europe. You can also see Hippopotamuses, which have bred many calves here, and next to them the much rarer Pygmy Hippopotamus, a much smaller and more solitary animal, found only in a few small areas in West Africa.

The bird collection at Whipsnade also contains some rarities. Probably the rarest bird here is the Manchurian Crane, which is both rare in the wild state and very unusual in zoos. There are many species of swan, duck and goose, and notice especially the Cereopsis or Cape Barren Goose of southern Australia, which nests here in winter; and the beautiful little Red-breasted Goose, a Siberian breeder which winters in Asia, and which is rare in the wild but breeds regularly here. Three species of flamingo are exhibited, the Rosy, a Caribbean species, the Chilean, from the cooler latitudes of South America, and the Greater Flamingo, which breeds in southern Europe, Africa and Asia. So far, only the Rosy Flamingo has bred at Whipsnade. You will also see three kinds of penguin including the King Penguin from Antarctica, the South African Black-footed, and Humboldt's Penguin from western South America. All the large flightless birds, the Ostrich, which is the largest, from Africa, the Emu from Australia, and its South American equivalent, the rhea, have bred here, the rheas breeding regularly each year.

The Park's latest major attraction is the Water Mammals Exhibit, which has a group of Bottle-nosed Dolphins from the Gulf of Mexico, which arrived in 1972. There is a large outdoor pool where shows are given, an indoor pool where the dolphins can be seen swimming under water, and a third pool, used for quarantine. The water is circulated through filters, giving a complete change of water every three hours. The three pools hold 130,000 gallons of water, kept at a temperature of 70°F, and you can see the pumping plant and filters opposite the indoor pool.

There is a children's zoo and farm where young animals can be handled, and you should not miss the Umfolozi railway which runs through several enclosures, including the White Rhinos' paddock.

The Whipsnade estate was bought by the Zoological Society of London in 1927, but because of legal difficulties it was necessary for a special Act of Parliament to be passed (The Zoological Society of London Act 1928) before the farm could be developed into a zoo. It was believed — correctly as it turned out — that tropical animals could become acclimatised to fresh air, and would do better than if they were kept in a hot-house atmosphere in London. The idea of an open-air zoo was completely new at the time, and Whipsnade was the first exhibition of its kind in the world when it was opened in 1931. The original idea was to provide a rest centre for some of the animals at Regent's Park, and although this was later abandoned as a regular policy, animals are transferred from Regent's Park when needed for breeding purposes. But the main purpose has been to provide plenty of space for herd animals and thus to enable them to breed. Most herd animals will not breed if kept in pairs or small groups, and the ability to show large groups of herd species has resulted in regular breeding which is impossible in the confined space of an urban zoo.

Until recently, Whipsnade has been essentially a farm with animal enclosures, as well as large numbers of wallabies, Muntjacs, and Chinese Water Deer which breed and live free in the Park. The latest development has been to group some of the animals geographically, and you can now see an Asian exhibit containing Bactrian-Camels, Onagers, Przewalski's Horses and Père David's Deer, and an African area next to the White Rhinoceroses, with zebras and Eland Antelopes. Many of the older enclosures are still among the most attractive to be seen in the country; do not miss the Chimpanzees, the European Brown Bear exhibit, the Lion and Tiger enclosures and the Wolf Wood. The Elephant Paddock now contains a young male African Elephant, the first male to be shown here for many years. Male elephants are dangerous when they reach maturity, and special handling facilities had to be installed before his arrival. He has settled down well with the five African and Indian females, but it will be some years before breeding can be expected.

Whipsnade offers enormous variety and interest in an attractive English setting with many fine trees, flowering shrubs and herbaceous borders. It was the first 'drive-in' zoo in the world, and except on the busiest days, when a one-way system has to be operated, you can drive round the Park at will, get out and walk wherever you wish, and see in every direction a vista of some splendid herd of animals grazing peacefully.

Woburn Wild Animal Kingdom

Woburn Wild Animal Kingdom is a safari park, opened in 1970 by the Duke of Bedford and Mr Jimmy Chipperfield. Woburn Park is the largest private park in the British Isles and the wild animal reserve occupies 350 acres, with ten miles of road through it. The Park specialises in large animals, mostly from Africa, and there are more than 400 here altogether. The dangerous species, Lions, Tigers, bears and Rhesus Monkeys, are enclosed in drive-through paddocks controlled by gates and park wardens. All the animals here are used to vehicles and will ignore them as long as car windows are kept closed.

There are several dozens of Lions, consisting of groups of males, females and their cubs, and these have considerable curiosity value since several large males are present in each group, a situation which does not normally occur in the wild. Wild Lions live in family groups, usually consisting of an adult male, several females, and cubs ranging in age from infants up to about two years old. Wandering males from outside the pride will be fought by the resident male, and such encounters are liable to end in the death of one or the other: this is because each pride has its own territory, containing herds of zebra or antelope which it kills for food. In a safari park, where food is supplied by man, there is no competition for food so there is less motive for fighting, although territorial squabbles cannot be entirely eliminated. In the wild all the hunting is done by the lionesses, the male Lions only appearing at a kill in order to eat, while the females and cubs wait patiently until the male has had his fill. Lionesses help each other to look after the cubs, and when a mother goes hunting she will leave her cubs with another female. Very young cubs are hidden in the bush by their mothers during the day and brought out in the evening. Lions are the only members of the cat family to be born with their eyes open. In captivity they live for up to 20 years, though in the wild their life span is probably several years less. Recent observations have shown that Lions in the wild spend 20 hours a day sleeping or resting.

Tigers are quite different from Lions in their family life. Adult animals only remain together during the breeding season, and the cubs stay with their mother until they are two or three years old. Adult males spend most of their time alone, often covering many miles on hunting expeditions. Like Lions, they only become dangerous to man when old or injured and incapable of killing wild game; they then turn to domestic cattle or human victims, which are easy to catch. Tigers

Woburn Wild Animal Kingdom. **Address** Woburn, Bedfordshire. **Telephone** Woburn 246. **Open** 10.00–18.00 summer, 10.00–dusk winter. **Catering** licensed restaurant, self-service cafeteria, snack bar, kiosk. Zoo shop and information centre. **Acreage** 500. **Car** 4 mls s. of M1/A5140 junction (13), off A5 between Woburn Sands and Dunstable. **Train** to Flitwick (5 mls) or Bletchley (8 mls). **Taxis** available. **Other facilities** dolphinarium, cabin lift, boating lakes. Public **not allowed** to feed animals.

Tigers at Woburn; adults remain to-gether only during the breeding season. Like Lions, they do not associate cars with people: so long as visitors remain in their vehicles (with the windows closed), there is no danger from the big cats.

love water and they will swim for pleasure. Like Lions, they kill about twice a week, gorging themselves and resting until roused again by hunger. An adult Tiger in the wild can eat 30 lb. of meat at one meal, although in zoos they are fed from 10 to 15 lb. of meat daily on six days a week, the seventh being a starvation day. The diet in captivity is varied with chickens and Rabbits, and vitamin supplements are given.

The drive-through paddocks also exhibit bears and Rhesus Monkeys. This monkey is common in India, although for several years past it has been exported in very large numbers to Europe and America for experimental purposes in medical research laboratories. This was the animal used in medical research to determine human blood groups: hence the term 'rhesus factor'.

You can also see herds of Bactrian Camels, bison, buffalo, native cattle, Eland, gnu, Yaks and Llamas.

The Bactrian or Two-humped Camel is now very rare as a wild animal, but it has been used as a beast of burden for centuries in northern Asia. The Yak, from Tibet, is also a traditional pack animal, and it is used for transport in other parts of Asia. It can breed with domestic cattle, and the domesticated form is smaller, often with colour variations. You can also see the African Buffalo, which is an exceedingly dangerous animal in the wild if disturbed, and the handsome Ankole Cattle, the domestic breed herded by the Watussi tribe of Uganda. The Eland is the largest of the African antelopes, and it can survive prolonged periods of drought owing to its preference for water-bearing shrubs; on which it browses. Because it needs large quantities of food owing to an inefficient digestive system, it absorbs enough moisture to enable it to withstand conditions which kill other species. It is farmed in several parts of South Africa, and it has been kept as a domestic animal in Russia for many years, on an experimental basis.

One of the most interesting animals exhibited here is the Bongo, a shy antelope from East Africa which is rarely seen in captivity. It is naturally timid, living in thick cover in groups of two or three. There is also a group of White Rhinoceros, which at the beginning of this century was close to extinction in South Africa. By careful conservation in Natal its numbers were increased, and it is now exported to zoos. White Rhinos are herd animals, living in small groups and browsing on shrubs and bushes. Their lips, adapted for grazing, gave rise to the Afrikaans name, meaning 'wide', and has nothing to do with the colour, which is grey.

The lake contains Hippopotamus, sealions, flamingos, and Chimpanzees on an island. To see these you must take the cabin lift in order to catch the safari boat. The only small animals exhibited are otters, Raccoons and squirrel monkeys, besides those to be seen in the Pets' Corner. There are also cranes and Ostriches, and a dolphinarium.

The Woburn Abbey Deer Park, opened to the public in 1955 and to which admission is separate, contains the herd of Père David's Deer established by the eleventh Duke of Bedford in 1895. This swamp deer from China, with its slanting eyes, is curious because the tines of the stag's antlers point backwards instead of forward, and because of its very long tail with a tuft of hair at the end. A herd of these deer was kept in the Imperial Hunting Park outside Peking, but when the Imperial Palace was sacked in 1894, the starving peasants killed all the animals for food. The remaining wild specimens were killed during the Boxer Rebellion in 1900. Fortunately, the eleventh Duke collected all the animals which had been sent to European zoos, and these formed the nucleus of the Woburn herd, which now stands at 300 animals. He sent small numbers for breeding purposes to several zoos in Europe and America, and without his foresight the species would almost certainly have become extinct. The deer owes its name to Père Armand David, a French missionary who first saw the Peking herd in 1865. The Deer Park also contains herds of black, white and the normal spotted Fallow Deer. Fallow Deer have been popular for centuries in private English parks, and they are found wild in many parts of the country. To come upon these two unusual colour phases as well as the spotted variety, running together, is a unique sight.

Visit also Woburn Abbey.

East Anglia ERIC DUFFEY

The wide, flat lands of East Anglia, with few hills and no rocky outcrops, may seem at first a rather unexciting landscape, but in fact no other part of England has had a more varied history since Neolithic man some 4,000–5,000 years ago. Although man has moulded and changed this countryside, particularly during the last 200 years, with inevitable losses of wildlife, these have been less than elsewhere in southern England, and we shall see that in other ways man has added greatly to its rich natural heritage.

On the northwest side the region is bounded by the great Fenland Basin of Cambridgeshire and Lincolnshire, where the long straight roads pass through

Eric Duffey was formerly the Nature Conservancy's Regional Officer in East Anglia. In 1962 he became head of a team of grassland ecologists at the Monks Wood Experimental Station, and is concerned with scientific research on wildlife management with the Institute of Terrestrial Ecology. He edits *Biological Conservation*, and has written several books.

some of the finest agricultural land in Britain, dark soils of peat or silt; a prairie landscape without hedge or tree. The brightness of the skies in this flattest of landscapes will delight travellers and remind them of the same horizons in the Dutch polders. But it is likely that most will hurry on to the Broads or coastline, forgetting that areas of great wildlife interest still survive round about.

If they have time to explore, they will find the famous Wicken Fen 12 miles north of Cambridge; and just below the edge of the clay upland lie the Wood-walton and Holme Fens NNRs, green oases surrounded by intensively cultivated farms. Along the rivers Nene and Ouse they will see the remarkable Washlands, which since the sixteenth century have been used for containing flood-water pumped from adjacent fields. The land has probably not been cultivated for a very long period, and has developed a rich pasture for cattle-ranching which is also a splendid habitat for aquatic birds. Today the Washlands fulfil another

View of part of Wicken Fen over the flat fenland landscape of the Isle of Ely, Cambridgeshire.

REFERENCE

Safari Park.....................

Zoo..............................

Bird Collection................

Aquarium........................

Dolphinarium...................

Farm Park.......................

Forest Nature Reserve......

National Nature Reserve....

Other Nature Reserve.....

National Trust.................

National and Forest Parks

10   5   0   10   20 MILES

10   5   0   10   20   30 KILOMETRES

NORTH

SEA

LINCOLN HEATH

Lincoln

Grantham

Boston

TF

TG

THE WASH

Welland

Scolt Head Island   Holkham Bay   Holkham

Holme Dunes   Titchwell   Brancaster   Wells-next-the-Sea   Cley Marshes   Beeston Regis Heath

Hunstanton   Kelling Park Aviaries   Cromer   Cromer Zoo

THE MARSH

Snettisham

Sandringham

Roydon Common   Lenwade Water   Barton Broad   Horsey

King's Lynn   Norfolk Wildlife Park   NORFOLK

Wisbech   East Winch Common   NORWICH   BROADS   Great Yarmouth

Swaffham   Strumpshaw Fen   Yarmouth Roads

Great Ouse

THE FENS   Downham Market   Hardley Flood   Lowestoft   Lowestoft Ness

Peakirk   Nene

Castor Hanglands   Thorney Wildlife Park   Welney Wildfowl Refuge   Waveney

Peterborough   East Wretham Heath   Banham Zoo   Suffolk Wild Life Park

Ouse Washes   Thetford Chase   Halesworth

Woodwalton Fen   ISLE OF ELY   Thetford   Kilverstone Wildlife Park   Diss

Rosswell Pits Ely   Dunwich Heath

Huntingdon   Ouse   Wicken Fen   Minsmere

Cam   Bury St Edmunds   Leiston

Grafham Water   TL   Newmarket   Ickworth   TM

St Neots Common   Cambridge   Bradfield Wood   Stowmarket   THE SANDLINGS   Alde

Nene   Wolves Wood   Ipswich   Havergate Island

EAST ANGLIAN HEIGHTS   Hollesley Bay

Bedford   Deben

Ouse   New Linton Zoo   Orwell

Stour   Sudbury   Stour

Saffron Walden   Harwich

Cam   Colne   THE NAZE

Luton   Mole Hall Wildlife Park   Colchester Zoo   Colchester

Bishops Stortford   Hatfield Forest   Braintree   Abberton Reservoir   Fingringhoe Wick

Lea   ST ALBANS   Colne   Clacton-on-Sea   Clacton Pier Dolphinarium

St Albans   THE RODINGS   Colne Point

VALE OF ST ALBANS   Harlow   Blakes Wood   Mersea Is   Blackwater

Chelmsford   Danbury and Lingwood Commons

EPPING FOREST   Crouch   Foulness Point   Foulness Is

Watford   Epping Forest   Brentwood   Roach   Maplin Sands

Chigwell   Basildon   Belfairs Great Wood

Aquatels Zoo   Vange Zoo   Southend Dolphinarium

GREATER LONDON   Leigh   Southend-on-Sea

SU   Thames   TQ   Thames Estuary   TR

Gravesend   ISLE OF SHEPPEY   Ramsgate

purpose apart from beef production and a safety valve in times of flood; they give protection to large numbers of geese, swans and wild ducks which shelter and feed there in the winter, and have enabled two rare breeding birds, the Ruff and Black-tailed Godwit, to re-establish themselves in this country after many years' absence.

Farther to the east, lying almost centrally in East Anglia across the border of southwest Norfolk and northwest Suffolk, are the light sandy soils of Breckland. The region covers 250 square miles and owes its distinctive character to deposits derived from glacial material overlying chalky rocks, and to a continental type of climate with low rainfall, cold winters and warm summers. In the early nineteenth century this was one of the few remaining haunts of the Great Bustard, and even today it is the stronghold of birds such as the Stone Curlew, which, like the Great Bustard, prefer dry open heaths with sparse vegetation. Breckland was regarded as a desolate area 300 years ago, almost a waste where little of value could be grown because the soils were so poor. The sand was easily disturbed and blown away by the wind, creating drifting inland dunes in some places.

For centuries the grasslands and heaths were used for grazing sheep — a special breed, the Norfolk Horn, able to live on the poor pasture and even to eat lichens, which most other sheep would find unpalatable. Beginning in the thirteenth century, and for many years afterwards, several large Rabbit warrens were created, a form of land management which, because of the continuous nibbling of these animals, had a profound effect on the vegetation. In some areas the sand is deep, poor in plant nutrients and rather acid because of the leaching effect of rain, so that a good deal of heather grows. Elsewhere the sand is shallower and is often mixed with underlying fragments of the chalk bedrock, making a much more calcareous soil. In these areas we find some of the many rare plants of Breckland, such as the spiked speedwell, maiden pink and Spanish catchfly.

Today you may well motor through the Breckland with scarcely a glimpse of heath because only fragments remain, but no other landscape has the characteristic lines of pine wind-breaks separating the fields, originally planted to prevent sand-blow. The impression is of cultivated land or dark coniferous forests. Extensive planting first began in the 1920s during a period of agricultural depression, the main purpose being to produce a supply of pit-props for the coal-mines. Today a very large part of Breckland — around 51,600 acres — is covered by plantations, forming one of the most extensive man-made forests in Britain. This has greatly changed the fauna in many ways, causing some heath-loving birds to disappear and allowing other animals such as deer to move in and increase as cover became available.

If we look at the map of East Anglia we will see a collection of over 40 lakes in the river valleys of the eastern part of north Norfolk — the famous Norfolk Broads. Thousands of people enjoy boating holidays on these waterways every year, including many who perhaps are not aware of their very great interest to the naturalist and conservationist. There is no doubt that the Broadland river fens are together the richest and finest example of the surviving freshwater marshes in this country. But the wildlife — exciting bird-watching, rare plants and insects and superb fishing — is not the only interest. The origin of the Broads is, in fact, so astonishing that many people at first find it hard to believe. Recent research has shown that they are enormous peat-cuttings, and not natural waterways at all. Before the early Middle Ages the few woods in this part of Norfolk could not supply the local people with sufficient fuel, so they depended on the large deposits of peat in the river valleys. The best peat was found at lower depths and it became the practice to excavate deep holes in the marshes alongside the rivers. In the twelfth and thirteenth centuries, however, the sea-level rose in relation to the land, and the flooding which followed gradually filled up the peat-cuttings to form the Broads.

In many places peat-cutting still went on, although the excavations were shallow. As they became flooded, plants colonised rapidly, silt and organic material accumulated, and the open water eventually disappeared. Most of the

Poppies in a barley field near Lakenheath, Suffolk: no other landscape has these characteristic lines of pine wind-breaks separating the fields.

The Broads. It is abundantly clear from recent research that the basins of the Norfolk Broads were hand cut, despite the almost incredible magnitude of the task. They have steep margins, are filled with loose muds quite unlike the material of the untouched 'ronds' adjacent, have rectangular profiles, and contain balks and islands of uncut peat reaching nearly to the present water level. The balks and straight boundaries have been found to correspond with the limits of properties shown on old tithe award maps, some strips crossing completely from one side of a broad to the other. Air photography, pollen analysis, and contemporary ecology all give evidence confirming this at first sight unlikely origin; and mediaeval church records indicate the existence of a peat-cutting industry of substantial magnitude and intensity.

H. Goodwin, Preface to *The Making of the Broads*, by J. M. Lambert, J. N. Jennings, C. T. Smith, Charles Green and J. N. Hutchinson. Royal Geographical Society Research Series No. 3, 1960.

Left: aerial view of Hickling Broad; like other broads it was formed by the subsidence and flooding of areas where peat was cut in the Middle Ages. The growth of reeds and other extensive vegetation makes them havens for wildlife.

Below: the beaver-like Coypu, which established itself in the waterways and marshes of East Anglia after escaping from local fur farms. This map of the numbers of Coypu killed in 1974 gives an idea of the animal's distribution in East Anglia; it is reproduced by courtesy of the Coypu Research Laboratory.

large Broads which remain for the enjoyment of the boating enthusiast and the naturalist were originally the deepest peat-cuttings. Before the last war most of the Broads were in private ownership and access was not easy, but today some of the finest are owned by the Norfolk Naturalists' Trust and the National Trust, including some which are National Nature Reserves. The most famous, perhaps, is Hickling Broad and Heigham Sound NNR, a very large area of shallow water which can be reached by boat from the River Thurne, and where anglers can enjoy some of the best Pike fishing in the country. Pike up to 36 lb. have been taken, and fish scaling over 20 lb. are regular.

The wide, open skies of the Broads with their glorious sunsets stretching across the horizon, their changing colours reflected in the dark waters, are amongst the most vivid memories of the visitor. But as your boat passes close to the reeds, listen for the strange sharp call of the Bearded Reedling, a very local bird characteristic of the Norfolk and Suffolk reedbeds; and during the spring and summer keep a watchful eye overhead for the Marsh Harrier, which in recent years has regrettably become irregular as a breeding species. In May you have a good chance of seeing Spoonbills at Hickling, while Black Terns are regular on passage, together with Ruffs, godwits, Redshanks and other waders. Nearby at Horsey Mere — another fine area for birds — and in the valleys of the rivers Bure and Ant there are several outstanding marshes, particularly Woodbastwick, Ranworth and Barton. At Hoveton Broad a fascinating nature trail has been laid out, which has the added attraction that it can only be reached by boat.

The Norfolk Broads are also known for that peculiar introduced animal, the Coypu or Nutria, a native of South America about the size of a Beaver. This creature was brought to Britain in the 1930s for breeding in fur farms but several managed to escape about the beginning of the Second War and rapidly found the waterways and marshes much to their liking. They increased greatly and in 1962 there were estimated to be 200,000. They began to destroy large areas of aquatic vegetation and damaged the flood-protection banks surrounding the Broads. They were also accused of disturbing some of the rarer breeding birds and of raiding the potato and sugar-beet fields in winter. Active control measures had little effect until the hard winter of 1962–63; then the Coypus suffered frost-bite on feet and tail, and died from eating frozen vegetation. Their numbers fell dramatically and by the summer of 1963 very few remained. A big effort was made to eliminate them, and although this was not successful, vigilance on the part of farmers and Ministry of Agriculture pest-control operators has kept the numbers at a low level. Nevertheless, the long succession of mild winters since

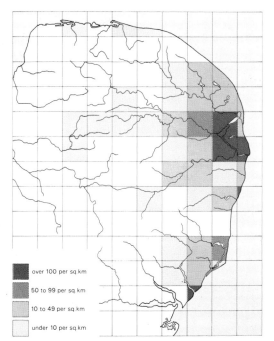

over 100 per sq.km

50 to 99 per sq.km

10 to 49 per sq.km

under 10 per sq.km

1963 may well enable the Coypu to increase, and perhaps spread to other parts of the country where it could do even more damage than it did in the Broads.

A second region of marshes and waterways bearing the name Broads is situated close to the coast in east Suffolk, but the total area of open water is relatively small and none of the Broads is accessible by boat from nearby rivers, so there is no tourist traffic. The best known of the other east Suffolk marshes is the Minsmere reserve where the RSPB has been very successful in protecting the Avocet and other rare marshland birds. Not far away, just south of the town of Southwold, lies a similar site, the Walberswick Marshes NNR. These splendid areas of reed-swamp and shallow lagoons are of recent origin and owe their creation to man, because prior to the last war, and probably for centuries before, they were drained cattle-grazed meadows. In the early 1940s they were deliberately flooded with seawater to prevent landings by enemy aircraft. Afterwards the enormous cost precluded reclamation, and as the water became less salty, reedbeds spread over extensive areas so that today Bitterns, Marsh Harriers, Bearded Reedlings and even the rare Savi's and Cetti's Warblers can be seen or heard. This magnificent landscape of marshes fringed by heath and forest makes it possible to recapture the atmosphere of a natural wilderness more easily than, perhaps, anywhere else in lowland England.

The Royal Society for the Protection of Birds' reserve at Minsmere, a carefully managed and versatile wetland.

Just inland from the east Suffolk marshes is another sandy region rather different from the Breckland because the soils, although of glacial origin, are not calcareous. These are the Suffolk Sandlings, extending from the River Deben to the River Blyth and consisting mainly of heather and grassy heaths. In the past they were used as sheep-walks and the type of farming was probably similar to that in Breckland. Several man-made coniferous forests dominate the landscape, some quite diverse and interesting and well worth a visit. For instance, in Dunwich Forest there are well-established herds of Red Deer which you can quite often see if you are energetic enough to take an early morning stroll along the woodland rides. The forests of Suffolk Sandlings and the Breckland also have the distinction of providing a home for the Red Squirrel, now very scarce in lowland England. This attractive native is better adapted to coniferous trees than the introduced Grey Squirrel which has replaced it over much of England, and the plantations of Norfolk and Suffolk have undoubtedly enabled it to hold its own and have slowed down the spread of the American intruder.

In spite of the fascination of heaths and marshes, many people still find the greatest pleasure in the East Anglian coastline. Certainly the region can claim to have one of the largest tracts of unspoilt coast anywhere in the southern half of England. Sand-dunes have a natural attraction for people who love the sea, but whereas on the south coast of England very few are free from development, Norfolk still has many miles of unspoilt dunes which are protected for their wildlife and scenery, and are yet accessible for public enjoyment. The greater part of the 34 miles from Holme to Cley, including Scolt Head Island NNR, Holkham and Blakeney Point nature reserves, is now protected either by the National Trust, Nature Conservancy Council, Royal Society for the Protection of Birds, or Norfolk Naturalists' Trust. The miles of dunes and saltmarshes are among the finest sights on the British coast, and are interesting and exciting places for seabirds and passage migrants.

Scolt Head Island NNR has one of the largest and most important breeding colonies of Sandwich Terns in the country, while the Holme and Cley Bird Observatories are probably the best observation sites on the east coast for migratory and wintering birds. Farther to the south there is Winterton Dunes NNR, and although a holiday camp on the south side means that it is frequented by a great number of people, there are still large areas which are scenically and biologically of very great interest. Dune systems are rather scarce on the coast of East Suffolk, partly because there is more shingle than sand but also because many areas are being eroded by the sea. Nevertheless, accretion is taking place

Scolt Head Island National Nature Reserve has one of the most important breeding colonies of Sandwich Terns in Britain.

Norfolk Horn Sheep. These hardy animals were often driven over 100 miles to London's Smithfield Market. Their flesh was valued for its flavour but, before the sixteenth century, sheep were kept primarily for their milk and wool. The milk was made into cheese and the old English name for a sheep dairy, 'wich', is remembered in the place-names Norwich and Ipswich. When mutton became important, quicker fattening breeds replaced the Norfolk Horn (a cross between it and the Southdown produced the modern Suffolk), and in 1968 the few remaining animals were moved to the National Agricultural Centre at Stoneleigh.

in some places and the best example is the magnificent shingle spit which runs south from Orfordness and forms part of the Orfordness-Havergate NNR. Shingle spits do not usually attract the same range of bird-life as sand-dunes, but both Little and Common Terns breed at Orford Beach.

The dunes of the Norfolk coast and the shingle banks of Suffolk are characteristic features of this coast, but there are also fine saltmarshes and mud-flats, particularly on the Norfolk side of the Wash. However, we find the best examples of such wildfowl habitats farther south along the sunken coastline of Essex, particularly at Hamford Water near Felixstowe, the Blackwater estuary, and south to Foulness and the much-publicised Maplin Sands. Inland are the great reservoirs of Abberton and Hanningfield, which also play a vital role as refuges for large numbers of ducks, including the scarce Red-crested Pochard. This vast complex of waterways, saltings, mud-flats and marshes is regarded by ornithologists and wildfowlers as one of the most important in Britain and has an enormous winter population of water birds. The Essex coast can claim the largest flocks of wintering Dark-bellied Brent Geese, from Novaya Zemlya and northern Siberia, now numbering about 40,000 and forming the greater part of the European population.

FENS AND WATERWAYS

Each of the three distinct groups of fens and waterways in Cambridgeshire, Norfolk and Suffolk has its own appeal, and together they can provide a long list of interesting birds. Cambridge is a pleasant city at which to begin a tour and is only half-an-hour's drive from Wicken Fen (NT). Its 640 acres include extensive sedge and reedbeds as well as much bush growth, mainly of alder and buckthorn, and a small mere of open water dug some 20 years ago. The fen is rich in the smaller song-birds, particularly Reed and Sedge Warblers, Blackcap, Garden Warbler, Nightingale, Willow and Grasshopper Warblers. Since the mere was dug, Little and Great Crested Grebes, Mallard, Shoveler, Tufted Duck and Pochard have become breeding species, and each winter Bearded Reedlings and Bitterns are recorded. Woodwalton Fen NNR, between Huntingdon and Peterborough, is more wooded than Wicken Fen, but also has reedbeds and a small recently completed mere in which the water has yet to reach its full level. The bird-life is similar but the Mallard is the only breeding duck, because waterside cover has not yet developed. Nevertheless, in 1974 an Osprey took up residence for three weeks, so the bird-watcher should always be ready for surprises.

A Little Tern settles on to its eggs, laid in a scantily lined scrape on the seashore; sensitive to the least disturbance, this tern's breeding performance is monitored and protected by local and national organisations.

Woodwalton Fen (left) where part of a bed of Phragmites *can be seen; this reed is the preferred nesting site for the Reed Warbler, seen (right) returning with food for its young.*

There have been no large stretches of open water in the vast fenland basin since 1851, when the 1,500 acres of Whittlesey Mere, lying adjacent to the present Holme Fen NNR, were drained. Everywhere is now rich farmland, and Holme Fen is a relatively dry birch wood. However, not far to the west, just on the clay upland eight miles from Huntingdon, is the Grafham Water Reservoir, 1,500 acres in area and filled to its present level since early 1966. The western shore is a nature reserve and there are parking areas and public footpaths for visitors. Many thousands of gulls roost there in winter and it has become an important feeding refuge for large numbers of ducks, Coots, Moorhens, grebes and waders. It is also a breeding site for the Little Ringed Plover.

As you travel east across the Cambridge fenland you should not miss a visit to the Ouse Washes, which run alongside the New Bedford River, and where more than two square miles of water-meadows are preserved by the RSPB, Wildfowl Trust and Cambridgeshire Naturalists' Trust. A hide, available to visitors, is situated on the south side near Welches Dam. In the winter months most of the area is flooded and spectacular numbers of wildfowl can be seen, including large herds of Bewick's Swans and flocks of Pintail which may exceed 3,000. When the flood-waters disappear in the summer the cattle-grazed pastures and muddy pools make an ideal breeding and feeding habitat for many birds. Over 60 species have bred but perhaps the most interesting are the Black-tailed Godwit, first recorded in 1952 and now numbering over 40 pairs, Ruffs, which first bred in 1963 and now have about ten nests annually, and occasionally Black Terns. All three had not bred regularly in Britain for a century or more, so their presence makes the Ouse Washes a unique place.

Continuing eastwards into Norfolk there are many small scattered fens and marshes in the river valleys, and a visit to the famous Breckland meres at East

Black-tailed Godwit settles on its nest; since 1952 this bird has bred annually in increasing numbers in the Ouse Washes.

View of a typical Ruff and Black-tailed Godwit breeding area in the Ouse Washes, and (below) the extravagantly feathered male Ruff, and the more sombre Reeve (the female), sitting on her nest.

Wretham Heath (Norfolk Naturalists' Trust) north of Thetford should not be missed; though there may not be water in them, because levels vary dramatically in these strange lakes. In some years there are broad expanses of water which afford the chance of seeing Garganey and Gadwall, while at other times they are dry apart from a muddy silt lying over the sand.

The Norfolk Broads, whose centre is the small town of Wroxham, are in some ways rather frustrating to the motorist because so few of the lakes can be approached by road. But you can get a splendid view of Ranworth Broad, part of the Bure Marshes NNR, from the top of Ranworth church tower. For a more intimate acquaintance it is essential to hire a boat. Travelling downstream from Wroxham, past Wroxham Broad, you come to the Hoveton Broad NNR nature trail. Hoveton Broad is private, and is in any case too shallow except for punts, but a good view of the marshes can be obtained from the trail vantage points. Farther on, the River Ant joins the Bure from the north and a detour should be made to the attractive reed-fringed Barton Broad (Norfolk Naturalists' Trust). Barton is a good place to see and hear the Bittern, whose resonant boom is such a characteristic sound of the marshes.

A second main tributary of the Bure, the River Thurne, takes you to one of the most exciting and interesting groups of waterways, Hickling and Heigham Sound NNR and Horsey Mere (NT). Both are favourite haunts of the Bittern and one of the best places to observe Bearded Reedlings and to hear their ringing metallic call-notes in summer, as your boat lies quietly among the reeds. Marsh Harriers are still seen from time to time but have not nested for several seasons. Montagu's Harrier has become even scarcer and no longer breeds in its old haunts at Hickling and Horsey. Breeding wildfowl include Tufted Duck, Pochard, Garganey, Gadwall and Shelduck, while in the woods are Long-eared and Barn Owls and three heronries.

Shallow water lagoons and wet meadows, particularly at Hickling, attract interesting wading birds during migration. Spoonbills are seen almost every year, while Ruffs, Black-tailed Godwits, Avocets and Black Terns are regular visitors. It comes as a surprise to the newcomer to find Common Terns nesting in the Broads, but a few do breed on Rush Hills at Hickling and there are over 50 pairs at Ranworth Broad, where rafts have been moored in open water to give them nesting sites.

Walberswick Marshes NNR, surrounded by bracken and heather-covered heath, lies on the south side of the Blyth estuary. The whole complex of over 1,200 acres of tidal mudflats, heath, woods, reedbeds and shallow freshwater lagoons forms one of the most eye-catching landscapes of southern England and attracts the artist as much as the naturalist. A hide for bird-watchers has been built by the Nature Conservancy Council on the marshes overlooking the mudflats of the Blyth and is open to all. All the Broadland reedbed birds can be seen and, in addition, the rare Savi's Warbler, which has a monotonous reeling song often preceded by low ticking notes. Wildfowl and waders visit the lagoons and mudflats where flocks of shore birds, especially Shelducks, can be seen easily from the footpath which follows the old narrow-gauge Blythburgh–Southwold railway line.

To the south, the heathland is hidden by the coniferous plantations of Dunwich Forest but the trees give way to the heather slopes of Westleton Heath NNR. Beyond the village, winding below the cut-back gravel terraces of Westleton Walks, flows the Minsmere River. A mile and a half from the coast it enters a wide, flat valley, formerly cattle pasture but now reverted to reed-swamps and pools by flooding. This is the famous Minsmere reserve of the RSPB. The total area of 1,500 acres has four main habitats – oakwood, sea-shore, heath and reed-swamp. Hides have been erected at selected points (including a public one by the shore) where visitors can watch Bitterns, Marsh Harriers, Avocets, Shelducks, Bearded Reedlings and the many waders, terns and ducks which come to rest and feed. Unlike the Norfolk Broads, Minsmere and nearby sites still have breeding harriers, both Marsh and sometimes Montagu's. A day at Minsmere is a day to remember, but cannot be enjoyed without a prior booking, so great is the demand.

The graceful Avocet is the symbol of the Royal Society for the Protection of Birds, who were largely responsible for its recolonisation of East Anglia since 1947.

Two famous and rare breeding birds of Minsmere: below, Bittern at its nest in the reeds; bottom, the female Marsh Harrier at a rather drier site.

145

SALTINGS, SHINGLE BANKS AND SAND-DUNES

We have already seen that the most extensive saltmarshes lie along the estuaries and inlets of the Essex coast, but bird-watching may be difficult because there are few roads. However, the new Leigh NNR on the north side of the Thames estuary between Southend and Canvey Island is probably the most readily approached. It consists of 643 acres of saltmarsh and mudflats on part of Two Tree Island. It is now an important feeding ground for Dark-bellied Brent Geese, but many other shore birds such as Curlew, Dunlin, Redshank, Grey Plover, Knot, Turnstone and Ringed Plover can be seen, especially during the migration months and in the winter.

Another island, Havergate (RSPB), is part of the Orfordness-Havergate NNR, and is situated on the Suffolk coast 16 miles east of Ipswich. It became famous in the 1940s as the first site where Avocets bred in Britain after an absence of over 100 years. It can only be reached by boat from Orford village, by prior arrangement with the RSPB. Orford shingle beach lies opposite Havergate Island on the other side of the River Alde and extends another four miles south as far as Shingle Street. It is of great physiographical interest and is well known for rare shingle plants particularly the sea pea and yellow horned poppy, but it also has a colony of Common and Little Terns as well as breeding Redshanks, Ringed Plovers and other birds.

The most interesting dune areas for the bird-watcher are Blakeney Point (NT) and Scolt Head Island NNR on the north Norfolk coast. Both show the same range of breeding birds, the former having the larger colony of Common Terns while the latter is one of the most important British breeding stations for the Sandwich Tern. Shelducks nest commonly in Rabbit holes on the dunes, and the adjacent marshes attract many interesting waders and wildfowl.

HEATHS AND SANDLINGS

Not much more than 6,600 acres of unreclaimed heath remain in the Breck, apart from abandoned farmland in the large military training area between Thetford and Watton. Of this total about 1,000 acres are protected in nature reserves. The most characteristic heathland birds of the Breck are Stone Curlew, Wheatear, Red-backed Shrike, Stonechat, Woodlark and Ringed Plover. All have declined in recent years, either because of reclamation and tree planting

Cavenham Heath National Nature Reserve (left) in Suffolk, a varied Breckland heath where the Stone Curlew (above) breeds.

or as a result of vegetation changes following the fall in the Rabbit population after the 1954–55 outbreak of myxomatosis. This event particularly affected the Wheatear (which nests in Rabbit burrows), Woodlark and Ringed Plover, although the thicker vegetation encouraged the Common Curlew to breed. The Stonechat is now an irregular breeding bird, and the Red-backed Shrike and Woodlark are very local. The Stone Curlew and Wheatear can usually be seen from the roadside at Weeting Heath NNR and Thetford Heath NNR, but it is best not to wander over their territories during the breeding season because disturbance can result in loss of eggs. When breeding is over, the Stone Curlews collect in flocks and often advertise their presence with a 'clamour' of loud melodious wailing calls and high-pitched metallic cries.

Cavenham Heath NNR, sloping down to the River Lark east of Barton Mills, is a much more varied heath with woods, heather, grassland and fen. Wheatears are present but Stone Curlews and Woodlarks are very scarce. A Great Grey Shrike is recorded in most years in the winter months. East Wretham Heath NNR has already been mentioned in connection with its meres, but is also well known for the Crossbills which are frequently seen in the pine trees. Redstarts, Nightingales, Nightjars and Hawfinches are recorded regularly.

The Suffolk Sandlings include part of the Minsmere reserve and Westleton Heath NNR, where Stonechats and Red-backed Shrikes can be seen on the gorse and heather slopes. In the north of Norfolk, however, are several important heaths, mainly on common land; one of the finest is Roydon Common (Norfolk Naturalists' Trust), not far from King's Lynn, a breeding site for the Curlew.

WOODLANDS

East Anglia is not rich in extensive deciduous woods, although in Cambridgeshire and Suffolk particularly there are many of great antiquity which are interesting for their plants. Staverton Park and The Thicks (privately owned) is an impressive relict forest with ancient oaks and hollies. However, since the surrounding heath was reclaimed the bird-life has lost some of its former interest, though the commoner woodland birds are still present. Many of the reserves already mentioned, such as Walberswick and Minsmere, include woods where Long-eared Owls nest and birds of prey such as Common and Rough-legged Buzzards are frequently seen in the winter.

Hayley Wood (Cambridgeshire Naturalists' Trust) is an attractive reserve

Ministry of Defence lands. The MOD owns nearly 800 sites varying in size from small-arms ranges to the 90,000 acres training area on Salisbury Plain. These properties encompass breckland, chalk downland, heath, woods, coastal cliffs, saltmarshes and sand-dunes. Some are effectively nature reserves for such rare creatures as Peregrine, Hobby, Chough, Stone Curlew, Dartford Warbler, Sand Lizard, Smooth Snake and Natterjack Toad, not to mention butterflies, dragonflies, orchids and other plants. The MOD has a Conservation Liaison Officer who works in close association with NCC, the County Trusts and other appropriate organisations.

Above: the colouration of the incubating Nightjar camouflages it in its nesting habitat.

Left: the Long-eared Owl breeds in various East Anglian woodlands.

famous for its oxlips and good for Nightingale, Blackcap, Garden Warbler and the woodpeckers. In the old county of Huntingdon, the best known of East Anglian woods is to be found in Monks Wood NNR, a profitable haunt of the entomologist for 150 years. It is said to have been one of the last nesting places for the Red Kite in England, but today its bird-life consists mainly of the familiar woodland species. A few miles to the north, Holme Fen NNR is now predominantly a birch wood and a good place to see Redstarts and Woodcocks and to hear the Nightjar. Castor Hanglands NNR, west of the expanding city of Peterborough, combines limestone grassland with dense scrub and some attractive regenerating oak/ash woodland. It has a long list of nesting birds including Long-eared Owl, Woodcock, the common warblers and the woodpeckers.

MAMMALS IN EAST ANGLIA

There are more species of mammals in the region today than for some time past, partly due to introductions and partly to the creation of suitable habitat. In the former category the best examples are Coypu and Mink, and in the latter, deer and Red Squirrel. Coypu, once again on the increase, inhabit the marshes, lakes and rivers of much of Norfolk and Suffolk and parts of the Essex coast. Their tracks, droppings and the damage to vegetation are clues worth looking for, and the animals themselves can often be seen. The Mink is so far only known along one or two Suffolk rivers, particularly the Deben. The Grey Squirrel has been making a strong bid to colonise those parts of Norfolk and Suffolk which are the natural home of the Red Squirrel. In the Suffolk Breckland two large blocks of coniferous forest have been set aside by the Forestry Commission for the conservation of the Red Squirrel. This delightful animal can also be seen in many of the wooded commons and parks of north Norfolk and in pine woods by the coastal town of Wells.

The new pine forests of Breckland and the Suffolk Sandlings have encouraged both Red and Roe Deer to increase remarkably. They are tolerated by the Forestry Commission provided they do no serious damage to the young trees. Roe Deer can often be seen elsewhere and one of the best places is Cavenham Heath NNR, where the birch scrub, fen woodland and marshes by the River Lark seem to have a special attraction for them. Fallow Deer occur in a number of private parks, notably Holkham in north Norfolk, and a wild herd is well established on the heath and in the woods of the Castor Hanglands NNR, west of Peterborough.

The Chinese Water Deer and the Muntjac Deer are two small species which have spread slowly in southern England since their escape from Woburn Park, Bedfordshire, where they were introduced between 1890 and 1900. The former is now found in several localities in the Norfolk Broads and also occurs in numbers at Woodwalton Fen NNR ten miles north of Huntingdon. It first appeared in the mid-1960s, and although it is not often seen, its tracks and droppings can be found almost everywhere. The Muntjac is much more local in East Anglia but the best chance of seeing it is perhaps in Monks Wood NNR, seven miles north of Huntingdon.

Badgers are generally scarce throughout East Anglia and none of the National Nature Reserves has permanently occupied setts. Foxes are scarce in the east but are commoner in the central and western parts and occur in most of the woodland nature reserves. The Otter has declined throughout the region in recent years, as it has elsewhere in the country.

The most familiar marine mammals are the Common and Grey Seals. The former frequents a wide stretch of the north Norfolk coast, although the Wash has the main breeding population. As many as 200 have been seen on the beach at Blakeney Point, but almost anywhere along the Norfolk coast one should look out for their characteristic dark shapes in the offshore water. The Grey Seal population is very much smaller, perhaps about 100. They breed on the Scroby Sands, producing their young in December and January. They are less frequently seen along the mainland coastline and one has a greater chance of spotting the broad 'roman' nose of this species if one takes a boat trip in the neighbourhood of the breeding colony.

After the escape of some individuals from Woburn Park in the 1960s, the Chinese Water Deer now flourishes in a wild state in several parts of East Anglia.

Scroby Sands are the East Anglian breeding headquarters of Common Seals, seen here lying out on the exposed sands in company with Grey Seals.

REPTILES, AMPHIBIANS AND SOME INVERTEBRATE ANIMALS

The rare Smooth Snake and Sand Lizard are not known in East Anglia, but the Grass Snake, Viper or Adder, Slow-worm and Common Lizard are all widespread. You should watch out for the Viper in marshy and heathy areas, especially in coastal regions. In the Broads marshes it is less common than formerly and has disappeared from places where it was abundant in the early part of the century. The Frog has also suffered a sharp decline in the western part of the region but is more widespread in Norfolk and Suffolk. The most interesting amphibian is the Natterjack Toad — known as the 'running toad' and immediately recognised by the pale yellow line down the middle of its back. Coastal dune slacks (marshy pools) are favourite sites, but it also occurs in fen ditches in some of the Broadland river valleys. Since 1930 it has disappeared from several of its former sites and many naturalists now regard it as an endangered species.

Natterjack Toad in full croak; an endangered species, this amphibian can be found at some sites in East Anglia.

It would need a large volume to describe the many interesting insects and other small creatures which make the East Anglian fauna so exciting to the biologist, and we can mention only a few. One of the best known is the Large Copper butterfly, which occurs only at Woodwalton Fen NNR and is on the wing in late June and July. In Holland it is called the 'Fire Butterfly', a name which aptly describes the brilliant bronze-coloured wings of the male.

In Britain, the Large Copper butterfly is found only at Woodwalton Fen.

The Large Marsh Grasshopper is green and brown with striking crimson and yellow legs. It is very rare in Britain but is known from five Broadland localities where there are wet fens with bog myrtle, sedges and rank grasses. It is full grown in August and September but very difficult to find amongst the dense vegetation. Three of the four British ground-hoppers also occur in the Broads, including the rare Cepero's Ground-hopper first found in this country in Surlingham Marshes in 1940. Unlike most of the grasshoppers, these species hibernate through the winter and appear as adults in the spring.

The rare Large Marsh Grasshopper is known in some broadland areas.

The Broadland marshes are particularly rich in dragonflies and the first to appear in spring is the Large Red Damselfly, followed by that powerful flyer the Hairy Dragonfly. In late May and June other equally attractive species appear over the waterways. A speciality of Broadland is the Norfolk Aeshna, its large brown body and dull wings distinguishing it from the much commoner Brown Aeshna. Many dragonflies are territorial, jealously defending their chosen waterways from rivals, and they often have clear preferences for water bodies of a certain size and depth and for different types of aquatic vegetation.

But the glory of these fenlands is undoubtedly the Swallowtail, one of the largest and perhaps the most attractive of Britain's native butterflies. It is not found outside this part of East Anglia but is still relatively plentiful there and is seen by many visitors in May and June. The Swallowtail overwinters as a pupa attached to a reed stem, suspended head down by a girdle spun the previous July or August. In the first warm sunny spell in May the butterflies emerge and search for wild flowers such as ragged robin and marsh valerian. They are strong flyers and cover considerable distances over the marshes and rivers, visiting garden blooms and other places away from the water. The eggs of the first brood are invariably laid on the milk parsley, a widespread plant in the wet fens. The young caterpillars are black with a broad band across the middle; as they grow older, they change to a bright green with black, orange-spotted rings. At this stage they are not difficult to find on the food-plant and when alarmed they erect a bright orange-coloured horn from just behind the head. Swallowtails used to occur at Wicken Fen, and it is said that they were generally smaller than those found in the Broads. At the present time an attempt is being made to re-establish a breeding colony there.

East Anglia's speciality, the Swallowtail.

Finally, there is the remarkable Raft Spider of Redgrave and Lopham Fens (Suffolk Naturalists' Trust). In body size it is one of the largest of our spiders and it is not known anywhere else in Britain. It is a rich brown colour with two pale cream stripes running along each side of the body. The patient observer will see it resting on the surface of a reedy pool, but a slight disturbance will cause it to disappear into the depths by running down the stem of a water plant. The survival of this spider is now threatened by a gradual drying-out of its habitat, and active management is needed to preserve the small shady pools where it lives.

Guide to wildlife habitats in East Anglia

This Appendix provides a selected but varied list of places of wildlife interest. It is emphasised that nature reserves exist primarily for the conservation of animals and plants and in some cases for environmental experiments and research. They are not 'public open spaces' in the recreational sense. Access to many is therefore restricted and some, because of their sensitivity to disturbance, have been omitted from this list, in deference to the wishes of conservation organisations. Even with 'open' reserves visitors are earnestly requested to keep to the paths and bridleways and so avoid damage to the habitat and undue disturbance to wildlife. *There is no public access to the enclosed farmland which is part of many National Trust properties.*

Application to visit a National Nature Reserve (NNR) should be made to the appropriate Regional Office of the Nature Conservancy Council (NCC) at the address given. Intention to visit reserves of the Royal Society for the Protection of Birds (RSPB) should be notified to the Warden (whose address is shown) as far in advance as possible. In all cases where an address is shown, it is wise to contact the Warden to avoid disappointment.

ESSEX

Abberton Reservoir TL 98 18. Waterfowl refuge and ringing station. 4 mls s. of Colchester B1026.

Belfairs Great Wood TQ 82 85. Deciduous wood in urban area. w. side of Southend-on-Sea, n. of Hadleigh and A13. Southend BC.

Blakes Wood TL 77 07. Hornbeam and sweet chestnut coppice. Hawfinches, woodpeckers. 5 mls e. of Chelmsford, n. of A414, access from Riffhams Lane, Little Baddow. NT.

Danbury and Lingwood Commons TL 78 05. Commons with birch, gorse, thorn scrub and some woodland.

Nightingales. 5 mls e. of Chelmsford, astride A414. Car park, trail. NT.

Epping Forest TQ 43 97. Remnant of Royal Forest of Essex. Hornbeam, oak, beech, birch, mixed and in pure stands, mostly coppiced or pollarded. 6000 a. (4000 a. woodland, 2000 a. open land). 'Black' Fallow Deer, Fox, Badger; Nightingale, Hawfinch. Extends from Wanstead Flats TQ 42 85 in south to the Lower Forest TL 47 03 beyond Epping in north, major part lying between Chingford and Epping in London Borough of Waltham Forest. Traversed by A11, Leytonstone–Epping. Parking, picnic places and other facilities at several points. Corporation of London.

Essex Naturalists' Trust, Fingringhoe Wick Nature Reserve, South Green Road, Fingringhoe, nr Colchester, Essex, CO5 7DN.

Fingringhoe Wick TM 04 20. Saltings and disused gravel-workings. Shore-nesting birds. 3 mls s.e. of Colchester, e. of B1025. Car park by lane opposite Fingringhoe Church. Interpretive centre, hides, trail. Essex Nats T.

Hatfield Forest TL 54 20. Remnant of ancient Royal Forest of Essex. Old coppices of oak/hornbeam with birch/hazel/elm, separated by open grassy 'chases', fine mature hornbeams in n.e., small lake and marsh in centre. 1000 a. Fallow Deer, Fox, Badger. Water Rail, Snipe, Woodcock, Hawfinch. 3 mls e. of Bishop's Stortford and 5 mls w. of Great Dunmow A120, at Takeley Street. Entrances at Bush End Gate and South Gate at Woodside Green. NT.

Leigh NNR TQ 82 85. Mudflats and saltmarsh on Two Tree Island, 634 a. Brent Geese, wildfowl, waders incl. Grey Plover, Knot, Turnstone. 4 mls s. of Rayleigh, between Southend and Canvey Island A13. Southend BC/NCC.

CAMBRIDGESHIRE

Bedfordshire and Huntingdonshire Naturalists' Trust, 23 St Cuthbert's Street, Bedford, MK40 3JR.

Cambridgeshire and Isle of Ely Naturalists' Trust, 1 Brookside, Cambridge, CB2 1JF.

Castor Hanglands NNR TF 12 01. Oolitic Limestone grassland and scrub, with oak/ash woodland, 221 a. Fallow Deer. 5 mls n.w. of Peterborough A47. (Permit required for parts other than Ailsworth Heath.) NCC.

Grafham Water TL 14 67. Reservoir with surrounding rough grassland and woods (w. shore is nature reserve). 1500 a. Big gull roost, waterfowl, Little Ringed Plover. 6 mls s.w. of Huntingdon, by B661 from Buckden on A1. Car park, hide (open Sun, Oct–March). Great Ouse Water Authority/Beds. and Hunts. Nats T.

Nature Conservancy Council, East Midland Regional Office, Monks Wood Experimental Station, Huntingdon.

Ouse Washes TL 48 88. Grazed meadows, flooded in winter, between Old and New Bedford Rs, 1687 a. Over 60 species of birds incl. Ruff, Black-tailed Godwit, Lapwing, Redshank, Gadwall, Shoveler, in winter Short-eared Owl, large herd of Bewick's Swans, flocks of Pintail, Wigeon and other ducks. 18 mls n.e. of Cambridge, 3 mls n.e. of Chatteris, e. of B1093, via Manea. Car park, 6 hides, information centre planned. (Note: no walking allowed on Washes in breeding season 31 March–1 July.) (Warden – Limosa, Welches Dam, Manea, March, Cambs.) RSPB.

Rosswell Pits, Ely TL 56 82. Flooded clay-pits, some with mature vegetation, and wet meadows. Great Crested Grebe, Coot, Moorhen, Kingfisher. 1 ml e. of Ely, on s. side of B1382; access via Springhead Lane; trail. Cambs. and Isle of Ely Nats T/Great Ouse R. Authority.

St Neots Common TL 18 61. Low-lying grassland, freshwater marsh. (Public access to Island Common and Lammas Meadow.) St Neots, off A1, between B1041 and R. Ouse. Car park. Beds. and Hunts. Nats T.

Welney Wildfowl Refuge TL 55 95. Part of Ouse Washes, 660 a. Bewick's and Whooper Swans, White-fronted Geese and various species of duck, breeding Ruff, Black-tailed Godwit, Garganey, Redshank, Snipe. E. of March B1100, e.

Mere, reedbed and bush habitat in Wicken Fen, a wildlife oasis in the flat agricultural landscape of Cambridgeshire.

of Welney, on n. side of A1101 between Old and New Bedford Rs. Observatory (incl. floodlit lagoon) and hides. Adm. fee. (Warden – Pintail House, Hundred Foot Bank, Welney, Nr Wisbech, Cambs.) Wildfowl T.

Wicken Fen TL 55 70. Undrained part of Great Fen, with extensive reedbeds, bush growth and mere, 730 a. Incl. Adventurers' Fen and Charles Raven Marsh Reserve. Coypu. Great Crested and Little Grebes, waterfowl, warblers. 10 mls n.e. of Cambridge A10, 1 ml w. of Wicken and s. side of A1123. (Access by permit only from Keeper's House, NOT Tues or Thurs.) NT.

Woodwalton Fen TL 23 85. Wooded fen with reedbeds and small mere. Chinese Water Deer. Large Copper butterfly. Marsh birds. 6 mls n. of Huntingdon, e. of A1 and 4 mls w. of Ramsey.

SUFFOLK

Bradfield Wood TL 93 57. Unique woodland with over 800 years continuous management as coppice-with-standards, supporting local industries. Ash/oak standards, ash/hazel coppice. 150 a. Woodcock, woodpeckers, Nightingales, woodland warblers and butterflies. 6 mls s.e. of Bury St Edmunds, by minor roads on e. side of A134. SPNR.

Dunwich Heath TM 47 68. Sandy cliffs, heath, shingle ridge on foreshore. Shore birds, Stonechat. 6 mls s. of Southwold, e. of B1125 (road off Westleton–Dunwich road ½ ml before Dunwich). Car park. NT.

Havergate Island TM 43 50. Island with lagoons at mouth of R. Alde, between coast marshes and Orfordness, with which it forms NNR. 267 a. Avocets, Black-headed Gulls, terns, Shelducks, Short-eared Owls. 1½ mls from Orford, 16 mls e. of Ipswich A12 – B1084. Adm. fee with permit, hides. (Warden – 30 Mundays Lane, Orford, Woodbridge, Suffolk.) RSPB.

Ickworth TL 81 61. House with formal garden and parkland and many cedars, redwoods and other exotic trees, woodland walk. 1792 a. 3 mls s.w. of Bury St Edmunds, on w. side of A143. NT.

Minsmere TM 47 67. Vast reed-swamp, lagoons with artificial islands, heath and woods; sand-dunes and shingle on shore. 1500 a. Marsh Harrier, Bittern, Shelduck, Gadwall, terns, Avocet, Stonechat, Bearded Reedling. Large variety of waterfowl and waders, late summer through to spring. 6 mls s. of Southwold B1125, via minor road e. of Westleton. Car park, toilets, information centre, adm. fee and permit needed for hides on reserve, public hides on shore. (Warden — Minsmere Reserve, Westleton, Saxmundham, Suffolk.) RSPB.

Suffolk Trust for Nature Conservation, St Peter's House, Cutler Street, Ipswich, IP1 1UU.

Wolves Wood TM 06 44. Deciduous wood, 92 a. Woodpeckers, Nightingales, warblers. 6 mls w. of Ipswich, 2 mls e. of Hadleigh, on n. side of A1071. Layby parking. RSPB.

NORFOLK

Barton Broad TG 36 22. Open broad with surrounding fen and carr vegetation. Heronry, Great Crested Grebe, Bittern, ducks, Bearded Reedling. Swallow-tailed butterflies. 3 mls n.e. of Hoveton, on e. side of A1151. (Access only by water, using public navigable channels.) Norfolk Nats T.

Beeston Regis Heath TG 17 42. Open and wooded heath, 108 a. 2 mls s.e. of Sheringham between A148 and A149, ¾ ml s. of West Runton station. NT.

Brancaster TF 80 45. Tidal foreshore, sand-dunes and saltmarsh, opposite Scolt Head Island NNR. 2150 a. 7 mls e. of Hunstanton A149. Access by Brancaster beach road (but flooded at high tide), also at Brancaster Staithe and Burnham Deepdale. Car park. NT.

Cley Marshes TG 06 45. Marsh, reedbeds and shingle, 435 a. Bittern, Bearded Reedling, migrant waders and waterfowl. (Cley Bird Observatory is nearby.) 1½ mls n. of Cley-next-the-Sea A149. Car park ¼ ml e. of Cley. Access via East Bank or beach only, visitors are asked not to enter the lagoon area. (Warden — Watcher's Cottage, Cley, Holt, Norfolk.) NT/Norfolk Nats T.

East Winch Common TF 70 16. Wet acid heathland. 5 mls s.e. of King's Lynn, 9 mls n.w. of Swaffham, on s. side of A47. Car park. Norfolk Nats T.

East Wretham Heath TL 91 88. Breckland reserve with two meres, 362 a. Roe Deer, Red Squirrels. Waterfowl and waders, Crossbill. 5 mls n.e. of Thetford astride A1075. Car park at n.e. corner of reserve. (Warden — Warden's Office, East Wretham Heath, Thetford, Norfolk.) Norfolk Nats T.

Hardley Flood and Chedgrave Common TM 38 99. Flooded marshland beside R. Chet. Great Crested Grebe, Common Tern, Gadwall and other waterfowl. 10 mls s.e. of Norwich, 2 mls e. of Loddon, on e. side of A146 at Loddon and Chedgrave. Car park at Hardley Hall Farm. (Inquiries — Norfolk Naturalists' Trust, 72 The Close, Norwich, NR1 4DF.)

Holkham NNR TF 90 45. Reclaimed coastal marshes and sand-dunes, some planted with Corsican pines, large saltmarsh and extensive mudflats. 9700 a. Terneries, Oystercatcher, Shelduck and other wildfowl. 11 mls e. of Hunstanton, 1 ml w. of Wells-next-the-Sea, on n. side of A149. NCC.

Holme Dunes TF 71 44. Sand-dunes, saltmarsh and foreshore, 400 a. Waterfowl, waders, migrants, incl. large flocks of Oystercatchers, Knots, Dunlins. (Holme Bird Observatory is nearby.) 3 mls n.e. of Hunstanton at Holme-next-the-Sea A149. Car park near The Firs, 1 ml e. of reserve entrance along Holme beach road. (Warden — The Firs, Holme, Hunstanton, Norfolk.) Norfolk Nats T.

Horsey TG 46 23. Horsey Mere, marshes and sand-dunes, 600 a. Coypu. Bittern, Bearded Reedling. 11 mls n. of Great Yarmouth, astride B1159. (No access to Horsey Hall and farmland, access to Mere by boat only.) NT.

Lenwade Water TG 10 18. Flooded gravel-pits and surrounding scrub. Great Crested Grebe, Tufted Duck, Kingfisher, warblers. 9 mls n.w. of Norwich A1067, at Lenwade and over the railway. Car park. Norfolk Nats T.

The National Trust, Eastern Regional Office, Blickling Estate Office, Norwich, NOR 09Y.

Nature Conservancy Council, East Anglia Regional Office, 60 Bracondale,

Norwich, Norfolk, NOR 58B.

Norfolk Naturalists' Trust, 72 The Close, Norwich, NR1 4DF.

Roydon Common TF 69 22. Dry and wet heathland with heather, bracken and sphagnum mosses. Nightjar, Stonechat. 3 mls n.e. of King's Lynn, 1 ml e. of junction of A148 — A149 with Roydon road. Norfolk Nats T.

Sandringham TF 68 28. Country Park, 740 a. 6 mls n. of King's Lynn A148 — A149, on n. side of B1439. Sandringham Estate.

Scolt Head Island NNR TF 80 46. Sand-dunes, saltmarsh and 4 mls long shingle ridge, 1620 a. Terneries, Oystercatchers, Shelducks, wintering Brent Geese, wildfowl and waders, Shore Larks, Snow Buntings. 10 mls e. of Hunstanton, 1½ mls n. of A149. Boat from Brancaster Staithe. (Restricted access from May to July.) NCC.

Snettisham TF 65 33. Mudflats, saltmarsh, shingle beach, flooded gravel-pits. 3250 a. Shelduck, Common Tern, Ringed Plover. In winter Snow Buntings and large wader flocks incl. Knot, Sanderling, Bar-tailed Godwit. 7 mls s. of Hunstanton, 10 mls n. of King's Lynn, w. of A149. Car park, hides. (Warden — School House, Wolferton, King's Lynn, Norfolk.) RSPB.

Strumpshaw Fen TG 34 08. Wet grazing meadows, fen carr and reedbeds, 310 a. Great Crested Grebe, Kingfisher, Reed and Sedge Warblers, Yellow Wagtail. 12 mls w. of Great Yarmouth, on s. side of A47 Blofield. RSPB.

Thetford Chase TL 87 84. State forest, mainly pines, on sandy Breckland heath. 48,360 a. Red Deer. Stone Curlew, Wheatear, Crossbill. Area to n. and w. of Thetford A11. Traversed by A134 Thetford–Mundford, A1065 Brandon–Mundford, B1107 Thetford–Brandon. Information centre, trails and picnic places at Santon Downham; camping/caravan sites at Thetford. For Comm.

Titchwell TF 76 44. Coastal reedbed and saltmarsh with sandy shore, 420 a. Little Tern, Oystercatcher, Ringed Plover, Bearded Reedling, migrant waders, Brent Geese and other wildfowl in winter. 6 mls e. of Hunstanton A149. (Warden — Three Horseshoes Cottage, Titchwell, King's Lynn, Norfolk.) RSPB.

Animal collections in East Anglia

Aquatels Zoo and Ecology Centre

This is a small Zoo with a general collection of mammals, birds, freshwater and marine fish and some reptiles. Several animals breed here regularly, including Lions, and Pumas and Leopard cubs have also been born here. The Zoo was opened in 1973.

Banham Zoo and Woolly Monkey Sanctuary

Banham Zoo and Woolly Monkey Sanctuary was started on a small scale in 1968, since when it has expanded to become an interesting small general collection, but specialising in New World monkeys and the rarer monkey species of the Old World. Its Woolly Monkeys now comprise one of the two major collections of this species in Great Britain (also see The Monkey Sanctuary, Looe, Cornwall).

The first animals you see are Malayan Sun Bears, wolves and Dingos. Sun Bears are the smallest of the bear family and the best climbers. They come from southeast Asia and their name is derived from the sun-shaped crescent on their chests. The Timber Wolf comes from North America, northern Europe and Asia, and it is rare in many areas, having been hunted for centuries. The Dingo is the wild dog of Australia, having been introduced originally by man. Dingos eat small mammals, kangaroos, and birds and they also prey on cattle and sheep. Like all wild-dog species they do not bark, but yelp or howl.

Opposite these exhibits are aviaries for Kenya Eagle Owls and Pallas' Sea Eagle, a fish-eating species from India and Burma. Next you see Red Foxes, natives of Great Britain, and Llamas, a member of the camel family, from South America. Llamas are domestic animals, used for centuries for their wool and meat and as pack animals. The other enclosure contains Indian Smooth Otters, a gregarious species from India and southeast Asia, and their expert swimming ability is well exhibited in their pool here.

You next come to the Chimpanzees, the Monkey House and the Woolly Monkey colony. Chimpanzees live in family troops in the rain-forests of central Africa and research has revealed that they use grass stems as a crude but effective tool to extract ants and termites from their nests. Also it was only discovered a few years ago that they eat meat in the wild in addition to their normal vegetarian diet, occasionally killing young monkeys or wild piglets. Chimpanzees mature at seven years of age, when they become ferocious and can inflict serious injuries with their teeth and hands. The Monkey House contains all the primates in the collection except the Woolly Monkeys and the colobus. You can see spider monkeys from tropical South America, which have long prehensile tails; and howlers from Central and South America, which have an enlarged voice-box which carries their morning and evening choruses for two or three miles; Vervet Monkeys from Africa; and five Asiatic species. There are Lar Gibbons which have bred here and have long arms like spider monkeys, but no tails; Spectacled and Silver Langurs, delicate leaf-eating monkeys from southeast Asia; Celebes Black Apes, from the island of Celebes; and Crab-eating Macaques, which feed on shellfish in the mangrove swamps of Malaya.

The Woolly Monkey colony is one of only six in Europe, and it is worth a special visit even if you see nothing else in the Zoo. Woolly Monkeys come from the rain-forests of the Amazon Basin and few zoos have kept them successfully or bred them. They are delicate and require specialised care, and the Zoo's

Aquatels Zoo and Ecology Centre. **Address** Aquatels Recreation Centre, Cranes Farm Road, Basildon, Essex. **Telephone** Basildon 25118. **Open** 10.00–19.00 summer, 10.00–17.30 winter. **Catering** unlicensed restaurant, self-service cafeteria, kiosk. Zoo shop. **Guided tours** by arrangement. **Acreage** 14. **Car** A127 London–Southend road, then A176 into Basildon, then 1st left into Cranes Farm Road A1235. **Bus** from Basildon town centre. **Train** to Basildon (2 mls), or Billericay (5 mls). **Taxis** available. **Other facilities** children's playground, lake, Aquatels Golf Driving Range. No pets. Public **not allowed** to feed animals.

Banham Zoo and Woolly Monkey Sanctuary. **Address** The Grove, Banham, Norwich, Norfolk. **Telephone** Quidenham 476. **Open** 10.30–18.30 summer, 10.30–17.00 winter. **Guide-book**. **Catering** licensed self-service cafeteria. Zoo shop. **Acreage** 20. **Car** 18 mls s.w. of Norwich on B1113; 7½ mls n.w. of Diss. Free car park. **Bus** irregular service from Norwich. **Train** to Attleborough (5 mls) or Diss (7 mls). **Taxis** available. No pets. Public **not allowed** to feed animals.

colony was brought by the Zoo Manager, Mr Dornbrack, who had kept them for several years before coming to Banham in 1971. Since then, the colony has grown and there are now more than 20 monkeys here. One female was delivered of two healthy babies after caesarian operations, the first ever performed on this species. Notice the monkeys' very strong tails, which are capable of taking their whole weight and are often used for swinging. The tip of the tail is bare and used as an extra finger to pick up objects. During the summer holidays, and on other Sunday afternoons, talks and lectures are given in the lecture room adjoining the Woolly Monkey House, and some of the monkeys are allowed out on these occasions, provided that this does not interfere with the life of the colony.

The other monkeys in the Zoo are Black and White Colobus, a handsome species with flowing hair from West Africa, and a related species, the Red Colobus. The latter are the only ones at present exhibited in Europe.

You next come to some paddocks for Ostriches, cranes, cattle and wallabies. Ostriches are the largest living birds, and being unable to fly, they rely on speed to escape from enemies. Males have black plumage and the females brown. Ostriches sitting on eggs lower their heads and necks to the ground to escape detection and do not bury their heads in the sand. In the paddock for Highland Cattle you may also see Crowned Cranes from West and East Africa, and Demoiselle Cranes, which come from southern Europe and Asia. There are two species of wallaby in the Zoo, the Dama Wallaby, which has bred here, from Australia and New Guinea, and Bennett's Wallaby from Tasmania, a race of the Red-necked Wallaby from the Australian mainland. The deer park contains Red Deer and two races of Sika Deer, the Japanese and the Formosan, the latter being found only on the island of Taiwan. The woodland walk is kept in its natural state except for a few enclosures and some waterfowl. This area will be developed during the next year or two, and it makes a pleasant diversion during your tour of the Zoo.

There is a group of well-designed smaller enclosures for mammals and birds, where you can see porcupines, Coypus, pelicans, penguins and sealions. The Crested Porcupine is a native of North Africa and southern Asia. It attacks by charging backwards, impaling its enemy with its sharp quills. If they come out, the unfortunate aggressor usually suffers a septic wound which cripples it. Related to porcupines, Coypus are South American rodents introduced into this country. They inhabit river banks and are good swimmers. In East Anglia they have increased to pest proportions, damaging crops and undermining river banks. White Pelicans are found in Europe, Asia and Africa. They fish in flocks, driving the fish into shallow water where they are scooped up in their capacious beaks. The penguins here are the little Humboldt's Penguin from the western coasts of South America, and the Magellan Penguin from the Falkland Islands and the coast of Patagonia. Other birds in this area are Chilean Flamingos, Cattle Egrets, which feed on ticks on the backs of hoofed animals, and herons. The sealions here are from the coast of Patagonia, the usual kind seen in zoos being the Californian Sealion.

There are more birds of prey in addition to those opposite the Sun Bears and Dingos, including the Indian Eagle Owl, Kestrels and Black Kites, and in adjoining aviaries are Golden and Silver Pheasants. The Black Kite is a relative of the famous rare Red Kite of Wales, and performs its useful scavenging of offal and carrion over almost the entire Old World. The Tropical Aviary contains jays, mynahs, Red-billed Blue Magpies, Sulphur-breasted Toucans, macaws, Budgerigars, Sulphur-crested Cockatoos and hummingbirds. There are also two species of hornbill here, the Wreathed and the White-crested, and one mammal, the Malabar Giant Squirrel, a handsome Indian species. In summer, the toucans are in an outdoor aviary near the Chimpanzees, and near these is an aviary for parrakeets, a very large group of small parrots.

Opposite the Zoo entrance is the Reeve Museum of Rural Bygones, an interesting collection of tools and implements used by East Anglian craftsmen. This and the Zoo itself, are well worth a return visit, since the progressive policy here ensures that the collection will develop and improve.

The Vervet Monkey, seen here with its baby, is found in Africa.

Basildon Wildlife Park, Vange Zoo

This small Zoo, with 18 species of mammal and 25 bird species, is intended for children with emphasis on the needs of school and family parties. The collection includes Leopards, Pumas, badgers, Red Fox, Arctic Fox, Bat-eared Fox, otter, Coypu, Celebes Ape, wallabies, porcupines, Barbary Sheep, goats and deer. There are also some swans, ducks, pheasants and peafowl. The Zoo was opened in 1973.

Clacton Pier Dolphinarium

This Dolphinarium, opened in 1971, in addition to Bottle-nosed Dolphins, exhibits Californian and Patagonian Sealions, Grey Seals, Common Seals, penguins, and has an Aquarium with local marine fish, tropical fish and crustaceans. This is an interesting open-air exhibition, and well worth a visit.

Colchester Zoo and Aquarium

Colchester Zoo has a general collection of animals and it is a good place in which to see and compare some of the big cat species, which are a speciality here. Lions and Leopards are regularly bred and you can also see Bengal Tigers, Cheetahs, Pumas, and the Caracal Lynx, a slender African species with the characteristic ear tufts of the lynx. Both spotted and black Leopards are exhibited, the latter being a colour phase usually found in Asia, while spotted Leopards come from both Africa and Asia. There are also Asiatic Black Bears, European Brown Bears and Striped Hyenas, which are nowadays seldom seen in zoos. These come from northeast Africa, India and Arabia, whereas the more commonly seen Spotted Hyena comes from East and South Africa. Smaller mammal species in the Zoo, either in outdoor enclosures or in the Nocturnal House, include palm civets, porcupines, pacas, acouchies, chinchillas and kangaroos.

There are Chimpanzees, Orang utans and gibbons, and the monkeys here include Mandrills, Celebes Apes, spider monkeys, Woolly Monkeys and Ring-tailed Lemurs. In the paddocks you can see Emus, Soay Sheep, Marabou Storks and Malayan Tapirs, Llamas, Jacob's Sheep and Ostriches. Also in this area are Grant's Zebras, camels, Highland Cattle, Ankole Cattle (a native African breed) and the sealion pool. Do not miss the Giraffe House, the White Rhinos (the larger of the two African species of rhino) and the elephants.

There is a lake with Black Swans from Australia and flamingos, a penguin pool, and bird of prey aviaries, showing Condors, large birds from the Andes, African Fish Eagles and Steller's Sea Eagles. Other aviaries exhibit pheasants, cranes, peafowl, guineafowl, Cattle Egrets, toucans, touracos, parrots and starlings. The Reptile House has monitors, pythons and Boa Constrictors, and there are giant tortoises in an outdoor enclosure in summer. There is also an aquarium. Pets' Corner, near the ruins of All Saints Church, has aviaries, a compound for Prairie Marmots, Pygmy Donkeys, Soay Sheep and a duck pond, while macaws, cockatoos and Fantail Pigeons are at liberty in the grounds.

Other attractions are an amusement arcade, an exhibition centre where you can see veteran cycles, antique guns, native spears, knives, shields and drums, butterflies, sea shells, portrait dolls, fans and iron work. There is also a model blacksmith's shop with bellows, a forge and other tools of the blacksmith's trade. The manor of Stanway was held by the Saxon king Harold, and the present house was built probably in the reign of Henry VIII and rebuilt in the seventeenth century. The Zoo was started in 1963 by Mr and Mrs Farrar, who travel far and wide each year, collecting animals.

The Basildon Wildlife Park, Vange Zoo. **Address** London Road, Vange, Essex. **Telephone** Basildon 553985. **Open** 10.00–19.00 summer, 11.00–½ hr before dusk winter. **Guide-book. Catering** self-service cafeteria. **Guided tours** by arrangement. **Acreage** 5. **Car** s. of Basildon on A13 Southend arterial road. **Train** to Basildon or Pitsea then bus. **Taxis** from Basildon and Pitsea. No pets. Public allowed to feed some animals with own food.

Clacton Pier Dolphinarium. **Address** Dolphin Pool, Clacton Pier, Clacton-on-Sea. **Telephone** Clacton 21115. **Open** daily shows from 11.30 to 19.30 summer, daily show at 15.00 winter. **Catering** self-service cafeteria, snack bar, kiosk. **Guided tours** by arrangement. **Acreage** 1. **Car** to Clacton Pier. All roads in town lead to sea-front and Pier. **Bus** stop in Pier Avenue directly above Pier. **Train** to Clacton (¼ ml). **Taxis** available. **Other facilities** first-aid post, children's playground. Public **not allowed** to feed exhibits.

Colchester Zoo and Aquarium. **Address** Stanway Hall, Colchester, Essex. **Telephone** Colchester 330253. **Open** 09.30–19.00 summer, 10.30–16.00 winter. **Guide-book. Catering** self-service cafeteria, kiosk. **Zoo shop. Acreage** 40. **Car** 3 mls w. of town on B1022. **Bus** 7, 5 or 2 from Colchester bus park. **Train** to Colchester North station then bus to Maldon Road. **Taxis** available. **Other facilities** first-aid post, exhibition centre, amusements, World's Smallest Railway. Public allowed to feed animals with food prepared at Zoo only.

Cromer Zoo

This Zoo was started by Mr Alex Kerr, who for many years trained big cats for circuses. When he retired from circus work, he tracked down all the animals with which he had worked and brought them to Cromer, so that he could look after them in their retirement. You can see Lions, Leopards, Pumas, bears, hyenas and some smaller mammals, such as porcupine, Kinkajou, Raccoon, wallaby, deer, and some Chimpanzees and monkeys, including Mandrills and baboon species. There are pools for sealions, penguins and pelicans, and the aviaries exhibit several kinds of parrot and birds of prey. The Lions breed here, and the Pumas have produced 30 cubs. The collection is added to annually. It was first opened in 1962.

Cromer Zoo. **Address** Howards Hill, Cromer, Norfolk. **Telephone** Cromer 2947. **Open** 10.00–19.00 summer, 10.00 –dusk winter. **Catering** snack bar. Zoo shop. **Acreage** 4. **Car** off A149 Sheringham coast road. **Bus** nearest stop 5 mins' walk to Zoo. **Train** to Cromer ($\frac{1}{2}$ ml). **Taxis** available. Public **not allowed** to feed animals.

Kelling Park Aviaries

Kelling Park Aviaries were founded in 1964 as a bird garden which became well known in the avicultural world for its large collection of lories and lorikeets. This has been maintained under the present management and you can see at least 25 species of these colourful small members of the parrot family. In addition to these, there are four species of flamingo – Greater, Lesser, Chilean and Caribbean – Crowned Cranes, Common Cranes, and Sarus and Demoiselle Cranes, and a good collection of ornamental pheasants and gamebirds. There are some 20 pheasant species here. Other animals exhibited are Ostriches and domestic animals.

Kelling Park Aviaries. **Address** Weybourne Road, Holt, Norfolk. **Telephone** Holt 2235. **Open** 10.00–dusk, Easter– Oct. **Guide-book. Catering** unlicensed restaurant, snack bar. **Guided tours** by arrangement. **Acreage** 14. **Car** 9 mls w. of Cromer, off A149. **Train** to Sheringham (4 mls). **Taxis** available. Public **not allowed** to feed animals.

Kilverstone New World Wildlife Park

As its name suggests, the New World Wildlife Park contains animals of the Americas, specialising in those found in Latin America. It was opened in 1973 by Lord Fisher, and the collection is still growing. There is a good collection of the predatory animals of North and South America, including the Jaguar, Puma, Bobcat, Margay, Tayra, Arctic Fox and Maned Wolf. Jaguars are a little larger than Leopards and they can be distinguished from them by the black spot in the centre of the rosettes on their coats, which the Leopard lacks. They like water and are good swimmers, sometimes attacking alligators and turtles, though their usual diet is wild pig, deer and other small mammals. They also like fish, which they scoop out of the rivers with their paws. Pumas, which breed readily in zoos, range from western Canada southwards to southern South America. The Puma is not dangerous in the wild unless attacked, and its voice is a high-pitched caterwaul. It is also called the Cougar and Mountain Lion. The Margay or Tiger-cat comes from South America, where it lives in thick forest, preying on small mammals, birds, frogs and reptiles. It is a good climber, hunting mainly at night. The Bobcat or Bay Lynx is smaller than the Lynx, and it is found in the southern United States. The Tayra, a large member of the weasel family, is found in Central and South America where it hunts for small rodents, eggs and young birds in woodland and grassland, often in packs. The Arctic Fox from northern Canada and Alaska feeds on carrion, fish and nesting birds and their eggs. The Maned Wolf, the rarest mammal in the Park, comes from the Argentine and Brazil where it lives on grassy plains. It is distinguished by its very long legs and shaggy coat, with a fox-like head. It is now rare in the wild and seldom seen in zoos, where it has been bred only a few times.

There is an equally good collection of smaller American mammals. Prairie Marmots, which live in colonies underground, are a kind of burrowing ground squirrel. They are active and inquisitive on the plains of Mexico and North

Kilverstone New World Wildlife Park. The Latin American Zoo. **Address** Kilverstone Hall, Thetford, Norfolk. **Telephone** Thetford 5369. **Open** 10.00–18.30 summer, 10.00–dusk winter. **Guide-book. Catering** self-service cafeteria, reduced catering in winter. Gift shop. **Acreage** 60. **Car** 2 mls n.e. of Thetford, off A11. Free car park. **Train** to Thetford (1$\frac{1}{2}$ mls). **Taxis** available at Thetford. **Other facilities** first-aid post, wheel-chairs, two picnic areas. Public **not allowed** to feed animals.

Kilverstone New World Wildlife Park specialises in animals from the Americas. Above: Chilean Flamingos; below; the collection's rarest exhibit is the South American plains-roaming Maned Wolf.

America, where the colonies may grow to several thousand animals. You can also see a closely related species, the Woodchuck, from Canada and the United States, where it is also called the Groundhog. Woodchucks hibernate in winter, by which time they are nearly double their weight, so that they can live on their fat while they sleep.

One of the most interesting exhibits is the Nocturnal House for burrowing animals, with observation indoors so that you can watch the animals from a darkened hall in their underground dens. There are badgers, skunks and three mammals from tropical South America, agouti, paca and viscacha. Skunks live on small animals, insects, fruit, eggs, frogs and crayfish. They defend themselves by squirting fluid from the anal gland, which will repel anything which smells it. They give fair warning of this, however, by stamping the feet and raising the tail. The agouti is a stout little nocturnal rodent from Central and South America, living in thick forest and burrowing in holes. It is a vegetarian and can swim, but cannot dive. The paca is larger and more heavily built, with large cheek pouches used for temporarily storing food. The viscacha, related to the chinchilla, lives in warrens on the grass plains of the Argentine. Its front feet have large claws used for digging its burrow.

Seven species of South American monkey are exhibited. There are two species of capuchin, the Brown and White-fronted. Capuchins are the commonest kind of monkey in this part of the world, and they live in troops, using their tails as an aid in climbing. They used to be seen quite frequently as the pets of organ-grinders, their name being derived from the fact that the short, straight hair on their heads was supposed to resemble the cowl, or 'capuche' of Franciscan monks. There are also spider monkeys which have very long prehensile tails, used for swinging between branches independently of arms and legs; and Woolly Monkeys, a close relation but more heavily built and with short, close fur and black faces and heads. The three smallest species exhibited here are the squirrel monkeys, marmosets and titi monkeys. Squirrel monkeys are about the size of a squirrel, with brightly coloured fur and large eyes; they live in troops in the tropical forests of South America, moving among the trees by night.

Marmosets, on the other hand, are active by day, living in large groups in the tree-tops. There are many species, all of which are becoming rare, owing to exploitation for research and the .pet trade, although they seldom thrive as pets. Titis belong to the same family as capuchins, spider and Woolly Monkeys, but they are much smaller. They have small eyes, are active by day and are found in northern South America.

Other interesting animals to notice are the Collared Peccaries, Brazilian Tapirs, Capybaras and Two-toed Sloths. The Collared Peccary is a wild pig found in Arizona, Texas, New Mexico and South America as far south as Patagonia. It differs in many ways from other wild pigs, one being the scent gland which gives off a strong odour. It lives in arid desert and woodland as well as in rain-forests, travelling in small herds and living on roots, grain, fruit and almost anything else it can find. It gets its name from the white band over its shoulders. The Brazilian Tapirs are fond of water; they are vegetarian and shy and inhabit thick jungle. Their enemies are alligators and Jaguars. The young have prominent stripes on their sides, which they lose after a short time. The nose is elongated to form a short trunk. The Capybara is the largest living rodent, weighing 120 lb. and looking like a guinea-pig the size of a small sheep. It comes from northern South America where it lives near water and eats vegetable matter. It is a fast runner and can also swim well. It is apparently quite harmless, its voice being a tiny bleat. Two-toed Sloths have long, curved claws on all four feet, which are used to grasp branches, usually high up. They find their favourite leaves to eat by smell — sight and hearing being poorly developed. Sloths are, as their name implies, slow movers, and they rarely come down to the ground. They are unusual in having two extra cervical vertebrae compared with normal mammals, and no front teeth.

The walled garden contains aviaries for King Vultures from the Andes, jays, guans, toucans, trumpeters and oropendolas, large tropical cousins of the oriole which nests in colonies. Three species of oropendola are shown, the Green, the Black-crested and the Olive, which is in the walk-through Aviary. This building, formerly used as a nectarine house, has been converted into a tropical house for touracos, quails, starlings, mynahs and the rarest bird here, Rothschild's Mynah, which is found only on the island of Bali.

Aquatic birds include flamingos, several species of North and South American waterfowl, the rarest being the Hawaiian Duck and Laysan Teal, and another pond for European waterfowl where several species of duck can be seen and Barnacle and Greylag Geese. There are aviaries for several parrot species, including Patagonian Conures, Military Macaws and Quaker Parrakeets, the only member of the parrot family which nests in colonies, where they construct large communal nests with many entrances.

The Riverside Park has paddocks for Fallow Deer, both the Japanese and the Formosan Sika Deer, Chinese Water Deer, Muntjac, Guanaco (related to the Llama and Alpaca) and the American Bison. You can walk round the paddocks and follow the path along the bank of the River Thet, where you may occasionally see Kingfishers, and so back to the boat house.

The Kilverstone Hall estate dates back to the time of Edward the Confessor. It became the property of William the Conqueror after the Battle of Hastings and remained a Crown possession until Henry I gave it to William de Albany. He presented it to Thetford Priory and it then became known as Monks Hall. After the dissolution of the monasteries by Henry VIII the estate was given to the Duke of Norfolk. It changed hands several times during the following centuries and the present house was built on the site of Monks Hall by Thomas Wright in 1620. It was bought in 1895 by Mr Vavasseur, a friend of Admiral of the Fleet Lord Fisher, with whom he had worked building up and arming the Navy. Mr Vavasseur left the estate to Lord Fisher's son. The Admiral had served several times aboard H.M.S. *Calcutta*, a wooden man-of-war, and he bought its figurehead from the Admiralty. The figurehead now stands at the end of the Admiral's Walk, the stretch of grass next to the yew hedge in the Flamingo Garden. The gardens were laid out by the second baron, the present Lord Fisher's father.

Three closely related South American mammals photographed at Kilverstone; top to bottom: Guanaco, adapted to high-altitude living; Llama, the domestic form of the Guanaco; Alpaca, bred for its wool.

Mole Hall Wildlife Park

This is a mixed collection of mammals and birds in the gardens and grounds of a moated Tudor manor house. There is a small ape and monkey collection consisting of Chimpanzees, Humboldt's Woolly Monkeys, capuchins, which breed regularly, Lion-tailed Macaques, a rare species, spider monkeys, mangabeys and Vervet Monkeys. Amongst the other smaller mammals you can see Dingos, coatis and Kinkajous, Red Foxes, Raccoons, Dwarf Mongoose, Arctic Foxes, and pools for groups of Indian and Canadian Otters. There are also Bennett's Wallabies and in the Park Field some Highland Cattle, Red Deer, Japanese Sika Deer, Shetland Ponies, St Kilda Sheep and donkeys.

In the 'flamingo moat' there are Caribbean and Chilean Flamingos, shelduck and several species of goose. The 'pelican pool' exhibits Indian Rose Pelicans and Pink-backed Pelicans from East Africa, and there are Humboldt's Penguins in another pool. The 'back moat' contains a large selection of waterfowl, including Black Swans, Black-necked Swans, and many species of goose and duck. The rarest of these are the Cereopsis or Cape Barren Goose, the Hawaiian Goose and the Laysan Teal, which is confined in the wild to one tiny island, Laysan, in the Hawaiian archipelago.

Other aviaries and enclosures exhibit hornbills, Cockatiels, starlings, conures, peafowl, Demoiselle and Sarus Cranes, Purple Gallinules, Razor-billed Currassows, ornamental pheasants, Snowy Owls, Great Spotted Eagle Owls, Kestrels and Indian Hawk Eagles. The Canadian Otters, all the deer, the wallabies, the Black Swans and the Sarus Cranes all breed regularly here. This is an interesting collection, which was opened by Mrs Pamela Johnstone in 1964.

Mole Hall Wildlife Park. **Address** Widdington, Saffron Walden, Essex. **Telephone** Saffron Walden 40400. **Open** 10.30–18.00 summer, 10.30–dusk winter. **Guide-book. Guided tours** by arrangement. **Acreage** 25. **Car** 3 mls s.e. of Newport, off A11 near Widdington. Free car park. **Train** Newport (3 mls). **Other facilities** picnic area. Public **not allowed** to feed animals.

New Linton Zoological Gardens

This general mixed collection aims to exhibit animals which are not commonly seen in most zoos, as well as to conserve those which are becoming rare. The stock is constantly being increased and you can see Lions, Pumas, black Leopards, bears, wolves, monkeys and a number of interesting small mammals, including agoutis, Kinkajous, Three-lined Civet, Indian Mongoose, genet, Binturong, deer mouse, African Field Rat, gerbil, Greater Egyptian Jird, field vole, Chinese Hamster and the less frequently seen Haired Hamster. Birds include a pair of Grant Hornbills, pheasants, waterfowl, and the birds of prey; and there are reptiles. Animals which breed regularly include the Red Foxes, badgers, genets, Red Deer, Jacob's Sheep and Pig-tailed Monkeys. The Zoo was opened in 1972.

New Linton Zoological Gardens. **Address** Mortimer House, Hadstock Road, Linton, Cambridge. **Telephone** Cambridge 891308. **Open** 10.00–19.00 summer, 10.00–dusk winter. **Catering** snack bar. Zoo shop. **Guided tours** by arrangement. **Acreage** 10½. **Car** 10 mls s.e. of Cambridge off A604 at Linton Village. Free car park. **Bus** nearest stop ½ ml, service from Haverhill, Saffron Walden or Cambridge. **Train** to Audley End or Cambridge. **Taxis** available. **Other facilities** first-aid post, lost children's room, picnic area. No pets. Public **not allowed** to feed animals.

Norfolk Wildlife Park and Pheasant Trust

The Norfolk Wildlife Park has the largest collection of European animals in the world, and a splendid record of breeding successes. Dedicated to the conservation of European animals, it breeds many more animals than it takes from the wild, which is one of the most important tasks of the modern zoo. Here, the first European Beaver ever bred in captivity in the British Isles was born and raised in 1973. Beavers are seldom seen in daytime in the wild, as they live in burrows in river banks, entered below water level, or in 'lodges' on lakes, built of mud and sticks. A replica of a Beaver's burrow has been built with underwater entrances, and the Beavers can be seen through windows in a darkened porch. The same principle is used to exhibit Badgers, which one would not normally see, since they are mainly active at night or in twilight. Badgers seldom breed in zoos, but a female cub was raised in 1973, and it was later introduced to a young male of the same age, and the two were released on an estate in Norfolk where

Norfolk Wildlife Park and Pheasant Trust. **Address** Great Witchingham, Norwich, Norfolk. **Telephone** Great Witchingham 274. **Open** 10.30–18.00 summer, 10.30–sunset winter. **Guide-book. Catering** (summer only) licensed cafeteria, kiosk. **Guided tours** by arrangement. **Acreage** 40. **Car** A1067, 12 mls n.w. of Norwich. **Bus** Eastern Counties 29, 402 stop near entrance. **Train** to Norwich (13 mls). **Taxis** available. Public **not allowed** to feed animals.

Badgers used to occur, but had been exterminated. They were fed by hand until they had learned to find their own food, and it is hoped to release more Badgers in Norfolk as they are bred in the Park.

You can also see the Brown Hare, which bred here for the first time in a British zoo, and the European Otters which have bred here, the first time this has been achieved in captivity in Britain for 89 years. Otters are now rare here, so the birth of three Otters is a significant achievement. There are enclosures for the Red Fox, still common in this country, and the Arctic Fox, from the European polar regions. It has a grey coat in summer to camouflage it against rocks, and in winter it turns white to match the snow. It preys on Arctic Hares and other small animals and it also scavenges the remains of seals killed by Polar Bears.

Other carnivorous European mammals to be seen here are the Wolf, Lynx, Wolverine, Raccoon Dog, Wild Cat, Polecat and Beech Marten. The Wolf became extinct in Britain when the last one was killed in Scotland in 1743. The race exhibited here is the Spanish Wolf, which is now nearly extinct there, being confined to remote mountain areas. The Lynxes are exhibited in a large grass enclosure, surrounded by high fences with a viewing platform, since they are powerful, agile animals which prey on small mammals and an occasional deer. They breed regularly here, and they have not been bred elsewhere in Britain for more than 30 years. The Wolverines are the largest members of the stoat family, attaining the size of a large cat. They come from the most northerly parts of Europe, where they are now becoming rare. The Raccoon Dog is a small animal with black facial markings, like a Raccoon, and its natural range extends from Siberia to Indo-China and Japan. Importations of the animal into Russia for its fur led to its spreading into Scandinavia and Germany, but it is seldom exhibited in captivity.

The Wild Cat, once common in Britain, is now found only in the remoter forests of Scotland. It has a thick coat, a flattened head and a thick, bushy tail marked with black rings. Wild Cats prey on small mammals and birds and they will breed with domestic cats. They are naturally fierce and have the reputation of being impossible to tame. The Polecat, another member of the stoat family, is still found wild in Wales, although it has interbred with domestic Ferrets and there are probably fewer pure-bred animals in the wild than there used to be. The Beech Marten is related to the Pine Marten and is a nimble tree climber, living a solitary life except in the breeding season, so the sexes have to be separated in captivity when not breeding to avoid fighting.

Another rare European animal is the Brown Bear, which used to be found all over western Europe, but is now confined to a few small areas in the Pyrenees, the Italian Alps, parts of Scandinavia and Russia. Like many wild animals, the male bear cannot be kept with the cubs, so the bears' pen is divided into two. A much larger enclosure is planned for the future, when the present one will be kept as a breeding area. Bears do not hibernate in captivity, since there is a regular food supply and therefore no need for them to stoke up for their winter sleep.

Both the Common Seal and the Atlantic Grey Seal are shown. Common Seals are found mainly off the east coast, their chief breeding area being the sandbanks in the Wash. Having been hunted for their fur in the past, they are now partly protected by law, culling being closely controlled. The Grey Seal prefers rocky coasts, and there is a large breeding colony on the Farne Islands, off the coast of Northumberland.

The pool for Coypus is an interesting exhibit, since this is really a South American animal which was introduced to this country for its fur, known in the trade as Nutria. Some of these animals escaped from fur farms and they are now classed as a pest in East Anglia. The Coypu looks a little like a large water rat, but its hind feet are webbed. It is a good swimmer and can stay under water for up to 20 minutes. Another interesting animal is the European Suslik, which burrows underground, where it lives in large colonies. It is related to the Prairie Marmot of North America and it hibernates in winter. They have bred here for the first time in Britain. There is also an enclosure for wild Rabbits which many

children may not have seen, since Rabbits became scarce after the myxomatosis outbreak of the 1950s. Also do not miss the Nocturnal House, in which European nocturnal animals are shown. There are Genets, Porcupines, Weasels, Stoats, Edible Dormice, voles, rats and lemmings.

There is a fine collection of hoofed animals, including Alpine Ibex, European Bison, Wild Boar, Mouflon and seven species of deer. The Alpine Ibex is a wild goat which was nearly exterminated in the mountainous regions of central Europe, but has been reintroduced into Switzerland, the Bavarian Alps and Yugoslavia. It is very rare in captivity and in 1971 the group shown here bred for the first time in a British zoo. The European Bison arrived here in 1973 and they can be seen in a two-acre enclosure. They are a valuable addition to the few herds in Britain, since fresh blood lines are needed to maintain healthy breeding stock. This is a forest animal which is now protected in a reserve in Poland. It no longer exists as a truly wild animal. The Wild Boar is still common in Europe, where it is hunted, but it was exterminated in Britain in the seventeenth century. There is a small breeding herd of Roe Deer, which is a woodland species, difficult to breed in captivity. The herd here is the only one regularly breeding in this country. You can also see Red Deer, the largest British land mammal, and Fallow Deer, which have been kept for centuries in parks, and are also to be found wild in many parts of the country. They came originally from southern Europe. The Reindeer is the most northerly species of deer in the world, and it has been semi-domesticated for centuries, the human inhabitants of the Arctic regions depending on its meat and hide for their existence. It was successfully reintroduced into Scotland about 20 years ago, where it is kept in a semi-wild state. The Reindeer in the Park were bred in Inverness-shire. Reindeer have very sensitive skins, especially to mosquitoes, and in the Park they are supplied with a fine water spray in hot weather.

Three other species of deer can be seen here which originated in Asia. The Sika, from eastern Asia and Japan, is a close relation of our native Red Deer, and the form shown here belongs to the Formosan race which is only found in Taiwan, where it is now very rare. Sika Deer were introduced into Britain and they are now found wild here, mainly in the south. Two small species originating in China can also be seen here, the Muntjac and the Chinese Water Deer. The Muntjac comes from tropical forests in southern China and was introduced here and elsewhere in Europe, where it occurs in a wild state. The male Muntjac has very small antlers and its canine teeth have developed like little tusks. The Chinese Water Deer also escaped from captivity in this country and it has colonised parts of southeast England. Unlike any other deer, it produces from two to six young in a litter, whereas other species bear only one young or rarely two. The Park also exhibits Mouflon, the only wild sheep of Europe, which is confined to Corsica and Sardinia.

The Park contains many attractive pools and small lakes where the large waterfowl collection can be seen. These include flamingos, Whooper Swans and many species of duck and goose: notice especially the fine group of Red-breasted Geese, a beautiful small goose which is a winter visitor to eastern Europe. Another outstanding exhibit is the Wader Pool, which represents the sandhills of the north Norfolk coast, planted with lyme-grass from the sea-shore. The birds here are Wigeon, Black-headed Gulls, Common Curlews and Stone Curlews. The Stone Curlews here are the only breeding group of this species in captivity. See also the European White Storks on their high platforms, which they prefer as nesting sites. The cleverly landscaped walk-through aviary has a good collection of British hedgerow birds, and some Alpine Choughs, which have bred here for the first time in Britain. There is also a small aviary for small perching birds and a collection of owls and eagles on Hawk Lawn, which are trained to hunt after being released and then return to their mews.

The Park grew out of the private collection of Mr Philip Wayre, a well known naturalist, author and broadcaster. He opened it to the public in 1961 and it is difficult to find an animal here which has not established one record or another. The country atmosphere has been preserved and the Park contains many fine flowering shrubs.

Above: Beech Marten, closely related to our native Pine Marten (see page 229); left: Wolverine, or Glutton, so called because of its great appetite; below: Norfolk Wildlife Park's Lynx and cubs.

It is also the home of the Pheasant Trust, owners of Mr Wayre's collection which was started in 1954 to begin captive breeding programmes for endangered species of wild pheasants. The Trust, founded in 1959, now owns the largest collection of rare pheasants in Britain, with many breeding successes. Many of the pheasant species in most danger of extinction in the wild have been bred regularly. Thirty Swinhoe's Pheasants were reintroduced in Taiwan in 1967 and released there as new breeding stock, and Cheer Pheasants were reintroduced in a forest reserve in India in 1971 and 1973. Other rare pheasants bred by the Trust include the Satyr Tragopan, Cabot's Tragopan (of which Mr Wayre has been developing a breeding stock since 1960, earmarked for wild 'replanting'), Koklass, White-crested Kalij, Himalayan Monal, and Mikado Pheasant, a bird confined to the mountains of Taiwan whose first scientific description was based on two tail-feathers out of a hunter's head-dress. The ultimate aim is to restock the natural homes of all these rare species. The Trust's 45 pheasant aviaries are on view to the public and they are well worth a visit.

A similar breeding programme has been very successful with European Eagle Owls, which have been returned to the forests of Sweden where they had become rare. Young birds are released from aviaries in the forest, where at first they are fed. Gradually, as they learn to hunt food for themselves, they become less and less dependent on their aviary rations, until finally they become completely wild birds.

In 1973, the Park and the Trust between them bred 277 birds and mammals more than they lost. A large proportion of these were species which are endangered in the wild, and this rate of increase gives added interest to the collection, as well as being important for conservation.

Peakirk Wildfowl Refuge

The Peakirk Wildfowl Refuge was established by the Wildfowl Trust in 1957. Its main purpose is to act as a reserve colony and breeding satellite for the Trust's main collection at Slimbridge, Gloucestershire. Nevertheless, this is an important waterfowl collection with 100 species of waterfowl and over 700 birds. Each year 400 birds are bred here and sent to Slimbridge, and more than 100 different species have been bred in the Gardens since they were opened.

The Gardens are arranged as a series of ponds in an attractive woodland setting. They are on a smaller scale than Slimbridge, but with a sense of seclusion which is as agreeable to visitors as it is necessary for the birds. Following the path beside the Long Pond, you come to pens for ducklings which are reared in summer by foster-hens. Then come some small pens for quarrelsome species or those which the Trust is specially anxious to breed. The Ring Pond pen has an island in the centre which is one of the main breeding areas in the Gardens, and from here you cross the ancient Cardyke to the new area where most of the geese are kept, consisting of a lake and an island and pens for Andean Geese, Chilean Pintails, Versicolor Teal, Lesser Magellan Geese, Chilean Teal, New Zealand Grey Ducks, Patagonian Crested Ducks and Ruddy-headed Geese. Returning via another path over the Cardyke past the Ring Pond you come to the House Pond, containing ducks and the winter shed for the flock of Chilean Flamingos. On the way back you complete the circuit of the Ring Pond, then turn left to see the Ten Island Pond which is the other important breeding area. Retrace your steps and keep left along the other side of the Ten Island Pond on your way back to the Gate House.

Species which breed regularly here include Trumpeter Swans and the rare White-winged Wood Duck. Other rare species are Hawaiian Geese, Cereopsis or Cape Barren Geese, Laysan Teal and Hawaiian Duck. Wild Shoveler and Teal are regular visitors in winter.

The 300-year-old duck decoy at Borough Pen, two miles away, is operated by the Trust and is open to members one weekend in summer. Members of the Trust have free entry to the Waterfowl Gardens.

Puma, the New World's big cat, can be seen at Thorney.

Peakirk Wildfowl Refuge. **Address** Peakirk, Peterborough, Cambs. **Telephone** Peterborough 252271. **Open** 09.30–17.30 (or 15 mins after sunset, whichever earlier) summer and winter. **Guide-book. Catering** snack bar (summer only). Gift shop. **Acreage** 17. **Guided tours** children's parties only, by arrangement. **Car** 7 mls n. of Peterborough on B1443. **Train** to Peterborough (7 mls). **Taxis** available. No pets. Public allowed to feed birds.

Snow Goose with goslings at Peakirk.

Southend Dolphinarium

You can see two fully trained Bottle-nosed Dolphins here, which give six shows daily, with a running commentary on all the feats performed. An educational lecture is also given on request, and this is worth having, since dolphins are fascinating animals with more ability than is demonstrated by their facility for performing tricks. The Dolphinarium was opened in 1969.

Southend Dolphinarium. **Address** Marine Parade, Southend-on-Sea, Essex. **Telephone** Southend 611846. **Open** 12.00–18.00 Easter–late Sept (6 shows daily on the hour), closed in winter. Gift shop. **Car** Marine Parade B1016, just e. of pier. Public **not allowed** to feed exhibits.

Suffolk Wild Life and Country Park

This is a small mixed collection with a Tiger, Lions, porcupines, wolves, Dingos, badgers, monkeys, a walk-through aviary, a lake with ornamental waterfowl, a children's corner, and a herd of Highland Cattle. There is also river fishing in season, and you can picnic on the sloping ground. The Park was opened by Mr L. F. Wright in 1969.

Suffolk Wild Life and Country Park. **Address** Kessingland, Nr Lowestoft, Suffolk. **Telephone** Kessingland 291. **Open** 10.00–18.00 (or 1 hour before sunset, whichever earlier) summer; 10.00–1 hour before dusk, winter. **Guide-book**. **Catering** self-service cafeteria. Zoo shop. **Acreage** 45. **Car** 5 mls s.w. of Lowestoft off A12 near Kessingland. **Bus** stops $\frac{1}{2}$ ml from Park. **Train** to Lowestoft (5 mls). **Taxis** available. **Other facilities** push-chairs, wheelchairs, children's playground. Public allowed to feed waterfowl with food prepared in Park only.

Thorney Wild Life Park

Thorney Wild Life Park was opened in 1968 with a general collection of the more popular animals, including elephant, Giraffe and some of the big cats. You can see Lions, Tigers, both spotted and black Leopards, and Pumas. Tigers are now endangered in the wild, and in India, which possessed some 40,000 Tigers only 30 years ago, it is estimated that there are only about 1,500 left. They are now legally protected. The Siberian Tiger is even rarer, and other races in southern Asia are also fast disappearing in the wild. Leopards, also numerous in Africa and Asia, have suffered heavy persecution to satisfy the fur trade, which has put a temporary embargo on certain cat skins, including Leopards. Black Leopards occur mainly in southeast Asia, the dark coat being merely a colour phase. The spots are just visible if you look closely. Pumas were formerly distributed over most of North and South America, and here again their numbers in the wild have diminished. They breed readily in captivity, however. The Zoo also exhibits Polar Bears, the only member of the bear family which is entirely carnivorous. They are insulated against the Arctic cold by their thick fur and a layer of fat under the skin.

Thorney Wild Life Park. **Address** Thorney, Peterborough. **Telephone** Thorney 221. **Open** 10.00–dusk summer, closed winter. **Catering** self-service cafeteria, snack bar, kiosk. Zoo shop. **Guided tours** by arrangement. **Acreage** 45. **Car** 7 mls n.e. of Peterborough on A47. **Bus** nearest stop 300 yds. **Train** to Peterborough ($6\frac{1}{2}$ mls). Dogs on leash only. Public **not allowed** to feed animals.

In the paddocks you can see Indian Elephants, Giraffes, camels, and Llamas, a domesticated member of the camel family from South America where it has been used for centuries for its wool, hide and meat and as a pack animal. Another interesting animal is the Barbary Sheep, which is found in the mountains of North Africa. It is in fact a wild goat rather than a sheep. You can also see Soay Sheep, a primitive breed from the island of Soay in the St Kilda group west of the Hebrides, and some Highland Cattle and ponies.

The small mammals exhibited here include kangaroos and wallabies, the African Crested Porcupine, Raccoons, coatis, otters, seals and the Dingo, the wild dog of Australia, which was introduced by man centuries ago. There are also some monkeys, including the Celebes Ape, from the island of Celebes. Birds in the Zoo include flamingos, pelicans, Crowned Cranes from Africa, Demoiselle Cranes from southern Europe and Asia, ducks and geese, including the Cereopsis or Cape Barren Goose, a rare species, and macaws, the largest member of the parrot family from South America, vultures and penguins. There is also a fish pond, an amusement arcade and a miniature railway.

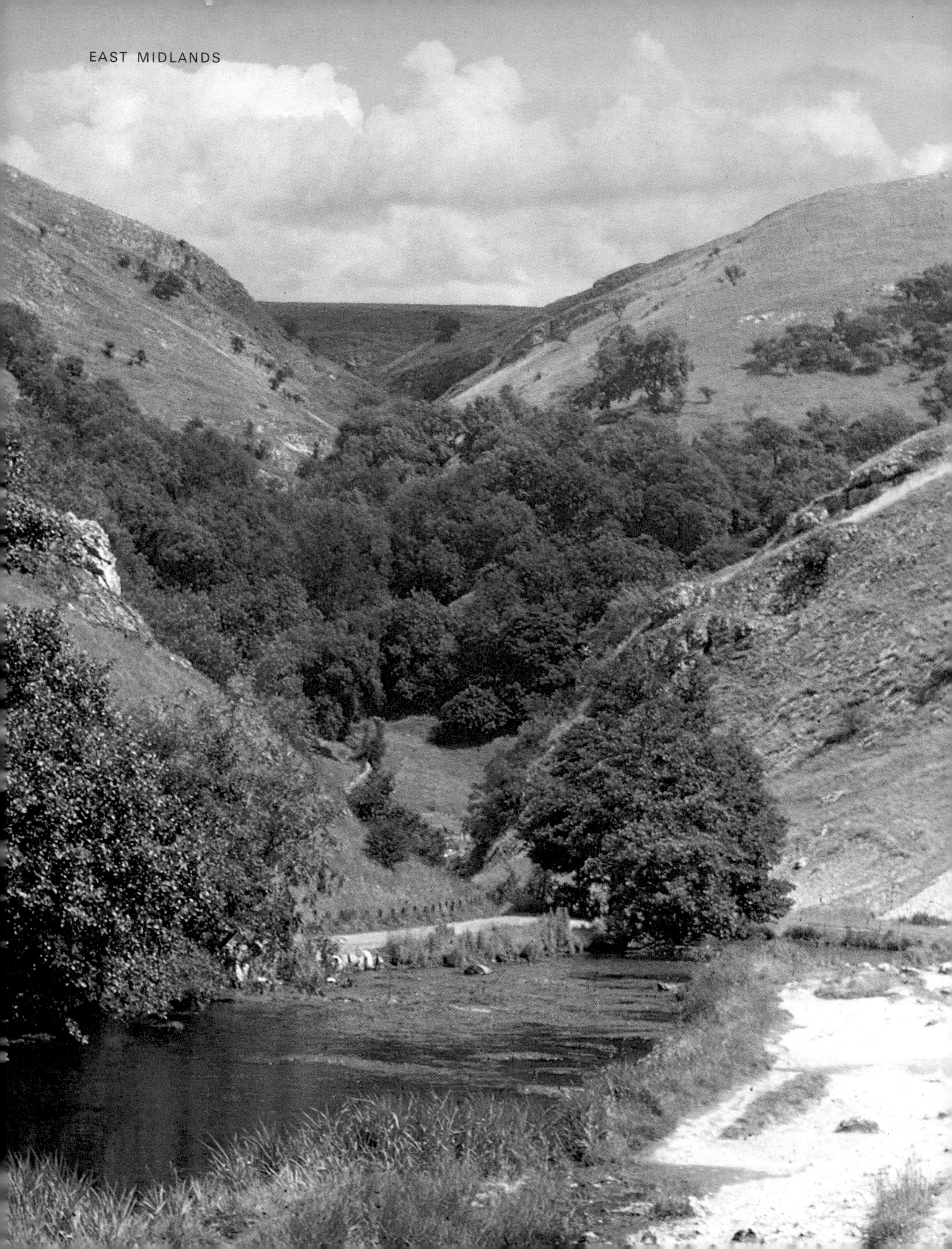

East Midlands RON HICKLING

Urban sprawl and factory farming — that could well sum up for many the East Midlands region. What could a naturalist find of interest in such country? An imaginary journey will show that this part of England has immense variety of landscape, much quiet beauty, and great richness of wildlife.

We will start our tour at its most spectacular — the Peak District National Park of Derbyshire. This falls into two parts; the gritstone moors of the north, and the limestone dales in the south. The massif of Kinder Scout and Bleaklow is a wild plateau of peat overlaying the dark grey Millstone Grit, kingdom of the Red Grouse and the Golden Plover. Bare cloughs thrust into this plateau, walled in by gritstone 'edges' like shattered battlements. These steep valleys, containing a few isolated hawthorns or rowans, or thin woods of twisted oaks where rocks have protected them from the woodman's axe, are the principal habitat of the Ring Ousel and the Merlin. The Raven has recently returned and pairs bred in 1968 and 1969. The Blue Hare, introduced from Scotland in the last century, still flourishes; a friend recently saw six in the partial white of their winter coats below Fairbrook Naze.

In the deeper valleys are tumbling rivers and streams, their twisting courses leaving rocky beds beloved of the Common Sandpiper. The Dipper feeds beneath the surface of the water where boulders create turbulence, and nests in the roots of the alders which line the banks. This mountain area, which towers above the Hope valley like the snout of a great black glacier, was formerly sacred to the shooting of the Red Grouse. Now it has been opened by access agreements and footpaths (the Pennine Way starts here), available to all who value wilderness and freedom. You could best discover the wildlife of the Dark Peak by taking the footpath from Edale northeastwards by Jagger's Clough to Ashop valley, and then to the summit of Kinder Scout by Blackden Brook.

South of the Hope valley lies the White Peak — the lovely green country of the limestone dales. Footpaths traverse many of these — Dovedale, Lathkill, Monsal Dale and the Manifold valley just over the county boundary. The rivers are wide and swift-flowing with shallow weirs built to provide the pools which the Brown Trout love; they are easily visible in the clear water, heads upstream, waiting for their prey. The Grayling is also fished in these rivers and the Grey Wagtail and Dipper breed. The walls of the dales are sculptured limestone cliffs, and where the slopes allow there are woods of ash and oak. The ashwoods of Dovedale NNR are the home of Wood Warbler and Redstart and occasionally the Pied Flycatcher, and Badgers disclose their presence by leaving broad trails through the dog's-mercury. On the stony slopes and in the dry-stone walls of the surrounding fields Wheatears nest, and the wetter fields are inhabited by Curlew, Redshank and Snipe.

The Ordnance Survey Map for Nottinghamshire bears, in bold capitals stretching from Nottingham to Worksop, the words SHERWOOD FOREST. Alas, there is nothing but a sad remnant of this great hunting forest of the Norman kings. Between Edwinstowe and Budby the last piece of original Sherwood is now a Country Park; the great oaks which might have been saplings when bold Robin operated in these parts are now decaying monsters, and the Major Oak itself is propped and chained to maintain some of its dignity in old age. It is sad that these ancient trees are not surrounded by a succession of younger trees of varying ages; but due to the care the forest now receives there are many saplings and plentiful regeneration is taking place. Woodland birds still abound, but the Woodlark, a distinguished resident of Sherwood until recently, seems to have disappeared and there have been no breeding records for several years.

The Norman kings and their successors allowed the oaks to be stripped from Sherwood, and encouraged settlement and development as farmland; they also rewarded their nobles or the Church with pieces of forestland. From the seventeenth century onwards these places were made into parks with splendid mansions. Thus the Duke of Newcastle 'humbly proposed' to Queen Anne in

Ron Hickling has served the British Trust for Ornithology (of which he is President) for nearly 30 years. He was a founder and first secretary of the Leicestershire and Rutland Trust for Nature Conservation and is honorary treasurer of the Society for the Promotion of Nature Reserves. He is currently writing a book on the birds of Leicestershire.

Two typical Peak District birds: above, the Golden Plover nests high up on the moorland tops; below, the Dipper inhabits turbulent streams lower down in the valleys.

Opposite: part of Dovedale National Nature Reserve in Derbyshire's Peak District.

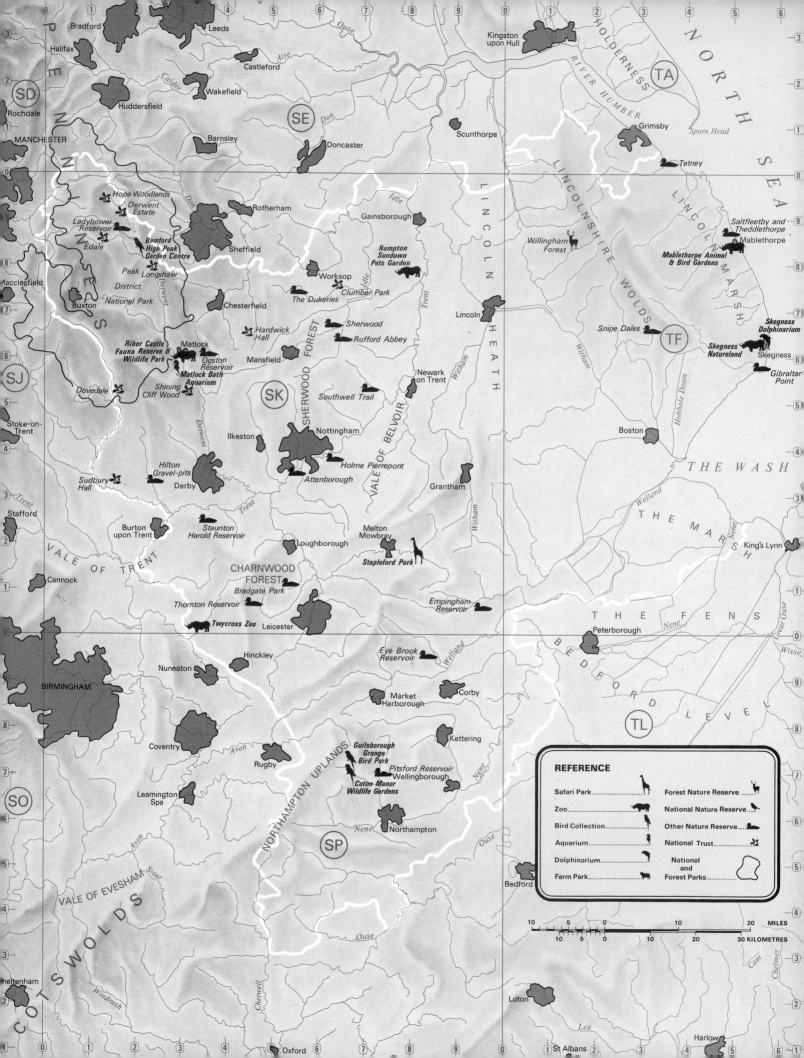

REFERENCE

Safari Park . . . .

Zoo . . . .

Bird Collection . . . .

Aquarium . . . .

Dolphinarium . . . .

Farm Park . . . .

Forest Nature Reserve . . . .

National Nature Reserve . . . .

Other Nature Reserve . . . .

National Trust . . . .

National and
Forest Parks . . . .

10   5   0   10   20   MILES

10   5   0   10   20   30   KILOMETRES

1707, 'for the better improvement and ornament of her Majestye's Forest of Sherwood', that 'a parke be made in the said forest containing at least 3,000 acres.' These great parks, the 'Dukeries', are now a refuge for wildlife and access is allowed at several: Clumber is National Trust property, Rufford is a Country Park, and Thoresby is open to the public regularly. Here the elusive Hawfinch breeds and the Nightingale is widespread; the lakes carry large flocks of Canada Geese and such wildfowl as Mallard, Teal, Tufted Duck, Coot and Moorhen.

The Trent valley is a great highway for migrating birds and has gravel-pits, as at the Attenborough Nature Reserve, which carry large numbers of wintering ducks and interesting breeding birds such as the Little Ringed Plover. Southwards lies Charnwood Forest in Leicestershire, an outcrop of the oldest series of rocks in Britain, the Pre-Cambrian, thrust out of the surrounding plain like the stump of an old tooth to form a miniature mountain landscape. This bit of wild country on the edge of major industrial areas is now carefully preserved and development is strictly controlled. Much is publicly owned or open to visitors, and the distinctive wildlife, so rich and varied compared with that of the surrounding Midlands plain, is available for all to enjoy.

Bradgate Park, home of the ill-fated Lady Jane Grey, has been an enclosed deer-park since at least the twelfth century. It has two herds; the native Red Deer, well fed and selectively bred, number about 100, and there are about 200 head of Fallow Deer. The bracken-covered slopes amongst the scattered and typically dwarfed oaks carry large numbers of heathland birds; Yellow-hammers and Reed Buntings, Whinchats and wintering Stonechats, Tree Pipits and Skylarks. The denser oaks of the river gorge with their many holes and cavities are the home of countless Jackdaws, with Nuthatches and Lesser Spotted Woodpeckers; the Redstarts, also hole-nesters, prefer the dry-stone walls.

A short distance away is Swithland Wood, the finest oakwood in Leicester-shire, haunt of Woodcock and Jay, Nuthatch and Treecreeper, Lesser and Great Spotted Woodpeckers and several species of tit. It is rich in summer warblers such as Blackcap and Garden Warbler, Chiffchaff, Willow Warbler and Wood Warbler, while Siskins come in winter. The open slopes of nearby Beacon Hill are worth searching for Adders or Vipers, Common Lizards and Slow-worms.

We go southwards again, into Northamptonshire, where there is yet another forest – the Royal Forest of Salcey. Much of this has never been clear-felled and there are many ancient trees. It is now in the care of the Forestry Commission, who have set out a picnic place and nature trail on the western side. A piece known as Little Straits is managed as a nature reserve by the two neighbouring County Trusts of Northamptonshire and Buckinghamshire. Salcey is famous for its woodland bird communities, but perhaps even more famous for its rare butterflies, now in considerable danger. As the late James Fisher wrote, 'The Purple Emperor's survival is now in doubt; the Large Tortoiseshell's status is precarious; the Black Hairstreak is vulnerable; the Wood White survives but the White Admiral is now rare.' So please take care to protect any butterflies you may see. At Salcey there are opportunities to encounter that tiny oriental deer the Muntjac, and you may see it from the nature trail, especially as it moves from ditch to ditch at dusk.

We now move quickly northeastwards along the quiet and beautiful River Nene, by boat or footpath from Thrapston to Oundle, home of Water Vole and Water Shrew, of Little Grebe and Heron, of Mallard and Moorhen; through the former county of Rutland (still fiercely independent) with its deep woods and rich valleys; by the workings for the new Empingham Reservoir, due to be completed in 1975 as the largest man-made lake in the country; along the limestone ridge into Lincolnshire, through the Ancaster Gap and over the fens to the chalk of the Wolds.

The Lincolnshire Trust's nature reserve of Snipe Dales, open to the public, is not actually in the Wolds but its wildlife is typical. Fallow Deer visit the valleys. There is at least one Badger sett, and a large population of voles which attract Kestrels and, in winter, Short-eared Owls. The marshy valleys are attractive to Woodcock, Snipe and Heron, and there is a colony of Sand Martins.

Outcrops of Pre-Cambrian rock thrust out of the land in Charnwood Forest, Leicestershire.

Salcey Forest straddles the boundary of Northamptonshire and Buckingham-shire.

And so to the holiday coast of Lincolnshire, where the sheer pressure of visitor numbers has driven away much of the wild shore-life. But two miles south of Skegness lies the great Gibraltar Point LNR managed by the Lincolnshire Trust for Nature Conservation, a magnificent example of what the whole of this coastline, with its wildlife, was like. A new visitor centre, attached to the Field Study Station, demonstrates graphically to visitors the mammals, birds and invertebrates of this 1,500-acre complex of mud-flats, beach, sand-dunes and saltmarsh. The dunes are clothed in prickly sea-buckthorn shrubs whose bright orange berries are the winter larder of vast flocks of Fieldfares from Scandinavia. The Little Tern and Ringed Plover, the main victims of disturbance around the coasts of Britain, still nest in small numbers, but are rarely successful because of the depredations of Foxes. Migrant birds from Scandinavia — warblers and flycatchers, thrushes and chats — pass through in great numbers and rest briefly after their crossing of the North Sea. Rarities like the Great Grey Shrike and Hen Harrier are almost regular. Vast flocks of wading birds feed on the mud-flats of the Wash in autumn and winter, and come into this reserve at high tide to rest on the sand-spits — Knots, Dunlins, Sanderlings, Turnstones, Curlews, Redshanks, Oystercatchers and Bar-tailed Godwits in their thousands. Seabirds of many kinds, auks, skuas and divers, pass by; flocks of Snow Buntings, Shore Larks and Twites are to be found on the beach in winter. The Common Seal breeds offshore and can frequently be seen resting on the sand-banks in the reserve.

Gibraltar Point is the northern tip of the Wash, with its mud-banks and saltmarshes supporting immense numbers of birds. It is difficult to explore these wild saltings but there are places between Skegness and Boston where side roads lead down to the shore. Here at high tide in winter one can see flocks of Brent Geese, and sea-ducks such as Common Scoters, Eiders and Goldeneyes will be just offshore. There are colonies of Black-headed Gulls, while Short-eared Owls and Redshanks also breed.

In the region reservoirs form one of the most important habitats for birds. There are some 20 major reservoirs and a number of smaller ones, the latter mainly canal-feeders. In Nottinghamshire the large lakes of the Dukeries replace the reservoirs. The Empingham Reservoir, now in the final stages of completion, is by no means the last, as others are proposed. Their rapid increase during this century, and especially since the end of the Second War, has had an enormous

A flock of waders wheels over a tidal lagoon at Gibraltar Point. Below: Short-eared Owls hunt over the saltmarsh at Gibraltar Point.

Male Snow Bunting in winter.

impact for good on our waterfowl populations. The reservoirs can indeed be said to have replaced the old fens which until they had been completely drained (the last one at the beginning of the nineteenth century), were the home of immense numbers of geese and ducks and other aquatic birds.

Nineteenth-century naturalists like Lord Lilford spoke only of small numbers of ducks and geese inland, and then only in the great river valleys during floods. One can only suppose that between the draining of the fens and the coming of the reservoirs the large wildfowl population wintered on the mud-flats and in the creeks of the Wash. Now every new reservoir seems to increase the wintering ducks, and peak numbers in the East Midlands must reach about 25,000. Some 70,000 gulls also use these waters for roosting, after they have fed at urban rubbish tips or on agricultural land. Small migrants such as warblers and wagtails, Swallows and Swifts, terns and waders, are all attracted to reservoirs on migration, some to remain for a lengthy stay, especially in the autumn since the spring birds are anxious to continue their journey. Storm-driven seabirds from the Atlantic, or vagrants from the Mediterranean, or wandering waders from America, turn up from time to time. Little wonder that bird-watchers spend so much time leaning over reservoir walls!

Reference to walls emphasises that reservoirs are easily and ideally observable from roads round or across them — such as at Pitsford in Northamptonshire, Eye Brook in Leicestershire, or Ogston in Derbyshire. The new reservoir at Staunton Harold has car parks placed at high vantage points. Empingham will have two shallow arms protected as nature reserves, with footpaths and public viewing 'hides' provided. Even those sited away from roads can be visited with permits, often obtainable with little trouble from the appropriate Water Authority.

A wetland habitat of a different type is provided by the canals, which lace the countryside with gentle waterways lined by overgrown towpaths. They mean walking, and freedom from cars, and the quiet conditions so necessary for natural history study. There can be few more pleasant occupations than a walk by the waterside on a summer's day, with its wealth of birds, mammals and insects. The present usage of canals is just enough to maintain the widest variety of habitat, from open water through beds of emergent vegetation to swamp. Bird-life is not confined to waterside species — Reed Bunting, Sedge Warbler, Kingfisher, Dabchick, Moorhen and Heron — but embraces many others. The mammals include that delightful creature the Water Vole, and the Water Shrew is not uncommon. In late summer the canal is bright with dragonflies and damselflies; recently an observer on a Leicestershire canal counted 13 different species! Frogs spawn in sheltered reaches and the Grass Snake is frequent. And if you will delve beneath the surface, using the simplest of apparatus — a strong net, a pie-dish, a magnifying glass and an identification book — you will discover a whole new and unsuspected world of nature.

To end this review we must consider the matrix in which all this richness is embedded — the fertile farmlands of the East Midlands. The modern pattern of farming, vast fields with no hedges, few grazing animals, monocultured barley, and no weeds, is spreading across the region from East Anglia. Nevertheless, there is still plenty of traditional farmland with generous hedges and standard trees, copses and spinneys, ditches and ponds, and sometimes waste places such as railway cuttings. This landscape has been influenced a good deal by the hunting and shooting propensities of many farmers. Let us not indulge in ethical arguments but enjoy what is left.

Farmland carries the greatest number of our bird species, from woodland birds like Robins, Chaffinches, Wrens, Dunnocks, Blackbirds and Song Thrushes, to birds of open country like Lapwings, Corn Buntings and Skylarks. Fox and Badger, Brown Hare and Hedgehog, Rabbit and the smaller rodents find ample food and shelter in such a countryside.

Farmland, we must remember, is private property, and we must use the footpaths and bridle roads, all now signposted (although, alas, some farmers plough across them). The tallest and most densely grown hedges will often be found along bridle roads. There is another type of track well worth discovering, the 'green road' or 'mere', narrow uncoloured roads on the map which seem to

A Moorhen, a typical canal-side species, settles on to its eggs.

The **Gibraltar Point** area is gaining land from the sea through the deposition of sand and silt against a shingle spit at the entrance to the Wash. No part of the Nature Reserve is more than 250 years old. The first stage is the development of a 'ridge and runnel' beach on which Little Terns, Ringed Plovers and Oyster-catchers breed. Gradually a mobile dune ridge builds, and when this is clothed with lyme-grass and marram, Skylarks, Meadow Pipits and occasional Shelducks colonise. Sea-buckthorn becomes established, giving song-posts for Reed Buntings and Linnets; as the cover becomes more extensive White-throats and Dunnocks quickly dominate the bird community. Strip-saltings, scoured by tidal action between successive ridges, harbour winter flocks of Snow Buntings, Shorelarks, Twites and mixed finches, feeding on the seeds of glasswort. Fieldfares and other thrushes eat the berries of sea-buckthorn. As the dunes become stable and the vegetation more varied, with occasional trees, so Magpie, Blackbird, Song Thrush, Blue Tit and other song-birds appear, the early colonists becoming fewer. But Skylarks, Meadow Pipits and Reed Buntings remain common on the salt-marsh, alongside Partridges, Pheasants and Short-eared Owls.

The rolling farmland scenery of Lincoln-shire; such habitats support a great variety of wildlife.

lead from nowhere to nowhere. They puzzle historians; to the naturalist they are a delight, for they usually consist of a narrow passage maintained by the occasional tractor through dense thickets of thorn and bramble. A superb example is the track which forms the boundary between Lincolnshire and Leicestershire; this ancient road, known as 'The Drift', runs from Woolsthorpe southward to Sproxton, and every creature of cultivated land can be seen there. At one point it passes the site of a Romano-British settlement. Was this the origin of the road? Whether it was or not, it does emphasise the debt we owe to our ancestors for the rich countryside in which we live, and the wildlife which surrounds us. It is our own generation which is endangering it.

BIRDS

The Great Crested Grebe is the most striking aquatic bird in the region. A survey in 1965 discovered nearly 800 adults in spring, among which there could well have been over 200 breeding pairs. There is a marked autumn movement of this species, which was nearly extinguished in the nineteenth century, when the black and chestnut head feathers were used by milliners. Its recovery was one of the first triumphs for conservation. The Little Grebe or Dabchick, a closely related but inconspicuous bird despite its noisy trilling calls, is even commoner; and whereas the Great Crested Grebe requires the larger lakes and reservoirs, the Little Grebe will breed in small pools, in quiet reaches of rivers, and along canals. A pair bred recently on the children's boating lake in a city park in Leicester.

Many people find the Heron attractive as it stands motionless by the water's edge, waiting to seize with lightning stroke some unsuspecting fish. Herons breed in colonies in the tops of tall trees, usually on private estates, and so are protected at a time when they are vulnerable to disturbance.

Several duck species breed in the East Midlands, in very small numbers except for the Mallard, which is common and widespread, and the Tufted Duck, now rapidly expanding. Many ducks winter at our reservoirs, where the Mallard and Wigeon are the most common. Peak numbers are often 1,000 or more of each at some waters. The talkative little Teal is still present in hundreds, and Shoveler, Pintail and the dull-plumaged Gadwall appear from time to time. These are all surface-feeding ducks, which spend most of the daylight hours just resting; in contrast the diving ducks are most active, constantly searching under the water for food. Commonest are the Tufted Duck and Pochard, and flocks of non-breeding birds are now often seen in summer as well as in winter. The Goldeneye, on the other hand, is more solitary, except during early spring when parties of birds, dominated by one or two black and white males, indulge in striking

Below: A Hedgehog tackles a hen's egg, one of its favourite delicacies. Bottom: drake Shoveler, a breeding duck of local distribution in the East Midlands.

display movements. The Goosander is now regular at some reservoirs, and at Eye Brook flocks often number up to 200. The closely related Red-breasted Merganser and the handsome white Smew are less common. There is always a chance of visits from sea-ducks, such as Scaup, Common and Velvet Scoters, Long-tailed Duck, and species of divers, all of which winter regularly off the coast of the Wash.

The Mute Swan is common and well loved everywhere; it has two wild relatives from the far north which are here in winter: Bewick's Swans come in large numbers to the Ouse Washes from north Russia; they wander a good deal, and often turn up at our larger waters. Whooper Swans, mainly from Iceland, are larger and show more yellow on their bills. Brent Geese occur in winter on the Wash, and the Pink-footed Geese come infrequently, although they were regular visitors until a few years ago. 'Grey Geese' only appear occasionally inland; but the black-necked Canada Geese, introduced from North America some 300 years ago to decorate private lakes, are now generally distributed and quite wild.

Of our birds of prey the Kestrel is widespread and is often seen by motorists hovering above motorway verges, where the long grass around the tree saplings harbours mice and voles. The Sparrowhawk, once our commonest predator, has been almost wiped out over most of east England, poisoned by toxic residues from the many chemicals used in agriculture and ingested by the small birds on which it preys. However, now that the conservationists have secured a ban on the worst of these chemicals, it is seen occasionally in the wilder parts of the region. On the northern moors that fierce little falcon the Merlin, the male grey-backed, the female dark brown, is found, although it has probably never been common. The related Hobby, a summer visitor with a southern distribution, and a prime target for egg-collectors, is here at the northern limit of its range; but it has bred in recent years in Northamptonshire and Leicestershire. Other birds of prey are winter visitors – the lordly Peregrine Falcon, the Osprey, the Buzzard (which has bred occasionally) and the Hen Harrier.

Guardian of the northern moors is the Red Grouse, whose loud voice warns you to *g'back-back-back*. In some parts of the Peak, particularly the Goyt valley, there are small colonies of Black Grouse, and the extraordinary arena

Male (top) and female Pochard, a duck most often encountered in this region in non-breeding flocks on open areas of water.

A female Kestrel, here seen about to alight, is a familiar hovering shape in the East Midland skies.

display of the males at their 'lek' is an experience eagerly sought by bird-watchers who do not mind being out at dawn. Pheasant numbers are artificially maintained, since shooting is big business nowadays. The Partridge, equally desirable to the sportsman, is not responsive to the same kind of encouragement, and probably because of changed farming methods is declining rapidly. It is now perhaps scarcer than the Red-legged Partridge, which has been spreading into the region from East Anglia for some time. The Quail is irregular in summer, a mere voice in the long grass, saying *wet-my-lips, wet-my-lips*; and so also was the hoarse Corncrake until it succumbed to changes on the farm. Water Rails are not infrequent in winter and breed in a few places; but this is a secretive bird, not often seen.

In the breeding season wading birds are widespread but not plentiful, except for the Curlew, which is found on the upland pastures and moors of the Peak. It has bred on a few lowland farms in Leicestershire in recent years. The Redshank and Snipe both nest in the wet upland fields, and used also to breed in wet pastures before efficient drainage took away their habitat. The highest moors of Derbyshire carry numbers of Golden Plovers, and on the wet summit of Bleaklow a few Dunlins breed. The Woodcock nests in the larger woods and recently I discovered a nest within a yard of a public footpath in Swithland Wood in Leicestershire. There is an influx of these birds from Europe in winter, judging by some of the large shooting bags. Since the Second War the Little Ringed Plover has colonised gravel workings, particularly in the Trent valley. It is good to note that the Lapwing or Green Plover is still a familiar breeding bird, and large flocks spend the winter on pastures and ploughland.

A familiar sight in winter is of various species of gulls, which feed at rubbish dumps, in town parks and on recreation grounds, or behind the plough, leaving at dusk in long skeins on the journey to reservoirs where they roost in dense, noisy packs well out on the water. Only the Black-headed Gull, the most numerous, breeds regularly in one or two small inland colonies, and in large numbers on the saltings of the Wash. There have been a few breeding occurrences of the Lesser Black-backed Gull, and flocks of non-breeding birds spend the summer months in some places. The others — Herring, Great Black-backed and Common Gulls — move to the coast or migrate to Scandinavia. The Little Gull, which breeds on the Continent, is visiting the Midlands increasingly, and the white Glaucous and Iceland Gulls of the far north sometimes occur, and are in fact fairly regular at Ogston Reservoir in Derbyshire. Both sea-terns and marsh-terns visit the reservoirs on migration, and gather in large numbers at Gibraltar Point, where they are often harried by passing Arctic Skuas.

Owl populations have to be judged mainly by what we hear at night, and the Tawny Owl is noisily concerned to keep us informed of his presence. The Barn Owl has always been a difficult species to census, but there is no definite evidence of a decline in the East Midlands. The Long-eared Owl is the most nocturnal, hunting in deepest darkness in dense woods, and its status is thus uncertain. The Little Owl, often seen just before dusk, was introduced to this country at the end of the last century; it increased at a frightening rate, then declined, and now seems to have stabilised at a reasonable level. The only diurnal member is the Short-eared Owl; it breeds in small numbers on the Derbyshire moors and on coastal marshes, and winters regularly at some of our reservoirs. Its numbers are geared to cyclical vole plagues, and when these destructive rodents are abundant it can rear large families. This is a lovely bird, as it quarters the ground with long-winged buoyant flight, its mottled plumage warm against the grey winter grasses.

Another bird of the night which seems to have almost disappeared is the Nightjar. Its decline is partly due to loss of habitat — it likes open heathy country — but the young Forestry Commission plantations which were so common at the end of the war and which suited it well have now grown up and are no longer ideal. A few birds can still be heard 'churring' on warm summer nights, mainly in the Dukeries, and in a few young coniferous plantations. One such is Morkery Wood in Lincolnshire, where a picnic place and forest walks enable one to get to know this extraordinary bird.

The Woodcock's mottled plumage camouflages it most effectively when it sits on its nest among dead leaves.

The Lapwing, a familiar breeding bird in the East Midlands.

Kingfishers are now regularly met with by river and canal, having quite recovered from the adverse effects of the last severe winter, 1962–63.

The great passerine order, the song-birds, comprises some 70 or so regular species in this region, and space forbids mention of many. The Skylark is everywhere common, and with the Meadow Pipit makes up the bulk of the bird population of the northern moors. In those areas will also be found the Twite: a Linnet-like bird with a cheerful twittering song. Woodland species often gather into large mixed flocks in winter, and it is worth while searching for them — the noisy gipsy band of tits and finches, Goldcrests, Treecreepers and woodpeckers. With them you may find the Nuthatch, but this has a curious distribution in the region; it is almost totally absent, for instance, from the woods of east Leicestershire. Recently it has spread into the limestone dales of Derbyshire.

The Whinchat is a summer visitor, now becoming scarce, for it delights in the rough weedy corners and the large headlands which modern farmers cannot tolerate; a close relative, the Stonechat, is frequently present in winter. The Nightingale is here at the northern limit of its range, and as with all species so placed, tends to fluctuate. Salcey and Yardley Chase are famous Nightingale haunts, as are the woods of east Leicestershire and the Nottinghamshire Dukeries. The Sedge Warbler is a common bird of the waterside and is spreading into farmland hedges; but the Reed Warbler is more confined, needing large beds of the common reed. The disused Grantham Canal is one of the very best places for it. Of the leaf-warblers the Wood Warbler is the least common, and its shivering song is the apotheosis of a woodland spring. In the Goyt valley a path runs level with the very tops of tall trees growing on a steep slope, and here the Wood Warbler sings on a level with one's eyes.

A number of winter visitors, the Great Grey Shrike, the Snow Bunting and rarer Lapland Bunting, can sometimes be met by reservoirs, or on coastal marshes. On the other hand that spectacular bird the Waxwing, which comes irregularly from Scandinavia when food shortage threatens, flaunts its unbelievable beauty on berried bushes in town gardens and trunk-road roundabouts.

Kingfisher with prey; a series of mild winters has favoured this bird's increase.

Barn Owls' nest-site in the gable of a barn: left, owlets (one swallowing a rat); right, fully grown owls.

173

MAMMALS

Mammals are common in our countryside, but as they are mainly small, and either nocturnal or secretive, they rarely come to the notice of the non-specialist observer. Small rodents, Moles and shrews, Rabbits and Brown Hares, Foxes and Badgers, are widely and generally distributed. There are exceptions. For instance the Yellow-necked Mouse, first described in 1894, has been recorded only once in Leicestershire in the last 40 years. A Dormouse obtained in 1960 beside a west Leicestershire canal was the first for 100 years, but two more have been found since. Harvest Mice have been recorded in several counties in the past few years — just odd animals here and there. But are these species as rare as the records suggest? Or is it rather scarcity of observers? The recording of mammals is scanty, and nothing like the voluminous county reports of birds is published.

The Grey Squirrel is probably our most conspicuous small mammal. It was introduced to several places in the last century and became a pest, especially in regions like ours where the forester is ever anxious for the care of his young trees. Our own Red Squirrel has suffered a serious decline — probably due to the loss of its specialised habitat as much as by direct competition with the Grey. In most of the region it has not been seen for 20 years or more, but a few are still to be found in the Peak and the north of Nottinghamshire, and it is still fairly plentiful in north Lincolnshire. There is a very good chance of finding it in Willingham Forest near Market Rasen, a Forestry Commission property with a public picnic area and nature trail. Just recently there have been signs that the Red Squirrel may be increasing; an inquiry carried out by Sheffield naturalists in 1973 found that numbers had recovered in that area since 1966. Their stronghold was in the Derwent valley and at two places just over the border in South Yorkshire.

The Red Squirrel, much scarcer than the Grey, is nevertheless to be found in scattered localities in the East Midlands.

Some interesting bat discoveries have been made recently. These are, of course, almost impossible to identify on the wing, though it is a fair assumption that the tiny ones we commonly see are Pipistrelle Bats, and the large ones frequently observed are Noctule Bats. Identification really depends on the occasional dead one found, or by the discovery of their roosts, so any bodies you find should be sent to the nearest museum. Two canal tunnels in Leicestershire have roosts of previously unrecorded species for that county, Daubenton's Bat at Saddington and Husbands Bosworth, and Natterer's Bat at the former place. Specimens of both have been found in Northamptonshire and Lincolnshire, and several colonies of Long-eared Bats are believed to exist. Caves are favourite roosting places, and it is disappointing that so far no bat roosts have been discovered in the limestone caves of the Peak.

The Red Deer is the only native species of deer found in the region, and these are in parkland herds, although escapes do occur and there are wild specimens at large in some places. The herd at Bradgate Park is well worth a visit. The Fallow Deer, much commoner as a parkland resident, is an introduced species which has a widespread distribution in Europe. There are records of introductions

Noctule Bat in flight and at rest; though this is the largest of the British bats, sure identification of these flying mammals can only be made in the hand.

Two waterside mammals swimming under water: left, Water Vole; right, Water Shrew.

from the fourteenth century, and there is a tradition that earlier ones were made by the Romans. A number of colour varieties exist, and it may be that the very dark ones are of the northern race, introduced from Norway. Even more than the Red Deer, escaped Fallow Deer now maintain wild populations. Quite recently I noted a small herd feeding in fields by the side of the M1 motorway near to Sherwood Forest.

Escapes of even more exotic species have occurred from Woburn, the Duke of Bedford's seat, but the only species which seems to have become established in the East Midlands is the Chinese Muntjac. There are numbers of this little deer in Salcey Forest, Yardley Chase and other woods in Northamptonshire, and single animals have been found in the grounds of the Northampton Technical College and at a factory in Wellingborough. Several records have come from Leicestershire and south Derbyshire, and it may become well established in the region.

Hunting interests have undoubtedly kept the Fox as a common mammal of our countryside; without the passionate zeal which farmers often show for the hunt it would have been exterminated as a pest. The Badger quietly maintains its numbers, and a survey in Leicestershire between 1960 and 1965 recorded at least 300 setts, many comprising several occupied holes.

Waterside mammals are most easily watched from canal banks, or along rivers such as the Nene which have towpaths and public access. The attractive Water Vole — wrongly described by many as a rat — is common and probably the most easy and rewarding to watch of our small mammals. The Water Shrew, largest of our three shrews, is not uncommon, and affects the same habitat. Otters are present, probably in very small numbers now, but you may see their signs, or the remains of a fishy meal, along river banks. The Mink, a ferocious waterside animal from North America, has escaped in some numbers from fur farms, and is firmly and dangerously established in some places. It prefers upland rivers, and there are numbers in the Ladybower area of Derbyshire.

One marine mammal occurs. The Common or Harbour Seal, which breeds on the sand-banks of the Wash, and hauls out at high tide at the Gibraltar Point LNR. The cows have their pups on sand-banks, the birth taking place between tides, and the pup is able to swim off when the water rises. Young pups are sometimes found on the beaches of Skegness and other resorts; they should be left for the experts to deal with, for if handled by humans they may not be accepted again by their parents. Dolphins and Porpoises can sometimes be seen offshore, and I remember a large dolphin — probably a False Killer Whale — coming in behind the sand-spit at high tide at Gibraltar Point, and having to roll and heave itself over a nearly submerged sand-bank to regain the sea.

The Rabbit is abundant in the East Midlands; but here as elsewhere its population is affected by periodic outbreaks of myxomatosis.

Left: Slow-worm; not a snake, but a legless lizard.

AMPHIBIANS AND REPTILES

Country-goers tend to ignore this group of animals — unjustifiably, for they are not difficult to observe and are full of interest. We have four common species of amphibians, the Smooth and Great Crested Newts, the Common Frog and Common Toad, and they are widely distributed. Unfortunately they are losing many habitats as field ponds disappear. In the past these have been major spawning sites, and therefore garden ponds, ornamental pools, and even reservoirs gain in importance. When Frogs and Toads journey to reservoirs they have to cross roads, and in recent years there has been heavy mortality from cars. Shallow reaches of canals are also extensively used, and Frogs may be found in moorland pools at high altitudes in the Peak — often quite temporary pools, such as large puddles on moorland tracks.

In the breeding season newts are most attractive, with dragons' crests along the back and tail, and orange and red underparts. There are two uncommon species in the East Midlands. The Palmate Newt — not easy to differentiate from the Smooth Newt — was originally an upland species, and tends to be found at higher altitudes. It is commonest in the Peak district, but in recent years several breeding stations have been discovered in Charnwood Forest in ponds above 650 feet.

The Natterjack Toad, distinguished by a yellow streak along its back, is now confined in the East Midlands to the Saltfleetby Nature Reserve on the Lincolnshire coast. It is mainly an inhabitant of sandy coastal areas, and as a matter of interest was first recorded as a British species in 1776 from Revesby Abbey in Lincolnshire, where it was locally called the 'Natter Jack'.

Our region contains two lizards: the Common or Viviparous Lizard and the Slow-worm. The former is common in dry upland areas and on heather moors, and is found on the Peak and in Sherwood, Charnwood and Salcey Forests, and in many parts of Lincolnshire. A quick rustle in dry bracken is often the only indication of its presence, but a warm spring day will reveal numbers to a quiet and watchful searcher. The Slow-worm likes sandy areas, and tends to hide under stones. It is worth searching for; the colour, often golden yellow, and the silky texture of the skin are a delight. On two occasions in Charnwood Forest I have found the uncommon southern blue-spotted form of this legless lizard.

Adders or Vipers are much more frequent than is supposed, and are timid creatures unless surprised. They can best be observed on open heathy hillsides, basking in April or May sunshine. One should move with care and examine likely spots, such as short grassy banks or smooth stones, in Charnwood Forest, the Peak and on dry heaths in Lincolnshire such as the Scotton Common Nature Reserve. The Grass Snake prefers lush vegetation and has a distinct liking for water. The canal-side is an excellent place to search for one, and it can often be seen swimming in the water.

Above: Common Toad; the filling in of field ponds destroys this amphibian's spawning-grounds, increasing the probability of their appearance in garden pools. Below: the Common Frog is now becoming scarcer as the result of the pollution of its water habitat.

Guide to wildlife habitats in the East Midlands

This Appendix provides a selected but varied list of places of wildlife interest. It is emphasised that nature reserves exist primarily for the conservation of animals and plants and in some cases for environmental experiments and research. They are not 'public open spaces' in the recreational sense. Access to many is therefore restricted and some, because of their sensitivity to disturbance, have been omitted from this list, in deference to the wishes of conservation organisations. Even with 'open' reserves visitors are earnestly requested to keep to the paths and bridleways and so avoid damage to the habitat and undue disturbance to wildlife. *There is no public access to the enclosed farmland which is part of many National Trust properties.*

Application to visit a National Nature Reserve (NNR) should be made to the appropriate Regional Office of the Nature Conservancy Council (NCC) at the address given. Intention to visit reserves of the Royal Society for the Protection of Birds (RSPB) should be notified to the Warden (whose address is shown) as far in advance as possible. In all cases where an address is shown, it is wise to contact the Warden to avoid disappointment.

DERBYSHIRE/WEST YORKSHIRE
Derbyshire Naturalists' Trust, 25 Rykneld Way, Littleover, Derby, DE3 7AT.

Derwent Estate SK 18 92. Deeply undulating moorland on e. bank of R. Derwent, rising to 1775 ft and overlooking Derwent and Howden reservoirs. 6468 a. 13 mls w. and n.w. of Sheffield, n. of A57. (Access by public footpaths only.) NT.

Dovedale SK 14 53. Farmland (private) and woods on both banks of R. Dove, from Biggin Dale at n. end to Ilam at s. end, 821 a. incl. (Derbyshire side) part of Cold Eaton Farm, Iron Tors, Mill Dale, Baley Hill, the Nabbs, Pickering

Tor and several plantations, and (Staffordshire side) Hall Dale, Bunster Hill, Hurt's and Dovedale Woods. 4–7 mls n.w. of Ashbourne, w. of A515. NT.

Edale SK 13 85. Lose Hill Pike SK 15 85, between Hope and Edale valleys; also Mam Tor and the Winnats Pass SK 13 83. 5–6 mls e. of Chapel-en-le-Frith, astride and n. of A625 near Castleton and Hope. (Access by public footpaths only.) NT.

Hardwick Hall SK 46 64. Country Park, 250 a. 5 mls n.w. of Mansfield, s. of A617 at Glapwell. NT.

Hilton Gravel-pits SK 25 32. Large and several small interconnected pools. Great Crested Grebe, Dabchick, Tufted Duck; various waders and waterfowl on passage. 7 mls s.w. of Derby, 10 mls e. of Uttoxeter, n. of A516 at Hilton. Entrance and car park on e. side of Sutton Lane SK 245 315. Derby. Nats T.

Hope Woodlands SK 14 94. Extensive moorland in Peak District. 16,000 a. 12 mls w. of Sheffield, 6 mls e. of Glossop, on n. side of A57. NT.

Ladybower Reservoir SK 18 86. Narrow reservoir in moorland setting. Mink. Waterfowl. 9 mls w. of Sheffield A57. Viewable from roads.

Longshaw SK 24 80 Moorland and woods, 1097 a. Incl. Padley Woods, Owlet Tor, and Froggatt Wood SK 247 770. 1–3 mls s.e. of Hathersage, on s. side of A625. NT.

Ogston Reservoir SK 37 60. Large reservoir attracting wildfowl and waders, especially in winter. 5 mls e. of Matlock, s. of B6014. Viewable from minor road.

Peak National Park, Mostly in Derbyshire, intruding into Staffordshire, Cheshire, Greater Manchester, South and West Yorkshire. 542 sq. mls. Comprises the 'Dark Peak' in the north, a gritstone plateau topping 2000 ft on Kinder Scout and Bleaklow, separated by Edale and Hope valleys from the 'White Peak', limestone upland with numerous wooded dales. Incl. Dovedale NNR, the Pennine Way (starts at Edale), Manifold valley, Hope Forest, the Tissington and High Peak Trails (former railway lines) and Goyt valley (traffic-free zone at summer weekends). Information centres at Bakewell (Market Hall, Bridge Street), Buxton (St Ann's Well, The Crescent), Castleton (Castle Street) and Edale (Field Head). Traversed by A515 Ashbourne–Buxton; A6 Matlock–Buxton; A623 Baslow–Chapel-en-le-Frith; A625 Hathersage–Chapel-en-le-Frith; A57 Sheffield–Glossop; A628 Stocksbridge–Hadfield; and many other

Sunset over the mud-flats of Kirton Marsh in Lincolnshire.

roads. Recommended leaflets: Walks in the Peak National Park, The Winnats, The White Peak Scenic Motor Route and Short Walks, Goyt Valley Traffic Scheme, Mountain Safety and the Pennine Way.

Shining Cliff Wood SK 34 53. Woodland on w. bank of R. Derwent, 200 a. 4 mls n. of Belper, 1 ml n. of Ambergate station, on w. side of A6. NT.

Staunton Harold Reservoir SK 37 23. Large reservoir attracting wildfowl and waders, especially in winter. 9 mls s. of Derby A514; traversed by B587. Car parks.

Sudbury Hall SK 16 32. Parkland, 193 a. 6 mls e. of Uttoxeter, 12 mls w. of Derby, s. of A50. NT.

NOTTINGHAMSHIRE

Attenborough LNR SK 53 34. Flooded gravel-pits with reedbeds and small islands by R. Trent, 240 a. Water Vole. Grebes, Common Terns, Little Ringed Plovers, Tufted and other ducks, Reed and Sedge Warblers. 3 mls s.w. of Nottingham, on s. side of A453 and railway. Car park, information centre, trail, key to hide available from warden. (Warden – 168 Long Lane, Attenborough, Nottingham.) Trent Gravels Ltd/Notts. T for Nature Conservation.

Clumber Park SK 64 75. Landscaped parkland on former heath bordering Sherwood Forest, 3784 a. Canada Geese and other waterfowl, Nightingale, Hawfinch. 2½ mls s.e. of Worksop, 4½ mls s.w. of East Retford, between A614 (three entrances) and B6005 (two entrances). A57 touches n.e. boundary at Manton Lodge gate. NT.

The Dukeries SK 57 74, SK 63 71. Landscaped parkland with lakes and waterfowl. Incl. Welbeck Park and Great Lake, and Thoresby Park. Canada Geese and other waterfowl, Nightingale, Hawfinch. 3 mls s. of Worksop e. of A60. (Restricted access to parts.)

Holme Pierrepont SK 62 39. National Water Sports Centre and Country Park incl. nature reserve with pool and woodland. 5 mls e. of Nottingham A52. Car and trailer parks, picnic area, toilets. Notts. CC.

The National Trust East Midlands, Regional Office, Clumber Park, Worksop, Nottinghamshire, S80 3BE.

Nottinghamshire Trust for Nature Conservation, High Pavement, Nottingham, NG1 1HB.

Rufford Abbey SK 64 65. Meadows, woods and lake forming Country Park. Canada and Barnacle Geese and other waterfowl, many song-bird species in The Wilderness. 15 mls n. of Nottingham, on e. side of A614 near Ollerton. Car parks. Notts. CC.

Sherwood SK 62 67. Country Park at heart of ancient Sherwood Forest, incl. magnificent oak woodland. 25 mls n. of Nottingham A614 – B6034, just n. of Edwinstowe. Car parks, visitor centre. Notts. CC.

Southwell Trail SK 70 54. 5½ mls of disused railway through Greet valley. 12 mls n. of Nottingham A614; 8 mls e. of Mansfield A617. Car parks at Southwell, Kirklington and Farnsfield (on w. side of A614). Picnic areas at the last two places. Notts. CC.

LINCOLNSHIRE

Gibraltar Point LNR TF 56 58. Accreting shingle ridges and sand-dunes, salt and freshwater marsh, sea-buckthorn scrub. 1500 a. Bird Observatory and Field Station. Common Seals. Winter flocks of Fieldfares, Snow Buntings, Shorelarks, Twites, seabirds on passage, breeding shore birds. 4 mls s. of Skegness on Wash littoral. Car parks, interpretive centre, nature trail. Accomm. at Bird Observatory by arrangement. Lincs. CC/ East Lindsey DC/ Lincs. T for Nature Conservation.

Lincolnshire Trust for Nature Conservation, The Manor House, Alford, Lincolnshire, LN13 9DL.

Saltfleetby and Theddlethorpe TF 48 90. Sand-dunes and freshwater slacks with sea-buckthorn and elder scrub. 3 mls n. of Mablethorpe A1031. Air Min./Lincs. T for Nature Conservation.

Snipe Dales TF 32 68. Steep-sided valleys fretted with streams, with rough grassland on higher slopes and marshy areas with alder/willow below. 120 a. Badger. Heron, Snipe, Woodcock, Kestrel, Short-eared Owl, Sand Martin colony. 4 mls e. of Horncastle A158 – A1115, 5 mls w. of Spilsby A1115 at Winceby. Car park on n. side of road, access to reserve by path through old churchyard. Lincs. CC/Lincs. T for Nature Conservation.

Tetney TA 36 03. Saltmarsh, dunes and sandy foreshore. Terns and other shore birds. 6 mls s. of Grimsby, on e. side of A1031. RSPB.

Willingham Forest TF 14 88. State forest. Red Squirrels. 1 ml e. of Market Rasen, on s. side of A631. Picnic area, trail. For Comm.

LEICESTERSHIRE

Bradgate Park SK 53 11. Remnant of ancient Charnwood Forest with herds of Red and Fallow Deer. Drive through leads to Cropston reservoir SK 54 11. Swithland Wood SK 54 13 and Swithland reservoir SK 56 14 are nearby. 4 mls n.w. of Leicester B5327, w. and n. of Anstey. Lies between B5327 and B5330, latter giving good views of Cropston reservoir and access to Swithland Wood. City of Leicester.

Empingham Reservoir SK 94 08. Largest man-made lake in England, over 3000 a., when flooding is complete in 1977. Comprises two main arms divided by Hambleton Hill 320 ft, with islands and 'bunds' to attract waders, terns and waterfowl. W. ends of arms and adjoining land will be nature reserve. 6 mls w. of Stamford, between Empingham and Oakham, on s. side of A606. Public footpaths, restricted access to hides. Anglian Water Authority/Leics. and Rutland Nats T.

Eye Brook Reservoir SP 85 95. Large reservoir attracting wildfowl and waders, especially in winter. 5 mls s. of Uppingham, w. of B6003. Viewable from minor road skirting n. half.

Leicestershire and Rutland Trust for Nature Conservation, 1 West Street, Leicester, LE1 6UU.

Thornton Reservoir SK 47 07. Reservoir attracting winter wildfowl. 4 mls s. of Coalville B585, turning e. at Bagworth. Viewable from minor road s. of Thornton.

NORTHAMPTONSHIRE

Pitsford Reservoir SP 76 69. Large reservoir attracting wildfowl and waders, especially in winter. 6 mls n. of Northampton, on e. side of A508. Traversed by road between Brixworth and Holcot.

Northamptonshire Naturalists' Trust, The Old Rectory, Stoke Doyle, Peterborough, PE8 5TH.

Animal collections in the East Midlands

Coton Manor Wildlife Garden

This is an old English garden of charm and beauty, in which you can see flamingos, waterfowl and various other tropical birds at liberty in the water gardens. There is also a Tropical House. Altogether there are 400 birds of 100 species. The gardens were opened in 1970 by Commander H. Pasley-Tyler, R.N.

Coton Manor Wildlife Garden. **Address** Coton Manor, Northampton. **Telephone** Guilsborough 219. **Open** 14.00–18.00 Thurs and Sun, April–Oct and special parties on other days by arrangement. **Guided tours. Acreage** 7. **Catering** tea room. Gift shop. **Car** 10 mls n.w. of Northampton, near Guilsborough, off A428. **Train** to Northampton (11 mls). Public **not allowed** to feed birds.

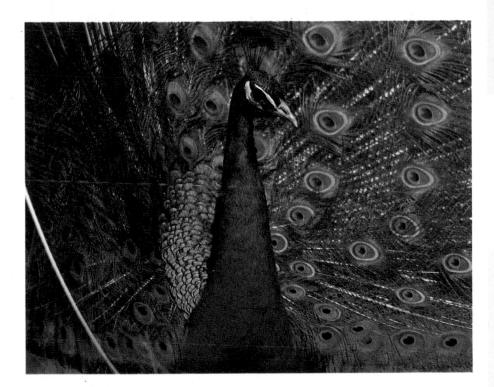

Left: Peacock in full display.

Guilsborough Grange Bird and Pet Park

This is mainly a bird collection, with waterfowl, parrots, Snowy Owls and other birds. There are a few mammals, including Fallow Deer, foxes and otters. Birds which breed here regularly include Diamond Doves, Quaker Parrakeets, Fischer's Lovebirds, Peach-faced Lovebirds and Zebra Finches. The Park was opened in 1971 by Major and Mrs S. J. Symington. This is a pleasant place in which to relax, with gardens, lakes and a stream. There is also a Pets' Corner containing domestic animals, where children can have pony and donkey rides.

Guilsborough Grange Bird and Pet Park. **Address** Guilsborough Grange, Guilsborough, Northamptonshire. **Telephone** Guilsborough 278. **Open** 11.00–18.00 28th Feb–31st Oct. **Catering** light refreshments. **Guided tours** by arrangement. **Acreage** 25. **Car** 12 mls n.w. of Northampton, off A428 on West Haddon road. **Bus** 326 to Guilsborough from Northampton and Market Harborough, then ¾ ml walk to Park. **Train** to Northampton (12 mls) or to Rugby (10 mls) or to Long Buckby (5 mls). **Taxis** available. **Other facilities** children's playground, pony and donkey rides. Dogs on leash only. Public **not allowed** to feed animals.

High Peak Garden Centre

The Garden Centre opened a small bird garden in 1973, having created an artificial stream from the River Noe nearby, which flows through a series of pools. The stream is stocked with trout, which you can feed with food provided by the management. The pools contain ornamental waterfowl. There are 15 aviaries exhibiting parrakeets, lovebirds, rosellas, Cockatiels, Budgerigars, quail, bantams and pheasants, cockatoos, macaws and a variety of small finches.

High Peak Garden Centre. **Address** Bamford, Derbyshire. **Telephone** Bamford 484. **Open** 10.00–dusk summer and winter. **Catering** snack bar. **Acreage** 2¼. **Car** 2 mls w. of Hathersage, 4 mls e. of Castleton on A625. **Bus** Castleton service from Sheffield stops outside entrance. No pets. Public **not allowed** to feed birds. Fish may be fed with pellets provided.

Mablethorpe Animal and Bird Gardens

This is a small mixed collection of mammals and birds, the emphasis being on animals which are often kept as pets. The aim is to show each species in pairs or family groups. Species which breed here include Moluccan Cockatoos, foxes and porcupines. There are about 40 mammals, and over 100 birds altogether, and half a dozen reptiles. The Zoo was opened in 1974 by Mr G. J. King.

Matlock Bath Aquarium

Matlock Bath Aquarium, once the site of the Hydro, was opened in 1963. The old Hydro's bathrooms and consulting rooms are now in the open air, where the Aquarium's tropical pool has an island and willow, with four powerful lamps below water level. The pool is fed by the original thermal spring, which is now enjoyed by a collection of large Mirror Carp, Higoi Carp, Golden Orfe, Green and Golden Tench, Goldfish, catfish and Rainbow Trout. The fish are fed every Sunday afternoon, between 3.30 and 5 p.m., from April to September, by divers who give them their food by hand. During August, feeding also takes place on Tuesday, Wednesday and Thursday mornings.

Natureland Marine Zoo

Natureland Marine Zoo specialises in aquatic animals and you can see seals, sealions, penguins and waterfowl in outdoor pools. There is also a Tropical House containing reptiles, a Floral House with tropical birds and more reptiles, a Children's Corner and an excellent Aquarium.

The Common Seals are in two seawater pools, and seal pups are often reared here, having been washed ashore as infants unable to fend for themselves. It is no easy matter to hand-rear a seal pup, but the experience gained here has resulted in a method being developed whereby 90% of the pups abandoned on beaches in the vicinity have been reared. The test of this is whether they have reached the weight at three months which they ought to reach in the wild. In theory, these young seals would be returned to the sea, but having been in captivity during the critical first few months of their lives, when they would normally learn to fend for themselves, they are unable to do so, and must therefore remain in human care.

The Common Seal is found round British shores in the Bristol Channel, the Wash, and along the east coast of Scotland, but the main populations are around the west and north Scottish coasts and islands. In the wild, pups are born in June, on dry land, but they immediately take to the water, becoming adult in four years. Adult females congregate for birth and rearing until August, when the males begin fighting before mating in September. Thereafter, males and females remain together until the following summer. Seals can sleep under water, remaining submerged for 15 minutes before drawing breath. While swimming, they surface to breathe every five minutes or so. They can swim at about 10 m.p.h., feeding on fish.

Sealions differ from seals in having jointed front flippers which enables them to move about more freely on land, and they have visible ears. Their skins, however, have no commercial value, and they are not slaughtered for fur, as are seals.

The penguins are Jackass Penguins, otherwise known as Black-footed or Cape Penguins. They live in South African waters, mainly around the Cape. Favourite foods in the wild are anchovies, squid and shellfish. In South Africa they are valued for their eggs and as producers of guano, the dung of fish-eating

Mablethorpe Animal and Bird Gardens. **Address** North End, Mablethorpe, Lincs. **Telephone** Mablethorpe 3346. **Open** daily 10.00–1 hour before dusk, Easter–2nd week in Oct. **Catering** snack bar. Zoo shop. **Car** 1 ml n. of Mablethorpe adjoining council car park (Quebec Road). **Bus** 52 stops 100 yds from Gardens. Public allowed to feed animals with food prepared in Zoo only.

Matlock Bath Aquarium. **Address** North Parade, Matlock Bath, Matlock, Derbyshire. **Telephone** Matlock 3624. **Open** 10.00–17.30 March–July, 10.00–21.00 Aug–Sept, 13.00–18.00 Oct–March Sat and Sun only. **Guided tours** by arrangement. **Car** 1 ml s. of Matlock on A6. **Bus** nearest stop $\frac{1}{4}$ ml. **Train** to Matlock Bath ($\frac{1}{2}$ ml). Public **not allowed** to feed exhibits.

Natureland Marine Zoo. **Address** North Parade, Skegness, Lincs. **Telephone** Skegness 4345. **Open** 10.00–19.30 summer, 10.00–16.00 winter. **Guidebook**. **Catering** kiosk (summer only). Zoo shop. **Guided tours** by arrangement, also recorded commentary. **Acreage** 1. **Car** to n. end of Promenade. **Bus** regular service to Zoo in summer. **Train** to Skegness station (1 ml). **Taxis** available. Public allowed to feed animals in Pets' Corner with prepared food.

Sea anemones live attached to intertidal rocks.

birds which is rich in nitrogen and valued as an organic fertiliser.

There are two more outdoor pools. The first is stocked with trout, rudd, perch, gudgeon, bream and orfe, and there is an island in the middle of it with a tree, which is the home of some Korean Chipmunks, a small species of striped squirrel. They produced six young in 1974. The second pool has Mandarin and Carolina Ducks, pintails, teals, shovelers, shelducks and a swan.

The Tropical House has a pool for Mississippi Alligators, which you see as you cross a bridge over a pool. The lighting here simulates a tropical night, and every few minutes there is an artificial rain storm, with thunder, lightning and cloud effects. Other exhibits here are owls, scorpions and pythons.

The 'Floral Palace' has a large collection of plants and flowers and it is divided into three sections, each with some kind of wildlife in it. The first room is a temperate area, with a pool for Chilean Flamingos and some African Grey Parrots. The middle room is a walk-through tropical aviary, with tanagers and Painted Quail flying free. Several species of tanager have bred here including Mrs Wilson's, Superb, Black-eared and Golden. The Painted Quail have also hatched young.

The Children's Corner has Rabbits, goats, calves and sheep.

In the Aquarium, there are tanks for tropical freshwater fish, many of which breed here, and an interesting collection of coral fish. A further range of tanks shows British seashore life: notice especially the excellent display of sea-anemones. There are two tanks here exhibiting invertebrate animals (without backbones) from British waters, and an enormous seawater tank which you reach via a separate entrance, in which the fish are fed under water each afternoon by a diver. The tank is 25 feet long and it contains Stingrays, sole, Turbot, dabs, skate, Cod, Edible and Shore Crabs, and lobsters.

The Zoo was opened in 1965 by Mr George Cansdale and Mr John Yeadon; Mr Cansdale was formerly Superintendent at London Zoo, and he has brought a wealth of experience to the creation of this interesting collection.

Riber Castle Fauna Reserve and Wildlife Park

This collection was opened in 1963, and it specialises in European and British animals. You can see Red and Fallow Deer, Wild Boar, Scottish Wild Cats, Polecats and an interesting group of Pine Martens, among other British species. One foreign exhibit here is the Raccoon, a North American species. There are aviaries for seabirds, owls and birds of prey, ornamental pheasants and waterfowl, rare breeds of poultry and farm livestock. Riber Castle is now a ruin, but the view from Riber Hill is worth seeing.

Riber Castle Fauna Reserve and Wild-life Park. **Address** Riber Castle, Matlock, Derbyshire. **Telephone** Matlock 2073. **Open** 10.00–19.00 summer, 10.00–16.30 winter. **Guide-book. Catering** snack bar, kiosk. Zoo shop. **Acreage** 12½. **Car** 1 ml s. of Matlock and s. of A615. **Bus** nearest stop Stalkhomes Road, Matlock. **Train** to Matlock (2 mls). **Taxis** available. No pets. Public **not allowed** to feed animals.

Left: the nocturnal Raccoon from North America can be seen at Riber Castle.

Skegness Dolphinarium

The Dolphinarium was opened in 1968, and there are two trained Bottle-nosed Dolphins which give six shows daily, each performance lasting for 30 minutes. A full commentary is given during each show, and this can be pitched according to requirements, with biological facts as well as facts of more general interest.

Skegness Dolphinarium. **Address** Tower Esplanade, Skegness, Lincs. **Telephone** Skegness 2523. **Open** 10.30–18.00 summer, closed in winter. **Guide-book. Guided tours** by arrangement. **Car** to Skegness sea-front, Dolphinarium opposite Tower clock. **Bus** stops at sea-front. **Train** to Skegness (1 ml). **Taxis** available. Public **not allowed** to feed exhibits.

Stapleford Park Lion and Game Reserve

Stapleford Park Lion and Game Reserve was opened in 1968 by Lord Gretton in the grounds of Stapleford Park. There are two drive-through reserves, one for Lions and one for monkeys. The Lions are exhibited in a group, as in safari parks, and you may not get out of your car, nor open the windows while in these two paddocks. This is an essential safety precaution, and it really is dangerous to ignore it. Like many wild animals, Lions appropriate a certain area as their own territory, and any intruder is chased away, or if necessary, attacked. Survival in the wild depends on successfully competing with rivals for the available food supply, and human intruders would be regarded as trespassers. The motor car is not regarded as a threat, since it is inanimate, and provided that the human occupants remain inside and cannot be smelt by the Lions, the car will not be connected with humans.

In the wild, Lions live in family groups consisting of an adult male and two or

Stapleford Park Lion and Game Reserve. **Address** Stapleford Park, Melton Mowbray, Leics. **Telephone** Wymondham (Leics.) 245. **Open** 10.00–18.00 Easter (except Good Friday)–26th Sept. **Catering** licensed restaurant, self-service cafeteria, snack bar. Gift shop. **Acreage** 50. **Car** 5 mls e. of Melton Mowbray off B676 Melton–Colsterworth road. Free car park. **Bus** Melton Mowbray to Saxby, then 1 ml to Park, or by tour buses Barton from Nottingham, Midland Red from Leicester and Birmingham, Lincolnshire Road Car from Grantham and Lincoln. **Train** to Melton Mowbray (5 mls). **Taxis** available. **Other facilities** children's amusements, picnic area, dog kennels, crazy golf. Public **not allowed** to feed animals.

Male Lion: these big cats are slow by wild animal standards, and the males are inclined to be lazy; nevertheless it is extremely dangerous for visitors to ignore the safety procedures laid down at Stapleford and at all other safari parks.

three females with cubs of different ages. The females do all the hunting, after which the male Lion eats first, followed by the females and lastly the cubs. By wild animal standards, Lions are slow creatures, and they mainly kill old, very young or sick animals, thus helping to improve the breeding stock of game animals. If Lions were quick, efficient killers, they would soon destroy their own food supply. In general, the more lethal a wild animal's natural weapons, the less often they are used.

The second reserve exhibits monkeys, and after leaving this you can leave your car and visit Animal Land, a small zoo mainly for children, which exhibits Himalayan Bears, monkeys, Lion cubs, Pumas and a variety of exotic birds.

Sundown Pets Garden

This is a Children's Zoo with about 200 animals. The wild animals here include monkeys, Raccoons, Kinkajous, foxes, squirrels and gerbils, and there is a variety of domestic animals such as chinchillas, Rabbits, guinea-pigs, dogs and farm livestock. You can also see a number of birds, including peafowl, pheasants, duck and geese, guineafowl, parrots, macaws, cockatoos, lories and Budgerigars.

The garden was opened in 1969 by Mr and Mrs J. Rhodes.

Twycross Zoo — see page 217 in the West Midlands section.

Sundown Pets Garden. **Address** Treswell Road, Rampton, Retford, Notts. **Telephone** Rampton 274. **Open** 10.00—dusk summer and winter. **Catering** tea gardens, snack bar. Zoo shop. **Acreage** 12. **Car** 5 mls s.e. of East Retford; from Rampton Village follow road to Cottam Power Station for ¾ ml. **Other facilities** children's playground. Public allowed to feed animals.

West Midlands COLIN RUSSELL AND ERNEST NEAL

As we ride through the countryside or gaze over it from some vantage point such as the Malvern Hills, it is hard to imagine that forest once covered all, and that fields and hedgerows have only become important features in the last few hundred years. It follows that the wildlife of this countryside are the creatures of the forest. It says much for their endurance and versatility that as the landscape changed so they changed, adapting their habits and way of life in order to survive. Those animals which became extinct, like the Brown Bear, Wild Boar and Wolf, did so only because man deliberately campaigned against them. The forests, mainly of oak and ash, have largely disappeared, but fragments can still be found in the Forests of Dean, Delamere and Wyre. These owe their survival to man's love of sport and to the royal obsession with the 'chase'. In fact, the original meaning of the word 'forest' was an area set aside for hunting. Animals such as deer and Fox have been encouraged, sometimes actually imported, for hunting. On the other hand, animals which man thought interfered with his pursuits have been persecuted and driven out into more remote mountainous areas. Eagle and Red Kite, Pine Marten and Polecat are some of the predators that met this fate.

So man not only creates the landscape but in some part determines what creatures will live there. Now the pressures are increasing again and certainly more animals are threatened with extinction. The pattern of agriculture today can take little thought of wildlife, and unfortunately the less obvious pressures of increasing country leisure pursuits are having an even more marked effect.

Colin Russell, zoologist, ecologist and teacher, responsible for a large Biology Department in a College of Education, believed in teaching his subject in direct contact with the living world of nature, and found his metier as Warden and Director of Studies at Preston Montford Field Centre near Shrewsbury. His untimely death, as this book was going to press, is a great loss to the wildlife conservation field in which he had been an active participant for many years.

Part of the Welsh Marches: a view over the Wye valley in Herefordshire towards the hills of Wales. Hereford cattle graze peacefully in the pastures.

Sparrowhawk and Otter have already shown an alarming decline in numbers over the whole of this region in the last 15 years. Let us hope that the gathering strength of County Naturalists' Trusts has come in time to avert disaster; those who care for our heritage of wildlife are urged to give their support and become members.

Yet there is still much to be seen in this region for the motorist who is prepared to park and walk a mile or two, and above all to be patiently observant. Because this is such a good region for the commoner mammals we have thought it worth while giving some hints on how you can find, and enjoy watching, some of the animals which still live amongst us. But first let us look more closely at the region by considering its wildlife treasures county by county.

THE WELSH MARCHES

The western county boundaries of Cheshire, Shropshire and Hereford-Worcester are also the national borders between England and the Principality of Wales. It is a line which still more or less follows the ancient earthworks which Offa, King of Mercia, built in the eighth century to fix the western limits of his kingdom. It is a line later followed by the Normans for their castles, and later still by Edward I and other monarchs in their attempts to contain the unruly Celts. There are abrupt and dramatic changes in land-form where the English lowlands meet the massive uplands of Wales. It is not surprising, then, that this is a region of sharp contrasts, from arable lands and orchards and rich pastures broken by hedgerows and game coverts, to wild moorland, hill sheep-walks and forestry plantations. It is an area rich in the remains of the past where two nations met to trade and fight.

Ernest Neal had a long and distinguished career as a schoolmaster, first at Rendcomb College, Cirencester, later as Senior Biologist and Head of the Science Department at Taunton, his old school. He broadcasts on natural history, particularly mammals, on radio and television, and his books include *The Badger*, *Woodland Ecology*, *Uganda Quest* and (in collaboration with his son Keith) *Biology for Today*. He is a member of the Statutory Advisory Committee for England of the NCC, and Chairman of the Mammal Society.

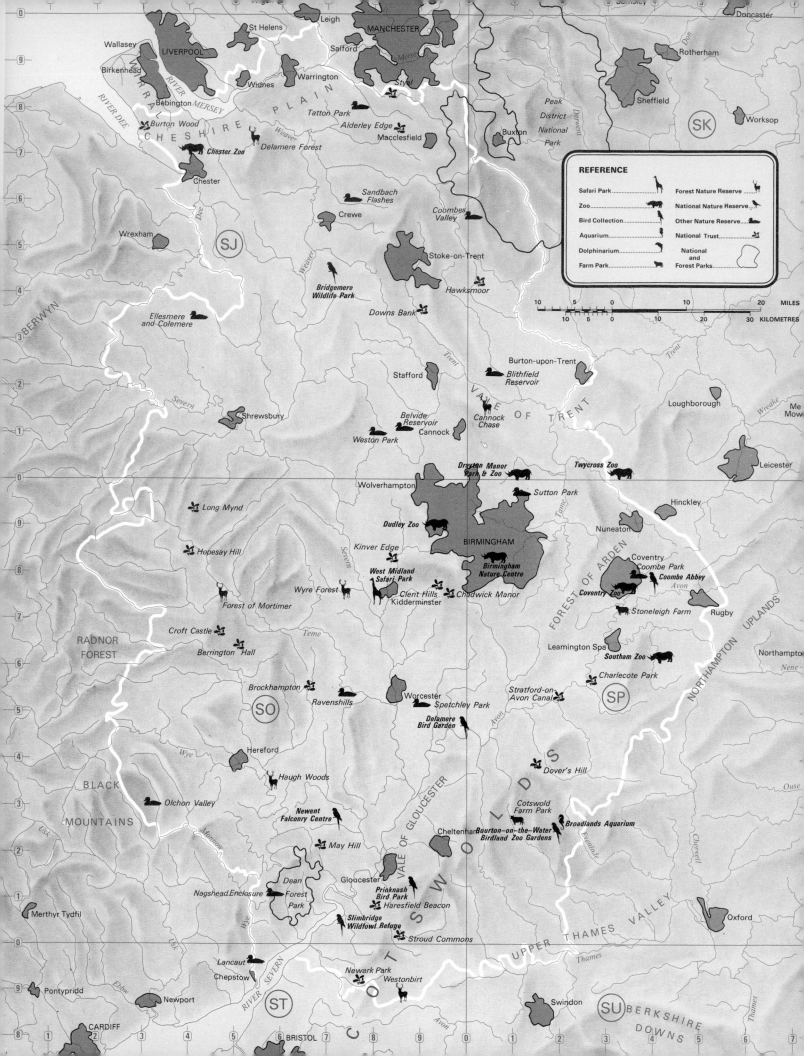

CHESHIRE

From the Welsh border and the estuaries of Dee and Mersey, Cheshire stretches eastwards till it meets the Pennine Chain. Most of this young landscape is a gently undulating plain formed from deep debris left by the retreating ice-sheets some 15,000 years ago. The older rocks are completely covered by a drift of clays, sands and gravels except where their higher peaks still protrude as sandstone hills. Lakes of varying size have developed where the moraine was left in hummocks. These 'meres' are popular centres for bird-watchers and botanists. Cheshire has become particularly noted for its ornithological sites, and some meres are so important that they have been made nature reserves and sanctuaries with restricted access. Others are used extensively for recreation, such as sailing, but are nevertheless of interest to the naturalist.

Within the 2,000 acres of Tatton Park, which has every facility for the visiting public, there are two meres with a good variety of wildfowl. Quite near is the famous Rostherne Mere NNR, haunt of Dabchick and Great Crested Grebe and several species of duck. A permit to make visits and use the splendid observatory is required from the Manchester Ornithological Society. Close to the M6 are the Sandbach Flashes which are particularly good for birds of the water's edge. Green and Wood Sandpipers, Spotted and Common Redshanks, Little Ringed Plovers and visiting Black Terns are regularly recorded. During the autumn migration rare visiting waders arrive, such as the Avocet, Grey Plover, Curlew Sandpiper and Little Stint.

Another important locality for waders and wildfowl is the Burton Marshes on the Dee; and, just above, Cheshire County Council have established an exciting new linear Country Park, called 'The Wirral Way'. It is 12 miles of good walking along an old disused railway line; seven miles of it run alongside the Dee estuary and provide good viewing of winter-visiting ducks such as Wigeon and Goldeneye, and a varied host of godwits, Knot, Dunlin, Curlew and other waders. The path also passes through open country with fine views across to the Welsh hills and a good chance to see the day-flying Short-eared Owl or the rare Hen Harrier. There are Badger setts, Fox earths and interesting little ponds with frogs and newts.

To the east of the richly historic city of Chester lies Delamere Forest. With frequent stops and short walks into the forest there is a good chance of seeing Grey Squirrels, perhaps Stoat and Weasel, and many woodland birds and butterflies. For the keen observer, there is the challenge of seeking out Fox and Badger signs. Cheshire County Council have established an imaginative long-distance walk leading from Delamere to the top of the Peckforton Hills; this 'Sandstone Trail' stretches for 16 miles through varied countryside including heath, oak-woods and sandstone cliffs. There are rewarding panoramic views, and the abundant wildlife includes the Wood Warbler singing his characteristic rattling song high in the leafy canopy. The trail ends at Duckington near to the Chester—Whitchurch road, the A41.

Alderley Edge, towards the eastern edge of the county, with its sandstone escarpments and extensive woodland, is well worth exploring. It is a good place for woodland birds in summer, especially the Redstart and the common warblers.

SHROPSHIRE

Shropshire is perhaps best known for its hills, but north of Shrewsbury is a land little changed from central Cheshire. There is the same fresh landscape of flat plains and small hillocks of glacial debris. Around the small town of Ellesmere are eight or nine water-filled hollows — the Shropshire Meres, varying in area from a few to over 100 acres. They are worth visiting not only for their beauty and tranquillity but also because of their interesting birds. Kingfishers regularly fish there and recently a new heronry has been established on the island at Ellesmere and can easily be watched from the road. In winter the wildfowl come in and are likely to include Pochard, Pintail, Goldeneye and Goosander. At other times terns come through and there are large resident flocks of Canada Geese, a massive roost of gulls and even Cormorants — looking out of place on trees.

A section of 'The Wirral Way' along the disused railway line, designated as a Country Park.

Canada Geese: adult behind, immature in front. Cheshire is one of the British strongholds of this goose, originally introduced in the eighteenth and nineteenth centuries from North America.

187

Some of the meres are private but there is good public access to Ellesmere and Colemere. A few of the shallower meres have become in-filled over the years and are now great areas of peatland called 'mosses'. They have unusual and fascinating plants growing on them and are fine sites for butterflies, especially the beautiful *philoxenus* form of the Large Heath and the distinctive early-flying yellow Brimstone. The mosses are excellent localities for Vipers, especially on a sunny day in spring when they are slow at sliding out of sight.

Offa's Dyke passes through the northwest corner of the county. This is a fascinating and little-known area and, not surprisingly, it is distinctly Welsh in character. The motorist must be content to explore its narrow lanes at a leisurely and careful pace, with constant reference to a good map. The landscape is determined by limestone and sandstone scarps with small fields of permanent pasture and much hillside scrub. The hills reach 1,000 feet in places and give fine views over the north Shropshire plain, and there are dramatic cliffs and quarries with a rich flora. The area is a stronghold for the Fox and the Rabbit, and is being reinvaded by the Polecat after a banishment of nearly 100 years. The new forestry plantations in Wales have suited this efficient little hunter and it has been pushing steadily eastwards again in recent years. Unfortunately the easiest place to see it is hanging on a gamekeeper's 'gibbet'. Buzzards are common and the border rivers such as Tanat and Vyrnwy are good places to look for Otter signs.

The hill country of south Shropshire is famous for its varied scenery and for the open country of the Long Mynd and Stiperstones Hills. In 1959 some 300 square miles, with Church Stretton at its centre, was designated an Area of Outstanding Natural Beauty. Wildlife is rich because of the great variety of semi-natural habitats. Patches of woodland cling to the valley sides and, where the soil is light, Badger setts are certain to be found. Woodland birds include the Redstart, Pied Flycatcher and Tree Pipit. Higher up, at altitudes of over 1,600 feet, moorland takes over and in places the scenery becomes almost mountainous. Croaking Ravens and mewing Buzzards are a common sight overhead, and you may see Wheatears and Stonechats although both species seem to be declining. Red Grouse are common in the heather and, if you follow one of the delightful little streams, you have a very good chance of catching sight of Grey Wagtails and Dippers, and just possibly the Ring Ousel.

To the east of the hills lies the long limestone ridge of Wenlock Edge, famous

A male Pied Flycatcher is seen here bringing food to its nest-hole in a decaying tree; the woodlands of the West Midlands are the English breeding stronghold of this bird.

The north Shropshire plain from the 900-foot-high Pontesford Hill.

Left: Yellow-necked Mice, larger and more colourful than the Wood Mouse. Right: the Silver-washed Fritillary is at home in the woodlands of Shropshire.

for its fossils of the wildlife of 400 million years ago! Near Ludlow in the extreme south is the Forest of Mortimer. There is a large herd of wild Fallow Deer in the forest, famous because there is a unique long-coated variety amongst them. Most of the forest is private, but the deer can often be seen crossing the road or grazing in the fields. Woodland in this area is still the home of one of the most beautiful of our butterflies, the Silver-washed Fritillary. In the centre of the county, eight miles from Shrewsbury, lies Earl's Hill, a nature reserve with an excellent nature trail managed by the Shropshire Conservation Trust. One can almost guarantee seeing or hearing the Green Woodpecker, and on a summer visit a total of 60 different birds and many butterfly species can be spotted within its 100 acres.

HEREFORD AND WORCESTER

The western boundary of the old county of Herefordshire is overshadowed by the Welsh mountains — in the north by Radnor Forest, and in the south by the Black Mountains. The Black Mountains are formed of Old Red Sandstone which out-crops in many other places in the county. One of the finest walks into the mountains is along the Olchon valley which begins just south of Hay-on-Wye. There are good routes to the Cat's Back and Red Darrens, giving superb hill walking and opportunities to see mountain birds. If you must stay in the car, then take the B4348 from Hay-on-Wye and follow the River Dore down the wide and fertile Golden Valley.

The Small Tortoiseshell, one of the commonest and most beautiful of all the British butterflies, is particularly attracted to purple and mauve flowers.

The Wye is Hereford's most famous river, flowing from the mountains of mid-Wales and wending its way to Hereford in the centre of the county. It passes through rich farmland and attractive rural landscapes of gently rolling hills with rich red soils. On the steeper slopes good woodland persists. Small mammals, secretive and nocturnal, are difficult to observe, but none more so than the beautiful Yellow-necked Mouse which lives in these woods. It is larger and more colourful than the Long-tailed or Wood Mouse and was first discovered in Herefordshire about 1894. The final reaches of the Wye have quite spectacular scenery, especially around Symonds Yat where the river cuts through hard Car-boniferous Limestone to create a dramatic gorge. Sections of these rich woods form part of the Forest of Dean, a haunt of Redstarts, Wood Warblers, Pied Flycatchers and a wealth of small song-birds.

Between the Wye and Severn there is less variety in the landscape, but dominating all is the nine miles of the Malvern Hills. The old county boundary with Worcestershire followed the spine of the hills which rear from the surrounding lowlands to over 1,000 feet. They are formed of ancient iron-hard Pre-Cambrian rocks with apt names like green hornblende, pink gabbro and black

Three butterfly species found in the woodlands of the West Midlands: left to right, Marbled White, Brown Argus, Comma.

diorite. Although woodland probably never covered the shallower soils of the upper slopes, the lower hills were part of the mediaeval hunting ground of Malvern Chase. There is good walking over its rough commonlands, and for the naturalist the main attraction is the profusion of butterflies in summer. About 36 of our native species are found there, some of them rare elsewhere. Wood and Marbled Whites, the Brown Argus and the High Brown Fritillary, can all be seen.

The Severn, the river of Worcestershire, dissects that erstwhile county as it passes through from north to south. Where it leaves Shropshire, near Bewdley in the north, is situated the Forest of Wyre. Lying on the edge of the Black Country and just 20 miles from the centre of Birmingham, this 6,000 acres of forest is an exceptional area for wildlife, despite the fact that industry over many generations has mercilessly exploited its resources. Now, although relics of industrial days are to be found everywhere, the forest is quickly healing. There are plenty of roads with ample parking and good open spaces. The streams are particularly delightful and provide pleasant dabbling for children (and fathers!). Lifting up stones from the stream-bed will reveal the little-known invertebrate fauna such as water snails, freshwater shrimps and even the remarkable Crayfish, a four-inch freshwater lobster. Equally fascinating are the numerous caddis larvae which build themselves protective cases made of tiny stones or sand-grains and even bits of twig. Fish like the Brown Trout and Miller's Thumb are abundant. If you should set out to investigate this rich stream-life do please replace the stones exactly as you find them, and so help to conserve these fascinating creatures.

The forest glades are good places for butterflies like the Brimstone, the white Orange-tip with orange splashes at its wing-tips, the wine-coloured Peacock, the Small Tortoiseshell, the Comma and even the southern High Brown Fritillary. This is one of the few remaining habitats in the British Isles of the Kentish Glory, a large, furry-bodied moth with wings beautifully patterned in brown, ochre and buff. Fox and Fallow Deer are common but not easily seen. Our only venomous snake, the Adder or Viper, occurs; although not generally realised, it is our commonest reptile and is widely distributed over drier habitats. Forest birds such as Redstart and Pied Flycatcher are well represented, and more unusual ones like the Woodcock can be flushed from damp hollows, or watched flying above the trees at dusk. Another strange bird still found in Wyre is the Nightjar which only spends three summer months with us; it also flies chiefly at dusk, making eerie 'churring' noises as it glides on extended wings.

About ten miles west of Worcester is the Ravenshill Woodland Reserve. These private woods, with signposted trails, have recently been opened to the public. Fox and Badger are in evidence, and Nightingales breed. It is an unforgettable experience to spend a May night in the woods listening to their rich song, perhaps whilst waiting in suspense for Badger cubs to come out of their sett to play.

In the southeast corner of the county the Avon flows in from Warwickshire to join the Severn at Tewkesbury. Before their confluence the Avon twists its way around the isolated mass of Bredon Hill; an outrider of the Cotswolds, it manages to reach 1,000 feet only with the help of a tower built on its summit.

Below: a Miller's Thumb, or Bullhead, is well camouflaged on the pebbles of a river-bed. Right: a Curlew, which breeds in the Pennine uplands, prepares to settle on to its mottled eggs.

The views are delightful and, although the land is private and devoted to rough grazing, there are numerous public footpaths. It has particular interest as a Badger stronghold for, where there are marlstone soils, there is good shrub and tree cover and setts are abundant. The west side of the hill is known locally as Badger Bank and without doubt this enchanting animal has lived there from time immemorial.

STAFFORDSHIRE

The Pennine Chain juts into north Staffordshire, bringing bare rocky hills and millstone grit which have weathered into sharp ridges and deep valleys. This is a countryside of stone walls, heather moors with nesting Twites and the ringing calls of Curlews. The Manifold valley, off the B5053 near Leek, has a nature trail which follows the old railway track, with beautiful and often dramatic scenery and especial opportunities to see hill and waterside birds such as the Dipper and Ring Ousel. On the moors the naturalist may have unimagined surprises, such as a grey-backed Merlin in hot pursuit of a Meadow Pipit, or a glimpse of a small herd of Red Deer. Until 1951 he might have come face to face with a grazing Yak! Perhaps even more surprising is the distinct likelihood of seeing wallabies grazing in the heather, for a few of these animals escaped from a private collection over 30 years ago and have been breeding successfully in the wild.

The central part of the county is a low-lying plain drained by the River Trent and its tributaries. One of these, the River Blithe, forms a reservoir near Abbots Bromley that is excellent for water birds. For the use of the bird-watching 'hides' a permit is required from the West Midland Bird Club, but the B5013 crosses the middle of the reservoir and provides adequate views of the grebes and the Mallard, Teal, Tufted and other ducks. Nearby is Blithfield Hall where the house and gardens are often open to the public, and the famous Bagot Goats are usually on view.

The southeast consists of a large upland plateau composed of Coal Measures and Triassic Sandstone. On the higher part lies the famous and ancient forest of Cannock Chase with its undulating landscape of heath, forestry conifer plantations, remnants of the ancient broad-leaved woodland of birch and oak, and picturesque little valleys. The Staffordshire County Council and the Forestry

Yak — In the 1930s a small private menagerie was established near Leek. At the beginning of the Second War it became impossible to maintain the fences and the small herd of Red Deer escaped and with them a single Yak. It survived on the moors until 1951.

Wallabies — A pair of Bennett's Wallabies were obtained from Whipsnade in 1936 for the Leek menagerie. They bred, and the family of five escaped in 1939. Numbers have increased and there are now about 20, but they do not seem to have extended their range beyond 15 miles or so. They live on heather moorland with bracken, grasses and bilberry and appear to eat all these plants, as well as pine and birch scrub, but mainly heather.

Bagot Goats — They actually belong to the Schwartzhals breed from the Rhône valley. They were brought home by Crusaders and were kept in the royal possession. During a visit to Staffordshire Richard II was so pleased with his day's hunting that he gave the herd to Sir John Bagot of Blithfield. From that time the herd was kept going and a goat's head became the family crest. They ran wild about the estate until it was broken up in 1961.

Commission are to be complimented on the way they have developed the area for public use. There is good motor access and parking, plenty of fine footpaths and picnic sites and, recently established, a large 'motorless zone'. This is the place to come and see the wild Fallow Deer which abound on the Chase. It is also one of the few remaining sites in the region where the pretty Red Squirrel can still be found in reasonable numbers. It is a well-known locality for butterflies, and in the summer months the Fox Moth and Oak Eggar Moth can be seen flying madly over the heathland. The Forestry Commission have a wildlife museum and offer the hire of a 'high-seat' from which Badger, Fox, Fallow Deer and Red Squirrel may all be watched.

WARWICKSHIRE AND WEST MIDLANDS

Industrialisation has had a great impact on this area, yet one feels that Warwickshire has put up a noble fight to contain the devastation of its countryside. There is still much squalor around Birmingham and the Black Country but, even within these boundaries, one can find rich pockets of wildlife. Most famous is perhaps Sutton Park lying north of the city of Birmingham. Although hemmed in on all sides by urban development, the 2,500 acres of woodland and open heath provide an oasis for many birds and mammals. Fox and Grey Squirrel are found in the park and the sandy heath is well known as a site for the colourful Brimstone and the beautiful Holly Blue butterflies.

An exciting and ambitious project has just been launched by the City of Birmingham Museums Department, a four-and-a-half-acre Nature Centre at Cannon Hill Park in the heart of the city. By extensive planting and landscaping, a range of wildlife habitats has been created. British wild mammals will be introduced and it is hoped that others will be attracted to the area. There is a mammal house, walk-through butterfly garden and bird house, and wild bird areas. Some of the pools are provided with underwater windows for viewing. This is a far more imaginative development than the old concept of a zoo and is a most commendable venture.

Coventry has several sizeable woods to the south, home for Badger and Fox and the naturalised Muntjac Deer, hardly more than 18 inches high. These deer escaped from Woburn Park in Bedfordshire nearly half a century ago and gradually spread northwards, entering Warwickshire about 1940. You should look out for their tiny 'slots' (footprints), about one and a half inches long and the width of a finger. To the east of the city on the A411 is Coombe Abbey Countryside Park. The nature trail borders a delightful lake with water birds and a sizeable heronry.

Warwickshire's river is the charming Avon which winds lazily through rich meadows and tiny hamlets as it flows towards Stratford. As the Avon passes through Charlecote Park, Herons can be seen feeding at its side and cattle and deer come down to drink. There is a fine Elizabethan house, owned by the National Trust, and a strong tradition that Shakespeare was caught poaching deer here! Certainly it was country he knew well enough, although there is little left of the Forest of Arden now, save for numerous place-names.

It is not a county known for hills, but those of Burton Dassett off the A41 south-east of Warwick are well worth a visit. There is a wildlife exhibition in the village. The only other hills are in the south where a road off the B4086 runs along the magnificent beech-lined escarpment of Edge Hill.

GLOUCESTERSHIRE

Gloucestershire is a county of rounded hills, gentle slopes and lush river meadows dominated by the famous Cotswold Hills, rolling arable uplands rising northwards and westwards from the upper Thames valley. It is ideal country for exploration by car, but offers splendid opportunities for wildlife discovery on foot along the 100 miles of the Cotswold Way footpath. The popular and beautiful village of Bourton-on-the-Water has a small park, Birdland Zoo Gardens, where some 600 species of birds can be seen, many flying freely around the visitor.

Between the steep southwestern scarp of the hills and the River Severn are

Aggressive posturing by an adult Heron (right) in defence of the young in its tree-top nest.

A White Admiral butterfly, a splendid inhabitant of English forests, settles on its principal food-plant, the blackberry flower.

A flock of White-fronted Geese in flight; the smaller birds are Starlings.

the rich pastures and stately elms of Berkeley Vale. The world-famous Wildfowl Trust is built on ancient reclaimed land near the village of Slimbridge, and is a good place to learn the different species of ducks and geese since it has the largest collection of wildfowl in the world. Flocks of White-fronted Geese, Bewick's Swans and an assortment of wild ducks can be watched from look-out towers overlooking the estuary during the winter months.

Between the Severn and the Wye lies the Royal Forest of Dean – Crown property since the year 1016. Its 35,000 acres are criss-crossed by roads, many of them unfenced, and there is now a clearly marked scenic drive. It is an open forest with numerous trails and picnic sites. Badgers and Foxes are common throughout the wilder parts and there are two herds of Fallow Deer. The list of breeding birds includes Willow Warbler, Blackcap, Garden Warbler, Wood Warbler, Grasshopper Warbler, Pied Flycatcher, Buzzard, Sparrowhawk and the woodpeckers. The unmistakable Crossbill, a settler from Scandinavia, can usually be encountered in the conifers – the male is red, the female green, and the young dull brown. Butterflies, too, are in abundance – Brown Argus, White Admiral, High Brown Fritillary and the delicate Wood White, among many others.

The Wood Warbler (right) is one of the characteristic birds of western woodlands such as the Forest of Dean (left).

WATCHING MAMMALS

Watching mammals can be a very exciting and rewarding pursuit, but it is not so easy as watching birds. Mammals are often more shy of man and consequently less easy to approach, and also the majority of British mammals are nocturnal.

To be successful at mammal-watching you need plenty of patience and enthusiasm, but little in the way of specialised equipment except binoculars. For night watching, binoculars with wide apertures such as 7×50 are ideal, as they concentrate whatever light is available, allowing you to see details which would be invisible to the naked eye under poor light conditions. It should be borne in mind that, unlike birds, which rely mainly on sight and hearing, mammals (especially nocturnal ones) rely far more on their sense of smell, although their hearing may also be acute. So it is more important to be downwind of your quarry and to be quiet than to worry about being seen. However, in some species such as squirrels, Foxes, Rabbits and deer, sight is good and any movement is easily detected, so it is as well to keep as still as possible.

Before trying to watch for a particular species you should do some detective work in order to find out the best places for watching. For example, most mammals have some kind of refuge — a place of comparative safety where they can sleep or breed. Foxes, Badgers, Rabbits and the smaller rodents have burrows, deer use dense thickets, squirrels make dreys or use hollow trees, and Hedgehogs shelter in thick vegetation. If you can find these hideouts you have a focal point for watching and you are much more likely to see them.

Most mammals pass along chosen paths to their various feeding grounds. These paths should be searched for. If a mammal has to leave its refuge before dark, concealment will be most important. You are more likely to see trails in woods, copses, hedgerows and scrub than across open fields. Trails made by the larger mammals are often found along the edges of woods and beside hedgerows, whilst the smaller ones often use the hedges themselves as their main highways.

If you find a trail, look out for footprints in the mud or on soft ground; and if the trail passes under barbed wire, look for hairs which may be caught in it. Droppings, traces of food and tooth marks on the remainders will help you to identify the animals and provide clues to the best places for watching them.

One of the easiest and most rewarding mammals to watch is the Badger. They are present all over the region, and in the most suitable areas there may be on average at least three setts to the square mile. A Badger colony, consisting of perhaps six to twelve animals including cubs, will often have more than one sett within its territory. Sometimes all may be living in one sett, at other times they may be occupying several.

A sett may have many entrances connected underground by a series of tunnels. During the day the occupants sleep in enlarged chambers which are lined with bedding such as hay or bracken. The bedding is brought in after dark in bundles, clasped by the forelegs and chin as the Badger shuffles backwards to the entrance. You can tell a Badger's sett by the larger heaps of earth outside and the traces of old bedding incorporated in the excavated soil. The entrance is not less than nine inches across and is often much wider due to wear and tear.

Any copse or piece of deciduous woodland is worth investigating as more than half the setts in the West Midlands are in such habitats. They are also found in hedgerows, coniferous woods, quarries and many other situations. Setts are often on private ground so permission to watch at night should be sought. Looking at a piece of woodland through binoculars will often reveal a patch of elders near one edge; these trees are very conspicuous in June with their white patches of flowers, and they often mark the position of a Badger's sett.

When going along a lane, look out for Badger paths, looking like tunnels, through the base of a hedge; or if there are high banks, search for 'up and overs'. These are bare slides down the banks which Badgers use regularly when crossing the lane. If you find one on one bank, you will usually find another on the opposite side. Similarly, if there are dry-stone walls, as in the Cotswolds, you can sometimes see that a few stones have been dislodged where Badgers have

Badger emerges from its sett.

Badger's hair caught on barbed wire, and a Badger's footprint in mud.

Badgers' sett in coppiced woodland; the claw-cleaning tree is in front of the sett.

An 'up-and-over', a Badger's regular crossing point of this bank.

clambered over; the moss will be worn away at such places. By following these trails into the woods you can often find a sett quite quickly.

Having found one, look first for signs of occupation. If an entrance is full of leaves or has cobwebs across it, it is unlikely to be in use, but if there are signs of recent digging, or you see flies going in and out of the entrance, these are good signs of occupation. In May, if cubs are present, the earth outside a sett may be trampled flat and hard by their playing.

To watch Badgers successfully you need to plan carefully. Between May and September they usually emerge just before dark, but after nightfall at other seasons. In secluded places they may be seen even before the sun has set during May and June, but it is usually only the cubs that come out as early as this. It is therefore advisable to get into a watching position about an hour before it is dark in spring and summer.

Watching from a comfortable position in a tree about 20–30 feet from a well-used entrance is as good a position as any, because if the wind is wrong, your scent may pass above the Badgers. Otherwise it is essential to be downwind and to sit or stand with your back to some bush or tree; in this way you are not silhouetted against the sky. You should avoid passing near a used entrance or standing near a Badger path when approaching your watching position, as the Badgers will detect your scent immediately they reach the place where you stood. After dark, a strong torch with a red filter may be used, or a weaker one without a filter. They take little notice of the light if it is not flashed into their eyes.

In spring and early summer it is possible to watch the adults and cubs playing together for half an hour or more after their emergence and before they go off to their feeding grounds. It is one of the most rewarding experiences of the countryside to see them playing their games of 'tag' or 'king-o'-the-castle', unconscious that they are being watched.

Badgers take a wide variety of foods. Their favourite is earthworms, and on damp nights when the worms are on the surface of the pasture, they will be eaten in

large numbers. They also feed on a great variety of invertebrates including beetles, slugs and the nests of wasps and wild bees. They also take the young of Rabbits, rats and other small mammals, and occasionally eat an adult Hedgehog. In summer and autumn they may glean in the cornfields and they are fond of fruits of all kinds, from blackberries to windfall apples. In October they may eat large quantities of acorns and are not averse to carrion or grass if other foods are scarce.

Foxes are widely distributed and generally common in the West Midlands, especially in the more hilly districts and in those parts where farmland is interspersed with woods and copses. To watch Foxes successfully you have to take into account the ways in which their behaviour varies according to the reproductive cycle and the time of year.

In the West Midlands, Foxes usually mate around mid-January. At this time the barking of the dog may be heard frequently, especially in the early evening. The cubs, usually four or five in a litter, are born below ground a little over seven weeks after mating. They remain in their earth for the first month where they are periodically suckled by the vixen. You see them for the first time above ground in April. At first they show little resemblance to the adult, as the head is more rounded, the ears small and the coat a chocolate colour. But within another two weeks or so the coat turns reddish, the snout elongates and the ears become more pointed and prominent.

In May, the activity of the cubs is centred round the earth. Remains of Rabbits, birds and other prey may often be seen near the entrance and the ground outside may be beaten flat by the playing of the cubs. The cubs become much more independent in June, and by July they usually abandon the breeding earth for good. They lie up during the day in good cover, often choosing a spot where the sun can reach them, and from which they can view a wide expanse of country. This habit of lying up above ground during the day is also characteristic of dog Foxes for most of the year, but vixens use earths much more regularly.

Although you may sometimes disturb Foxes from their resting places during the day, they are mainly active at night. However, during the summer when nights are short you can frequently see them in the late evening or early morning. During April and May when the cubs are small the vixen may hunt in daylight, and the cubs may be seen playing or sunning themselves near the entrance of the earth.

From these variations in behaviour it follows that there are two main ways of watching Foxes successfully. The first is to watch at an earth in the same way as for Badger-watching. You can do this at most times of the year. The Fox, usually a vixen, should emerge just after dark, and to help observations a dim torch may be used. The second, and by far the best way of watching, is to observe a breeding earth during daylight in April or May. If at all possible you should choose a high vantage point some distance from the earth, and use binoculars. A Fox's senses of smell and hearing are excellent and eyesight is good, especially for detecting movement and any unusual silhouette, so it is well to approach your vantage point with great care. Dawn is an excellent time to arrive, for in the early hours of daylight you may see the vixen (and possibly the dog too) bring back food for the cubs, and you can enjoy the scrapping as each cub struggles to get a share.

But first you need to find the earth and recognise that it is occupied. Foxes make their earths in rather similar places to Badgers. They often enlarge Rabbit burrows, especially if these have been made between the roots of a large tree; this gives them greater security. The earth differs from a Badger's sett by having far less soil, and there is no bedding mixed with it. Sometimes, however, Foxes will use unoccupied Badger setts as breeding earths, or take over part of one which is occupied. You can tell if a Fox is in residence by getting down on your knees and sniffing at the entrance; a Fox's smell is rank and easily distinguished from the faint musky odour of a Badger.

Otters are scarce in the West Midlands, as they are in most parts of England today, but it is just possible to see them occasionally. Although mainly nocturnal, chance sightings may be had during the day in secluded places, especially in

Fox cubs are born with snub noses; within a few months the snout becomes longer and pointed.

An adult Fox prowls round a chicken-run in broad daylight.

the late evening – but these, unfortunately, are rare events. However, it is not so difficult to find signs of their presence if they are around. The best places to look are the shores of lakes and reservoirs and beside streams, especially slow-moving ones.

Otters are constantly on the move, sometimes covering five or more miles on a single night within their extensive territories. However, they tend to follow regular trails and this makes it fairly easy to find signs of their presence. Their tracks in soft mud or sand can be recognised by the five toes with webbing between, although on harder ground neither the fifth toe nor the webbing may be visible. Sometimes their trails may be followed across fields – for example, from a river to a marshy feeding area; where Otters enter the water there is often a muddy slide down the bank. Occasionally you may find fish scales on the bank, or on a small island, where Otters have been feeding.

Otters mark their trails with their dung, or 'spraints' as they are called. These act as smell signals which enable other Otters to recognise who has passed that way. Spraints also act as territorial markers to warn others that the region is occupied. When fresh, these spraints are black and slimy, but as they dry they become grey and powdery. If soaked in water, or merely broken up when dry, bones of various fish and other animals they have eaten may be recognised. Special places are chosen for sprainting, and sometimes scrapes are made, and each Otter passing that way will leave its visiting-card. The best places to look for these spraints are on boulders in a stream, on the ledges under bridges and on half-submerged logs. If there is an obstacle to an Otter's progress, such as a weir or sluice, it will scramble up the river bank just downstream of the obstacle and leave its spraint in a prominent place on top of the bank. Another good place to search is where a side-stream enters a main one.

Otters may breed during any month, but probably most often in the late winter or early spring. The breeding den, or holt, is often a dry shelter among the

Above, an Otter's slide down a river bank; left, two adult Otters playing.

Otter's scrape, covering its spraint.

roots of a riverside tree or in dense vegetation near a lake or stream, or on a small island. If you are fortunate enough to find a breeding holt this provides the best possible focal point for watching, as the mother makes regular sorties for food, and when the cubs are old enough they are extremely playful and are marvellous to watch. The greatest care should be taken not to disturb them, and watching should only take place from a distance. Night watching can be successful once you have become familiar with the area and the habits of the resident Otters. It needs much patience, and a moonlight night is very desirable. However, you are more likely to hear their fluting whistles than to see the animals.

Otters need all the protection they can be given as their numbers have declined dramatically over the past decade. They do little harm to fishing interests as they much prefer coarse fish and Eels to Salmon and Trout. They also help to keep stocks healthy, as they usually catch the weaker fish. They occasionally feed on Moorhens and other waterfowl and take Crayfish if these are available.

Mink have been breeding wild since their escapes from fur farms in the 1950s.

Mink may be seen in similar situations. They were imported from America and kept in fur farms, but many escaped. Since 1956 they have been breeding wild, in recent years on a big scale, and are now to be found in most counties. You can see them by day, but more usually in the evening or at night. They are much smaller than an adult Otter, dark brown all over, with a much more furry tail. Their tracks are rather similar to an Otter's, but smaller. However, when moving fast they go in a series of bounds, so their tracks are found in groups of four, up to two feet apart. Mink spraints have a rank, musky smell compared with an Otter's, which are sweet smelling. Mink feed on a great variety of small animals, especially Water Voles, fish, frogs and waterfowl; they will also take insects, earthworms and various fruits. They have their young in spring and early summer, up to seven in a litter.

The other large mammals you can watch out for are deer. All deer have very acute senses of smell and hearing, and their ability to see the slightest movement is remarkable, so to watch them successfully is quite a challenge. You will need binoculars, and it is wise not to try to get nearer than 50 to 100 yards, or you may disturb them. It is not unusual to see them during the day; but more often at this time they are hiding up in the woods and thickets. In the late evening they come out to feed in grassy glades or meadows bordering woods. Deer habitually use certain trails which lead to their feeding areas, so you should wait concealed and downwind in a strategic place. You can also watch them very well from 'high-seats'. These are sometimes erected near deer feeding grounds in forestry plantations. They have the advantage of allowing your scent to pass above the deer.

Common Shrew, active by day or night.

Dawn is another excellent time for watching deer, but you then have to stalk them with the greatest stealth as they may still be out in the open on their feeding grounds. Once you have seen them, you should move forward only when their heads are down.

The smaller mammals are often overlooked, but they can also be extremely interesting to observe. One of the best techniques is to go for a walk after dark, choosing the edge of a wood or alongside a thick hedgerow, especially one on a bank. You need to have a torch with a red filter, and must wear soft shoes and have the wind in your face. You should only go a few yards at a time, pausing for long periods to listen and watch. Hedgehogs are often seen in this way as they leave their daytime shelters and search for insects, slugs and worms. Shrews, voles and Wood Mice also frequent these places and Dormice are a possibility, especially in woods with coppiced hazel. All these animals are usually heard before they are seen.

If you find a good place for voles or mice you can have some entertaining watching by putting small piles of grain near their runways. This should be done for several consecutive evenings before watching begins. It is best to put out the grain at dusk so that the birds do not discover it first.

Watching mammals can be great fun, and if some species are difficult, then success is all the more satisfying. With patience and ingenuity much can be accomplished.

The Bank Vole is an agile climber.

Guide to wildlife habitats in the West Midlands

This Appendix provides a selected but varied list of places of wildlife interest. It is emphasised that nature reserves exist primarily for the conservation of animals and plants and in some cases for environmental experiments and research. They are not 'public open spaces' in the recreational sense. Access to many is therefore restricted and some, because of their sensitivity to disturbance, have been omitted from this list, in deference to the wishes of conservation organisations. Even with 'open' reserves visitors are earnestly requested to keep to the paths and bridleways and so avoid damage to the habitat and undue disturbance to wildlife. *There is no public access to the enclosed farmland which is part of many National Trust properties.*

Application to visit a National Nature Reserve (NNR) should be made to the appropriate Regional Office of the Nature Conservancy Council (NCC) at the address given. Intention to visit reserves of the Royal Society for the Protection of Birds (RSPB) should be notified to the Warden (whose address is shown) as far in advance as possible. In all cases where an address is shown, it is wise to contact the Warden to avoid disappointment.

CHESHIRE

Alderley Edge SJ 86 77. Wooded sandstone escarpment, incl. Alderley Beacon, Dickens Wood and Wizard of the Edge Inn, 219 a. 4½ mls n.w. of Macclesfield, s.e. of Alderley Edge, astride B5087. NT.

Burton Wood SJ 31 75. Scots pine woodland, 21 a. Goldcrests, Coal Tits. 9 mls n.w. of Chester, at Burton on w. side of A540. NT.

Cheshire Conservation Trust, 2 Pear Tree Lane, Acton Bridge, Northwich, Cheshire.

Delamere Forest SJ 55 72. State forest. 5 mls w. of Northwich A556, traversed by B5152 from Delamere to Kingsley. Parking bays on B5152 and the Switchback road. Information centre, trails. For Comm.

Sandbach Flashes SJ 76 61. Large subsidence pools noted for migrant sandpipers and waterfowl. 10 mls s.e. of Northwich A533, 7 mls w. of Congleton A534. M6, exit 17 (A534). Viewable from roads.

Styal SJ 83 83. Long wooded stretch of the Bollin valley, 252 a. 1½ mls n.w. of Wilmslow. NT.

Tatton Park SJ 76 83. Parkland, gardens, woods and Tatton Mere. 2086 a. Waterfowl. 13 mls s.w. of Manchester, 4 mls n. of Knutsford, entrance on A5034 just n. of junction with A50. Car park, trail. NT.

SALOP

Ellesmere and Colemere SJ 41 35. Meres with islands. Ellesmere heronry, gull roost. 7 mls n.e. of Oswestry, e. of Ellesmere and A495, viewable from A528. (Colemere is 2 mls s.e. SJ 43 33.)

Forest of Mortimer SO 49 73. State forest. Fallow Deer. 1 ml s.w. of Ludlow, on w. side of A49 and B4361. Information centre, trails. For Comm.

Hopesay Hill SO 40 84. Moorland sheepwalk. 3 mls w. of Craven Arms, 1 ml n. of B4368. NT.

Long Mynd SO 41 94. Moorland rising to 1700 ft affording views of Shropshire and Cheshire Plains, 4530 a. Also Minton Hill, 755 a., on s. side. Badgers. Buzzard, Red Grouse. 15 mls s. of Shrewsbury A49 to w. of Church Stretton, approached from Church Stretton (e. side), Ratlinghope or Asterton (w. side). NT.

The National Trust West Midlands, Regional Office, Attingham Park, nr Shrewsbury, Salop, SY4 4TW.

Nature Conservancy Council, West Midland Regional Office, Attingham Park, Shrewsbury, Salop, SY4 4TW.

Shropshire Conservation Trust, Bear Steps, Shrewsbury.

STAFFORDSHIRE

Belvide Reservoir SJ 86 11. Reservoir, wintering wildfowl, also at Gailey Pool nearby, SJ 93 11. 7 mls w. of Cannock, s. of A5.

Blithfield Reservoir SK 06 24. Reservoir attracting wildfowl, especially in winter. (Bagot's Park is nearby at SK 08 27.) 3 mls n. of Rugeley, traversed by B5013.

Cannock Chase SK 00 15. State forest, pines and deciduous, and much open heath. Access to 3100 a. Fallow Deer, Red Squirrels. Woodcock, Nightjar, Redstart, Tree Pipit and other woodland birds. Skirted on n. by A513 Stafford–Rugeley, on e. by A460 Rugeley–Cannock, on w. by A34 Cannock–Stafford. From M6 by exits 12 (A5) or 13 (A449), via Penkridge. Traversed by minor roads. Many car parks, picnic areas, trails. Information centre and toilets at Milford Common SJ 973 212. Forest Centre and Deer Museum and trails at Ladyhill SK 025 174. For Comm/Staffs. CC.

Coombes Valley SJ 06 53. Wooded valley, 261 a. Badgers. Woodpeckers, Kingfisher, Dipper, Redstart, Pied Flycatcher. 3 mls s.e. of Leek, 10 mls n.e. of Stoke-on-Trent, and 2 mls s. of A523. Car park, information centre, trail. (Warden – Six Oaks Farm, Bradnap, Leek, Staffs.) RSPB.

Downs Bank SJ 90 37. Moorland traversed by stream. 1 ml s.e. of Barlaston, 1½ mls n. of Stone, between A34 and A520. NT.

Hawksmoor SK 03 44. Undulating woodlands and open area. 1½ mls n.e. of Cheadle, on n. side of B5417. NT.

Staffordshire Nature Conservation Trust, 5 Harrowby Drive, Newcastle, Stoke-on-Trent.

Weston Park SJ 81 10. Wooded parkland with lakes, pets corner, aquarium. Special facilities for children. 7 mls w. of M6/A5 junction 12 between Cannock and Oakengates, 10 mls n.w. of Wolverhampton A41. Adm. fee. Refreshments, educational visits. Earl of Bradford.

WEST MIDLANDS

Chadwick Manor SO 97 76. Woodland

on a n. extension of the Lickey Hills, incl. Spring Poole and Highfield, 873 ft 526 a. Country Park. 8 mls s.w. of Birmingham, 4 mls n. of Bromsgrove, astride A38. NT/Birmingham MDC.

Clent Hills SO 93 80. Commonland and woodland in Clatterbach valley, 362 a. Country Park. 3 mls s.w. of Halesowen, between A456 and A491 at Clent. NT/Hereford and Worcester CC.

Coombe Park SP 39 79. Parkland and Coombe Pool, 290 a. Country Park. 4 mls e. of Coventry centre, on n. side of A427. Coventry MDC.

Sutton Park SP 10 97. Heathland and variety of woodland types, with large shallow lakes. 3000 a. 6 mls n. of Birmingham, e. of A452 and B4138, to w. of Sutton Coldfield.

WARWICKSHIRE

Charlecote Park SP 26 56. Parkland with famous 'Shakespeare' herd of deer and flock of Spanish sheep, and fine cedar avenues. 4 mls e. of Stratford upon Avon, on n. side of B4086. NT.

Stoneleigh Farm SP 33 73. Farm and woodland walks, bee centre, rare breeds of sheep, special educational areas for children. Between Coventry and Leamington Spa e. of A444. Refreshments, car park, trail, displays, toilets, etc. Roy. Agric. Soc. of Eng./Rare Breeds Survival T.

Stratford upon Avon Canal 13½ mls of the canal from Kingswood Junction, Lapworth, through Lowsonford and Wilmcote to the Memorial Theatre gardens, Stratford. (SP 187 707 – 204 552). NT.

Warwickshire Nature Conservation Trust, c/o The County Museum, Market Place, Warwick.

HEREFORD AND WORCESTER

Berrington Hall SO 51 64. Park with 14 a. lake by Capability Brown. 3 mls n. of Leominster, on w. side of A49. NT.

Brockhampton SO 68 55. Typical Herefordshire farmland (private) and woods. 1895 a. 1–2 mls e. of Bromyard, mostly on n. side of A44. NT.

Croft Castle SO 46 66. Castle and estate, incl. spectacular Iron Age hill-fort. 1375 a. 5 mls n.w. of Leominster, 9 mls s.w. of

Ludlow A49. Approach from B4362 turning n. at Cock Gate between Bircher and Mortimer's Cross. NT.

Haugh Woods SO 58 36. State forest. 5 mls s.e. of Hereford B4225, 1 ml e. of Mordiford. For Comm.

Herefordshire and Radnorshire Nature Trust, Community House, 25 Castle Street, Hereford, HR1 2NW.

Kinver Edge SO 84 83. High heath and woodland. Kingsford Country Park nearby to s. 4 mls n. of Kidderminster, 1½ mls w. of A449. NT.

Olchon Valley SO 30 30. Moorland and wooded country. 6–9 mls s. of Hay-on-Wye, 9 mls n. of Abergavenny A465, turning n. at Pandy.

Ravenshills SO 74 54. Woodland. Fox, Badger. Nightingale. 6 mls w. of Worcester, 1½ mls s. of A44 from Knightsford Bridge. Trails.

Spetchley Park SO 89 53. Gardens and parkland. Red and Fallow Deer. Exotic waterfowl. 2 mls e. of Worcester, on s. side of A422. Adm. fee.

Wyre Forest SO 75 76. State forest, incl. fine deciduous woods. 5 mls w. of Kidderminster and w. of Bewdley between A456 and B4194. Information centre, trails. For Comm.

Worcestershire Nature Conservation Trust, Fox Hill, Ullenhall, nr Henley-in-Arden, Warwickshire.

GLOUCESTERSHIRE

Cotswold Farm Park SP 11 27. Farm Park with rare domesticated breeds incl. ancient White Cattle, Warwickshire Longhorn and Old Gloucester Cattle, Manx Loghtan and North Ronaldsay Sheep, Jacob and Portland Sheep. Bemborough Farm 3 mls n.e. of Guiting Power, 3 mls s.e. of Ford and 1 ml s. of B4077. Car park, cafeteria, information centre, open 17th May–30th Sept. Adm. fee. Private/Rare Breeds Survival T.

Dean Forest National Park SO 55 05. Ancient Royal Forest, mainly oakwoods and planted conifers. 35,000 a. Incl. Tintern Forest, 4902 a., Blackcliff and Wyndcliff FNR, and other woodlands in Wye valley. Traversed by A466 Monmouth–Chepstow, B4266 Cinderford–Coleford and other B roads in area. Camp site s. of Symond's Yat SO 55 16, car parks. For Comm.

Dover's Hill SP 13 39. Natural amphitheatre on a spur of the Cotswolds overlooking Vale of Evesham. 1 ml n.w. of Chipping Camden on s. side of B4035 s.e. of Weston Subedge. NT.

Gloucestershire Trust for Nature Conservation, The Church House, Standish, Stonehouse, Gloucestershire, GL10 3EU.

Haresfield Beacon SO 82 08. Hill and woodland on n. edge of Cotswolds. Incl. Standish Wood, part of Randwick Wood, Ring Hill and Haresfield Beacon, 713 ft. 2–3 mls n.w. of Stroud, between A46 and B4008. Topograph on viewpoint at SO 828 085. NT.

Lancaut ST 54 96. Cliffs, scree, salt-marsh. 1 ml n. of Chepstow, on w. side of B4228. Glos. Nats T.

May Hill SO 69 21. Hill and viewpoint over ten counties. 9 mls w. of Gloucester, 1 ml n. of A40. NT.

Nagshead Inclosure SO 61 09. Part of Forest of Dean; oakwood, nest-boxes, 368 a. Nuthatches, Redstarts, Pied Flycatchers, Wood Warblers. 3 mls s.e. of Coleford, 5 mls e. of Monmouth, e. of B4431. Car park, information centre, trail. For Comm/RSPB.

The National Trust Severn, Regional Office, 35/36 Church Street, Tewkesbury, Gloucestershire.

Newark Park ST 78 93. Farmland and woods on a spur of the Cotswolds. 1½ mls e. of Wotton-under-Edge, 1½ mls s. of junction of A4135 – B4058. NT.

Slimbridge Refuge SO 72 05. In addition to collection, has wild Pintail, Gadwall, Shoveler, Pochard and Bewick's Swans in winter, Shelduck, Teal and Wigeon. Observation towers overlooking flocks of White-fronted Geese on New Grounds. Beside R. Severn at Slimbridge w. of M5, leave by interchange 13 (Stroud A419) from n. or 14 (Falfield) from s. Car park, education centre, observatory, hides. Adm. fee. Wildfowl T.

Stroud Commons. Incl. Minchinhampton Commons SO 85 01, Rodborough Common SO 850 038, and smaller areas. N. of Nailsworth between A46 and A419.

Westonbirt ST 86 90. Magnificent pinetum and arboretum. 3 mls s.w. of Tetbury, w. of A433. Car park. Information centre. For Comm.

Animal collections in the West Midlands

Birdland Zoo Gardens

This is a beautiful little garden with a big collection of birds, opened in 1957 by Mr L. W. Hill in this picturesque Cotswold village. Many of the birds are at liberty, and a feature of the garden is the sight of flights of macaws wheeling overhead. The main attractions here are the Tropical House and adjacent Tropic Hall, where you can see a good collection of hummingbirds and other nectar-feeders, and the large glass-sided penguin pool, in which the penguins can be seen swimming under water, especially when they are fed. The garden itself is beautifully planted and maintained and whether you are a tourist or an expert, you should not miss a visit to this excellent collection.

The Birdland Zoo Gardens. **Address** Bourton-on-the-Water, Glos. **Telephone** Bourton-on-the-Water 20689. **Open** 10.00–dusk summer and winter. **Guide-book. Car** 3 mls s. of Stow-on-the-Wold on A429 Cirencester road.

Birmingham Nature Centre

Opened in 1975 by the Natural History Department of Birmingham Corporation's City Museum and Art Gallery, this collection is devoted to British animals, animals introduced to this country, and European animals which were once found wild here. Mammals exhibited include the Badger, Fox, Wild Cat and small rodents, and there is also a bird collection. A selection of fish is displayed, as well as aquatic molluscs and crustaceans, and there are some amphibians and reptiles, an apiary (beehives) and a walk-through butterfly enclosure. All living animals shown are supplemented by museum exhibits with explanatory notices and displays. There is a farm section containing rare breeds of sheep and old agricultural machinery. The grounds are laid out to create as many habitats as possible, such as deciduous woodland, coniferous woodland, marshland, pasture and moorland, each with its own animal and plant communities.

The Nature Centre replaces the small zoo which formerly occupied this site and entry to it is free.

Birmingham Nature Centre. **Address** Cannon Hill Park, Pershore Road, Birmingham. **Telephone** Birmingham 472 7775. **Open** 10.00–18.00 Easter to May and Aug to Sept, 10.00–20.00 June to Aug, 10.00–16.00 Oct–Easter (Sun 13.00–16.00). Closed Tues all year round. **Admission free. Guide-book. Guided tours** by arrangement for schools. **Acreage** $4\frac{1}{2}$. **Car** The Nature Centre is adjacent to Cannon Hill Park, Edgbaston; s. of Birmingham on the A441 Pershore road, opposite BBC centre, Pebble Mill. **Bus** 41, 45, 47 stop outside Nature Centre from city (John Bright Street). **Train** to New Street station. **Taxis** available. No pets. Public **not allowed** to feed animals.

Bridgemere Wildlife Park

When Mr J. W. Norden opened this Park to the public in 1972 he exhibited waterfowl and a few exotic species of bird in aviaries. Since then, he has added European mammals, more tropical birds and birds of prey. The main interest of the Park lies in beautifully laid out ponds and pools for waterfowl, where a large and growing collection, including some rare species, is likely to become an important one. Mr Norden is one of the few people in this country with a regularly breeding flock of Red-breasted Geese, a beautiful small species which breeds in northern Siberia and which is now becoming rare in the wild.

Bridgemere Wildlife Park. **Address** Bridgemere Hall, Nr Nantwich, Cheshire. **Telephone** Bridgemere 223. **Open** 10.30–dusk summer, closed Nov–March. **Guide-book. Catering** self-service cafeteria. Information centre and zoo shop. **Acreage** 35. **Car** 6 mls s.e. of Nantwich on A51 Nantwich–Woore road. **Train** to Crewe (8 mls). Public **not allowed** to feed animals.

Chester Zoological Gardens

Chester Zoo has the largest collection of wild animals in the country after London Zoo, and it is impossible to appreciate fully all it has to offer, in a single visit. Although the Zoo is approaching its fiftieth anniversary, it is in many ways one of the most up-to-date exhibitions in Great Britain. The feeling of spaciousness here, and the delightful setting do full justice to the importance of the collection, numbering about 4,000 specimens, which give pleasure to a million people every year. You need a full day to walk around the Zoo, and it is best to follow the map so as not to miss any of the exhibits.

Starting at the south entrance, you pass the Peacock Enclosure and the Wapiti Paddock. The Wapiti is the largest of the deer family, standing five feet tall and weighing up to 1,000 lb. Related to the British Red Deer, they are found in the Rocky Mountains of North America and in central and northeastern Asia. They have also been introduced into South Island, New Zealand. Near these are the Red or Lesser Pandas. The Red Panda is an attractive animal with bright chestnut fur and a ringed tail, found in the Himalayas. It is a forest animal, sleeping during the day in the top branches of trees, coming down at night to search for roots, eggs, insects and grubs. Two races of the Brown Bear are exhibited, the European and the Syrian. The European race, common all over Europe at one time, is now restricted to a few mountainous areas in Europe, and is rare. In the wild, it hibernates in winter, building up a store of fat during the summer months on a mixed diet of flesh, fruit, grubs and honey, but in captivity it remains active all the year round, since there is a constant supply of food. The Syrian race, also now rare, is a lighter, creamy-brown colour.

There is an excellent Aquarium, with an interesting collection of tropical freshwater fish, and a few marine species. One of the most interesting freshwater fish is the piranha, from the rivers of tropical South America. Piranhas are vicious, carnivorous fish, feeding on other fish, but also attacking any other animal which is wounded and bleeding. The largest piranhas are no more than two feet long, but they attack in shoals, and with their sharp teeth they can consume quite a large animal in a short time. There are records of animals weighing 100 lb. being reduced to a skeleton within a minute. Three species of catfish are exhibited, the Talking Catfish of the Amazon, the Congo Catfish, and the curious Upside-down Catfish of tropical Africa. This swims upside-down at the surface, where it eats floating food, the mouth being positioned on the underside of its head. When feeding on the bottom, it turns the right way up. Notice also the Congo Tetra, a beautiful little fish which has some elongated rays in its tail fin. Another dangerous species here is the Freshwater Stingray, with sharp spines which can cause a fatal infection when they pierce the skin. For this reason they are feared even more than the piranha by the Indians of South America.

There is a large specimen of the African Lungfish. Unlike other fishes, which extract oxygen from water, most lungfishes breathe air, and they die if held under water. The African Lungfish wriggles down into the river mud at the beginning of the dry season, making a tunnel to the surface. When the river dries up it has access to the air, becoming comatose until the rains soften the mud again and fill the river. During its hibernation, the lungfish breathes in and out only about once every two hours. It lives off its muscle tissue, and may lose half its weight during the dry season.

In the marine tanks you can see the sea-horse, which swims in an upright position, with its body encased in armour and its mouth at the end of its long snout. When the female spawns, she places her eggs in a pouch under the male sea-horse's tail, where they are incubated for about six weeks. The male then wriggles his body and expels the young fish, about 100 in number, which are immediately able to feed themselves on shrimps. You can also see both black and white forms of the Axolotl, which can remain in the larval form throughout its life. In certain conditions it undergoes a complete transformation from an aquatic to a terrestrial existence, when it becomes the Tiger Salamander.

The Electric Eel, from tropical South America, is the largest of about 250 species of fish which have the ability to discharge electricity. It is a freshwater fish, and it uses its electric current as a form of radar to locate fish and frogs, which are its prey. Once the prey is located, the eel produces a high-voltage discharge which stuns the prey. Electric Eels can grow to more than nine feet long and produce an electric shock of 650 volts. The front part of its body contains all its internal organs, the backward four-fifths of its length consisting of the specialised tissue which produces the current. Its eyes atrophy with age, and it breathes air, coming to the surface every few minutes.

Chester Zoological Gardens. **Address** Upton-by-Chester, Cheshire. **Telephone** Chester 20106. **Open** 09.00—dusk summer and winter. **Guide-book. Catering** licensed restaurant, un-licensed restaurant, self-service cafeteria, snack bar, kiosk. Zoo shop. **Acreage** 3,500 (including farm land). **Car** 2 mls n. of Chester off A41 at Upton-by-Chester. **Bus** C40 and C6 stop at south entrance gate. **Train** to Chester (2 mls). **Taxis** available. **Other facilities** first-aid post, nursing mothers' room, lost children's room, push-chairs, wheel-chairs. Public **not allowed** to feed animals.

Congo Tetra (opposite), and the Discus from South America (below): two fish which can be seen at Chester Zoo.

Two other interesting species are the Climbing Perch and the Discus. The Climbing Perch of southeast Asia is not a true perch, and although it can climb a few inches, its main feature is its ability to migrate across land from one piece of water to another, wriggling along with the aid of its gill covers at ten feet a minute. The Discus of South America is interesting for its breeding habits. When its eggs are hatched, the fry are attached by the parents to the stems of under-water plants, where they fan themselves for two or three days, after which they attach themselves by threads to the parents' bodies, which have a secretion in the skin on which the young fish feed.

The Parrot House contains a couple of dozen species of parrot, macaw and cockatoo, which are among the most brightly coloured birds in the world. Parrots are found practically throughout the tropics, while macaws occur only in Central and South America, and cockatoos in Australia and southeastern Asia. Parrots and related species are all distinguished by their strong, hooked bills, and by the ability to hold a piece of food in one foot while they take bites out of it. The feet have opposing toes, so that they can also grasp branches when climbing. Several species of parrot have been bred here, and they thrive in captivity. You can see here the Gold and Blue, Gold and Yellow, Red and Blue, Military and Hyacinthine Macaws, and an equally good selection of cockatoos, including the largest species, the Great Black or Great Palm Cockatoo from New Guinea and northern Australia, which is 2 feet 7 inches long. The Black Cockatoo differs from the White Cockatoo in leading a solitary life, or in groups of two or three. One of the most interesting species in this house is the Kea, one of only two species of parrot found in New Zealand. The Kea comes from South Island, nesting in holes and cracks in the rocky highlands. In winter it descends to the farmlands, where it scavenges, even killing sheep by pecking their backs to get at the kidney fat. An aviary at the end of the house contains a mixed group of tanagers, babblers and white-eyes, and the Rufous-sided Crake, a small wader of the marshlands in southeast Asia which belongs to the rail family.

The Free Flight Aviary exhibits some of the larger species of wading bird, including ibises, Cattle Egret, curlews, Weka Rail, herons and the Purple Gallinule. Also shown here is the Brahminy Kite, a medium-sized bird of prey found in India, southeastern Asia and Australia. There are four species of ibis here, the Scarlet, Glossy, Sacred and Indian. The most striking is the brilliantly coloured Scarlet Ibis, found in Venezuela, southwards to Brazil and sometimes in the West Indies. It requires protection, being in demand for its feathers and meat, but it is prized for its beauty in zoos. The Sacred Ibis, revered by the ancient Egyptians as the god Thoth, is found in Africa and Madagascar, and the Glossy Ibis, a small species widely distributed throughout southern Europe and Asia, America, the East Indies and Australia, has a beautiful greenish sheen on its wing feathers. The Cattle Egret, or Buff-backed Heron, is native to southern Europe and Asia and northern Africa, but it has colonised Guyana and the warmer parts of the United States. It is well known for its habit of foraging in the company of ruminating animals, perching on their backs to remove ticks, and around their hooves in search of insects. Three species of heron are exhibited, the Night Heron, Eastern Purple Heron and Grey Heron. Night Herons are visible in the daytime, although they do most of their hunting by night, the young birds migrating in all directions in search of new territory before heading southwards. The largest group of herons includes the Grey Heron of Europe and Asia, and the Purple Heron, which is also found in Africa. These stand four or five feet tall. Herons belong to one of the groups of birds which have powder-downs, a special type of feather which is never moulted. It grows continuously and frays at the edges into a powder, which the bird uses for dressing its other feathers. The Purple Gallinule, a New World relative of our familiar Moorhen, has bright purple plumage and red feet and legs.

The Ape House contains breeding colonies of Chimpanzees and Orang utans, with large indoor rooms joined by corridors to their outdoor islands, surrounded by shallow water. The Orang utans have one room containing waterfalls, with a background of climbing plants. Chimpanzees are sociable animals, and in the wild they live in large family groups of all ages, but with the composition of the groups changing often as individuals join other groups. They travel considerable distances in search of seasonal fruits, sometimes killing young baboons or wild pigs, and they also use grass stems or twigs to probe into ants' nests, picking the ants off the stem as a delicacy. Orang utans have a more solitary social life in twos and threes, and they live in the high forest canopy, rarely coming down to the ground. Their numbers in the wild have dwindled alarmingly owing to poaching and forest clearance. Both species breed in captivity, and several have been born in the Zoo.

Near the Ape House is the Tuatara exhibit. The Tuatara is a lizard found only in New Zealand, and is the only living member of its scientific order, and the oldest surviving type of reptile. It grows to 2 feet 6 inches in length, but so slowly that it apparently takes 50 years to reach its full size. Once common, it is now confined to small uninhabited islands and is legally protected.

Next you come to the peccaries, the bird of prey aviaries, jackals and hyenas, porcupines, Coypus (see p. 140) and Beavers. The peccary is the small wild pig of South America, where it replaces the Wild Boar of Europe. In the wild it lives in small groups on forest and open scrub. There are two aviaries for birds of prey, one of which is reserved for Condors, which are found in the high Andes of South America. The condors are the largest of the predatory birds, with a wing span of 10 or 11 feet. The Zoo attained distinction in 1939 when a pair of Griffon Vultures hatched and reared a chick for the first time in captivity in any zoo. The Black-backed Jackals and Spotted Hyenas are both animals of the African plains, and both are scavengers, following lions to feed on the kills but also catching small game. Hyenas also hunt on their own account, often taking new-born antelopes when the opportunity offers. Female hyenas burrow into the ground to give birth to their pups, and they have to guard their litters from marauding male hyenas which have no compunction in eating them if they get the chance. Porcupines, Coypus and Beavers are all rodents, but while porcupines are strictly land animals, the other two spend much of their time in the water. The Beaver constructs 'lodges', entered from below water level, in lakes and streams. The water is dammed with logs cemented together with mud, to maintain the water level. The Beavers here are supplied with timber to enable them to pursue their activities, but it is necessary to watch them so that they do not build their way out of the enclosure.

The Giraffe House contains a breeding group of Giraffes, and it is interesting to recall how this very large building was reconstructed. It was needed in a hurry and funds were limited at the time. The most expensive part would be the roof, so this was made first. The walls were then built a few feet high, the completed roof was hoisted on top and lifted up on one side with three 5-ton lorry jacks. The wall on that side was then built up a further 18 feet and the roof lowered on. The process was then repeated on the other side, and continued until the eaves were 20 feet from the ground. The apex of the roof is 40 feet high, and the building was completed without the use of scaffolding in 1954. The whole project took five months at a cost of under £2,000, yet it remains one of the most practical buildings for Giraffes in the country.

The Camel House exhibits both Arabian and Bactrian Camels, the one-humped and two-humped species respectively. The Arabian Camel, or Dromedary, is still used as a pack animal, the racing camel being a breed developed for riding. The Bactrian Camel is a more heavily built animal, used for transport in central Asia. It has a thick coat which is shed in the summer. Arabian Camels were imported into Australia as pack animals during the building of railways in the nineteenth century, and when these were completed the camels were turned loose, so that the species still exists there as a semi-wild animal.

The Tropical House is one of the largest zoo buildings in the world, being 240 feet long, 200 feet wide and 40 feet high. It contains a zoo-within-a-zoo. It is well worth the separate admission charge, and one can easily spend an hour or two here. The house is completely landscaped with tropical plants and trees, and the well-established banana trees, which reach to the roof, bear fruit each year. At liberty in the house there are about 200 small tropical birds, including

The Black-backed Jackal, a scavenger of the African plains, often follows larger carnivores to feast on their leavings.

The Spotted Hyena of Africa, the largest and strongest of the scavengers, also hunts and kills on its own account, particularly new-born antelopes.

starlings, touracos, waxbills, whydahs, weavers and mynahs. There is a 30-foot waterfall, and a gallery at first-floor level containing aviaries, from which you obtain a view of the whole house. At ground level there is accommodation for Gorillas, Pygmy Hippopotamus, the echidna, giant tortoises, tropical pools for crocodilians, a reptile house and a nocturnal house.

This is the only zoo in the country where you can see both the Lowland and the Mountain Gorillas. Gorillas come from the dense rain-forests of tropical West Africa and central Africa, living in family groups and sleeping in a different place each night. They are strict vegetarians, being specially partial to bitter-tasting plants such as wild celery. At night the females and young construct nests of branches and leaves low down in the trees, the heavier males remaining on the ground. Both species are now rare in the wild, and here one can compare the Lowland species, which is usually exhibited in zoos, with the shaggy-coated Mountain species, the only examples in Great Britain. These came from the mountain ranges on the borders of Zaire, and the species was not discovered by western scientists until 1901. The Gorillas have access to two island enclosures outside, and there is also a Chimpanzee colony attached to this house with a large island enclosure surrounded by shallow water. There is an electric fence in the water which is an effective barrier, although a Chimpanzee has been known to earth the wire with a stick. But Chimpanzees do not like water and they prefer to remain on their grass-covered island.

The Pygmy Hippopotamus comes from Liberia, Guinea and Sierra Leone, living in dense forests near river banks. Unlike its large cousin, the Pygmy Hippo does not live in large herds, preferring a more solitary existence, and it spends less time in the water, browsing on land at night and lying up during the day in thick cover near the river. The species is endangered in the wild, and a studbook for captive animals is maintained at the Basle Zoo, Switzerland, which has bred them regularly. The echidna, or spiny anteater, is a difficult animal to exhibit, as it spends most of the day sleeping in a hollow log, coming out in early morning and late evening to dig for beetles, ants, termites and grubs. In the wild, it hibernates in winter, shedding its spines and fur in the spring to grow a new coat. The echidna is a monotreme, which means that it lays an egg, and then suckles its young after hatching. The long claws are used for digging, and the long, tubular snout and sticky tongue for reaching ants. When danger threatens, it digs itself into the ground, leaving only the tips of its spines sticking up above the surface. The species shown here comes from Australia.

Most giant tortoises come from the Galapagos Islands in the Pacific and the Aldabra Islands in the Indian Ocean. Once common in these isolated regions, they were reduced in number by sailors who killed them for food, though they are now protected by law. Each island has developed its own species. Giant tortoises have developed their great size owing to the climate and lack of predatory animals in their natural home. They can reach a weight of 300 lb. and a length of 4 feet, and they may live for 200 years.

Five members of the crocodile family are exhibited, all of which are becoming rare in the wild. The largest of these is the Nile Crocodile, found in African rivers, which can reach a length of 18 feet. A foot or two less when adult is the Mississippi Alligator, from the southeastern United States. The False Gavial grows to 15 feet and its natural home is Borneo and Sumatra, while the West African Broad-nosed Crocodile and the Siamese Crocodile of Java and Siam are smaller species, reaching only six and seven feet in length respectively. The Mississippi Alligator has a very broad snout, rounded at the tip, while the Nile and Siamese Crocodiles have less sharply shaped snouts. The Broad-nosed Crocodile has a very short, broad snout, and the False Gavial has a long, narrow snout, like a saucepan handle.

The Reptile House inside the Tropical House has a good collection of snakes, iguanas and lizards, and a Matamata Turtle. This last is one of the most curious looking of turtles, with projecting points on its shell plates, a long tubular nose and small eyes placed unusually far forward. It comes from the rivers of Brazil and the Guyanas, feeding mostly on fish. Several species of iguana are exhibited, including the Rhinoceros Iguana, so called because of the three blunt horns

Giraffes, photographed wild in Africa.

205

African Elephant, photographed here in the wild adopting an aggressive posture; it is considerably more difficult to manage in captivity than the Indian species, the traditional passenger-carrying and circus elephant.

on its snout, which is found only in Haiti and Puerto Rico and is now endangered in the wild state. Two interesting lizards are here, the Gila Monster (pronounced 'Heela') and the Mexican Beaded Lizard. The Gila Monster has a pink and black body and a short tail, used for storing fat, and it comes from Arizona and New Mexico. The Beaded Lizard is pale yellow and black with a black head and longer tail; it is found in Mexico and Central America. Both species live in deserts, are venomous, and are regarded as dangerous; they are rare in the wild, but still appear fairly often in good reptile collections. Several venomous snakes are shown, and there is a collection of seven species of python. The largest of the pythons is the Royal, of eastern India and Malaysia, which can reach a length of 33 feet, although this is the maximum and the average length is about 22 feet. Next come the Indian Python at 25 feet, and the African Rock Python at 20 feet, but both the last species average about 18 feet long. The Indian Python is now an endangered species in the wild.

The smaller mammals can be seen in the anteater enclosures, near the tigers in the Mammal House, and in the Small Mammal House which is near the Elephant House. These include the Giant Anteater, the rarest of the anteaters in the wild, which comes from Central and South America; and the Chinchilla, a native of the Andes in Peru, which was so sought after for its fur in the early part of this century that it was almost exterminated there, though now it enjoys legal protection. You can also see the Cream-coloured Giant Squirrel, which grows to a foot long and comes from the forests of Malaya; the Capybara, from South and Central America, the largest living rodent; and the American Badger which is similar to the British species but smaller and with less conspicuous head markings. There are also several small carnivorous animals, such as the Blotched Genet, the Common Palm Civet, the Banded Mongoose and the Jaguarondi. The Blotched Genet is the commonest species of genet in Africa. This is a small cat-like creature which stalks its prey at night, mostly small mammals and birds. The Common Indian Palm Civet has a long tail and it used to be known as the Toddy Cat, because it was in the habit of sipping palm wine in the cups attached to trees which were being tapped. It has a scent gland, used like the skunk's in repelling enemies. The Banded Mongoose, found in Africa south of the Sahara, lives on small rodents, lizards, fruit, snakes and birds' eggs. The Jaguarondi is a small cat species, mainly found in central and northern South America. This lives on small mammals and birds, reptiles, frogs, fish and insects.

After the Mammal House, you pass the Gibbon Island, and come to the Flamingo Pool and waterfowl enclosures. The rarest species of waterfowl in the Zoo is the Laysan Teal, which originated on Laysan Island, 900 miles from Honolulu. It nearly became extinct by 1912, when only seven individuals were known to exist. It has since been bred satisfactorily in captivity and is no longer in any danger of extinction, although it remains rare in the wild. It has unremarkable brown plumage, but can be distinguished by the white area around the eye.

The penguin and otter enclosures each have glass-fronted tanks in which the animals can be seen swimming under water. The otters exhibited here are Indian Small-clawed Otters from the hill streams in the foothills of the Himalayas. They live mainly on mussels, crabs and snails when wild. Their enclosure here has a slide covered with running water into the pool. The penguins exhibited are the Rockhopper, Humboldt and Jackass or Cape Penguin. The Rockhopper is found in the temperate sub-Antarctic regions, and it is noted for being the most aggressive species of penguin, attacking intruders vigorously. The Humboldt's Penguin comes from islands off the west coast of South America where the Humboldt current flows. Its nesting grounds are exploited for guano deposits, which are rich in minerals. The Cape Penguin lives in the seas of South Africa, mainly around the Cape, and also produces guano, for which reason it is protected. Near this exhibit are the sealions, in a large pool which enables them to display their exceptional powers of swimming.

The enclosures for Polar Bears, Tigers, Lions, Cheetahs and Malayan Bears are all within a short distance of the Oakfield Restaurant. The Polar Bear pool is one of the largest in the country, and was built in 1945 from concrete road blocks used during the Second War and from Portland stone. The Zoo got permission from the War Office to remove all the tank traps and pill-boxes for several miles around, and these formed the basis of the retaining walls. The large blocks of Portland stone used for the waterfall and the island arrived as the result of a local contractor's order for one block of Portland stone. Owing to a mistake in the order, a whole train-load of stone arrived, which the contractor could not use, so the Zoo took over the consignment. The Tigers breed regularly in their spacious paddock, and the Lions, which also breed freely, can be seen both from ground level and from a raised terrace. The Cheetahs are from Africa, as are all Cheetahs in zoos, since the Indian Cheetah is now extinct in the wild, and the

Blotched Genet, an African species which stalks its prey at night, may be seen at Chester Zoo.

American Badger digging: this New World cousin of our own Badger (see page 194) is smaller and less strikingly marked.

African Cheetah is becoming rare. The Malayan Bear is the smallest of the bear family, and the best tree climber. It lives on insects, honey, small animals and fruit. The Kamchatka Bears, opposite the Elephant House, are a race of the Brown Bear from eastern Siberia, where they are occasionally attacked by Wolves and Tigers, although these are their only natural enemies. Brown Bears breed freely in captivity, and are even becoming something of a problem in zoos, since only a limited number of establishments have bear enclosures and can accept surplus animals.

The eastern and western halves of the Zoo are divided by a canal system, which is unique in British zoos, and by taking the waterbus you can rest your feet (and your children) and see some of the big paddock enclosures as you glide past in comfort. Near the waterbus kiosk is one of several enclosures for wallabies, and from the canal you can see the Zoo's fine herd of Red Lechwe, whose natural range is from Botswana to western Zambia. This is a handsome chestnut-coloured antelope which follows rivers in flood, feeding on water plants. Other antelope species in this area of the Zoo are kudu, which breed here, Eland, the largest of the African antelopes, a breeding herd of Blackbuck, a graceful small Indian species, and Arabian Gazelles, the rarest antelopes in the collection. These are natives of the Sinai Peninsula, where they have become almost extinct owing to the depredations of motorised hunting parties of soldiers and oil men, who have virtually exterminated all wildlife in the desert areas of the Middle East. Two species of zebra are exhibited, the Grévy's Zebra from Ethiopia, Somaliland and northern Kenya, which is the largest of the zebra family, and Grant's Zebra, from approximately the same area but ranging southwards into Tanzania. This species has broad, well-defined stripes like the Grévy's, but with the stripes continued under the belly, whereas the Grévy's has a white underbelly. The deer you can see include the Red, Sika and Père David's Deer. The Sika are of the Formosan race, which is an endangered subspecies on the island of Taiwan, but it breeds readily in captivity. Père David's Deer is extinct in the wild, but before that happened at the turn of the century enough animals had been collected in captivity to ensure its survival. It is a swamp deer from China, with the characteristic splayed hooves adapted to marshy ground, but it has certain curious physical characteristics, one of which is its very long tail. Other paddocks exhibit Ankole Cattle, a domestic breed kept by the Watussi tribe in Uganda, Llamas and Alpacas which share an enclosure with Prairie Marmots. Llamas and Alpacas are domesticated species from South America, the latter being much prized for its wool. Prairie Marmots, from the western plains of the United States and Mexico, are small burrowing rodents, active by day, which live in huge underground colonies.

At the northern end of the Zoo you come to the Elephant House, where you can see both African and Indian Elephants, of both sexes. Very few zoos keep bull elephants because they are difficult to handle when adult. But Chester Zoo would like to breed elephants, and they have the space in which to do it. The Elephant House also accommodates Hippos, which have an outdoor mud wallow, and this they greatly appreciate. They have bred here, and they maintain friendly relations with the elephants in the adjoining enclosure. Both the Malayan Tapir and the Brazilian Tapir are exhibited, the Malayan species being black and white, and somewhat the larger.

Passing via the paddocks for Emus, cranes and storks, you come to the Cat House, containing the smaller cat species. These include Jaguars and Leopards, which breed here, and Amur Leopards, a Chinese race which also breeds in the Zoo. The rarest species here, and one not so often seen in zoos, is the Clouded Leopard, a much smaller animal than the true Leopard, with a mottled coat. It comes from Nepal, southern China, Malaya and Borneo. Another species here is the Ocelot, a beautifully marked small cat from South America, which has for long been a favourite in the fur trade.

There are more paddock enclosures containing American Bison, and two more antelope species, the Beisa Oryx which often live in association with zebras and gazelles in Africa, and the White-bearded Gnu, a rare sub-species of the Brindled Gnu, from Tanzania. The Rhinoceros House has both the Black

Above: American Bison, of which vast herds used to roam the North American plains.

Ankole Cattle, a domestic breed kept by the Watussi tribe in Uganda.

Coombe Abbey Bird Gardens. **Address** Coombe Abbey Regional Park, Brinklow Road, Coventry, Warwicks. **Telephone** Coventry 453500. **Open** 10.00–dusk summer and winter. **Catering** (available in the Regional Park during summer only), snack bar, kiosk. Gift shop. **Acreage** 10. **Car** 6 miles e. of Coventry, off A427. **Bus** from Coventry to Brinklow road. Special bus service from Coventry in summer. **Train** to Coventry (6 mls). **Taxis** available. **Other facilities** first-aid post, lost children's room, children's playground, Nature Trail, boating. Public allowed to feed birds with own food.

and White Rhinoceros. The White Rhino, once rare in southern Africa, has now been bred successfully in game reserves and it is exhibited in many zoos. It is a herd animal and it grazes, whereas the Black Rhino, now becoming rare in Africa, is more solitary in its habits and it browses on bushes and small trees. Studbooks of animals in captivity for both species are kept in the West Berlin Zoo. When a telegram from Africa announced the impending arrival of the Zoo's first rhinos in three weeks' time, the maintenance staff worked almost non-stop to build their house, and it was completed on time – a wonderful effort which is nevertheless almost routine in this remarkable zoo.

The Monkey House has a good selection of African monkeys, as well as some from Asia and South America. The largest groups represented here are the guenons, which are widely distributed in Africa. Among these you can see the Vervet Monkey, distinguished by the white band across its forehead. Several races exist, and they inhabit woodland and savannah country. Two guenons which are very much alike are the Moustached Monkey and the Red-eared Nose-spotted Monkey. Both have long, red-haired tails, but the latter has (as you might expect) red ears. Two more very similar guenons are the Diana and the Mona Monkeys. The former has a white beard, and less chestnut-coloured hair on its back. Another guenon is the Sykes Monkey, a race of the Blue Monkey, found east of the Rift Valley, and the Talapoin is the smallest of all African monkeys, active during the day in the swampy forests of West Africa, and a timid species. Another group of African monkeys are the mangabeys, and here you can see the Sooty and the Cherry-crowned Mangabey. Found in western and central Africa, mangabeys live in the lower parts of forest trees in small troops. They move more slowly than guenons, and are very noisy. The most colourful of the baboons is the Mandrill, a large West African species with blue and scarlet face markings and on the hind parts. This decoration has sexual significance, and it is confined to males. An endangered species here is the Lion-tailed Macaque, a shy monkey from the mountainous forests along the west coast of southern India. Lastly, there are three species of spider monkey, the Geoffroy's, Red-faced and Black-faced. Spider monkeys have short bodies and very long arms, used for rapid swinging from tree to tree in the tropical forests of South America, where they correspond to the gibbons of Asia.

Chester Zoo was founded in 1930 by Mr George Mottershead, who wished to develop his ideas for exhibiting animals without the use of bars. He opened the Zoo in 1931 on nine acres around Oakfield House, which now houses the Oakfield Restaurant. In 1934 the North of England Zoological Society was formed to take over the Zoo, and several lean years followed until attendances increased during the Second War. After the end of the war development was incredibly rapid, thanks to Mr Mottershead's genius for improvisation and his flair for exhibiting animals to the best advantage. He is still Director of the Zoo, and it is now one of the major collections in Europe. The gardens and hot-houses, where exotic plants of all kinds are propagated for the animal houses, are also famous in horticultural circles, and you will always see a magnificent display in the herbaceous borders, and tens of thousands of bulbs in spring. More than any other zoo in the country, this is the creation of one man, who has transformed a few bare fields into a fascinating animal collection in a delightful setting. Members of the Society have a restaurant, library, meetings and lectures.

Coombe Abbey Bird Gardens

This is a bird collection set in natural surroundings, consisting of woodland, a lake and a stream. Many birds are at liberty, including pelicans, cranes, parrots, macaws and cockatoos. You can also see flamingos, swans, geese, ducks, cassowaries, parrakeets, magpies, jays, peafowl, pheasants, guans, ibises and finches. There are also some birds of prey – eagles, vultures and owls – and some rare breeds of poultry and a Pets' Corner. The collection was opened in 1972 by Mr and Mrs K. Deacon.

Coventry Zoo Park

Coventry Zoo Park has a mixed collection of animals, with about 80 species of mammal, 50 bird species and a small number of reptiles. Mammals which breed regularly include Lions, Leopards, Pumas, bears, monkeys, Dingos and Heidesnucki Sheep, a very rare Danish breed. There is also a dolphinarium. The Zoo, originally opened in 1966, is now owned by Messrs W. J. and J. W. F. Chipperfield.

Delamere Bird Garden and Reptilia

This is a small Bird Garden with a reptile house which contains a good collection of reptiles, including crocodiles and alligators. It was opened in 1951 by Mr R. W. Harding.

Drayton Manor Park and Zoo

The Zoo is part of an entertainment park and it has a mixed collection. You can see Lions, Leopards, Pumas, bears, Chimpanzees, about 50 monkeys, sealions, penguins, pelicans, waterfowl, about 60 tropical birds, flamingos, birds of prey, storks, cranes and peafowl, and a zoo farm, complete with a scaled-down piggery, milking parlour and hatchery. In this area there are paddocks for deer, sheep, Llamas, wallabies and Highland Cattle. There is a good Reptile House, with Mississippi Alligators, several snake species and lizards, of which the house geckos and Giant Zonures have bred recently. Fish and turtles are also displayed here. The Zoo was opened in 1957.

Dudley Zoo

Dudley Zoo is the main urban zoo in the industrial part of the West Midlands, with a good general collection of animals, including all three great apes, elephants, Lions, dolphins, a Reptile House and an Aquarium. You can also see flamingos, birds of prey, penguins and the smaller tropical birds in the Bird House. The Zoo does not specialise in any particular group of animals, but there are a few rarities here, and about 1,100 animals in all, including fish.

The large carnivorous animals exhibited include Lions and Tigers, in large rocky ravines, and the Bear Ravine contains Asiatic Black Bears, otherwise called Himalayan Bears. This part of the Zoo has been mined for limestone for generations, and where surface quarrying has taken place it was possible to adapt the excavations as enclosures for dangerous animals. Tigers are now endangered in the wild, and in India, where the Tigers exhibited came from, they are now protected in reserves. The group of Lions here breed regularly. There is a large Polar Bear pool, which is one of the original barless enclosures constructed when the Zoo was built. Other big cats here are Leopards and Pumas. The Zoo has both spotted and black Leopards, the latter being merely a colour phase of the spotted Leopard, and you can just make out the spots on their dark-coloured coats. Black Leopards are mainly found in India and southeast Asia, the spotted form being found in Africa as well as Asia. Pumas are the largest of the big cats in South America and the southwestern United States. There are some smaller carnivorous animals in the Zoo, including various small cat species, wolves and Spotted Hyenas. The Spotted Hyena comes from North and central Africa, and hunts in packs, also scavenging on the prey of other animals. The two other hyena species are the Brown Hyena, a rare animal from South Africa, and the

Coventry Zoo Park. **Address** Whitely Common, Coventry, Warwick. **Telephone** Coventry 301772. **Open** 10.00–19.00 summer, 10.00–dusk winter. **Guide-book**. **Catering** self-service cafeteria, snack bar, kiosk. Zoo shop. **Car** 1½ mls s.e. of city centre s. side of London Road A423. **Bus** 22 or 27 from city centre. **Train** to Coventry (1 ml). **Taxis** available. **Other facilities** first-aid post, children's playground. Public allowed to feed monkeys with food prepared and sold in Zoo only.

Delamere Bird Garden and Reptilia. **Address** Hill Furze, Nr Pershore, Worcs. **Open** 10.00–dusk summer and winter. **Acreage** 1½. **Car** 3 mls n.e. of Pershore off B4084 towards Bishampton. **Train** to Evesham (4 mls) or Pershore (3 mls). No pets. Public **not allowed** to feed animals.

Drayton Manor Park and Zoo. **Address** Nr Tamworth, Staffs. **Telephone** Tamworth 68481. **Open** 10.30–18.00 Easter–Oct, closed in winter **Catering** licensed restaurant, self-service cafeteria, tea rooms, kiosks. **Guided tours** by arrangement. **Acreage** 160. **Car** 2 mls s. of Tamworth, off A5 on A4091 at Fazeley. **Bus** National 198 (Midland Red). **Train** to Tamworth (3 mls). **Taxis** available. **Other facilities** first-aid post, entertainment park with chair-lift, boats, trains, amusement park, garden centre. No pets. Public **not allowed** to feed animals.

Striped Hyena, a smaller animal with long hair on its sides, from India.

There is a breeding group of Giraffes in the Giraffe House, and also breeding regularly here is the Brazilian Tapir, which lives in dense jungle in tropical South America. It swims well and lives on leaves and aquatic plants in rivers. Its chief natural enemy is the Jaguar. On the hill near the Zoo entrance is a group of Mouflon, the wild sheep of Corsica and Sardinia, and you can also see Barbary Sheep, natives of the mountainous regions of North Africa, in their man-made rocky enclosure. Barbary Sheep are really wild goats, and you can distinguish the males by their larger and heavier horns. Another sheep here is the little Soay Sheep, the most primitive breed of sheep, resembling the Mouflon. Most of the members of the camel family are represented — the Arabian Camel, with one hump, being the one used for riding, is a much less heavily built animal than the two-humped Bactrian Camel, the pack animal of central Asia. The Zoo has three of the four South American members of the family, the Llama, domesticated for its wool and for carrying loads; the Alpaca, another form domesticated for its wool and meat; and the Guanaco, a wild form. The fourth camel cousin is the Vicuna, a much smaller wild form, much prized for its wool for which it has been extensively hunted. It is now protected in Peru, and may not be exported to zoos. There is also a ban on the export of its wool from Peru.

Other hoofed animals exhibited here are the Nilgai, the largest kind of antelope in India; the Axis Deer of India and Ceylon; our native Red Deer; and a herd of Arabian Gazelles. These are the rarest animals in the Zoo, and they are in danger of extinction in the wild, having been hunted mercilessly by motorised parties armed with automatic weapons in the Near East. The first three gazelles to be received were not enough to form a herd, but some more came from an R.A.F. sergeant stationed at Aden, who rescued them from the cooking pot. They were flown to England by R.A.F. Transport Command, and divided between Chester Zoo and Dudley Zoo. Only three other zoos in the country exhibit this graceful animal. You can also see American Bison, and three species of wild pig — the peccary of South America, the European Wild Boar, once common in Britain, and the Red River Hog from Africa, the only specimen in the country. There is a wooded walk-through enclosure called the Australian Safari, containing Red Kangaroo, the largest kangaroo species, Bennett's Wallabies from Tasmania, pelicans, Emus, Australian Black Swans, and Dingos, the wild dog of Australia which went wild after being introduced by man centuries ago.

The dolphins here are of the species used for performing in zoos, the Bottle-nosed Dolphin, a shoalwater animal found in all warm seas but caught off the coasts of Florida for exhibition. Their pool is eight feet deep and it contains 40,000 gallons of water, to which seven tons of salt are added. Other aquatic mammals in the Zoo are the sealions, from California, seals, which are natives of British waters, otters, and Coypus (see p. 140). There are also various exhibits in the Zoo for small mammals such as squirrels, Raccoons and porcupines.

The first birds you see on entering the Zoo are the Caribbean or Rosy Flamingos, in an attractively landscaped enclosure with a pool and waterfall. There is also a pool for Black-footed Penguins which are found off the shores of South Africa. There are outdoor aviaries for parrakeets, macaws and cockatoos, while the circular Bird House, built in 1936, is also devoted mainly to members of the parrot family, and small, delicate species such as sunbirds. The pools round the perimeter of the castle ruins contain waterfowl — geese, Mallard, teal, shelducks and pochard. Various species of soft-billed birds, birds of prey and pheasants are located in other aviaries around the Zoo.

The Aquarium is built in the crypt under the ruins of the castle chapel, and it contains a good collection of tropical freshwater and temperate freshwater fish and a smaller number of marine fish. The Reptile House, built in 1956, exhibits crocodiles, alligators, pythons, Boa Constrictors, and a number of poisonous snakes, such as cobras, Puff Adders and rattlesnakes, as well as some amphibians. There are also giant tortoises, which are exhibited out of doors during the summer months.

There are numerous other attractions in and around the Zoo, including a Children's Farm, and a Contact Paddock, where domestic animals mingle with

Dudley Zoological Society. **Address** 2 The Broadway, Dudley, West Midlands. **Telephone** Dudley 52401. **Open** 10.00–17.30 summer, 10.00–dusk winter. **Guide-book. Catering** licensed restaurant with waitress service, un-licensed restaurant, self-service cafeteria, snack bar, kiosk. Zoo shop. **Guided tours** by arrangement. **Acreage** 40. **Car** 6 mls s.e. of Wolverhampton on A461. **Bus** stops 4 mins' walk from Zoo. **Train** to Wolverhampton then WMPT bus, or Dudley Port then 74 bus. **Taxis** available. **Other facilities** first-aid post, lost children's room, push-chairs, children's playground. Public **not allowed** to feed animals.

Old male Orang utans, like this one at Dudley, develop cheek pouches in maturity.

visitors; and a chair-lift, which takes you from the Zoo entrance to the top of the hill for a smallish fee, so that you can walk downhill as you see the animals. There is also a funfair, a miniature railway, a dry ski slope open throughout the year, and, under the castle, the Dudley Caverns which have an exhibition called 'Land of the Dinosaurs'. Here you can see life-sized models of prehistoric animals such as Stegosaurus, Triceratops, *Tyrannosaurus rex*, pterodactyls and the Cave Man Village.

The Zoo was founded by Lord Dudley and Mr E. E. Marsh in 1937 in the grounds of Dudley Castle, which was mainly built between the twelfth and eighteenth centuries but is mentioned in Domesday Book. The keep dates from 1300, but the fortifications were destroyed by Cromwell. The kitchen wing was burnt down in 1750. The original zoo buildings are subject to a preservation order, which makes it difficult to modernise them. The Dudley Zoological Society Ltd, the company which originally owned the Zoo, was bought by Scotia Investments Ltd in 1971. The members of the Society, who are its shareholders, have a members' restaurant in the Fellows' Club.

Peregrine, one of the falcons trained at the Falconry Centre.

The Falconry (and Bird of Prey) Centre

The Falconry Centre, established by Mr and Mrs P. Glasier in 1967, has a superb collection of birds of prey, including eagles, falcons, hawks, owls and others, and many of the birds are trained for falconry. The Hawk Walk, or weathering ground, contains the trained birds, each in its own shelter, and each is flown during the course of the year. One of the Centre's aims is to breed birds of prey, apart from those suitable for falconry, and the aviaries display a good collection of these. Some of them have been released to the wild, in the cause of conservation. Birds which breed here include Common Kestrels, Merlins, Lanner Falcons, caracaras, Eagle Owls, Tawny Owls, Barn Owls and the Ferruginous Buzzard. Weather permitting, visitors can see birds being exercised on the flying ground, and for those interested in falconry, 12-day courses of instruction are run during the winter months. Advice is given on all aspects of falconry and on the breeding of birds of prey, either by telephone during office hours or by letter, on receipt of a stamped addressed envelope. There is an interesting museum, where you can see photographs, prints, models and various displays covering all aspects of the art of falconry and the conservation of birds of prey.

The Falconry (and Bird of Prey) Centre. **Address** Newent, Glos. **Telephone** Newent 820286. **Open** 10.30–17.30 summer, 10.30–dusk winter. **Guide-book**. Information centre, gift shop. **Guided tours** by arrangement. **Acreage** 12. **Car** 9 mls n.w. of Gloucester, off B4215 on Cliffords Mesne road. Free car park. **Bus** from Newent. **Train** to Gloucester (11 mls). **Taxis** available. No pets. Public **not allowed** to feed birds.

Marine and Freshwater Aquarium

The Aquarium displays tropical marine and temperate freshwater fish, the freshwater species all being caught locally in lakes and rivers. The Aquarium has its own carp fishery with two lakes of 3 and 16½ acres. The collection was opened in 1962 by Mr T. Farnworth.

Marine and Freshwater Aquarium. **Address** Broadlands, Bourton-on-the-Water, Glos. **Telephone** Bourton-on-the-Water 20462. **Open** 10.00–18.00 summer, closed Oct–March. **Car** the Aquarium is just off village High Street. Public **not allowed** to feed exhibits.

Prinknash Bird Park

Prinknash Bird Park was established in 1974 by Mr Philip Meigh next to Prinknash Abbey, and stocked with his private collection of waterfowl. Although the area is small, Mr Meigh has already built up an impressive collection of 750 birds, of 70 species.

The Park is divided into several areas, the main one being the lake and its surroundings, where you can see swans, geese and the larger ducks. The geese on the lake include Pink-footed Geese and Barnacle Geese, which winter in Scotland, Taverner's Canada Geese and Bar-headed Geese from China. The

Prinknash Bird Park. **Address** Prinknash Abbey, Cranham, Glos. **Telephone** Painswick 812727. **Open** 10.00–18.00 summer (possibly opening at weekends in winter). **Guide-book. Catering** self-service cafeteria, kiosk. Gift shop. **Guided tours** by arrangement. **Acreage** 9. **Car** 4 mls s.e. of Gloucester off A46 near Cranham. **Bus** 564 stops at entrance to Abbey. **Train** to Stroud (5 mls) or to Gloucester (4 mls). **Taxis** available. No pets. Public allowed to feed birds with food prepared in Park.

ducks here, among others, are Laysan Teal, a species which was close to extinction early in this century but which has since been saved by captive breeding, and the Ruddy Shelduck and Patagonian Crested Duck, both aggressive species.

In an enclosure near the lake are Greenland White-fronted Geese, which breed in Greenland and winter in Gloucestershire, and the Swan Goose, ancestor of the domestic Chinese goose, which breeds in northern Russia and winters in China. Also there are teal and wigeon, including the Chiloe Wigeon and the Argentine Shoveler, both South American species. Beyond the lake is a range of pens containing Carolina or Wood Ducks from North America, Ruddy and Paradise Shelducks and Mandarin Ducks, natives of China, Japan and eastern Asia, which have been established wild in parts of southern England and Scotland.

Across the lake there is a breeding area for geese and a pheasantry. The pheasants here are Mikado, Copper, Reeves', Lady Amherst's, Silver and Golden; and two rare species, Elliot's and Hume's Bar-tailed Pheasants. Below the dam are ponds for Ross's Geese and Red-breasted Geese, another rare species in the wild, Black Swans from Australia and the native British Mute Swan. At the waterfall begins a range of stream pens for sea-ducks, with eider, Barrow's Goldeneye, Tufted Duck and, farther along, whistling ducks. There are also more geese in this area, including the Giant Canada Goose, the largest of the 17 forms of black goose.

Many of the waterfowl are at liberty, including a flock of 30 Snow Geese and Black-shouldered, Indian and white Peafowl, this last being an albino form. There are also Crowned Cranes from Africa and some Pygmy Goats from Nigeria. More expansion is planned, including a secret garden for more exotic birds and a Pets' Corner.

Prinknash Abbey and Pottery are also open to the public.

Slimbridge Wildfowl Refuge

Slimbridge is the headquarters of the Wildfowl Trust, founded to study and preserve wildfowl throughout the world. Here you will see the world's largest display of ducks, geese, swans and flamingos. There is a resident population of about 2,500 birds, but one of the attractions of the Trust is that you will also see about 2,500 fully winged wild and semi-wild birds which visit the grounds seasonally. Out of the 247 species and sub-species of wildfowl known to science, Slimbridge has 170 species, including all six forms of flamingo. For the specialist or knowledgeable amateur, of course, this collection is a rare feast, but even if you do not know much about wildfowl you will find a visit here a fascinating experience, not only because of the variety of birds to be seen but because of the delightful setting which displays them to the best advantage.

You enter the Main Hall which has a picture window with a splendid view of the Big Pen, which is the first outdoor exhibit. This building is the Research Centre, and on its ground floor there are displays presenting the case for wildfowl conservation and some of the results of the research work done here. It is well worth looking at these before you go outside, as they will give you a good idea of what the Trust does, and why it is there. It is also well worth your while to buy a copy of Peter Scott's *Coloured Key to the Wildfowl of the World*, from which you can identify the birds you will be seeing. The pens have been landscaped according to the arrowed route, and numbered according to the guidebook.

The Big Pen contains several species of geese, including Barnacle Geese, which winter in Scotland and Ireland, Snow Geese, which occasionally appear in the British Isles, and a large flock of Hawaiian Geese, a species which the Trust has saved from extinction. The Hawaiian, or Ne-ne Goose, breeds only on the main island of Hawaii, where it nearly disappeared. In 1952, only 42 of these birds were known to exist in the wild, and three were sent to Slimbridge, where they began to breed. Since then, more than 800 have been bred, of which 200

Above: Ringed Teal at Prinknash.

Below: Whooper Swan at Slimbridge.

Slimbridge Wildfowl Refuge. **Address** The Wildfowl Trust, Slimbridge, Glos. **Telephone** Cambridge (Glos.) 333. **Open** 09.30–18.30 (or 15 mins after sunset, whichever earlier) summer and winter, visitors admitted up to 1 hr before closing time. **Catering** licensed restaurant, self-service cafeteria, snack bar (summer). Gift shop, information centre. **Guide-book. Acreage** 443 (100 on exhibition). **Guided tours** for schools by arrangement. **Car** 12 mls w. of Stroud off A38 and M5 junction 13. **Bus** main Gloucester–Bristol service on A38. Bus service to The Patch ($\frac{1}{4}$ ml) twice daily. **Train** to Stroud (11 mls), Gloucester (12 mls). **Taxis** available. **Other facilities** special observation hides and towers, observatory, wheelchairs. No pets. Public allowed to feed birds.

have been returned to the wild and a similar number sent for breeding to 40 major zoos and private wildfowl breeders. Protected on Hawaii itself, another colony of the species has been established on the Hawaiian island of Maui, and the bird's world population is now well over 1,000. It is no longer regarded as endangered, although it must still be considered rare. The Hawaiian Geese at Slimbridge now breed so freely that the Trust has been able to leave some of the birds full-winged, and to offer a limited number for sale. The full-winged birds are males, whose families have pinioned wings, so that the fully winged birds will remain in the vicinity. Slimbridge is thus the only place in the Old World where Ne-ne Geese can be seen in flight. Farther along the Big Pen you will see two rare flamingo species, the Andean and the James's. The flamingos at Slimbridge spend the winter under cover in sheds with indoor pools. Flamingos are related to wildfowl, and in the wild they are usually found on brackish or saltwater lakes and inlets. They congregate in huge flocks, and the shape of their bills is designed for their unusual method of feeding. The bill is held upside-down under water, water and food being sucked in, pumped by the tongue. The water is then expelled, leaving behind the food, which is retained by filtering structures in the bill. The food is then pushed down towards the gullet by the tongue. The bill is also used to scoop soft mud into a cone-shaped mound upon which the eggs are laid. At Slimbridge, four species of flamingo have been bred, and to stimulate breeding a number of artificial nests have been made in their enclosures.

After the Big Pen, you pass a series of pens containing pairs of birds which are either bad mixers with other species or are being kept there specially for breeding purposes. There is a series of pens containing birds from particular geographical areas, and the first of these is the North American Pen. These often contain wild birds from other areas, so the *Coloured Key* is useful here to identify the resident inhabitants. One rare form here is the Aleutian Canadian Goose, which probably breeds only on Buldir Island. It is one of 12 recognised sub-species of Canada Goose, and one of the smallest. There are breeding pens for all the swan species, and one of these, the Trumpeter Swan, is now rare. It used to breed all over North America, but now does so only in Alaska, Alberta, British Columbia, Montana and Wyoming, and there are probably no more than 1,500 birds in the wild. It has bred here, as have all the swans except the Whistling Swan, another North American species. These two can be identified by their black bills, the Trumpeter being the largest of all the swans.

The South American Pen contains South American Sheldgeese and a flock of Chilean Flamingos, which also breed here. One of the South American swans, the Coscoroba, really belongs to a different tribe, and it looks much more like a goose. Among the interesting ducks from this area are the Bronze-winged Duck, which is rare in captivity, the Black-headed Duck, which lays its eggs in other birds' nests like a cuckoo, and the Peruvian Ruddy Duck, from the mountain lakes of Peru and Bolivia. The Tower Pen contains the Acrow Tower, 51 feet high, from which you get a good view of the Severn Estuary, where flocks of White-fronted Geese and Bewick's Swans come to feed in winter on the Dumbles.

The Australian Pen contains some interesting birds, including the Cereopsis or Cape Barren Goose, from the islands off the southern coast of Western Australia and South Australia. Its wild population is estimated at about 6,000 birds. In captivity, the Cereopsis is aggressive towards other birds, and you will usually see it by itself in wildfowl collections. One curious-looking species is the Magpie Goose, from southern New Guinea and Arnhem Land in Northern Australia. It is also called the Semi-palmated or Pied Goose, and both sexes have a knob on top of their heads, the male's knob being larger than the female's. The Pink-eared Duck, a nomadic species from the Australian interior, has a soft flap at the tip of its bill, the bill being very long for the size of the bird. The Australian Pen also includes the Tropical House, opened in 1968 for delicate tropical birds which require protection in the British winter. Besides tropical waterfowl you can also see tanagers and hummingbirds here, one of which was bred in 1969, which is a rare occurrence in captivity. The house has three ponds at different levels, the highest being at eye level with an observation window.

Above: White-faced Tree Duck, found wild in South America and southern Africa.

Left: Pink-footed Goose which breeds in the sub-arctic and winters in Britain and Europe.

Below: a pair of Black-necked Swans, natives of South America.

A feeding trough is placed here, so that you can see ducks feeding just below water level. The plants in the house come from the Royal Botanical Gardens, Kew, and the pillars are covered with cork bark, while overhead piping provides artificial rain at intervals.

The African Pen contains the Guinness Aviary, which is also used for delicate species. These have heated winter quarters, and the pond is equipped with a water impeller which cuts in automatically when the water temperature drops to 35°F. The warmer water at the bottom is stirred up, and part of the pond is thus kept free of ice. One interesting species here is the Maccoa Duck from eastern Africa, which bred here in 1974. This is the first record of the species breeding outside its natural home. The successful breeding was probably partly due to the preparation of a nesting site identical to the one made for European White-headed Stiff-tail Ducks in 1973, which bred for the first time in captivity in that year. The sea-duck exhibit has two pools at different levels and a waterfall, where you can see various species bred in the collection. All the ponds at Slimbridge are artificial, most being three feet deep; but where diving ducks are kept the water is more than ten feet deep. It has been found necessary to surround the ponds with stone or rough concrete to prevent erosion, and also to prevent the birds from picking up lead pellets in the soil, left from the days when the New Grounds were shot over. Lead pellets swallowed by waterfowl are fatal, and some birds are fatally poisoned by a single pellet. All the ponds are well stocked with fish, mostly Rudd, with smaller numbers of roach, orfe, Tench and eels. The Tump Pool and Swan Lake are stocked with Mirror Carp, some of which weigh 7 lb. or more.

Passing through the attractive Tump and Water Garden, you come to the New Zealand Pen. Two rare ducks from that country are the Brown Teal, now dangerously rare, which became extinct in the Chatham Islands in about 1915, and the Blue or Mountain Duck, which is confined to mountain streams in a few remote localities. The European Pen has most of the duck species which can be seen wild in the British Isles. Two ducks in the collection which occasionally appear in these islands are the King Eider and the Atlantic Harlequin Duck. The King Eider breeds in fresh water near Arctic coasts and the northern islands of Europe, Asia and America. The male has a prominent knob above the bill, blue plumage on the head, green cheeks and a pale yellowish breast, while the female is a uniform brown. The Harlequin Duck lives in Iceland, Greenland and Labrador, and it occasionally leaves their coasts in winter to visit Great Britain. The drake has a chestnut streak from above the eye to the back of the head and a white spot behind the eye. The female also has a white spot on the head, but the plumage is greenish brown.

In the Asian Pen are two interesting species, the White-winged Wood Duck of Assam, Malaya, Sumatra and Java, which is rare in the wild, and the Spotted Whistling Duck of the East Indies, which is rare in captivity. It was bred here in 1973 for the first time in Great Britain for several years.

You now come back to the Big Pen, and from the restaurant terrace you see the Orchard Pen with its magnificent flock of Caribbean Flamingos. These made history when a chick was hatched and reared here in 1968: it was the first flamingo of any species to be bred in Great Britain. Flamingos require a certain amount of seclusion for breeding, an important factor here being the high wall of shrubbery around three sides of the enclosure, which gives the birds a sense of security. In subsequent years, four other flamingo species bred, and this is a remarkable record. No other British collection, apart from Whipsnade, has so far bred flamingos. From here you can visit the Gazebo Tower, where a good view of the duck decoy is obtained; this is used for catching wild ducks in order to ring them. From there you pass through the Wood Pen into the Rushy Pen containing the Holden Tower, which is open in winter for the observation of the wild swans and geese on the Dumbles.

You look across the Rushy Pen to Swan Lake, to which the wild Bewick's Swans come every winter from October to March. They breed in northern Russia, migrating in winter to the British Isles, northern Europe, the Caspian Sea and central Asia. The Slimbridge migrants form one of the largest winter

215

colonies in this country, and Sir Peter Scott has developed a method of identifying each bird by its beak conformation, which varies from one individual to another. In this way he has been able to record the return of each bird every year, as well as its mate, and all losses and replacements during the breeding season in Russia. Visitors are restricted to the southern end of the wild swans' enclosure in winter to avoid disturbance, and special observation hides have been built so that visitors can study the birds. At the far end of the Rushy Pen is the rearing area where large numbers of young birds are on view during the summer months.

The New Grounds at Slimbridge were chosen as the Wildfowl Trust's head-quarters because wild geese have wintered here for centuries, protected by the Berkeley family who are the owners of the land. The saltmarsh and water meadows bordering the River Severn are controlled as a wildfowl refuge, together with a large area of tidal sand and mud. Winter visitors to be seen here are European White-fronted Geese between October and March, the numbers rising to more than 5,000 in January and February, during the coldest part of the continental winter. All the wild geese recorded in Great Britain came here, and there are six observation towers and 15 hides in the sea-wall for visitors. Other wildfowl to be seen in winter are the Lesser White-fronted Goose, the Red-breasted Goose, Wigeon, Teal, Pintail, Shoveler, Tufted Duck, Shelduck, Pochard and Gadwall. Another attraction of this site is the duck decoy, which is in a wood. It was built in 1843 and it is shaped like an egg, consisting of a small pond with four curved ditches, hooped and netted over. Ducks are enticed into the ditches, running along to the blind end of each ditch into a detachable 'tunnel net'. More than 2,000 may be caught each year, after which they are ringed and released.

The Trust was founded by Peter (now Sir Peter) Scott in 1946, and at first it was called The Severn Wildfowl Trust, but it became so well known for its conservation programmes that 'Severn' was dropped in 1954. H.M. The Queen became the Trust's patron in 1950.

The Trust is a non-profit-making charity, and the research programme is supported by Government grant. Its object is to study the biology of wildfowl and their habitats, including the botanical aspects. There are experimental aviaries in the grounds and three ringing stations are maintained in Essex, Northamptonshire and Suffolk. Two research workers are seconded to Loch Leven, Kinross, which is the centre of the main wintering populations of Greylag and Pink-footed Geese. The ringing programme assists the study of wildfowl populations, their distribution and migration patterns. Part of the scientific work is pure research — for instance, the study of bird navigation, food and feeding behaviour, the incidence of disease and its treatment. Behaviour studies on the bird collection is also an important part of the work, and much attention has been paid to courtship and the behaviour of newly hatched young. The Trust acts as adviser to the Nature Conservancy Council, and a network of wildfowl refuges have been established all over Great Britain. Members of the Trust have free admittance to its collections, and the use of the Rushy Pen observatory in winter. A research library and conference facilities are also available.

A visit to Slimbridge is well worth while at any time of year, but for the enthusiast the winter months are perhaps the most rewarding, when the migrants are there and all the wildfowl are in full plumage.

Southam Zoo

This small Zoo has a good collection of cat species, including Bengal and Sumatran Tigers, the latter being particularly rare in the wild. Animals which breed here regularly include Lions, Leopards and Pumas, and a Chimpanzee. Spider monkey and De Brazza Monkey have also been bred here. This is a mixed collection with about 200 mammals and a similar number of birds. There is a Pets' Corner and a Chimpanzee tea party is held at 4 p.m. on Sundays, weather permitting. The Zoo was opened in 1961 by Mr and Mrs Clews.

Southam Zoo. **Address** Daventry Road, Southam, near Leamington Spa. **Telephone** Southam 2431. **Open** 10.00–dusk summer, closed 31st Oct–Easter. **Catering** snack bar. Zoo shop. **Acreage** 7. **Car** 13 mls s.e. of Coventry, on A425 $\frac{1}{2}$ ml from Southam. **Bus** from Southam to Zoo. **Train** to Leamington Spa (7 mls). Public allowed to feed animals with food prepared and sold in Zoo only.

Three of the African monkey species among those which can be seen at Twycross: De Brazza Monkey (top left), Diana Monkey (left), Black and White Colobus Monkey (above).

Twycross Zoo

Twycross Zoo Park has a general collection, but it specialises in apes and monkeys, especially gibbons and the South American species of which it has the best examples in Britain. You can see here family groups of the three great apes, Gorilla, Orang utan and Chimpanzee. Bongo and Joe, the Gorilla pair, arrived in 1965 and they are now approaching maturity. Although they look frightening and can be formidable when excited, beating their chests to scare away intruders, Gorillas are naturally shy animals. Adult males have scaled 600 lb. in zoos, although in the wild they are usually lighter. The Gorillas here belong to the Lowland form, and notice the silvery-grey colour of the male's back, indicating adulthood. Their house, built in 1971, contains every modern convenience, including underfloor heating, separate sleeping dens, a sunken bath — which the male especially enjoys, playing with the soap suds — and colour television. The Chimpanzees which share the house appear to enjoy viewing more than the Gorillas, their favourite programmes being Westerns. The outdoor enclosure, surrounded by glass screens, enables visitors to take photographs, while shielding the animals in windy weather.

The group of Orang utans has bred here and, like the Gorillas, they have a modern house, opened in 1973, also with a glass-fronted enclosure which is modelled on the Gorilla enclosure at Frankfurt Zoo. Fewer than 5,000 Orang utans are left in Sumatra and Borneo, their only home in the wild. This is partly because of hunting in the past, but more recently because of the destruction of the thick forest in which they live. They are legally protected, but comparatively few are born in zoos, and they are officially rated as an endangered species. Whereas Gorillas live on the ground, Orang utans live high up in the trees, building nests for sleeping and rarely coming down to the ground. The Sumatran race has longer hair than the Bornean, and both races are exhibited at Twycross.

There is a large colony of Chimpanzees here, and several have been bred. Unlike Gorillas and Orang utans, Chimpanzees are noisy and excitable, and they live on the ground, travelling in loosely knit groups whose members often leave to join another group, later returning to their original group. They build nests in the lower branches of trees, and within recent years it has been discovered that they use twigs for capturing and eating ants and termites, and are thus one of the very few wild animals to use a crude tool. They are mainly vegetarian, but occasionally they will catch and eat young monkeys. Twycross Chimpanzees have appeared in two feature films, a Searchlight Tattoo at the White City, and they have appeared regularly in television commercials advertising Brooke Bond tea. One even took part in the *Daily Mail* Air Race from London to New York. Notice the red Chimpanzee, a colour freak rarely seen anywhere in the world. She has had a baby which, however, has natural black hair like its father. Chimpanzee tea parties are held in the summer.

Six species of gibbon are exhibited in this Zoo, the largest collection of this group in the country. Gibbons are the smallest members of the ape family, and they are easily distinguished by their long arms, used for swinging from tree to tree. When on the ground they run or walk erect, with their hands scarcely touching the ground. They come from southeastern Asia, from India and Malaysia, Java and Sumatra. The rarest species here is the Pileated or Black-capped Gibbon. The Lar Gibbon has white hair round its face and on its hands and feet, while the Agile Gibbon looks very much like it but without the white markings. All these have bred here. The Silver Gibbon is silvery grey, and the Siamang has a throat sac which inflates to enable it to give its very loud and long-lasting call. The Black Gibbon, rarely seen in captivity, has erect hairs on the top of its head. Gibbons all have loud calls and they are very active by day.

Two other Asiatic species, both exhibited here and rare in captivity, are the Spectacled Langur and the Douc Langur. The thumb and toe is shorter in the langurs than in their African counterparts, and they live on leaves. They are not easy to keep in zoos, but they have bred at Twycross. Like the gibbons, langurs live in trees, taking enormous leaps from branch to branch. The Spectacled Langur gets its name from the white markings encircling its eyes. The babies are born bright orange which changes to a blue-grey colour at five months old. The other langur shown here is the Douc, from the forests of Indo-China. It has a brown head with a bright chestnut band under the ears, and chestnut legs. The body is grey, and it has white whiskers, tail and rump, and a bright yellow face. This also is a leaf-eating species, and rarely kept in zoos. Another monkey which is only kept in one or two zoos in the world is the Proboscis Monkey, from Borneo. The adult male has a large bulbous nose which is very long, though less developed in females. It is an active species by day, living in small groups. Both the females here produced young before the male died and they were the first to be bred in Britain.

The African monkeys represented here include the Black and White Colobus, a beautiful animal with long, silky hair, black on the body, and white on the face, sides and tail. It lives in trees, only coming to the ground to seek mineral salts. The long hair acts as a brake as it leaps from tree to tree. Because of its fine fur the Colobus has been hunted extensively, and it is no longer common in the wild. Another central African species is the De Brazza Monkey, a handsome species with an orange and white patch on its forehead and white beard. The equally handsome Diana Monkey has a white band across its brow, a black face and white beard. The markings of these two species act as a camouflage as they move through the trees. There is also a fine group of Ring-tailed Lemurs, found only in Madagascar and, like all the lemur family found there, it is in danger of disappearing owing to timber felling. This species lives in rocky country, with palms and soles adapted to holding on to slippery rocks. Its black and white banded tail makes it easy to recognise.

The rarest of the South American monkeys at Twycross are the Red Uakaris. The Red Uakari, of the Amazon region, has a bright red face and almost naked head, giving it the appearance of a wizened old man. It is a tree-dweller, running along the branches but not leaping from tree to tree. It is probably rare in the wild, and very seldom seen in captivity. It took the Zoo several years to find a young male to join the female, and it is hoped that they will breed when he reaches maturity. There is a thriving colony of capuchin monkeys, a forest species with long tails used to grasp branches. When a baby is born, all the members of the group take turns in carrying it on their backs until it is old enough to move about on its own.

Another larger species from the Amazonian forests is the Humboldt's Woolly Monkey, which also has a very strong, thick tail used in grasping branches. Woolly Monkeys, as their name suggests, have thick, woolly fur, and they are heavily built and immensely strong. The thumb is better developed than in other monkeys, and their agility is increased by the tail, which acts as a fifth limb. The colony at Twycross has bred, and this is seldom achieved in captivity. The much smaller squirrel monkey, from northern South America, has a squirrel-like face and large eyes. It climbs along the sides of trees as well as leaping along branches when travelling at speed, and the father often carries the young. This species breeds regularly here.

The breeding colony of marmosets here represents the smallest group of South American monkeys. They have a long tuft of black or white hair on the ears and a banded tail, and they have claws instead of nails. The tail is not used for gripping, and they depend on their sharp claws as an aid to travel in the tree-tops. They live in small family groups and the father takes a hand in feeding and tending the young. The spider monkey of Central America is the American counterpart of the gibbons in Asia. Its long tail is prehensile and, like the gibbons, it has a light, short body and legs, and very long arms. The group here breeds regularly.

The Zoo also exhibits families of Giraffe, Llama, its close relation the smaller and more graceful Alpaca, the Dromedary and Brazilian Tapir, which has bred here. You can also see the Asiatic Tapir, a black and white species from Malaysia. There are also Lions, Tigers, Cheetahs, Bobcats, sealions, Giant Anteaters and Maras, a long-legged rodent related to the guinea-pig which hops like a rabbit and comes from Patagonia. The African Elephant shares its indoor quarters

with porcupines and Aldabra Tortoises, one of the giant species of tortoise.

Another interesting exhibit is the Indian Smooth Otter, which first bred here in 1972, the first time in captivity for this species in the Western world, after their enclosure had been specially designed for them. Too many zoos build an otter pool before they even know which of the 16 species of otter they are going to exhibit, not realising that each species has its own special requirements. For instance, some otters live in groups, while others live mostly alone, like the European Otter; all are good swimmers, but the little Asiatic Clawless Otter spends far less time in the water than other species. This exhibit is a good example of how trouble taken to ensure that the environment was exactly right resulted in breeding. An unusual exhibit is the Cuscus, the largest kind of Australian possum. The size of a cat, with a long prehensile tail, it lives in trees, moving slowly about eating leaves and fruit, but occasionally catching roosting birds and small lizards. The group here is the only one in Britain.

The Reptile and Tropical House has an alligator pool and a fine collection of snakes, lizards, small tortoises and amphibians. Notice especially the Rhinoceros Iguana, a large lizard with a horn on its snout.

Although this is chiefly a mammal collection, those who are interested in birds will see some fine specimens of Crowned Hawk Eagle, Golden Eagle, Imperial Eagle, Eagle Owls and Griffon and Ruppell's Vultures. The water birds include Humboldt's Penguins, which have bred, pelicans and flamingos. There is a good collection of macaws and parrots in the Parrot House. A wide variety of colourful small birds will be found in the attractively landscaped walk-through aviary.

This is one of the most delightful of country zoos, with wide expanses of lawn separating the spacious enclosures for the larger animals, and flower-beds surrounding many of the animal houses. You can go inside the larger buildings, and elsewhere all the animals can be seen through windows when they are indoors. Do not miss a visit to the Rural House, a fascinating collection of ancient farm implements and early machinery, beautifully displayed. You will find this behind the Giraffe House.

The Zoo was started here in 1963, and it has become one of the most successful in the country, thanks to the dedication of its owners, Miss Badham and Miss Evans. Many animals, particularly those breeding for the first time, will not raise their own young, and these are reared indoors at Twycross, which for young monkeys involves bottle-feeding every two hours for the first few weeks. It is easy to see that the inmates come first here, resulting in healthy animals, nearly all in happy family groups and with plenty of room to exercise. One can learn more about animals here than in many older zoos with cramped cages, where exhibits are far less interesting. Since 1972 the zoo has been a registered charity, with all profits being ploughed back for the benefit of the animals.

Arabian Camels in the West Midland Safari Park.

West Midland Safari Park. **Address** Spring Grove, Bewdley, Worcs. **Telephone** Bewdley 402114. **Open** 10.00—dusk (last admission 18.00) summer. Possibly opening on Sun during winter. **Guide-book. Catering** self-service cafeteria, kiosk. **Acreage** 240. **Car** on A456 Kidderminster–Bewdley road. Free car park. **Bus** 192 stops outside main entrance. **Train** to Kidderminster (1½ mls). **Taxis** available from station. **Other facilities** pets' corner, aviary, first-aid post, amusement area, bird garden, Friendly Animal Forest, aquarium. No pets. Public **not allowed** to feed animals.

West Midland Safari Park

This Safari Park, set in undulating parkland on the edge of Wyre Forest, has a general collection which includes Lions, Tigers, bears, wolves, White Rhinoceros, Giraffe, Eland Antelope, gnu, zebras, camels, elephants, deer, Chimpanzees, baboons and sealions. Many Lion cubs are bred. You pay extra to go into 'Bird Paradise' where there are 600 birds. There is also an Aquarium with 200 fish; a children's zoo called 'Friendly Animal Forest', containing flamingos, pelicans, Muscovy Ducks, lambs and goats; and a safari boat trip on which you see Chimpanzees on an island and flamingos. There is also a garden centre. The Park was opened in 1973.

Wales PETER SCHOFIELD

THE WILD WALES OF BORROW

Wales is remarkable for its diversity of scenic beauty. Every bend in the road, every crest of a hill produces a new vista often dramatically different in colour and texture from the previous one. Windswept coast and mountain-tops, sheltered, wooded, steep-sided valleys, tumbling, rushing rivers, mountain lakes and coastal marshes, rushy fields and heather-clad moors are but a few of the features which contribute to wild Wales. Land is often difficult to plough, so the extension of arable land has not been widespread throughout the centuries.

The direct effects of industry, centred on the coal-fields, are limited mainly to the southeast and northeast, and to isolated regions where rocks are suitable for mining or quarrying. Nuclear power stations and hydro-electric schemes have occasionally been dropped into a backcloth of mountain or coast. The rest of industry is of a more subtle nature, vast commercial forests or water-regulating reservoirs located on rolling hills, moors and in magnificent valleys. The most significant change brought about by both agriculture and industry has been the depletion of vast areas of native forests which formerly extended from the coasts to well up into the mountains.

Unlike much of lowland Britain, the wildlife in Wales is distributed over large areas of countryside, so there are fewer Minsmeres and Ouse Washes where large concentrations of birds can be seen at close quarters from special 'hides'. Most of this section, therefore, will describe the birds and animals of the countryside rather than of specific locations. Highlights of the bird species in the Principality are Red Kite, Bittern, Chough and Roseate Tern, all with a limited distribution in Britain. In recent years a number of interesting birds have nested again or nested for the first time in Wales and these include Red-breasted Merganser, Goosander, Tystie or Black Guillemot and Twite. There are stories of Golden Eagles over the Carneddau 250 years ago. Alas, they have long disappeared; but, with a more enlightened attitude now prevailing towards conservation, we are anticipating that they may return, as they have done to the English Lake District.

Three mammals in Wales are rather special: the Polecat, Pine Marten and the unique Skomer Vole. Many rare insects are found, among them Bee Beetle, Snowdon Beetle, Conformist Moth, Ashworth's Rustic Moth and Mazarine Blue butterfly. Several fish, such as Gwyniad in Bala Lake and the Llyn Padarn Char, are unique.

GEOLOGY OF WALES

Three features above all others influence the Welsh landscape and the distribution of the plants and animals: geology, the Atlantic, and man. The geology is complex and varied. It has excited scientists, including Charles Darwin, and delighted or distressed travellers throughout the ages. The story it tells is too intricate to explain in more than a brief outline, but for those who would like more information there is an excellent geological display in the National Museum of Wales in Cardiff. The Welsh mountains were formed in the oldest geological periods. Since the early sedimentary rocks were laid down there has been much volcanic activity. In later times great ice-sheets sculptured dramatic rock faces, jagged mountain-tops, knife-edge ridges and upland lakes.

The spectacular, much-folded South Stack cliffs on the Isle of Anglesey are of Pre-Cambrian age, the oldest known rocks. Great mountain ranges in the north — Snowdon, Glyder, Carneddau, Rhinog and Cader Idris — are formed of Cambrian and Ordovician slates, grits and volcanics, later modified by ice action. There was less volcanic activity in the Ordovician rocks which form mountains farther east and south in the broad band of more rolling land stretching from the north coast, through the Berwyns and Bala to Llandeilo and St Bride's Bay.

More gentle hills of Silurian age were laid down as sediments and are now

Peter Schofield joined the Nature Conservancy in North Wales in 1968. A founder-member of the Mid-Cheshire Ornithological Society, he has served on the Cheshire Conservation Trust Council and is now President of the Cambrian Ornithological Society and is on the council of the Bardsey Bird Observatory.

Roseate Tern breeds in Wales.

Drake Red-breasted Merganser.

Opposite: Snowdon, the highest Welsh mountain, seen from the south.

located in an arc from Clwyd (Denbighshire) to the Dyfed (Pembrokeshire) coast. Nowadays these are seen as mudstones, shales and slates. In the southern border counties fertile red and rich brown plough lands, at their broadest in southern Powys (Breconshire) and narrowing towards Dyfed, are part of the Devonian Old Red Sandstone series. Several outcrops of Carboniferous rocks occur as the South Wales and Clwyd (Flintshire) coal-fields with their associated mining and industrial developments, or as spectacular cliff scenery near Llangollen, or on Great Orme, Puffin Island, the northeast coast of Anglesey, Gower and parts of Dyfed. Part of the Glamorgan coast and the Vale of Glamorgan are the product of the newest solid rocks and give the countryside its own special character.

THE ATLANTIC

The Atlantic has an effect on Wales well known to regular travellers and holiday-makers. Generally the Principality experiences cool summers, mild winters and high rainfall, over 200 inches a year on higher mountains. One feature is the contrast between mountain rainfall and that on Lleyn, Isle of Anglesey, Gower, Preseli and south Pembrokeshire and parts of the border country within the rain-shadow, which have between 30 and 35 inches of rain in most years. The Atlantic maritime climate gives a special character to many Welsh woodlands, especially those in narrow, steep-sided valleys in the west which are often rich in ferns, mosses and lichens. In some more humid valley woodlands great clumps of ferns grow on tree trunks and branches. The Vale of Ffestiniog and Maentwrog woodlands in Gwynedd are particularly fine in this respect. It is in these situations, which abound in insect-life, that the Pied Flycatcher is common. The mild winters frequently bring large increases of wading birds and wildfowl to west-coast estuaries, particularly Conwy Bay, those in the Isle of Anglesey, Dyfi (Dovey) and Burry Inlet, when their feeding grounds farther east in Britain and Europe become frozen over — a good reason for extending holidays to the quiet of the 'off-season'!

MAN AND THE WELSH ENVIRONMENT

For over 4,000 years man has wandered over the Welsh countryside, first settling on some of the drier coastal plains or moving up the larger rivers and settling on their banks. Evidence left in cave homes, particularly from Clwyd, Gower (Goats Hole and the Red Lady of Paviland) and Dyfed, suggests that Wolves, Brown Bears, Mammoths, and Woolly Rhinoceroses roamed the lowlands, which would be covered with thick forest, mainly oak and birch, mixed scrub, alder swamp and bog. Frequently early man would pass through and settle on lower mountain slopes above 1,000 feet, a compromise between exposed cold mountain-tops and wet inhospitable forests. The remains of many hut circles, villages and cromlechs are found at these altitudes.

The first inhabitants hunted wild animals and birds and gathered fruits and vegetation; later, they cultivated ground and raised stock with increasing efficiency. Forest was felled, a process which has continued until the present day, so that there are now relatively few woods containing native oak, birch, alder and hazel. Farm stock grazed most types of vegetation, including tree seedlings, so that grassland eventually replaced trees. Wild Boar, Wolf and Brown Bear, all of which featured in Celtic culture, were exterminated. The Nant Ffrancon, the 'Valley of Beavers', suggests that this animal was once present in Wales; Giraldus Cambrensis, in his famous book *Itinerary through Wales*, reported deer on the Black Mountains of Monmouthshire, while Roe and Red Deer were still found in Gwynedd 450 years later in the 1570s. With the exception of a few escaped Fallow Deer which breed in small numbers in border forests and some parts of Gwynedd and Dyfed, and the occasional deer escaping from parks, these larger mammals have long since disappeared from the Welsh scene.

Because of the waterlogged nature of much of the ground, man's next major landscape alteration would be to drain the wetlands, a process started in the eighteenth century and continuing today. Birds such as the Bittern must have

A sessile oakwood in Snowdonia; mosses and lichens thrive in the humid maritime climate.

A characteristic habitat of the Common Sandpiper (above) is the gravel beds of the River Ogwen (below) in Nant Ffrancon.

Two of Wales's most splendid birds of prey: left, the carrion-eating Red Kite, whose breeding sites are carefully protected by the RSPB; right, Peregrine male at its cliff eyrie, an old Raven's nest.

disappeared at an early date. Although small numbers have returned to breed, even in the 1970s several Welsh Bittern sites are threatened. Another threat to rarer Welsh breeding birds is the attentions of egg-collectors who seem particularly attracted to the Peregrine, Red Kite, Raven, Buzzard, Merlin, Hen Harrier, Chough, Roseate Tern and Little Tern. After Peregrines have hatched from the eggs there have been many successful but deplorable attempts to take young birds for falconry.

CONSERVATION

Forty per cent of Wales lies over the 820-foot contour. In addition, lower lands are often on poor, shallow soils, or exposed to high winds, so that agriculture has not been intensive and the wildlife heritage is rich. There are many wildlife conservation organisations. The Nature Conservancy Council's Welsh Headquarters and North Regional Office are in Bangor, with other Regional Offices in Aberystwyth and Cardiff. The Council has 31 National Nature Reserves in Wales covering some 23,500 acres, and has designated nearly 650 Sites of Special Scientific Interest on account of their important flora, fauna or geological and physiographical features. There are five County Naturalists' Trusts and they also own and manage many nature reserves for the conservation of habitats, plants and animals. The Royal Society for the Protection of Birds has four reserves — Ynys-hir, Gwenffrwd and Dinas, Grassholm, and Ramsey.

Many National Trust properties and Ancient Monuments contain parks or estates of great beauty and much natural history interest. The Trust has also designated several reaches of Heritage Coast, some of which has been purchased from Enterprise Neptune funds. There are three National Parks — Snowdonia, Brecon Beacons and the Pembrokeshire Coast; and four Areas of Outstanding Natural Beauty — the Wye Valley, Gower, Lleyn and Anglesey. The Prince of Wales' Committee, stimulated by European Conservation Year 1970, made the need for conservation within the Principality more clearly understood.

The RSPB, the NCC and the 'Kite Committees', together with local farmers, have saved the Red Kite, one of Britain's most magnificent birds of prey, from extinction. There are only about 20 pairs breeding in Wales. The Red Kite is particularly susceptible to disturbance and motorists are asked not to go looking for it in the breeding season. However, it can often be seen from the roads in mid-Wales, as it glides over upland sheep-walks — a large Buzzard-size rufous bird with a distinctive deep cleft in its long tail. Another pressing conservation problem is the protection of tern colonies. These fork-tailed 'sea-swallows' nest on several Welsh coasts which are attractive to holiday-makers, so please be

Protection of Red Kites. By the end of the nineteenth century the Red Kite's range was reduced to the mountainous country of central Wales, where they lived on Rabbits and the carrion of the upland sheep-walks. The first of several Kite Committees for their protection was formed in 1903, but with gamekeepers and egg-collectors active in the area there were hardly ever more than a score of birds, and occasional good seasons (like 1954, when 15 young were reared from 12 nests) were interspersed with disastrous years of almost total failure. The RSPB supported the early work, and took a more active rôle from 1958, at a time when myxomatosis (decimating the Rabbits) and dieldrin (used in sheep dips) introduced new hazards.

H. Morrey Salmon in *Welsh Wildlife in Trust,* NWNT, 1970.

particularly careful not to disturb them. If, when enjoying a picnic, you see or hear a bird which looks or sounds agitated, then you are probably sitting in its nesting territory; if you move 50 to 100 yards away you will perhaps save the brood. Common Sandpipers, Dippers and Grey Wagtails on river banks and lake-sides frequently suffer disturbance in this way.

MAJOR ZONES IN WALES

Wales can be conveniently divided into environmental zones such as sea, coast, offshore islands, agricultural lowlands, foothills, uplands or mountains, river systems and urban and industrial areas. Each is subjected to different types of impact from human beings, some long-standing, others more recent. A combination of geological and physiographical features, location, altitude, temperature, rainfall and land-use have produced features characteristic of each zone, and largely govern the prominent types of vegetation, animals and birds associated with them.

In the sea round the Welsh coasts are concentrations of Guillemot, Razorbill, Puffin, Manx Shearwater, Storm Petrel and, in winter, sea-ducks, particularly the black Common Scoter. Whales, Porpoises, dolphins and Atlantic Grey Seals are frequently seen.

Stack Rocks, part of the Pembrokeshire coast National Park, where Razorbill (below) and Common Guillemot (bottom) are among the breeding seabirds. The percentage of Guillemots that are 'bridled' with a white streak round and behind the eye increases with latitude.

The coastal zone is the most varied in terms of land-form and land-use, and in its vegetation, animals and birds. There are many types of cliff, some of igneous rock, others of limestone or sandstone. Seabirds, many of which come ashore only to breed, can be seen in large numbers at places such as Great Orme, South Stack, Trwyn Cilan and Carreg y Llam, all in Gwynedd; Bird Rock, Dinas Island and Stack Rocks in Dyfed. Sand-dunes and saltmarshes, estuaries and mud-flats, pools and lagoons — each has its own range of bird and animal species.

Unlike Scotland, islands are few off the Welsh coast. Most can be visited if trips are well planned. Welsh islands are small and much exposed to winds, which limit the climax vegetation to shrubby heath and close-cropped herb-rich grassland. Seabird colonies and Atlantic Grey Seals are attractions. Many islands such as Skokholm, Skomer, Grassholm, Ramsey, Cardigan Island and Bardsey are well known as reserves or as Bird Observatories; others, such as Caldy, St Margaret's, Ynys Gwylan Fawr and Fach, St Tudwal's, Skerries and Puffin Island afford protection for plants, animals and birds because of their relative inaccessibility.

The agricultural lowlands extend for varying distances inland and form inroads into the hill country from the Welsh borders or Marches. Depending upon the viability of the land for agricultural crops, this zone stretches from sea-level to between 500 and 1,000 feet, and many birds and animals have survived in the remnants of woodland, or have adapted to live in hedgerows and uncultivated patches. Our common birds such as Blackbird, Song Thrush, Robin, Dunnock and Chaffinch are at their most numerous in such situations. The Mole and Hedgehog, formerly woodland animals, are also numerous and widespread. Important habitats in this zone are fens, mires, bogs and lakes which have survived the reclamation of more extensive wetlands for agriculture. Two of the most spectacular are Cors Fochno and Cors Tregaron NNRs. The Isle of Anglesey, with its gently undulating ground, has many lakes and mires, such as Llyn Llywenan, Cors Goch, Cors Erddreiniog, and Llyn Bodgylched (Bulkeley Lake), while Llangorse Lake in Powys is important in southeast Wales.

The foothill zone is frequently difficult to distinguish from the higher parts of the agricultural zone but is characterised by its more undulating nature and steeper slopes, often with deep, steep-sided, wooded valleys, coarser areas of unreclaimed grassland and rushes, with many moorland areas up to about 2,000 feet. Hawthorn and birch scrub is a widespread feature. Foxes, common throughout Wales, are still found at these altitudes, as indeed they are amongst

Red Kites. Kites scavenged in London throughout the Middle Ages. Charles Clusius, the Flemish botanist, thought there were as many there in 1517 as in Cairo (but these were a different species, Black Kites). They picked up garbage from the streets, even from the Thames, and stole food from unsuspecting children. They were widespread over Britain (but not in Ireland), and their decline was rapid when London became hygienic and country landowners sought to protect their gamebirds from avian predators. London's last Red Kite was observed flying over Piccadilly on 24th June 1859 — and the only kites seen in and around the metropolis since have been the paper toys named after them.

James Fisher, *Natural History of the Kite*, RSPB, 1949.

The Welsh Mountain Pony (left) is a familiar sight in Gwynedd's foothills; in winter Wild Goats (right) come down from the mountain slopes.

The undulating and wooded landscape of the Aber valley in the foothill zone (above), typical hunting country of the Buzzard (below).

mountain-top boulders and screes up to 3,000 feet. Hares, Welsh Mountain Ponies and Stoats are there throughout the year, and in winter Wild Goats will leave the more exposed mountain slopes and graze the foothills, in Snowdonia and Rhinog particularly. The foothill zone is the home of the mewing Buzzard, the hoarse Raven, and in restricted areas Red Kites and Choughs. In some parts of Wales Red Grouse are reasonably common, but they are nowhere as abundant as on the Pennines or in Scotland. In a few areas the Merlin and Short-eared Owl hunt above the heaths and moor-grasses, and the Hen Harrier, when not persecuted, still quarters the ground in search of voles. Dunlin and Golden Plover breed occasionally in remote parts.

Less disturbed by agricultural activities, Lapwings flourish, beating the air with pied rounded wings, and on wetter ground the bubbling call of the big, long-billed Curlew and the 'drumming' of the Snipe are part of the spring and summer scene. The season is often short, with Curlews which have returned to the foothills to breed in April departing again in July. The Cuckoo is still widespread at these altitudes, although it seems to be scarcer in the lower fields. Skylarks and Meadow Pipits make up the great bulk of birds, the latter in particular providing foster-parents for the Cuckoo and food for the Merlin.

Where there is scrub or open woodland the more richly plumaged Tree Pipit, the fiery-tailed Redstart and the Yellowhammer are regularly distributed, and if gorse is widespread the Stonechat and the Whinchat are frequently seen and heard. Wherever there are boulder-strewn grasslands the Wheatear will probably appear, a buff-breasted grey bird with black eyestripe and a white flash in the tail. The Wheatear has been recorded breeding at over 3,400 feet on the Carneddau mountains — perhaps Wales' highest breeding bird.

The mountain zone, over 2,000 feet, is one of heather and bilberry heaths, mountain grasslands and mossy tundra-like communities interspersed with stony summits, steep rocky slopes, cliffs and screes. For much of the year the high mountains present such an inhospitable climate that few birds or mammals remain there for long; by October most animal life has left and will not return until the following May.

On many of the steep scree slopes are Ring Ousels, Blackbird-like in size and behaviour but with a whitish crescent on the chest, their clear songs carrying far through the mountain air. The tiny brown Wren, so common throughout all the zones, is often heard singing or scolding an intruder from crannies in cliffs, old trial-levels or mine-shafts, or from under the larger boulders in some vast scree or land-slip, even in the middle of winter. The Peregrine hunts from cliff-faces from which he can survey the surrounding countryside.

In May migrating Dotterels can often be located against a background of Meadow Pipit and Skylark song. By June many of the lower-level breeding crows, Rooks, Jackdaws and Choughs, move up to the high grasslands to feed on insects. Ravens and Kites also search for the more weakly of the season's lambs which have died on the mountain, such carrion being a staple food source when they have nestlings to feed.

Most Welsh rivers are fast flowing, rising as small streams high up in the mountains and coursing through an alternating series of steep gradients and terraces to the sea. They are characterised by their 'flashiness', that is, the way they rapidly increase in depth, often in width, and certainly in speed of flow following heavy rain. Animals and birds have to be able to survive these rapid changes. On the sections of steep gradient the Dipper is most at home, bobbing on stones in mid-stream, or submerging to walk along the river-bed. On the terraces, as on the shingle shores of lakes, the Common Sandpiper appears in April and is frequently found in the greatest density of all riparian species. The Grey Wagtail — showing more yellow than grey and flirting an inordinately long tail — is common along many such stretches. In recent years there has been an increase in breeding Red-breasted Mergansers in the northern part of the Principality. The head and neck of this diving duck are bottle-green in the male and rufous in the female, and both exhibit large white wing-patches when in flight.

Where it is not hunted to near extinction, the Otter is still to be seen, or more commonly heard, and the diminutive Water Shrew is sometimes observed crossing even the swiftest-flowing rivers.

The urban and industrial areas are not renowned for their wildlife. There are, however, several sites well worth a passing visit, particularly during autumn bird migration, and in some cases throughout the winter. Aberystwyth harbour, Bangor harbour, Shotton Steelworks Pools, Swansea Bay and Blackpill, and Penarth Flats at Cardiff are places where ornithological pilgrimages are often made from far afield.

Three species of crow. Top: the Rook nests in colonies at fairly low altitudes, and moves up into the hills after breeding. Above: a Raven, the biggest British crow, attends its young at the enormous crag-side nest. Left: Welsh and Manx speciality, the Chough, inhabitant of rocky coasts and mountain sides.

FAUNA OF WALES

Invertebrates, especially the more spectacular ones like butterflies, moths, dragonflies, beetles, grasshoppers, bees and wasps, are numerous in species and numbers; children should be encouraged to search for them in every habitat, even on the verges of country lanes and in hedgerows. There are excellent pocket guide-books which will help with identification. The relative lack of use of toxic chemicals in agriculture has enabled a richer insect fauna to survive in Wales than in most of England.

There are five amphibia which are common in the right habitat – Crested Newt, Common Newt, Palmate Newt, Common Toad and Common Frog; and there are four common reptiles – Slow-worm, Common Lizard, Grass Snake and Adder or Viper.

The wooded mountain and hill country is the stronghold of the secretive Pine Marten. The great increase in forestry in the last 50 years has helped this animal and it is probably expanding its range from mid-Wales to both north and east. The Polecat is even more Welsh than the Pine Marten and, although it is not often seen, increasing numbers are now found dead on roads, giving some indication of its distribution and spread. It occurs throughout Wales, with the exception of parts of the south coast, in a wide range of habitats from sand-dunes at Ynyslas on the Dyfi to hill areas up to 1,650 feet.

The Skomer Vole is a special island race of the Bank Vole which, due to its long separation from mainland animals, has developed unique characteristics. Wild Goats, former domesticated animals which have long since returned to the hills, are found on the Snowdon, Glyder, Carneddau, Rhinog and Cader Idris groups of mountains and in smaller numbers on Yr Eifl and Great Orme. Most other common British mammals, with the notable exception of the deer family, are generally widespread throughout Wales, but the difficulty from the watcher's point of view is that so many are nocturnal. An exception is the Atlantic Grey Seal, to be seen off many rocky coasts, particularly those of northern Anglesey, Lleyn, Preseli and south Pembrokeshire.

Woodland remnants, bracken-covered hillsides and upland heath, scrub and moor-grass habitats and the fast disappearing hedgerows, banks and dry-stone walls provide food and shelter for Hedgehog, Common Shrew and Pygmy Shrew, Bank Vole, Short-tailed Vole and Rabbits. Two former woodland animals, the Mole and Hare, now live over much of the grassland; and while the Red Squirrel still survives, the Grey Squirrel is now widespread, having reached Anglesey in 1966 and more recently some of the wooded river valleys on the north Gwynedd coast.

With so much wetland and rivers, Otters, sleek black Water Shrews and the larger and browner Water Voles are widespread. The Dormouse and Yellow-necked Mouse occur in several districts and have reached Snowdonia. The diminutive Harvest Mouse, thought to be confined to the Welsh border counties, may be more widespread than suspected, since the remains of one were found in the pellets of a Barn Owl in Vaynol Park near Bangor.

With so many smaller mammals to feed upon, predators such as Stoat, Weasel and Fox are also common and widespread. Foxes have become plentiful in Anglesey, where they were little encountered formerly, and hill-walkers are often surprised to see them on screes and boulder-strewn grassland at over 3,000 feet above sea-level. The Badger is also widespread and common, as is the Welsh Mountain Pony.

Relatively little is known about our bats. The Lesser Horseshoe Bat is found in west Wales and the rare Greater Horseshoe Bat in the south. Whiskered Bats are found mainly in the border counties but also occur in some of the northern wooded areas. Pipistrelle, Natterer's, Long-eared and Noctule Bats are common and widely distributed.

Most visitors seeking wildlife in Wales come for the plants or birds. It is perhaps easier to deal with birds by giving an outline of the main features of each new county, concentrating on those areas which contain the greatest diversity of bird-life and the largest extent of National Parks and nature reserves.

The wooded mountain and hill country is the stronghold of the secretive Pine Marten.

The rare Polecat is found in Wales.

Skomer Vole, unique to Skomer island.

Part of the Herring Gull colony on Puffin Island (left); the Menai Strait can be seen in the background. Young Herring Gulls (right) take four years to attain the full grey and white adult plumage.

GWYNEDD: LAND OF SEA, COAST AND MOUNTAIN

Gwynedd is the new county formed from the old counties of Anglesey, Caernarfon and Merioneth. It is convenient to divide it into three distinct natural areas; Isle of Anglesey, Lleyn peninsula and Snowdonia. The Snowdonia National Park dominates the central and southern parts. The Anglesey and Lleyn coastal AONBs also give an indication of the diversity and scale of the beauty within the county.

The National Trust has many properties in Gwynedd including Aberglaslyn Pass, Cemaes and Cemlyn (both sites now have views of Wylfa Nuclear Power Station), Coedydd Maentwrog NNR, and the mountain areas around the Ogwen valley, to name but a few. It is not surprising that half of the Welsh NNRs are in Gwynedd: Newborough Warren and Ynys Llanddwyn, Cwm Idwal, Snowdon and Cader Idris are great attractions to holiday-makers, naturalists and scientists. The North Wales Naturalists' Trust has a number of reserves, and under the charge of the Forestry Commission there are many rare and interesting species in both the Gwydyr and Beddgelert Forests.

When in Gwynedd it is worth stopping at any of the lakes, cliffs, woods, marshes, rocky shores, and indeed any part of the uncultivated countryside. The key sites are obviously important for the conservation of flora and fauna but the areas in between are often just as worthy of a visit. It is possible to see over 70 species of birds in a day; and for those interested in mammals, amphibia, reptiles or invertebrates the scope is also good. In your quest for bigger things don't overlook the multitude of rock-pool animals or the dune and woodland insects.

Coastal sites and wetlands predominate in the Isle of Anglesey. The north coast has many vantage points, among them Cemlyn (NT and NWNT) which has a summer tern colony, breeding Red-breasted Mergansers and many winter visitors to the seaweed-covered rocks and shingle beaches. Wigeon whistle as they swim offshore, while small groups of Turnstones and Purple Sandpipers rest on the wave-splashed rocks. At times of high wind, Gannets, Manx Shearwaters and Storm Petrels pass close inshore. Recently Long-tailed Ducks, the drakes especially handsome in their brown and white livery, have made a winter appearance on the lagoon; they are becoming more frequent as winter visitors to North Wales.

Point Lynas is one of the many good vantage points from which to watch passing seabirds such as Great and Arctic Skuas, Guillemots, Razorbills, Manx Shearwaters and Gannets. Farther east, Red Wharf Bay has several road access

A pair of Fulmars, primitive tube-nosed seabirds, on their nesting ledge.

points giving good views of wader flocks. Beyond, the limestone cliffs afford opportunities to see Kittiwakes, the daintiest of all the gulls, and the long-necked Cormorants and Shags. As one approaches the northern end of the Menai Strait there is a possibility of seeing the Tystie flashing his broad white wing-patches — a bird common in parts of Scotland but only recently resident in Wales. Puffin Island (Priestholm or Ynys Seiriol, as it is sometimes known) still supports a respectable colony of Puffins and has many other nesting seabirds including Guillemots, Razorbills, Fulmars and a vast colony of Herring Gulls which can often be seen flying in the Strait.

In the autumn and winter the many small bays between Penmon and Beaumaris provide excellent wader-watching — with the Grey Plover, a portly, round-headed wader with dappled back and white underparts, one of the attractions. At high tide the pools at Trwyn y Penrhyn are worth looking at, while the hedges and shrubs between road and shore provide good cover for finches, sometimes including the colourful white-rumped Brambling.

The south coast of Anglesey is equally varied but quite different. In the southeast corner is the magnificent Newborough Warren NNR. Shore-nesting birds such as the terns have come under tremendous pressure from beach visitors and the wardens need all the help they can get to protect the few that remain. As an ornithological site the area comes into its own in the autumn and winter with several interesting wildfowl, including such ducks as the black-and-white Tufted, the Pintail, Teal, Shoveler and Wigeon. Occasionally there are Brent and Greylag Geese. Llyn Rhos Ddu, the Cob Pools at Malltraeth and the Cefni estuary are the most favoured parts of the reserve and here Greenshanks and Spotted Redshanks are regular visitors.

Bird-watching along the rest of the coast to South Stack is tremendous and visitors come from far and wide. The best advice is to stop and explore at every lake, marsh, river, dune and stretch of rocky coast. A good walk takes you through the dune grassland and gorse towards Llyn Coron. Great Crested Grebes, Moorhens, Coots, Canada Geese and a variety of ducks are to be seen on the water, whilst russet Stonechats abound in the gorse. In winter Greylag Geese, Wigeon, Cormorants, Snipe and Dabchicks add to the tally, while Ravens regularly roam the dunes. Farther west the fields beyond Aberffraw often contain considerable flocks of Golden Plovers, Lapwings and Curlews.

Female Shoveler, whose bill is the most massive of all the British ducks, and is used to sift food from shallow water.

Cob Pools in Anglesey, with Snowdonia in the background.

It is worth a detour to Llyn Maelog, but then take the road to Valley where a left turn to Four Mile Bridge often reveals Common Terns, Arctic Terns, the occasional Sandwich Tern and, if you are lucky, a Roseate Tern.

South Stack is most rewarding in summer for there are good cliff-faces for Guillemots, Razorbills and Fulmars, while the path to the lighthouse provides an occasional Puffin and Rock Pipit and, in the early morning, perhaps a Peregrine Falcon. On the return the Penrhos Reserve and Beddmanarch Bay at the east end of the Stanley Embankment are often rewarding.

Lakes and wetlands abound — Llyn Coron, already mentioned; Llyn Llywenan, easily seen from the road; Llyn Alaw, occasionally visited by Little Gulls and Black Terns; and Llyn Bodylched, reached by the public footpath from near the Bulkeley Memorial. Apart from all the common or widely distributed water birds, Water Rails, Shovelers, Whooper Swans, Bewick's Swans, Bearded Reedlings and White-fronted Geese are strong possibilities in autumn and winter.

The Lleyn peninsula is an area of beautiful contrasts. The rural peace of gently undulating agricultural land, interspersed with fen and bog, is interrupted by fortresses of rock such as Yr Eifl rising to 1,849 feet and steep cliffs falling into turbulent seas. Rocky shores and inviting beaches alternate with the cliffs. St Tudwal's Islands, off Abersoch, also provide seabird nesting sites. Narrow, winding country lanes with sheltered banks clothed in flowers often lead to cliff-top heaths with golden gorse and purple heather haunted by twittering Linnets and scolding Stonechats. In every direction the views of big skies, vast seas or distant mountains provide a superb setting. The quietest solitude of much of Lleyn is often only broken by the crying of gulls and Curlews, the 'drumming' of Snipe and the unceasing song of Skylarks.

The rare Chough — a jovial crow with scarlet legs and down-curved beak — feeds on the short-cropped grassland on several cliff-tops, and on Bardsey Island. In winter, flocks of Golden Plovers, lacking their black fronts at this season but still with golden-spangled backs, feed in the fields between Tudweiliog and Rhydlios. Curlew and Snipe are common and there are several breeding stations for Kittiwake, Fulmar, Razorbill and Guillemot.

Foryd Bay is just to the south of Caernarfon; over the River Seiont, a minor road follows the coast where many shore birds can be seen from the car, especially the pied Oystercatchers, demure Ringed Plovers and excited Redshanks. Cormorants, Red-breasted Mergansers and Shelducks are all resident. In summer the terns — Little, Common, Arctic and Sandwich — frequently fish offshore. Towards the middle of the east bank of the Foryd are some patches of ground suitable for finches, buntings and warblers. It is always worth remembering that Sparrowhawks are relatively common in Wales, particularly in the lower lying areas where there is some tree cover, and may sometimes be seen hunting small birds in such places. Mynydd Mawr (NT) is a good spot from which to view Bardsey and look for Stonechats in the gorse, and Choughs calling *chwee-ar* as they sport in the up-currents against the cliffs.

Bardsey, lying two miles off the southern tip of Lleyn, can be approached by boat from the picturesque village of Aberdaron. Bird-watching holidays can be arranged at the Bird Observatory which has done invaluable work for over 20 years and has recorded many rarities in the migration season, often birds from France like the Woodchat Shrike and Melodious Warbler. Fulmar, Shag, Kittiwake, Raven, Chough and Stonechat are amongst the breeding birds and the Manx Shearwaters are estimated to number about 2,500 pairs.

Trwyn y Ffosle (NT) affords good views of Porth Neigwl or Hell's Mouth. Seabird colonies can be seen by walking towards the tip of the peninsula at Trwyn Cilan.

The land of mountains stretching from Dyfi (the Dovey estuary) to the north coast of Wales boasts the highest mountain in England and Wales — Yr Wyddfa, or Snowdon. Ravens and sandwich-seeking Herring Gulls visit its summit and the other 13 peaks over 3,000 feet in height. The main mountain blocks of Snowdon, Glyder and Carneddau are separated by steep-sided, flat-bottomed glaciated valleys, the Nant Ffrancon, Llanberis Pass and Nant Gwynant, making

Male Stonechat with a beakful of food: this small member of the chat family is associated with gorse.

Great Spotted Woodpecker brings food to its young in the nest-hole.

the mountains appear even higher. Lesser mountains — Moel Siabod, Moel Hebog and the Moelwyns — lie to the south, and still farther south, between the Vale of Ffestiniog and the Mawddach, are the rugged, heather-covered Rhinogau. The most southerly of the ranges is the impressive Cader Idris with its fine corries and escarpments. Rushing rivers, wooded valleys, large expanses of wet rushy hillsides, coastal plains, sand-dunes, estuaries and the Lavan Sands, a proposed LNR just outside the Park, make up one of the most exciting areas in Britain.

The birds in lowland Snowdonia are similar to those over much of Anglesey and Lleyn. Waders and ducks abound in winter on Lavan Sands, but to people on holiday in late July and August a trip to the mouth of the River Ogwen should reveal terns and skuas, a large flock of Red-breasted Mergansers and the occasional turquoise and emerald Kingfisher. Not far away is the Aber Valley NNR, a mixed woodland with Pied Flycatchers, yellowish-green Wood Warblers, Redstarts, Blackcaps, sombre-tinted Garden Warblers and all three woodpeckers (Green, Great Spotted, and Lesser Spotted), with perchance a broad-winged Buzzard circling overhead. As you progress towards the magnificent waterfall, Rhayader-fawr, the valley assumes a more montane appearance of scrub woodland and gorse with Tree Pipits song-flighting from one high point to another, and Yellowhammers, Stonechats and Whinchats often sitting in full view on top of the gorse. On the crags and screes the Wheatear, Ring Ousel, Cuckoo, Raven and Kestrel can be heard or seen, the last hovering at a fixed point as his keen eyes search the ground below.

Maentwrog NNR has a woodland nature trail which demonstrates many features of Welsh sessile oakwoods. At Penrhyn Castle (NT) with its superb views and delightful parkland, one can find woodpeckers or a Treecreeper climbing a trunk like a small brown marionette pulled by an invisible string. Bodnant (NT) gardens are amongst the finest in Wales and have fine views of Snowdonia. Nuthatch, Jay, Heron, Sparrowhawk and Buzzard may be seen at both places.

A drive down the Conwy valley to Gwydyr Castle, then turning up the roads through the forests to the Nant Plateau and along Llyn Geirionydd, can be rewarding on a summer evening. If you are lucky Black Grouse may be feeding at the woodland edge, and at dusk 'roding' Woodcocks will be flying above the trees. You may hear the reeling song of a Grasshopper Warbler, or see a Peregrine on swept-back wings pursuing some unfortunate small bird.

Skylark beside nest with young: while breeding, each pair establishes a territory which the male defines in his glorious song-flights; outside the nesting season, however, Skylarks band together in flocks.

Afon Caleddwr, one of Snowdonia's rivers, rushes through a wooded valley.

CLWYD: COUNTY OF ESTUARIES, RIVERS AND MOORLAND

Flintshire and Denbighshire were joined together by the 1974 Local Government reorganisation to form Clwyd. Low beaches, estuaries and rivers give way to flat agricultural land backed by massive moorlands. Industry threads through the area with coal-mining, chemicals and steel along the Dee estuary and inland to Ruabon and Wrexham. The coasts of Clwyd have been largely taken over by holiday-makers. Caravan sites and holiday towns such as Abergele, Rhyl and Prestatyn spill their visitors on to the beaches, so the bird-watcher has little joy in the height of summer.

In autumn and winter Rhos Point, the Clwyd estuary, Point of Air, Mostyn Bank and Tan Lan, although not the most beautiful of sites, provide good bird-watching. The Dee estuary is of international importance for the numbers of winter wading birds which feed there, but access is often difficult. It is the third most important estuary in Britain for waders after Morecambe Bay and The Wash.

Inland there are two main attractions, moorlands and river valleys for which the Clwyd has been described as 'The Eden of Wales'. Bird-life is not so rich as in the more varied Gwynedd, but the moors are the home of exciting birds such as Raven, Hen Harrier, Merlin, Kestrel, Short-eared Owl, Red Grouse, Golden Plover, Dunlin, Ring Ousel and Buzzard. Where pine plantations cover the slopes the Black Grouse is sometimes found.

Several lakes and reservoirs, such as the Nant-y-Ffrith, Llyn Bedydd, Hanmer, Cilcain and Llyn Gwerydd, support some ducks, though none can be said to compare with the Shropshire meres in the variety or numbers of waterfowl they hold; but Mallard, Teal, Tufted Duck, Shoveler, Pochard and Goldeneye are often seen and Whooper Swans and Goosanders have been recorded. Black-headed Gull colonies, Great Crested and Little Grebes, Moorhens and Coots (with up to 300 present on Llyn Helyg in some winters) can also be seen.

In the more fertile valleys, Curlew, Lapwing, Skylark, Snipe and the occasional Redshank fill the summer air with their calls. The valleys, especially those with well-wooded sections, contain the greatest number of bird species in the county, although there are few really well-known sites and no NNRs. In the southern part of former Denbighshire the Afon Tanat has a typical selection of river birds including Dipper, Grey Wagtail, Common Sandpiper, Kingfisher and, in the woodlands, Buzzard, Redstart, Wood Warbler and Pied Flycatcher. A little farther north the Ceiriog valley and Glyn Ceiriog (NT), situated eight miles northwest of Oswestry, contain a similar selection of birds. Five acres of meadow and a mile of the Glyn valley tramway, south of Ceiriog on the east side of B4500, provide a public walk. The Yellow Wagtail, a scarce summer visitor which does not occur regularly to the west of Flintshire, may be encountered, but care in identification is necessary since the equally bright yellow Grey Wagtail is common on most of the faster-flowing streams throughout Wales; but it has a grey, not olive-brown, back and an unusually long tail, and the male has a black triangular bib.

There are many vast new conifer forests in Clwyd and several interesting woodland species can be seen, including Sparrowhawk, Buzzard, Tawny Owl, and Great Spotted and Green Woodpeckers. On the edges of wood and moor, Tree Pipits and Whinchats may be encountered, and where there are patches of alder one should look and listen for the melodious flight-calls of Lesser Redpolls.

POWYS: REMOTE, HILL, FOREST AND THE MARCHES

Alas, Montgomeryshire, Radnorshire and Breconshire are no more; giant Powys has swallowed them up into one of the largest administrative areas in England and Wales, with perhaps the smallest population. The northern part of Powys stretches from the English border to Machynlleth in the west. It is a land of soft mountain landscapes, large man-made reservoirs such as Clywedog and Vyrnwy, pools, bogs and grasslands where farmsteads are few and far between.

There is a wonderful solitude of a different kind from that experienced on the plateau of the Carneddau, little explored by naturalists but nevertheless offering great scope for the bird-watcher, mammal-tracker and botanist. Mile after mile

Contrast in Clwyd's landscapes: the Denbigh Moors (above), and the slate-strewn Ceiriog valley (below).

of undulating land and winding river valleys, much longer than those in the north and west, enfold unexpected farmhouses and lonely shepherds — not that they lack comfort from birds and animals. The Berwyns merge with the south Denbigh moors in the north and the rolling afforested areas of the west extend to Plynlimon. Natural oakwoods abound and many claim that the northern parts of Powys contain some of the best woodland in Wales, although neighbours in Gwynedd might dispute that!

The Radnor section of Powys is the most sparsely populated part of Wales; this is hardly surprising as only a small area in the lower Wye valley is below 500 feet and there are nearly a hundred hills over 1,650 feet. The southern reach is dominated by Brecon Beacons and the main part of the mountain range, including Pen y Fan (NT). Two other major mountain blocks, Carmarthen Van and Black Mountains, form a chain across the county. Many river valleys dissect the uplands and there are now several large reservoirs along the Elan valley. The Brecon Beacons National Park was established in 1957 and there are several NNRs in the southern part of the county.

Mountain and moorland birds are well distributed but they have to be looked for, and many hours can be spent before you come across them. The rewards, however, can be great, with the chance of Hen Harrier, Merlin, Red Grouse, Golden Plover, Short-eared Owl, Raven, Ring Ousel, Wheatear, Whinchat and numerous Buzzards. Craig y Cilau NNR has typical mountain birds and is spectacular for its geology, scenery and vegetation. Woodlands in the valley contain Pied Flycatcher, Redstart, Wood Warbler, Tree Pipit and Marsh Tit.

There are many wetland sites in Powys. Leighton Flats south of Welshpool, and Camlad valley near Montgomery, are well known for their winter wildfowl, but river drainage work has made much of the low-lying flood meadows less attractive to birds. Many of the reservoirs, like Clywedog, Vyrnwy and Elan, are too deep to make good habitat, but occasionally Bewick's Swans, Red-breasted Mergansers, Goosanders, Goldeneyes, Tufted Ducks, Pochards, Mallards and Cormorants visit them.

The more natural lakes, at both low and high level, are usually more profitable with waders and waterfowl present, and where there are reeds and alders, many small song-birds are often seen. Trips to many of these lakes will take you up remote lanes and mountain tracks, but the results are often worth the arduous ascent. Rhosgoch Common, Pwll Gwy Rhoc near the Craig y Cilau NNR, and Dderw Pools by the side of the A4079 road from Llyswen to Aberllynfi are some of these sites. The County Naturalists' Trust have acquired as reserves Brechfa Pool and Ty Mawr Pool, two miles southeast of Brecon. Pride of place should go to Llangorse Lake but its popularity is not confined to wildlife. Great Crested Grebe, Little Grebe, Tufted Duck and Mute Swan are resident and the lake has gained a reputation for autumn migrations of waders and terns, while its reedbeds have Sedge Warblers and Reed Buntings.

For those who like to combine natural history with country house and garden visits, Leighton Park, three miles southeast of Welshpool, is worth exploring. Here the Charles Ackers Redwood Grove has awe-inspiring stands of Californian coast redwoods and wellingtonias 130 years old, many over 120 feet tall, with red trunks like the columns of a great cathedral. There is a fine pinetum too at the mediaeval Powis Castle (NT) just south of Welshpool.

DYFED: MAGNIFICENT COASTS, ISLANDS AND ROLLING HILLS

Dyfed, formerly Cardiganshire, Carmarthenshire and Pembrokeshire, has several distinct ecological areas. Islands, diverse coastlines, varied river systems with their banks and bogs, woodlands and remote rolling hills give the naturalist plenty of variety.

The Pembrokeshire islands have the most important seabird colonies in south-west Britain. Large numbers of Gannets breed on Grassholm, 15,500 pairs at the last census in 1964. Manx Shearwaters, Puffins and Storm Petrels inhabit Skokholm and Skomer, which lie closer to the magnificent mainland cliffs, where Fulmars and aerobatic Choughs are a frequent sight and Grey Seals loll on the rocks. Shags, Kittiwakes, Choughs, Guillemots and Razorbills are on

Redwoods. The Charles Ackers Redwood Grove, owned by the Royal Forestry Society, is dominated by coast redwoods brought from California in pots and planted out in 1858. They are surrounded by younger redwoods planted in 1935. About 50 originals remain, in three impressive groups, mostly over 120 feet tall and 12 feet in girth. Some redwoods are growing as coppice shoots from stumps of old trees blown down in 1923; and one windthrown monster is now rooted at both ends and its lateral stems have become nine separate trees! There are also many fine Sierra redwoods or wellingtonias, dark green spires rising over 130 feet. This awe-inspiring wood shimmers with Goldcrest song.

The Brecon Beacons; part of the National Park.

Part of the vast Gannet colony at Grassholm, off the Dyfed coast, and a close-up of the adult's head and dagger-like bill. Across the top and down the right-hand column, a sequence of six dramatic photographs shows a hunting Gannet check in mid-flight, then dive like an arrow to below the surface of the sea, and emerge a moment later with the fish for which it had aimed.

Ramsey also. Cardigan Island and St Margaret's Island are good seabird stations, and Caldy Island has a large Herring Gull colony.

Two features of the coast provide very different bird-watching opportunities: large estuaries, and rocky headlands and cliffs. In the north, Dyfi (Dovey) estuary, from Ynyslas to Ynys-hir, forms a complex of dunes, mud-flats, saltmarsh and open water rich in bird-life. A large raised bog, Borth Bog, and some good undulating land with woods and bracken-covered slopes provide additional habitat on which Nightjars breed. On the Ynys-hir (RSPB) section of the estuary there is a heronry and Red-breasted Mergansers have recently begun to nest. Many waders, including Curlew, Lapwing, Bar-tailed Godwit, Oyster-catcher and Redshank, are frequent, and there are several species of ducks and geese of which Wigeon are usually the most numerous.

Moving south along the coast of Dyfed we come to several more estuaries and flat coastal sites, some small and others fairly large. Aberystwyth harbour and sea-front frequently have Oystercatchers, Redshanks and many gulls, while in winter the Turnstones and a few Purple Sandpipers can be seen on the rocky reaches. The Teifi estuary near Cardigan, Nevern estuary, Fishguard harbour (particularly in rough weather in winter), the Cleddau estuaries and Gann Flats off Milford Haven, and the Tywi-Gwendraeth complex opening into Carmarthen Bay, are all good value for migrant and winter-visiting waders and ducks.

Of the rocky cliff coasts, Bird Rock southwest of New Quay Head, and Lochtyn Farm (NT), with one and a half miles of cliff near the village of Llangranog, have splendid views of Cardigan Bay. Both sites have Razorbills, Guillemots, Kittiwakes, Fulmars and Herring Gulls galore. There is a chance of seeing Chough, Raven and Stonechat on the brows. The Pembrokeshire Coast National Park extends from the old Cardigan border to that of Carmarthenshire and has 170 miles of footpath. There are superb bird sites along this rocky coast with its many fine sandy beaches. The National Trust, largely through Enterprise Neptune funds, owns large areas of the Pembrokeshire section of Dyfed coastline.

Other good sites are Dinas Head, sometimes known as Dinas Island, and Needle Rock, Strumble Head, St David's Head and, on the south Pembrokeshire coast, the stretch from Stack Rocks to St Govan's Head. Apart from the cliff-nesting birds, many small species such as Stonechat, Blackcap and Reed Bunting can be heard or seen, and there is always the chance of a Peregrine Falcon. Terns and skuas pass along the coast in a southerly direction on autumn migration, and on rare occasions a school of Killer Whales moves by offshore.

There are several inland reserves which should be included in every motorist's itinerary. Cors Tregaron NNR is a truly remarkable example of a raised bog which can be seen from the Tregaron to Pontrhydfendigaid road B4343: its plant and animal life are exceptional. Cormorant, Heron, Mallard, Teal, Gadwall, Wigeon, Whooper Swan, Buzzard, Sparrowhawk, Red Kite, Hen Harrier, Montagu's Harrier, Merlin, Kestrel, Red Grouse, Water Rail, Snipe and Curlew are just some of the birds from a formidable list, and it provides a wintering ground for Green-land White-fronted Geese. After a visit to Tregaron a slow journey takes you to Devil's Bridge where there is a nature trail, then down the Vale of Rheidol where Buzzards and Ravens abound.

Farther south in the Carmarthenshire part of Dyfed, the RSPB has a splendid reserve in two parts: Dinas, a sessile oakwood with Wood Warblers, Redstarts and many Pied Flycatchers, the last two at unusually high density because so many nest-boxes have been provided; and the Gwenffrwd with the same species but including moorland and mountain birds, such as Ring Ousel, Buzzard and Merlin.

THE GLAMORGANS: VALLEYS AND VALE AND BEAUTIFUL GOWER

Unlike the rest of the old Welsh counties, Glamorgan, instead of being amal-gamated with its neighbours, was divided into three — Mid, West and South. Most of the population of Wales resides in the Glamorgans, in the valleys and towns like Swansea, Bridgend and Cardiff. One-fifth of the area is occupied by urban or industrial buildings. The Vale of Glamorgan and Gower are not

Gannet. This magnificent seabird has undergone a remarkable increase in Britain and Ireland in this century, from fewer than 50,000 pairs at 8 colonies in 1902 to more than 140,640 in 17 colonies by 1975. The increase was slow at first, but has been explosive since 1950. The latest census was organised by the Seabird Group as part of its 'Operation Seafarer' programme between 1968 and 1970. Grassholm gannetry, founded between 1820 and 1860, had rocketed to 16,128 pairs by 1969; the one at St Kilda, already in existence in the ninth century, is much the biggest colony with 59,000 nests on Boreray and its attendant rocks Stac an Armin and Stac Lee. The smallest and newest, reported to have four nests with young in 1975, is on the Dronga stacks off Fair Isle. Other new colonies in this century are Noss (1914) and Hermaness (1917) in Shetland; Great Saltee (1929) off Co. Wexford; Bempton Cliffs (1937), still small and the only one in England; and Roareim (1969) in the Flannan Islands. During the same period Gannets from Britain have settled the northern coast of France and Alderney in the Channel Islands, and have established four stations on the coast of Norway. They have also increased in Iceland and the Newfoundland–Quebec region. Formerly birds were taken for food on both sides of the Atlantic, and it is thought that the end of persecution sparked off this rapid population growth. It is at least probable, however, that the climatic amelioration which reached its height in the 1930s, leading to an abundance of surface-shoaling fish such as Mackerel and Saithe, was an important contributory cause.

industrialised and now the land above the valleys is being changed from rough grazing into forest.

From a natural history standpoint, the Gower AONB with Oxwich NNR and the Burry Inlet National Wildfowl Refuge are the highlights. Oxwich has pools, dunes, beach and woodland which can provide a varied list of birds at most times of the year. The National Trust has several properties purchased largely through Enterprise Neptune funds. Llanrhidian Marsh, Nicholaston Burrows, Port Eynon Point, Rhosili Downs, Whitford Burrows and Worms Head give a great variety of habitat for birds and animals. The Gower peninsula is unique and any walk across the heaths or along the coasts and cliff-tops will be rewarding.

In the more industrialised part of Glamorgan's coast, Kenfig Pool and Dunes should be visited, and although plants are the main attraction the dunes and pools hold some interesting insects and birds. In autumn and winter the occasional rare bird has visited the pool: Red-necked Grebe, Hen Harrier, Glaucous Gull, Little Gull and Great Grey Shrike are amongst them.

GWENT: SOUTHERN GATEWAY TO WALES

Gwent is perhaps one of the least interesting, ornithologically, of the Welsh counties. Most travellers will be passing west through the county for the Dyfed peninsulas or north along the Wye valley to Monmouth and then on into mid-Wales.

Along the southern route several short detours will take the motorist to the banks of the Severn estuary with its water-meadows and low-lying land, but for the casual visitor this is only rewarding during the autumn passage, or perhaps the winter months and spring passage. The first spot is Nedern Brook and water-meadows near Caldicot. Farther west the Monmouthshire Naturalists' Trust reserve at Magor and the Undy water-meadows lie in a large area of reclaimed land which is now mainly farmland. Farther west still are the mud-flats and saltings near Goldcliff on the eastern side of the Usk estuary. On the west side of the Usk and towards the River Rhymney are several sites for ducks and waders, with wet meadows, reedbeds, mud-flats, ditches and banks.

The most profitable places are Peterstone Wentlooge and Rhymney but the whole area is subject to land-drainage operations which can alter the distribution of birds from year to year. Along the southern coast the bird-watcher is likely to encounter Heron, Mallard, Teal, Garganey, Gadwall, Wigeon, Pintail, Shoveler, Pochard, Shelduck, Mute and Whooper Swans, Grey and Golden Plovers, Green and Common Sandpipers, Redshank, Greenshank and Dunlin. Wherever such species congregate there is always likely to be the rare wader such as the Curlew Sandpiper and Little Stint, and, of course, in winter Merlin and Peregrine come here in search of living prey.

For travellers taking the delightful road up the Wye valley through Chepstow, past Tintern Abbey and on to Monmouth, the river and woodlands provide a continual supply of river species and woodland birds such as the Wood Warbler, Pied Flycatcher, Redstart, Treecreeper, Nuthatch and the woodpeckers and tits. This is the area of the Dean Forest where old deciduous stands alternate with planted conifers inhabited by Coal Tits and Goldcrests, and sometimes by nomadic Crossbills.

The varied habitat at Oxwich National Nature Reserve in the Gower peninsula supports a good range of bird species.

Two duck species to be seen in the coastal parts of Gwent: left, a duck and two drake Garganeys; right, a drake Pintail.

Guide to wildlife habitats in Wales

This Appendix provides a selected but varied list of places of wildlife interest. It is emphasised that nature reserves exist primarily for the conservation of animals and plants and in some cases for environmental experiments and research. They are not 'public open spaces' in the recreational sense. Access to many is therefore restricted and some, because of their sensitivity to disturbance, have been omitted from this list, in deference to the wishes of conservation organisations. Even with 'open' reserves visitors are earnestly requested to keep to the paths and bridleways and so avoid damage to the habitat and undue disturbance to wildlife. *There is no public access to the enclosed farmland which is part of many National Trust properties.*

Application to visit a National Nature Reserve (NNR) should be made to the appropriate Regional Office of the Nature Conservancy Council (NCC) at the address given. Intention to visit reserves of the Royal Society for the Protection of Birds (RSPB) should be notified to the Warden (whose address is shown) as far in advance as possible. In all cases where an address is shown, it is wise to contact the Warden to avoid disappointment.

GWYNEDD

Aberglaslyn Pass SH 60 47. Incl. famous viewpoint of Pont Aberglaslyn, and wooded bank Bryn-y-Felin. 14 mls s.e. of Caernarfon A4085, extending s. for 1½ mls from Beddgelert. (Note: the old mine-workings are dangerous.) NT.

Beddgelert Forest SH 57 50 State forest, mainly conifers, in Snowdonia National Park, 3000 a. W. of A4085 between Beddgelert and Waenfawr. For Comm.

Bodnant SH 80 72. Magnificent garden with pinetum and arboretum. 8 mls s. of Colwyn Bay via A55–A470. Entrance by Eglwysbach road, car park. NT.

Braich-y-Pwll SH 14 25. Headland with fine views of Bardsey. Near Aberdaron, via minor roads w. of B4413. NT.

Cader Idris NNR SH 71 13. Mountain of Ordovician rocks, 2927 ft, and high lakes, 969 a. Arctic-alpine flora, moorland birds. 4 mls s. of Dolgellau, w. side of A487, n. of B4405. Restricted access in foothill woods. NCC.

Carnedd SH 66 66. High valley farms and moorland, 15,860 a. Incl. Llyn Ogwen, head of Nant Ffrancon Pass and several mountains over 3000 ft, e.g. Carnedd Dafydd and n.w. slopes of Carnedd Llywelyn and Foel-fras. 10–15 mls s.e. of Bangor, astride A5 between Bethesda and Capel Curig. NT.

Cemlyn SH 33 93. 2 mls of coast, incl. bird sanctuary, mainly for winter wildfowl. 7 mls w. of Amlwch, 2 mls w. of Cemaes Bay A5025, on n. coast of Anglesey. NT.

Coedydd Maentwrog NNR SH 67 42. Ffestiniog Woodlands, steep oakwooded slope in valley of Afon Dwyryd. Maentwrog, 6 mls e. of Porthmadog A487. NT/NCC.

Cregennan SH 66 14. Hill farms and moorland with 2 lakes. 6 mls s.w. of Dolgellau, 1 ml e. of Arthog A493, approached by steep winding road. NT.

Cwm Idwal NNR SH 65 59. Northern slopes of Glyder Fawr 3279 ft and Glyder Fach enclosing high valley containing Llyn Idwal. Wild Goats. Raven, Ring Ousel, Dipper. 3–4 mls w. of Capel Curig, on s. side of A5. NT/NCC.

Derlwyn SH 70 26. Heather moorland with small lakes. 6 mls n. of Dolgellau, 2 mls n.w. of Ganllwyd, on w. side of A470. NT.

Dolmelynllyn SH 72 22. Park and sheep-walk on slopes of Y Garn and Y Llethr (3 mls w.) rising to 2475 ft, incl. spectacular waterfall Rhaiadr Ddu on the Gamlan ¼ ml n. of the hall. 4 mls n. of Dolgellau, on w. side of A470. NT.

Gamallt SH 74 44. Moorland with 2 small lakes. 3 mls n. of Ffestiniog, access by track 1¼ mls along B4391. NT.

Gwydr Forest SH 78 55. State forest, mainly conifers, in Snowdonia National Park. 20,000 a. This is n.w., w. and s.w. of Betws-y-Coed traversed by A5 Betws-y-Coed–Capel Curig, A470; Betws-y-Coed–Dolwyddelan, B5106; Betws-y-Coed–Dolgarrog. Information centre at Gwydyr-Uchaf SH 795 609, between A470 and B5106. For Comm.

Hafod Lwyfog SH 65 51. Moorland overlooking Llyn Gwynant. 5 mls n.e. of Beddgelert, ½ ml e. of A498. NT.

Llanengan SH 29 25. Cliffs rising from e. arm of Porth Neigwl (Hell's Mouth). 10 mls s.w. of Pwllheli, 3 mls s.s.w. of Abersoch. NT.

Mynydd-y-Graig SH 23 27. Coastal. headland rising 800 ft to Gwynedd Rocks. 10 mls s.w. of Pwllheli via A499 – B4413 and unclassified road, 3 mls e. of Aberdaron. NT.

National Trust for North Wales, Regional Office, Dinas, Betws-y-Coed, Gwynedd.

Nature Conservancy Council, Welsh Headquarters, Penrhos Road, Bangor, Gwynedd, LL57 24Q.

Newborough Warren (Ynys Llanddwyn) NNR SH 40 64. Recent sand-dunes, slacks and Llanddwyn Island, also part of Newborough Forest, 2300 a. Wildfowl, waders and gulls. Isle of Anglesey, 10 mls s.w. of Menai Bridge A4080. Malltraeth Cob pools are viewable from road. For Comm/NCC.

North Wales Naturalists' Trust, 154 High Street, Bangor, Gwynedd, LL57 1NU.

Penrhyn Castle SH 60 71. Woodland, native and exotic trees. 1 ml e. of Bangor, between A5 and A55. (Seasonal, adm. fee.) NT.

Snowdonia National Park, Gwynedd. 845 sq. mls. Reaching from Aberdyfi and Machynlleth in the s. to Conwy in the n. and embracing the mountain fastness of North Wales. High ranges separated by deep glacial valleys, with peaks above 3000 ft incl. Carneddau, Glyder Fawr and Fach, Snowdon 3560 ft and (in the s.) Cader Idris 2927 ft. Upland lakes and reservoirs incl. Llyn Ogwen, Llyn Padarn, Llyn Cwellyn and

Lakes Trawsfynydd and Bala. Coastline from Aberdyfi n. to Tremadog Bay, with estuaries of Afon Dyfi, Afon Mawddach and Afon Glaslyn. Many fine oak woodlands and Forests of Dovey, Aberhirnant, Coed y Brenin, Beddgelert, Gwydyr and Snowdonia National Forest Park (For Comm). Information centres at Aberdyfi (The Wharf), Bala (Old British School, High Street), Blaenau Ffestiniog (Queen's Bridge), Dolgellau (Bridge End), Harlech (Gwyddfor, High Street), Llanberis (Craig Afon, Snowdon Road) and Llanrwst (Glan-y-Borth). Flanked on n.e. by B5106 Conwy–Llanrwst; n. by A55 Conwy–Bangor; w. by A487 – A496, Maentwrog–Harlech–Barmouth, and A493 Dolgellau–Tywyn–Aberdyfi–Machynlleth. Traversed by A487 – A470 Machynlleth–Dolgellau, and B4405 Tywyn–Tal-y-Llyn Lake (embracing Cader Idris); A498 Beddgelert–Pen-y-Gwyrd, then A4086 w. through Pass of Llanberis, and A4085 past Beddgelert Forest and Llyn Cwellyn (embracing Snowdon); A5 Betws-y-Coed–Bethesda through Nant Ffrancon, between Glyders and the Carneddau; and other main and minor roads. Recommended leaflets: Snowdonia National Park (details of landscape trails).

Ynysgain SH 48 38. 1 ml of coast incl. mouth of Afon Dwyfor. 1 ml w. of Criccieth, s. of A497. NT.

Ysbyty Ifan SH 84 48. Hills and valleys lying to w. of Ysbyty Ifan village, incl. Llyn Conwy at 1488 ft. 25,820 a. S. of Betws-y-Coed, on s. side of A5 and A470, and astride B4406 and B4407. NT.

CLWYD

Afon Tanat SJ 15 24. Wooded river valley. 12 mls s.w. of Oswestry A483 – A495 – B4396, 3 mls n. of Llanfyllin, B4391 – B4580 – B4386.

Llyn Helyg SJ 11 77. Lake in mixed woodland. 5 mls w. of Holywell on s. side of A5151, via Tan-yr-allt and footpaths through wood.

Point of Air SJ 13 84. Estuarine mudflats; excellent for waders approaching high-tide. 3 mls e. of Prestatyn, leaving A548 at SJ 114 834, then crossing sand-dunes to coast.

DYFED

Bird Rock SN 38 60. Seabird cliffs. 1 ml s.w. of New Quay, via path through Penrhyll Farm SN 379 597.

Cleddau Estuary SM 96 12. Tidal mudflats between wooded banks of West Cleddau. Wildfowl refuge, many wader species. 3 mls s.e. of Haverfordwest, via minor roads to Hook.

Dinas 'Island' SM 82 22. Promontory 463 ft, 400 a. Grey Seals, seabirds, Oystercatcher, Raven, Stonechat. 4 mls e. of St Davids, A487, on coast s.e. of Solva, reached from Cwm-y-eglwys SN 015 400. Car park. W. Wales Nats T.

Dolaucothi SN 66 42. Woodland in Cothi valley, incl. hill of Allt Dynbeth. Pumpsaint, 9 mls s.e. of Lampeter A482. Picnic site adjoining old gold mine at Carreg, Pumpsaint. NT.

Grassholm SM 60 09. Island, 23 a. Seabirds, incl. big gannetry (c. 16,000 pairs). 10 mls w. of Dyfed coast. RSPB.

Gwenffrwd/Dinas SN 79 47. High open sheep-walks with sessile oakwoods on steep valley sides, 1366 a. Buzzard, Kestrel, Raven, Red Kites visiting, oakwood nest-boxes attract Redstarts and Pied Flycatchers. Rhandirmwyn, 9 mls n. of Llandovery. Car park, Information centre, trail at Dinas. (Warden – Troedrhiwgelynen, Rhandirmwyn, Llandovery, Dyfed.) RSPB.

Lochtyn SN 32 55. 1½ mls of cliffs, beaches and hill-top Pen-y-Badell with views of coast. 12 mls n.e. of Cardigan A487, n.e. of Llangranog. NT.

Lydstep Headland SS 09 97. Carboniferous limestone promontory. Grey Seals. Fulmars, Cormorants, Shags, Stonechats. 4 mls s.w. of Tenby A4139, 1½ mls e. of Manorbier, reached by footpath from Lydstep. Car park (members) SS 087 978, trail. NT.

Marloes SM 79 08. Cliffs on s. arm of St Bride's Bay, opposite Skomer, Middleholm and Gateholm. 524 a. Grey Seals. Seabirds, Raven, Chough, Stonechat. 13 mls s.w. of Haverfordwest B4327, minor roads to Marloes and Martin's Haven. Car park at Runwayskiln Farm SM 78 08, trail, also at Kete SM 80 05 with access to 1 ml of coast. NT/W. Wales Nats. T.

National Trust for South Wales, Regional Office, 22 Alan Road, Llandeilo, Dyfed, SA19 6HU.

Nature Conservancy Council, Mid Wales Regional Office, Plas Gogerddan, Aberystwyth, Dyfed, SY23 3EB.

Pembrokeshire Coast National Park, Dyfed. 225 sq. mls. Wonderful range of coastal scenery from near Tenby north to St Dogmael's – 168 mls. Incl. s. and n. shores of Milford Haven, Dale Peninsula, St Bride's Bay, St David's Head, Strumble Head, Dinas Head and Cemaes Head. Inland sections embrace the Prescelly Hills (Mynydd Prescelly) in the north, and the complex estuarine system of the Cleddau in the south. Information centres at Broad Haven (Countryside Unit), Fishguard (Town Hall), Haverfordwest (County Museum), Kilgetty (Kingsmoor Common), Milford Haven (Town Hall), Pembroke (The Drill Hall, Main Street), St David's (City Hall) and Tenby (The Norton). Access to coast path by many B and minor roads, especially B4319, B4320 from Haverfordwest; and from A487 on s. and n. sides of St David's, and e. of Fishguard. Mynnyd Prescelly is flanked by B4313 Fishguard–Maenclochog, and traversed by B4329 Greenway–Crosswell. Minor roads serve Cleddau Estuary south of A40 east of Haverfordwest; east of A4076 – A477, Haverfordwest–Neyland; and north of A477 – A4075, eastwards from Pembroke Dock. Recommended leaflets: Guided Walks, Accompanied Walks and Lectures, Pembrokeshire Coast Path.

Ramsey SM 72 25. Island, 596 a. Seabirds, Buzzard, Raven, Chough. Off St David's Head, 3 mls w. of St David's A487. Boat from St Justinian. (Warden – Ramsey Island, St David's, Haverfordwest, Dyfed.) RSPB.

St Bride's Bay Coast between Carn Nwchwn and Nine Wells SM 78 24, St Elvis immediately to e. of Solva harbour SM 81 24, and between Upper Solva and Cwm Bach Newgale SM 80 24. 9–12 mls n.w. of Haverfordwest, 2–5 mls s. of St David's, s. of A487. NT.

St David's Head SM 74 28. Coast between Tywyn Fach and Carn Llids 595 ft. Also Whitesands Bay to Porth-Clais SM 73 23. 2 mls n.w. of St David's A487. NT.

Sandy Haven SM 86 07. Estuarine mudflats and saltmarsh. Wildfowl and waders. Incl. Gann Flats, via beach n. of Dale

SM 82 07. 9 mls s.w. of Haverfordwest, on s. side of B4327 by minor roads.

Skomer NNR SM 72 09. Island, 759 a. Grey Seals, Skomer Voles. Seabirds incl. Manx Shearwaters, Puffins, Raven, Chough, Buzzard, Short-eared Owl. Boat from Martin's Haven SM 760 092, 12 mls w. of Haverfordwest B4327. Car park. Cliff walks on mainland. Restricted access to parts of the island, landing fee (mid Mar.–mid Oct.), trail. NCC/W. Wales Nats T.

Strumble Head SM 89 41. Cliffs with seabirds. 5 mls n.w. of Fishguard A40, via minor roads from Goodwick to Lighthouse.

Teifi Estuary SN 16 50. Mudflats and saltmarsh. Wildfowl and waders. 3 mls n. of Cardigan at end of B4548.

Tywi-Gwendraeth Estuary SN 37 12. Mudflats and saltmarsh. Waterfowl and waders. 7–8 mls s.s.w. of Carmarthen, on w. side via B4312, Llanstephan–Pantyrathro, and on e. side at Ferryside via minor road w. of A484 at Llandyfaelog.

West Wales Naturalists' Trust, 4 Victoria Place, Haverfordwest, Pembrokeshire, Dyfed.

POWYS

Brecknock County Naturalists' Trust, Byddyn, Llanhamlach, Brecon.

Brecon Beacons National Park, Southern Powys, intruding into Gwent in e. Mid Glamorgan and Dyfed in s. and w. 519 sq. mls. Wild moorland country from Black Mountains 2660 ft (Gwent) in east to Black Mountain 2022 ft (Dyfed) in west. Highest point of Beacons is Pen y Fan 2906 ft. Mostly sandstone, also picturesque limestone region with anciently occupied cave system. Hills intersected by valleys with farming, and high reservoirs such as Taf Fechan and Tal y bont. Glas Fynydd and other forests (For Comm) and some deciduous woodlands (NT); fine waterfalls in s. and a 32-ml stretch of canal. Information centres at Abergavenny (Lower Monk Street), Brecon (6 Glamorgan Street), Libanus (Mountain Centre, Cae Harn SN 97 26) and Llandovery (8 Broad Street). Flanked by A40 Brecon–Llandovery, on n. side. Traversed by A40 and B4558 Brecon–Crickhowell, thence A40 to Abergavenny, with Sugar Loaf (NT) 1955 ft to n.; A465 – B4423 – minor road through Vale of Ewyas, Abergavenny–Hay-on-Wye, with Black Mountains to w.; A479 – A40 Talgarth–Crickhowell–Abergavenny; B4560 Talgarth–Bwlch–Ebbw Vale; A470 Brecon–Merthyr Tydfil through Glyn Tarell, with Brecon Beacons to east; A4067 Sennybridge–Ystradgynlais, over Fforest Fawr; A4069 Llangadog–Brynamman, along Afon Sawdde and over Black Mountain (Dyfed). Recommended leaflet: Brecon Beacons National Park.

Cors Tregaron NNR SN 68 63. Raised bog, moss and carr. Wintering Whitefronted Geese. 10 mls n.e. of Lampeter, 2 mls n.e. of Tregaron A485 – B4343. Permit required, but viewable from B4343. (Permits and Leaflet from NCC, Plas Gogerddan, Aberystwyth, Dyfed.) NCC.

Herefordshire and Radnorshire Nature Trust, Community House, 25 Castle Street, Hereford, HR1 2NW.

Henrhyd Falls and Graigllech Woods SN 85 12. 140 a. N. of Coelbren Junction, 11 mls n. of Neath, midway between A4067 and A4109. Car park. NT.

Powis Castle SJ 22 06. Mediaeval castle and grounds, with fine pinetum and arboretum. S. side of Welshpool off A483. NT.

Royal Society for the Protection of Birds, Welsh Headquarters, 18 High Street, Newtown, Montgomeryshire.

Upper Taf Fechan SO 05 15. Reservoir. Wintering wildfowl. 4 mls n. of Merthyr Tydfil, n.e. of A470. Car park at SO 055 145. Hide (members) at n.e. end. Brecknock County Nats T.

Vale of Rheidol SN 70 77. River valley, field and woods, leading to sessile oakwoods near Devil's Bridge. Narrowgauge railway, Aberystwyth – Devil's Bridge, 12 mls. Nature trail booklet. Brit. Rail/W. Wales Nats T.

Ynys-hir SN 68 96. Mixed woods, farmland, mudflats and saltmarsh on estuary of R. Dyfi, 630 a. Heron, Buzzard, Sparrowhawk, Pied Flycatcher, Whitefronted Geese, ducks and big wader flocks in winter. 10 mls n.e. of Aberystwyth, 8 mls w. of Machynlleth via A487 – B4353. Car park, trail. (Warden – Ynys Edwin, Eglwysfach, Machynlleth, Powys.) RSPB.

WEST GLAMORGAN

Glamorgan County Naturalists' Trust, 39 Harle Street, Neath, SA11 3DN.

Llanrhidian Marsh SS 49 93. Extensive saltmarsh on n. coast of Gower, 1271 a. 6 mls w. of Swansea B4295, w. of Crofty. NT.

Oxwich NNR SS 50 86. Sand-dunes and fen, 542 a. 10 mls w. of Swansea A4118. Restricted access. NCC.

Pennard Cliff SS 53 86. Coastal cliffs from Pwlldu Head in e. to Southgate in w. also Nicholaston Burrows SS 53 88, cliffs, sand-dunes and beach. 7 mls s.w. of Swansea, on s. side of A4118. NT.

Port Eynon SS 47 85. Contiguous series of Carboniferous Limestone cliffs, 250 a. Fulmars, Kittiwakes, Ravens, Stonechats. 12 mls w. of Swansea, 1 ml s. of Port Eynon at end of A4118. Car park. NT/Glamorgan County Nats T.

Rhosili Downs SS 42 90. Gorse and bracken-covered hill, 531 a. Also Ryers Down on n. side SS 45 92. 15 mls w. of Swansea A4118 – B4247, 1 ml n. of Rhosili. NT.

Whitford Burrows SS 45 95. Sand-dunes and saltmarsh, 670 a. 15 mls w. of Swansea A4118 – B4271 and minor road to Llanmadog. NT.

Worms Head SS 42 87. Island and headland at s.w. corner of Gower Peninsula. Incl. cliffs from Rhosili to Mewslade Bay. 1004 a. 15 mls w. of Swansea A4118 – B4247, s.w. of Rhosili. NT.

MID GLAMORGAN

Dane Valley SN 98 03. Country Park, 400 a. W. of Aberdare A4059. Cynon valley DC.

Nature Conservancy Council, South Wales Regional Office, Summit House, Windsor Place, Cardiff, CF1 3BX.

GWENT

Gwent Trust for Nature Conservation, 40 Melbourne Way, Newport, NPT 3AF.

Sugar Loaf SO 27 18. Hill 1955 ft and commonland overlooking the Usk valley. 3 mls n.w. of Abergavenny, on n. side of A40. NT.

Animal collections in Wales

Cardiff Zoo

This Zoo has a mixed collection of about 100 mammals and 30 birds, and a small number of reptiles. There is an Indian Elephant, deer, Brazilian Tapirs, Chimpanzees, Mandrills, baboons and Rhesus Monkeys, and Bengal Tiger, Lions, Leopards, Pumas and bears. The smaller mammals include Dingos, porcupines, Coypus and badgers. The birds include white Emus – an unusual colour phase – cassowaries, penguins, flamingos, parrots and vultures. The reptiles consist of Royal and Rock Pythons, Boa Constrictors and tree snakes. Snake-handling demonstrations are given throughout the summer months, and Mr George Palmer enters the cat cages to demonstrate his control over them. There are also pony rides for children in the summer. The Zoo was started by Messrs Hugh and George Palmer in 1962.

Cardiff Zoo. **Address** Weycock Road, Barry, Glamorgan, Wales. **Telephone** Barry 4687. **Open** 10.30–19.00 summer, 10.30–dusk winter. **Guide-book. Catering** snack bar. Zoo shop. **Guided tours** by arrangement. **Acreage** 11. **Car** 2 mls n.w. of Barry, n. side of A4226. **Train** to Barry. **Taxis** available. **Other facilities** first-aid post, lost children's room, children's playground. Public **not allowed** to feed animals.

Penscynor Wildlife Park

Penscynor Wildlife Park is mainly a bird collection, with flamingos, penguins, many members of the parrot family, a large walk-through Aviary and a Tropical Bird House, but there are also a few mammals, including deer, sealions, monkeys, otters, foxes and badgers. There is also a small aquarium. A mountain stream with a 35-foot waterfall runs through the gardens, supplying all the pond enclosures, and the flower gardens make an attractive setting for the animals.

In a paddock beside the entrance you can see Sika Deer, Llamas, donkeys, a pair of rheas, the flightless birds of South America, and some pheasant runs. Beyond these, there is a sealion pool, and near this, a pool containing waterfowl and 500 Rainbow Trout which rise to receive the pellets sold in the Zoo with which you can feed them. Some aviaries for parrots and macaws lead you to the penguin pool and the pelicans. Opposite these is the Aquarium, with both freshwater and marine tanks. A fine big aviary for wading birds contains Eurasian Spoonbills, Sacred Ibises, the brilliantly coloured Scarlet Ibises and Purple Gallinules. The stream running towards the main garden area flows through a waterfowl pool and you come to aviaries exhibiting toucans, hornbills, Crowned Pigeons, Occipital Blue Pies, Grey Hornbills, Eclectus Parrots and White-throated Jay Thrushes. Eclectus Parrots, from the South Pacific islands, are curious in that the sexes are quite different, the male being bright green and the female plum-coloured. There is a large walk-through aviary with toucans, parrakeets, lorikeets, touracos, glossy starlings, Necklaced Doves and many species of small perching birds. A big flight aviary for macaws and cockatoos enables you to get a close look at these birds; others are at liberty in the gardens.

The Tropical Bird House has a stream and waterfall, with hummingbirds, tanagers, finches, barbets, hoopoes, pittas, starlings and a Sun Bittern, all flying free. At one end is an indoor cage for marmosets, and the other end has cabinets in which you can see crickets and mealworms used for feeding the birds. The flower garden has some very large flight aviaries for hornbills, eight kinds of toucan, Green-winged Trumpeters and aracaris. Other aviaries in this garden display White-crested Jay Thrushes, Pileated Jays, White-cheeked Touracos, Blue-crowned Motmots, doves, fantails and a further selection of macaws, parrots, parrakeets, conures, lories and lorikeets. There are two rare species of parrakeet in the collection, the Splendid and the Turquoisine. The flower garden also exhibits some mammals; there are Woolly Monkeys, Rhesus Monkeys and a fox enclosure, and on the patio under a rain shelter you can see gerbils, hamsters, Rabbits and tortoises, as well as Painted Quail, Hill Mynahs and

Penscynor Wildlife Park. **Address** Cilfrew, Neath, Glamorgan. **Telephone** Neath 2189. **Open** 10.00–dusk summer and winter. **Guide-book. Catering** restaurant (summer only), cafeteria, snack bar. Zoo shop. **Guided tours** by arrangement. **Acreage** 15. **Car** 2 mls n.e. of Neath, off A465 towards Cilfrew. **Bus** from Neath to Cilfrew stops outside Park. **Train** to Neath (2 mls). **Taxis** available. **Other facilities** first-aid post, lost children's room, children's playground. No pets. Public allowed to feed some animals with food prepared and sold in Zoo only.

Japanese Sika stag and hind; this animal is closely related to our native Red Deer (see page 24).

newly hatched chickens. The large aviaries for birds of prey show King Vultures, Bateleur Eagles and yellow-billed Black Kites. Another monkey exhibit for Diana Monkeys will be found opposite the Tropical Bird House.

Continuing through the gardens you come to a lawn where there is a flock of 30 Chilean Flamingos. A pond with soft mud has been made for them, where it is hoped they will breed. Finally, there are two more mammal exhibits, for Malayan Small-clawed Otters and European Badgers. The Badgers have an indoor den with a window, through which they can be seen when you press a button which lights up the den.

The Park was opened in 1970 by Mr and Mrs Idris Hale, who have travelled widely, filming birds in the wild. Mr Hale is a particularly successful breeder of parrakeets, of which he has a large collection.

St Catherine's Island Zoo

This little Zoo is housed within and around a fort built by Lord Palmerston as a defence against possible attack by Napoleon III, and it was completed in 1870. The Zoo is divided into sections: the Pet Room, Bird Room, Small Mammal Room and Information Room, with the larger mammals out of doors. The mammals to be seen here are baboons, marmosets, squirrel monkeys, bushbabies and macaques; civet, genet, coati, fox, otter and ferret; porcupine, chipmunk, chinchilla, gerbil, rats and guinea-pigs; St Kilda Sheep and Rabbits. Birds include parrots and related species, finches, mynahs, starlings, toucans, Barn Owl and Little Owl. There are also some reptiles, including iguanas, Eyed Lizard, plated lizard and turtles, and Giant Toads. On the island you can see Shags, Cormorants and Puffins, while seals and dolphins visit the waters around it. The Zoo, started in 1968, is now owned by Mr and Mrs Perry.

St Catherine's Island Zoo. **Address** St Catherine's Island, Tenby, Dyfed, Wales. **Open** 09.20–dusk (at low tide only) summer, open by appointment only, winter. **Catering** local cafes and restaurant available. **Acreage** 3. **Car** park at Castle Beach, Tenby. The island is accessible on foot at low tide. **Other facilities** first-aid post, lost children's room. No pets. Public **not allowed** to feed animals.

Tropicana Aquarium and Mini-Zoo

This is a small collection of small animals, and you can see monkeys, chipmunks, gerbils, hamsters, mice, porcupines and goats. There are also some small birds, lizards, snakes and a crocodile, and some tropical fish, which are the primary exhibit in the collection. This exhibition was opened in 1961.

Tropicana Aquarium and Mini-Zoo. **Address** above the Queen's Supermarket, Sussex Street, Rhyl. **Telephone** Rhyl 53306. **Open** 10.00–18.00 Whitsun bank holiday to mid Sept. **Guided tours** by arrangement. Public **not allowed** to feed animals.

Welsh Mountain Zoo

The Welsh Mountain Zoo was opened in 1963 by Mr Robert Jackson at the top of a wooded hill overlooking Colwyn Bay, and you can see here a mixed collection of animals, including the big cats, bears, Chimpanzees, monkeys, sealions, an elephant and some hoofed animals. There are many aviaries, a good collection of birds of prey and a small aquarium and reptile house. As befits the best zoo in Wales, the labels on each exhibit are in English and Welsh, which represents quite a linguistic feat with some of the more exotic animals; in fact, this is the only British zoo with bi-lingual labelling.

The big cats here are Lions, in a family group which you can see from the balcony of the Treetops Safari Restaurant, often with their young cubs, and Leopards and Pumas. All are excellent specimens of their kind, and the camouflage effect of the Leopard's spots is well illustrated in the Leopard cage, where they merge into the branches of their trees. A short walk through the water gardens brings you to the apes, monkeys and the small mammals enclosures. There are Chimpanzees, from tropical Africa, which live in loosely knit family groups, feeding on fruit, plants, insects and occasionally young baboons or wild pig; Lar Gibbons, another member of the anthropoid apes, with no tails, which come

Welsh Mountain Zoo and Botanic Gardens. **Address** Colwyn Bay, Clwyd, Wales. **Telephone** Colwyn Bay 31660. **Open** 10.00–19.00 (or dusk whichever earlier) summer, 10.00–16.00 winter. **Guide-book. Catering** unlicensed restaurant, licensed self-service cafeteria, kiosks. Zoo shop, information centre. **Guided tours** by arrangement. **Acreage** 37. **Car** 1¼ mls s. of town centre on B5113 Llanrwst road. **Bus** special service runs (Whitsun–Sept) from Colwyn Bay Pier Head to Zoo. **Train** to Colwyn Bay (1¼ mls). **Taxis** available. **Other facilities** first-aid post, lost children's room. daily falconry and sealion displays. No pets. Public **not allowed** to feed animals.

from the tropical jungles of southeast Asia, and live mainly in trees, through which they can swing very rapidly with their long arms; spider monkeys from South America, which also swing along branches, but with prehensile tails which they use as a fifth limb; and Olive or Anubis Baboons, a species found north of the equator in Africa, but south of the Sahara. Baboons live in troops on the ground, usually in rocky country, sleeping at night in rock clefts as protection from Leopards. One or two young males are posted as sentries, and any marauding Leopard will be attacked, which often ends in the death of both the baboons and the Leopard.

The enclosure for small mammals exhibit Raccoons from North America, Prairie Marmots, burrowing rodents of the American grasslands, Crested Porcupines from Africa, and two native species, the Pine Marten and a related species, the Polecat (see p. 229). Two more monkey species can be seen in the Pets' Corner, the Rhesus Monkey, still common in India although huge numbers have been exported in recent years for medical research, and Woolly Monkeys, another South American species which has a very strong prehensile tail which it uses for grasping branches and even swinging from them. Pets' Corner also has Rabbits, guinea-pigs, chickens, white rats, Budgerigars, mynahs, goats, calves and Vietnamese Pot-bellied Pigs, an immensely fat breed with short legs.

The bears here are Syrian Bears, which breed in the Zoo. This is a race of the European Brown Bear from Asia Minor, which is now very rare in the wild. It has a lighter, creamier coat than the ordinary Brown Bear. Do not miss the young Indian Elephant or the Californian Sealions, which perform tricks when they are fed. The Seven Acre Paddock contains Llamas and Fallow Deer, both of which breed here, wallabies, and the rarest animals in the Zoo, Przewalski's Horses. These are the last of the truly wild horses, which come from Mongolia, although it is doubtful if there are any left in the wild. They are bred regularly in captivity, and there are now about 200 in zoos all over the world. You can also see the attractive little Welsh Mountain Ponies here, which are so much more suitable for children to ride than the tubby Shetland, which was only intended to pull a cart. The larger Welsh pony breed was crossed with the Arab and other thoroughbreds, which has made it one of the most graceful of pony breeds.

In the Reptile House you can see a selection of snakes, lizards, tortoises, terrapins and amphibians. Snakes which have bred here include European Grass Snakes and Florida King Snakes, and the European Wall Lizards and Green Lizards have also produced young. Two other interesting lizards are the tegu, a carnivorous South American lizard which eats chickens and is hunted for its flesh, and the Rhinoceros Iguana, which has three blunt horns on its nose. It is found only in Haiti and Puerto Rico, and it eats small animals, berries, vegetables and flowers. The Aquarium exhibits Mississippi Alligators in a tropical pool and some tanks with tropical freshwater fish.

The birds in the Zoo are one of its best features. There is a large flight aviary for macaws, the largest members of the parrot family, and the Parrot House has a selection of parrots, cockatoos, parrakeets and conures. More parrakeets and conures can be seen in the Temple aviaries, including Red-rumped Parrakeets, which have bred here. Other aviaries exhibit Cockatiels, Painted Quail, Pekin Robins, Red-billed Weavers, Red-headed Buntings and Japanese and Bobwhite Quail, both of which have been bred. There are two pools, beyond the sealions, where you can see pelicans, waterfowl and Humboldt's Penguins. There are cassowaries, the large and fierce flightless birds of New Guinea, in a paddock. In the wood, you come to a range of pheasant aviaries, and the birds of prey. There is a pair of condors, the largest predatory birds in the world, which live in the high Andes, and an interesting collection consisting of the Wedge-tailed Eagle, King Vulture — another South American species — Black Kite, Mexican Goshawk, Roadside Hawk, Lagger Falcon, and Kestrels, which have bred here. The owl aviaries exhibit Spotted and Kenya Eagle Owls, European Eagle Owls, which have bred, and our native Barn Owl and Tawny Owl. Falconry displays, using hawks, falcons, eagles, vultures, and even the condors, are given in summer, and these are well worth seeing.

The estate on which the Zoo now stands is thought to have acquired the

Among the reptiles which can be seen at the Welsh Mountain Zoo are Florida King Snake (above), and Green Lizard (below).

The Rhinoceros Iguana is so named because of the 'horn' on its snout.

name of Flagstaff Gardens when local nonconformists rioted in 1886 in protest against paying tithes to a church to which they did not belong. Flags were flown from local hill-tops as part of the demonstration, and this hill being the most prominent it was probably used as a signalling station. There are telescopes on the observatory on the roof of the Lookout Café and from here you get magnificent views of the surrounding countryside.

Whitson Zoological Park

Whitson Zoo is in the grounds of Whitson Court. The animals exhibited here are bears, monkeys, birds and over 60 varieties of tropical fish. The rarest exhibits are Blue Crowned Pigeons, and the most regular breeders are the Rhesus Monkeys, which produce young every year. There are also a few reptiles on exhibition. The Zoo was opened in 1965 by Mrs O. J. Maybury, and Whitson Court, built by Nash, may be seen by appointment.

Whitson Zoological Park. **Address** Whitson Court, Nr Newport, Gwent. **Telephone** Newport 72515. **Open** 10.30–18.00 summer and winter. **Catering** snack bar (summer only). **Guided tours** by arrangement. **Acreage** 20. **Car** 5 mls s.e. of Newport. **Bus** 5 stops at Park. **Train** to Newport (5 mls). **Taxis** available. **Other facilities** children's playground. Public allowed to feed animals with food supplied by Zoo only.

North West England JOHN WILSON

The outstanding feature of the northwest is the variety of the landscape. The scenic but barren uplands contrast sharply with the flat, featureless, fertile plains, the expansive sandy estuaries with precipitous sea-cliffs, the placid rivers of the plains with the tumbling streams of the hills. Variety can be found in the coniferous and broad-leaved woodland, inland waters large and small, moorland and bog, saltmarsh, sand-dunes and offshore islands. Some parts have been drastically changed by man; others, because of the difficult terrain, have so far suffered less from his activities than most parts of the country. This diversity produces a corresponding variety of wildlife to delight the careful observer.

A long coastline is deeply indented by five major estuaries — the Mersey, the Ribble, Morecambe Bay including the Lune, the Duddon and the Solway Firth. Here the twice-daily ebb and flow of the tides produces an ever-changing world of water, sand and mud teeming with invertebrate animals which provide sustenance for one of the largest concentrations of birds to be found anywhere in Britain, or indeed in Europe. This complex supports over a third of the estuarine wading birds wintering in Britain as well as large numbers of wildfowl and gulls; it also provides an essential stopping-off place or refuelling halt for many other birds on their migrations to and from their wintering grounds to the south

John Wilson has lived in North Lancashire all his life. Since 1964 he has been Senior Warden at the RSPBs Leighton Moss Reserve, and now has the added responsibility of their extensive Morecambe Bay Nature Reserve. He has been a prominent member of the team of biologists who have investigated the possible effects of the proposed Morecambe Bay Barrage. He has published a number of articles, booklets and scientific papers on the natural history of northwest England, and in particular on wading birds.

and their breeding areas in the Arctic. At high tide the birds are concentrated on the extensive saltmarshes or shingle beaches, providing an unforgettable spectacle as they mass together in their thousands, or suddenly lift as a flock, twisting and turning, rising like animated puffs of sudden smoke on the wintry shoreline.

Other than industrial pollution, which is mainly confined to the Mersey, man has had little effect on these vast intertidal areas; he has only nibbled at the edges with small-scale land reclamation schemes. But with ever-improving technology the threats are increasing, and current proposals include possible estuarine barrages across Morecambe Bay, the Duddon and the Solway. If implemented, they would transform large sections of each estuary into freshwater reservoirs, displacing large numbers of estuarine birds — especially waders — although perhaps attracting more wildfowl, unless water-based recreational activities make them untenable. Fortunately large areas of intertidal sandflats are now reserves, over 14,000 acres on the south bank of the Ribble forming the Southport Sanctuary, while 9,000 acres of the Wyre-Lune are similarly dedicated. Both areas are National Wildfowl Refuges designed to protect roosting geese, ducks and waders. Over 6,000 acres of saltmarsh and intertidal flats have been acquired by the Royal Society for the Protection of Birds to protect three of the major wader roosts on the east side of Morecambe Bay. Wildfowling is practised all along the coastline, especially on the estuaries, but it is strictly controlled by the various clubs, several of which have set aside some areas as sanctuaries.

The Lakeland hills form a backdrop for Morecambe Bay, Britain's most important estuary for wintering waders.

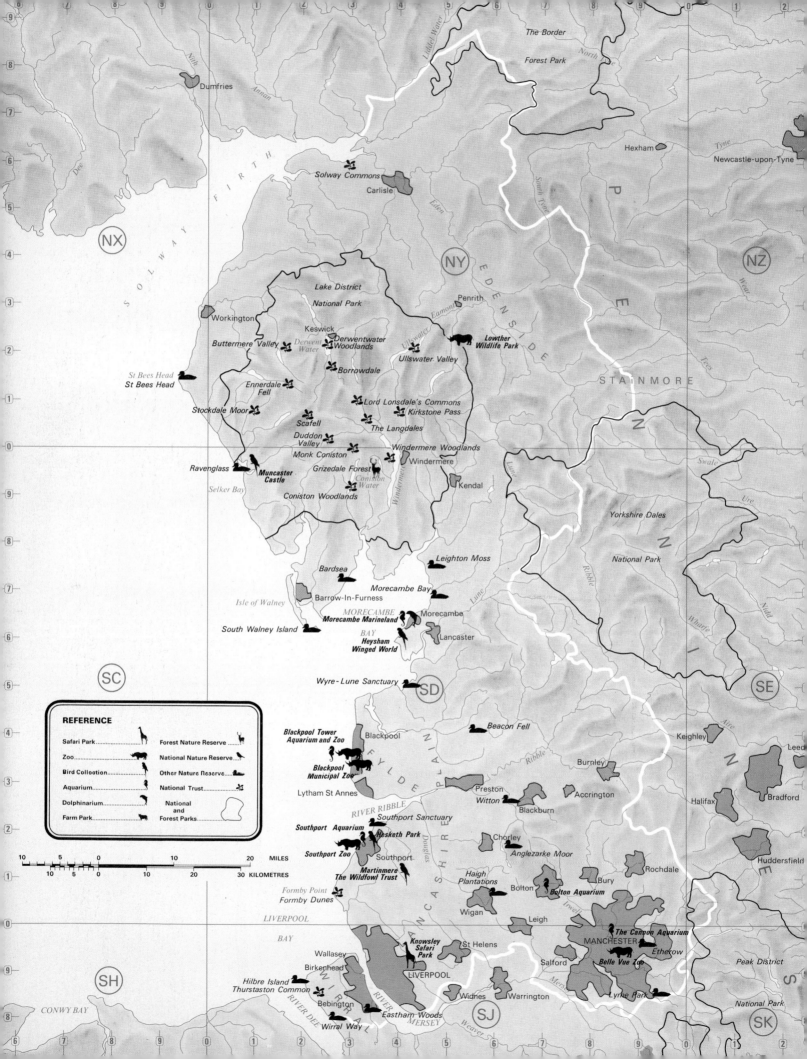

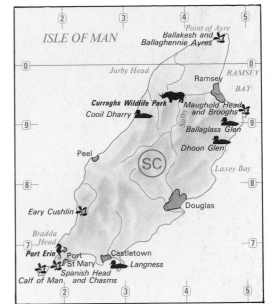

Sand-dunes flank most of the estuaries, although many have disappeared — especially in south Lancashire — under a rash of bungalows, golf-courses and holiday-camps. The Ainsdale NNR and the Lytham St Annes Reserve protect much of the remaining undeveloped areas. The formerly large seabird colonies have long since gone, while recently a low water-table, possibly aggravated by increased water abstraction, has seriously reduced the breeding success of Frogs, Natterjack Toads and other amphibia. Farther north, on the Cumbrian coast, the sand-dune reserves of South Walney and Ravenglass protect important areas rich in plant-life and supporting colonies of terns and gulls. Sandy beaches outside reserves are very much under recreational and tourist pressures, and the most popular have lost their breeding birds.

Except for the sandstone headland of St Bees near Whitehaven (RSPB) all the major sea-cliffs are in the Isle of Man, where Maughold Head, Peel Hill and the Calf of Man hold important auk and Kittiwake colonies, as well as Ravens and Choughs, and an occasional Peregrine's eyrie.

Arable farming is only important on the fertile drained 'mossland' of south Lancashire and north Cumbria where the stubble and potato-fields provide rich pickings for large numbers of geese and other wildfowl during the autumn and early winter. Elsewhere dairying and stock-rearing are practised, with sheep-walks on the hills. Changes in agricultural practice have been much slower than in the eastern counties; hedge removal has been on a small scale, and on the lower ground many miles of predominantly hawthorn hedges remain. On the higher ground these give way to the dry-stone walls so characteristic of upland areas. Both hedges and walls provide shelter and food for birds and small mammals, and act as highways along which they are safe from predators. The use of pesticides and herbicides has also been on a limited scale although there have been isolated cases of wildlife kills. The modernisation of farm-buildings, or their replacement by hygienic structures of steel and concrete, has reduced the available nest-sites and food supply for birds such as the Barn Owl, Swift, House Martin and Swallow.

Small woods and copses of trees are very much a feature of the northwest, extensive woodlands being restricted to south Lakeland and north Lancashire. Commercial planting of soft-woods by the Forestry Commission and the Water Undertakings has been on a large scale, and many plantations are now maturing, providing cover and sanctuary for our larger mammals and a rather restricted group of birds. Despite extensive felling and in some places replanting with exotic conifers, large areas of the native broad-leaved woodlands remain, especially in the Rusland valley, on the east side of Coniston, and in the Arnside-Silverdale area. Sessile oak and birch predominate on the higher and more acid soils, with ash and yew dominant on the limestone.

Many of our smaller woods, especially those on high ground, are subject to heavy grazing by sheep which remove the secondary growth and prevent natural regeneration, so that as trees are blown down or die there are no replacements. This is probably the most pressing conservation problem in the region, and speedy and widespread action will be needed in the near future or this denuding of the landscape will accelerate over the next few decades. Replanting and other positive management is being undertaken only on a small scale. In limestone areas another threat is the commercial removal of stone to supply the demand for rockeries in suburban gardens; this removal often destroys many rare and interesting plants, while in some cases the tree cover is felled to facilitate quarrying.

The region is well endowed with fresh water, although many of the lakes and tarns are rather unproductive due to their great depth or altitude. A few of the shallower lakes do have some bird and mammal interest and these include Esthwaite, Rydal, Bassenthwaite, Elterwater and Grasmere.

The most productive inland waters from the naturalist's point of view are on the periphery of Lakeland and in lowland Lancashire. In the latter area, drainage during past centuries has completely changed the landscape, for much of the Lancashire plain was covered by shallow meres and fens before man extended his agricultural activities. The last part to succumb was the formerly extensive

The Redstart (above) is a familiar bird of small valley woodlands such as this one (below) at Lodore Falls in Borrowdale.

249

Part of the RSPB's reserve at Leighton Moss, in June; the carefully managed reedbeds form an important breeding habitat for a variety of waterside birds such as the shy and secretive Water Rail.

Martin Mere inland from Southport. It is pleasing that the Wildfowl Trust is restoring a small section on a new reserve named after the ancient mere. The Leighton Moss Reserve (RSPB) was originally fen, but was completely drained in the early nineteenth century. After 70 years as farmland the 400 acres were flooded when difficulties during the First War brought about the stopping of the steam-powered pump. Reedbeds and willow scrub gradually encroached on the shallow water, creating an outstanding refuge for wildlife.

Mining subsidence has formed several freshwater 'flashes', especially around Wigan, Leigh and Workington, providing excellent wildfowl and wader habitat. Scotmans and Pennington Flashes in the Wigan area are probably the most interesting, although both now have sailing dinghies on them. Many reservoirs are also invaluable wildlife resorts, especially those in east Lancashire where Rivington, Belmont, Doffcocker and Foulridge are the most productive. Another excellent haunt is Cavendish Dock near Barrow-in-Furness, which provides cooling water for the nearby power station and so remains unfrozen even in the coldest spells, giving sanctuary at such times to many hard-pressed waterfowl.

The numerous streams and rivers vary greatly in character, from the small

A section of the River Lune, with a sand cliff suitable for breeding Sand Martins.

Cumbrian streams which tumble from the fells, to the larger rivers which meander through the plains. Of the latter, the Eden, Lune, Wyre and Ribble are the most interesting; periodic floods have formed shingle beds and in places have cut steep sandy banks which afford nesting sites for Sand Martins and Kingfishers, while Sedge Warblers, Whitethroats and many other birds inhabit the alders and willows which frequently line the banks. On the fells the streams are often a focal point for wildlife, the eroded valleys providing shelter and cover.

In historic times the fells were well wooded, but clearance for charcoal burning, timber, fuel and eventually to provide grazing for sheep and other domestic animals has almost completely removed the trees. The present heavy grazing precludes any regeneration. The trees were replaced by heather and fescue grasslands with cotton-sedge and bog-moss on the damper areas. Over-grazing has brought about degeneration into poor mat-grass pasture or bracken. In Lakeland, heather has now largely disappeared, although it remains plentiful on the grouse moors of the Pennines where it is regularly burned to promote fresh growth.

The scenic mountain ridges and the 'high tops', so beloved by the fell-walker and mountaineer, have only a limited range of bird and mammal species, the extreme exposure to wind and rain and the short growing season allowing survival of only a few hardy creatures. Historically the high fells and mountains provided sanctuary for predatory birds such as Golden Eagle and Peregrine, and hard-pressed larger mammals such as deer. These remote areas were difficult of access, while the sparse human population and limited game preservation were further advantages.

A pair of Sand Martins attend their young in the hole they have excavated in a sand cliff.

MAMMALS

Despite the depletion throughout history of our native fauna, the northwest still holds a variety of mammals which find sanctuary in the varied habitats or co-exist with man. The patient observer will see much to delight him, especially on dawn and dusk visits to the wilder valleys and uplands.

It comes as something of a surprise to most visitors to learn how widespread are Red Deer in Lakeland. Another surprise, especially to those conditioned to Scottish haunts, is the preference of many Lakeland Red Deer for woodland. They thrive in the extensive and now maturing plantations of the Forestry Commission and the Water Undertakings. Although widespread and probably increasing slowly throughout Lakeland and north Lancashire, the largest group is based on the eastern fells, England's only deer forest. Outlying groups extend to the limestone country from near Kendal to Morecambe Bay, where in spring a group of hinds and young stags frequent the reedbeds at Leighton Moss (RSPB).

Roe Deer are true forest-dwellers and are well distributed throughout much of Lakeland and north Lancashire, where they are the most numerous of our deer. This highly territorial animal has increased rapidly during the last 30 years with the growth of the new forests, though some stock has been introduced. Numbers in the plantations reach a peak when the undergrowth is thick, but decline as the canopy closes and kills off the ground vegetation. In some areas special clearing and replanting have been done to retain the Roe. Such techniques have been pioneered by the Forestry Commission in Grizedale Forest where an enlightened deer management policy has successfully reconciled commercial forestry, sport and conservation. Deer-watching 'hides' are provided on request, with dawn and dusk recommended as the best times for occupation. Similar facilities, together with a museum, are also offered at the Hay Bridge Deer Sanctuary in the lower Rusland valley where Red and Roe Deer live in the extensive woods and mosses. Introduced Sika Deer are well established in Bowland, with outlying groups in the Lune valley, while a few escaped Fallow Deer breed in the woods of the Arnside-Silverdale area.

Despite man's relentless persecution, the Fox remains common throughout the region, excepting the Isle of Man. This universally successful predator ranges from the expanding suburbs of the Lancashire plain to the wild crags of the high fells, and is equally at home foraging in urban dustbins or hunting voles on the hillsides. Mainly a nocturnal hunter, it lies up during the day in woodland or in

Moles are common throughout north-west England, despite trapping and poisoning operations.

a hole in a crag. In limestone country Foxes and Badgers often live in close proximity, occasionally sharing the same sett. Throughout the mainland the Badger is only patchily distributed, partly due to misguided persecution in some areas and lack of suitable terrain in others. Let us hope that the recent Badger Act will put a stop to this senseless persecution. Its strongholds include the Ribble valley, the Arnside-Silverdale area and the Eden valley.

Otters are perhaps the most difficult mammals to locate and study. They have recently declined in south Lancashire due to river pollution and disturbance, but from the Wyre northwards and throughout Lakeland they remain widely though thinly distributed on most river systems. Otter-hunting is still practised, with some success, by the Kendal and District Otter Hounds, who have their kennels at Milnthorpe. The most likely place to see Otters is Leighton Moss where they not infrequently hunt during daylight. Eels, which they catch with ease in the shallow weedy meres, seem to be their main prey. Up to five Otters have been seen together, though sightings of one or two are more usual.

Stoats and Weasels are most often glimpsed as they dash across the road. Both hunt regularly for rodents in dry-stone walls and hedgerows and are widely distributed. They are surprisingly numerous in many of the higher valleys and on the fells, and at such altitudes Stoats in their winter ermine coats are quite common. There is a marked similarity between these two animals and you should look at the tail tip; if it is black, then you are watching a Stoat.

Following escapes from fur farms, the North American Mink is now well established on most Lancashire rivers and is spreading to some Cumbrian ones, including the Eden. Despite an intensive eradication campaign, it continues to thrive. Past persecution has all but wiped out the Pine Marten and its present position is extremely precarious; it has been reported very occasionally in recent years.

Everyone knows the Hedgehog, if only from the frequent road casualties. It is widely spread throughout the region, including the Isle of Man, although mainly on low ground. Rabbits are now slowly recovering from the major setback of myxomatosis, but are still absent from many areas where they used to be numerous. This is especially the case on the higher ground. Brown Hares are also rather uncommon on the uplands, but are plentiful on the lush lowland pastures and in most woods.

Visitors from the south will be surprised to learn that the Grey Squirrel is absent from much of the northwest, while our indigenous Red Squirrel is still well distributed. Greys have reached the Ribble valley, but to date have failed to penetrate farther north — possibly the combination of inhospitable moorland and the recently completed M6 holds them at bay. Red Squirrels can be seen in many woods, both coniferous and broad-leaved. Numbers fluctuate from year to year but strongholds include Freshfield near Southport, Arnside-Silverdale, Whitbarrow Scar and Grange-over-Sands in the south, and Windermere, Grasmere, Thirlmere and Hawkshead in Lakeland.

Molehills are a common sight on marginal land throughout the region despite trapping and poisoning by farmers and professional mole-catchers to protect the quality of the pastures.

Few species of mammal occur on the Isle of Man, but mention should be made of the primitive Loghtan Sheep which are preserved by the Manx Museum and National Trust on the Calf of Man and at Cregneash in the south of the island. Both sexes have horns, the ram two pairs, of which one pair points upwards and outwards, while the other curls inwards towards the throat.

BIRDS

The upland birds are rather sparse in numbers and variety; however, several interesting species can be sought by those with good lungs and sureness of foot. Precipitous crags are favoured nesting sites for Ravens and Peregrines. The early-nesting Raven is well distributed throughout Lakeland and the Isle of Man; Peregrines used to be widespread, but they declined catastrophically during the 1950s and 1960s due to a build-up in their body fats of toxic chemicals such as dieldrin and DDT-based compounds ingested from the prey they caught, mainly

A Stoat struggles to drag a dead Rook.

Isle of Man. There is a great diversity of wildlife habitat within its 220 square miles; but the sea-barrier restricts the variety of animal species. The northern alluvial plain comprises the sand-dunes and raised beaches of the Bride Ayrelands, backed by rough fields and hummock-heath. Oystercatchers, Ringed Plovers, Redshanks, Lapwings and terns are its breeding birds. Nearer the hills are the tiny fields and dense willow-and-alder carr of the Ballaugh and Sulby Curraghs. The central mountain mass is pierced by numerous glens. South of the low-lying fields and 'gareys' of the Douglas—Peel gap are South Barrule and neighbouring hills, extending to impressive coastal cliffs and steep 'brooghs'. Here the Chough is a familiar sight, and Peregrines are breeding after many years' absence. The grey-backed Hooded Crow replaces the Carrion Crow and in this and other attributes the natural history of Man parallels Ireland's. The characteristic sessile oakwood birds of Wales and Cumbria are scarce or absent; no natural woodland remains, the present tree-cover dating from the Great Plantation Period of the early nineteenth century. There is a wide variety of coastal habitats, and Man has its own offshore island in the Calf, the site of an important Bird Observatory.

A crag in the Westmorland Pennines: the cliff is a Raven's nest-site. But the commonest breeding bird of the fells is the Meadow Pipit, seen above feeding a young Cuckoo whose mother substituted her egg for one of the pipit's.

in their wintering areas. Since restrictions on the use of certain pesticides were introduced there has been a slow recovery, together with a marked improvement in breeding success. One pair of Golden Eagles has nested each year since 1969: the secret location is guarded by a team of RSPB wardens. No more than one young has been reared in any year, so any future increase will be slow. Inexperienced visitors often confuse Golden Eagles with the smaller Buzzards which are widespread throughout the Lakes, and can often be seen soaring over the fells. Merlins prefer the heather moorland and although thinly distributed, having decreased for much the same reasons as the Peregrine Falcon, they are commoner on the Pennines than in Lakeland.

The commonest breeding bird of the fells is the Meadow Pipit, being found wherever there is open ground with rough grass; it is the regular host-species of the Cuckoo, which is quite common on the hills. Another common breeder is the handsome and conspicuous Wheatear, which occurs wherever there are stone walls or rocky outcrops to provide nest-sites and song-perches. Ring Ousels are our upland Blackbirds and they are not uncommon on the more broken ground, especially on the Pennines, which are also the headquarters of that carefully preserved gamebird the Red Grouse. The Twite has a surprising distribution, being common on the fells of east Lancashire and in the southern Pennines, but rare elsewhere. This small brown bird (the male has a bright pink rump) nests on the open moors but tends to take most of its food from seeding grasses in fields near the upper limit of agriculture. Dotterels have recently shown signs of recolonising the 'high tops', while Hen Harriers have also become re-established on the heather moors.

Both Dunlin and Golden Plover have declined as breeding birds but can still be found on the Pennines. The buff-breasted Whinchats are widely distributed on the lower fells and, following the recent succession of mild winters, the darker and more rufous Stonechat has returned to many former haunts from which it disappeared after the severe winter of 1963.

Maturing coniferous woodland is rather poor in bird numbers and species, but Goldcrests and Coal Tits have increased and spread into the new forests and small numbers of Siskins and Crossbills are now breeding. By contrast the young plantations quickly attract a good variety of scrub-loving birds, especially Willow Warblers, and often Whinchats, Stonechats, Cuckoos and Short-eared Owls.

The broad-leaved woods are much more productive, especially in the lowlands, where a good variety of warblers, tits, finches and woodpeckers will be found. All three of our native woodpeckers have spread northwards over the

A male Whinchat removes its young's faecal sac from the nest.

253

River Lune. Northern rivers are astonishingly rich in bird-life. In 1975 members of Lancaster and District Bird-Watching Society made sample counts along the R. Lune for the B.T.O. Waterways Bird Survey. Eighteen species were found holding territories. (Approximate densities of some of the commoner ones, in pairs per 10 km of river, are given in parentheses.)

Heron, Mallard (27), Goosander, Shelduck, Canada Goose, Mute Swan, Moorhen, Oystercatcher (30), Ringed Plover (8), Common Sandpiper (19), Dunlin, Kingfisher, Sand Martin (several colonies), Dipper (6), Pied Wagtail (27), Yellow Wagtail (7), Grey Wagtail (9), Reed Bunting (8). Lapwing, Curlew, Snipe and Redshank inhabited the riverside fields.

The counts showed a gradual change in species composition proceeding upstream, Ringed Plovers and Canada Geese fading out, Yellow Wagtail and Redshank becoming much scarcer, Common Sandpipers increasing, with Dippers and Moorhens commonest in the middle reach.

Female Red-breasted Merganser on nest; the drake (see page 221) is much gaudier.

last few decades, although the Lesser Spotted Woodpecker is still scarce. No woodpeckers have yet colonised the Isle of Man. The high-pitched cries of the grey and russet Nuthatch are regular only in the extreme south, apart from an occasional breeding territory in Lakeland. The sessile oakwoods of the hills have as their typical species Chaffinch, Pied Flycatcher, Redstart and Wood Warbler. These may be heard and seen in Grizedale Forest and the National Trust woodlands of White Moss near Ambleside and Glencoyne near Ullswater, where many Pied Flycatchers nest in boxes provided by the Cumbria Naturalists' Trust. Tree Pipits breed in the more open woodland and spread out on to the fell-side wherever there are trees to sing from, sometimes overlapping the duller Meadow Pipits. Even the smallest wood has its quota of Tawny Owls which have increased and spread to other habitats, including suburbia. The other woodland owl, the Long-eared, has declined markedly and has disappeared from many former haunts; it replaces the Tawny Owl in the Isle of Man. Sparrowhawks are well distributed in most of the larger woods and spread out into open country in winter. Buzzards also are regular nesters in Lakeland and north Lancashire.

Fast-flowing streams and rivers are very much a feature of the northwest and each has its quota of Dippers, Grey Wagtails and Common Sandpipers. A summer walk along any Lakeland stream will produce all three species, while farther south good places for finding them include the Devil's Bridge at Kirkby Lonsdale on the River Lune, Cromwell's Bridge on the Hodder and Mytton Bridge on the Ribble. The Kingfisher is reasonably common on the main Lancashire rivers and the Eden, but it is uncommon in the Lakes. Pairs are often located on the lower reaches of the tributaries rather than on the main river itself. Sand Martin colonies will be found wherever rivers have formed steep sandy banks, the lower reaches of the Lune having the highest density. Oystercatchers and Ringed Plovers have recently colonised the shingle banks of the larger rivers, especially the Lune, while another recent arrival, the Goosander, is rapidly establishing itself on the upper reaches of several streams.

Great Crested Grebes nest where there is sufficient cover as on Esthwaite Water, Belham Tarn and Pennington Flash. A recent colonist, the Red-breasted Merganser, now breeds on several lakes and tarns, including Windermere and Coniston. The shallow meres and extensive reedbeds of Leighton Moss (RSPB) support an exceptional variety of birds, several of which breed nowhere else in the northwest. Bitterns returned in the late 1940s and nine or ten pairs now breed annually, the spring 'booming' call of the male carrying far across the reeds from late January to mid-June. Another recent arrival is the Bearded Reedling which first bred in 1973. Reed, Sedge and Grasshopper Warblers nest in large numbers, as do Reed Buntings and Water Rails. Breeding wildfowl include Garganey, Gadwall, Tufted Duck, Pochard and Shoveler, while Osprey, Marsh Harrier and migrant waders occur on passage in spring and autumn.

In winter many waters hold concentrations of wildfowl, although the deeper lakes and those at high altitudes have at most only a few diving ducks. The largest concentrations are to be found in south Lancashire and on the Solway coast, feeding on the stubble and potato-fields of the drained mosslands. Over 10,000 Pinkfooted Geese winter in south Lancashire, centred on Martin Mere (Wildfowl Trust), but flighting out to roost on the intertidal mud of the Ribble within the Southport Sanctuary. Large numbers of Pintail and Wigeon also winter in the same area. On the Solway the biggest concentrations of geese occur in the New Year as many move from the Scottish shore to feed on farmland and coastal marshes.

Other wildfowl haunts include Cleveley Mere where Tufted Duck, Pochard, Goosander and wild swans winter. The reservoirs of east Lancashire and the 'flashes' farther south also support numbers of Whooper Swans and other wildfowl, with Doffcocker, Belmont, Foulridge and Pennington Flash holding the largest numbers. During cold spells Cavendish Dock attracts Wigeon, Pochard, Coot and swans which have been frozen out of inland haunts.

South Walney (Cumbria Naturalists' Trust) holds the largest colony of gulls in Europe; recent counts suggest that a total of 50,000 pairs of Lesser Black-backed Gulls and Herring Gulls, in roughly equal numbers, nest on the sand-dunes and gravel workings, along with about 30 pairs of Great Black-backed Gulls. Among them nest some 400 pairs of Eiders which arrived as recently as 1949. Walney is still their only breeding place on the west coast of England. Other breeding birds include Shelduck, Oystercatcher, Ringed Plover and Stone-chat. Terns alternate between Walney and the other islands in Morecambe Bay and in recent years all five species — Common, Arctic, Sandwich, Little and Roseate — have nested, although the total has rarely exceeded 400 pairs, mainly of Common, Sandwich and Little Terns. In winter the reserve is an important roost for Oystercatchers. Turnstones and Redshanks, while numbers of Wigeon, Teal, Eider and Mallard regularly frequent the bay at the southern tip.

Over 10,000 pairs of Black-headed Gulls nest on the Ravenglass Reserve at the southern tip of the sand-dunes, along with numbers of Sandwich, Common and Little Terns and other species such as Oystercatcher, Ringed Plover, Red-breasted Merganser and Stonechat. A little farther to the north, St Bees Head (RSPB) has big colonies of Guillemots, Razorbills, Kittiwakes, Fulmars and Herring Gulls, along with smaller groups of Puffins and Tysties or Black Guillemots. The last-named are the only birds of this species breeding in England.

A wintering herd of swans. Two species are seen: the Mute, and the smaller Bewick's.

Two types of seabird nest-site: left, St Bees Head, where Kittiwakes nest on narrow ledges of the dramatic sandstone cliff; right, the Black-headed Gull prefers flat terrain on which to nest.

Waders fly in dense flocks to their feeding grounds. Among species whose winter activity centres on estuarine coasts are, above top to bottom: Oystercatcher; Bar-tailed Godwit; Dunlins and the larger Knot.

There are smaller gull and tern colonies on the saltmarshes of the Solway, at Morecambe Bay and the Ribble, along with good numbers of Redshanks, Oystercatchers and Skylarks.

The Manx sea-cliffs, especially on the Calf of Man and at Maughold Head, have seabird colonies. Besides the numerous Guillemots, Razorbills, Fulmars, Kittiwakes and Shags, smaller numbers of Puffins, Tysties and Cormorants nest. The Manx Shearwater has recently recolonised the Calf in small numbers after the success of measures taken to reduce the population of its chief enemy, the Brown Rat. In our region, the Chough is restricted to the Isle of Man, where it nests on many sections of the rocky coast, as well as at ruined mine-shafts inland.

Outside the breeding season the seabird colonies are deserted and interest switches to the estuaries and offshore waters. Vast congregations of waders assemble on the estuaries from late July until mid-May, throughout the winter, feeding at low water on the extensive sand and mud-flats, and roosting at high tide on the shingle beaches and saltmarshes. Spring tides are the best for watching these wader 'spectaculars' as the birds assemble. The larger Oystercatchers,

The spectacular high-tide wader roost in Morecambe Bay: Oystercatchers and gulls in the background; Dunlins and Knots in front.

Curlews and Bar-tailed Godwits arrive first, often up to three hours before high tide, followed by Knots and Redshanks and finally the small Dunlins, Ringed Plovers and Sanderlings. The first to come are also the last to go since they feed well down the intertidal zone and have to wait until their feeding grounds are exposed. There are high-tide roosts at many points along the coast and suggested vantage points include Crossens north of Southport on the Ribble, the Cockerham Marshes on the Lune, Hest Bank on the east and South Walney on the west of Morecambe Bay, Langness on the Isle of Man and Moricambe Bay on the Solway. Offshore movements of seabirds can best be observed at Formby Point, Morecambe stone jetty, South Walney and St Bees Head.

AMPHIBIANS, REPTILES AND BUTTERFLIES

Frogs occur throughout the area, although numbers have declined recently in south Lancashire; they regularly spawn at considerable altitudes in Lakeland, often in small temporary pools. Toads are also widespread, breeding in deeper water than the Frogs. Natterjack Toads occur on many of the coastal sand-dunes, and the Sand Lizard is still to be found in south Lancashire. Adders or Vipers and Grass Snakes are patchily distributed and their numbers seem to fluctuate from year to year.

Butterflies are restricted by the distribution of the food-plants of the caterpillars. One of our most interesting species is the small Mountain Ringlet which usually occurs only above 1,800 feet and flies on fine days in late June and early July; the caterpillars feed on mat-grass. The Green Hairstreak is common on moorland in May. In broad-leaved woods many fritillaries occur, including the Pearl-bordered and Small Pearl-bordered, High Brown and Dark Green Fritillaries, while the delicate Orange-tip is common in clearings and at woodland edges. On the mosses the Large Heath is abundant, the larvae feeding on the white-beaked sedge. In limestone areas one can search for the elegant little Duke of Burgundy Fritillary, the caterpillars of which feed on cowslips, while the rock-rose provides food for the larvae of the Brown Argus. The Grayling and Common Blue butterflies are abundant on the sandhills.

At the present time a rapidly increasing number of people who live in or visit the northwest find great delight in watching and studying wildlife, and there is an increasing concern for conservation. Our rapidly changing world continues to pose threats. In the lowlands, an increasing human population demands more homes, and an increasing industrialisation provides more jobs. Better road communications and more intensive farming are to some extent detrimental to wildlife. In the Lake District and the Isle of Man, the pressures are on a much smaller scale, and here the main threat comes from recreation and tourism, as more people and cars converge on the mountains, fells and coast along the new roads. The Local Authorities, through their Planning Departments, are fully aware of the problem, especially within the Lake District National Park.

Many of our major wildlife sites are already established nature reserves where the habitat can be protected from disturbance and development and managed for the benefit of birds, mammals and the plants and invertebrates on which they depend. The several organisations administering reserves in the northwest area include the Nature Conservancy Council, RSPB, Wildfowl Trust, the Cumbria and Lancashire Naturalists' Trusts, and the Manx Museum and National Trust. Most of these reserves can be visited by making arrangements with the organisation concerned.

More reserves are needed in different parts of the country to protect other vulnerable sites or rare species. There is also the need to extend the reserve network to include habitats which are not fully represented at present — in particular, good examples of our broad-leaved woodland and heather moor. Wardening schemes to protect fragile habitats or rare species also have a part to play, as the National Park wardens, the National Trust and the RSPB have shown.

Green Hairstreak, common on moorland.

Superbly camouflaged Grayling butterfly.

Grass Snake and its eggs, which are joined together in clusters by a secretion from the oviduct.

Guide to wildlife habitats in North West England

This Appendix provides a selected but varied list of places of wildlife interest. It is emphasised that nature reserves exist primarily for the conservation of animals and plants and in some cases for environmental experiments and research. They are not 'public open spaces' in the recreational sense. Access to many is therefore restricted and some, because of their sensitivity to disturbance, have been omitted from this list, in deference to the wishes of conservation organisations. Even with 'open' reserves visitors are earnestly requested to keep to the paths and bridleways and so avoid damage to the habitat and undue disturbance to wildlife. *There is no public access to the enclosed farmland which is part of many National Trust properties.*

Application to visit a National Nature Reserve (NNR) should be made to the appropriate Regional Office of the Nature Conservancy Council (NCC) at the address given. Intention to visit reserves of the Royal Society for the Protection of Birds (RSPB) should be notified to the Warden (whose address is shown) as far in advance as possible. In all cases where an address is shown, it is wise to contact the Warden to avoid disappointment.

CUMBRIA

Borrowdale NY 27 16. Watendlath Tarn and hamlet and surrounding fells, 955 a., Seatoller Farm and fells reaching to top of Honister Pass NY 24 14, 963 a., Grange Fell incl. King's How 1363 ft and Borrowdale Birches NY 26 17, 311 a. 9 mls s. of Keswick on minor road off B5289. NT.

Buttermere Valley NY 15 20. Buttermere 230 a. and shore woodlands NY 18 15; Crummock Water 623 a. and Lanthwaite Wood 69 a. NY 15 20 (and woods between), Loweswater 160 a. and Holme Wood on s. side 122 a., NY 12 21. 10–15 mls s.w. and w. of Keswick B5289. NT.

Coniston Woodlands Coniston Hall SD 30 96, 1 ml s. of Coniston astride A593, Nibthwaite Woods and Peel Island SD 29 91, at s. end of lake, Park-a-Moor SD 30 92, on e. shore, 412 a. NT.

Cumbria Naturalists' Trust, Low Cartmell Fold, Crosthwaite, Kendal, Cumbria, LA8 8HS.

Derwentwater Woodlands. Brandelhow NY 25 20, on w. side of Derwentwater under Cat Bells 108 a., Castle Crag NY 25 16 between Rosthwaite and Grange incl. Low Hows Wood 253 a., Coombe Allotment and Troutdale NY 26 17 on e. flank of Borrowdale adjoining Grange Fell 184 a., Great Wood Keswick NY 27 21 along e. side of Borrowdale road 1 ml s. of Keswick 238 a., Manesty Park NY 25 19 at s. end of Derwentwater between Brandelhow and R. Derwent 107 a., Ashness NY 27 18 3 mls s. of Keswick off B5289 straddling Watendlath road 179 a., Cockshott Wood NY 26 22 stretching 1½ mls between Crow Park and Ashness Gate 139 a., Johnny's Wood and High Doat NY 25 14 in heart of Borrowdale 80 a. NT.

Duddon Valley NY 25 03. Fell country on s. side of Wrynose Bottom in Duddon valley reaching to Grey Friar and the Carrs (Cockley Beck and Dale Head Farms 1215 a.) adjoining Monks Coniston in the e. and on the n. side stretching from Three Shires Stone to top of Hard Knott Pass, Crinkle Crags and Pike of Blisco (Blackhall Farm 2700 a.), and over to head of Eskdale NY 24 05 and summit of Bow Fell 2960 ft (Butterilket Farm 3328 a.). 9 mls w. of Ambleside A593 – B5343 and Wrynose Pass. NT.

Ennerdale Fell NY 15 12. State forest and fell country incl. Pillar 2927 ft, Steeple 2687 ft, Caw Fell 2187 ft, Haycock 2618 ft, Red Pike 2629 ft, and over Black Sail Pass to Kirk Fell 2630 ft and w. slope of Great Gable 2949 ft. 8 mls e. of Gosforth A595, on minor road via Greendale, Wast Water and Wasdale Head, or 6 mls e. of Cleator Moor A5086 on minor road via Ennerdale Bridge. For Comm./NT.

Grizedale Forest SD 35 95. State forest of conifers and oakwoods, streams, artificial lakes with wildfowl, Red and Roe Deer. Wood Warbler, Pied Flycatcher and other song-birds. 3 mls s. of Hawkshead, the countryside between Windermere and Coniston Water. Car parks, picnic/camping areas, Visitor and Wildlife Centre SD 37 95, Deer Museum, tree-top hides, trails, and the 'Theatre in The Forest'. For Comm.

Kirkstone Pass NY 41 09. Fells and farmland, incl. Brotherswater, from Hart Crag to Kirkstone Pass and adjacent moorland, extending to Troutbeck Park Farm and summits of Ill Bell, Froswick and Thornthwaite Crag. Also Scandale Fell NY 38 19. 3900 a. 6–9 mls n. of Windermere, astride A592. NT.

Lake District National Park, Cumbria. 866 sq. mls. Highest mountain country in England with Scafell Pike 3210 ft, Scafell 3162 ft, Helvellyn 3118 ft, Skiddaw 3053 ft and many peaks over 2000 ft. Large lakes incl. Windermere, Ullswater, Derwentwater, Thirlmere, Bassenthwaite, and innumerable small 'waters' and mountain tarns. Grizedale and Thornthwaite Forests (For Comm) and extensive deciduous woods, many owned by NT. Fine exposed passes such as Wrynose and Hard Knott. Numerous archaeological, historic and literary sites. National Park Day Visitor Centre at Brockhole, Windermere NY 389 010. Information centres at Ambleside (Old Court House, Church Street), Borrowdale (The Barns, Seatoller), Bowness (Caravan, The Glebe), Keswick (Moot Hall) and Windermere (District Bank House, High Street). Flanked by A6 Kendal–Penrith (and nearby M6) in east; A595 Broughton-in-Furness–Calder Bridge in southwest. Traversed by A592 Newby Bridge–Penrith, alongside Lakes Windermere and Ullswater; A591 Kendal–Keswick, via Windermere, Grasmere and Thirlmere; A66 Cockermouth–Penrith, via Bassenthwaite and Keswick; A593 Broughton-in-Furness–Coniston–Ambleside; B5289 Keswick–Cockermouth through Borrowdale, Honister Pass and Buttermere; B5292 Cockermouth–Keswick, over Whinlatter Pass. Large areas in north, southwest and southeast are devoid of even minor

View across the tarns to Black Fell, in the National Trust Lake District property of Tarn Hows.

roads. Recommended leaflets: Geology and Scenery, Mines and Minerals, Placenames, Literary Associations, Viewpoints and Sites of Historic Interest, A Circular Motor Tour, Sites for Caravans and Tents. Series of simple guides on natural history subjects, and many leaflets describing forest and nature trails and waymarked walks.

The Langdales NY 28 06. Fell country of Little Langdale, Great Langdale and Langdale Pikes 2323 ft, incl. Dungeon Ghyll, Blea and Loughrigg Tarns. 2356 a. 5–8 mls w. and n.w. of Ambleside A593, astride B5343 from Skelwith Bridge. NT.

Lord Lonsdale's Commons NY 33 12. Fell country from Seat Sandal 2365 ft, Fairfield 2863 ft and Rydal Fell 2022 ft, w. to head of Great Langdale and Langdale Pikes, incl. Easedale and Stickle Tarns. 16,842 a. 6 mls n. of Ambleside, 9 mls s. of Keswick, astride A591. NT.

Monks Coniston NY 32 00. Fell country from Coniston n. to Little Langdale and w. to Wetherlam 2502 ft and Broad Slack 2630 ft, adjoining Duddon valley estate; incl. Tarn Hows and High Tilberthwaite. 4067 a. 5 mls s.w. of Ambleside, 2 mls n.e. of Coniston, astride A593. NT.

The National Trust North West, Regional Office, Broadlands, Borrans Road, Ambleside, Cumbria.

Nature Conservancy Council, North

Regional Office, Merlewood Research Station, Grange-over-Sands, Cumbria, LA11 6JU.

Ravenglass SD 07 96. Sand-dunes at mouths of Rs. Esk, Irt and Mite. Terneries, Black-headed Gulls, shore birds. 16 mls s. of Whitehaven, on w. side of A595. Muncaster Estate/Cumberland CC.

St Bees Head NX 96 13. High sandstone cliffs for 3 mls. Seabird colonies include Puffins, Tysties, Fulmars, Kittiwakes. 4 mls s.w. of Whitehaven, on w. side of B5345. (Note: it is dangerous to leave the footpath inside the cliff-top fence.) RSPB.

Scafell NY 20 06. Highest mountain in England, Scafell Pike 3210 ft NY 21 07, Lingmell 2649 ft, Broad Crag 3054 ft and Great End 2984 ft, extending e. to Bow Fell. Over 2000 a. 10 mls s. of Keswick, s. of B5289 via Seatoller and Seathwaite. NT.

Solway Commons NY 20 60. Commonland, Burgh Marsh and 12 mls of coast on s. side of Solway Firth. Nearby is Glasson Moss Nature Reserve NY 26 61. 12 mls w. of Carlisle between Bowness and Anthorn along coast road. NT.

South Walney Island SD 23 62. S. point of island. Vast colony of Herring/Lesser Black-backed Gulls, wintering wildfowl.

Permit essential. (Secretary – 82 Plymouth Street, Walney, Barrow-in-Furness.) Cumbria Nats T.

Stockdale Moor NY 10 08. Fell country rising to Caw Fell 2187 ft, n. of R. Bleng. 2508 a. 3–5 mls n.e. of Gosforth A595. NT.

Ullswater Valley NY 40 20. Gowbarrow Park incl. Aira Crag 1579 ft, Aira Force and 1 ml of lake shore, 754 a. Red and Fallow Deer on fells. Also fell country of Glencoyne Park w. of head of Ullswater NY 36 18, rising to Stybarrow Dod 2766 ft and Raise 2885 ft, 2692 a. Glencoyne Wood NY 38 17, 189 a., contains many ancient oaks. 9–12 mls s.w. of Penrith A592, near junction with A5091 and s. to Glenridding. NT.

Windermere Woodlands Claife SD 38 97, 2 mls s.e. of Hawkshead B5285, along w. shore of n. half of Windermere, from Ferry Nab to Wray Castle, 750 a., Kelsick Scar NY 38 03, 2 mls s.e. of Ambleside, s. of Wansfell e. of A591, 215 a., Wansfell NY 39 03, 1 ml s.e. of Ambleside on e. shore of lake, A591, 190 a. NT.

ISLE OF MAN

Ballakesh and Ballaghennie Ayres NX 44 04. Shore, sand-dunes, raised beach. Terns and shore birds. 8 mls n. of Ramsey A10. Car park, picnic site, nature trail. Manx Museum and NT.

Calf of Man SC 16 65. Island, 616 a. Bird Observatory. Loghtan Sheep, Grey Seals. Seabirds, Ravens, Choughs, migrants. Boat from Port St Mary or Port Erin. Accomm. at farmhouse by arrangement with Manx Museum and NT, Douglas, I. Man.

Cooil Dharry SC 32 90. Wooded glen 1 ml long incl. deep river gorge. E. of Kirk Michael A3, above Glen Wyllin. Access by track from Glen Wyllin village to Baaregarrow–Ballaleigh road. Manx Nature Conservation T.

Eary Cushlin SC 22 76. Cliffs and heath. Seabirds, Choughs. 382 a. 5 mls n. of Port Erin, w. of A36. Car park. Manx Museum and NT.

Langness SC 28 66. Coastal rocks, salt-marsh, fields. Wintering waders and wildfowl, Ravens, Choughs, migrants. By Derbyhaven, 2 mls e. of Castletown A12. Car park. Manx Museum and NT.

Manx Glens. Well-wooded glens usually with fine waterfalls, leading to rocky coasts and shingle beaches, can be found at several points e. of A2 Douglas–Laxey–Ramsey and Manx Electric Railway stations named below from s. to n. Groudle SC43 78, Garwick SC 44 81, Dhoon SC 46 86, Glen Mona SC 46 88, Ballaglass SC 47 89. Isle of Man Forestry, Mines and Lands Board.

Manx Nature Conservation Trust, St Maur, Agneash, Lonan, Isle of Man.

Maughold Head and Brooghs SC 49 92. Cliffs and heath. Seabirds, Ravens, Choughs. 114 a. 3 mls s.e. of Ramsey A15. Shelter. Manx Museum and NT.

Spanish Head and Chasms SC 18 66. Cliffs and heath. Seabirds, Ravens, Choughs. It is s.w. of Port St Mary A31. Shelter/picnic area at Chasms SC 19 66. Manx Museum and NT.

LANCASHIRE

Anglezarke Moor SD 64 17. Adjacent Anglezarke SD 61 16 and Rivington SD 63 13 reservoirs lie on w. side and Belmont reservoir SD 67 17 is on e. side. Waterfowl, especially in winter. 2 mls s.e. of Chorley, on e. side of A673 via minor roads; 4 mls n. of Horwich on minor road via Rivington and 6 mls n.w. of Bolton near Belmont A675 for eastern approach to moor.

Bardsea SD 30 74. Woodland and shingle beach overlooking sandflats. Country Park. Wader roost at high tide. 2 mls s. of Ulverston A5087. Car park at Bardsea shore SD 299 740. Cumbria CC.

Beacon Fell SD 57 43. Woods and moorland rising to 873 ft, 269 a. Country Park. Large Starling roost. 8 mls n. of Preston A6, 3 mls e. of Garstang via minor roads. Car park SD 569 428. Lancs. CC.

Lancashire Naturalists' Trust, Samlesbury Hall, Samlesbury, nr Preston, Lancashire, PR5 0UP.

Leighton Moss SD 48 75. Vast reedbeds and mere below limestone hills, 321 a. Bittern, Bearded Reedling, Shoveler, Garganey, Water Rail, migrant ducks and waders in spring and autumn. Near Silverdale, 8 mls n. of Lancaster, to w. of A6 on minor road via Yealand Redmayne. Car park, information centre, hides. (Warden – Myers Farm, Silverdale, Carnforth, Lancs.) RSPB.

Martin Mere Refuge SD 43 15. Large artificial lake with decoy waterfowl to attract wild ducks and geese, waterfowl gardens, also 262 a. of marshland. Roosting/feeding area for Pink-footed Geese, breeding Ruffs, Dabchicks, Dunlins. 2 mls e. of Southport A565, turning s. at Mere Brow. From M6 by interchange 27 (Burscough B5239) and 28 (B5248–A59–A565). Car park, education centre, picnic area by mere, hides, tea room, shop, Adm. fee. (Curator, Wildfowl Trust, Martin Mere, Burscough, Nr Ormskirk, Lancs.) Wildfowl T.

Morecambe Bay SD 47 67. Vast expanse of estuarine mudflats, part of internationally important wader/wildfowl wintering area and spring assembly ground. 6000 a. Great flocks of Knots, Sanderlings, Dunlins, Curlews, Bar-tailed Godwits at high-tide roosts. Hest Bank, 4 mls n. of Morecambe, on w. side of A6. Car park, walk over level-crossing to upper marsh, at or near high tide. (Warden – as for Leighton Moss.) RSPB.

Southport Sanctuary SD 35 20. National Wildfowl Refuge on sand and mudflats, 14,000 a. Wildfowl and waders incl. Pink-footed Geese, massed flocks of Knots, Dunlins and Bar-tailed Godwits at high-tide roost. 2 mls n.e. of Southport on w. side of A565. Viewable from Marshside to Crossens road SD 352 205.

Witton SD 66 28. Woods and parkland, 250 a. Country Park. W. of Blackburn, on n. side of A674. Car park SD 656 277. Entrance Buncer Lane. Blackburn DC.

Wyre/Lune Sanctuary SD 43 52. National Wildfowl Refuge on sand and mudflats, 9000 a. Wildfowl and waders incl. Pink-footed Geese roost, large flocks of Knots, Dunlins and Bar-tailed Godwits at high tide. 8 mls s. of Lancaster on w. side of A588, between Cockerham and Pilling. Best observation point and car park is at Fluke Hall overpass SD 388 500.

MERSEYSIDE

Eastham Woods SJ 36 82. Woodland, 71 a. Country Park. 9 mls n.w. of Chester, between A41 and Eastham Ferry on R. Mersey. Wirral MDC.

Formby Dunes SD 28 08. Sand-dunes and foreshore, 450 a. Oystercatcher, Ringed Plover, other waders, 9 mls s. of Southport A565, w. side of Formby. NT.

Hilbre Island SJ 17 87. High-tide island; at low tide surrounded by mudflats. Vast flocks of Oystercatchers, Knots, Dunlins and other shore birds from autumn to spring. Bird Observatory. Offshore adjacent to West Kirby and Hoylake A540.

Thurstaston Common SJ 24 85. Commonland, 175 a. Views over the Dee estuary. 2 mls s.e. of West Kirby, ½ ml n. of Thurstaston, on e. side of A540. NT.

Wirral Way SJ 28 77. 12 mls disused railway track, 7 mls of which gives views of Dee estuary mudflats. Badgers. Wigeon, Goldeneye and other ducks, flocks of Knots, Dunlins, Bar-tailed Godwits. Access at Burton SJ 30 75 or Neston SJ 29 77, on w. side of A540. Merseyside Metropolitan CC.

GREATER MANCHESTER

Etherow SJ 97 91. Country Park beside R. Etherow. Dipper, Grey Wagtail, woodland birds. 6 mls e. of Stockport and 2 mls n.e. of Marple, w. of A626.

Haigh Plantations SD 60 08. Woodland, 250 a. Country Park. 2 mls n. of Wigan, n. of B5238, s. of B5239. Wigan MDC.

Lyme Park SJ 96 82. Park and moorland, 1321 a. Large herd of deer. 7 mls s.e. of Stockport, at Disley on s. side of A6. NT/ Stockport MDC.

Animal collections in North West England

Belle Vue Zoo Park

Belle Vue Zoo Park has a general collection of animals, and besides being one of the major zoos in the northwest of England it is the oldest commercial zoo in the British Isles. There are about 650 mammals, birds and reptiles, and a similar number of fish in the aquarium. The Zoo has a good collection of apes and monkeys, big cats, elephants, Hippos and rhinos, Giraffes and antelopes and a particularly good aquarium and reptile house. One of its most modern exhibits is the Tropical River House, and there are daily sealion performances, an unusual feature in British zoos. Although it is part of the extensive Belle Vue entertainment complex, the Zoo is concentrated in one area, and modernisation of many of the animal exhibits during the past few years has made it one of the major attractions of the Manchester region.

The big cats are exhibited in large outdoor enclosures with plenty of trees, grass and shrubbery, which form a natural background for them. This is the only zoo in the heart of a large city with cat enclosures on this scale, and looking at them it is easy to forget that you are in Manchester. You will see Lions, Tigers, Leopards and Pumas here. Lions are still fairly common in Africa but they have disappeared in Asia, except for a small population in the Gir Forest, a reserve in the State of Gujerat in northwestern India. Tigers, once common in India and southeast Asia, have declined in numbers owing to hunting, poaching and the destruction of forest — and with it the disappearance of game animals which are their natural prey. Lions live in family groups, usually composed of an adult male and two or three females with cubs of various ages. Tigers are more solitary, hunting alone or in couples. Leopards, because of the demand for their fur, have decreased greatly in numbers in the wild, both in Africa and Asia. They live in open, rocky scrubland in Africa, either dropping on their prey from trees or hunting in pairs, or even sometimes in larger groups. Pumas, sometimes called Cougars or Mountain Lions, are Leopard-sized cats from South and Central America and the southwestern United States, which prey on deer and smaller animals. In the wild they are not aggressive towards human beings. The Lions, Tigers and Pumas all breed regularly in the Zoo.

A pack of Canadian Timber Wolves can be seen in the Wolf Wood, which is equipped with log-cabin sleeping quarters. Wolves have been hunted by man mercilessly and pointlessly for centuries, although they are not aggressive towards humans unless attacked. There is an authentic case of a couple of prospectors, hopelessly lost in the forests of Ontario, who met a pack of Wolves and, although the Wolves were obviously hungry, they led the two people back to the main road, involving a trek of several hours.

The Aquarium and Reptile House is one of the most modern buildings in the Zoo. The Aquarium contains some 50 tanks exhibiting a fine collection of tropical fish, both marine and freshwater, and the dioramas of coral reefs in the tropics are particularly attractive. The small tanks in the first hall are for tropical freshwater fishes, such as angels, Swordtails, Neon Tetras and black mollies, as well as rarer species like the pompadours, Electric Eels and elephant fish. The second hall is entitled 'Fishes of the Coral Seas', and here you can see some of the most colourful fish in the collection, including the Pennant, puffer fish, Clown Trigger, bat and lion Fish. In the third hall, British fish are displayed, both freshwater and marine. Then comes a row of tanks displaying fish which live near the water surface in search of insect food, or which come out of the water on to dry land, such as the Climbing Perch and the mudskipper. These represent the transitional stage in evolution of fish to amphibian.

Linked to the aquarium is the Reptile House, and in the first section you can see the large snakes, such as pythons and Boa Constrictors, and a good collection

The rarest monkey at Belle Vue, the Lion-tailed Macaque of India.

Belle Vue Zoo Park. **Address** Hyde Road, Manchester. **Telephone** Manchester 223 1331. **Open** 10.00–dusk summer and winter. **Guide-book. Catering** licensed and unlicensed restaurants, self-service cafeteria, snack bar, kiosk. Zoo shop. **Guided tours** by arrangement. **Acreage** 35. **Car** 2½ mls s.e. of city centre on A57 Hyde road. **Bus** stops outside Belle Vue main entrance, routes 33, 34, 53, 125, 204, 205, 206, 210, 211. **Train** to Manchester Piccadilly (3 mls). **Taxis** available. **Other facilities** first-aid post, lost children's room, children's playground. Public **not allowed** to feed animals.

A female Rhesus Monkey and her baby.

of desert monitors, iguanas and other lizards. The main hall is landscaped as a tropical forest, with rocks covered in creepers, dense foliage and a waterfall flowing into a pool. As you cross the bridge over the pool, you see crocodiles and alligators. It was here, for the first time in a European zoo, that the Mississippi Alligators mated and laid eggs, although the eggs proved to be infertile. Alligators require plenty of dry land with cover to induce them to reproduce, and the temperature of both water and air is also important. If either is too cold, the alligators become sluggish. In the last section, the smaller reptiles are exhibited, such as small lizards and snakes, tree frogs and chameleons. The rarest species here are the Indian Gavial, a narrow-snouted crocodile, and the Galapagos Tortoise, a giant tortoise from those islands. Other species which have bred are the Royal Python and the Thailand Water Lizard. The Zoo was also the first in Europe to breed the Indian Cobra in 1953.

On the Bear Terraces you can see the Polar Bears, Asiatic Black Bears displaying the distinctive white V on their chests, a characteristic of this species from the Himalayan region, and two races of the Brown Bear — the European Brown Bear and the Syrian Bear. These two are similar in appearance, but the Syrian Bear is a much lighter creamy-brown colour. Both races are now rare in the wild but they breed readily in captivity. The Polar Bears have bred here, which is a less usual occurrence in zoos, and they are now rare in the wild. Facing the bears are the Marsupial Paddocks, exhibiting the Great Grey Kangaroo, one of the largest of the kangaroo family, and two groups of wallabies, the Dama and Bennett's Wallabies. The latter breed here regularly.

There are two elephants in the Elephant House, both females from Ceylon. There are two races of elephant in Ceylon, both of which are now rare. Unlike the Indian race, they are usually tuskless. Also in this house is an indoor pool for Hippopotamus, heated in winter, with an outdoor summer pool. Flanking one side of the Elephant House is a range of aviaries called 'Birdcage Walk', where you can see a good collection of parrots, parrakeets, cockatoos, lories and conures, all of which are members of the parrot family.

The Tropical River House, completed in 1970, displays tropical birds, both in aviaries and flying free, three pool enclosures for aquatic mammals and more aviaries for birds. When you enter, you see an exhibit for wading birds such as ibises and spoonbills and these share the aviary with laughing jay thrushes, touracos and Crowned Pigeons which have bred here. The main part of the building introduces you to the twilight conditions found beneath the canopy of a dense tropical forest, where sunlight seldom penetrates. Two large pools are divided by a central raised path, and on one side you look down at a pool containing Pygmy Hippopotamus, the smaller cousin of the Common Hippopotamus in the Elephant House. In the background, cleverly simulated rockwork with plants growing out of it adds to the impression of jungle. On the opposite side of the path is an enclosure for Malayan Tapirs which have a pool fed by a waterfall. Both Pygmy Hippos, which frequent the rivers of West Africa, and tapirs, which live in the jungles of southeast Asia, spend much of their time on dry land to feed, but both are good swimmers and never stray far from water. Beyond these are two more pools for aquatic animals, such as Capybaras, the largest of the rodents, which live in the jungle rivers of South America. At the end of the house is a large aviary for Indian Hornbills, which are fruit-eaters.

The Monkey House has both indoor and outdoor cages where you can see a selection of African and Asiatic species, such as the Rhesus Monkey and the Lion-tailed Macaque of India, and the Mona, Patas, Green, Sykes' and Diana Monkeys of Africa. The Lion-tailed Macaque is the rarest of these in the wild, and both it and the Diana Monkeys breed here regularly. Do not miss the large gibbon cage elsewhere in the Zoo, in which a fine group of these tree-dwelling apes can be seen swinging acrobatically. Gibbons come from southeast Asia and they are the smallest of the man-like apes. The Great Ape House contains all three of the largest species — Gorillas, Orang utans and Chimpanzees. Seen from a central viewing area, the apes can pass from their outdoor enclosures via underground passages into their heated indoor quarters, seen through armour-plated glass. The Lowland Gorillas and Orang utans, from Central and West

Africa, and Borneo and Sumatra respectively, are now both endangered in the wild. The groups of Orang utans and Chimpanzees here have bred, and the Zoo is hoping that the Gorillas will follow suit when they reach maturity.

The Giraffe, Camel and Rhino House contains two races of Giraffe, the Masai or Vine-leaf Giraffe, so called because of the pattern of its coat, and the Reticulated Giraffe, whose pattern is bolder. These breed here regularly. You can see both the Bactrian Camel, a heavily built animal of central Asia used for centuries as a beast of burden, and the more slenderly built Arabian Camel or Dromedary, which is still used both for riding and as a pack animal. The rhinos here are Black Rhinoceros, one of the two-horned species of Africa which is now rare in the wild although it breeds fairly frequently in zoos.

The Small Mammal House is divided into two sections — the first containing animals which are active in daytime, such as squirrels, coatis and agoutis, and the second for nocturnal animals which are mainly active at night, or at dawn and dusk. These include galagos or bushbabies, lorises, Kinkajous, armadillos, Pottos and Tree Porcupines. The rarest of the animals here is the Potoroo, a species of rat-kangaroo which is fairly common in Tasmania but rare in Australia, being confined to the extreme southwestern part of Western Australia. This little animal is about a foot long and it proceeds in a series of zigzag bounds. It is nocturnal and, like the kangaroos, it is a marsupial, carrying its young in a pouch. On the Rocky Mountain enclosure is a herd of Barbary Sheep, in fact a species of wild goat from North Africa. There is also an otter pool, where these active animals can be seen swimming expertly. There are 16 species of otter, some of which live singly or in pairs in the wild, while others live in family groups.

The hoofed animals in the Zoo are mainly to be seen in the Paddock Range and Ruminant Enclosure. Among others you may see here are Père David's Deer, a species of swamp deer from China, first discovered by a French missionary and brought to Europe before it became extinct in the wild in 1900; the Sika Deer, of which there are two races here, the Japanese Sika and the Formosan Sika, the latter being a rare species in the wild in Taiwan; Fallow Deer, natives of Asia and Europe; and the Brindled Gnu or Wildebeeste of Africa. The Ruminant Enclosure contains Ankole Cattle, a domestic species from Uganda; American Bison; Llamas and Alpacas, both South American members of the camel family; and Burchell's Zebra, two races of which are still found in Africa. The zebras here are regular breeders.

There are paddocks for flightless birds including Ostriches which are natives of Africa, and Emus which come from Australia and New Guinea. Smaller than these are the rhea of South America and the kiwi of New Zealand. All the members of this group depend on the father to care for the newly hatched chicks, and the Emus in the Zoo breed quite regularly. The Square Pool enclosure exhibits a mixture of water birds, including pelicans, Black Swans, an Australian species, and several kinds of goose and duck. The bird of prey aviary contains White-headed Vultures, and the pheasant aviaries, facing the Paddock Range, have a collection of pheasants, including some rare species, such as the Chinese Monal, Swinhoe's Pheasant and Elliot's Pheasant. You can also see some less rare but equally colourful pheasants here, including Golden, Silver, Lady Amherst's and Reeves' Pheasants. All pheasants are natives of Asia and the game Pheasant familiar in this country was introduced, possibly by the Romans. There is a penguin pool, and in the crane pen you can see the Sarus Crane, Lilford's Crane, the graceful little Demoiselle Crane and Crowned Cranes as well as guineafowl, peafowl and curassows.

Do not miss the Sealion House where the sealions perform daily, both in a large swimming pool and on dry land. Lastly, a variety of domestic animals can be seen in the Children's Zoo and Farm.

The Zoo was founded by Mr John Jennison, who bought the Belle Vue Inn, having prospered as the owner of a tea garden at Stockport where he exhibited a small collection of monkeys and parrots. He took his animals with him when he moved to Belle Vue, and the Zoo was opened in 1836. Two years later he bought most of the animals in the Broughton Zoo at Salford when it closed down. At that time Belle Vue was still in the country, but Jennison foresaw that

Père David's Deer may be seen at Belle Vue; the species has been extinct in the wild for over three-quarters of a century.

Chapman's Zebra: the stripes of zebras break up the animal's outline, and camouflage it from its predators.

there would be opportunities to expand. He bought more land, and when the North Western Railway to Manchester was opened, Belle Vue had its own station, which brought more visitors to the Zoo. As Jennison's business prospered, he acquired cattle, his own brewery and printing works, his own gas works and even an ice-storage business. He also built an electrical generating plant before electricity was brought to Manchester. The Jennison family sold out in 1925 and a few years ago the company was bought by Trust Houses Forte Ltd. Over the years, the Zoo has maintained its position as one of the best collections in the north·of England, and it was one of the first zoos in the British Isles to keep its monkeys in the fresh air instead of in over-heated houses. In spite of atmospheric pollution, the health record of the animals at Belle Vue has remained good, and the most recent animal buildings and enclosures compare favourably with those in other major British zoos.

Blackpool Tower Aquarium and Zoo

The Aquarium in Blackpool Tower is one of the largest and best in the country, and it exhibits more than 225 species of fish, with 2,000 fish in all. The collection is noted for its British marine species, and for fish from the coral seas. There is also an excellent collection of freshwater fish, including both cold water and tropical. The Tower Company has its own boat which goes on collecting trips each year to the waters around the Isle of Man, and the results can be seen in some enormous seawater tanks here. Blackpool has seawater mains, and the marine tanks are supplied from these.

The Aquarium was opened in 1874, 20 years before the Tower itself was built on top of it. There is also a small zoo on the top floor, also opened in 1874, where a selection of mammals and birds is on view. Having paid admission to the Tower, there is no extra charge for the Aquarium and Zoo.

Blackpool Tower Aquarium and Zoo. **Address** Promenade, Blackpool. **Telephone** Blackpool 25252. **Open** 10.00–22.00 summer, closed in winter. **Catering** self-service cafeteria, snack bar, kiosk. **Car** s. of North Pier, on Promenade (A584). **Bus** direct to Tower. **Train** to Blackpool ($\frac{1}{4}$ ml). **Taxis** available. Public **not allowed** to feed animals.

Blackpool Zoological Gardens

Blackpool Zoological Gardens were opened to the public in 1973, and they already have an interesting general collection of animals, including Lions, Tigers, elephants, rhinoceroses, Gorillas, sealions, hoofed animals and a magnificent tropical bird house. The Zoo is the most modern in Great Britain, and one of the major collections in the northwest. The enclosures are planned on a zoo-geographical basis, with animals from each part of the world grouped together. There are sections for American animals, and those from Europe, Asia and Australasia. The 32 acres developed at present are only the first phase of a much larger area, and the geographical divisions may not be as obvious as they will be in the future. Most zoos in the world are financed by public funds, except in Great Britain where municipal zoos are the exception rather than the rule. But this zoo is owned by Blackpool Corporation, and a special Act of Parliament had to be passed to enable it to be built.

Not far from the entrance is the Children's Section, with Shetland and Gotland Ponies, calves, lambs and goats. There is a 'village pool' and green for Chinese Geese and waterfowl, and next to this is the Animal Nursery, where young animals and zoo orphans which need special care are kept. Naturally, the population here varies from time to time, but some other small animals are often kept here, such as Kinkajous, squirrel monkeys and Aldabra Tortoises. The Kinkajou is an agile animal adept at climbing, which comes from Mexico and Central and South America. It eats small animals, fruit and insects, hunting mainly at night, and it is unusual among carnivorous animals in having a prehensile tail, which is strong enough for it to hang by at seven weeks old. Squirrel monkeys are small, living in troops in the tropical forests of South America. Aldabra Tortoises are of the rare species of giant tortoise found on Aldabra Island in the Indian Ocean.

Blackpool Municipal Zoological Gardens. **Address** East Park Drive, Blackpool. **Telephone** Blackpool 65027. **Open** 10.00–dusk summer and winter. **Guide-book**. **Catering** licensed restaurant, self-service cafeteria, snack bar, kiosk. Zoo shop. **Guided tours** by arrangement. **Acreage** 32. **Car** on approaches to Blackpool follow signs 'Zoo'. **Bus** 21 direct to Zoo from town centre, or 23 from Talbot Road bus station to Victoria Hospital, then $\frac{1}{2}$ ml to Zoo. **Train** to Blackpool ($2\frac{1}{2}$ mls). **Other facilities** first-aid post, push-chairs and wheel-chairs. Public **not allowed** to feed animals.

One of the most interesting of the Asiatic animals here is the Arabian Gazelle, a graceful animal whose natural range is Arabia, Syria, Palestine down to Aden, and some of the Red Sea islands. It is a denizen of treeless desert and mountain, and it has been hunted almost to the point of extinction by motorised parties of soldiers and oil men. Blackpool is one of only 11 zoos in the world where this species can be seen. Gazelles in the wild live in small herds or family groups, expectant females forming their own herd to raise their young. Both sexes have horns, and the gestation period is about six months. The gazelles are breeding regularly in the Zoo, and there should be a fine herd here in a few years' time. Another Asiatic species shown is the Bactrian Camel, the heavily built two-humped cousin of the Arabian Camel or Dromedary. The Bactrian Camel comes from central Asia, where it is used for transport across desert and semi-arid regions. It has a thick coat which is shed in summer.

The largest Asiatic species of cat is the Tiger, and the ones exhibited here, next to the Lions, are Bengal Tigers. Tigers used to be common in India, and 30 years ago it was estimated that there were 50,000 in the country, but hunting, poaching, and the destruction of their forest habitat in order to graze cattle has reduced their numbers drastically. It is now estimated that there are only about 1,500 Tigers in the whole of the Indian sub-continent, and they are now protected by law in a number of reserves. Tigers love water and are good swimmers. Their favourite prey is wild pig and they also eat deer and, occasionally, fish.

The largest of the Asiatic apes is the Orang utan, found only in Borneo and Sumatra. It is a solitary animal in the wild, living in dense forest and rarely coming to the ground. The adult male develops enormous cheek growths which almost envelop the head. This is another species which is endangered in the wild, and there are now only about 5,000 left. Orang utans breed fairly regularly in zoos. Another species from southeast Asia is the Siamang, the largest species of gibbon. Gibbons are the smallest of the man-like apes, with short, tailless bodies, short legs and long arms used for swinging through the trees. Siamangs have the ability to expand their voice-boxes, resulting in a piercing cry. These animals can be seen on the gibbon islands, where they are kept in couples. If adult males are kept together they fight, being fiercely jealous of their territory, so in captivity they are segregated in family groups.

Above: Chamois, in the wild a superb climber in its rocky hillside habitat.

Right: Arabian Gazelle, an endangered species of the Middle East.

Below: Doria's Tree Kangaroo from Australasia.

In the Ape House you can see young Lowland Gorillas and Chimpanzees, the anthropoid apes of Africa. Both the Lowland and the Mountain Gorilla are now rare in the wild, and it is only in the past 20 years that they have been bred in zoos. (The only Mountain Gorilla born in a zoo is in Antwerp Zoo.) They are shy, unaggressive animals living in family groups and feeding on plants, leaves, fruit and insects. They build nests at night, the females and young climbing into the low branches of trees, and the heavier males making theirs on the ground. Chimpanzees are gregarious, travelling in loosely knit groups, individual animals often changing their allegiance from one group to another. They are better climbers than Gorillas, but spend a lot of time on the ground.

The Lions are the largest of the African cat species, and they differ from other cats by living in family groups or prides. The Lion is also the only member of the cat family whose young are born with their eyes open. Lions were once common all over Asia Minor and India as well as Africa, but in Asia they are now found only in the Gir Forest in northwest India, where they are protected. In the wild it is the lioness who does the hunting, the male Lion merely appearing at the kill and taking first pick at the carcass.

The African hoofed animals in the Zoo include the White-tailed Gnu or Black Wildebeeste, an antelope found in South Africa though now rare, having been extensively killed for meat in the nineteenth century. They are aggressive animals, and both sexes carry horns. There are two species of zebra here, the Grévy's Zebra, which is the largest species, found in Ethiopia, Somaliland and northern Kenya, and the Damara, or Chapman's Zebra, a much smaller animal with 'shadow' stripes between the main stripes on its creamy-brown coat. There is also a fine group of Barbary Sheep, a species from the Atlas Mountains in North Africa which breeds regularly in the Zoo. In fact, these are wild goats, living solitary lives except in the breeding season, when they congregate in

herds. The males are distinguished by their heavy horns and long mane of hair on the neck and chest.

The animals of the American continent to be seen here include the American Bison, once numbered in millions on the grassy plains of the United States, which was almost wiped out by hunters before legislation to protect it saved it in the 1920s. Since then, the bison have increased in reserves and they are quite commonly exhibited in zoos. An American representative of the cat family here is the Puma, the largest of this family in the New World. Its range is from British Columbia to southern South America. Its natural prey is the agouti, peccary, deer and monkeys. They are not aggressive in the wild towards man, and there is no authentic case of a man being attacked by a Puma. You can also see Llamas and tapirs here, Llamas being a New World member of the camel family. Llamas have been used as beasts of burden for 1,000 years in their native Peru and Bolivia. They breed regularly in the Zoo. The tapirs here are the Brazilian species, a native of Columbia and Venezuela, Paraguay and Brazil. It lives in wooded grassland near rivers, feeding at night on aquatic plants. Young tapirs have broken horizontal stripes and spots on their bodies, which disappear in about eight months. There is a thriving group of Californian Sealions, which are found around the northern Pacific islands as well as along the western coastline of America. Sealions differ from seals in having external ears, and the hind flippers turned forwards so that they can move across land, impossible for seals.

There is a good collection of marsupials, or pouched animals, in the Australian area, and you can see Bennett's Wallabies, Doria's Tree Kangaroos and Long-nosed Rat Kangaroos. The 11 species of wallaby are medium-sized kangaroos found in Australia, Tasmania and New Guinea, where they inhabit woodland and coastal scrub. Tree kangaroos, found in northern Australia and New Guinea, divide their time between the ground and the lower branches of trees, which they climb in order to feed and sleep. They normally climb down a tree tail first, but can take great leaps if disturbed. The Long-nosed Rat Kangaroo, or Potoroo, lives in thick grassland and dense low scrub, favouring damp places. It is Rabbit-sized, sometimes hopping like the kangaroo, otherwise moving on all fours.

A European animal not often seen in British zoos is the Chamois, the wild goat of the Alps, Apennines, Carpathians and Asia Minor. This is an expert climber, frequenting mountains on and above the tree line. It is much less common than it used to be, though not as rare as the Alpine Ibex. The coat is light brown in summer, turning dark brown or black in winter.

Near the Children's Section you will see the first of the bird exhibits in the Zoo. There is an aviary for Budgerigars, and next to it another for macaws and Silver Pheasants. Budgerigars are grass parrakeets from Australia, one of the small members of the parrot family. In the wild, the natural colour of their plumage is green, the blue variety having been bred in domestication. Macaws are the largest members of the parrot family, from South America, where they live in flocks in tropical forest. The cranes in the Zoo include the Crowned Crane, with its halo of stiff golden feathers. The East African race has a grey neck, and the West African race a black neck. You can also see Demoiselle Cranes, the smallest of the crane family, which is found in southeastern Europe and central Asia. It winters in North Africa and India. On the lake you will find flamingos, pelicans and a variety of ducks and geese, including Blue-winged Geese, Emperor Geese, Andean Geese and Red-breasted Geese. There are also Black Swans from Australia, and Black-necked Swans, which are otherwise white, from South America. The ducks exhibited include the Carolina or Wood Duck, from the eastern United States and southern Canada, and the Mandarin Duck of eastern Asia, which has been introduced into this country and is well established in southern England and Scotland. The two species of penguin here are Humboldt's Penguin, from the western coasts of South America, and the South African Black-footed Penguin.

The most colourful tropical birds will be found in the Toucan House and the Free Flight Bird Hall. Toucans feed on small fruits and berries, insects and eggs. Their large bills are light in weight but very strong. Food is seized in the bill and the toucan tosses its head upward, throwing the food backwards into its throat.

The Free Flight Bird Hall is a remarkable construction, made of heavy PVC supported by air pressure, and it is the only bird house of its kind in Europe. Inside, it is delightfully landscaped with rockwork, and a pool and waterfall to represent a tropical valley. There are about 300 species here, including wading birds, such as the Scarlet Ibis and the bittern, rails, Crowned Pigeons, fruit pigeons, doves, touracos, Rothschild's Mynahs — a rare species — trumpeters, Purple Gallinules, whydahs, Fairy Bluebirds and pittas. One of these, Van den Bosch's Pitta, breeds here regularly. You will also see a great variety of tropical and sub-tropical plants growing in this hall, gathered from Mexico, Costa Rica, Brazil, Ethiopia, Madagascar, South Africa, Australia, Tasmania, India and Polynesia.

Large numbers of trees have been planted in the Zoo, labelled with their names for those interested. On the right of the Zoo entrance is the main station for the miniature railway with its scale model engine, which runs through woodland areas of the Zoo, past some of the animal enclosures. The central station is near the Llama and Tapir House, with a second station near the Toucan House. You may get off the train at either of these points. The Zoo is still expanding, and for regular visitors to Blackpool a return visit to this interesting collection will always be rewarding.

Bolton Museum Aquarium

The Aquarium exhibits freshwater fish, mainly British and European species. Among the fish you can see here are roach, rudd, carp, Tench, bream, Perch and Pike, and an impressively large eel. There are also some tropical fish, including Tinfoil Barbs, Oscars and Jack Dempsey, and there is a small collection of reptiles and amphibians. These include terrapins, tortoises, salamanders, iguanas and other lizards, pythons, frogs and toads. One interesting exhibit is the Axolotl, the larval form of the Tiger Salamander. One mammal, the gerbil, is also exhibited.

There are plans in the not-too-distant future to have a marine exhibit, with both vertebrate and invertebrate species (animals with and without a backbone). Evening lectures on a variety of subjects are held for Friends of the Museum and Art Gallery. The Aquarium, operated by the local authority, was opened in 1947 and admission is free.

Cannon Aquarium and Vivarium

The emphasis here is on reptiles, of which 16 species are exhibited, rather than on fish. The main attractions are the Dwarf Crocodiles from the Congo, and American Alligators, both of which are rare in the wild. The alligators have mated successfully, producing a clutch of eggs, although no young have been reared as yet. The mating took place in March 1969, and the eggs were laid at the end of June. This is an unusual occurrence in captivity, and elsewhere it has been achieved only in Belle Vue Zoo, Manchester, in recent years. The Aquarium and Vivarium were opened in 1964 in Manchester Museum, which is operated by Manchester University, and admission is free.

Curraghs Wildlife Park

Curraghs Wildlife Park was opened in 1965 by the Isle of Man Government. Twenty-four species of mammal are exhibited, among which the rarest is Père David's Deer, which breed here regularly. You can also see Red Deer, Sika Deer, South American tapirs, Llamas, and some smaller mammals, including White-

Bolton Museum Aquarium. **Address** Bolton Museum, Civic Centre, Bolton. **Telephone** Bolton 22311 ext. 384. **Open** 10.00–18.00 Mon–Sat, summer and winter. **Admission free. Guidebook. Catering** snack bar. **Guided tours** for school parties only, by arrangement. **Car** drive to Bolton city centre. **Train** to Bolton ($\frac{1}{2}$ ml). **Taxis** available. No pets. Public **not allowed** to feed exhibits.

The Cannon Aquarium and Vivarium. **Address** The Manchester Museum, University of Manchester, Manchester. **Telephone** Manchester 273 3333. **Open** 10.00–17.00 Mon–Sat (except Wed 10.00–21.00) summer and winter. **Admission free. Guide-book. Guided tours** by arrangement. **Car** 1 ml s.e. of city centre on Oxford Road. **Bus** from city centre. **Train** to Manchester Piccadilly, or Manchester Victoria (1 ml). **Taxis** available. Public **not allowed** to feed exhibits.

Curraghs Wildlife Park. **Address** Ballaugh, I.O.M. **Telephone** Sulby 323. **Open** 10.00–18.00 Good Friday–Easter Monday and 4th May–28th Sept. Closed in winter. **Guide-book. Catering** cafeteria. Gift shop. **Acreage** 26. **Car** from Douglas ($17\frac{1}{2}$ mls) follow T.T. route to 18th milestone (4 mls from Ramsey). **Bus** from Douglas or Ramsey to Park. No pets. Public **not allowed** to feed animals.

Opposite: two buck Eland in conflict at Knowsley Safari Park.

throated Capuchins, a sturdy monkey species from tropical South America, Kinkajous, chinchillas and Red-necked Wallabies. There are nearly 800 birds of 90 species, including numerous species of waterfowl.

This is an open-air zoo in pleasant surroundings.

Hesketh Park Aviary

The Hesketh Park Aviary, which is operated by the Local Authority, exhibits peafowl, pheasants, waterfowl, parrots, canaries, Budgerigars, mynahs and other tropical birds — about 50 species altogether. There has been considerable success in breeding peafowl. Entry is free.

Hesketh Park Aviary. **Address** Hesketh Park, Southport, Merseyside. **Telephone** Southport 34024. **Open** 09.00—dusk summer and winter. **Admission free. Catering** self-service cafeteria. **Acreage** ⅓. **Car** to Park Road 1 ml n.e. of town centre on A565 Preston Road. **Bus** stops 150 yds from Park. **Train** to Southport (1 ml). **Taxis** available. **Other facilities** children's playground. Public allowed to feed birds with own food.

Knowsley Safari Park

Opened by Lord Derby and Mr Jimmy Chipperfield in 1971, this Safari Park has six drive-through reserves arranged on a five-mile circuit. You can see Bengal Tiger, about 40 Lions, Cheetahs, 70 baboons with three species mixed together, and herds of large African game animals in mixed groups. These include Giraffe, zebra, Eland, kudu, gnu, elephant, White Rhinoceros, Hippopotamus, and Ostriches, cranes and waterfowl. You can also see Red Deer and large herds of camel and buffalo. There is also a dolphinarium and a children's zoo. The Cheetahs here have bred.

Knowsley Safari Park. **Address** Prescot, Merseyside. **Telephone** Liverpool 426 2167. **Open** 10.00—18.00 summer, 10.00—16.00 winter. **Guide-book. Catering** licensed self-service cafeteria, kiosks. Gift shops. **Acreage** 450. **Car** 8 mls e. of Liverpool off A58 at Prescot. **Other facilities** pets' corner, dolphinarium, children's amusement park. Public **not allowed** to feed animals.

Lowther Wildlife Country Park

The Park was opened in 1969, and you can see here a good collection of deer, old breeds of cattle, sheep and goats, a waterfowl lake, some small mammals, members of the parrot family and some cranes at liberty. The emphasis is on British and European animals, with some introduced species and exotic waterfowl added to the waterfowl collection. The Red Deer here are descended from the herd originally enclosed in the Park when Edward I granted a licence to Sir Hugh de Louther to enclose 200 acres of land to make a deer park, in 1283. You can also see Fallow Deer, the Formosan and Japanese races of the Sika Deer, and Chinese Water Deer. The old English domestic breeds are Longhorn and Highland Cattle, Manx Loghtan, St Kilda and Jacob Sheep, and Lord Bagot Goats.

The wild British mammals here are the Red Fox and Scottish Wild Cat, both of which breed in the Park, the Badger, European Otter, Polecat and Beech Marten, a species seldom exhibited in this country. There are also some European Wild Boar, Mouflon which are the wild sheep of Corsica and Sardinia and Wolves, which are still found wild in parts of Europe.

Snowy Owls and Eagle Owls are represented and they breed here. The decoy pond exhibits eight species of goose and 18 species of ducks and their allies. You can also see Black Swans from Australia, and Rosy and Chilean Flamingos. Common Cranes, Sarus Cranes and Demoiselle Cranes are at liberty in the Park, and in the woodland walk there are aviaries showing parrots, parrakeets, cockatoos, lories, conures and rosellas. Also at liberty here are free-flying macaws.

The Lowther family, whose head is Lord Lonsdale, has lived in north Westmorland since the reign of Henry II, and the ruins of Lowther Castle can be seen in the Park. There are ancient oak, beech and sycamore trees, and you have magnificent views of the Lakeland fells to the west and of the Pennines to the east.

Lowther Wildlife Country Park. **Address** Hackthorpe, Nr Penrith, Cumbria. **Telephone** Hackthorpe 392. **Open** 10.00–17.00 April–mid Oct (late closing July and Aug 18.00), closed in winter. **Guide-book. Catering** self-service cafeteria, kiosk. Gift shop, garden centre. **Guided tours** by arrangement. **Acreage** 130. **Car** 4 mls s. of Penrith on A6. **Bus** long distance and local buses from Penrith to Kendal stop near entrance. **Train** to Penrith (4½ mls). Public allowed to feed some animals.

Marine Biological Laboratory

The Aquarium, operated by the Department of Marine Biology at the University of Liverpool, exhibits marine species found in the waters around the Isle of Man. The size of the collection of fish and invertebrates (animals without backbones) varies according to availability. The Aquarium was opened in 1887, and is thus one of the oldest in the country. Entry is free.

Marine Biological Laboratory. **Address** Port Erin, I.O.M. **Telephone** Port Erin 83 2027. **Aquarium open** 10.00–17.00 Mon–Fri summer and winter. **Admission free. Car** to Breakwater, Port Erin. **Bus** to Port Erin. **Taxis** available. Public **not allowed** to feed exhibits.

Marineland Oceanarium and Aquarium

Marineland was opened by Morecambe and Heysham Corporation in 1963. It consists of an outdoor dolphinarium, with Bottle-nosed Dolphins, and outdoor pools for sealions, Grey Seals and penguins. From mid-May until mid-October there are daily performances by the dolphins and the sealions, but all the exhibits are on view during winter. Indoors, there is an excellent aquarium, with 40 tanks displaying cold freshwater and tropical freshwater fish, tropical marine and local marine fish. There are also two enclosures for alligators and turtles, and a reptilium containing various lizards, such as monitors, iguanas and tegus.

Marineland Oceanarium and Aquarium. **Address** Stone Jetty, Morecambe, Lancs. **Telephone** Morecambe 414727. **Open** 10.00–19.00 summer, 10.00–17.00 winter. **Guide-book. Catering** licensed restaurant (summer only), self-service cafeteria. Zoo shop. **Guided tours** by arrangement. **Acreage** 2. **Car** to Stone Jetty opposite Morecambe station. **Bus** stops 2 mins' walk from Aquarium. **Train** to Morecambe Promenade, station opposite Aquarium. **Taxis** available on Promenade. Public **not allowed** to feed exhibits.

Martin Mere Wildfowl Refuge

Martin Mere was opened by the Wildfowl Trust on 1st March 1975, with over 1,000 individual birds of 76 species and sub-species, illustrating all the tribes of water-

Martin Mere Wildfowl Refuge. **Address** Burscough, Ormskirk, Lancs. **Telephone** Burscough 895181. **Open** 09.30–18.30 (last admission 17.30) summer, 09.30–dusk winter. **Guidebook. Catering** light refreshments. Shop and information centre. **Acreage** 363. **Car** 1¾ mls w. of A59 Liverpool–Preston road at Burscough Bridge station towards Mere Brow (Redcat Lane). **Bus** nearest stop 1½ mls. **Train** to New Lane station (½ ml) or to Burscough Bridge (1½ mls) or to Burscough Junction (2 mls). **Other facilities** Education Department with staff and Field Study Centre, special observation hides, wheel-chairs. No pets. Public allowed to feed most birds.

Clown Triggerfish at Marineland.

Muncaster Castle and Bird Gardens. **Address** Ravenglass, Cumbria. **Telephone** Ravenglass 614. **Open** 14.00–17.00 April–Oct, Sun, Tues, Wed and Thurs, closed in winter. **Guide-book. Catering** unlicensed restaurant, self-service cafeteria, snack bar, kiosk, Gift shop. **Acreage** 77. **Car** 6 mls s.e. of Gosforth on A595 near Ravenglass. Free car park. **Bus** 13 Millom–Whitehaven. **Train** to Ravenglass (1 ml). Public **not allowed** to feed birds.

fowl. Special emphasis is placed on European species, although some exotic waterfowl endangered in the wild are also here, including Hawaiian Geese, Hawaiian Duck, Cereopsis or Cape Barren Geese, Laysan Teal and White-winged Wood Duck.

There is a wild refuge with a marsh and a large lake adjacent to the collection, and this is visited by several thousand wild Pink-footed Geese, over 2,000 Pintail and Teal, and many other waterfowl. The area is also a popular visiting place for waders, and several thousand Snipe are resident there. The wild refuge can be viewed from a number of hides which have covered approaches. It is hoped that most of the British species of waterfowl will rear their own young in the grounds.

The visitors' centre has a large exhibition illustrating the work of the Trust, as well as subjects of general and local conservation interest. Members of the Trust have free entry.

Muncaster Castle and Bird Gardens

Muncaster Castle Bird Garden was opened in 1970 by Sir William and Lady Pennington-Ramsden in the courtyard and grounds of the Castle. The bird collection is mainly composed of small exotic species, flamingos, waterfowl and pheasants, and one large mammal exhibit for Asiatic Black Bears.

There are several aviaries in the courtyard containing various species of finch, toucans, weavers, Red-crested and Virginian Cardinals, a group of finches from Central and South America and the warmer parts of North America; Paradise Whydahs and Pouter Pigeons. There are several small members of the parrot family, including Cockatiels, Peach-faced Lovebirds, and Ring-necked and Moustached Parrakeets. Macaws and Jacobin Pigeons are at liberty in the grounds, and they have nest-boxes in buildings in the courtyard. There is one small mammal exhibit here, for chipmunks, a small burrowing rodent of North America, with striped sides and cheeks. The colony here has bred, and they are usually active during the day.

Walking through the gardens you come to a lake with two islands for Lesser Flamingos, kept with various waterfowl. The Lesser Flamingo is one of the smaller of the six forms of flamingo, and it nests in the rift valleys of Africa. Flamingos live in huge colonies on brackish or salt lakes, and their oddly shaped beaks are used to scoop up minute organisms out of shallow water. The bill is held upside-down, and the food is siphoned through filters in the beak, the water and soft mud being expelled by the tongue. Flamingo chicks are reared by a group of adult birds in nursery colonies before they join the main flock. The waterfowl here are Snow Geese, Barnacle Geese, Egyptian Geese and two species of ibis, the Sacred Ibis and Wood Ibis. Ibises are wading birds found in most warm climates, with no feathers on their faces and little or no voice. The Sacred Ibis of Africa and Madagascar was venerated by the Ancient Egyptians as the god Thoth, who had the duty of recording the history of all human beings. The Wood Ibis or Wood Stork is a larger bird from Peru, Argentina and the southeastern United States. Next to the lake enclosure you can see a pair of Sarus Cranes, a tall graceful bird from India, Burma and Thailand.

There is a range of aviaries for pheasants, with Golden Pheasants and Reeves' Pheasants from the central Chinese highlands, Silver Pheasants of southeast Asia, Blue-eared Pheasants, and Swinhoe's and Hume's Bar-tailed Pheasants, two species which are now rare in the wild. You can also see here some Abyssinian Ground Hornbills, which feed on snakes, lizards, locusts and grasshoppers in the wild, nesting on rocks or tree stumps near the ground; and Blue-crowned Pigeons from New Guinea. Crowned Pigeons are the largest members of the pigeon family, which used to be hunted as food, but are now protected by law. Beyond these aviaries is a large paddock for rheas, peafowl and guineafowl. The rhea is a flightless bird of South America, where it replaces the Ostrich of Africa. It is much smaller than the Ostrich, and in the wild it eats vegetable matter, with a few insects and small mammals. The male collects a harem of half a dozen hen birds, and when they lay, he drives them off and incubates the eggs himself. The Common Peafowl, a native of India and Ceylon, have been semi-domesticated for centuries, although they are quarrelsome and do not mix well with other birds. The large ornamental feathers used in courtship display to attract the female are elongated tail covert, and not proper tail feathers. Guinea-fowl come from Africa, and are often found in flocks numbering hundreds, which disperse during the breeding season when the birds pair off. There are Demoiselle Cranes in an adjoining paddock, an attractive small species from southern Europe and Asia.

The Asiatic or Himalayan Black Bear ranges in the wild along the Himalayas and eastwards to China. In hot weather it climbs to 12,000 feet, and in winter it descends to lower altitudes or hibernates. This is the largest bear found in Asia (the others being the Sloth Bear and the Honey Bear), but it is considerably smaller than the Polar Bear or the Grizzly. Asiatic Black Bears breed less readily in captivity than Brown Bears; in the wild they give birth to one or two cubs in winter, which are independent by the following autumn, reaching maturity at three years old.

Young Asiatic or Himalayan Black Bear, the largest bear found in Asia.

Southport Aquarium

The Aquarium exhibits freshwater fish, including fish of temperate zones, such as Japanese carp, Goldfish and Shubunkins, and a good collection of tropical fish, including Blind Cave Fish, and piranhas, the carnivorous river fish of South America. You can also see both black and white Axolotls, the larval form of the Tiger Salamander, and there are some clawed frogs and terrapins. There is also a small reptile collection, with some large Burmese pythons, up to 14 feet long,

Boa Constrictors, small crocodiles, Speckled Zonures, Tokay Geckos, Common Lizards and Sand Lizards, which have bred here, and some stick insects. There are some Common Iguanas, which come from tropical South America, where they are eaten, and these have been photographed while laying eggs by the Curator of the Aquarium, a most unusual occurrence. One curious exhibit here is the series of small aquaria in the shape of kettles, teapots, cars, wheelbarrows, lamps and barrels.

Free advice on home aquaria and all aspects of fish-keeping may be obtained here. The Aquarium is owned by the Local Authority, and it was opened in 1964.

Southport Aquarium. **Address** Marine Parade, Southport. **Telephone** Southport 32553. **Open** 09.00–21.00 summer, closed in winter. Information centre for home aquarists. **Car** drive to sea-front for Marine Parade. **Bus** stops ½ ml from Aquarium. **Train** to Southport (¼ ml). **Taxis** available. Public **not allowed** to feed exhibits.

Southport Zoo

The Zoo has a small mixed collection of mammals, birds and reptiles, and a small aquarium. You can see Lions, Pumas, Leopards, a monkey collection, including gibbons, Pig-tailed Macaques, Mandrills and Sykes' Monkey, and some other small mammals such as Crested Porcupines. There is a mixed bird collection with many species of finch, and a parrot house, in which the Grand Eclectus Parrots have bred. There is a Pet's Corner, with domestic animals, including Pygmy Donkeys, and in summer there are pony rides for children.

The Zoo was first opened in 1953, and the present owners, Mr and Mrs Douglas Petrie, have made many improvements in recent years.

Southport Zoo. **Address** Princes Park, Southport, Merseyside. **Telephone** Southport 38102. **Open** 10.00–between 18.00 and 20.00 summer, 10.00–16.30 winter. **Catering** snack bar. Zoo shop. **Car** drive to sea-front – Marine Drive. **Bus** main station ¼ ml from Zoo. **Train** to Southport (½ ml). **Taxis** available. Public allowed to feed animals with food sold in Zoo only.

Winged World

Winged World was opened in 1966 by the Morecambe and Heysham Corporation, and it is well worth a visit for anyone interested in tropical birds. The collection is housed in one building, designed on the same lines as the bird halls in Frankfurt Zoo, with 400 birds of 150 different species. The house is divided into three sections, the first being a series of glass-fronted cabinets displaying hummingbirds and other nectar-eaters. The main hall has 11 large glass-fronted exhibits for tropical soft-billed and insect-eating birds, each exhibit being cleverly and beautifully landscaped with tropical plants and flowers. There is also a large open-fronted exhibit for birds such as spoonbills, ibises and Cattle Egrets. The principle here is that the birds are in a lighted compartment, while the viewing area is darkened, and the birds remain voluntarily in the lighted area. This technique was developed in Antwerp Zoo, and it works.

The third section is a free flight hall, which you enter from the main hall through a bead curtain. Again, there is no other barrier, and birds seldom stray. Amongst a profusion of palms, rubber trees and other exotic plants, there are grackles, starlings, fruit pigeons, flamingos and many other large colourful birds. Among the species which breed here are the Kiskadee Flycatcher, Green Wood Hoopoe, Blue-crowned Motmot, Spurwinged Plover, Yellow-breasted Fruit Pigeon, Bristle-crowned and Andaman Starlings, Painted Bush Quail and Rufous-chinned Laughing Thrush. The rarest species here is Rothschild's Grackle, found only on the island of Bali. Many species have bred here for the first time in captivity in the British Isles, and this is one of the best collections of soft-billed birds in Europe.

Adjacent to Winged World is a small children's zoo, with Llamas, wallabies, monkeys and other small mammals. There are also some aviaries, including European Eagle Owls, which have bred here.

Winged World. **Address** Heysham Head, Heysham and Morecambe, Lancs. **Telephone** Heysham 52391. **Open** 10.00–18.30 summer, 10.00–18.00 winter. **Guide-book**. **Catering** self-service cafeteria, snack bar, kiosk. No catering in winter. Information centre, zoo shop. **Acreage** 29. **Car** 3 mls s.w. of Morecambe on B5273. **Train** to Morecambe (50 yds). **Taxis** available. **Other facilities** first-aid post, lost children's room, children's playground, fairground, rose garden, theatre, Olde English Village, kart racing. Public **not allowed** to feed exhibits.

North East England A. M. TYNAN

After the flat lands of Humberside the rocks of the north pick themselves up and challenge the weather. The Pennine chain, rippling up from Derbyshire, shields Yorkshire and her northern allies from many of the wet winds which blow in from out of the west, creating lush colours in the Lakes that are absent in the northeast. The higher land of the Pennines forms vast tracts of sheep-farming country, bleak moorland, often difficult of access but in many ways far more rewarding for the wildlife enthusiast than the lower terrain, where a softer climate, albeit supporting a greater variety of habitat, allows man to exploit the land more intensively. Wildlife and places of great interest still abound, but somehow one cannot escape from the feeling that they are present by grace and favour; although there are, of course, areas specially set aside – nature reserves, where wildlife takes priority. Great skill in management is needed to keep the right balance in such areas so that the wildlife flourishes whilst people still get the chance to thrill to the sight of it.

The edge of the seemingly barren uplands is gashed by many fast-growing, fast-flowing rivers, the haunt of the Dipper, the Grey Wagtail and the Common Sandpiper. Up these valleys the fertile farmlands of the plains extend their fingers, but the upland flavour persists. In some places the rivers cut narrower valleys through harder rock and the steep sides of these, frequently wooded, present yet another habitat.

Because of the marginal quality of much of the land in northeast England, extensive tracts have been planted with conifers by the Forestry Commission and private organisations. The primary aim of these operations is to produce timber for profit, and in the past scant regard was paid to the wildlife interest. In recent years, however, as the demands of a leisure-rich public have been recognised, greater attention is being paid to amenity, and more diverse woods are attracting a greater variety of birds and mammals. This is probably most true of Northumberland which includes part of the Border Forest, said to be the largest man-made forest in Europe. Dense thickets of Sitka spruce have little appeal for wildlife, but continuous timber operations produce plantings of all ages. Some of these are proving attractive to a number of exciting birds, like the Hen Harrier and Short-eared Owl. Similarly the Grasshopper Warbler, once a rarity, now 'reels' away merrily in dozens of places where the young trees are a few feet high.

Man the hunter, thousands of years ago, probably had little effect on wildlife; but the entry of man the farmer, clearing the forests, undoubtedly began to have an impact. It is becoming more and more evident that there were probably considerably greater numbers of folk around doing their thing than we thought. The same can be said of later periods. Clearly, these forebears of ours used their wit and concentrated on the development of land with potential – down by the rivers, for example, but not so close as to make for problems of drainage. The uplands in those times would probably have been relatively undisturbed. Then, as now, one would take to the hills for peace and quiet. The arrival of the Romans must have given something of a boost to the economy, even if it was relatively shortlived. Their road systems, for instance, allowing easier access to lands at one time thinly populated, must have had just the same kind of effect that a new motorway has upon an area previously avoided by many motorists because of their hatred of congested rural roads. The establishment of a Roman frontier in Northumberland probably set the theme of development in that county for many centuries to come. The Normans and their mediaeval successors were enthusiastic hunters and we owe many of our great forests to their love of the chase. In the northeast of the region there were few, if any; but there were forests a-plenty in the lowland river plains, now alas gone beneath the plough, but still immortalised in some village names like Sutton-on-Forest near York.

The period of greatest impact must surely have been around the Industrial Revolution. Coal had been dug for centuries, but it was not until iron and iron-masters appeared upon the scene demanding coke for furnaces and coal for

A. M. Tynan is Curator of Newcastle University's Hancock Museum of Natural History. He was born and bred in the city of York, studied geology at the University of Reading, and worked at Maidstone Corporation Museum (where he became founder-secretary of the Kent Bird Club), before moving on to the National Museum of Wales at Cardiff. Since his return to northeast England in 1958 he has been much involved in the development of nature trails and countryside museums, and is an active member of the Society for the Promotion of Nature Reserves.

A hill burn cascades through Northumberland's Border Forest.

Opposite: Goredale, one of Yorkshire's limestone dales, with yew and ash trees clinging to the scar.

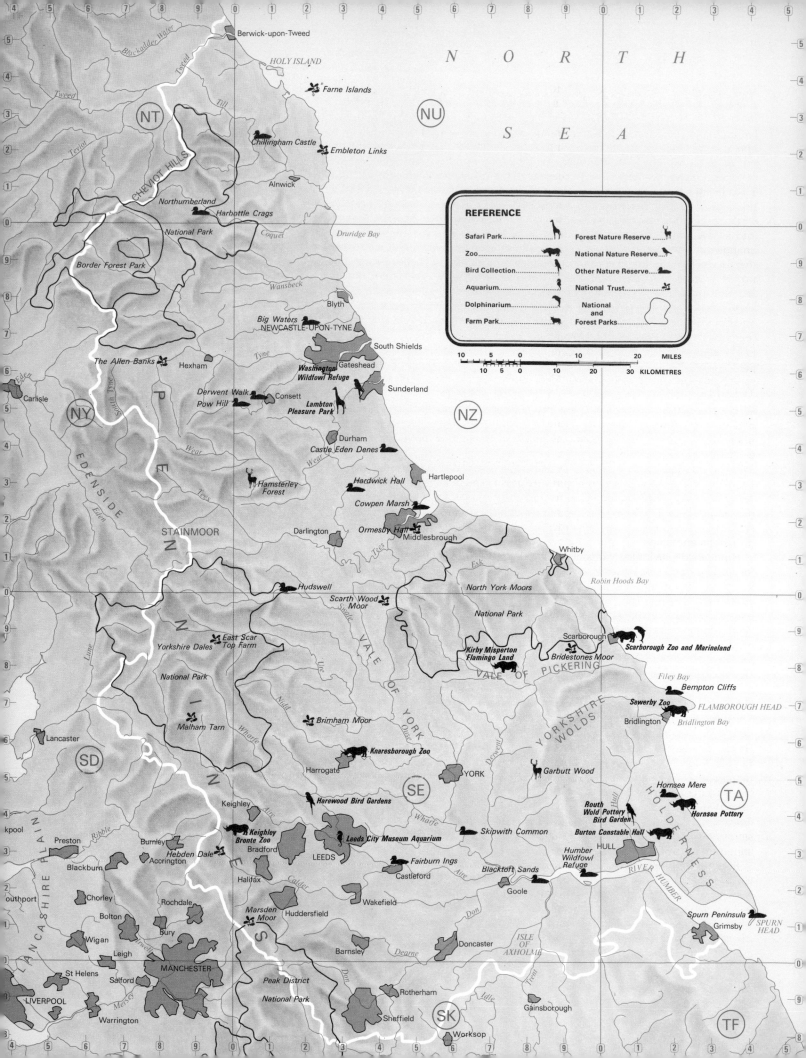

steam boilers that man really began to rive the black diamonds from the bowels of the earth. Although, on a regional scale, the physical impact of mining is fairly restricted, this new-found prosperity stimulated population growth. This, in turn, led to the development of industry and commerce, the intensification of farming and a greater investment in land, bringing radical changes in the landscape and the wildlife.

What we look at today in northeast England is the cumulative effect of all these various human endeavours. The burning question of the moment concerns the future. Does modern society differ dramatically — or indeed at all — from those of the past which created the landscapes we know so well? Have we moved into a new era of discovery, of demands, of pursuits which will in time subtly change our attitudes and inevitably our landscape and its wildlife? If we suspect that this is the case should we, in fact, oppose such changes? I believe we should, not in any cranky fossilising way, but by pointing out the vital truth that the environment in which we live is the product of evolution, a superb and complex system of relationships, each animal, each plant relying for survival upon a multitude of others — relying also upon a system of other precise physical factors, soil and water are examples. The world we live in is not one gigantic accident; it has developed over millions of years, and we tamper with the balance at our peril.

YORKSHIRE AND HUMBERSIDE

Where shall we go? Where shall we start? We are talking about the greater part of the ancient kingdom of Northumbria which once stretched from the Humber to the Forth. The administrators and the bureaucrats have so meddled with long-established boundaries recently that one must forgive confusion in the mind of many an honest lover of his native patch. Our particular patch stretches from Humberside in the south, takes in three Yorkshires, a Cleveland, a Durham and a Northumberland, squeezing in a new-born Tyne and Wear *en route*. Only human beings are worried by all this. No one has yet sent the wildlife a circular, so let's start in the south and wander up towards the Border, making frequent diversions and stops.

Humberside, its industry increasing rapidly as in all major estuaries, is notable for its birds and the fantastic hook-shaped peninsula of Spurn Head with its important Bird Observatory. There is always a special fascination about the coast, but at Spurn, with Lincolnshire skulking in the mists of the Humber, there is an unbelievable sense of mystery, of the battle between land and sea, which is very special. Oystercatchers and Ringed Plovers nest on the shore, and a small colony of Little Terns survives, one of the few in the land. The hinterland of scrub, ditches, reedbeds and dunes boasts all kinds of breeding birds, from Carrion Crows in old thorn bushes to Sedge Warblers in the reeds. The real thrill of Spurn is, of course, the migrants passing through, a list of enormous length including, for instance, 14 or more different species of warbler.

The Wolds, great rolling expanses of chalk hills, build up to the north and west, finding a dramatic final expression in the towering white cliffs of Flamborough Head. The drama is not just in the scenery, for hordes of Guillemots, Razorbills, Puffins, Fulmars and Kittiwakes gather here to breed, while Bempton Cliffs just to the north have England's one and only gannetry. I recall with nostalgic pleasure my childhood holidays at Bridlington, just south of the Head, and the thrilling discovery of white pebbles which abounded on the beach, washed south from Flamborough. No longer did we need to purloin the blackboard chalk to set out our hop-scotch squares! With a bagful of such pebbles one became an important person, a trader with great resources.

Before Flamborough — and what a fabulous place it is for seabirds — lies Hornsea Mere, a great irregular sheet of water, famous for its monstrous Pike and huge flocks of Coot. This miniature Yorkshire broadland with its fringing reedbeds, woods and meadows has much to offer; in summer migrant warblers set up house there, and during the spring and autumn migrations the chances of seeing rare visitors are very real. Ospreys pay an annual visit. The winter months are notable for the great flocks of ducks, some driven in from the sea, which find

Bempton Cliffs, with a snow flurry of its breeding Kittiwakes.

The widely distributed Ringed Plover nests on flat coasts.

Denaby Ings, in Yorkshire: river and winter-flooding water-meadows.

Below: Jay, whose raucous cries are a woodland warning system.

relative peace and quiet in the enclosed waters: Goldeneye, Pintail, Garganey and Gadwall have all been recorded. This is the obvious place to seek the Bittern. Turning inland now, dropping down the chalk escarpment to the Vale of York where the Ouse, gathering in its children Wharfe, Nidd, Ure, Swale, Derwent and the rest, meanders gently through rich farmland, we find the landscape is attractive enough in a peaceful kind of way. Hedgerows abound, also networks of country lanes, long spinneys planted for shelter, and bigger pieces of woodland probably put there originally as cover for Pheasants.

This is a common enough agricultural setting throughout the land, but for a brief, time-filling jaunt into the countryside what could be better? The hedges are mostly old, with deep ditches, and still thickly grown with all the colourful old favourites — Jack-by-the-hedge, dead-nettles, willowherb, celandine, a different splash of colour as month follows summer month. Hedgerows are, in fact, long thin nature reserves. They probably represent some part of the last remnant of the scrub which, many centuries before, man the farmer systematically cleared and burnt to make way for his crops and cattle. The Yellowhammer is a characteristic bird, but finches of all sorts abound, and Magpies nest in the high old thorns, making untidy globes of twigs. The Pheasants share their woods with Jay and Kestrel, Sparrowhawk and Woodpigeon. Beside the rivers are extensive water-meadows, 'ings' they are sometimes called, as at Clifton, on York's north-western boundary. These are pastures of great age, what the botanist calls 'herb-rich', containing not just thoroughbred grasses developed by scientists, but a plethora of attractive flowers of all kinds. In the winter they frequently flood and the temporary lakes make attractive feeding places for all kinds of wading birds and ducks.

The Ice Age left its mark in the Vale, extensive deposits of sand and clays which frequently form low ridges and hills. Some of these areas of acid and poorly drained land have not been taken into farming and remain as extensive tracts of lowland heath — Strensall and Skipwith Commons are good examples. There are occasional patches of birch scrub with rowans and Scots pines, the home of Nightjars. Dominated by heather with scattered marshy hollows they retain a wildlife interest of their own. Vipers are there, and with them Slow-worms and Common Lizards; butterwort and sundew grow in the wet places, with the beautiful rare ultramarine marsh gentian. The Emperor Moth, with eyes painted on all four wings, survives, and every small pond has its fluttering troupes of damselflies, of different bright colours. On a hot day Common Shrews rush about amongst the heather stems, shrieking at one another. What a varied scene, and what a good thing we had an Ice Age!

Male (left) and female Emperor Moth.

Over to the west the hills start, Yorkshire South and West, the valleys of the Calder and the Don, with Halifax and Huddersfield and other great mill-towns. Keighley is to the north, Brontë country, looking down on the Aire valley. Ilkley always seems to me to epitomise this kind of Yorkshire with its bleak high grass-lands and great sandstone bluffs — weatherbeaten and rugged, a bit like the folk (only a Yorkshireman born and bred could say such a thing). It is more rewarding to seek out any one of the great dales and investigate it thoroughly. It is not possible to say that 'this' or 'that' is the 'best' dale, there is no such thing; they are all so different, and each has its own character and delight. That great man Alfred J. Brown described and eulogised them so well that any attempt by me would be total impertinence, so read his book *Broad Acres* for the real thing. For me the attraction of the dales lies in the riversides. Fast, then slow, rocks and shingle, always changing. Dipper and Grey Wagtail, Kingfisher and Common Sandpiper, they are all there if you have the heart to seek them quietly. Malham Cove is, of course, fantastic, a sheer grey-white cliff, where House Martins nested long before there were houses, and still do. Go out of season or in mid-week, for only then can you stand and let the sheer size overcome you. Remember

Malham. Considering its altitude, this section of the Pennine Way is a wonderfully varied region. Malham Tarn, at a height of 1,230 feet, has adjoining fen with alder and willow carr, and perhaps the finest example of a raised bog in England lifting in a low dome of heather and sphagnum mosses to the west. It echoes to the calls of Curlew and Lapwing, the 'drumming' of Snipe and the whirring wingbeats of Red Grouse. On the Tarn swim Little and Great Crested Grebes, Tufted Ducks in abundance, Mallard, Teal and Shoveler. The outlet stream disappears into a sink-hole on the moor a little way to the south and does not see the light again until it flows out of the foot of Malham Cove. East of the Tarn the wet Mires attract Redshanks, and Yellow Wagtails haunt the grassland. Rising above the woodland which shelters the Field Studies Centre on the northern shore are the white cliffs of Highfolds Scar, with classic 'limestone pavement' stretching away towards the moorland habitat of Wheatear, Ring Ousel and Golden Plover. Gordale Beck has its Dippers and Grey Wagtails, and plunges from the moor near Malham village in a craggy ravine every whit as spectacular as Malham Cove. It is magnificent country and worth a day of anyone's leisure life.

Left: Malham Cove in the Pennine Hills.

The River Tees flows over a sill of igneous rock at High Force, and forms the boundary of County Durham and North Yorkshire.

this is limestone country, and saxifrages and other lime-loving plants are found, and I recall, as a child, blood-red cranesbill under the ash trees along the path to the cove.

Although I have lumped these western dales together, one calls for special mention, if only because I know it best. It was also the site of the greatest conservation battle of all time, when the chemical giants of industrial Teesside sought — and got permission — to build a reservoir at the head of the valley. Teesdale is really special only at its head, at Cow Green where an assemblage of rare plants grows on the lime-rich soil. The plants are left-overs of a vegetation which flourished when the retreating glaciers still held icy sway. Many of them are tiny and unobtrusive, and because they stood in the path of progress large areas of them were sacrificed. What remains of the special area is now a National Nature Reserve, with restricted access, but the enthusiast can still go and rhapsodise over most of the rarities and cast glances of venom at the dam. Downstream is Cauldron Snout, and lower still is the splendid High Force, where the Tees flows over a sill of igneous rock, and half the glory goes to North Yorkshire and the other half to Durham.

From Richmond on the Swale or Middleham on the Ure look east over Northallerton's head at the rising escarpment of the Hambleton Hills. Over the crest are the North Yorkshire Moors, to the north are the Cleveland Hills and to the south, round the corner so to speak, are the Howardians. All the rocks belong to the Jurassic, a younger system than the hard coal-rich Carboniferous of the west, and older than the soggy chalk of the Cretaceous of the Wolds.

In the valleys, the enrichening effect of lime is well in evidence, and Ryedale and Bilsdale above Helmsley, steep-sided and heavily wooded, are completely different from the dales of the west. The rocks are softer, even the accent seems

Grayling may have been introduced by mediaeval monks into Yorkshire streams.

softer, and to me there seems to be a softer 'feel' about the whole scene. The noble ruins of Rievaulx Abbey show that the monks knew where the soil was good and the water clear and fish-bearing. Besides holding fine Trout, the Rye, in common with other rivers, also has Grayling in it. It was thought at one time that these were actually introduced by the monks to give variety to their Friday diet. Speaking of abbeys, Yorkshire has some rather good ones — Fountains, for instance, perhaps the greatest in all England; and Bolton, not far from where the Wharfe boils through the narrow crevasse of the Strid.

What of the coast? From the dune-like shores of Redcar via Saltburn and Staithes, Runswick to Whitby, the coast is rocky and the fishing communities, large and small, seem to crouch at the foot of the cliff. The rock pools make marvellous hunting-grounds for mussels, winkles, whelks and other gastronomic delights, and there's the excitement of the darting blenny and similar tiny fish, and the fascination of tide-tossed egg-cases of dogfish or Skate. Whilst occasional Fulmars and several kinds of gull nest along the cliff, Rock Pipits are regular companions along the beach, and during the migration periods Turnstones, Redshanks, Oystercatchers and other waders frequent the shores.

South of Whitby is Ravenscar, the amphitheatre and the great undercliff. This is a fascinating place to visit and whether your interest be with plants, birds or insects, your visit will be worth while. Many years ago I found a paddle of a fossil sea-lizard jutting out of the shale; the light was going and the tide was rising fast, and I had to go. In spite of careful searching I never found it again. That is, of course, the heart of the matter — every trip we make to the beach, to the countryside, is unique. Rare is the day that we return without some kind of memory well worthy of storing.

DURHAM

Durham, dominated by cathedral and castle, is set proudly four-square on a tight bend in the River Wear. A county and a city small in size in relation to its neighbours north and south, it is nevertheless packed with great interest and charm and diversity of scene. The Great North Road snakes gently through the middle, for most of the way appearing to mark off industrial from agricultural Durham. The Tees forms the county boundary and Teesmouth is a splendid place at any time of the year for the keen bird-watcher. Like all great estuaries it started as a bewilderment of mud-flats and creeks, many acres of potentially flat land not impossible to reclaim and offering great scope for development and growth. Each year refineries and petrochemical complexes thrust their tanks and lunar pipeworks and hissing valves farther and farther out over land prised from the sea. Remarkably enough, the flocks of waders and wintering wildfowl strike back and retain muddy footholds.

In addition to huge flocks of Knots at such places as Coatham Sands, and Dunlins on Seal Sands, rarities come in plenty and variety, Little Stints in the autumn, with Curlew Sandpipers and Spotted Redshanks. Skuas — the Arctic, Great and Pomarine — are regular passage migrants in autumn, and flocks of Snow Buntings grace the coastal dunes and beaches in winter. There is even a centre, in the middle of all this, for the reception and education of school parties. The most impressive introduction for the newcomer is from the south, up and over the escarpment of the Cleveland Hills on the road from Scarborough — especially at night. Like all such places it combines the spectacular with the horrific. Moving northwards up the coast, a new rock takes over, the yellow magnesian limestone, sometimes forming quite spectacular cliffs especially near Sunderland, the classic locality. Here the great arched stump of Marsden is thick with nesting seabirds, including Kittiwakes, Fulmars, Herring and Lesser Black-backed Gulls. If you walk along the shore, keep an eye on the rock; some of this looks, for all the world, like great masses of kingsize ball-bearings welded together, and there are other weird shapes.

Slashing down to the sea are the denes — steep-sided crevasses, heavily wooded, damp and thick with ferns. The stream flowing in the bottom is an anticlimax, barely a trickle, clearly unable to gouge out such a feature alone even if the rock is soft; help must have come from somewhere, doubtless the massive

Redshank (top) in breeding plumage, and a migrant Curlew Sandpiper from Siberia.

A pair of Lesser Black-backed Gulls.

flows of water from melting glaciers. Castle Eden Denes NNR is probably the most famous; it lies within the boundaries of the Peterlee New Town, which authority is responsible for its welfare. At one time that most spectacular of our orchids, the lady's slipper, grew there. Alas, so beautiful, it wrote its own death warrant, being picked and uprooted until today it survives as the occasional plant at a secret site in Yorkshire. The Castle Eden Argus, a pretty little butterfly, hangs on by its feelers. Hawthorn Dene, a few miles to the north, is much smaller in extent and was bought some years ago by the Durham County Conservation Trust. Like Castle Eden Denes, the steep sides are well wooded in an area where mature deciduous woodland is something of a rarity. Not surprisingly, such woodland contains a high percentage of older trees which provide nesting-holes for Tawny Owls, Jackdaws, several titmice and Nuthatches to name but a few. At the mouth are pieces of old grassland on limestone soil, another disappearing habitat in the county, supporting a variety of plants not found elsewhere, including the frog, fragrant and early purple orchids.

Male Whitethroat attends to its hungry young; their brightly coloured gapes trigger a food-providing response in the parent.

There are other information centres in the county either in operation or in various stages of development. The Forestry Commission has one at Hamsterley Forest and the Durham County Conservation Trust has started work on a similar project in a disused Methodist chapel at Bowlees, a tiny hamlet in Teesdale about four miles upstream from Middleton. In the Wear valley the Trust has a nature reserve at Witton-le-Wear, some 80 acres of old gravel workings by the river. The disused farmhouse has been restored and equipped for displays and demonstrations. This is well worth a visit; Coot, Mallard and Tufted Duck all breed there, and the gravel beds attract Oystercatchers, Little Ringed Plovers and Common Sandpipers. The mature alder wood included in the reserve attracts Kestrels and Tawny Owls, whilst the reedbeds and scrub provide nesting sites for Whinchat and at least seven species of warbler including Blackcap, White-throat and Chiffchaff. Nearer to Sunderland, in Washington New Town, the Wildfowl Trust has transferred part of its world-famous collection of ducks, geese and swans — including the once-threatened Ne-Ne or Hawaiian Goose and the Laysan Teal — to a new Wildfowl Refuge specially landscaped on the north side of the Wear.

The valley of the Derwent, to the north of Weardale, was dammed a few years ago to meet the ever-growing demand for water from Wearside. The upper end of the reservoir has been declared a nature reserve and its development is carefully monitored. In a matter of a few years Common Sandpiper, Coot, Mallard, Tufted Duck, Little Ringed Plover and Yellow Wagtail have nested successfully. In autumn and winter, big flocks of ducks gather there, including Mallard, Teal, Tufted, Wigeon and Goldeneye. The Goosander appears to be increasing on the upland rivers and flocks of up to 40 have been seen during the build-up in March. Herons visit the reservoir: I once had the unbelievable experience of surprising 27 which were resting on the shore. Picnic sites have been established and a 'hide' built in a strategic position overlooking one of the bays where wildfowl congregate in large numbers during the winter. Sailing and fishing are other leisure pursuits which have been catered for. Downstream from the reservoir, where the river still makes the county boundary with Northumberland, lies Consett with its famous iron foundry. Below this, in the wooded Chopwell area, a disused railway line is being developed as a public footpath which will surely have much to attract anyone with an interest in wildlife, such as Roe Deer, Badgers and Foxes and a rich variety of woodland birds like Pied Fly-catchers and Green and Great Spotted Woodpeckers. Much of it is now in the new Metropolitan County of Tyne and Wear.

Buck (left) and doe Roe Deer in grey winter coats.

Weardale, if followed to its source, crosses the boundary with Cumbria, passing on the way the gigantic Eastgate cement works. It is possible to continue along this road and drop down into the South Tyne valley, via Alston. An alternative route, turning north over twisting moorland roads, would land the traveller in the Allendales — superb miniatures of the bigger South Tyne.

At Lord Barnard's Raby Castle near Staindrop there is a flourishing herd of Fallow Deer which can often be seen from the roadside, grazing in the park around the castle. The smaller native Roe Deer is now a common animal, but is

shy and feeds mainly at dawn and dusk. It is not often seen unless a determined effort is made to visit the right place at the right time. Squirrels deserve a mention. It is an odd and inexplicable fact that the American Grey Squirrel introduced into Britain about 80 years ago has not moved, in any numbers, north of the Tees. There are a few, but they have only penetrated a few miles. This seems to have been the situation for over 40 years, which suggests that they are going to stay within those limits. The native Red Squirrel is by no means abundant and seems to fluctuate dramatically in numbers. There are quite extensive conifer plantations, especially on the west side of the county, and this delightful little animal, like the Roe Deer, has probably benefited from these. Dense regiments of foreign conifers are not exactly the best of habitats for a wide variety of wildlife, but situations do develop when some of our native species would be hard pressed without them.

NORTHUMBERLAND

Northumberland has sometimes been called the connoisseurs' county, and this is fair. Before the reorganisation of local government boundaries it was fourth in the size league — and that's big, with plenty of room for variety of landscape and wildlife, not to mention the coast. The southeastern corner, now partly absorbed into the Metropolitan County of Tyne and Wear, is the focus of industry. Up came the coal and with it immeasurable quantities of spoil, and down went the land. These subsidence hollows represent a new generation of ponds, sometimes of considerable size, and marvellous for the birds. The marshy edges of some, like the Big Waters Nature Reserve a few miles north of Newcastle, have been taken over by Sedge Warblers, Reed Buntings and Dabchicks. In the extensive reedbeds Great Crested Grebes nest and there have been reports of visits by Bitterns. Ospreys moving to and from their Scottish nesting sites pay

After leaving the Pennines, the River Tees (pictured here near Middleton) flows through a gentler agricultural landscape.

Male Reed Bunting: the female lacks the striking black on the head.

annual visits, and Herons are commonplace. In the winter big flocks of Mallard, Coot, Tufted Duck, Wigeon, Teal and Pochard assemble. The sight of perhaps 100 Whooper Swans coming in against a sky of pinks and greys is not easily forgotten. All this, remember, is within a few miles of the Tyneside conurbation.

To the north of this industrial corner a strip of relatively low-lying land up the coast to Scotland is farmed quite intensively. One rapidly moves on to higher ground where the regimes are quite different. The western quarter of the county was declared a National Park in 1956 and a substantial stretch of the coast received the accolade of an Area of Outstanding Natural Beauty some years later.

In choosing a route out of Tyneside it is perhaps best to go first to the west towards the southern end of the National Park, following the line of Hadrian's Wall — and, for most of the way, General Wade's 'emergency' road to Carlisle. Arable farming begins to wane quite soon and our road goes between the Whittle Dene complex of reservoirs. Any large expanse of open water is always worth more than a passing glance, so stop and have a look round; a courtesy call at the keeper's house first is always a good idea. Depending on the time of year, look out for Grey, Pied and Yellow Wagtails, Goosanders, Herons, Dabchicks, with Whooper Swans grazing in the fields — and the flies of trout-fishers on the back-cast! The road begins to climb to a peak to the south of Stagshaw. Here one gets the first view of the Cheviots to the north with the Simonsides nearer. The land is mainly rough grazing; stone dykes have almost entirely replaced thorn hedges, Curlews call and Snipe 'drum' over marshy hollows. This is the Wheatear belt, barely more than half-an-hour's drive from Newcastle.

The road drops steeply quite soon, down to Chollerford and over the River North Tyne. The waters are still and ponded back by a weir just below the bridge.

The Pied Wagtail often uses man-made structures as nest-sites.

A typical Cheviot scene, looking from Hadrian's Wall across one of the many waters, always attractive to wildfowl.

In the shallow broken water tearing across the gravels at the tail of the weir, dozens of Black-headed Gulls wash and feed, down from their nesting colonies on upland loughs. Pied and Grey Wagtails and Common Sandpipers flit around nervously and, with luck, a Kingfisher or a Heron could appear. There is an option here — turn left, following the Wall into west Northumberland and the several loughs of the Wall country, or carry on up the valley of the North Tyne. If you go west, make for the National Park information centre at Once Brewed, then cut off up the hill to Steel Rigg and walk the Wall to Crag Lough. Wheatear and Meadow Pipit will be your constant companions, Jackdaws will spring out of the crags — not a rich variety of wildlife, but the sheer drama of the walk will delight. North of the Wall the countryside is thick with conifer plantations, but sprinkled with upland loughs like Greenlee and Broomlee. Travel farther west to the Milecastle and walk down the burn by the public footpath into Haltwhistle, along the old mineral line from Cawfields Quarry to the railway in the river valley below. Cawfields is now restored as a picnic site.

Should your choice be the route into North Tynedale the way will wind through well-wooded farmland and the river will hardly be seen until upstream from Bellingham. If time is on your side, try a walk up the Hareshaw Dene, beginning in the village of Bellingham, a lovely deep ravine, mainly deciduous woodland, rich in plants and all kinds of woodland birds, with the added bonus of a spectacular waterfall in a sandstone chasm thick with Jackdaws. In the spring you will surely see Goosanders on the river, startlingly beautiful drakes seeking mates before disappearing for the summer, often into the oblivion of some tiny burn. As the conifer forests close in on the road, the National Park becomes the Border Forest Park.

A small museum at Lewisburn, now ten years old, describes the natural history of the Park; it was the first of its kind in the country. A few miles upstream the Forestry Commission has an exhibit in Kielder Castle, mainly dealing with the forestry aspects of the area. There are forest roads for the walker, but choose those which lie near one of the many beautiful burns for the real rewards. A scenic drive over the watershed into Redesdale starts at Kielder, giving access to splendidly remote areas where Red Grouse, Blackcock, Hen Harrier and Merlin reward the energetic. Up on the tops are Wild Goats but be prepared for a full day's hike, take a spare sweater, and don't put your foot on a Viper (or Adder). This county has plenty, but always remember that in spring they are still a bit drowsy, while in summer they are quicker and fear you more than you need fear them. The bite is rarely lethal but is most painful and can lead to a couple of weeks in a hospital bed. Grass Snakes are virtually absent; in other words, if it's a snake, it's going to be a Viper.

There are a few pairs of Ravens on isolated crags, but their numbers seem to be dwindling. Peregrines are seen occasionally, Short-eared Owls come and go as the Short-tailed Vole population rises and falls. Foxes are numerous, and the Badger and the very rare Otter complete the 'big' mammal contingent. Except, of course, for the Roe Deer. These abound in the forest but you will see their slot a hundred times more often than the animal itself. The only Fallow Deer in the county are in parkland near Alnwick and at Chillingham. The Chillingham Wild White Cattle should be visited. This strange remnant of our past is still of unknown origin, but it seems highly likely that it descends from our native wild cattle. They are far from tame! Look back from Chillingham to the Cheviot and Hedgehope. The gullies and crags of the Henhole and the Bizzle of the north side are more exciting; approach them from the College Valley, but don't forget your permit from the Estate Office in Wooler. To the south of the Cheviot the Breamish Valley is worth a visit if only for the information centre at Ingram and the walk up to Linhope Spout. In the same general area is the World Bird Research Station at Glanton.

Keep moving south; drop in on the Forestry Commission's mature woodlands at Thrunton for splendid views of hill and dale, and then go across the moors to Rothbury and the Coquet (call it Coke-it) valley. Try the Simonsides, great slabs of sandstone on the south side of the river, for Ring Ousels; press on up to Harbottle to the information centre, walk up to the Drake Stone and admire the

The pattern of diamonds running the length of the Viper's back distinguishes it from non-poisonous British snakes.

Chillingham Wild White bull: this strange remnant from our past may be descended from native wild cattle.

The Farne Islands, off the north Northumberland coast, present within a comparatively small area diverse possibilities for breeding birds and seals: above left, ground-nesting terns of more than one species panic aggressively when their colony is approached; above right, cliffs and pinnacles provide nesting ledges for auks and Kittiwakes; below, Grey Seals, which breed on the archipelago, rest on the stony shore.

view. Green Woodpeckers occur by the river but this is a rare bird in the county, where the Great Spotted Woodpecker seems better favoured. Farther up the valley, beyond Alwinton, above the steep grassy slopes of the andesite rocks which spilled out of Cheviot volcano perhaps 300 million years ago, I once saw seven Kestrels playing in the rising air currents. They looked better, bigger, prouder there than their adapting cousins along the flanks of motorways.

Let's go now to the coast, if only briefly. The Farne Islands are an attraction at any time. Find Billy Shiel or one of his friends at Seahouses, pay your fare and sit back for an experience which makes safari parks in Africa a waste of your money. If seabirds excite you, there are 13 species breeding here, including four terns (only the Little is absent), Guillemot, Puffin, Kittiwake, Cormorant, Shag and Eider. If the terns are nesting wear a hat: their brave attacks will give you a sore head! The Grey Seals breed from about November and December, but be prepared for a cold day and landing restrictions. Eiders will bob around you, and the footballs with eyes and snorting disappearances are Grey Seals. If you can fit in a winter trip, say December, you'll see the whole family. When you've had enough of the rocky islands — and when could that be? — watch the tides and go to Lindisfarne. In the summer the dune slacks are a blaze of colour and the village itself is sheer fascination. Take the coast to the south to Dunstanburgh and Craster for kippers, to Cullernose for Fulmars and House Martins nesting where God intended, on the cliffs. Go on south to Howick Haven and say a little prayer of thanks to Operation Neptune and enlightened landowners.

What else could be said of the county which would not fill three volumes and more! I have hardly mentioned Hexham and the 'Shire', as the area to the south of this charming town is known. The Allendales have received scant attention, as has Redesdale. In mid-Northumberland, the National Trust maintains the Trevelyans' Wallington Hall, surrounded by beautiful woodland and lakes; Nuthatches are there, near the northern limit of their range. The County Council has a country park at Bolam Lake, less than 20 miles from Newcastle.

Where shall I stop? It is, as I said, for the connoisseur: the weather can be vicious (the North Tyne endured over 20 degrees of frost in June 1974) or glorious, so come prepared for both. For the wildlife enthusiast there is everything, but you must work for it. The people who belong here call it God's own county — I do believe they are right.

Guide to wildlife habitats in North East England

This Appendix provides a selected but varied list of places of wildlife interest. It is emphasised that nature reserves exist primarily for the conservation of animals and plants and in some cases for environmental experiments and research. They are not 'public open spaces' in the recreational sense. Access to many is therefore restricted and some, because of their sensitivity to disturbance, have been omitted from this list, in deference to the wishes of conservation organisations. Even with 'open' reserves visitors are earnestly requested to keep to the paths and bridleways and so avoid damage to the habitat and undue disturbance to wildlife. *There is no public access to the enclosed farmland which is part of many National Trust properties.*

Application to visit a National Nature Reserve (NNR) should be made to the appropriate Regional Office of the Nature Conservancy Council (NCC) at the address given. Intention to visit reserves of the Royal Society for the Protection of Birds (RSPB) should be notified to the Warden (whose address is shown) as far in advance as possible. In all cases where an address is shown, it is wise to contact the Warden to avoid disappointment.

NORTHUMBERLAND

The Allen Banks NY 80 63. Hill and river scenery with walks among wooded banks and crags, near confluence of Rs. Allen and Tyne. 3 mls w. of Haydon Bridge, ½ ml s. of A69. Car park, picnic site. NT.

Big Waters NZ 23 73. Lake and swamp caused by mining subsidence. 4 mls n. of Newcastle upon Tyne, ½ ml w. of A1 at Brunswick village. Northumberland Nats T.

Border Forest Park NY 70 90. A number of state forests, mainly spruce, and fells on either side of English-Scottish border. 300 sq. m. Bordered by Liddesdale B6357 in w. through Newcastleton, and by Redesdale A68 through Kielder to Carter Bar in n. Camp site and forest centre at Kielder village NT 62 93. For Comm.

Chillingham Castle NU 06 25. Park with herd of ancient Wild White Cattle. 12 mls n.w. of Alnwick, n. of B6346; 5 mls e. of Wooler, s. of B6348 at Chatton. Private.

Embleton Links NU 26 22. Sand-dunes, foreshore and golf links, 494 a. Incl. Newton Pool Nature Reserve. 7 mls n.e. of Alnwick A1. (Access on foot only, from Craster on s. side or across golf course from Embleton and Dunstansteads on n. side.) NT.

Farne Islands NU 23 37. About 30 islands from 2 to 5 mls offshore from Bamburgh. Grey Seals. Seabird colonies incl. Fulmars, Kittiwakes, terns, Eiders, Shags, Guillemots, Razorbills, Puffins. By boat from Seahouses, e. of A1 by B1341 – B1340. Access to Inner Farne and Staple Islands only from end March to end Sept. Prior booking essential at information centre, Seahouses Harbour, landing fee. (Warden/Naturalist – The Sheiling, 8 St Aidan's, Seahouses.) NT.

Harbottle Crags NT 92 04. Heather moorland in Upper Coquetdale, 390 a. 7 mls w. of Rothbury, w. of B6341 at Flotterton. For Comm. car park on Alwinton side of village. Northumberland Nats T.

The National Trust North East, Regional Office, Cambo, Morpeth, Northumberland.

Northumberland National Park, Northumberland. 398 sq. mls. High moorland stretching 40 mls from Wark Forest in the south to the Cheviots in the north; threaded by the Pennine Way; highest points Cheviot 2676 ft and nearby Hedgehope Hill; numerous burns and wooded valleys of Rs. North Tyne, Coquet and Grasslees Burn. Incl. Redesdale, Harbottle Crags, Simonside Hills, Hadrian's Wall with Roman Forts of Housesteads and Carrawburgh. Information centres at Ingram in the Cheviots NU 020 163, Byrness in Upper Redesdale NT 765 028, and Once Brewed near Bardon Mill NY 753 669. Traversed by B6318 Low Brunton–Greenhead (along Hadrian's Wall); B6320 Bellingham–Otterburn; A68 Otterburn–Byrness and beyond Catcleugh Reservoir to Carter Bar; B6341 Elsdon–Swindon; and minor roads except north of Coquetdale. Recommended leaflets: The Roman Wall, The Northumberland Coast, The Pennine Way, and series of natural history leaflets. Handbook 30p.

Northumberland Wildlife Trust, The Hancock Museum, Barras Bridge, Newcastle upon Tyne, NE2 4PT.

DURHAM

Castle Eden Denes NZ 43 39. Steep wooded denes. 5 mls n.w. of Hartlepool, s. of Peterlee A1088 – B1281. Peterlee Corporation.

Derwent Walk NZ 10 52 – NZ 20 62. 10 mls walk along grassed track of former Derwent Valley Railway, incl. four viaducts, two crossing R. Derwent, and access to woods. Between Consett and Whickham, parallel with A694. Access at Ebchester station NZ 107 549 (information centre, picnic area), 1 ml e. of Shotley Bridge NZ 104 535 (picnic area, toilets), and Rowlands Gill NZ 166 582 (picnic area). Durham CC.

Durham County Conservation Trust, 17 Highwood View, Durham City, DH1 3DT.

Hamsterley Forest NZ 05 29. State forest. 1100 a. 7 mls n.w. of West Auckland, 3 mls w. of A68 at Witton-le-Wear. Information centre, forest drive, trails, picnic areas, toilets. For Comm.

Hardwick Hall NZ 35 29. Landscaped park, deciduous woods and conifer plantations, fen carr and serpentine lake. Country Park. 9 mls w. of Hartlepool, 9 mls e. of Bishop Auckland A689, near Sedgefield (junction A177), 2 mls e. of A1(M)/A689 interchange. Car park, trail. Durham CC.

Pow Hill NZ 01 52. Sheltered valley above Derwent reservoir. Country Park. Waterfowl, waders. 8 mls s. of Hexham B6306, 8 mls n. of Stanhope B6278. Car park, picnic area, toilets, hide beside reservoir. Durham CC.

Limestone pavement and grassland at Scar Close in Yorkshire's Pennines.

TYNE AND WEAR

Washington Wildfowl Refuge NZ 32 57. Landscaped area sloping to n. bank of R. Wear with pools and pens for collection of about 80 species exotic waterfowl, and sanctuary for wild ducks, waders and terns. At Pattinson, District 15, Washington New Town, approached from A1(M) by A1231, n. along A182, then e. by A1231, following District 15 and Refuge signposts. Information centre and shop, refreshments, adm. fee. Wildfowl Trust/Washington Development Corporation.

CLEVELAND

Cowpen Marsh NZ 51 25. Salt and freshwater marsh, 160 a. Snipe, Common Tern, Yellow Wagtail. Migrant ducks and waders. 2 mls n. of Middlesbrough A178. Car park. (Warden – 315 Wolviston Back Lane, Billingham, Cleveland.) RSPB.

Ormesby Hall NZ 53 17. House and parkland, 273 a. 3 mls s.e. of Middlesbrough, s. of A174. NT.

NORTH YORKS

Bridestones Moor SE 87 93. Heather moor and upland pasture with deep ghylls and spectacular outcrops 'The Bridestones'. 625 a. Roe Deer, Fox, Badger. Sparrowhawk, Kestrel, Jay. 6 mls n.e. of Pickering via A170 turning n. at Thornton-le-Dale and taking Dalby Forest Drive. Car park at SE 880 904, footpath opposite. NT/Yorks. Nats T.

Brimham Moor SE 21 65. Open moorland with spectacular rock formation, 362 a. 8 mls s.w. of Ripon, approached from B6265; 8½ mls n.w. of Harrogate, approached from B6165. NT.

East Scar Top Farm SD 95 89. Farmland (private) and moor from valley to summit of Addleborough, 1564 ft, affording fine view of the whole of Wensleydale. 1 ml s.e. of Bainbridge A684. NT.

Fairburn Ings SE 47 28. Open water fringed with reeds and scrub, resulting from mining subsidence. 620 a. Great Crested and Little Grebes and other waterfowl. 1 ml n.e. of Castleford, on w. side of A1 at Fairburn. RSPB.

Garbutt Wood SE 51 83. Boulder-strewn bracken slopes with birch/hazel scrub, Gormire Lake and birchwood, and Whitestone Cliff. Red, Roe and Fallow Deer, Fox and Badger. Great Crested Grebes. 4 mls e. of Thirsk A170, at Sutton Bank. Access footpaths from car park at Cooper Cross on hill-top or from Sutton Bank SE 514 830. For Comm./Yorks. Nats T.

Hudswell NZ 15 01. Woodlands beside R. Swale, 134 a. Between Richmond and Hudswell, just s. of A6108. NT/Richmond Corporation.

Malham Tarn SD 89 66. Tarn at 1316 ft and surrounding moorland, limestone pavement, calcareous marsh, raised bog, fen carr and planted woods. 3088 a. Moorland and wetland birds. 6 mls n.e. of Settle or 10 mls n.w. of Skipton A65 via minor roads. On Pennine Way. NT.

The National Trust Yorkshire, Regional Office, 32 Goodramgate, York.

North York Moors National Park, North Yorkshire. 553 sq. mls. Rugged coastline with highest cliffs on east coast (Boulby); heather-moors of Cleveland and Hambleton Hills; fishing villages of Staithes, Runswick and Robin Hood's Bay; valleys of Rs. Derwent, Dove, Esk and Rye. Incl. Cleveland Way (93 mls), Roman Road (Goathland Moor SE 81 97), Dalby and Pickering Forest Drives (For Comm), Bridestones Moor (NT), Rievaulx and Byland Abbeys. Day Visitor Centre, March–Oct, at Danby Lodge, Danby, Whitby. Flanked by A170 Scarborough–Thirsk; A173 Stokesley–Guisborough; A171 Guisborough–Whitby. Traversed by A171 Whitby–Scarborough; A169 Sleights–Pickering; B1257 Helmsley–Stokesley; and many minor roads. Recommended leaflets: Farndale, Walks around Goathland.

Scarth Wood Moor SE 46 99. Moorland near Cleveland Hills, 257 a. 8 mls n.e. of Northallerton via A684 and A19; between Osmotherley and Whorlton A172. NT.

Skipwith Common SE 66 37. Lowland heath with small pools and reed-swamp; regenerating Scots pine and birch, oak and willow. Fallow Deer, Black-headed Gull colony, Nightjar, woodpeckers, wintering waterfowl. 9 mls s.s.e. of York A19, via minor road Escrick–Skipwith, 4 mls n.e. of Selby and Barlby A19 – A163. Car parks and access at SE 669 378 and SE 642 374. Yorks. Nats T.

Yorkshire Dales National Park, North Yorkshire. 680 sq. mls. High Millstone Grit moors rising to Ingleborough 2373 ft, Whernside 2419 ft, Pen-y-Ghent 2273 ft and Darnbrook Fell 2048 ft; limestone scars and pavements of Craven; dales of Rs. Swale, Ure, Aire, Wharfe and Ribble. Incl. Malham Tarn (NT), Hardraw and Aysgarth Forces. Information centres at Aysgarth, Wensleydale; Clapham (Reading Room) via Lancaster; and Malham (alongside the car park). Traversed by A684 Sedbergh–Hawes–Leyburn, through Wensleydale; B6255 Ingleton–Hawes; B6479 Settle north through Horton-in-Ribblesdale; B6160 Grassington–Aysgarth; and many minor roads. Recommended leaflets: Mines, The Pennine Way, Walks in Wharfedale, Clothing and Footwear for the Dales, Guided Walks, A Motorist's Dales.

Yorkshire Naturalists' Trust, 20 Castlegate, York, YO1 1RP.

WEST YORKS

Hebden Dale SD 97 30. Hardcastle Crags and woods along n. bank of Hebden Water. Also High Greenwood Wood and Black Dean, w. and s. of Hebden Water, and Gibson Wood on w. bank. 5 mls n.w. of Todmorden A646, 2–3½ mls n.w. of Hebden Bridge, w. of A6033. NT.

Marsden Moor SE 02 10 – 06 11. Open moorland, 5685 a. 8–9 mls s.w. of Huddersfield, on n.w. and s. of Marsden, stretching from Buckstones Moss (A640) astride A62 to Wessenden Moor (n. of A635). NT.

HUMBERSIDE

Bempton Cliffs TA 20 74. Chalk cliffs 300 ft high with England's only gannetry (90 pairs), Fulmars, Kittiwakes and auk colonies. 4 mls n. of Bridlington B1255–B1229. Information centre. (Note: it is dangerous to leave the footpath along the cliff-top.) RSPB.

Blacktoft Sands SE 84 23. Large brackish reedbed bordered by saltmarsh, 460 a. Water Rail, Shelduck, Short-eared Owls, Bearded Reedling, Reed and Grasshopper Warblers. 7 mls e. of Goole at confluence of Rs. Trent and Humber, via A161 to Swinefleet and minor road through Reedness. Hide. (Warden – Hillcrest, High Street, Whitgift, Goole, S. Humberside.) RSPB.

Hornsea Mere TA 19 47. Large shallow lake with reedbeds and wooded fringe, 580 a. Coot, Reed Warbler. Variety of wintering wildfowl, migrants. 13 mls n.e. of Hull, w. of Hornsea and s. of B1244. (Warden – The Bungalow, the Mere, Hornsea, N. Humberside.) RSPB.

Humber Wildfowl Refuge SE 96 22. Tidal mudflats of R. Humber between Brough and Trent Falls incl. Read's Island. Pink-footed Geese, Wigeon and other waterfowl, waders. N. of A1077, Winterton–Barton upon Humber. Permit needed off roads. Humber Wildfowl Refuge Committee.

Spurn Peninsula TA 42 12. 3½ mls long sand and shingle spit at mouth of R. Humber, 280 a. above H.W.M. and 477 a. foreshore and mudflats. Famous resting place for migrant birds, and Bird Observatory. 20 mls s.e. of Hull A1033 – B1445, via minor road Easington–Kilnsea. (Warden at Warren Cottage near reserve entrance TA 417 151.) Yorks. Nats T.

Animal collections in North East England

Brontë Zoo

This is a small open-air Zoo with mammals and birds. The collection is still being expanded, and at present it contains Pumas, Coyotes, Dingos, Raccoons, porcupines, monkeys, deer and a selection of birds, including parrots, parrakeets, cockatoos, pheasants, doves, pigeons and waterfowl. There are also some Shetland Ponies and other domestic animals. The Zoo is set in a pretty valley with views of the surrounding hills. It was opened in 1972.

Burton Constable Hall and Bird Gardens

Burton Constable Hall and Bird Gardens has a small children's zoo containing a selection of wild mammals and birds, including Rabbits, foxes, gerbils, a few monkeys, macaws, parrakeets, Budgerigars and owls. The wild Rabbit, now reduced in numbers since the myxomatosis epidemic in the 1950s is by nature a burrowing animal, though for several years after the introduction of the disease, it avoided the old warrens which were infected.

Our native Red Fox is by nature a daylight hunter, but has become largely nocturnal as the result of foxhunting. Of all predatory animals the Fox has survived the most successfully and in recent years has learned to scavenge on the edge of towns. The natural diet is Rabbits and other small mammals, insects, birds' eggs and wild fruit. For much of the summer, Foxes live on a vegetarian diet, and they will only take chickens if these are not properly enclosed.

One interesting little animal exhibited here is the gerbil, a small burrowing rodent from the hot, arid regions of Asia and Africa. There are 106 species of gerbil and they mostly have hairy tails and silky fur. They are active animals, constantly enlarging their underground system of tunnels. They feed on roots and seeds.

Several species of ornamental pheasant are kept, of which 48 species are recognised. Sixteen of these are in danger of extinction in the wild, and because they live in thick cover they are difficult to observe, so that there are considerable gaps in our knowledge of their natural habits. Pheasants were probably introduced into Great Britain by the Romans, and by the twelfth century they were eaten regularly, and established in the wild by the sixteenth century. Nearly all pheasants originated in Asia, and all our domestic poultry are descended from wild jungle fowl, which are members of the pheasant family. Wild pheasants feed on insects, seeds and worms, and some species mate for life while others, including our Pheasant, are polygamous.

There are 315 members of the parrot family of which the macaws of South America are the largest. Macaws usually live in pairs, flying from one feeding ground to the next in tropical jungle. There are 15 species, all brightly coloured and with very long tail feathers. Parrakeets, also long-tailed, are small parrots, found in Malaysia and Indonesia. They travel in flocks, eating fruit and grain. Budgerigars are grass parrakeets, natives of Australia, which are coloured green in the wild state.

The owls of the world are divided into 133 species, found virtually throughout the world. They are distinguished by their large, forward-facing eyes, short necks and distinctive calls, which have made them objects of superstition and fear in the folklore of many peoples. Sight and hearing are well developed in owls, and many species hunt by day rather than by night. Their large ears are hidden by feathers, and in a number of species the ears are of different size, as a device for locating the sound of the small animals on which they feed.

Brontë Zoo. **Address** Station Road, Oakworth, Keighley, Yorks. **Open** 11.00–dusk summer and winter. **Catering** licensed restaurant, kiosk. Zoo shop. **Guided tours** by arrangement. **Acreage** 1½. **Car** 2½ mls s. of Keighley on B6143. **Bus** 17 via Oakworth. **Train** to Oakworth (25 yds). Private railway running from station most of the year at weekends also Wed during summer. **Taxis** from Keighley or Haworth. Public allowed to feed animals.

Burton Constable Hall and Bird Gardens. **Address** Burton Constable Hall, Humberside. **Telephone** Skirlaugh 62400. **Open** 12.00–18.00 from Easter Saturday at weekends until spring bank holiday, then daily except Mon and Fri, until end of Sept (but open bank holiday Monday). **Guide-book. Catering** self-service cafeteria. **Guided tours** by arrangement. **Acreage** 150. **Car** 9 mls n.e. of Hull on A165 to Bilton, then to Sproatley, turn left on to Marton Road. **Bus** Hull–Sproatley, then 1½ mls to Hall. **Train** to Hull. **Other facilities** children's playground. Public **not allowed** to feed animals.

Flamingo Land. **Address** The Rectory, Flamingo Park, Kirby Misperton, Malton, North Yorkshire. **Telephone** Kirby Misperton 287. **Open** 10.00–dusk summer and winter. **Guide-book. Catering** licensed restaurant, self-service cafeterias, snack bar, kiosk. Zoo shop. **Guided tours** by arrangement. **Acreage** 320. **Car** 2½ mls s. of Pickering, off A169 near Malton. **Bus** stops outside Zoo. **Train** to Malton (6 mls). **Taxis** available. **Other facilities** first-aid post, lost children's room, push-chairs, wheel-chairs, children's playground. Dogs on leash only. Public **not allowed** to feed animals.

Flamingo Land

Flamingo Land is a large zoo with a mixed collection, requiring a day's visit if you are to see everything. All the big cats are represented, as well as Cheetahs, and Gorillas, Orang utans, which have bred here, and Chimpanzees. Monkeys include the rare Lion-tailed Macaque and gibbons, Barbary Apes and Hamadryas Baboons, all of which have bred. The baboons are displayed on a large 'baboon island'. You can also see Polar Bears, Brown Bears, wolves and hyenas, and there is a good selection of hoofed animals, including the rare Père David's Deer and Arabian Gazelle. The camel family is represented by Arabian Camels, Llamas and Alpacas, and there are American Bison, tapirs, and Indian Elephants, wallabies and Giant Anteaters. There is a dolphinarium, and the Zoo was the first in this country to exhibit dolphins. In fact, it claims to be the biggest importer of dolphins in Great Britain.

The bird collection is a varied one, with birds of prey, waterfowl, tropical birds, including free-flying macaws, pelicans, penguins and, of course, flamingos. The Tropical House and Aquarium also exhibit reptiles, including crocodiles, alligators, snakes, giant tortoises from the Seychelles, and a collection of invertebrates (animals without a backbone), including scorpions.

You can take a Jungle Cruise on a raft, which is accompanied by sealions, and on the banks of the lake there are Disneyland-type models of wild animals, a dinosaur, Red Indians and Tarzan. Other attractions are a fairground, Cowboy City, Children's Farm, model railway, Garden Centre, Ocean World, mini-circus, and at weekends displays by the Armed Forces and gymkhanas. The Zoo has over 700 mammals and 700 birds, and the policy is to assemble as large a collection as possible, so that it can say 'You name it — we've got it'. Opened in 1961, the Zoo is now owned by Scotia (Pleasure Parks) Ltd.

Harewood Bird Gardens

This Bird Garden was opened by Lord Harewood in 1970 in the grounds of Harewood House. You will find it in part of the Lakeside Walk south of the stable block, set in the garden which was laid out over 200 years ago by the famous landscape architect, 'Capability' Brown. This is the best collection of exotic birds in the northeast, with penguins, flamingos, cranes, pheasants and waterfowl. There is a Tropical House and many aviaries, including a large walk-round aviary.

The first exhibit you see is the Penguin Pool, with a colony of Humboldt's Penguins, which breed here regularly. They have little igloos in which they lay two eggs on a nest of pebbles and straw. This species comes from the coasts of Peru and Chile. When you go out into the Gardens, you can see the penguins in their glass-fronted pool, swimming under water.

In the paddock enclosures leading down to the lake are Emus, the flightless birds of Australia, and Paradise or Stanley Cranes, a large member of the crane family from South Africa, and Crowned Cranes. There are two varieties of these, the black-necked ones from West Africa and the grey-necked from East Africa. Next to these is the large flock of Chilean Flamingos. Flamingos are gregarious birds, living in huge flocks, sometimes numbering millions. The oddly shaped beak is specially adapted for feeding on minute organisms in the water, which are scooped up with the beak held upside-down. The flamingo's tongue is used to pump out the water and mud and the food is drawn in through special filters, called lamellae, and sucked down the bird's throat.

There are Barnacle Geese in the Flamingo Paddock and the waterfowl in the lakeside pens include many species of geese and ducks. The rarest goose here is the Cereopsis, or Cape Barren Goose, which breeds here regularly. You will also see Black Swans from Australia, and Black-necked Swans from South America. Many waterfowl are permanent residents on the lake, such as Tufted Duck,

Crowned Crane: this is the grey-necked form from East Africa.

Harewood Bird Gardens. **Address** Harewood, Leeds. **Telephone** Harewood 238. **Open** 11.00–18.00 Easter–31st Oct, 11.00–dusk winter, Sat and Sun only. **Guide-book. Catering** unlicensed restaurant, self-service cafeteria, kiosk. Zoo shop. **Acreage** 4. **Car** 7 mls s. of Harrogate on A61. **Bus** service passes the Gardens every 15 mins between Leeds and Harrogate. **Trains** to Leeds City (7 mls) or Harrogate (7 mls). **Taxis** available. **Other facilities** first-aid post, wheel-chairs, children's playground. Public **not allowed** to feed birds.

Above: the beautiful Victoria Crowned Pigeon, the largest of the pigeons. Below: Blue and Gold Macaw.

Pochard and Great Crested Grebes, and migrants such as Whooper Swans and Goldeneye. There is also a flock of between 300 and 400 Canada Geese, which are counted and ringed each year by the Canada Goose Club of Yorkshire, whose headquarters is at Harewood.

Near the flamingos you can see a variety of macaws which fly about freely in the gardens. Besides the handsome Red and Blue and the Blue and Gold Macaw, you can also see the rare Hyacinthine Macaw, the largest macaw species, which is only found in Brazil. There are several other aviaries for other members of the parrot family, including parrakeets, cockatoos and lovebirds. The rarest parrakeets here are the Turquoisine Parrakeet and the Splendid Parrakeet. There are three aviaries through which a little stream runs into the lake, and in the first of these there are some Ypecaha Wood Rails, a wader from southeastern Brazil, Uruguay, Paraguay and Argentina. They have been bred here for the first time in Great Britain.

In the aviary for weavers there is constant activity, with nest-building going on all the time. Weavers are found mainly in Africa, making communal nests which often cover the trees. Two species of owl are exhibited, the Snowy Owl, which has bred here, and the European Eagle Owl. The Snowy Owl comes from the Arctic regions, and the European Eagle Owl is found in the forests of Scandinavia and western Asia.

There are particularly good collections of jays and magpies and starlings. These include Hunting Cissas, Pileated Jays, the Red-billed Blue Magpie and the White-crested Jay Thrush; and among the starling species, the Wattled Starling, which breeds here, the Superb and Amethyst Starlings, and Rothschild's Grackle, a very rare member of the starling family which is pure white and is only found on the island of Bali. Other aviaries exhibit lorikeets, touracos, toucans and crowned pigeons, the largest member of the pigeon family. They come from New Guinea where their plumes are prized by the natives. There is also a good collection of rare pheasant species, nearly all of which breed regularly in the gardens. These include the Mikado, Brown-eared, Blue-eared, Swinhoe's, Elliot's and Hume's Bar-tailed Pheasants. There is an attractive enclosure for Scarlet and Sacred Ibises, which are among the most colourful of wading birds. They come from Central and South America.

The largest aviary in the gardens is the walk-round aviary, opened in 1971. It is attractively landscaped with a pool and waterfall, and you can see Grey-headed Gallinules, which breed here, Bush Quail, Rain Quail, Vermilion Cardinals, six species of mynah, and last but not least, touracos, which are seen at their best when in flight, with their crimson wing-patches showing. Lastly you come to the Tropical House, kept at 70°F., where you can see hummingbirds, sugarbirds, sunbirds, tanagers, manakins, Pekin Robins and the graceful Sun Bittern. The tropical vegetation growing here includes palms, banana trees, passion vines and orchids. The latest addition is an exhibition of butterflies.

This is a superb collection, beautifully exhibited, and for those who are keen ornithologists there is an ornithological library which is open to the general public by appointment.

Hornsea Pottery

The Mini-Zoo attached to Hornsea Pottery contains some aviaries, monkeys and domestic animals. The birds you can see here include parrots, macaws, cockatoos, parrakeets, lovebirds, and many other small species of finch. There are also some pheasants and free-flying pigeons. The monkeys here are Rhesus and there is one marmoset. The other attractions are Crazy Golf, pony rides, children's playground, and of course the guided tour round the Pottery, which was established in 1949. The Mini-Zoo was started in 1960.

Knaresborough Zoo

This is a small mixed collection, the main attraction being twelve specimens of the big cats, and what is claimed to be the world's largest snake in captivity, a Reticulated Python from Malaya which is 27 feet long and weighs 220 lb. You can also see monkeys, bushbabies, genets, fruit bats, Llamas, wallabies, goats, and sealions, which are fed twice daily. There is also a mixed collection of birds, including macaws; a tropical aquarium, a monitor and an alligator; and a Pets' Corner. The Zoo was opened in 1965, and it is now owned by Mr Nyoka, many of whose animals have appeared in films and television commercials.

Lambton Pleasure Park

Lambton Pleasure Park is a safari park with a walk-about section in the middle. The drive-through section contains Lions, Giraffe, gnu, Eland, Ostrich and other animals from Africa. The animals one visits on foot are in the moated and fenced enclosures, and these include zebras, American Bison, elephants, camels, bears and baboons. The plans for this section are to exhibit animals from the Old and the New World. The Lions, Giraffe, antelopes, zebra and several monkeys all breed regularly here.

Other attractions are the western-style donkey rides, a children's zoo, an adventure playground and a veteran aircraft museum. The Park was opened by Lord Lambton in 1972 and future plans include a reptile collection.

Hornsea Pottery. **Address** Hornsea, North Humberside. **Telephone** Hornsea 2161. **Open** July–Aug, Mon–Fri 09.00–19.00, Sat 10.00–18.00, Sun 10.00–19.00. Sept–June Mon–Fri 09.00–17.00, Sat and Sun 10.00–17.00. **Admission free. Catering** self-service cafeteria. Pottery shop. **Guided tours** by arrangement. **Car** s. of Hornsea on B1242. **Bus** from Hull nearest stop 300 yds, from Bridlington or Beverley nearest stop ¾ ml. **Other facilities** pony rides, children's playground, garden centre, picnic area, crazy golf, go-karts. Public allowed to feed animals with food prepared in Zoo only.

Knaresborough Zoo. **Address** Connyingham Park, Knaresborough, Yorks. **Telephone** Knaresborough 2793. **Open** 10.00–dusk summer and winter. **Catering** snack bar. Zoo shop. **Acreage** 2. **Car** 3 mls n.e. of Harrogate on A59. **Bus** from High Bridge, Knaresborough, then 5 mins' walk to Zoo through Park. **Train** to Harrogate (3 mls). **Other facilities** first-aid post, lost children's room. Public allowed to feed animals.

Lambton Pleasure Park (incorporating Lambton Lion Park.) **Address** Lambton Park, Chester-le-Street, Co. Durham. **Telephone** Fencehouses 3311. **Open** 10.00–17.00 (last car admitted), March–Oct. **Catering** licensed restaurant, self-service cafeteria, snack bar, kiosk. Zoo shop. **Guided tours** by arrangement. **Acreage** 212. **Car** 7 mls n. of Durham off A183 near Chester-le-Street. **Bus** to Chester-le-Street depot, then Sunderland 775 or 776 to entrance. **Train** to Chester-le-Street, then local bus. **Other facilities** 'Walkabout Zoo' section in Safari Park, adventure playground, pets' corner, veteran aircraft collection, picnic area, first-aid post, overnight caravan stop, dog kennels. No pets. Public **not allowed** to feed animals.

Female (left) and male Ostrich, by far the largest bird in the world.

Leeds City Museum Aquarium

This small Aquarium is part of the Leeds City Museum. It displays tropical freshwater fish, and sea fish both tropical and temperate. The cold-water marine tanks contain representative marine life of the Yorkshire coast. There is also a small number of amphibians and reptiles. The Aquarium was opened in 1952 and entry is free.

The Wildlife Youth Service of the World Wildlife Fund meets here monthly throughout the year for lectures, films and outings.

Leeds City Museum Aquarium. **Address** Caverley Street, Leeds 1. **Open** 10.00–18.00 summer and winter except Sun. **Admission free. Car** next to Town Hall in city centre. **Train** to Leeds ($\frac{1}{4}$ ml). Public **not allowed** to feed exhibits.

Scarborough Zoo and Marineland

The Zoo specialises in marine mammals, and visitors are conducted on a tour consisting of a series of shows. The first of these is a dolphin performance lasting 35 minutes. You then see a Chimpanzee tea party, followed by a visit to the farmyard where children are given free bottles of milk with which to feed the lambs and goats. Then comes a sealion performance, where children are provided with fish for the sealions. You then see the March of the King Penguins, and this is followed by a return visit to the dolphin pool to see a diver feeding the dolphins. Lastly, you watch a performing Chimpanzee.

The tour lasts one and a half hours, after which you are free to walk round the rest of the Zoo, which includes a children's zoo and an aquarium, and about 250 birds. The Zoo was opened in 1969 by Mr Don Robinson.

Scarborough Zoo and Marineland. **Address** North Bay, Scarborough. **Telephone** Scarborough 64401. **Open** 10.00–dusk summer. Winter opening times vary. **Guide-book. Guided tours** by arrangement. **Acreage** 10. **Car** to North Bay, Scarborough. **Bus** to Corner Cafe, North Bay. **Train** to Scarborough ($\frac{1}{2}$ ml) then buses every 15 mins to Zoo. **Taxis** available. Public allowed to feed animals with free food provided.

Sewerby Zoo

This small zoo, opened in 1946 by the Local Authority, has a collection of mammals and birds. There is a breeding herd of Formosan Sika Deer, a breeding group of Bennett's Wallabies, some Llamas and some smaller mammals, including monkeys and porcupines, as well as ponies and small domestic animals. The birds include Humboldt's Penguins, flamingos, Crowned Cranes, peafowl, macaws, cockatoos, parrakeets and small aviary birds, and a collection of ornamental pheasants and waterfowl. The old English walled garden and the grounds are of considerable botanical interest, and there is a 12-hole golf-course, archery, bowls, croquet, putting and a Children's Corner, with band concerts on summer Sundays.

Sewerby Zoo. Address Bridlington, North Humberside. **Telephone** Bridlington 3769. **Open** 09.00–19.30, summer and winter. **Guide-book. Catering** licensed restaurant, self-service cafeteria, snack bar, Clock Tower Tavern. No catering in winter. **Acreage** 8½. **Car** 3 mls n.e. of Bridlington along B1255 (Marton Road, Martongate) to junction with Sheeprake Lane and Church Lane. Entrance is 300 yds along Church Lane, Sewerby. **Bus** from Bridlington bus station to Sewerby Park (EYMS routes, 83, 83a every ½ hour during summer months, every hour winter). **Train** to Bridlington (3 mls). **Taxis** available. Public **not allowed** to feed animals.

Washington Wildfowl Refuge

Washington Wildfowl Refuge was opened in May 1975 and it is managed by the Wildfowl Trust in conjunction with Washington Development Corporation. Over 800 birds of 80 species are kept here, including Hawaiian Geese, Hawaiian Duck, Cereopsis or Cape Barren Geese and Laysan Teal, all of which are rare in the wild. The aim is to specialise in North American species to emphasise the link with Washington D.C. George Washington's family originally came from this area. Visitors will be able to see seven species of swan and several large flocks of geese, and American visitors will soon recognise such birds as the Hooded Merganser, the Emperor Goose and the Black Brant.

There is a wild refuge adjacent to the collection, containing a number of ponds and a large lake for wading birds, of which at least 13 species were recorded in the first year. Hides have been built to allow the viewing of wild birds at close quarters, and visiting species include Mallard, Teal, Pochard, Shoveler, Goldeneye, Goosander and Whooper Swans. Two nature trails have been planned through small woods.

The entrance building has a large picture window overlooking the ponds in the collection area, and there is an exhibition room with information on the Trust's work and on wildlife in the region. Members of the Trust have free entry.

Washington Wildfowl Refuge. Address The Wildfowl Trust, Middle Barmston Farm, Pattinson, Washington 15, Tyne and Wear. **Telephone** Washington 465454. **Open** 09.30–18.30 (or 15 mins after sunset whichever earlier) summer and winter. **Guided tours** by arrangement. **Acreage** 103 (collection 30 acres, remainder is wild refuge with public hides). **Car** 1 ml e. of Washington on the n. bank of the Wear to Pattison District of the New Town. **Train** to Newcastle (10 mls) or to Durham (12 mls). **Taxis** available. **Other facilities** wheelchairs, educational services to schools, special observation hides. No pets. Public allowed to feed birds.

Wold Pottery Bird Garden

The opening of this Bird Garden to the public in 1974 arose from the personal hobby of the owner, Mrs Joyce Dixon. The emphasis is on pheasants, many of which are at liberty in the garden. These include Elliot's Pheasants and Swinhoe's Pheasants, both of which are rare in the wild, Himalayan Monal and Nepal Kalij, as well as Golden and Yellow Golden Pheasants. There are many peafowl, guineafowl and bantams at liberty, and in aviaries you can see more pheasants, white peafowl, finches, conures, doves, laughing thrushes and some ducks. Three African Pygmy Goats are also at liberty here, and there is a donkey. The owner's house has been scheduled as being of historical and architectural interest.

Wold Pottery Bird Garden. Address Wold Pottery, Routh, Nr Beverley, Humberside. **Telephone** Leven 42236. **Open** 10.30–17.00 summer, 10.30–dusk winter. Zoo shop. **Guided tours** by arrangement. **Acreage** 2½. **Car** 4½ mls e. of Beverley on A1035 to Hornsea road; at Routh turn down lane signposted Meaux, Wawne, Sutton and Wold Pottery. Pottery and Bird Garden 250 yds on right, past Church. **Bus** from Beverley–Hornsea stops at top of lane, 250 yds from Gardens. **Train** to Beverley (4½ mls). **Taxis** available. No pets. Public **not allowed** to feed animals.

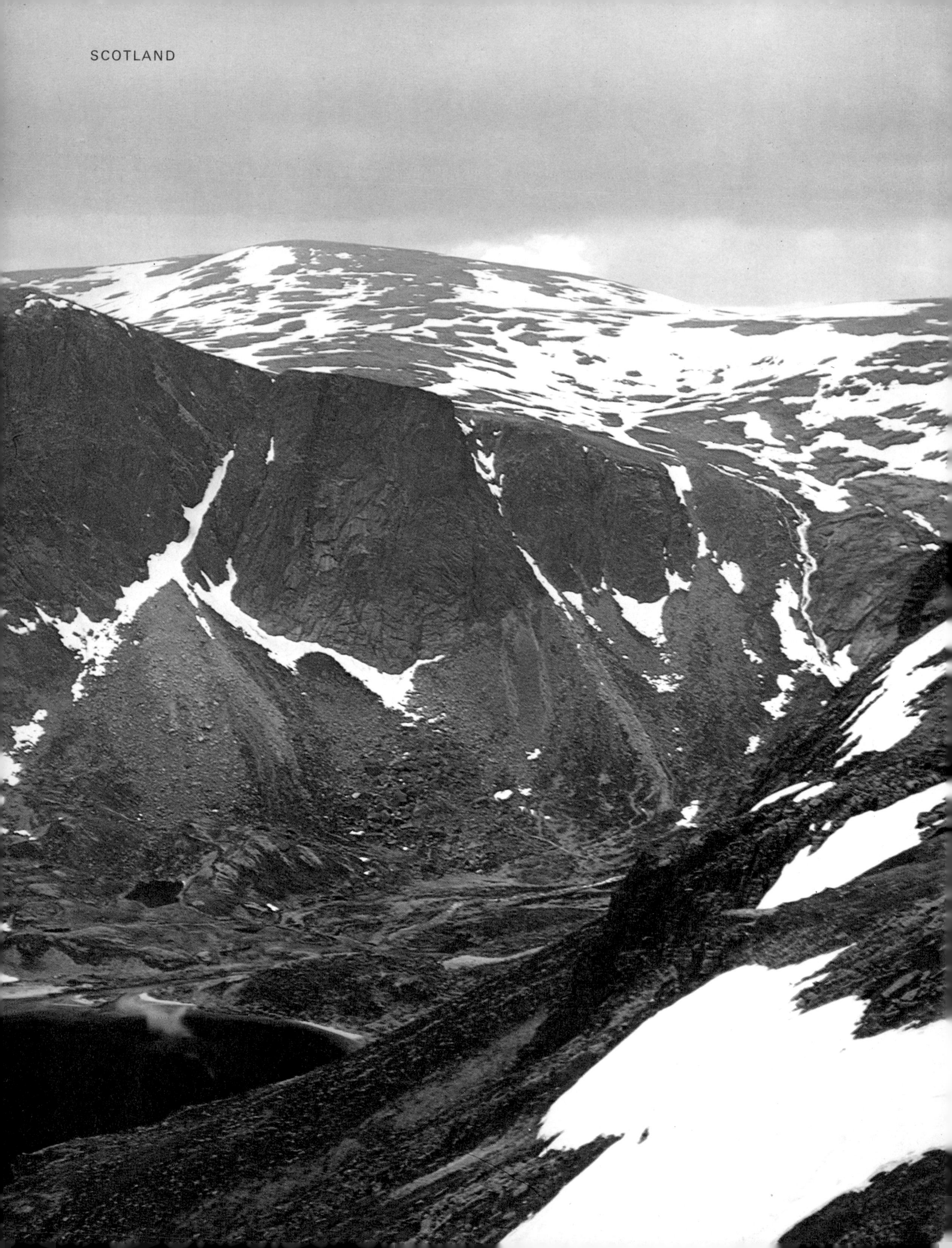

Scotland TOM WEIR

THE CAIRNGORMS

A day in May. Warm sun and sparkling visibility. It is only 10 a.m. and we are at 4,000 feet on top of Cairngorm, the Roof of Scotland. Far below lies Loch Morlich in the Glenmore Forest Park. We were walking by its yellow sands only an hour ago. Thanks to the ski-road and the chair-lift we are now in a world of frost-shattered granite and big snow patches that could be the Arctic — on the edge of the biggest stretch of high land in Britain, the Cairngorm plateau, giving us a flashback into prehistory. For this is the greatest surviving remnant of the vast plateau from which the land we call the Scottish Highlands was carved by millions of years of weathering and glaciation.

Up there the exhilarating walking is a lot flatter than on the lower ground. But take care as you set off wandering, for no road spans this second biggest nature reserve in Europe. Have a map and compass and plot your movements, for mists can descend and storms blow up quickly in this country of the Ptarmigan and the Dotterel where Golden Eagles hunt.

There is a jingle of Wheatear and Meadow Pipit song on the moor towards Ben Macdhui, and now and then the monotonous *whee-whee-whee* of a Ring Ousel comes from the corrie below. Distances are hard to judge. The hidden bumps take time and produce unexpected things — a Dunlin giving out its ecstatic reeling note from green patches among large snowfields, a cock Snow Bunting flitting about a likely nest-site among some screes, a Dipper flirting a stumpy tail, its white breast throbbing as it sings. The highest song I have heard was at the source of the Dee at 4,000 feet on Braeriach.

This is the home of the Ptarmigan, the mountain grouse which turns white to match the winter snow, but in summer is almost exactly like the lichen on the boulders. I have had a hen run right up to my hands to distract me from her ten yellow chicks. In August it is a common experience to find yourself driving a flock of grey Ptarmigan before you, moving over the stones in orderly fashion, as tame as domestic hens. The careful-stepping birds give a marvellous impression of stealth. It is all part of an inherent reluctance to fly and reveal their presence.

Finding the elusive Dotterel is not so easy. This rare plover of the Eurasian Arctic tundra prefers tripping about the stones to flying, and its disruptive pattern of mingled chestnut, cinnamon and white makes it difficult to see unless you spot it flying in to alight, pirouetting daintily, wings stretched high above its head for a second or two as it taxis along on racing legs. The cock looks bright until you see a hen, which is bigger and has a sharper edge to her colours. Nature has decreed that she must lay the eggs, but the duller cock has to do the work of sitting on them and rearing the chicks. No doubt this is to conserve the resources of the hen in such a hostile environment. Breeding success is low, the average being no more than 0·2 to 0·4 chick per pair of birds — so, please, do not disturb any Dotterel at a nest.

Golden Plovers with their spangled backs and black fronts send out lonely whistling notes beside the stream of Feith Buidhe in its grassy hollow below Ben Macdhui. Following it to where it disappears into snowfields like a glacier, we have the luck to see a Golden Eagle, the finger-ends of its broad wings spreading and narrowing as it hangs like a black cross in the sky, its lumpy head turning from side to side, searching the ground with telescopic vision. Golden Eagles are by no means a rare sight in the Cairngorms. That bird was perhaps after Ptarmigan, but Blue Hares and Red Grouse are more likely prey, though they will lift deer calves as well as Fox cubs, and even the poisonous Adder or Viper. Tree eyries in Caledonian pines are not uncommon in the Cairngorm country.

Rothiemurchus and the Loch an Eilein nature trail two miles from Aviemore make a fine introduction to this Caledonian pine forest of distinctive trees, each an individual of gnarled pink bark with umbrella canopy of bottle-green needles.

Tom Weir lives on the south shore of Loch Lomond and is an author, journalist, mountaineer and photographer. He is interested in the whole land-form of his native country and recent books include *The Western Highlands* and two volumes on *The Scottish Lochs*.

The Ptarmigan's plumage changes with the season to camouflage it within the prevailing landscape colours.

Opposite: The 'Roof of Scotland', the Cairngorm Mountains, a world of frost-shattered granite where snow patches lie even in midsummer.

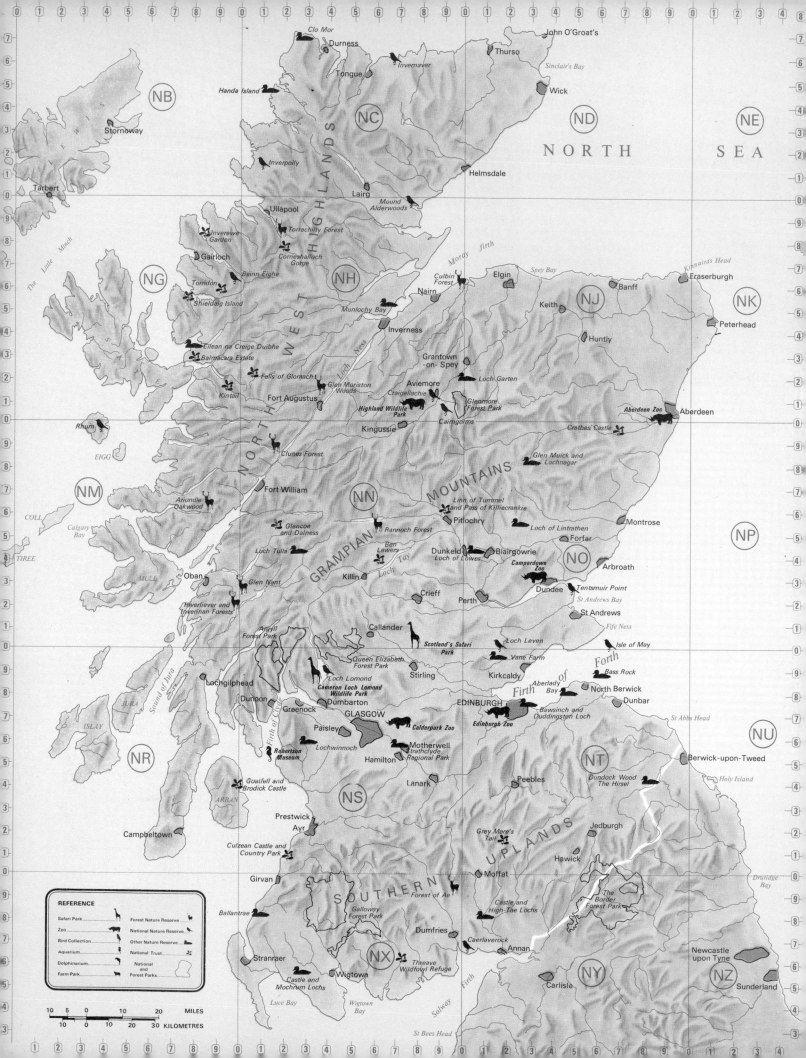

The forest dates back 9,000 years, when the tundra of alpine plants which followed the last advance of ice was colonised by alder, willow and hazel, giving way to climax forest of Scots pine, birch and juniper. As the trees grew up animals from Europe moved in, and were cut off from any retreat when the English Channel was formed. The first men to penetrate Rothiemurchus where the trees then grew to an altitude of 3,000 feet must have met a rich diversity of wildlife, some of it frightening. Wolf packs preyed on Red and Roe Deer, Reindeer and Elk. Brown Bears prowled, Northern Lynx stalked and Wild Boars grubbed. Beavers had their dams in streams, sharing the woods with Polecats, Pine Martens and Wild Cats. There were wild Oxen and Horses to be tamed.

Think of these animals as you walk the fine paths of Rothiemurchus, listening for the trilling Crested Tits and the metallic *clink* of Scottish Crossbills, distinctive birds which arrived with the pinewoods and have become different from their continental counterparts. Like the native Red Squirrels and the Roe Deer, the Wild Cat and the Red Deer, they managed to survive in this and some other fragments of primaeval highland forest which escaped the destructive hands of men. The native Capercaillie was extirpated, and any you see swerving through the trees, big as Turkeys, are descendants of birds introduced from Sweden in 1837 at a time of extensive tree planting by many landowners.

In a sense man began destroying the forest from the moment he came to live in Scotland, but the clearing for his agriculture, and even burning to exterminate Wolves, were nothing until trees became money. From the fifteenth century onwards Scotland's natural forests went up in smoke to smelt iron, or went sailing down the rivers Dee, Tay and Spey as rafts of logs to make the timbers and masts of ships. Timber was a good investment after the Jacobite risings of 1715 and 1745. Highland estates were forfeited and companies were formed in England to exploit the northern forests. Destruction went on at an ever-accelerating pace as 'bloomeries' by the score were set up from the Loch Lomond shores to as far north as Sutherland.

The natural forest could still have recovered, but for an alien animal introduced in tens of thousands into the Highlands — sheep. They displaced the Highlanders whose economy had been founded on cattle. Then came the buying up of the sheep ground to create deer forests and grouse moors. Over 4 million acres of the Highlands became deer forest a century ago, and although this had the paradoxical effect of preserving too many deer, it could be said that the forests became by accident something akin to nature reserves.

The wooded glens of Mar, now part of the Cairngorms NNR, were royal deer forest as long ago as the sixteenth century — perhaps the first stretch of high mountain country to be conserved for the specific purpose of deer-hunting. It is still deer forest, as is Glen Feshie on the Spey side of the Cairngorms. The Glenmore Forest Park on the north side has become a big attraction to campers and caravanners who enjoy a superb site beneath the ski-tows and chair-lifts which rise above Loch Morlich. The holiday complex known as the Aviemore Centre attracts ever-increasing numbers of skiers and tourists. The Centre has plenty of indoor attractions, but the accent is on the outdoors, for pony-trekking, hill-walking, bird-watching, mountaineering, canoeing, sailing and organised natural history studies. We must keep a balance between accessibility and inaccessibility if nature is to survive. Loch Morlich, for example, used to be one of the best places in the Cairngorms for seeing wildlife, but nowadays you are more likely to see hundreds of people on the beach and sailing dinghies peppering the waters.

It is well known, however, that Red Deer will move down to graze after the tourists have gone home to dinner. The richest prizes go to those who get up early and stay out late. Go out when the Blackcock are 'bubbling' at the lek, their communal display arena near the edge of the woods, and the chances are you will meet Roe Deer feeding by the roadside as you go. Nor do hill Badgers wait until darkness to come out in remote places. I know a sett where they lie, tummies turned to the sky, to enjoy the last hour of sun on June evenings. And just above that sett is a Golden Eagle's eyrie which I photographed a few years ago when it contained an eaglet with black wing feathers sprouting through its

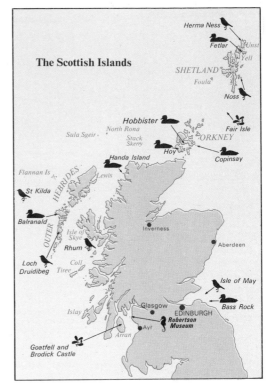

The Blackcock (male Black Grouse) uses its lyre-shaped tail in aggressive display.

299

The tree eyrie of a Golden Eagle gives a splendid look-out over its 15 square miles of hunting territory.

Female Siskin at its nest in a spruce.

white down, a heavily speckled egg which had failed to hatch, two Fox cubs, one leg of lamb, and a partly feathered grouse. When I climbed above the rocks of the eyrie I almost stepped on a tiny Red Deer calf; curled up and lying very still, it merely blinked at me with brown eyes. No prey could have been handier to an eyrie, yet I doubt if an eagle would see it, because parent birds coming to the nest are so concerned to make an invisible approach that they have eyes only to ensure that the coast is clear of enemies.

By contrast to the woods and hills, the marshes of Loch Insh, where the Spey loses itself for a time, are of special interest. One morning I saw three Otters at play near Kincraig, backs arched like Porpoises, though at times all you could see was the sharp ends of tails or whiskery faces as they dived and cavorted. A careful look will usually disclose a Goosander or a Short-eared Owl, and always there are waders. Temminck's Stints have nested here, Green and Wood Sandpipers have been heard singing in recent years. The Royal Society for the Protection of Birds has a reserve at the western end, a great haunt of Whooper Swans from winter into spring.

Craigellachie NNR, quickly reached by path from the Aviemore Centre, offers not only a most enjoyable bird walk, but from its little peak one looks over the Spey valley to the whole northern sweep of the Cairngorms. Not only are the birches a delight in themselves, but in early summer they ring with the songs of birds like Redstarts, Tree Pipits, Siskins and Redpolls. It is not uncommon to see Kestrel and Buzzard on the walk, and with luck even a Peregrine Falcon.

Then, of course, there is Loch Garten, which became famous overnight in 1954 when Ospreys nested for the first time for many decades; and 21 years later the eyrie is still in use, thanks to RSPB protection. Visit the hide (signposts point the way) and look through the powerful binoculars if you would see the birds. From this beginning, quite a few pairs of Osprey are breeding in the Highlands now. At least 16 sites were known in 1973, when 10 pairs reared a total of 21 young.

To see deer on Speyside, the best plan is to walk the right-of-way up Glen Feshie beyond the shooting lodge through fine meadows and Caledonian pines where Red and Roe Deer love to loiter. It is also a good place to see Eagle and Merlin, to glimpse a Greenshank, and have the company of 'roding' Woodcock and 'drumming' Snipe as each performs its strange nuptial flight at dusk or

Left, Red Deer stags in evening sunshine in Glen Feshie; right, Osprey perched close to its tree-top nest.

Blue Hare, which turns white in winter to gain concealment in its snow world.

dawn. The Glen Feshie path goes all the way through to Deeside, whose best centres for wildlife-watching are Ballater and Braemar. This is the quiet side of the Cairngorms, with fine walking approaches by the roadless glens of the Quoich, the Derry and the Lui, each pine-clad and haunted by deer.

Much more accessible, however, and as good as anywhere in the Cairngorms, is Lochnagar going up from Ballater by way of Glen Muick to the car park at Spittal. This is part of H.M. the Queen's Balmoral Estate, and under a deed of agreement it has become a Scottish Wildlife Trust Reserve. This is possibly one of the easiest places in all the Highlands for seeing Red Deer, since the road leads into the very heart of the forest beneath the crags of Lochnagar. Climb up to the vast summit of the mountain by a good path, wander over the tops, and you will find everything that is special to these hills, even to Water Voles breeding above 3,000 feet. Late April is an exciting time to go there, when the snowfields have broken and the Ptarmigan are squabbling for territory with strange squeals and croaks.

Ask me the question, which side of the Cairngorms do I prefer, Dee or Spey, and I find it hard to answer. Basically they have their similarities, but each is different. Deeside around the Pass of Ballater and the Old Bridge of Dee I find enchanting. I also love the Glentanar pinewoods behind Aboyne, not to mention Dinnet oakwood with its fine mixture of old and young trees so good for wildlife. Then there is the heathery country stretching north of Ballater beyond Morven, and continuing over the richest grouse moors in Scotland to the Gairn, Cock Bridge and the Lecht. That is country with Blue Hares in such density that keepers think nothing of killing 800 in a day.

Speyside is perhaps better for family walks. There is the chair-lift out of

Glenmore on to the 'high tops'. The Caledonian forest is quickly accessible and offers shelter from the wind and delightful paths on poorish days. Then there are the lochs, Morlich and Insh, Alvie and Pityoulish, where you might see an Osprey splash-diving after a fish — and that is a considerable thrill! Also, the Crested Tit with its barred crest and trilling call is commoner on Speyside; indeed, it is only recently that it has spread to Deeside. For animals, however, especially Red and Roe Deer, I think Deeside is better. You have a greater chance of seeing birds of prey too, especially Golden Eagles, Hen Harriers and Merlins. But whether you go to Dee or Spey or both, keep an eye open for Goshawks which are being seen more often in both valleys; it seems only a matter of time until they too establish themselves, as the Ospreys have done. The Greenshank is on the fringe of its range in the Dee valley, so it is thrilling to find it in the wet flows where it breeds, flying with quick darting flight and loud ringing calls so much more staccato than a Redshank's. Speyside still has a breeding population, but the Sutherland flows are really its stronghold.

THE HIGHLAND REGION

The Pine Marten has been mentioned as an animal that held out, as did a few native Polecats, through the period of forest destruction by retreating to the least accessible parts of the Highlands. It is to the main stronghold of the Pine Marten that we go now, to the northwest, to bare rocky mountains thrusting up from low-lying glens tailing into fjords — drowned valleys invaded by the sea when the ice-sheets melted.

Yet these spectacular mountains of Torridon and Assynt were hacked out of the same plateau as the Cairngorms, except that we are down to the very foundations here. The bedrock Lewisian Gneiss is 2,500 million years old, and the pink sandstone terraces building the peaks had been desert and sea-bed before being thrust upwards and denuded to their present form. Glen Torridon and Loch Maree are the places where this formation can be seen most spectacularly, and have the added merit of providing exceptional wildlife interest. Here a substantial fragment of Caledonian forest remains, and its importance can be judged from the fact that when the Nature Conservancy was formed it became part of Britain's very first nature reserve by declaration in 1951. The Ben Eighe NNR was established to perpetuate the native pinewoods of Coille na Glas Leitire, where Glen Torridon edges Loch Maree in what has been called 'the oldest floor in the world'. Much has been done to allow the visitor to share its scenic delights, for there are fine mountain and nature trails, and an interpretive centre just north of Kinlochewe on the A 832. All this is deer forest, and the landowners work closely with the Nature Conservancy Council to cull the stock after agreeing figures for stags for the whole area of 90,000 acres. By killing not more than a sixth of the total number, the herds are maintained at a strength which the resources of the ground will support. This is conservation in action.

The observant traveller should not merely walk the laid-out trails, but make frequent stops and use binoculars carefully while motoring anywhere in the neighbourhood. Loch an Iasgaich can be glassed from the Torridon roadside and is a good place for seeing Greenshanks. Loch Clair has a pair of Black-throated Divers surfacing on it often enough. Eagles and Peregrines are shapes that can be glimpsed on the crags where the Kinlochewe River goes into Loch Maree, and in the alderwoods the Redwings — new colonists in Scotland — sing their attractive song.

Litter bins are good places to see Pine Martens: so park your car near one before dusk and wait quietly, headlights switched off. So secretive are these slim, cat-like, cinnamon-brown animals, with yellow bib and pale pointed ears, bushy tail and clawed feet, that it took the Ben Eighe warden-naturalist, Dick Balharry, three years to find his first den. This is Wild Cat country too, so look out for them as you drive in dusk or darkness.

The coastal region is the best place for seeing Otters, and in my experience this applies to the whole of the Highlands and Islands. Perhaps this is their only stronghold in Britain. I have had many sightings, the best when one swam

Crows. During the last Ice Age the European Crow population was forced to retreat southwards to 'refugia' in the Balkans and the Iberian peninsula. These isolated groups developed striking plumage differences, the grey-and-black Hooded Crow in the east, and the all-black Carrion Crow in the west. There was, however, no change in voice and general behaviour, so that when the glaciers retreated and the separate groups expanded and met in middle Europe, they were able to interbreed and produce fertile hybrids, but only over a very narrow zone of overlap. The climatic amelioration of the early part of this century has caused a marked shift in the position of this zone in Scotland, the Carrion Crow making the greatest advance in the agricultural east, and the Hoodie holding its own in the highland country of the west.

Adult Golden Eagle.

View over Loch Clair to Liathach and Ben Eighe on the right: Golden Eagle and Wild Cat country.
The ringed tail is a distinguishing feature of the Wild Cat, larger and more striped than the domestic tabby — and considerably fiercer!

close to where I was sitting on the rocky shore, landed with a crab in its whiskery mouth, and made a meal of it with crunches that came noisily to me across the short distance separating us.

Glen Torridon is well blessed in its owners, with the 14,100-acre estate of the National Trust for Scotland marching across the summits of Liathach and Ben Alligin, west of Ben Eighe, to Loch Torridon, where close to an audio-visual visitor centre the warden-naturalist maintains a collection of live animals taken from the hills. The road to Shieldaig round Loch Torridon and on north to Applecross is of outstanding interest, twisting over low hills good for deer, and threading a coastline of fine bays where Eider Ducks float with Red-breasted Mergansers and Tysties. Herons are sea-cliff nesters on a small offshore island, and beyond the fluttering Arctic and Common Terns you may glimpse Manx Shearwaters skimming far out over the waters.

The 30 arms of the Atlantic which penetrate so deeply into the western Highlands are not only unique to Britain, but to a naturalist are the most delightful feature of the coast. Loch Torridon takes the form of a wide mouth angling to a narrow end, as do Lochs Carron, Duich, Hourn, Nevis, Sunart, Linnhe and Etive. Covetous eyes of oil-men were quick to see the advantages of these lochs for the building of platforms. The attraction to industry is the deep water for floating away these monstrous artefacts. West of the platform building-site at Loch Kishorn the sea reaches its greatest depth anywhere off the coast of Britain, at over 1,000 feet. Fortunately, in wildlife terms, the damage caused by oil-related developments is slight. Such a prediction cannot be made on the actual exploration sites of the rigs in the North Sea, where there must always be a fear of spillage in an as yet unknown technology — a disaster which could take the lives of thousands of seabirds.

Loch Broom, biggest of the sea lochs, was fortunately spared from platform building, and Ullapool makes a fine base for exploration of the Coigach peninsula. Coast and inland road systems make possible an exciting 50-mile car circuit round the fringes of an almost uninhabited country of lochs, bogs, remnant birchwoods and strange monolithic peaks, the last crumbled fragments of the ancient plateau. Driving north, the first stop should be 12 miles from Ullapool to take a turn round the Knockan Cliff geological trail, which sets the background of your tour and climbs over the very bones of the earth to look down on

The Coigach Hills in the heart of the Inverpolly National Nature Reserve.

the strangest of loch and mountain landscapes. Go into the visitor centre and take a copy of the Inverpolly Motor Trail which interprets your route and tells you what to look for. Notice the greenery of the limestone soil at Inchnadamph — like Inverpolly, part of a National Nature Reserve. All this is Salmon fishing and deer forest country, with narrow tracks leading to the coast where crofting villages are dotted above the sea. No coast gives more to enjoy than the sinuosities and bays stretching north from Loch Broom, but the exploring motorist must be prepared for wary driving on narrow, single-track roads.

At Scourie a diversion should be made to Handa bird island, an RSPB reserve easily reached by boat. It is a tiny grassy pancake rising gradually and then plunging suddenly in sea-cliffs thronged with Razorbills, Guillemots, Puffins, Fulmars and Kittiwakes. The sheer concentration of shouting life on the stepped ledges is exciting as you stand on the brink looking across to the cylindrical Stack of Handa, sandwiched between gully walls where the sea lunges. Great and Arctic Skuas advertise their presence, and Red-throated Divers nest on the small loch.

From Durness, by ferrying across the Kyle from Keoldale, you can take a minibus to Cape Wrath lighthouse, beyond which there is nothing but ocean stretching to Arctic ice and the North Pole. It is worth while walking back part of the route. My advice is to get off the bus at the Kervaig burn about five miles southeast of the Cape, take the croft-house path to the shore to enjoy the rock stacks, then follow up the edge of the rising cliff to look down the full height of the Clo Mor for the sight of ledges packed with seabirds, the effect of dizzy height emphasised by the criss-crossing of their flight-paths seen through 500 feet and more of plunging verticality to the bursting waves. Golden Eagle and Peregrine also nest on these frightening cliffs.

In contrast to the far northwest, the northeast tip of Scotland is agricultural land and heather moorland with shallow lochs spattered here and there, where you get Common Scoters breeding alongside Red-throated Divers, and where Black-tailed Godwits have nested. The most spectacular scenery is at the seabird cliffs at Reay and Dunnet Head — the most northerly point on the British mainland and well worth a visit. The Great Skua is increasing here, and Badgers have recolonised after a lapse of over a century.

South, down the Moray Firth, the gentleness of the scenery with its long muddy estuaries belies the excitement of its wildlife, for this is one of the great assembly points for wildfowl and waders. Counts along the coast between Golspie and Burghead at 15 sites in six winter seasons to 1972 showed an annual peak of 20,000–30,000 ducks and 400–500 wild swans. It is a main arrival point for birds from Iceland and Scandinavia, so the Dornoch, Cromarty, Beauly and Inner Moray Firths have an international importance. The invertebrates of sand and mud-flats supply rich feeding for vast numbers of waders which use the fields as well as the shore. So keep a sharp look-out between Golspie and Inverness for a great variety of visitors. The little estuary at Loch Fleet, the Kyle of Sutherland, Edderton Sands and Morrich More at Tain are of outstanding interest, though Nigg Bay is best of all with its winter diversity of Wigeon and Goldeneye, Common and Velvet Scoters, Bar-tailed Godwits and even Greenshanks. Man is faced with a big challenge here to equate the need for work and economic survival with wildlife conservation, for this is a major industrial growth area with problems of pollution discharges and atmospheric contamination by petrochemicals and other substances.

Inverness is a splendid centre, backed by fine mountains and glens. To the Firth, hundreds of Canada Geese come from Yorkshire to moult their feathers, and fly off again in late June once the flightless period is past. Cross the Firth north from Inverness and you are on the Black Isle. Munlochy Bay has a large heronry on its southeast tip, and it is likely you will see Wild Goats on the way. Take the A 862 and you are on the old road to Fort Augustus, running through a strange country of lumpy little hills with lochs where Slavonian Grebes have their Scottish stronghold. Head for Glen Affric, A 831, and you will find yourself in natural forest of birch and Caledonian pine, in a lochscape of sharp peaks, haunt of all the animals of the deer forest.

Three of the wildest birds of the lochs and lochans of the Highland region: top to bottom, Black-throated Diver, Red-throated Diver, Slavonian Grebe.

THE GRAMPIAN REGION

Eastwards along the A 96 lie the Culbin Sands, now a Forestry Commission plantation of Corsican pines stretching to the mouth of the Findhorn. The forest grows over the roofs of houses and farms of a barony which was completely buried in the seventeenth century when sand began to blow and created a miniature Sahara. With difficulty it was afforested, and now it is a haunt of Crested Tits and Scottish Crossbills. Some dunes remain, with saltmarsh, shingle and even a small loch, so there is the rich variety you would expect from such an exciting habitat. Then there is Findhorn Bay itself, clamouring with waders at low tide, while on nearby Loch Flemington you have a good chance of seeing an Osprey fishing.

East of the mouth of the Spey stretch the cliff villages of the fisherfolk of the Moray Firth. Gardenstown is one of the most exciting. Try to get a lobsterman to sail you round the base of the big Troup Head cliffs to enjoy the clamouring Kittiwakes, Razorbills, Puffins and Guillemots. Shags seem to be crowding every cave of this fine-weather coast.

South of Fraserburgh is the unusual Loch of Strathbeg, northern limit of the Great Crested Grebe in Britain and a wonderful goose and duck haunt, where no less than 500 wintering Whooper Swans have been seen together. The loch was once a tidal lagoon, until sand blocked out the sea 300 years ago and the brackish water became fresh. But for the efforts of conservationists, this rich habitat would have been despoiled by development. This flat country, windswept and bare, is known as treeless Buchan, but in the Ythan valley the Rook reaches its greatest concentration in Britain, with something like 70 nests to the square mile. Scientists of the Aberdeen University Field Station at Culterty near Newburgh have been studying these birds for many years, together with much else on the River Ythan which winds its way along the edge of the Sands of Forvie NNR to the sea and is one of the richest estuaries in all Scotland for wildlife.

Newburgh can be confidently recommended for family bird-watching, for distances are short, the channel is narrow at low tide, and the ducks and waders are used to the proximity of people; so you have Eiders, Shelducks, Red-breasted Mergansers, swans and gulls all competing for your attention. Over 1,500 pairs of Eiders nest on the Sands of Forvie. Sandwich, Common, Arctic and Little Terns breed in a strange terrain and the stranger company of Red Grouse and Great Crested Grebes. Winter or summer it is impossible to be disappointed here, and advice is always there for the asking at Culterty.

Eiders: top, drake; above, duck settling on to nest; below, hundreds resting on the Sands of Forvie at the mouth of the River Ythan.

Hermaness, Shetland, an important site for breeding seabirds, including Gannets, seen here on ledges.

A Hooded Crow scavenges for food in a Shetland rubbish-tip.

THE SHETLAND ISLANDS

Aberdeen is the boat terminal for Shetland, and the motorist who puts his car aboard in the afternoon can expect to wake up bright and early next day in Lerwick, capital of our most northerly islands. They are justly famed for their wildlife, and here too is the Shetland Pony, the tiny breed closest to the wild race which inhabited Scotland before the coming of man. At Clickhimin Loch the town's rubbish-tip is a swirl of Ravens and Hooded Crows competing for scraps with the quarrelsome gulls, often with the odd Glaucous or Iceland Gull amongst them. Lerwick is nearer to Bergen in Norway than it is to Aberdeen, and north Shetland has the same latitude as south Greenland, so it is not surprising that some of the birds have an Arctic affinity. The importance of Shetland can be judged from the fact that it has no fewer than five nature reserves of national status, and these do not include Fair Isle where more 'first records' of vagrant birds have been recorded than anywhere else in Britain.

You need go no farther than Noss, outside the larger island of Bressay which shelters Lerwick harbour, to get the authentic flavour of wild Shetland. Ferries shuttle back and forth to Bressay, then you must walk two miles or so to a jetty on the far side for another short sea-crossing. Visiting days are Sundays,

Mondays and Thursdays, unless by special arrangement. The great spectacle on Noss is its 600 feet of Old Red Sandstone cliff, the ledges thronged with Gannets. Skuas dart about your head, anxious for their nests as you climb the moor, and on the detached stack known as the Holm of Noss you will see the biggest colony of Great Black-backed Gulls in Britain.

Hermaness NNR, at the northern tip of Unst, includes Muckle Flugga with its lighthouse and the Outstack where in autumn the Atlantic Grey Seals haul out and have their pups, and in summer myriads of seabirds crowd the ledges. Gannets began nesting here in 1914 and the colony now comprises over 4,000 pairs. As on Noss, you may be lucky enough to see a pair of Great Skuas harassing a flying Gannet in the hope of robbing him of fish; and prepare to be dive-bombed when you visit this most northerly of our nature reserves, for there are about 400 pairs of these aggressive birds together with about 100 pairs of Arctic Skuas on the moor. Red-throated Divers nest on the lochans, Whimbrels and Dunlins in the hills, and Redshanks and Black-tailed Godwits on the low marshy ground.

Fetlar, where Snowy Owls nest on Vord Hill, is one of the most fertile of the Shetland Islands, with ponies around the crofts and moors loud with Whimbrels and Golden Plovers. These Snowy Owls, which have nested since 1967 and feed mostly on Rabbits, can be watched from the RSPB warden's hide. Nearby Hascosay also has much to delight the heart of the island-goer. Mainland is no less interesting, especially in the Rona's Hill NNR and around Loch Spiggie, a winter haunt of Whooper Swans near Sumburgh Airport. Not far away is the tiny offshore island of Mousa with a Storm Petrel colony nesting in the walls of its prehistoric broch. Sumburgh and Fitful Heads have fine seabird cliffs, and from their tops on a clear day you can see the remote Foula of 'Edge of the World' film fame, where a small community still hangs on to a precarious livelihood. Its great cliff, the Kame, is the second highest sea-cliff in Britain.

The other island you can see, to the south, is Fair Isle which has a well-equipped Bird Observatory offering comfortable accommodation. Isolated between Shetland and Orkney, Fair Isle can be reached by plane in 15 minutes from Sumburgh on Saturdays, or you can sail across the 25 miles of the Sumburgh Roost in the island's mail-boat, *The Good Shepherd*, which plies from Grutness pier three times a week. The island has fine colonies of seabirds and skuas, and its own special Field-mouse and Wren. The National Trust for Scotland took it over in 1954, but the Bird Observatory, established in 1948 to study bird migration, is run by a separate Trust and is visited by about 300 people each year.

On Fair Isle, a crofting community midway between Shetland and Orkney, more vagrant birds, blown by strong winds from varying directions, are recorded than from anywhere else in Britain.

Snowy Owl, an Arctic bird which colonised Fetlar in 1967.

The two breeding skuas of Britain, which nest in both Shetland and Orkney: top, Great Skua; above, Arctic Skua, whose elongated central tail-feathers are distinctive in flight.

Orkney is the best place to see breeding Hen Harriers; here a female prepares to settle on to her eggs.

THE ORKNEY ISLANDS

The Orkney Islands are most easily accessible to the motorist by driving north to Thurso on the Pentland Firth and ferrying from Scrabster to Stromness on the daily boat service. Apart from the hills of Hoy, Orkney is a greener and more agricultural country than Shetland, for the rock is mainly Old Red Sandstone which breaks down into good soil. Nowhere in Scotland is it so easy to watch Hen Harriers and Short-eared Owls as on the Mainland of Orkney. A vision comes to mind of an entire tern colony attacking and driving off a Hen Harrier in a screaming, diving flock of over 100 birds, the brown harrier with white rump almost lost in the snowflake whirl of angry terns. Watch the graceful wavering flight of the Hen Harriers as they skim so buoyantly, balancing on thrown-back wings for a moment, pouncing and quartering. The cock birds are pale as seagulls with ebony primaries and owl-like face masks. They are so common that it is easy to take them for granted, but this was almost their last breeding stronghold before the Forestry Commission plantations in northern Scotland gave them new habitats among the seedling trees where the long grass was colonised by voles — a main food-source for harriers as well as for Short-eared Owls, Kestrels and Buzzards. Nor should the Orkney Voles be taken for granted, for they are very special to the islands, being larger and darker than

the Short-tailed Vole of mainland Britain. It is a relict species, more closely allied to an older continental species, *Clethrionomys nageri*, long banished from the rest of Britain.

The Atlantic Grey Seal is the most obvious mammal of Orkney, with a big breeding population on the remoter holms where cows and bulls haul out in late autumn when the pups are born and mating and moulting take place. Common Seals are also present in these waters, as they are elsewhere round the Scottish coast. Their pups take to the water almost immediately after birth in summer. The size of the adults is a good guide to species, Common Seals being smaller than Grey Seals, which have broader heads with nostrils set farther apart.

Mainland, with its freshwater lochs and causeways over the sea-sounds to the tip of South Ronaldsay, offers a very good sample of the best of Orkney: of an archipelago where Corncrakes rasp in the fields, Arctic Skuas wheel over the moors, and seabirds throng the cliffs. Indeed, in Orkney and Shetland everybody is interested in, and lives close to, wildlife.

The Corncrake's rasping call is still to be heard in the fields of Orkney; but here too it is threatened by the farming methods which have eliminated it as a breeding species in much of Britain.

THE HEBRIDES

It is difficult to be brief about the 550 islands which shield the Western Highlands in two groups known as the Inner and Outer Hebrides, whose St Kilda outliers form the greatest rock stacks and highest sheer cliff in the British Isles, and where more Gannets now breed than anywhere else in the northern hemisphere. St Kilda has its very special races of Wren and Field-mouse, also the result of long isolation, and its long-legged Soay Sheep related to the wild Mouflon. The National Trust for Scotland organise annual cruises round these and other Atlantic islands at remarkably low cost. Accommodation is in dormitories and there are guest-lecturers aboard to accompany shore expeditions. Details can be obtained by writing to the NTS, 5 Charlotte Square, Edinburgh.

Strange things happen on some of these Inner Hebrides. Something like 60,000 Manx Shearwaters fly into the mountain-tops on Rhum at night,

Fulmars at their nest-site on Hirta, the main island of the St Kilda group. In the background can be seen Stac an Armin, Stac Lee and Boreray, collectively the largest colony of breeding Gannets in the world.

seeking their nesting burrows, having waited patiently in huge rafts at sea for darkness to fall. Shearwaters also nest below the Sgurr of Eigg, Rhum's neighbour to the south, an island with Tysties swimming in its harbour and song-birds in the coppiced hazel woods. In Rhum NNR, Red Deer are studied and efforts are being made to rehabilitate the moorland with native trees and shrubs. It has a unique breed of ponies, and like Canna to the north its rich moth and butterfly fauna bears witness to the mildness of the climate. Beyond Canna rise the Red Hills and the impressive Cuillins of Skye, the only isle of the Inner Hebrides where the Fox occurs.

You can take the ferry from Uig in Skye to Lochmaddy in North Uist, a commanding islandscape of wide skies, fresh and brackish water and stark rocks on whose open west coast the Atlantic casts up great quantities of seaweed along miles of sand fringing the dunes or 'machair'. There is an interesting RSPB reserve with a variety of marsh and shore birds, as well as Grey Seals, at Balranald. Loch Druidibeg NNR in South Uist, to which you can drive via Benbecula, is famous for its breeding Greylag Geese, and in summer it is a delight to see the parents and goslings swimming, flighting and cropping the grass against the background of Ben Mhor and Hecla, the highest of the Uist hills and home of Golden Eagles and a group of lightweight Red Deer. Compared with the Uists with their abundant wildlife, the peat moors of Lewis and the big hills of Harris seem dull; yet in treeless country the plantations of Stornoway, and even the town rubbish-dump where scores of Ravens forage, can be rewarding.

Anyone who goes amongst the islands, or the mouths of the big sea lochs facing them, should keep an eye open for small whales, and not only the fat bouncing Porpoises, but dolphins 12 feet long which leap nearly their own length out of the water when at play. They may be White-beaked or White-sided Dolphins, but Risso's and the Bottlenosed also pass by. More deadly are the Killer Whales which occasionally come close to land, frightening the seals. Lazy, big-finned Basking Sharks also float in the water; they are inquisitive and, like the Killer Whales, are best given a wide berth if you are in a small boat.

The Black Guillemot, or Tystie, breeds along most of Scotland's western coastline and islands.

The peaks of Hecla and Ben Mhor form a backdrop for Loch Druidibeg (left) in South Uist, famous for its breeding Greylag Geese (right).

THE FORTH AND CLYDE

Not all the exciting bird islands are in the remote north and west. In the Firth of Forth off North Berwick rises the Bass Rock, a miniature St Kilda sea-stack from which the Gannet gets its scientific name, *Sula bassana*. Take a sailing excursion round it from North Berwick and you will get all the thrills of the best sea-cliffs, with Gannets packing the ledges in their thousands and as many wheeling and diving around you in a blizzard of wings, as the boat noses past ledges and caves crowded with head-shaking Shags and growling auks.

Farther out in the Firth of Forth lies the Isle of May NNR, quickly reached from the fishing harbour of Anstruther in Fife, a rocky platform thronged with summer seabirds, and at its most delightful in late May or early June when the thrift is in pink bloom amidst a froth of white bladder campion. On a one-day sail you can explore this almost Hebridean island, and watch scurrying Puffins and soaring Fulmars from its cliff-tops. Bad weather sometimes causes thousands of birds to drop in at the Isle of May at migration time. In such a rush I handled my only Pine Grosbeak, caught in one of the traps, the first to be taken at any Bird Observatory.

The Forth indeed has vast riches, with the big bird-cliffs of St Abbs an easy walk just beyond Coldingham Bay north of Eyemouth, and the estuary delights of Aberlady along the shore to Gullane Point — at its best as the tide begins to go out. Late August can really be thrilling here, when the wading birds are in veritable clouds. From the car park on the Edinburgh–North Berwick road, the footbridge over the Peffer Burn is indeed a gateway to enchantment. Great numbers of Sandwich Terns haunt the estuary at this time, often pursued by parasitic skuas which give you fine aerial displays when robbing the terns of fish they have caught.

Edinburgh itself is virtually a city in the country, dominated by its own mountain, Arthur's Seat, from which the whole reach of the Forth can be seen on a clear day. Holyrood is a Royal Park containing an exceptional bird sanctuary in Duddingston Loch where a marvellous variety of water birds congregate in the reeds. This is no ornamental pond, but offers a rich enough variety of wild birds to whet the skill of any observer.

The Clyde estuary, while not so exciting for birds as the Forth, has Highland hills on its northern shore, the peaks and lochs of the Argyll Forest Park. Westward rises the Isle of Arran, a miniature of the Isle of Skye, with Red Deer, Golden

Shags on the guano-whitened ledges.

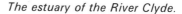

The estuary of the River Clyde.

View across Loch Lomond to the Queen Elizabeth Forest Park.

Eagles, Red-throated Divers, Hen Harriers, Short-eared Owls, Nightjars and all the best things of river and shore. Ferries from Gourock and Ardrossan give easy access: Gourock for the Forest Park, Ardrossan for Arran. The visitor wishing to continue north from Arran can take the car-ferry from Lochranza across to Kintyre, thus taking in the islands of Gigha, Islay and Jura. Islay is an especially good place in winter for Barnacle Geese, and the Rhinns and Mull of Oa cliffs are the best sites in Scotland for Choughs.

CENTRAL REGION AND TAYSIDE

From Glasgow, hub of the Clyde, a rich variety of contrasting scenery opens up. Northward, less than an hour away by car, lies the eastern shore of Loch Lomond, roadless beyond Rowardennan. Balmaha, where you first touch the loch coming from Drymen, is a good place to take stock, park your car, and ask the boat hirer to put you across to the nearby island of Inchcailloch within the Loch Lomond NNR. There is a fine nature trail through lovely oakwoods alive with the songs of Willow, Wood and Garden Warblers. From the summit you can look to the mouth of the River Endrick where it enters the loch through marshes and wetland scrub, where the shallows are good for ducks and the wet grassland for Lapwings, Redshanks and Curlews. The feral American Mink has been colonising the Endrick since 1964, and Ospreys are frequent visitors to this part of the loch.

North of Balmaha you enter the Queen Elizabeth Forest Park, with its nature trails, but the most exciting bit of the loch lies between Rowardennan and Inversnaid. Here you are on rough tracks, away from motor traffic; the hills close in on the deepest part of the loch where Goosander, Dipper, Common Sandpiper, Grey Wagtail, Buzzard and Raven live by the bays, burns and crags of the wild shore. The most inaccessible part of Ben Lomond lies above, haunt of Red Deer and Wild Goat. Badgers have setts and Pied Flycatchers nest by streams where Seatrout come to spawn in autumn. Vipers or Adders and Slowworms are sometimes met with on this shore and Stoats get a good living from the numerous Short-tailed Voles.

The Queen Elizabeth Forest Park stretches over Ben Lomond into the Trossachs, a miniature Lake District most easily reached from Aberfoyle or Callander. This country is not only scenically exciting, but over the last 35 years of tree planting has become much richer in wildlife. The high road mounting up

The Short-tailed Vole's unfortunate but important position in the food-chain influences the populations of its predators, which include nearly all birds and mammals of prey.

Autumn colours in the valley of the River Tay near Pitlochry, an area justly popular for its fine scenery.

The long shaggy coat of the Highland cow protects it from the sometimes inhospitable Scottish Highland climate.

from Aberfoyle is a fine way into it, and a stop should be made at the David Marshall Lodge to take in the wildlife exhibit and learn about some of the things you might see in the park. It can be said that the recently planted areas are best for birds, because the trees are tiny, and such raptors as Short-eared Owl, Hen Harrier, Merlin, Buzzard and Sparrowhawk are more easily spotted. Jays are common among the mixture of birch, oak, larch and spruce which make up the main forest. Watch out for Green and Great Spotted Woodpeckers, and listen for the curious 'reeling' song of the Grasshopper Warbler. Altogether there are something like 170 miles of forest tracks, 40 of them waymarked, so there is plenty of scope for walkers to work out long or short routes from the Duke's Pass, the hill road which is virtually a linear car park.

Loch Lomond drains to the Clyde, but the Trossachs drain to the Forth. North of these neighbouring regions the Highland hills rise higher and drain into the Tay. Ben Lui is the source of the Tay in wet Highland Cattle country. These tawny-coated hairy Highlanders with the dour looks and wide spread of horns are as close as we get in Scotland to the wild cattle of primaeval times and are hardy enough to stay out in any conditions. Their savage looks belie their sweet natures, but take care never to get between a cow and her calf!

Following the Tay eastward, the climate gets drier by an estimated inch for every mile, so the grassland quickly gives way to woods and heather once Loch Tay is behind. Pitlochry is the hub of the Garry, Tummel and Tay regions, justly popular for its setting in fine river, loch and hill scenery. Just south of it is Dunkeld and the Loch of the Lowes where visitors may enter the Scottish Wildlife Trust 'hide' and look across to the breeding Ospreys' eyrie. The Slavonian Grebe is another exciting bird of this loch.

Loch Rannoch, due west of Pitlochry, has the famous Black Wood, a fine fragment of Caledonian forest, where marked walks have been laid out; while westward of it lies Rannoch Moor with only the bleaching bones of long dead trees to tell of its former forest cover. Lochs and boulders and vast skies suggest desolation, but in early summer it is a thrilling place for seeing Red Deer in the wildest setting, where Snipe 'drum' and Golden Plovers and Greenshanks 'flute'. No road crosses the moor for ten miles west of the railway line. The part which is a National Nature Reserve can be quickly reached from Rannoch station, where the B846 ends.

The western strip of Rannoch Moor is easily reached by the Glencoe road, the A82, which crosses between two of the moor lochs backed by the biggest corrie in Scotland, Coire Ba of Clachlet. Pull in, use your binoculars, listen for sounds or walk a little along Loch Ba. An eagle over Clachlet, Red Deer in the corrie, Dunlin in the heather, Black-throated Divers on the loch, Wheatears chuckling and Skylarks singing are only some of the possible rewards for small effort.

Another good ploy is to swing away from the A82 at Bridge of Orchy for the west side of Loch Tulla on the old Glencoe road. This leads through another fragment of ancient pine forest, with Capercaillie, Roe and Red Deer, Blackcock, Whinchat, and a good mixture of Highland birds, including Goosander and Black-throated Divers on the loch and exciting waders in the western marshes. By comparison with the Loch Tulla shore at Inveroran the moorland hills seem bare of life, but they are the haunt of Fox, Wild Cat, Badger, Otter and Golden Eagle, with Ring Ousels here and there.

The first half of June is the best time for the Western Highlands, not only for drier weather and more sunshine, but for the sheer volume of life as the birds' nesting grounds pulsate with wader sounds and the deer hinds run with their spotted calves in the corries.

DUMFRIES AND GALLOWAY

For easy coastal bird-watching nothing beats Carsethorn below the peak of Criffel, facing out to Moricambe Bay across the Solway, a village of fisher cottages where waders come on to the street, and huge rafts of Pintail and Scaup anchor in the bay where the Nith enters. And just south round the coast lies Southerness, favourite haunt of Barnacle Geese, and always a good place for Common Scoter and Wigeon and wading birds.

But the real Barnacle Goose ground is Caerlaverock, reached from Dumfries by driving down the Nith. Go there at Easter when the maze of intertidal sand-banks is thronged by up to 15,000 grey geese, and as many as 3,000 Barnacles, not to mention silver flashes from the wings of Knots and Dunlins as they turn in flocks of thousands. It is also a good place for Natterjack Toads. The whole coast, from the bird-cliffs of the Mull of Galloway to Caerlaverock, takes a very long time to explore and is sure to produce some surprises, even for the most

Barnacle Geese which breed in Spitzbergen graze the Solway pastures in winter.

Criffel looms over the water from Caerlaverock National Nature Reserve, regular winter quarters for Barnacle Geese.

sophisticated. The Willow Tit is commoner here than elsewhere in Scotland, and migrant warblers tend to come earlier. Nesting Gannets on the Scar Rocks of Luce Bay, and breeding Cormorants at freshwater Mochrum Loch are only two of the unexpected things hereabouts. To hear a Nightjar 'churring' at dusk, try Glenapp south of the bird-cliffs of Ballantrae.

Nature has not confined her varied wildlife bounty to northern Scotland, for in the southwest where the Rhinns and the moors of Galloway swell from the bird-rich Solway shore rises a granite cauldron of plateau like a miniature of the Cairngorms. This is a country of peace, quiet roads, fine coast and scenic glens, and a good exploration base is Newton Stewart, meeting place of two rivers, the Cree and the Penkil. From there you have an estuary rich in bird-life to the south, and northward gentle hills rising in green waves through Galloway Forest Park to the brown crest of the Merrick, at 2,770 feet the highest point in Galloway. See it in May when the oaks are yellow, breaking bud against the dark conifers, and primroses button the russet of last year's bracken. Here it is easy to combine a day on the 'high tops' with an evening's birding in Wigtown Bay, exchanging the haunts of Golden Eagle, Red Deer, Wild Goat, Roe Deer and Peregrine for mud-flats beloved of waders. Thanks to forestry operations, the Hen Harrier is now a breeding bird of the hills, Short-eared Owls and Sparrowhawks have increased, Buzzards are in exceptional density and are often mistaken for eagles, Golden Plovers and Dunlins nest sparingly in the Snipe and Curlew country. The flanks of Cairnsmore of Fleet are particularly rewarding, and a delightful back road leads from Creetown following the line of the old railway and descending by the Water of Fleet to Gatehouse.

Above, male; below, female Crossbill; the beak of this finch has crossed mandibles, efficient tools for extracting the seeds from pine-cones.

There is so much you can discover for yourself in this not yet too popular backwater, but narrow duck-haunted Loch Ken, stretching from New Galloway for ten miles, is something not to be missed. Nor must it be rushed, for careful watching will disclose plenty in the bays and on the banks and hills. Few inland regions are better in the whole of Scotland. To list everything would only be monotonous in a country of Crossbill and Kingfisher, where Greenland White-fronted Geese gather for the winter.

This all too brief introduction to the wildlife of Scotland singles out some of the most rewarding places where it may be sought, but makes no pretence to be exhaustive. For example, nothing has been said of the Borders, from the Tweed to the orchard country of the Clyde valley, nor any details given of such notable freshwater lochs as Awe, Shiel, Tay, Arkaig, Garry, or secret oakwoods like Ariundle above the Strontian River draining into Loch Sunart. Wander in this fragment of sessile oakwood, haunt of Roe Deer, Wild Cat and Buzzard, and you have the privilege of being in a precious fragment of the kind of deciduous forest that man destroyed. Somehow, 400 acres managed to survive here, and now it is being conserved and seedling oaks are growing up where hitherto they had no chance because of sheep.

In the space available it has been possible to pick out only the distinctive places most likely to reward the patience of the seeker: and patience is the essence of all wildlife-watching. To those who can sit still, observe, listen, watch and wait come the highest rewards. Just to see your own Red Squirrel, Stoat or Pine Marten is infinitely more memorable than seeing the rarest bird or animal in the world on television. The Grey Seals on the Atlantic rocks, the panic of rising Red Grouse before a soaring Golden Eagle, Red Deer stags with antlers thrown back crossing a Highland ridge, Fox cubs playing at the mouth of a den, a Wild Cat with twitching upright tail in the heather, a Dipper flying into its moss-domed nest in the spray of a waterfall — these are things once seen you will never forget.

But it is the intensity of the moment of 'seeing' which is the true delight. There is ego in it too, for you know you have won the precious moment by the stealth of your observation and your fieldcraft.

Guide to wildlife habitats in Scotland

This Appendix provides a selected but varied list of places of wildlife interest. It is emphasised that nature reserves exist primarily for the conservation of animals and plants and in some cases for environmental experiments and research. They are not 'public open spaces' in the recreational sense. Access to many is therefore restricted and some, because of their sensitivity to disturbance, have been omitted from this list, in deference to the wishes of conservation organisations. Even with 'open' reserves visitors are earnestly requested to keep to the paths and bridleways and so avoid damage to the habitat and undue disturbance to wildlife. *There is no public access to the enclosed farmland which is part of many National Trust properties.*

Application to visit a National Nature Reserve (NNR) should be made to the appropriate Regional Office of the Nature Conservancy Council (NCC) at the address given. Intention to visit reserves of the Royal Society for the Protection of Birds (RSPB) should be notified to the Warden (whose address is shown) as far in advance as possible. In all cases where an address is shown, it is wise to contact the Warden to avoid disappointment.

SHETLAND

Fair Isle HZ 22 72. Bird Observatory. Crofts, moorland, fine sea-cliffs. 774 a. Grey Seals. Seabird colonies, skuas on moor, rare migrants. Wren and Field Mouse subspecies. Boat *The Good Shepherd* from Grutness Pier, by Sumburgh, 22 mls s. of Lerwick, or Loganair flight from Sumburgh Airport. Accomm. at Bird Observatory (March–Nov), shop, post office. NTS.

Fetlar HU 60 92. Rough hill country with breeding skuas, Red-throated Diver, Whimbrel, Dunlin, Eider and Snowy Owl. Boat from Mid Yell. (Warden – Bealance, Fetlar, Shetland.) RSPB.

Hermaness NNR HP 60 15. Northernmost cliffs and stacs in Britain. 2383 a. Gannetry and other seabird colonies, Red-throated Diver, Great and Arctic Skuas, Whimbrel, Dunlin. Around Burrafirth, Unst, at n. limit of A968 – B9086. NCC.

Noss NNR HU 55 40. Island with Old Red Sandstone cliffs 592 ft. Gannetry and other seabirds incl. Great Black-backed Gulls and skuas. Boat from Lerwick to Bressay, walk across Bressay, ferry to Noss. NCC.

ORKNEY

Copinsay HY 61 01. Island memorial to late James Fisher, 375 a. Seabird colonies incl. Tysties. 2 mls s.e. of Point of Ayre, from Kirkwall via A960 and B9050. Boat from Deerness. (Warden – Easter Sower, Orphir.) RSPB.

Hobbister HY 40 07. Moorland, marsh, freshwater and sea lochs, low cliffs, 1875 a. Hen Harriers, Kestrels, Short-eared Owls preying on Orkney Voles, Tystie, Common Gull and several species of duck. 5 mls s.w. of Kirkwall A964. (Warden – as for Copinsay.) RSPB.

Hoy ND 25 95. Island with fine Old Red Sandstone cliffs incl. Old Man 450 ft stac. Seabird colonies, skuas. Boat from Stromness. Private.

WESTERN ISLES

Balranald NF 71 71. Sand-dunes, machair, lochans and marsh. 1500 a. Breeding wildfowl and waders, Corncrake. Tysties nest on offshore islets. On n.w. coast of North Uist, w. of A865. Visitors to contact Warden at Hougharry. RSPB.

Loch Druidibeg NNR NF 80 37. Moorland, sand-dunes, machair, loch and shore. Greylag Geese, shore and hill birds. By Stilligary, A865 from Lochboisdale, South Uist, also along B890. Access controlled in breeding season (April–June). NCC.

St Kilda NNR NF 10 99. Islands of Hirta, Dun, Soay, Boreray and Stacs an Armin and Lee, about 3000 a. Grey Seals, Soay Sheep. Immense gannetry and puffinries, seabirds incl. Manx Shearwaters, Storm and Leach's Petrels. Wren and Field Mouse subspecies. Cruises and working-parties arranged by NTS, inquire 5 Charlotte Square, Edinburgh. NTS/NCC.

HIGHLAND

Ariundle Oakwood FNR NM 85 65. Sessile oakwood on steep slope above Strontian R. Roe Deer, Wild Cat. Buzzard and song-birds. It is n.e. of Strontian, n. of A861. Dep. Ag. & Fish. Scot./NCC.

Balmacara Estate NG 80 30. Moorland, covering most of the Kyle of Lochalsh–Drumbuie–Plockton coast and hinterland to Beinn Raimh 1466 ft. 6400 a. N. of A87 between Kyle of Lochalsh and Kirkton. Visitor centre (June–Sept) at Balmacara village. NTS.

Beinn Eighe NNR NH 00 60. Lowland to alpine country of Beinn Eighe 3309 ft, with birch and alderwoods s.e. of Loch Maree and Caledonian pine forest remnant on slope of Meall Ghiubhais. 10,507 a. Red and Roe Deer, Pine Marten, Wild Cat. Golden Eagle, Ptarmigan, Greenshank. It is s.w. of Kinlochewe A896. Car park, picnic area, camp site, trails. 1 ml n.w. of Kinlochewe A832. Visitor centre at Aultroy. NCC.

Cairngorms NNR NN 92 97. Immense dissected granite plateau around 4000 ft. Caledonian pine forest remnant (Rothiemurchus) through birchwoods and moorland to Ben MacDui 4296 ft. 64,118 a. Arctic-alpine flora; Red and Roe Deer, Blue Hare, Wild Cat, Red Squirrel. Golden Eagle Capercaillie, Ptarmigan, Dotterel, Snow Bunting, Crossbill, Crested Tit. It is s.e. of Aviemore and e. of Kingussie A9, via A951 to Coylumbridge and B970 to Loch Morlich. Chair-lift. NCC.

Clo Mor NC 30 73. Highest mainland cliff 800 ft. Seabird colonies, Peregrine. Ferry across Kyle of Durness from A838 at Keoldale. (No vehicles other than minibus.)

Clunes Forest NN 15 89. State forest, mainly conifers, on n. shore of Loch Arkaig. 20 mls n. of Fort William B8005. For Comm.

Corrieshalloch Gorge NH 20 77. Spectacular mile-long wooded gorge 200 ft deep, incl. Falls of Measach 150 ft. Braemore at junction of A832 – A835, 12 mls s.e. of Ullapool. NTS.

Craigellachie NNR NH 88 12. Birchwoods and moorland to 1600 ft. Hill birds, song-birds. 1 ml w. of Aviemore A9. NCC.

Eilean na Creige Duibhe NG 82 33. Small island wooded with Scots pines. Heronry, Eiders. Plockton Bay, by boat from Plockton A87. Ross and Cromarty CC/SWT.

Falls of Glomach NH 00 25. Moorland with 370 ft waterfall. 2200 a. They are 13 mls e. of Kyle of Lochalsh, A87 to Ardelve, then n. to Killilan, Glen Elchaig. From there it is $1\frac{1}{2}$ hrs arduous climb. Alternatively, continue A87 to Croe Bridge, where there is a steep 7 mls path via Dorusduain. NTS.

Glenmore Forest Park NH 97 07. Relict Caledonian forest and planted pinewoods rising through birchwoods and scrub to peaks of Cairn Gorm and Cairn Lochain, incl. Loch Morlich, 6200 a. Reindeer herd on tops, other mammals and birds as for Cairngorms NNR. N. of Cairngorms NNR, e. of Aviemore A9 via Coylumbridge, A951 – B970. Camp site at Glen More, trails, and information centre. For Comm.

Glen Moriston Woods NH 31 12. Caledonian forest remnant, Scots pine/birch/oak. Roe Deer, Red Squirrels. Black Grouse. Between Invermoriston and Torgyle Bridge A887. For Comm.

Handa Island NC 13 48. Spectacular Torridonian Sandstone cliffs and stacs. Rough pasture and peat bogs with lochans. Seabird colonies, Great and Arctic Skuas, Rock Dove, Twite. Offshore from Scourie A894. Unpredictable boat service, excl. Sundays, from Tarbert. (Warden on island, Apr–Sept.) RSPB.

Inverewe Garden NG 87 82. Magnificent garden beside sea loch. Exotic trees and plants; song-birds. N. of Poolewe A832. Restaurant (April–Sept), snack bar, car park. Visitor centre (April–Oct). Caravan/camp site between Garden and Poolewe (April–Sept). NTS.

Invernaver NNR NC 68 61. Shell-sand beach and high dunes, 2 mls w. of Bettyhill A836. Privately owned/NCC.

Inverpolly NNR NC 12 13. Glaciated plateau of Lewisian Gneiss with Torridonian Sandstone 'butte' mountains (Stac Pollaidh 2009 ft, Cul Mor 2786 ft) lochs and birchwoods. Red Deer, Pine Marten, Wild Cat. Golden Eagle, divers, Ptarmigan. 13 mls n. of Ullapool surrounding Loch Sionascaig, w. of Knockan A835. Restricted access to Drumrunie Forest throughout the year, and to remainder of reserve Aug–Oct. Visitors should contact Wardens. Privately owned/NCC.

Kintail NG 98 15. Mountain country to over 3000 ft incl. Five Sisters and Beinn Fhada, also Loch a' Bhealaich. 12,800 a. Red Deer, Wild Goats. Golden Eagle and hill birds. 14 mls s.e. of Kyle of Lochalsh n. of A87 through Glenshiel. Morvich caravan/camp site by Loch Duich off A87, visitor centre. NTS.

Loch Garten NH 98 19. Pinewoods by Loch Garten, lochans and moorland, 1500 a. Osprey, Capercaillie, Black Grouse, Siskin, Crested Tit, Crossbill. 3 mls e. of Boat of Garten off A95 near junction with A9, via B970. Layby parking, information centre, hide, trail. Open mid April to mid Aug. RSPB.

Mound Alderwoods NNR NH 76 98. Alder swamp at head of Loch Fleet. Salmon leaping under A9 road-bridge in autumn. Inner Loch Fleet, w. of Mound Station, on s. side of A839. Privately owned/NCC.

Munlochy Bay NH 67 53. Wildfowl refuge. Wild Goats. Heronry, waders. 9 mls e. of Muir or Ord A832, near Munlochy. Ross and Cromarty CC.

Nature Conservancy Council, North Scotland Regional Office, Caledonia House, 63 Academy Street, Inverness.

Rhum NNR NM 36 96. Island with castle and planted woods, new plantations of native trees; extensive moors with lochs rising to 'cuillins' over 2500 ft, with vast colony of Manx Shearwaters. 28,000 a. Red Deer, Celtic Ponies, Highland Cattle, Wild Goats, Grey Seals. Golden Eagles, Red-throated Divers, seabirds. Boat from Mallaig, A830 from Fort William. Shop, post office, camp site at Loch Scresort (permit required) but access controlled elsewhere. NCC.

Shieldaig Island NG 82 55. Small island wooded with Scots pines. Loch Torridon, w. of Shieldaig A896. NTS.

Torrachilty Forest NH 18 84. State forest, mainly conifers, with arboretum. 10 mls s. of Ullapool A835. Car park, picnic area, trails. For Comm.

Torridon NG 90 58. Mountain country incl. Liathach 3456 ft and Beinn Alligin 3232 ft. 14,100 a. Red Deer, Wild Cat, Pine Marten. Golden Eagle, Ptarmigan. N. side of A896 through Glen Torridon. Visitor centre at junction of A896 and Diabeg road in Torridon village. NTS.

GRAMPIAN

Crathes Castle NO 69 98. Castle, magnificent gardens and woodland. 595 a. 14 mls w. of Aberdeen A93, n. of Banchory via A980. Car park, restaurant, trails (April–Oct). Adm. fee. NTS.

Culbin Forest NH 98 62. State forest, mainly Corsican and Scots pines, binding sand-dunes. 7546 a. Capercaillie, Crested Tit. Waterfowl and waders in nearby Findhorn Bay. N. side of A96 between Nairn and Forres. For Comm.

Glen Muick and Lochnagar NO 30 80. Mountain country up to Lochnagar 3800 ft with lochs, corries, blanket-bog, heather-moor. Blue Hares, Red Deer in Glen Muick. Golden Eagle, Ptarmigan, Red Grouse. Balmoral Estate. From Ballater along Glen Muick to car park at Spittal. From s. footpath from Glen Clova B955 off A926 at Kirriemuir. HM The Queen/SWT.

TAYSIDE

Ben Lawers NN 65 41. Ben Lawers 3984 ft (views from Atlantic to North Sea), Meall Garbh 3661 ft and Meall Greigh 3280 ft. 8000 a. Arctic-alpine flora. Buzzards and hill birds. 9 mls n.e. of Killin A827, on n. side of Loch Tay. Visitor centre, car park, trail (May–Sept). NTS.

Countryside Commission for Scotland, Battleby, Redgorton, Perth, PH1 3EW.

Linn of Tummel and Pass of Killiecrankie NN 93 62. Banks of Rs. Tummel and Garry, and wooded gorge. Red Squirrels. Dipper, Grey Wagtail. 3–4 mls n. of Pitlochry, on w. side of A9. Visitor centre at Killiecrankie NN 92 64 (Easter–mid Oct), trails. NTS.

Loch Leven NNR NO 15 03. Migrant and wintering wildfowl incl. 4 species of

View across Loch Linnhe to the snow-capped Ben Nevis.

geese. E. of Kinross off M90. Public access at 3 points only. (See also Vane Farm.) NCC.

Loch of Lintrathen NO 27 55. Reservoir and surrounds, 400 a. Wildfowl refuge incl. Greylag Geese, Whooper Swans. 6 mls w. of Kirriemuir B951. Access at Balnakeilly, car park, hide available to public on special 'open days'. E. of Scotland Water Board/SWT.

Loch of Lowes NO 05 44. Glacial 'kettle hole' loch and margins, with reedbeds. Ospreys, grebes and wildfowl. 2 mls e. of Dunkeld A923. Visitor centre, car park, hide. SWT.

Rannoch Forest NN 55 57. Includes Black Wood of Rannoch, Caledonian pine forest remnant and planted pinewoods. Red Squirrel. Capercaillie, Black Grouse, Jay, Crossbill. Camp site and trails. On s.w. shore of Loch Rannoch, via Kinloch Rannoch, off A9 by B8019 — B846, 2 mls n. of Pitlochry. For Comm.

Vane Farm NT 16 99. Farmland beside Loch Leven, a feeding and roosting area for over 10,000 wild geese in winter; also up to 400 Whooper Swans and several species of ducks. Teal, Gadwall, Shoveler and Tufted Duck breed. Hillside birchwoods. Red Grouse and Curlews on moor. S. shore of Loch Leven, e. of Kinross off M90, via B9097. Car park, picnic area, Loch Leven Nature Centre, hide, trail. (Warden — Vane Farm, Kinross.) RSPB.

FIFE

Isle of May NNR NT 66 99. Bird Observatory of Midlothian Ornithological Club. Seabird colonies incl. Kittiwakes, Puffins, Herring Gulls, migrants. Boat from Anstruther A917, permit required. Commissioners of Northern Lights/NCC.

Tentsmuir Point NNR NO 50 28. Coastal accretion of dunes and slacks, open shore. Geese and waders on Abertay Sands. 6 mls e. of Dundee, 3 mls e. of Tayport A914 — B945. NCC.

CENTRAL

Queen Elizabeth Forest Park NS 45 97. State, mainly conifer, forests of Loch Ard, Achray and Rowardennan, incl. Ben Lomond 3192 ft. 60 sq. mls. Adjoins Ben Venue 2393 ft and The Trossachs. Fine oakwoods along Craig Rostan shore of Loch Lomond accessible by footpath Rowardennan–Inversnaid. E. side of Loch Lomond n. of Drymen B837. Caravan/camp sites at Cobleland (Aberfoyle) and Rowardennan (10 mls n. of Drymen). Traversed by A821 Aberfoyle–Trossachs and B829 Aberfoyle–Inversnaid. For Comm.

STRATHCLYDE

Argyll Forest Park NS 15 95. State forest, mainly conifers, and lochs, mountain country to over 3000 ft. 63,000 a. W. side of Loch Long and Loch Goil. Traversed by A815 Strachur–Ardbeg, along e. shore of Loch Eck, and A880 to Ardentinny. In the n. A83 – B828 – B839 Arrochar–Lochgoilhead. For Comm.

Ballantrae NX 08 82. Shingle spit 1000 yds.long and lagoon. Shore birds. 13 mls s. of Girvan A77. SWT.

Culzean Castle and Country Park NS 23 10. Parkland, walled garden and aviary, farm and woods. 565 a. 12 mls s. of Ayr A719. Restaurant, shop, exhibition at Home Farm. Adm. fee. Ayrshire CC/Ayr and Kilmarnock TCs./NTS.

Glencoe and Dalness NN 18 56. Mountain country incl. Buachaille Etive Mor 3345 ft, Buachaille Etive Beag 3029 ft and Stob Coire nan Lochan 3657 ft. 13,400 a. Red Deer, Wild Cat, Golden Eagle, Ptarmigan, Dotterel. 4–10 mls e. of Ballachulish, traversed by A82 through Pass of Glencoe. Visitor centre (mid May–mid Oct) with information on walks, car park. NTS.

Glen Nant FNR NN 03 27. Wooded gorge, coppiced oak/ash/hazel/birch. Buzzards, songbirds. 1–4 mls s. of Taynuilt, traversed by B845. For Comm/NCC.

Goatfell and Brodick Castle NS 00 38. Ridge walks in 7300 a. mountain country incl. Goatfell 2866 ft, Glen Rosa, Cir Mhor 2618 ft. Red Deer. Golden Eagle and hill birds. Isle of Arran, by steamer from Ardrossan. Restaurant at Brodick Castle and Gardens 2 mls n. of Brodick pier A841. Adm. fee. NTS.

Inverliever and Inverinan Forests NM 98 15. State forests, mainly mature conifers, beside Loch Awe. 13,000 a. N. shore of Loch Awe 10 mls s. of Taynuilt A85, via B845 to Kilchrenan

and minor road to s.w. joining B840 at Ford. For Comm.

Loch Lomond NNR NS 41 90. Inchcailloch and other islands, wet pastures and woods between Endrick mouth and loch shore. Oakwood and wetland birds, migrants. Boat from Balmaha, 4 mls w. of Drymen B837. Picnic site and trails on Inchcailloch, access to Endrick mouth restricted. NCC.

Loch Tulla NN 29 43. Loch with native Scots pinewoods on s.w. shore. Red and Roe Deer. Golden Eagle, Black-throated Diver, Black Grouse. 2 mls n. of Bridge of Orchy A8005 leaving A82. Private but viewable from road.

Lochwinnoch NS 36 58. Wildfowl refuge, incl. Barr Loch and Aird Meadows, 388 a. 15 mls e. of Largs A760. (Warden – The Barony, Kirkland Road, Kilbirnie, Ayrshire.) RSPB.

Nature Conservancy Council, South West Scotland Regional Office, Loch Lomond Park, Balloch, Dunbartonshire.

Strathclyde Regional Park NS 73 56. Wildfowl refuge, bird sanctuary at Bothwell. Hamilton, on w. side of A74. Hamilton Burgh C.

LOTHIAN

Aberlady Bay LNR NT 45 81. Dunes, beach, tidal flats. 1439 a. Waders, geese and wildfowl, migrants. 12 mls e. of Edinburgh A198 or B1348, on w. side of Aberlady. Car park by Peffer Burn NT 47 81. E. Lothian CC.

Bass Rock NT 61 87. Historic gannetry and other seabird colonies. Boat from North Berwick A198. Permit required. Private. (Contact F. Marr, 24 Victoria Road, N. Berwick, Lothian.)

Bawsinch and Duddingston Loch NT 28 72. Wildfowl refuge and bird sanctuary adjoining high amenity area of Arthur's Seat and Holyrood Park. City of Edinburgh. Can be viewed from n. (Holyrood Park) side of loch. Royal Parks/SWT.

The National Trust for Scotland, 5 Charlotte Square, Edinburgh, EH2 4DU.

The Nature Conservancy Council, Scottish Headquarters, 12 Hope Terrace, Edinburgh, EH9 2AS.

The Nature Conservancy Council, South East Scotland Regional Office, 12 Hope

Terrace, Edinburgh, EH9 2AS

Royal Society for the Protection of Birds, Scottish Headquarters, 17 Regent Terrace, Edinburgh, EH7 5BN.

Scottish Wildlife Trust, 8 Dublin Street, Edinburgh, EH1 3PP.

BORDERS

Dundock Wood, The Hirsel NT 83 41. Mature planted woodland with lake and fine show of rhododendrons and azaleas in early summer. Bird Sanctuary. N. side of A697, immediately w. of Coldstream. Car park.

DUMFRIES AND GALLOWAY

Caerlaverock NNR NY 05 66. Meadows and 'merse' saltmarsh, flocks of wintering geese incl. Barnacle Geese. 7 mls s. of Dumfries B725, e. of Bowhouse. NCC.

Castle and Hightae Lochs LNR NY 08 81. Wildfowl refuge. By Lochmaben, 8 mls e. of Dumfries A709. Annan and Eskdale DC.

Castle and Mochrum Lochs NX 30 53. Wildfowl refuge. Greylag Geese, inland Cormorant colony. 8 mls w. of Wigtown, on n. side of B7005 at Culshabbin.

Forest of Ae NX 98 93. State conifer forest. Birds incl. Sparrowhawks. Ae village road linking A701 – A76, 10 mls n. of Dumfries. For Comm.

Galloway Forest Park NX 40 80. State conifer forest, mainly spruce, pine and larch, Loch Trool with relict oakwoods, open moorland rising to Benyellary 2360 ft and Merrick 2770 ft, with lochs on e. side. 200 sq. mls. Red and Roe Deer, Wild Goats. Hill and forest birds incl. birds of prey. 8 mls n.w. of Newton Stewart, A714, access n. of Bargrennan NX 36 78, along Bargrennan–Straiton road. Forest village, car parks, caravan/camp sites, trails. For Comm.

Grey Mare's Tail NT 18 14. Moorland rising to 2696 ft, with spectacular 200 ft waterfall and Loch Skeen, 2383 a. Wild Goats. Hill birds. 9 mls n.e. of Moffat, on w. side of A708. NTS.

Threave Wildfowl Refuge NX 75 60. Roosting/feeding area for wild geese and ducks by R. Dee. 2 mls s. of Castle Douglas A75. Visitor centre at Threave House Gardens, trail. Controlled access Nov–March. NTS.

Animal collections in Scotland

Aberdeen Zoo

The Zoo has a general collection, with some 200 mammals, 400 birds and a small number of reptiles and fish. British and European mammals are well represented, and you can see Scottish Wild Cats, which breed here, Pine Martens, squirrels, Grey Seals, Red Deer and Roe Deer. Other mammals include Wild Boar, wolves, porcupines, Malayan Short-clawed Otters, Kinkajous, Chimpanzees, Pig-tailed Monkeys, Pumas, Bennett's Wallabies, Dingos and Guanacos. The otters, wolves, wallabies and Guanacos (which are related to the Llama) all breed here regularly.

Among the birds you can see ravens, cranes, peafowl, pheasants, pelicans, Black Swans – an Australian species – birds of prey and owls. The Barn Owls also breed in the Zoo. There are a number of birds at liberty here, and you will find small collections of fish, amphibians and reptiles in the aquarium and the Reptile House. There is also a children's zoo showing various domestic animals.

The Zoo is owned by the Aberdeen and North of Scotland Zoological Society, founded in 1962. The Society opened the Zoo in 1966, with the assistance of the City of Aberdeen. There is a Senior Zoo Club, which meets each month for illustrated talks, and a Junior Zoo Club, which has monthly talks, nature rambles and other activities.

Aberdeen Zoo. **Address** Hazlehead, Aberdeen. **Telephone** Aberdeen 39369. **Open** 10.00–20.30 summer, 10.00–dusk winter. **Catering** kiosk. Zoo shop. **Guided tours** by arrangement. **Acreage** 3. **Car** 2 mls w. of city centre at Hazlehead Park on A944, Queens Road, direction Alford. Zoo at entrance to Hazlehead Park. **Bus** 4 (Hazlehead bus) from town centre stops 200 yds from Zoo. **Train** to Aberdeen Joint (2 mls). **Taxis** available. **Other facilities** children's playground, first-aid post. Public **not allowed** to feed animals.

Aquarium and Robertson Museum

AT THE UNIVERSITY MARINE BIOLOGICAL STATION

The Aquarium of the Marine Biological Station is controlled by the Universities of London and Glasgow. It was opened in 1896, and is one of the oldest in the British Isles. The exhibition specialises exclusively in the marine life found in the Firth of Clyde, and you can see Soft Corals, fan worms, lobsters, prawns, shrimps, as well as hermit crabs, Shore Crabs, spider crabs and starfish – brittle stars and Feather Stars. Other marine creatures here are sea-urchins, sea squirts and, occasionally, sea cucumbers. The fish exhibited include Cod, dogfish, scorpion fish, wrasse, blennies, gobies, anemones and an octopus.

The Marine Station's main functions are research, the teaching of marine biology and the supply of specimens.

Aquarium and Robertson Museum at the University Marine Biological Station (Universities of London and Glasgow). **Address** Marine Station, Millport, Cumbrae, Scotland. **Telephone** Millport 581. **Open** 09.30–12.30 and 14.00–17.00 Mon–Sat summer, Mon–Fri winter. **Guide-book**. **Guided tours** by arrangement. **Car** to Largs then Cumbrae Car Ferry to Millport. **Bus** local service from Cumbrae Ferry stops at Aquarium. **Train** to Largs. **Taxis** available. Public **not allowed** to feed exhibits.

Calderpark Zoo

Calderpark Zoo is in the process of rapid expansion after many years of comparative stalemate, and regular visitors are likely to see many exciting developments over the next few years. At present there are about 400 bird and mammal species and about 50 reptiles. This is a general collection with representatives of most animal families, and the majority of these are now exhibited in attractive modern enclosures, mainly in the open air. There are also some important indoor exhibits – the Tropical House, the Nocturnal House, the Small Primate House and the Tapir and Elephant House.

The paddock along the entrance drive exhibits Parma or White-throated Wallabies, which breed regularly here, and a variety of ducks as well as Barnacle Geese and Swinhoe's Pheasants. You can also see American Bison, once numerous on the American prairies, and five species of deer. There are Red Deer, still numerous in Scotland and in English parks. The Fallow Deer, kept for centuries in England and now found wild there, share a paddock with Soay Sheep. All these species breed here regularly. The Two-wattled Cassowaries, colourful flightless birds of northern Australia and New Guinea, have laid eggs in the Zoo but have not yet reared young. They are aggressive birds, striking out with their powerful claws, and they are unusual in having no tail feathers and in that the female is larger than the male; otherwise the sexes look alike. Other paddocks exhibit European Wild Boar, Chinese Water Deer (a small animal with no antlers), Muntjac (a primitive deer of southeast Asia), Llamas, and Barbary Sheep, which are in fact wild goats from the Atlas Mountains of North Africa. There are mixed paddocks exhibiting wallabies, deer and birds. The first contains Red-necked Wallabies from southeastern Australia. These share their enclosure with Golden Pheasants and with Demoiselle Cranes — the smallest of the crane family which are found in southeastern Europe and central Asia, wintering in India and North Africa. The other mixed paddock has peafowl, more Water Deer and Dama Wallabies, a small shy species which inhabits dense scrub in Australia. It is probably the first Australian marsupial ever seen by a European, having been recorded by a Dutch navigator in 1629. One of the rarest hoofed animals in the Zoo is Père David's Deer, a swamp deer from China which became extinct in the wild in 1900. First seen by a French missionary in 1865, enough animals were taken to European zoos to ensure its survival, and it now exists only in captivity. The other very rare animal is Przewalski's Horse, the wild horse of Mongolia. This is probably extinct in the wild but it is preserved in zoos, being named after the Russian cavalry officer who discovered it in 1870. Behind the Tropical House is a paddock for donkeys and Shetland Ponies, which give rides to children in the summer.

There are a number of smaller mammal exhibits in the Zoo for African Crested Porcupines, Grey Seals, Polecats, Striped Skunks, Red Foxes, and two interesting small marsupials, Bruijn's Pademelons and Potoroos. The Potoroo is a rat-kangaroo, of which there are several species no larger than a Rabbit, which lives in low vegetation, and carries bundles of grass wrapped round its tail for nest-building. Pademelons are small scrub wallabies found in Australia and New Guinea, and the group in the Zoo regularly produces young. The Crested Porcupine of southern Europe, North Africa and tropical East Africa has long, easily detached quills which stick into an enemy when the porcupine charges at it backwards. Grey Seals are found off British coasts. The Striped Skunk is an American species which ejects evil-smelling fluid from its anal gland as a form of defence. The fluid will burn exposed skin, though it is not used against another skunk. The Red Fox, a British species, is common and probably increasing in numbers, having learned to scavenge in and around urban areas. Also see the Vietnamese Pot-bellied Pigs, short-legged, fat animals with compressed snouts which breed readily in the Zoo.

The Tropical House, opened in 1969, is mainly a reptile house, but with a number of aviaries and other exhibits for small creatures. At the entrance is a glass-fronted exhibit for Jackass or Cape Penguins which are found in the wild around the coasts of South Africa. There are two tanks opposite it for tropical freshwater fish, and the central area of the house is planted, with a Goldfish pond and waterfall at the far end. The reptiles shown include the Mississippi Alligator and the Estuarine Crocodile, a southeast Asian species which swims in the sea as well as in rivers. Both are endangered in the wild. You can also see the much smaller Siamese Crocodile. There are several species of tortoise, lizard, skink and gecko, the rarest of these being the Blue-tongued Skink and the Rhinoceros Iguana, which has horns on its nose. The house geckos have bred here, and so have the Slow-worms, a harmless British species which looks like a snake. The snakes here are the Indian Rock Python and the King Snake. You can also see Giant Indian Fruit Bats, which live in colonies, roosting in trees by day and feeding at sunset. There are aviaries for lovebirds, Banded Aracaris and Swainson's Toucans, and the Leopard Cat, a small jungle species of southern Asia, Sumatra, Java and Borneo, and the African Civet, a thick-bodied nocturnal animal which preys on small mammals. Some species of civet are valued for their musk which is used to make cosmetics.

Calderpark Zoo. **Address** Uddingston, Glasgow. **Telephone** Glasgow 771-1185. **Open** 09.30–17.00 (or 19.00 depending on the month) summer and winter. **Guide-book. Catering** snack bar, kiosk. Zoo shop. **Guided tours** by arrangement. **Acreage** 35. **Car** 6 mls s.e. of centre of Glasgow on A74. **Bus** from Glasgow, Anderson Cross bus station, 40, 44, 56, 240, 241; or Buchanan bus station, 52, 53, 54, 55. **Train** to Glasgow Central or Queens Street stations, then bus or taxi; or to Uddingston station (2 mls) buses every 15 mins to Zoo. **Taxis** available. **Other facilities** first-aid post, push-chairs, children's playground. No pets. Public **not allowed** to feed animals.

A squirrel monkey from South America can be seen at Calderpark Zoo.

The Nocturnal House, built in 1968, exhibits the Musang, or Common Indian Palm Civet, a smaller animal than the African Civet, which exudes a strong odour in defending itself, like the skunk; and two galagos or bushbabies — Demidoff's Galago, a small primate from tropical Africa, and the Thick-tailed or Great Galago, a large member of the same family found in South and East Africa. You can also see the Tree Porcupine here, a species with barbed quills which work themselves more and more deeply into the attacker's flesh.

The Small Primate House contains squirrel monkeys, White-throated Capuchins and Cotton-top Tamarins, all South American species; Patas Monkeys, a species of the plains of northern central Africa; and Ring-tailed Lemurs from Madagascar. All the lemurs are now endangered in the wild, since their habitat in Madagascar is threatened by forest clearance. Elsewhere in the Zoo you can see Rhesus Monkeys, the commonest monkey in India, although it has been exported in huge numbers in recent years for medical research; and the Barbary Ape, the only monkey found in Europe, with a colony on the Rock of Gibraltar. The Small Primate House also exhibits young Chimpanzees, the only one of the three large anthropoid apes not in danger of extinction in the wild.

There are large outdoor enclosures for Lions and Tigers, and in the Cat House you can see Leopards, Pumas, which breed regularly, and four smaller cat species: the Serval, Caracal, Northern Lynx and Temminck's Golden Cat. The Serval is a long-legged, short-tailed African species with stripes and spots. The Caracal or Desert Lynx, widely distributed in Africa, the Near East and northern India, lives in grassland and semi-desert. The Northern Lynx is a more heavily built animal with a stubby tail, rare in Europe, but also found in northern Asia and Siberia. Temminck's Golden Cat is a species of southeast Asia, a little larger than the European Wild Cat. The other animals kept in this house are Raccoon Dogs, an undog-like member of the dog family with a bushy coat and short legs, found in Japan, Korea and China; and Binturongs, members of the civet family from southeast Asia. This is a slow-moving tree-dweller with shaggy black hair and a long bushy tail which is prehensile. The Binturongs here bred three young in 1972, an unusual event in a zoo. The other large carnivorous animals in the Zoo are the Polar Bears. Their pool is one of the Zoo's original constructions, which has been recently renovated with improvements to the indoor dens to enable the bears to breed. Also, do not miss the Tapir and Elephant House, where you can see Brazilian Tapirs and an Indian Elephant.

Other birds you can see in the Zoo are Dalmatian and Brown Pelicans, Secretary Birds, a long-legged snake-eating bird of Africa, several pheasant species, the Cereopsis or Cape Barren Goose, a rare species, and Sarus Cranes, a tall handsome species found in India, Burma and Thailand. There are also aviaries for macaws, the largest of the parrot family from South America, and for birds of prey. The species exhibited are Barn Owls, Tawny Owls and Long-eared Owls, and Kestrels, all of which are native British species.

There is a small children's showground, with a separate entrance at the side of the Zoo. Whether or not you have a special interest in animals, you will find Calderpark Zoo a pleasant place in which to spend a day. The Zoo is operated by the Zoological Society of Glasgow and West of Scotland. The Society was founded in 1937, but it was not until 1947 that the Zoo was opened. The gardens were planned during the 1950s and the Zoo receives grants from Glasgow Corporation, Lanark County Council and other local authorities. The Society's chief object is 'to promote, facilitate and encourage the study of Zoology and Animal Psychology, and to foster and develop among the people an interest in and knowledge of animal life'. There is plenty of land on which the Zoo can be expanded, and the rate of development has been accelerated in the past few years, thanks to progressive management. The collection is being developed as a complement to Edinburgh Zoo's collection rather than in competition with it. Membership of the Society entitles one to complimentary tickets to the Zoo, use of the members' room in the restaurant, regular meetings for both adult and junior members, and a free copy of *Zoo Life*, a lively bi-monthly magazine. It will not be many years before this becomes one of the major zoos in Great Britain, worthy of the importance of the City of Glasgow.

Above: Caracal Lynx, an inhabitant of arid regions of Africa and Asia. Below: Demidoff's Galago, a bushbaby.

323

Cameron Loch Lomond Wildlife and Leisure Park

Cameron Loch Lomond, originally opened as a bear park in 1972, was re-designed in 1975 by Mr Patrick Telfer-Smollett, owner of Cameron House, with a wider range of animals. You can now see four types of bear, and a number of hoofed animals, small mammal species and waterfowl, all within sight of Loch Lomond, the largest lake in Great Britain and one of the most beautiful.

The bears are exhibited in two reserves which are visited by car and, as in all safari parks, you may not get out nor open the car windows while you are in these areas. Bears are both inquisitive and uncertain-tempered, besides being extremely strong. One reserve contains two species of black bear, the Asiatic and the Canadian, and the other contains two sub-species of Brown Bear, the European and the Grizzly. The Asiatic or Himalayan Bear, also sometimes called the Moon Bear, is found in the Himalayas, China and Japan, the bears in Japan being considerably smaller than those in the Himalayas. It has a distinctive white V across its chest, and is slightly smaller than the Brown Bear, but it is a better climber. In winter, this bear will sleep for a good deal of the time, often finding a hollow poplar tree near a river and sleeping in the tree about 15 feet from the ground. Its diet is mixed, favourite foods being fish and fruit. The American or Canadian Black Bear is usually black, but the colour can vary to brown, sometimes with white on its chest. It is still fairly common in the northern United States and Canada, and in the Rocky Mountains. Like the Asiatic Black Bear, this species is smaller than the Brown Bear and it is also a better climber. It is considered less dangerous than the Brown Bear. A lot of its time in winter is spent sleeping, and as in all bears of the northern hemisphere, the cubs are born in the winter den shortly before the spring. The American Black Bear's fur was used for the bearskin hats of British Guardsmen until recently, but it has now been replaced by man-made nylon fur. The Grizzly Bear is a large race of Brown Bear, now mainly confined to the Canadian Rocky Mountains. It is a huge animal measuring up to eight feet tall when standing on its hind legs, and it is extremely dangerous. Its enormous claws used to be made into necklaces by Red Indian tribes. Grizzlies feed on game, honey, fruit, and salmon, which they scoop out of rivers.

The third drive-through enclosure is called the Highland Reserve, the aim being to exhibit animals from high altitudes around the world, which are more suited to the climatic conditions of Scotland. You can see American Bison, Red Deer, Fallow Deer, Yaks and Muntjac, as well as a variety of geese and cranes. The American Bison bull weighs more than a ton, and both sexes have horns. Originally, Bison roamed all over the prairies of the United States, and in the eighteenth century there were over 60 million of them, often in herds of a million or more. But the Plains Indians depended on them for food, and they were hunted by white settlers as a means of controlling the Indians. Besides their food value, Bison were also hunted for their hides, and they were exterminated east of the Mississippi River by 1820. The only survivors of the great western herds by 1885 were 75 animals. Eventually they were given legal protection, and there are now several thousand animals in reserves.

The Red Deer is the largest native British mammal, and it was once common throughout the forests of Europe and Asia. The deer of the Highlands are smaller than the animals usually seen in English parks, since they are more truly wild and they have a harder life on the hills. Stags live alone in summer, joining the hinds in autumn when their antlers are grown and the velvet has been rubbed off them. The velvet is a covering of furry skin over the growing antlers. Stags collect their hinds during the rutting season in late September and October, bellowing and fighting other stags. Calves are born in May and June. Fallow Deer originated in the Mediterranean area, and they are spotted in summer, later turning a uniform grey. The rut follows the same pattern as in Red Deer. The Muntjac, of which there are several races, is found in India and all over southeast Asia. It favours dense forest, and in the Himalayan foothills it lives at

Cameron Loch Lomond Wildlife and Leisure Park. **Address** Alexandria, Dunbartonshire, Scotland. **Telephone** Alexandria 57211. **Open** 10.00–18.00 summer, closed Nov–Feb. **Guide-book**. **Catering** self-service cafeteria. Zoo shop and information centre. **Guided tours** by arrangement. **Acreage** 220. **Car** 5 mls n. of Dumbarton, off A82, near Balloch and Alexandria. **Bus** to Balloch bus station, 20 mins' walk from Park entrance. **Train** to Balloch ($\frac{1}{2}$ ml). **Taxis** available in Balloch and Alexandria. **Other facilities** giant astraglide, splash cats, boats and playground, dog kennels. No pets. Public **not allowed** to feed animals.

The Smooth Indian Otter hunts in both fresh and salt water.

altitudes of up to 6,000 feet. It is a small animal with short, pointed antlers and elongated, tusk-like canine teeth which are visible. It does not have a fixed rutting season, and can breed all the year round.

The Yak belongs to the cattle family, and it is still found wild in Tibet and China at altitudes of from 14,000 to 20,000 feet. In Tibet Yaks have been domesticated for hundreds of years by nomadic tribesmen, as riding and pack animals, for their milk and meat, and for their dung, which is used as fuel. Domesticated Yaks are smaller than wild ones, and their coat colour varies, whereas the truly wild Yak is black.

The birds to be seen in the Highland Reserves are Emperor Geese, Greater and Blue Snow Geese, Barnacle Geese, Canada Geese and Common Eider. Four species of crane are exhibited: the Common Crane of Europe and Asia, which migrates southwards in winter to South Africa; the Sarus Crane, a tall bird with a red head and grey plumage, from India, Burma and Thailand; the little Demoiselle Crane of southern Europe and Asia; and the Crowned Crane of Africa. The Crowned Cranes here are the grey-necked race from East Africa, the West African race having black necks. You can see more waterfowl on the pond near the restaurant, including Red-crested Pochard, Carolina and Mandarin Ducks, Soft-billed Ducks, Indian Whistling Duck, African Red-billed Teal, and Black Swans from Australia.

The smaller mammals exhibited at present are Raccoons, chipmunks, Arctic Foxes, Smooth Indian Otters and Binturongs. Raccoons are found in many parts of North America, and they are active tree climbers. They eat rodents, frogs, fruit and insects, often washing their food in water. Chipmunks are also North American animals, and there are dozens of different forms, all with stripes on their backs and faces. They are gregarious, burrowing animals, some preferring open ground and others woodland. The ones in the Park have bred here. The Arctic Fox comes from northern Canada, Greenland and Iceland, Scandinavia and northern Asia. Its white winter coat turns to grey in summer, though some foxes of Arctic Canada grow a grey winter coat, for which they are bred on fur farms as the Blue Fox. In the wild they live on fish, hares, lemmings, Ptarmigan and seabirds, but sometimes hunt on the pack-ice for seal carrion left by Polar Bears. The Smooth Indian Otter lives by lakes and streams, also hunting in creeks and estuaries, even swimming in the open sea after fish. But it also travels long distances overland in search of food or water. This is a gregarious species, often fishing in family parties. The Binturong is related to the civet and mongoose but it is a larger, slow-moving animal, living in trees in the thick tropical forests of southern Asia. Being slow, it is mainly vegetarian, although it will eat meat. The largest member of the civet family, it is the only mammal in the Old World with a prehensile tail, used for grasping branches as it climbs.

Beyond the waterfowl pond is a pets' garden and farm, where children can see Rabbits, guinea-pigs, goats, lambs and donkeys. There is also a walk-through aviary with doves and various other birds.

The Park is still being developed and expanded, and other animals are being added to the collection, particularly northern hemisphere species which are suitable for the Highland Reserve. This is an interesting collection, and well worth a visit for tourists in the vicinity of Loch Lomond.

Cameron House is well worth a visit.

North American chipmunks have bred in captivity at Cameron Loch Lomond.

Binturong, an inhabitant of the dense tropical forests of southern Asia.

Camperdown Wildlife Centre

The Camperdown Wildlife Centre was established by the Parks and Recreation Department of Dundee Corporation in 1968, and its policy is to provide country-side education as well as spectator appeal. Most of the exhibits are of British native mammals and birds, but there are a few wild animals from other parts of the world. Most of the animals here are in a large walled garden with a few aviaries and enclosures grouped round it in the Park. You can see Red Deer and Fallow Deer, and several species of small mammal, including Red Squirrels, and a good

Camperdown Wildlife Centre. **Address** Camperdown Park, Dundee. **Telephone** Dundee 580368. **Open** 10.00–20.00 summer, 10.00–dusk winter. **Catering** unlicensed restaurant, snack bar, kiosk. Zoo shop. **Guide-book. Guided tours** by arrangement. **Acreage** 7. **Car** 4 mls n.w. of Dundee on A923 Coupar Angus road. **Bus** 28 from city centre — nearest stop 5 mins' walk. **Train** Dundee station. Public **not allowed** to feed animals.

collection of the weasel family – Pine Martens, Polecats, Weasels and Stoats, which make an interesting comparison. The foreign species here are European Brown Bears, which were once native to Great Britain, various species of squirrel, wallabies and Kinkajous. The Kinkajous have been very successful in breeding and rearing their young here. This is an open-air collection, the only indoor exhibit being a nocturnal house.

The bird collection include eagles, buzzards, Kestrels, Snowy Owls, which are very occasional visitors to British shores, and three native species of owl – the Tawny, Long-eared and Barn Owl. The crow family is well represented, with Ravens, Rooks, Carrion Crows, Magpies and Jackdaws, and there is a collection of British finches, doves, swans and waterfowl. The foreign birds exhibited include insect-eating species, finches, parrots, parrakeets, macaws, pheasants and peafowl. There are a few fish, amphibians and invertebrates (animals without backbones) on display, and plans are envisaged for a reptile house.

There is a children's section showing varieties of sheep, goats, ponies, poultry, Rabbits and guinea-pigs. The Park also contains more waterfowl ponds and a nature trail, while another nature trail, 12 miles away at Belmont, is run by the Parks Department. This is an interesting and well laid out collection, well worth a visit.

The tree-climbing Kinkajou.

The North American Beaver can be seen at Edinburgh Zoo.

Edinburgh Zoo

Edinburgh Zoo is the largest zoo in Scotland, as well as being one of the major British collections. Set on the slopes of Corstorphine Hill, it offers visitors the option of taking the zoo bus to the Viewpoint at the top of the hill and then walking down, or of seeing everything on foot, which provides plenty of exercise. The Zoo has a good collection of monkeys and apes, the larger carnivorous animals, many small mammal species, hoofed animals, tropical birds and waterfowl, and it is famous for its penguin collection, which is the largest in the British Isles. There is also a good aquarium and reptile house, and a children's farm, and you can spend a full day here in all kinds of weather.

The Carnegie Aquarium has two floodlit ponds in the entrance hall containing Golden Orfe and Goldfish. The original wild Goldfish was a dull brown, until the Chinese began breeding them for colour in the tenth century. There are now many fancy varieties exhibiting the familiar reddish orange which bear little resemblance to their ancestors. From here you enter two large halls with seawater tanks containing a variety of marine fishes, Conger Eel, lobsters, Edible Crabs, and two species of marine turtle, the Green and the Hawksbill. The Green or Edible Turtle has long been prized for its greenish fat, which is used to make turtle soup. Commercial demand has reduced its numbers but it is now being raised in turtle hatcheries, where the young turtles are kept until they are old enough to be released at sea. The Hawksbill Turtle was also killed for its shell, the well-known tortoiseshell. Demand decreased with the invention of plastics, but in recent years there has been renewed exploitation in Japan, so this species must continue to be regarded as endangered.

The freshwater tanks in the aquarium have an interesting collection of brilliantly coloured fish, both tropical and freshwater, including the Giant Salamander, Electric Eels and lungfish. The Electric Eel gives off a low pulsating current by means of specialised tissue occupying four-fifths of its body, to locate its prey. A much stronger shock is then produced to stun the prey. The lungfish burrows into the mud of dried-up streams, leaving a tunnel to the surface through which it breathes air. It sleeps during the dry season, breathing very slowly, and it only reverts to its gills when the rivers fill up again.

The Carnegie Aquarium was opened in 1927 with a grant from the Carnegie United Kingdom Trust.

As you walk round the Zoo, you will see many enclosures for the smaller mammals, many of which are landscaped to exhibit their natural environments in the wild. The Crested Porcupine is one of several porcupine species found in

Edinburgh Zoo, Royal Zoological Society of Scotland. **Address** Scottish National Zoological Park, Murrayfield, Edinburgh. **Telephone** Edinburgh 334 9171. **Open** 09.30–19.00 summer, 09.30–17.00 (dusk) winter. **Guide-book**. **Catering** licensed restaurant, self-service cafeteria, snack bar, kiosk. Zoo shop, information centre. **Acreage** 80. **Car** 3 mls w. of city centre on A8 Glasgow road at Murrayfield. **Bus** from Princes Street, 12, 26, 31. **Train** to Waverley (3 mls) or Haymarket (2 mls). **Taxis** available. **Other facilities** first-aid post, lost children's room, push-chairs, wheelchairs. Public **not allowed** to feed animals.

Africa, southern Asia and some parts of Europe. Porcupines rattle their tail quills to warn an approaching intruder, and they attack by rushing backwards and piercing the enemy with their sharp quills protruding from their backs. Many large carnivorous animals, such as Tigers, have become man-eaters after being crippled in this way, so that they are forced to attack domestic cattle or human beings, which are easy to catch. Porcupines are nocturnal rodents, eating vegetable matter and fruit.

One of the most attractive exhibits is of Prairie Marmots, the short-tailed burrowing ground squirrels of the North American prairies. They live in large underground communities, excavating the earth in a large cone which drains rainwater away from the burrow. Two aquatic mammals which burrow underground are the Coypu and the Beaver. The Coypu burrows in river banks, spending much of its time in the water. It is a South American rodent, and it was once nearly exterminated for its fur, known in the fur trade as Nutria. The Canadian Beaver, another rodent once extensively hunted for its fur, has a broad flat tail used for balancing as it carries sticks and mud with which it builds its dam or 'lodge' to maintain water level above its burrow. Trees are felled by gnawing with great rapidity, and logs and branches are cemented into place with mud. Two other aquatic mammals exhibited here are the Malaysian Otter and the European Otter. Otters are expert swimmers with webbed feet, and they live on fish, molluscs, eels, and other small water creatures. There are 16 species of otter, some of which live in family groups while others, like the European Otter are solitary in habit.

Two tree-climbing animals are the Raccoon and the Wolverine. Raccoons are related to bears, and they come from North America. They have the habit of dipping their food in water before eating it. The Wolverine, a solitary predator, is reputed to be fearless, and it has been persecuted for its destructiveness as it will kill anything it meets, even deer. Because of its large appetite it is also sometimes called the Glutton. Wolverines are found in North America and the cold regions of northern Europe and Asia.

The Ratels, or Honey Badgers are natives of Africa, India and parts of the Middle East. They are good tree climbers and burrowers, living on small animals, frogs, insects and honey.

The Pine Marten, a member of the weasel family, lives in coniferous forests in Europe, hunting on the ground for Rabbits, hares, small rodents, birds and soft fruit. The Polecat is also a member of the weasel family, and it favours woodland and rocky ground, hunting small animals, birds' eggs and fish. The Ferret is a domesticated species, which has interbred with Polecats in Wales, and is used for flushing Rabbits out of their burrows. The Kinkajou, an attractive tree climber from Mexico and South America, is a nocturnal animal which lives on fruit and small animals. It is unusual in having the ability to use its tail for holding on to branches. The genet is a slender cat-like animal, preying on small animals and insects. It is found in parts of southern Europe, but most species of genet live in Africa, and all have beautifully marked coats.

The Monkey House, completed in 1972, is one of the most modern buildings in the Zoo, and you can see all the primates here except the Chimpanzees, Orang utans and gibbons. There is a representative collection of monkeys from Africa, Asia and South America. The Ring-tailed Lemur, unlike most lemurs which all come from Madagascar, lives in sparse woodland country. It lives largely on the ground, but like all lemurs it is a good tree climber, and its beautifully marked tail is used as a balancing aid. The Great Galago or Bushbaby is another denizen of thinly wooded country in southern and eastern Africa. It is the largest species of galago, 2 feet 6 inches long, including the tail, and it can leap 20 feet from tree to tree. Most galagos are nocturnal, but this species is mainly active by day. Another African species, the Green Monkey, common throughout most parts of Africa, lives in dense forest and thick bush but forages in open grassland. There are two species of baboon, the Anubis, of northern central Africa, and the Chacma of southern Africa. The Anubis Baboon, also known as the Sacred Baboon, because it was a species revered by the ancient Egyptians, is olive-green in colour, while the Chacma is a dark greenish brown

Above a normally coloured Leopard at rest.
Below: A Crab-eating Macaque swimming.

327

and more slenderly built. Both carry their tails in the 'broken' position, held erect from the hind quarters and then drooping. Another monkey from West Africa is the Moustached Monkey, an animal with a blue face and a long reddish tail. Three Asiatic species here are the Rhesus Monkey of northern India, Burma and China, which is sacred to the Hindus but now used in large numbers for scientific research; the Pig-tailed Macaque and the Crab-eating Macaque. The former is the largest of the macaque family, and in Sumatra and Burma it is sometimes trained to climb palm trees and throw down the coconuts; the latter is a Malayan species which lives in mangrove swamps and feeds on shellfish. The four South American species in the Monkey House are one of the capuchins, the squirrel monkey, the spider monkey and the Woolly Monkey. Capuchins are the commonest South American monkeys, stocky animals with a prehensile tail. Squirrel monkeys are nocturnal, living in dense tropical forest in large troops. Spider monkeys, another gregarious animal, have short bodies and long arms like gibbons, but unlike gibbons they have a prehensile tail, used as a fifth limb when swinging from branch to branch. The Woolly Monkey, related to the spider monkey, also has a powerful prehensile tail, but it is a much heavier animal and moves more slowly. It also has a well-developed thumb.

The Lar Gibbons are in a large outdoor cage, where they can be seen swinging rapidly along its whole length. Gibbons are the smallest of the apes, and they are found in southeast Asia. They live mostly in trees in the wild, but they run upright along the ground, the arms being used for balancing. The Ape House contains the Zoo's Chimpanzee colony and its three Orang utans. The Chimpanzees used to be kept singly or in pairs here, but a recent development has been to establish groups of them living together, as they do in the wild. Many animals, especially the higher primates, become bored in captivity, and when this happens they develop all kinds of stereotyped behaviour as a result of lack of stimulus. The Edinburgh Chimpanzees were given a variety of toys, ropes in the outdoor cages, and nesting material at night, and their activity and alertness improved at once. Not only has this proved beneficial for the Chimpanzees, but they are more interesting to watch. In the wild they use their hands a lot, and even use grass stems to probe into ants' nests, withdrawing the stem and eating the ants crawling on it. The Orang utans are less sociable than the Chimpanzees, normally living alone or in small family units. They seldom come to the ground, spending their time high in the forest canopy, and nesting in tall trees at night.

This is one of the few zoos in Great Britain which breeds sealions and you can see these in their very large pond, excavated from natural rock. There is also a pond for Grey Seals, which are found off the coasts of Great Britain. Sealions and seals are flesh-eaters, intelligent and easy to tame. Sealions have external ears, and their hind flippers are turned forward so that they can move across land. Both species spend most of their time in the water, coming ashore only to breed and to sunbathe.

The Children's Farm is a farmyard in miniature, complete with farmhouse, stables and pens for calves, lambs, kids, pigs and bantams. In the centre of the farmyard is a pond and dovecote, fenced in to make a run for Rabbits, guinea-pigs, chickens and ducklings. All the farm implements are scaled down, and the buildings are modelled on a South African farm built in the Dutch style. This is a great improvement on the usual zoo pets' corner, and far more interesting for city children.

The Zoo exhibits both kangaroos and wallabies, which are regularly bred here. The Grey Kangaroo is the next largest member of the kangaroo family after the Red Kangaroo. Wallabies, which are simply small species of kangaroo, are divided into many species, the ones exhibited here being Bennett's Wallaby from Tasmania, a race of the mainland Red-necked Wallaby; the Dama Wallaby, the first Australian marsupial ever recorded in 1629; the White-throated or Parma Wallaby, and the Rottnest Island Wallaby or Quokka. This is much smaller than other wallabies, and it has a hairless, rounded tail. When first seen by a European in 1696 it was thought to be a kind of rat.

Three kinds of bear are in the Zoo, the Brown Bear, once common all over Europe but now confined to a few mountainous districts, where they are rare;

Bactrian Camel.

the American Black Bear and the Polar Bear. Polar Bears, unlike most other bear species, are carnivorous, living mainly on seals. They also have hair on the soles of their feet to stop them slipping on ice, and for warmth. The hollow hairs of their coats and the layer of fat under their skin insulate them against the cold; and also against heat, so that they can live comfortably in warm weather in zoos.

Most of the other carnivorous animals are in the rock enclosures up the hill. The Lion House contains Lions and several other large members of the cat family, and the Lion Rock is a naturalistic exhibit, moated at the front to give an unobstructed view of the Lions. There is a similar large barless enclosure for Tigers, and smaller rock exhibits along the path leading to the Tiger enclosure. The cat collection includes Leopards, Jaguars, Pumas and the rare Clouded Leopard, which does not often breed in captivity. The normal-coloured Leopards, Lions and Tigers all breed regularly in the Zoo.

The Scottish Wild Cat, in a separate exhibit, is found in central and southern Europe, but in the British Isles it is now confined to northern Scotland in mountainous districts. The Wild Cat is larger than a domestic cat, and it has a thick tail which does not taper at the end like a domestic cat's tail. Other species in the rock enclosures are the African Hunting Dog, a large animal with big rounded ears and blotched markings on the body; the Red Fox, increasingly common in the British Isles; and Spotted and Striped Hyenas. The Spotted Hyena is the largest of the three hyena species, and it is found throughout Africa wherever there are antelopes, zebra and Giraffe. The more lightly built Striped Hyena has a longer coat, striped with black markings, and it is found in India, southwestern Asia and North Africa. Hyenas scavenge after Lions and Leopards, but they also hunt on their own account, usually in small packs. They have powerful jaws, capable of crushing large bones, but contrary to popular belief they are not cowardly animals. Like most predatory wild animals they are opportunists, intent on making as easy a living as possible, but they will fight if cornered.

You can also see the Indian Elephant, Grant's Zebras, the South American tapir, which lives near rivers in tropical jungle, the European Wild Boar, still common in the forests of central Europe, and the Pygmy Hippopotamus. This is a pig-sized cousin of the Common Hippo from the rivers of West Africa. Unlike the Common Hippo, which congregates in large herds, the Pygmy Hippo lives in ones and twos, spending much of its time grazing on dry land.

In the Camel House you can see the one-humped Arabian Camel or Dromedary, and its two-humped cousin the Bactrian Camel, from central Asia. This is a beast of burden, whereas the Arabian Camel is used both as a pack animal and for riding. Other members of the camel family here are the Llama and the Guanaco. The Llama is a domesticated species, kept for transport and for its wool and meat in South America, the Guanaco being a wild species of the same family.

There are three Giraffes in the Zoo, of which there are several sub-species in Africa. One of the rarest of these, the Northern Nigerian Giraffe, was exhibited here until its death in 1961. This was the only one of its kind ever exhibited in captivity. There are three species of deer here, the Red Deer, which is common in the Scottish Highlands and in many English deer parks; the Roe Deer, a woodland species which is not easily bred in captivity; and Père David's Deer, a swamp deer from China, which was discovered in 1865 by Père David, a French missionary. It became extinct in 1900 during the Boxer Rebellion, but not before several animals had been sent to European zoos. These were collected by the eleventh Duke of Bedford, who bred a herd at Woburn, subsequently sending groups of the animals to zoos. This is a curious animal, since it has an unusually long tail and the stag generally grows two sets of antlers each year. It breeds regularly in the Zoo.

Other cloven-hoofed animals exhibited are the American Bison, Highland Cattle, Blackbuck, a small graceful Indian antelope, and the Nilgai, the largest of the Indian antelopes. Both these species breed regularly here. The Zoo also has a fine group of Red Lechwe, an African antelope which prefers swampy ground and spends much time standing in water feeding on aquatic plants. One of the

329

most interesting exhibits is the breeding group of Maxwell's Duiker, a small species from western Central Africa, which rarely breeds in zoos. However, a thriving herd has been built up here, the largest to be seen in the British Isles. Another animal rarely seen in the British Isles is the Saiga Antelope, from the steppes of southern Russia. It is a desert species, living in small groups until autumn, when it migrates southwards in herds to avoid the snows. The peculiar bloated form of its muzzle enables it to warm very cold air before drawing it into its lungs. There are two species of sheep, the Soay, a native of Soay Island in the St Kilda group, and the Barbary Sheep, in fact a large wild goat from the Atlas Mountains in North Africa. The male has fine, curving horns and a mane of hair over its throat and chest, and there is a thriving herd in the Zoo.

The pride of the Zoo's bird collection is the penguin colony. The first penguins arrived soon after the Zoo was opened, and others were brought back each year from the Antarctic by Messrs Christian Salvesen, the Leith whaling firm, thus enabling the Zoo to build up a good potential breeding stock. From its beginnings, the Zoo has exhibited King Penguins, the second largest of the 17 species of penguin, and in 1919 the first King Penguin ever hatched and successfully reared in captivity was produced here. This bird died in 1925 and is now exhibited in a glass case in the Mansion House, in the centre of the Zoo. In 1952 another species, the Ringed or Chinstrap Penguin, was the first of its kind ever to be reared in Great Britain, and a further record was set in 1964 when 13 Gentoo Penguins were reared to maturity from 22 eggs. The species exhibited at present are the King Penguin, the Gentoo and the Rockhopper. The King Penguin is three feet tall and it breeds on Antarctic and sub-Antarctic islands, where a single egg is incubated by both parents in turn. The adult birds feed on squid and sprats, regurgitating food to feed the chick, which grows rapidly, reaching the adult weight of up to 40 lb. within three months but retaining its infant down until its first moult. The Gentoo Penguin is a small, inquisitive, intelligent species, which lays two eggs in a nest of pebbles, and it has bred regularly here. The Rockhopper is the most aggressive of penguins, and lays two eggs in a nest of grass or pebbles in temperate sub-Antarctic regions. Penguins mate and breed following the annual moult, but a record was created when a pair of Gentoo Penguins reared a chick while still awaiting the plumage change. In the wild, they moult in March and April, nesting in October and November. But in Edinburgh, April and May is the laying season and the moult takes place in August and September. The change of season causes an 18-month delay in moulting for newly arrived birds, but in 1964 the unmoulted Gentoo pair nested and reared their chick. The penguins parade through the Zoo at 3.30 p.m. every summer afternoon, weather permitting, and this is a sight not to be missed.

The other birds in the collection include the Emu and cassowary, Crested and American White Pelicans, three species of stork — the Maguari, Marabou and White — and many waterfowl and wading birds. Notice the Bewick's Swans, which in the wild are winter visitors to the British Isles from northern Russia. This swan is not often seen in zoos, and it is smaller than the Whooper Swan, also in the collection, which winters here and breeds in Iceland, northern Europe, Asia and Japan. There is a free-flying colony of Night Herons in the Zoo, started by three pairs of herons which escaped from their aviary in 1939 but stayed to nest in the trees nearby. They breed every year and there are now about 60 birds in the colony. They visit ponds and rivers around Edinburgh each night to fish, returning in the morning to their trees beside the sealion pool. The Night Heron is found in southern Europe, Asia and Africa, and wild birds rarely visit this country. The birds of prey exhibited include the Kestrel, Sparrowhawk, vultures, eagles and the Secretary Bird, which lives on snakes and small animals in Africa. The rarest bird of prey here is the New Guinea Harpy Eagle, one of the very few in captivity. In the wild it preys on monkeys and other small mammals and, as far as is known, it lays only one egg in a clutch.

The Parrot Garden has aviaries arranged along its walls, with a variety of macaws and cockatoos, parrakeets, Cockatiels and Senegal Parrots. Other aviaries contain canaries, weaver birds, turtle doves and touracos. The smaller birds requiring artificial heat in cold weather are in the Tropical Bird House, with

Edinburgh Zoo has a fine collection of penguins: above, Gentoo Penguin; below, Chinstrap Penguin.

access to outdoor aviaries. Here, you can see many species of finch, African touracos and plantain eaters, hornbills from Malaya, toucans from South America, parrots, lories and lorikeets. One interesting bird here is the Kookaburra or Laughing Jackass of eastern and southern Australia. This is a species of forest kingfisher which lives on insects, reptiles and amphibians, and occasionally small birds and mammals. Its weird cry, heard when roosting at night and again in early morning, occurs so regularly that the Kookaburra is known as the 'bushman's clock'. In the nectar-eating Bird House you can see hummingbirds, sunbirds and tanagers, which feed either on nectar from flowers or on soft fruit. In captivity, the nectar-eaters take a specially prepared syrup from glass tubes suspended in their aviaries.

The Reptile House adjoins the Tropical Bird House, and here you can see crocodiles, alligators, monitors, geckos, skinks, lizards and iguanas. There is also an interesting collection of the large constricting snakes, and a few venomous species.

Edinburgh Zoo, or, to use its correct title, the Scottish National Zoological Park, belongs to the Royal Zoological Society of Scotland which was founded in 1909. Its purpose was to advance the study of zoology, and to establish a zoo to encourage public interest in animal life. When the Corstorphine Hill House estate came up for sale in 1912, not enough money had been raised to buy it, so Edinburgh Town Council bought the property and leased it to the Society. The Town Council is still represented on the Society's council, and since 1954 Edinburgh Corporation has made the Society an annual grant. A royal charter was granted to the Society in 1913 and the Zoo was opened in the same year. The barless enclosures hewed out of the whinstone rock at the top of the gardens were modelled on those at Hamburg Zoo, which had been opened in 1907. The Zoo was inaugurated with many animals hired for the first three months from the private zoo of Sir Garrard Tyrwhitt-Drake in Kent. His animals arrived by special train, just in time for the opening day.

The sloping ground in the gardens has been used to lead running water through many of the animal enclosures, and from the Viewpoint at the top of the Corstorphine Hill one can see the Pentland Hills and the Firth of Forth on a clear day. Members of the Society are entitled to free entry, six free tickets, lectures and film shows in the winter. The Members' Club has a restaurant, bar and library.

Immature Rockhopper Penguin: like most penguins, this species is confined to Antarctic and sub-Antarctic waters.

Highland Wildlife Park

The Highland Wildlife Park, opened in 1972, is one of the most interesting collections of wild animals in the country, its theme being to show the wild life which has existed in the British Isles since the last Ice Age. Many of these, such as the Bear, Wolf, Lynx, Beaver and Bison, became extinct, while others, including the Red Deer, Wild Cat, Badger, Pine Marten, Capercaillie and Ptarmigan, have survived. You can therefore see our native fauna as they exist today, side by side with many animals which have not existed in the Highlands for hundreds, or even thousands, of years. When you go into the main building you will find a fascinating exhibition in pictures illustrating wild life since the Ice Age, and why some of the animals disappeared.

Twelve thousand years ago, as the Ice Age was breaking up, the hills in northern parts of Great Britain were still covered with glaciers, which melted a little more each summer. When the ground was free of ice, herds of Reindeer, Saiga Antelope, Musk Ox and Wild Horses grazed on the lichens and mosses, and they were followed by Wolves and Polar Bears, Arctic Foxes and hares, lemmings and Snowy Owls. Later, the valleys were covered with forests of birch, pine, aspen and juniper, and the Arctic animals moved on; the Polar Bear and Musk Ox went north and the Saiga Antelope went eastwards. After another cold spell the forests changed, with oak, ash, lime, alder and elm trees replacing birch and pine. Man had arrived by then, and 10,000 years ago he was sharing

Highland Wildlife Park. **Address** Kincraig, Kingussie, Inverness-shire. **Telephone** Kincraig 270. **Open** 10.00—18.00 (or 1½ hours before dusk, whichever earlier) summer, closed Nov—Feb winter. **Guide-book. Catering** self-service cafeteria, snack bar. **Acreage** 260. **Car** 7 mls s.w. of Aviemore, 5 mls n.e. of Kingussie on A9. **Train** to Aviemore (7 mls) or to Kingussie (5 mls). **Taxis** available. Dog kennels available. No pets. Public **not allowed** to feed animals.

these rich forests with Wood Bison, Elk, Aurochs, the primaeval wild cattle, and Wild Boar. By that time many smaller animals had appeared, including Beavers, Otters, Lynx, Wolves, Bears, and many birds of prey. The country became an island at about 6000 BC, when the sea-level rose with the melting of the ice-sheets. Thereafter, the Romans and the Vikings cleared and burnt large areas of Scottish forest, and domestic flocks increased, resulting in the extermination of the Aurochs, Lynx and Bear. Beavers were hunted to extinction for their fur, but the Wild Boar was domesticated.

In the mid-eighteenth century, Cheviot and Blackface Sheep were imported in millions, and the forests were converted into bare deserts. Animals which lived in forests, such as the Polecat, disappeared, and hunting and trapping exterminated the White-tailed Eagle (see p. 335), Osprey and Red Kite.

The Park is divided into two sections. To begin with, you drive round a two-mile circuit containing most of the hoofed animals. You can stop on the road, and there is a layby half-way along it. It is worth hiring binoculars at the Park entrance, as this is a large area and the animals merge into the scenery. After this, you come to the walk-round section containing the carnivorous animals, the smaller mammals, and the game birds, birds of prey and waterfowl.

In the drive-through section you see Red Deer, Roe Deer, Soay Sheep, Wild Goats, Highland Cattle, Wild Horses and European Bison. The Red Deer is the largest wild animal left in Great Britain, and the population on the Scottish hills is estimated at 185,000. They have to be controlled by shooting which takes place in late summer and early autumn for stags, and in the winter months for hinds. Deer stalking is an important local source of employment, and $1\frac{3}{4}$ million pounds' worth of venison is exported annually, mostly to Germany. The Red Deer in the Park came from the surrounding hills, and they are smaller than the animals seen in English parks since they have to subsist in a more truly wild state on Highland grazing. The Park's policy is to increase their size by selective breeding, to produce an animal more like the great beasts which lived on the lusher vegetation of earlier times. Stags live separately from the hinds during the summer, and the calves are born in June. The stags cast their antlers in March and April, and these are replaced fully by July, but still covered in velvet, a furry covering of skin. The velvet is rubbed off in August, and the rutting season starts in late September, when the stags rejoin the hinds and compete with each other, roaring and sometimes fighting.

Roe Deer are indigenous in this part of Scotland, living in small groups or alone. They prefer woodland and are therefore not often seen. The planting of new forests in the Highlands has enabled them to increase, and although they damage trees they are not now shot, as they were until recently. Soay Sheep come from the island of Soay in the St Kilda group of islands, west of the Hebrides, where there is a wild population. They are thought to be descended from the earliest breed of sheep domesticated in Europe during the Bronze Age. They resemble the Mouflon, the wild sheep of Corsica and Sardinia, but they are smaller and carry more wool. The wild Alpine Goats are not a native breed, having probably been imported originally from the Mediterranean area. However, they are now wild in Scotland, and the population is estimated at 4,000. A herd of Wild Goats can sometimes be seen from the main road at the Slochd, between Carrbridge and Tomatin, and from the Newtonmore to Laggan road at Creagdhu. Highland Cattle are one of the oldest breeds of domestic cattle, and they may be partly descended from the primaeval Aurochs. Though they are now chestnut-brown in colour, 200 years ago they were usually black. At that time, Highlanders used to demand cattle from Lowland farmers in return for not burning their farms and crops, and the old Scottish word 'mail' meaning rent, gave rise to the word 'blackmail'.

The Wild Horses here were not of Scottish origin, but they are the only Wild Horses in existence. This is Przewalski's Horse from Mongolia, one of the rarest wild animals in the world. There are only about 250 left in zoos and parks, and they may now be extinct in the wild.

When Great Britain was covered with forest after the last Ice Age, Bison were common, but now they have been extinct here for thousands of years. After the

Above: Reindeer in the Highland Wild-life Park; this species is being reintro-duced into the Cairngorms. Left: Canadian Timber Wolf. Below: this form of the Arctic Fox turns from grey to white in winter.

First World War they nearly became extinct in Europe, but have been preserved in zoos and there are now over 1,000 animals in captivity. The last wild ones in Europe are animals that were reintroduced into Poland, but the last survivors of a Caucasian race were shot during the Second World War. European Bison live in small groups, and they have begun to breed in the Park.

Having completed this circuit, you park your car and continue on foot. The first enclosures here exhibit the Red Fox, Wild Cat and Badger, all species which still exist in the wild. There is also an enclosure for Roe Deer, so that you may take a closer look. The Red Fox has always been persecuted by man, yet it has survived owing to its cunning and adaptability and it is on the increase. The hill fox of the Highlands is larger than the English animal, and often greyer in colour. It takes lambs in the Highlands, although seldom if ever in the English lowlands. The Wild Cat has been persecuted by man, and by the end of the nineteenth century it had disappeared in Scotland, except for the remoter parts of Inverness-shire, Sutherland and Wester Ross. The development of Forestry Commission plantations has enabled it to spread and increase, and foresters welcome it as it kills Rabbits and voles.

Badgers have always lived around the Park, and they are fairly common in the Highlands, though seldom seen. The shelter belts of trees round the Park have Badger gates in their fences, and Badgers can be seen in daylight in May and June here, when the nights are short. Another small native species which lives wild in the Park is the Brown Hare. There are also semi-tame Mountain Hares, which in summer are sometimes mistaken for Rabbits. The Mountain Hare normally lives at higher altitudes in the hills around, seldom coming down to the Park, which is 900 feet above sea-level. It is really an Arctic species, having been left behind on the mountains when the ice-fields retreated from Scotland. It is common on Speyside but is seldom seen in the Lowlands, since it does not thrive at lower altitudes. Like the Ptarmigan, it turns white in winter.

You next come to one of the most extraordinary looking animals, the Saiga Antelope, which was a native of this country at the end of the Ice Age. The function of its bulbous nose is to warm the icy air before it is drawn down into the antelope's lungs. It is still found wild on the Russian steppes, and because of its ability to withstand very low temperatures it is virtually the only animal which can survive the winter months on the steppes. By the end of the Second War the Saiga had dwindled to a few hundred animals, but it was then protected and there are now millions on the Russian steppes. In captivity the Saiga has never flourished, since it has usually developed septicaemia in its nose from polluted air in northern zoos. It is hoped that Saiga can be maintained in the Park, where the Highland air is still pure.

The next range of exhibits is devoted to carnivorous animals — the Pine Marten and Polecat, the birds of prey, and the Bears, Wolves and Lynx. The Pine Marten, like the Wild Cat, became extremely rare in Scotland, but it has increased with the growth of forest plantations. It is an agile tree climber and preys on small animals, including the squirrel. Pine Martens were common in the Middle Ages, and there was a thriving export trade in their skins. Closely related to the Pine Marten is the Polecat, which still exists in some wild parts of Britain. Polecats exude a pungent smell, which accounted for their ancient name of Foumart, or 'foul marten'.

The birds of prey here are the European Eagle Owl, the Snowy Owl, the Golden Eagle, White-tailed Eagle, Buzzard, Merlin and Peregrine Falcon. The Eagle Owl is the largest of the European owls, but it no longer occurs as a native species. It probably died out in Scotland before the beginning of human settlement here, and it is still rare in Europe, occurring mainly in Scandinavia. Only a few wild specimens have been recorded in Scotland during the past 200 years, but a pair nested in southwestern Scotland in the 1920s. Eagle Owls need a large amount of territory in which to hunt, preying on deer calves, small mammals, gamebirds and song-birds. The Snowy Owl is an Arctic bird, coming to Scotland in winter when food is scarce farther north. It occasionally summers in the Cairngorms, and a pair wintered four years running about 40 miles from the Park. Since 1967 a pair has bred annually in the Shetlands. The Golden Eagle, another native inhabitant which has been persecuted by man, is now legally protected and is increasing again. The latest threat to it was the use of poisons in sheep-dips, but these are now banned. The eagle is traditionally the symbol of power, and Highland chieftains wear three eagle feathers in their bonnets as a badge of authority. The White-tailed Eagle, or Sea Eagle, is now only an occasional visitor to the Highlands, and it has not bred here since 1912. It was once as common as the Golden Eagle, but its hunting areas were nearer human settlements and it was hunted persistently by sheep farmers. The Buzzard is a smaller bird than the eagle, and it is now the commonest bird of prey in the Highlands. Buzzards can often be seen over the Park. The Merlin is the smallest of the falcons, and it frequents Highland moorlands, preying on small birds and insects and depending on its swift flight to catch its victims. The Peregrine Falcon, some four inches taller than the Merlin, lives along coastal cliffs and hills, preying chiefly on seabirds, waders and pigeons.

The European Brown Bear was once common all over the British Isles, but it was exterminated in about the tenth century, probably being hunted for its meat. The Romans exported 'Caledonian bears' for the spectacular and bloody shows in the Coliseum in Rome. Now rare in the wild, Brown Bears are confined to a few mountain areas in the Pyrenees, central Europe and the Abruzzi district of Italy.

The Wolf pack here are breeding in their rocky enclosure, and you may have to look carefully before you spot them, well camouflaged against their natural background. Wolves used to be so numerous in Scotland that they were greatly feared; the dead were often buried on islands so that the graves would not be disturbed by wolves, and shelters were put up for travellers to protect them at night. In the fifteenth century laws were passed requiring landowners to hunt Wolves four times a year, and to organise Wolf hunts during the whelping season. The last Wolf in Scotland is reputed to have been killed in 1743, not far from the Park, by a hunter called MacQueen, whose descendants still own the farm which he was given as a reward. The Northern Lynx, which you can see in a large enclosure built around the natural outcrops of rock in the Park, probably became extinct in Scotland before regular human settlement. It is a forest animal, and it was probably common in prehistoric times. Lynx bones have been found in a Neolithic cave in Sutherland.

The next exhibits show Alpine Ibex, Wild Boar and Reindeer. The Ibex is a wild goat which shared the barren hills with Wild Horses and Saiga Antelope at the end of the Ice Age, moving eastwards when the North Sea was still dry land as the climate became wetter in Scotland. Ibex were hunted on the Continent until they were confined to the Pyrenees and the Italian Alps by the end of the nineteenth century. They have since been protected and reintroduced into Switzerland, Bavaria, Austria and Yugoslavia. The Wild Boar was probably exterminated in Scotland during the eighteenth century, and domestic pigs were bred from wild stock, although the modern pig has been developed from another ancient Chinese strain. Wild Boar are still common in many parts of Europe, especially in France and Germany where they are hunted for sport. Reindeer occurred as wild animals in Scotland until about the twelfth century, the last ones being hunted in Caithness and Sutherland by the Earls of Orkney. In the 1950s Reindeer were reintroduced in the Cairngorms by Mr Utsi, who supplied the animals in the Park.

Above the Reindeer paddock you come to the Viewpoint, the highest point in the Park, where you have a magnificent panoramic view of Highland scenery in the Spey valley. From here you walk downhill until you come to the enclosures for Arctic Foxes and Otters. The Arctic Fox probably pre-dated the arrival of man in Scotland, moving northwards with other Arctic animals when climate and vegetation changed. It is smaller than the Red Fox, and it has rounded ears and thick, dense fur. The European Otter, now rare in England, is still fairly common in the Highlands, and in the nineteenth century Otter skins were in demand for the making of sporrans. Otters are by nature daytime hunters, but persecution by man made them become largely nocturnal.

Next, you come to a range of outdoor runs for Scottish gamebirds — Black

One of the Chimpanzees at Scotland's Safari Park.

334

Grouse, Red Grouse, Ptarmigan and Capercaillie. Black Grouse are fairly common in the eastern Highlands, and they have elaborate courtship behaviour, the males gathering in special places known as the lek. The male is called the blackcock and the hen the greyhen. The Red Grouse has great economic value in the Highlands as a gamebird during the shooting season, which starts on 12th August, and local county councils charge rates on the number of grouse shot. The restaurants of London and New York provide a ready market for grouse, which fetch high prices. Ptarmigan are seldom seen by tourists since they live at about 3,000 feet above sea-level. In winter their plumage changes to white as camouflage in the snow. The Capercaillie is a large bird which became extinct in Scotland in about 1770 owing to the disappearance of its pine forest habitat. It was reintroduced in 1837–38, by which time conifer forests had again been planted. It soon became established again, and is now common in the Highlands. The cock bird has black plumage with green breast feathers, but the hen is much smaller and reddish brown in colour, with mottled plumage.

As you approach the lake, you pass the pen for Common Cranes, which would have been a native species in Saxon times, although they have not bred in Great Britain since the fifteenth century. They are still found wild in northern and eastern Europe. On the lake you may be lucky enough to see the European Beaver, or the Canadian Beaver, a similar race with darker fur. Beavers were probably exterminated in the sixteenth century in Scotland, partly owing to hunting and partly because forests were cut down. Their natural food is the bark and leaves of the native aspen, birch and willow. The European Beavers in the Park were imported from Russia. There is a good variety of waterfowl on the lake, all the species here being either indigenous or winter visitors to Scotland. The species of goose here are Greylag, Bean, Pink-footed, Brent and Barnacle; and the White-fronted, Greenland White-fronted and Lesser White-fronted Goose. The smaller waterfowl include Shelduck, Gadwall, Wigeon, Pintail, Shoveler, Pochard, Scaup, Common Teal and Eider. A short walk from the car park brings you to the children's park, which has a selection of tame animals and rides for children on Shetland Ponies.

Keen bird-watchers should keep a lookout for the many wild birds which nest in the Park. Moorland birds here include the Wheatear, Meadow Pipit and Skylark, Lapwing, Snipe, Curlew and Oystercatcher. Less common species are Whinchat, Ring Ousel, Red Grouse, Black Grouse and Teal. Duck often fly over the Park, and in spring and autumn you will see flocks of geese. Birds of prey to be noticed are Buzzard and Kestrel. Other birds commonly seen here are Black-headed Gulls, pigeons, Swifts, Swallows, Sand Martins, Crows, Rooks, Jackdaws and Ravens and migrant finches. Nobody visiting the Highlands who is interested in wild life, and the part it plays in the Highland landscape, should miss seeing the Park. It offers a fascinating glimpse into the distant past, as well as a plea for conservation in the future.

Scotland's Safari Park

Scotland's Safari Park was opened in 1970 by Sir John Muir and Mr Jimmy Chipperfield. As in other safari parks, most of the animals here are African. There are two drive-through reserves for Lions, one of which is for about 50 cubs, and another for Siberian Tigers, a species now very rare in the wild. Another, called Monkey Jungle, contains Rhesus Monkeys, an Indian species, with Grant's Zebras and African Elephants; and a fifth reserve is for camels and Giraffes. The Giraffes have produced 13 calves here. There is also a Hippopotamus pool and a boat safari, on which you can see Chimpanzees on an island. A Chimpanzee was born here during a blizzard in January, but it has survived.

There is a dolphinarium, which is under cover, with dolphin performances, and a Pet's Corner containing a walk-in aviary, a 'Goat Tower' and various farm animals. Other attractions include a garden centre, a playground with a Giant Astraglide and a whisky kiosk.

White-tailed Eagles. In 1975 the Nature Conservancy Council announced a project for re-establishing the White-tailed Eagle — the 'Erne' which figures in many Gaelic place-names — on Rhum NNR. Four eaglets were brought from Norway under licence and put in large cages in the open, and will be released after a period of acclimatisation. Since young eagles wander for four or five years before settling, the experiment will be repeated annually for several years in the hope that the species will once again become a regular breeder in western Scotland. It was commoner than the Golden Eagle on Rhum (and in the coastal regions of Scotland generally) 120 years ago; but following the evictions and the rise of sheep rearing it was heavily persecuted, and the last birds of native stock disappeared from Skye and Shetland about 1916. It is possible that climatic change, causing a northwards retreat of the fish stocks on which it largely depends, hastened the end. An unsuccessful attempt to re-establish the species at Fair Isle was made in 1968.

Scotland's Safari Park. **Address** Blair Drummond, By Stirling, Scotland. **Telephone** Doune 456. **Open** daily 10.00–18.00 (last admission), mid-March–end Oct. Closed winter. **Guide-book. Catering** licensed restaurant, self-service cafeteria, snack bar, kiosks. Gift shops. **Acreage** 120. **Car** 5 mls n.w. of Stirling on A84 Stirling–Doune road. **Bus** from Stirling to Park. **Train** to Stirling (5 mls) then bus to Park. **Taxis** available. **Other facilities** safari boat trip, pets' corner, picnic areas, giant astraglide, dolphin shows, first-aid post, safari bus available for visitors without cars. Public **not allowed** to feed animals.

Index

Acknowledgments

The publishers wish to thank the following organisations, agencies and individuals from whose collections photographs have been reproduced:

A. C. Aldridge/Ainsdale Sand Dunes NNR 149 top; Heather Angel 4 left, 25 bot, 31 bot, 62 top, 65 top left, 75, 149 above cent, 151, 176 bot, 258 bot left, 280 bot; J. F. Archibald 30 bot, 32, 33 bot; Ardea London 19; Keith Atkin 168 bot/cent, 227 top, 281 cent; J. A. Bayley/Ardea London viii; R. Balharry 17 bot, 228 cent, 303 bot; J. and D. Bartlett/Bruce Coleman Ltd 262; Ian Beames/Ardea London 34 bot, 98 cent, 99 cent, 229 cent, 238 bot left, 323 bot rt; S. C. Bisserot F.R.P.S. 174 top/bot left; S. C. Bisserot/Bruce Coleman Ltd 52 bot, 99 bot, 174 bot rt, 202 top, 207 top, 245, 251 bot; Blackpool Zoo 266–7 top; V. Blankenburgs 275; R. J. C. Blewitt/Ardea London 250 top rt; Joe B. Blossom/The Wildfowl Trust 214 top, 215 top; Anthony and Elizabeth Bomford 170 cent, 175 bot, 189 top left, 196 cent, 198 cent/bot, 224 left, 225 rt top/bot, 228 bot, 236 top cent/rt column, 252; Mark N. Boulton/Bruce Coleman Ltd 89 bot, 204 top, 263; Ian Bradshaw 24 bot, 81 top, 82, 91 bot, 121 bot, 308 bot, 333 bot; Dennis Bristow 6 bot, 15 bot, 98 top, 106 bot, 107, 171 top/cent, 187 bot, 230 bot, 231 top, 238 bot rt; Elizabeth Burgess/Ardea London 244 top; Jane Burton/Bruce Coleman Ltd 44 bot, 53 bot, 90–1 top, 101, 160 top, 175 top left/rt, 179, 197 bot left, 202–3 bot, 244 bot, 264 top, 282 bot, 325 top; Bob Campbell/Bruce Coleman Ltd 291; R. I. M. Campbell/Bruce Coleman Ltd 323 top; Kevin Carlson 6 top, 66 bot rt, 104 top left, 105 top, 143 top/bot rt, 144 rt cent/bot, 169, 172 top/bot, 193 bot rt, 232 bot, 251 top, 309 bot; Frank Clafton 13 top, 256 cent rt; Antony Clay/RSPB 141, 192 top; Phillip F. Coffey/Jersey Wildlife Preservation Trust 41, 47; Brian J. Coates/Bruce Coleman Ltd 266 bot, 292 top; Bruce Coleman/Bruce Coleman Ltd 43 bot, 92, 110, 140 bot, 267 bot, 325 bot, 327 bot, 332 bot; Richard Cooke 48–9; Cornwall Naturalists' Trust 15 top left, 20; Cotswold Farm Park 18 top; Robin Crane Films 62 bot, 69 bot left, 73 bot, 136–7; Gerry Cranham 330 top; Werner Curth/Ardea London 145 bot; Richard Davies/*The Illustrated London News* 94, 102, 193 bot left; John Doidge 216 top/bot, 217; Dudley Zoo 211, 272; Francisco Erize/Bruce Coleman Ltd 326 top, 330 bot; Philip Evans 220, 235; F. R. Evers-Swindell/The National Trust 233 bot; The Falconry (and Bird of Prey) Centre 212; Crispin Fisher 167 bot; Geoffrey Fisher/The Wildfowl Trust 213 bot; Robin Fisher 165 top/bot, 191, 228 bot left; Robin Fletcher 30 top, 58, 63, 64, 65 top rt, 66 bot left/cent rt, 67 top, 68 top, 100 cent, 149 bot, 176 cent, 189 top rt, 190 top left/bot, 192 bot, 278 bot; Dr Bruce Forman 7, 27 top, 69 bot/rt, 70–1, 140 top, 149 cent bot, 164, 184–5, 274, 279, 280 top, 286 top left; Neville Fox-Davies 24 top, 36, 319; Michael Freeman/Bruce Coleman Ltd 322; Roy A. Giles/*The Illustrated London News* 129 bot; Robert Gillmor/Bruce Coleman Ltd 229 bot; David A. Gowans 304, 311 bot left; G. Haines 157 bot, 158 cent; Dr J. P. Harding 181 bot; Roy A. Harris and K. R. Duff 98 bot, 148 top, 234 bot, 242; Pamela Harrison F.R.P.S. 59, 73 top, 193 top, K. W. Harvey/Birdworld Zoological Bird Gardens 79; Morley Hedley F.R.P.S. 311 bot rt; Pierre Henriot 104 bot, 227 bot; Ron Hickling 167 top; Highland Wildlife Park/Braemar Films Ltd 12 top; Peter A. Hinchcliffe/Bruce Coleman Ltd 194 top; Eric Hosking endpapers, 18 bot, 29 bot, 67 bot, 106 cent, 145 cent, 146 top, 170 bot rt; Howletts Zoo Park 85 top/bot; Ken Hoy/Ardea London 4 rt; R. Hussey 176 top, 190 top cent/rt, 196 top, 258 top/cent/bot rt; Neil Jinkerson 162 top; M. Johnson 196 bot; Edgar T. Jones/Ardea London 254 bot; Peter Kaminski/Stagsden Bird Gardens 130; Kilverstone New World Wildlife Park 157 top, 158 top/bot; Frank W. Lane 271, 327 top; Peter Laub/Ardea London 144 top; Leonard Lee Rue/Bruce Coleman Ltd 207 bot, 208–9 top; Ake Lindau/Ardea London 9 top, 301 top; Eric Lindgren/Ardea London 52–3 top; Michael Lyster/Zoological Society of London 54–5, 87, 118–19, 119 top, 120 bot, 120–1, 122–3, 124–5, 124 bot, 125 bot, 126–7, 128–9, 132–3, 328–9; Iain L. P. Malin 249 cent; Marineland Oceanarium and Aquarium, Morecambe 181 top; John Markham/Bruce Coleman Ltd 68 bot, 313 bot; Christopher Marler/Flamingo Gardens and Zoological Park 114–15; Bob Marsh 28, 29 top left, 168 top, 230 top rt, 246–7, 250, 255 top, 257; Marwell Zoological Park 89 top; John Mason 31 top, 71 rt top/cent/bot, 143 bot left, 189 top; J. L. Mason/Ardea London 14; Hugh Maynard/Bruce Coleman Ltd 331; E. R. Meadows/The National Trust 284 bot; Derek Middleton/Bruce Coleman Ltd titlepage, 297 cent; Pat Morris/Ardea London 44 cent, 99 top, 115 top; Norman Myers/Bruce Coleman Ltd 86, 116–17; C. K. Mylne 9 bot, 297 bot, 300 top, 301 top left/rt, 302, 305 top/bot, 306 bot, 310 top/bot, 312 bot; Chris Mylne/Ardea London 224 rt; Nature Conservancy Council 72, 142, 146 bot, 288, 296; Dr Ernest Neal 194 cent/bot, 195 top/bot, 197 top; D. Nicholson/Marine Biological Association of the U.K. 45; Norman Orr A.R.P.S. 65 top rt, 66 top, 256 top rt, 281 cent, 282 top; D. J. Pannett 188 bot; A. E. McR. Pearce 34 top; G. D. Plage/Bruce Coleman Ltd 205; Allan G. Potts F.R.P.S. 100 top, 171 bot, 173 top, bot left/rt, 236 cent left, 253 bot, 277 bot, 299, 312 top; Prinknash Bird Park 213 top; R. J. Raines 3, 29 top, 256 left; Dr Derek Ratcliffe 8 bot, 13 bot, 100 bot, 139, 144 bot left, 147 rt, 223 top, 249 bot, 253 top left, 283 top, 297 top; Dennis Reed 17 top; Hans Reinhard/Bruce Coleman Ltd jacket, 69 top, 161 top, 182, 204 bot, 206, 229 top; Michael W. Richards/R.S.P.B. 145 top, 284 top; Ralf Richter/Ardea London 27 bot; Betty Risdon/Tropical Bird Gardens, Rode 292 bot; S. Roberts/Ardea London 332–3 top; Ann Rooper/Bentley Wildfowl Collection 78 top/bot, 214–15; Colin Russell 197 bot rt; B. L. Sage/Ardea London 221 top; Peter Schofield 223 bot, 227 top, 230 top left, 231 bot, 234 top, 238 top; Bob Scorer 286 top rt; Phillippa Scott 162 bot; Victor J. Scott 16; Seals Research Division IMER NERC 148 bot, 286 bot; Jack Sheldon 223 cent, 255 bot left, 256 bot rt, 278 cent, 281 bot, 283 bot, 306 top; James Simon/Bruce Coleman Ltd 326 bot; Brian Sinfield/Cotswold Wildlife Park Ltd 112–13, 324; Peter Steyn/Ardea London 44 top; Richard Tilbrook 42–3, 134–5, 183, 208, 218–19, 269, 294, 334; Tony Tilford/Dennis Avon/Ardea London 8 top; Norman Tomalin/Bruce Coleman Ltd 90 bot; Simon Trevor/Bruce Coleman Ltd 154; Bobby Tulloch 26, 236 top left, 306 cent, 307 top/bot, 309 top/cent; University of Durham, Dept of Photography/The Chillingham Wild Cattle Association Ltd 285 bot; W. G. Vanderson/Chessington Zoo 80–1; Joe Van Wormer/Bruce Coleman Ltd 90, 198 top; Wales Tourist Board 225 left; K. C. Walton 226 left/rt; © Philip Wayre/Norfolk Wildlife Park 160–1; A. J. S. Weaving/Ardea London 88; Tom Weir 10 left, 10–11, 303 top, 311 top, 313 top, 314 top, 315 bot; John Wightman/Ardea London 221 bot; Kenneth Williamson 5 bot, 308–9, 314 bot; John Wilson 250 top left; P. J. Wilson 5 top, 12 bot, 15 top rt, 21 top/bot, 95, 170 top, 177, 188 top, 233, 236 bot left, 285 bot; Wirral Country Park 187 top; Tom Wright/The National Trust 260; Yorkshire Naturalists' Trust 278 top; J. F. Young 25 top, 33 top, 103 top, bot/left/cent/rt, 104 top rt, 105 bot, 106 top, 147 bot, 232 bot, 253 top rt, 254 top, 255 bot rt, 300 bot, 305 cent, 315 top, 316 top/bot.